55°E   60°E

Aral Sea

Shelpe

Nukus   **UZBEKISTAN**

Dzhebel   T U R K M E N I S T A N   Galaasiya   40°N

Ashkhabad

Minudasht   Ouchan   Meymaneh

Mashhad   35°N

Torbat-e Heydariyeh

ran   I R A N   Herat

ahan   Birjand

Yazd   **AFGHANISTAN**

Abadeh

Rafsanjan   Kerman   30°N

Sirjan   Zahedan

Bam

Bandar
Abbas

Str. of
Hormuz

amah   25°N

Dawhah

Abu   Gulf of Oman
Dhabi★   **Muscat**

U.A.E.

OMAN

Al Khaluf

Arabian Sea

Salalah

Ghaydan

Suqutra

55°E   60°E

FIFTH EDITION

A HISTORY OF THE
ARAB–ISRAELI CONFLICT

Ian J. Bickerton
University of New South Wales, Australia

Carla L. Klausner
University of Missouri–Kansas City

PEARSON

Prentice
Hall

Upper Saddle River, New Jersey 07458

Library of Congress Cataloging-in-Publication Data

Bickerton, Ian J.
    A history of the Arab-Israeli conflict / Ian J. Bickerton, Carla L. Klausner. — 5th ed.
        p.   cm.
    Includes index.
    ISBN-10: 0-13-222335-X
1. Arab–Israeli conflict.   2. Palestine—History—1917–1948.   3. Arab–Israeli
    conflict—1993—Peace.   I. Klausner, Carla L.   II. Title.
    DS119.7.B49 2007
    956.04—dc22

                                                              2006012877

Editorial Director: Charlyce Jones-Owen
Executive Editor: Charles Cavaliere
Editorial Assistant: Maria Guarascio
Marketing Manager: Emily Cleary
Marketing Assistant: Jennifer Lang
Production Liaison: Marianne Peters-Riordan
Manufacturing Buyer: Ben Smith
Art Director: Jayne Conte
Cover Design: Bruce Kenselaar
Cover Illustration/Photo: Raffi Garabedian/Ian
  J. Bickerton

Director, Image Resource Center: Melinda Patelli
Manager, Rights and Permissions: Zina Arabia
Manager, Visual Research: Beth Brenzel
**Manager, Cover Visual Research &
  Permissions:** Karen Sanatar
Image Permission Coordinator: Frances Toepfer
Composition/Full-Service Project Management:
  GGS Book Services/Chitra Ganesan
Printer/Binder: RR Donnelley & Sons Company

Credits and acknowledgments borrowed from other sources and reproduced, with permission, in this textbook
appear on appropriate page within text.

Pearson Education LTD.
Pearson Education Singapore, Pte. Ltd
Pearson Education, Canada, Ltd
Pearson Education–Japan
Pearson Education Australia PTY, Limited

Pearson Education North Asia Ltd
Pearson Educación de Mexico, S.A. de C.V.
Pearson Education Malaysia, Pte. Ltd
Pearson Education, Upper Saddle River, New Jersey

10 9 8 7 6 5 4 3 2 1
ISBN 0-13-222335-X

And thus is the way of the world.
No, rather thus is the way
we have made the world.
                    —Anonymous

CONTENTS

3   WORLD WAR II, JEWISH DISPLACED PERSONS, AND THE PARTITION OF PALESTINE

7   HOLY DAYS AND HOLY WAR: OCTOBER 1973   155

8   THE SEARCH FOR PEACE, 1973–1979   178

9 LEBANON AND THE INTIFADA   205

10 THE PEACE OF THE BRAVE   237

11 THE PEACE PROGRESSES

TABLES, CHARTS, AND MAPS

TABLES

CHARTS

MAPS

DOCUMENTS

PREFACE

In the fifteen years since we wrote the first edition of this book, there have been far-reaching changes in the Arab-Israeli conflict, and significant shifts in the way it has been written about. Relations between Israel and the Arab countries have altered, the dynamic between Israel and the Palestinians has been in constant flux, alternating between periods of relative calm and outbreaks of explosive bitterness and hostility, and, at present, the entire Middle East appears to be in the midst of major political and religious upheaval, as the repercussions of the United States-led war against Iraq are being felt throughout the region.

The way the participants, including their respective historians, view, speak, and write about themselves and each other has also significantly shifted since the first edition of this book. The discourse between Palestinians/Arabs and Israelis and within each group—especially among Israelis—has matured and moderated with the passage of time, and we still believe that a majority on both sides recognize that specific goals are more attainable through peaceful means than by warfare. We acknowledge that there are extremists on both sides. Nevertheless, Israel is now recognized and accepted as a reality by most Arabs, and most Israelis are ready to accept the almost certain possibility of a Palestinian state. With this new awareness, new questions have arisen, new frameworks through which the past and present can be viewed have been constructed, new histories have been written. Of course, the circumstances that produced the Arab–Israeli conflict have not changed, nor have old enmities disappeared. Historians cannot ignore or change past events or sentiments. We simply see things differently in the twenty-first century than we did in earlier years. Time provides alternative perspectives with which to interpret events. The Arab–Israeli conflict continues to surprise pundits and commentators, however. It even appears to defy the participants themselves. Recent events, such as the death of Palestinian leader Yasser Arafat in November 2004, the dismantling of Jewish settlements and the withdrawal of Israel from the Gaza Strip in August, 2005, the sudden departure from the scene of Israeli Prime Minister Ariel Sharon because of a life-threatening stroke, and the unexpected victory of Hamas in Palestinian elections in January 2006, have enveloped the conflict in uncertainty, and have transformed the relationship between Israel, the Palestinians and the Arab states. It is difficult to know what to make of it all, and events unfold so quickly as we write that, at times, we ourselves have not always agreed on how to interpret them. We fluctuate between optimism and despair.

In this fifth edition of *A Concise History of the Arab–Israeli Conflict* we have tried to reflect the changes outlined above. Our narrative and chronologies have been updated, and we have reviewed how we interpret many of the events preceding these startling, rapidly changing, and somewhat unpredictable happenings. We have also considered new accounts and interpretations and have included many in the bibliographies at the end of each chapter. In the last chapter of this edition and in the conclusion, we have attempted to present and explain the meaning of recent frenzied and chaotic events.

The genesis of this book was a history colloquium we team-taught on the Arab–Israeli conflict at the University of Missouri–Kansas City. We discovered that, like the general public, our students had lots of opinions but only fragmentary knowledge. They lacked background information and approached the subject with preconceptions and emotional biases. Our students required knowledge of the events, but they also needed ready access to the documents most relevant to the issues, they needed maps, and they needed guidance as to their future reading.

We found no single book that met these requirements, so we decided to write this text to fulfill that need. The book is basically a chronological narrative; however, within that framework, we have tried to highlight certain themes that we regard as central to the conflict.

As in past editions, we have attempted to achieve some balance and objectivity about a subject upon which most people feel it necessary to adopt a partisan point of view. Throughout the narrative, we have tried to present both sides of the issues, although we realize that even the selection of material to be included reveals some subjective judgment on our part. If the book succeeds in provoking thoughtful discussion of the Arab–Israeli conflict, we will have achieved our goal.

We hope the additions and revisions in this edition will enhance the book's timeliness and usefulness, and that this updated account will be of interest to a wide audience, since the Middle East is an area of significance and importance not only to students but also to an educated public.

We would like to acknowledge the assistance of the University of New South Wales and the University of Missouri–Kansas City, from which we received faculty research grants. We are also appreciative of the detailed and constructive comments and criticisms of Professor Arthur Goldschmidt, Jr., who read the original manuscript for the publisher. We also wish to thank the following reviewers of later editions for their insights and helpful suggestions: John O. Voll, Georgetown University; Sanford R. Silverburg, Catawba College; Stephen L. McFarland, Auburn University; Robert Olson, University of Kentucky; Ronald Davis, Western Michigan University; John Calvert, Creighton University; Caroline T. Marshall, James Madison University; Paulis Lazda, University of Wisconsin—Eau Claire; Malik Mufti, Tufts University. Thanks are also due to Judy Echin, "Flexigraphics" Sydney, Susan Baumgart, Bill Clipson, Arthur J. Fisk, Roni Kresner, and Rhonda Roosa who helped with maps; Patrick Burgess, who assisted us with the pronunciation guide; our history department office staffs; and the editorial and production staff of this edition and previous edition at Prentice Hall, especially Steve Dalphin, Bayani Mendoza de Leon, Katy Bsales, Sally Constable, Jenny Moss, Jean Lapidus, Charles Cavaliere, Mary Araneo, Emsal Hasan, Charlyce Jones-Owen, Maria Guarascio, Emily Cleary, Jennifer Lang, Marianne Peters-Riordan, Ben Smith, Jayne Conte, Melinda Patelli, Zina Arabia, Beth Brenzel, Karen Sanatar, and Frances Toepfer. Finally, we thank Jenny, Tibor, our families, friends, and colleagues for their patience and support.

Ian J. Bickerton
Carla L. Klausner

Note: The photograph on the cover of this book, by Jerusalem photographer Raffi Safieh Garabedian, shows the Western Wall and the Dome of the Rock, symbols of the religious and nationalist dimension of the conflict.

Introduction

The Middle East is a puzzle to most people, and the Arab–Israeli conflict is perhaps the most confusing dimension of the modern history of the area. Almost daily, television news projects into our living rooms images of Israelis and Palestinians engaged in a futile, seemingly out-of-control cycle of terror raids, suicide bombings, assassinations, and brutal repression that leads to despair and plays into the hands of extremists on both sides.

This constant reportage and the seemingly never-ending violence go to make understanding the conflict involving Israel, Palestinians, and neighboring states more urgent than ever. The situation is becoming even more confusing and alarming, if that is possible. Just what is going on, however, is hard to fathom in the short sound bites that commercial TV imposes on daily news coverage. And much of what the viewer sees appears at odds with what the participants say about events. Using increasingly bitter and hard line rhetoric, Israeli and Palestinian spokespersons blame the other side for every escalation of violence that occurs and refuse to accept any responsibility themselves. The "peace process" that held out such hope only a short decade ago seems to have been forgotten or abandoned. Can these and the other apparent inconsistencies be explained, and what do they reveal about the conflict and the prospects for its peaceful resolution? Attitudes on both sides appear to have hardened, and the path toward peace is strewn with more fatalities and casualties, making reconciliation even more difficult.

We should begin by making it clear that the term "Arab–Israeli conflict" used throughout this text is the generic label most people apply to the struggle centered on the area of the Middle East that in the years prior to the establishment of Israel was known as Palestine. For a period of around seventy-five years before May 1948, the confrontation was essentially one between Palestinian Arabs and Jews over the future disposition of that territory. After the creation of the state of Israel, however, the localized dispute widened to include many other nations both inside and outside the Middle East. The Arab states saw the Jewish state as an enemy to be destroyed. However, although they provided economic and moral support for the Palestinian cause, the majority engaged only indirectly in military operations against Israel. The major protagonists in the six or so major wars or confrontations between 1948 and 2000 were limited to Israel and the contiguous states of Jordan, Egypt, Lebanon, and Syria, as well as Iraq. During the period called the Cold War, both sides received military and economic assistance from the major world powers. As Egypt and Jordan signed peace treaties recognizing the Jewish state, the conflict again began to focus more narrowly on the disputes between Israel and the Palestinian Arabs. Thus, while Israelis describe themselves as involved in an "Arab–Israeli conflict," Palestinians regard the term as quite inappropriate. They see themselves as involved in a "*Palestinian*–Israeli conflict," in which Israel is supported against them by Jews worldwide.

Another problem with the term Arab–Israeli conflict is that it is used inclusively to apply to larger ongoing conflicts, like those in the Persian Gulf, that are only peripherally related to the conflict between Israel and its neighbors. The term might suggest to some that Israel is part of the broader regional conflicts taking place. For at least the past half century the countries of the Middle East have undergone tremendous changes, as they threw off their colonial pasts and tried to cope with the unimagined wealth that oil has brought to some of them. These changes have frequently resulted in wars over territory. By far the greatest conflicts within the Middle East during this period centered on the Persian Gulf area: the horrendous eight-year-long war between Iran and Iraq, the extraordinary high-tech Gulf War following Iraq's invasion of Kuwait, and the current U.S.-led war against Iraq. Although those wars were fought over resources (oil), territorial boundaries, and for regime change, they were sustained by religious and ethnic hatreds as well. Israel has figured in these events, but not as a central actor. Nevertheless, we find the term Arab–Israeli conflict the most usable term to apply to the events this book describes.

Many see the Arab–Israeli conflict as the present-day extension of enmity that has existed since biblical times. This is because the issues underlying the conflict strike at the very heart of the identity of the peoples involved. In the case of Israelis and Palestinians, both parties regard sovereignty over the same territory as essential to their existence as a people. It is a case of two peoples with common national aspirations vying for the same piece of land. While this, in itself, is not unique, the area of Israel/Palestine is geographically so small that how both sets of aspirations can be met has been impossible so far to work out. As if that were not enough, much of the area is both resource-poor and water-poor; these scarcities have added to the intensity of the conflict.

In addition to being the contemporary expression of a historic territorial battle over Palestine between two traditional ethnic rivals, Jews and Arabs, the Arab–Israeli conflict involves two great world religions, and the outcome is of major concern to Jewish, Islamic, and Christian communities throughout the world. To Jews and Judaism, the establishment of Israel is the pivotal event of the past 2,000 years of Jewish history. To Islam and to Muslims, the existence of a Jewish state in the midst of the Muslim world poses a great challenge and is difficult to accept.

The Christian world is fascinated by the Arab–Israeli conflict for a number of reasons. The land, its names and places, are familiar to most Christians through their reading of the Old Testament, and the fate of the Holy Land is a central issue in Christian theology. Sites associated with the life of Jesus are especially significant to Christians, and some indication of the high value Christians place on the Holy Places can be seen in the importance placed on the visit to the area by Pope John Paul II in March of 2000, the first such visit by a pope in modern history. The insistence that Christians have some say in the future of Holy Places in and around Jerusalem has made resolution of the issues surrounding that city even more complex.

Also, Christians have had, and retain, a love-hate relationship with Jews. As we shall see, for most of its history, Christianity has persecuted and discriminated against Jews, and, following the Holocaust, Christians now observe Jews working out their own destiny in a Jewish state. Christian attitudes toward Arabs and Muslims for the most part have been—and to a considerable degree remain—based on ignorance and fear.

If we add to these considerations the fact that the Middle East is the location of much of the world's oil supplies and reserves, and that as a result the region became caught up in the great-power rivalries of the Cold War and continues to be an area of concern and contention, it is easy to see why the Arab–Israeli conflict has absorbed so much of the world's attention in the past half century.

The primary objective of this book is to make the Arab–Israeli conflict more intelligible without the distortions that result from oversimplification. This involves tracing the broad sweep of the history of the region and the perceptions both parties have of each other. Both the Arabs and the Israelis are locked into the histories they have created for themselves—into the dreams of their pasts. Both have sought and some still seek to set in our minds favorable cultural images and symbols of themselves and unfavorable ones of their opponents. Remember, legitimizing one's position is an essential element in any international conflict, and that task sometimes results in intentional or unintentional falsification of the past, as well as vilification of one's enemies. That is one reason why the Arab–Israeli conflict is so passionately argued over, by participants and observers alike. The distinction between the past and the present, while real enough in one sense, is in part an artificial one. While we are aware of and conscious of the past, only the present exists in experiential terms. Constructing and controlling "the truth" about the past to justify one's actions in the present is an important function of all states and all political activity. An important task of a student of history is to separate the rhetoric designed by both sides to create a usable, legitimizing, and heroic past from the reality of past events. The primary sources included in this book will provide the opportunity for readers to reach their own conclusions as to the issues involved and the way they are portrayed by both sides.

Neither side in the conflict should be seen as a monolith; there are divisions and tensions within both sides along ethnic, religious, class, and gender lines that lead to many different political attitudes. One aim of this book is to assist you in sorting out the various groups and their opinions, assessing which ones are more likely to lead to peaceful rather than violent solutions. As David K. Shipler points out in *Arab and Jew: Wounded Spirits in a Promised Land:* "The time has passed when Jews and Arabs could face each other in simple conflict. They live together now in rich variety. There is no single Arab–Jewish relationship; there are many, and they require an elusive tolerance that must somehow run against the forces of war, nationalism, terrorism and religious certainty."

Defining the Question

How, then, can the Arab–Israeli conflict be explained? Is it a religious war between the followers of Islam and Judaism in which the protagonists are driven by deep-seated suspicions and hostilities concerning the Divine instructions to each other? Is it an ethnic war between traditionally rival groups, reflecting changing demographic patterns? Is it a war of nationalist aspirations in which rival militant nationalisms are seeking to establish a state and thereby find their "place in the sun"? Is it a war of self-defense in which a newly established state is defending itself against the determination of its neighbors to destroy it? Is it a war of territorial expansion in which one state is attempting to expand its borders at the expense of its neighbors? Is it an imperial war reflecting the history of the rivalries and ambitions of the imperial states of Europe—and more recently the United States and the Soviet Union—in the Middle East? Is it the inevitable consequence of the disruptive process of transition from traditional society to modern state taking place in the Middle East? Or is it simply a series of random, unconnected events that have had tragic and unforeseen consequences for the people involved?

All these elements are present in the Arab–Israeli conflict, but to single out any one of them as the explanation for the events that make up the conflict is to oversimplify a situation that has developed over the past century. As we shall see, the tragedy of the Arab–Israeli conflict is that it is the collision of two sets of historic and moral rights of groups over the same land. Both portray themselves as victims—victims of outsiders as well as of each other's violence.

The opposing claims differ, of course. In Shipler's words: "To draw the boldest outline of the past is to make Israel's basic case. To sketch the present is to see the Arab's plight."

Who are the Arabs and Jews?

We must begin with a definition of Arabs and Jews. Both terms have a historical and cultural meaning. Mythically, Arabs and Jews have a common origin. Thus, some regard Noah's eldest son, Shem, as the ancestor of the Hebrews and Arabs. Arabs as well as Jews see themselves as descendants of the patriarch Abraham, and therefore as inheritors of the Promised Land. Arabs trace their lineage to Ishmael, Abraham's first son born of Hagar, Sarah's handmaiden, while Jews trace themselves to Isaac, son of Abraham and his wife, Sarah. In the Hebrew Bible, known to Christians as the Old Testament, the term *Arab* referred to the nomadic inhabitants of the central and northern Arabian Peninsula. Over the centuries, these nomadic tribes, headed by a sheikh who acted as a first among equals, developed a structure shaped by the harsh deserts and dependent on the camel. Survival depended upon the strength and solidarity of the tribe, and on obedience to custom and an unwritten code of honor called *muruwwa*. We can learn more about Arab values and the Arab experience during the period just before Muhammad through the heroic poetry they spoke and sang in the sixth and early seventh centuries. The greatest of these poems are the so-called "Suspended Poems" or "Mu'allaqat," the most famous of which is that of Imru al-Qays, ruler of an ephemeral pre-Islamic desert kingdom in the sixth century. When the Arab conquest of the Middle East occurred in the seventh and eighth centuries of the common era (C.E.),* following the founding of Islam, Arabic became the language and Islam the religion of the region. The term *Arab* acquired a new cultural definition that lasted during the period of Arab hegemony until the Mongol sack of Baghdad in 1258. Not all the inhabitants adopted the new language and religion, however. Some remnants of early Christianity remained: Nestorians in Persia and Iraq, Christians in Syria, and Maronite Christians in Mount Lebanon (who use Syriac in their liturgy but recognize Rome as the head of the Christian Church), and some Greek Orthodox. And, of course, Jews resisted the religion of the new conquerors.

Arabs today do not form one nation-state although, like Jews, they consider themselves a people and national group. They constitute a majority in many modern nation-states (Algeria, Bahrain, Egypt, Iraq, Jordan, Kuwait, Lebanon, Libya, Morocco, Oman, Qatar, Saudi Arabia, Sudan, Syria, Tunisia, the United Arab Emirates, North Yemen, South Yemen). Today there are close to 300 million in the region from Morocco to Iraq who consider themselves Arab. Nor are Arabs a race in the commonly understood sense. Neither are they a religion, for many Arabs—about 9 million in the Middle East and 30–35 million world-wide—are Christian. And only about one-fifth of the world's 1.2 to 1.4 billion Muslims are Arab. Indeed, the largest concentration of Muslims in the world is in Indonesia. In the final analysis, Arab can be applied to those who use Arabic as their language and identify with Arab culture and Arab causes.

The term *Jew* is as difficult to define as the term *Arab*. Jews trace their history to the Semitic tribe or groups of tribes who claimed descent from Abraham through his son Isaac who were known as Hebrews or Israelites. Although Jews consider themselves a people, as do the Arabs, Jews are not simply a nationality, are not a race, and are more than a religion. They are at once an ethnic group, a religious group, and a cultural group. Even identifying as Jews those who use Hebrew as a language does not help us much as it is the spoken language of only about one-third of the inhabitants of Israel, and many who identify themselves as Jews

---

*The term C.E. (Common Era) is preferred by Muslims and Jews to the corresponding designation A.D. (the year of our Lord) used by Christians.

have little or no familiarity with the language. According to *halacha*, Jewish religious law, the term *Jew* can be applied to those who have a Jewish mother, or who have converted to Judaism.

One problem facing Europeans in discussing Arabs and Jews is to free themselves from the distorting lens of two destructive ideologies: anti-Semitism (in the sense of anti-Jewishness), and Orientalism. Irrational suspicion, fear, and hatred of Jews—as Jews—have characterized European history for centuries, leading to almost uninterrupted oppression and persecution of Jews throughout all the countries of Europe. Anti-Semitism—the term was first used by the German racist Wilhelm Marr in 1879—in its modern form defined and attacked Jews in terms of race rather than religion and relied on pseudo-scientific Social-Darwinist theories in attempting to prove the superiority of the "Aryan" race over the "inferior" Semitic Jews. These twisted ideas found their ultimate expression in the Holocaust, Hitler's attempt to exterminate the Jews of Europe.

Americans and western Europeans have also exhibited a contempt, disregard, and sense of arrogance toward Arabs and Muslims and have failed to recognize the intrinsic value and contributions of Arabs and Muslims to history. These assumptions, or more correctly, limitations, were defined by one scholar, Edward Said in his book *Orientalism*, as "Orientalism." Said described Orientalism as the racist way the western world views the inhabitants of the Orient, including the Middle East. The West, Said argued, has tried to establish the idea that Europe, by defining the political, economic, and cultural characteristics of the people of the Orient as inferior to those of the West, has the right to hegemony or dominance over the Orient. Thus non-Middle Easterners have come to regard the Middle East as politically despotic, economically backward, and culturally decadent. As a result, there is a tendency to overlook completely the contributions of the Middle East to the development of Western European civilization and, in restructuring the realities of Middle Eastern life and history, to distort them. The cultural or intellectual assumptions that Occidentals bring to their study of Jews and Arabs make an understanding of the Arab–Israeli conflict considerably more difficult.

More serious as far as solving the conflict is concerned, Jews and Arabs bring their own prejudices and negative stereotypes—exaggerated by past and recent history—to bear upon each other. For Jews, the most pervasive stereotype of the Arab, according to Shipler, is "the fearsome violent figure of immense strength and duplicity. . . . Capable of great cruelty, given to fanatical disregard for human life, he murders easily, either out of a crazed lust for blood or as an emotional animal easily incited and manipulated by murderous leaders." Arab stereotypes of Jews are remarkably similar to those of their Jewish counterparts. Jews are seen by Arabs as violent and cowardly. Ignoring the ancient ties of the Jews to Palestine, the Arabs regard them as aliens, as outsiders, as interlopers who do not belong. Needless to say, these prejudices add significantly to the passions of the participants in the conflict.

The Religious Dimension: Judaism and Islam

Much of the Arab–Israeli conflict is secular, involving issues of territory, security, and ethnic and cultural differences. In many respects the sources of tension are nonreligious, resembling those of any conflict. But religious identification is a central element in the conflict and adds an extra dimension and sense of inevitability to the unfolding events. Despite the fact that only a minority of Arabs and Jews are strictly observant religiously, religion has been, and continues to be, a focal point for the peoples involved in this conflict. Religion significantly shapes the attitudes of the protagonists toward each other. Furthermore, high-profile religious extremists and their inflammatory statements attract widespread press and public attention which is, no doubt, why the conflict is sometimes described as a religious war. All this is somewhat ironic given how much both religions share in common.

Judaism is the oldest monotheistic religion and foreshadows both Christianity and Islam. Judaism refers to the faith and ceremonies of Jews and is a faith that is revealed by God and interpreted by religious teachers, namely rabbis. In its widest sense, Judaism is the entire Jewish tradition and way of life. Central to Judaism is the belief that God acted personally in history through a Chosen People, the Jews (the people called Israel), and that God entered into a Covenant with them that if they obeyed God's teachings God would, through them, save all mankind. God's instructions to the Jews are contained in the Torah (literally teachings), or Pentateuch, which consists of the Five Books of Moses. The Torah contains the laws God revealed to the Jews, including the Ten Commandments. It also includes the message to establish an independent society based on Divine precepts, which are elaborated in great detail. One finds in the Torah, as well, God's promise to Abraham, Isaac, and Jacob, the three Jewish patriarchs, that God will give the Jews the land of Israel—the Promised Land—the state in which they will live in truth, justice, and peace. Throughout the Torah, the boundaries of the "Promised Land" vary (see Genesis 15:18–21; Numbers 34:1–12; Deuteronomy 1:7–8), but the borders were greater than those of the state of Israel even after the 1967 war. In the minds of many religious Jews today, the Torah is more than just a "Bible"; it is a blueprint for existence and should be the constitution of any Jewish state.

Judaism has gone through several stages in its long history. The first stage could be said to be that described in the Hebrew Bible, which consists of the Torah, the books of the Prophets, and a collection of other writings such as Kings, Chronicles, Ruth, Esther, and the Song of Solomon. It tells of the Jews' search under Moses for the land promised them by God after their expulsion from Egypt (the Exodus) and describes the Kingdoms of David and Solomon. The boundaries of Solomon's kingdom around 1,000 B.C.E.,* with Jerusalem as its capital, included the areas called Judea and Samaria, and extended from Aqaba and the Negev beyond Beersheba in the south, to beyond the Litani River and Golan Heights in the north, to areas of present-day Jordan on the east. Extreme religious and nationalistic groups today insist that these biblical boundaries of *Eretz Yisrael*, or the Land of Israel, especially Judea and Samaria, or the West Bank of the Jordan River, must remain under Jewish control.

The northern part of the kingdom, or Samaria, was conquered by the Assyrians in 721 B.C.E. The Jews of the southern kingdom, or Judea, were exiled to Babylonia in 586 B.C.E., after the destruction of the First Temple built by Solomon in Jerusalem, which had become the center of Jewish worship until it was destroyed by the army of King Nebuchadnezzar. Restored to Palestine by the Persians, the Jews built a Second Temple in Jerusalem and lived autonomously under a succession of foreign rulers until 70 C.E. when the Romans destroyed the Second Temple and dispersed the Jews (the Diaspora). One of the last strongholds to fall to the Romans was the hillside fortress known as Masada. The Israeli slogan "Masada shall never fall again" has come to symbolize Israel's determination to fight to the death to maintain its national sovereignty. It is thus significant that recruits of the Israel Armoured Corps swear their allegiance at Masada.

Following the destruction of the Temple and the disappearance of the priestly class, synagogues (places of worship, study, and community gathering) came into existence throughout the Jewish world, and teachers, or rabbis, interpreted the law. This oral law of the rabbis was later codified in a work known as the *Mishnah*. The accumulated mass of law and lore based on the Torah and Mishnah and known as the Talmud was then codified by about 500 C.E. In subsequent centuries, living under Muslim or Christian rulers, Jewish thinkers and teachers continued to study and interpret their traditions. In the Middle Ages, Moses ben Maimon, or Maimonides (1135–1204), a Jew living in Islamic Spain, emigrated to Egypt, where he served as a physician at the court of the Muslim rulers. Recognized as the most learned and authoritative Jewish

---

*The term B.C.E. (before the Common Era) is used throughout the text and corresponds to the designation B.C. (before Christ) used by Christians.

figure of his age, Maimonides codified Talmudic law up to his time in the *Mishneh Torah* and dealt with fundamental theological and philosophical questions in the *Moreh Nebuchim*, or *Guide for the Perplexed*. Maimonides distilled 13 articles of the faith and enumerated 613 positive and negative commandments found in the Torah that form the basis of Jewish law and faith.

Jews who lived in Spain, or Sepharad, as well as those who lived elsewhere under Islamic domination, are known generally as the *Sephardim*. In the Islamic world, Jews had lived for hundreds of years as *Ahl-al-Dhimma*, or people of a contract or covenant, with the Muslim rulers. As *Dhimmis*, Jews, like Christians, were given the status of second-class citizens. They were subject to heavy land and poll taxes (*jizyah*) and discriminatory social regulations and were forbidden to exercise control over Muslims, although these restrictions were sometimes ignored. A "tolerated minority," Dhimmis were allowed to worship freely, to live under their own laws, and to enjoy a large measure of self-government. There were no restrictions on their travel or economic life. Although there were occasional massacres, attacks against them, and sometimes even forced conversions, no Islamic ruler ever instituted a policy of wholesale expulsion or extermination of the Jews. Arabized Jews tended to take on the characteristics of their surroundings. Defined in terms of their religion, they tended to think of themselves primarily as a religious group.

In the eighteenth and nineteenth centuries, the Jews of Western Europe (European Jews in general were known as *Ashkenazim*) were gradually emancipated, and many older customs and rituals were rejected to enable Judaism to accommodate the modern world. Reform Judaism, Zionism, and secular Yiddish culture emerged. Today, the largest Jewish communities are in the United States, the former Soviet Union, and Israel. Devout Jews maintain traditional Jewish observances in their individual and familial practices, including attendance at synagogue, observing special holy days, periods of fasting, and other rituals. The Jewish return to Jerusalem and to Zion (Mount Zion, which came to stand for the Holy City and the Holy Land) became a central part of Jewish ritual and ceremonial practice. Although divided into Orthodox, Conservative, and Reform branches of Judaism, the vast majority of Jews throughout the world support the existence of the Jewish state of Israel.

Islam asserts that God has revealed Himself several times in history, and it accepts the validity of scriptural religions like Judaism and Christianity. Muslims believe that the transmitter of God's final revelations to mankind was Muhammad, a member of the Quraysh tribe of the trading city of Mecca. Muhammad was born about 570 C.E. and is regarded by Muslims as the last of God's prophets, in a line that includes Abraham, Moses, and Jesus. Not much is known about Muhammad's life, except that he came from a poor family of the clan of Hashim, married Khadija, a wealthy widow fifteen years his senior, became a successful businessman, and was also deeply spiritual. According to tradition, the angel Gabriel (the same archangel who appeared to Mary in Christian tradition) appeared to Muhammad and revealed the word of *Allah* (*al-Illah*, or The God), whom Muhammad accepted as the One True God—the same monotheistic deity of the Jews and Christians.

Around the year 610 C.E., Muhammad began to preach the word of God, and the passages of rhymed prose that he uttered were copied down and later collected to form the *Qur'an* (or Koran), the holy book of Islam, considered by pious Muslims to be the divine word of God. Within a few years, and especially after his flight, or emigration (*Hijra*, or Hegira), from Mecca to Medina in the year 622 C.E.—the year 1 of the Muslim calendar—Muhammad was the acknowledged religious, political, and military leader of a new community of believers, or *Umma*, as it was called. In 630 C.E., after he had taken over Mecca and reconsecrated the *Kaaba* (a cubelike structure that had previously housed 360 idols) to Allah alone, delegations of tribes from all over Arabia accepted Muhammad's authority. The precepts of the Qur'an became, theoretically, the law of a new religious-political entity.

Although the Kaaba became the focal point of Muslim worship, and a pilgrimage to Mecca, the *Hajj*, is one of the Five Pillars of Islam (the others being the profession of faith that there is no God but Allah and that Muhammad is his messenger; prayer; fasting; and charity), Jerusalem also occupies a special place for Muslims. Sura (or chapter) 17 of the Qur'an recounts a mystical night journey of Muhammad to a spot known today to the Jews as the Temple Mount, the platform upon which Solomon's and later Herod's Temple once stood, and to the Muslims as the Noble Sanctuary, or the *Haram al-Sharif*. From there, he ascended to heaven for a vision of Allah. The Western Wall, all that remains today of Herod's Temple, and the Muslim shrines known as the Dome of the Rock and the al-Aqsa Mosque that were later built on the platform, are important symbols for both Jews and Muslims and have made Jerusalem a focal point of the Arab–Israeli conflict.

Muhammad died in 632 C.E., and it was left to his successors, the *caliphs* (who inherited his manifold functions but not his power of revelation), to put down revolts of recalcitrant tribes and then to lead Muslim Arab armies out of Arabia to conquer, within a century, an area extending from the Pyrenees in the west to the Punjab in the east and the borders of China in the north. Arabic soon became the language of the entire Middle East and Islam the dominant religion, and it remains so today.

Islam means "submission," and for Muslims the primary purpose of existence is to submit to the will of God as revealed in the Qur'an. Muslims, like Jews, believe that the state should exist to do God's will; the Qur'an, covering all aspects of living, therefore, became the foundation of a legal system for a community in which religion and politics (or "church" and "state") were one and the same thing. The *Sharia*, or "straight path," the corpus of Islamic law that developed over about three centuries, consists of the Qur'an, the traditions of the Prophet Muhammad (*Hadith*), and, for Sunni Muslims, legal points derived from analogous situations (*Qiyas*), and material often based on local traditions and customs accepted by the consensus (*Ijma*) of the community or, more accurately, by the learned men or jurists. The entire Sharia, once compiled, was considered to be divine; it continues to form the basis of the legal system in many Middle East countries today.

Islam is no more unified than Christianity, and conflicts over the question of leadership in the early community led to a schism between the Sunnis, the followers of tradition, who insisted on an elective element to the position of caliph, and the *Shia* or *Shiites*, the party, or partisans, of Ali, the fourth caliph, Muhammad's son-in-law and the father of Muhammad's only two grandchildren to survive into maturity, Hassan and Hussein. Regarding the leadership of the Umma, the Shiites insisted on the principle of designation in the house of the Prophet through Ali's family. They called their leaders *Imams*. This dispute, which continues into the present day, began as a political rather than as a theological one. The great majority of Muslims, however, are Sunnis; the Shiites constitute about 10 to 12 percent of Muslims (about 150 to 170 million), although they are a majority in Iran, Iraq, Bahrain, and Yemen.

Islam has no centralized authority, no overall clergy; a religious elite, the *ulema* (learned theologians, jurists, and teachers), wield authority. Islam is more than a religion as such. It is a sense of belonging to a cultural tradition and a kind of "secular" identity that, for many Muslims, is closely related to being an Arab. The major problem faced by Islam today is to bring about change within sanctified tradition without going against those traditions. As in Judaism, there is no division in Islam between the secular and sacred, or the temporal and the spiritual realms. Indeed, more rigorous adherents of Islam, such as members of the largely Sunni *Hamas* and *Islamic Jihad*, or the Shia *Hizbullah* groups, believe they have an obligation—which they frequently act upon—to overthrow secularist and nationalist regimes in order to create a "true" Islamic state governed according to the Sharia.

The expansion of Europe in the nineteenth century challenged the power of Islam. Because Islam had established and maintained various empires for centuries, accepting other political and religious structures on equal terms was a major problem; Muslims were especially confounded by the military and economic superiority of European colonialism. Israel is seen by Muslims and by Arabs as the creation of Western colonialist and imperialist powers, and their response to the establishment of the Jewish state was, in part at least, an example of the difficulties Muslims have in accepting the political sovereignty of a previously "tolerated minority." The sense of Islamic community that all Muslims share had been weakened by the impact of Western colonialism, but since World War II, some Muslims believe that Islam helped them in their struggle to gain political freedom and independence. Most states with Muslim majorities have created modern political and economic infrastructures and are in the often slow and painful process of accommodating Islam to modern social patterns.

Given their historical background, it is not surprising that a number of striking similarities exist among Judaism, Christianity, and Islam. They all believe in the existence of the same God. All three religions believe in a final Day of Judgment; all have prophets, in many cases the same ones; and all are intolerant of what they regard as deviation. Where they differ is in their historical experience. Thus, Christianity and Islam became universal religions whereas Judaism remained the religion of a single group. This has led to the particularism or exceptionalism that characterizes Judaism, but it is probable that had the Jews of Palestine had a different historical experience, had they taken an imperial path, for example, they too would have adopted the universalistic principle of Christians and Muslims that all mankind could—indeed should—belong to their religion.

The major departure of Islam and Judaism from Christianity stems from their different attitudes toward Jesus. Muslims and Jews do not believe the claim, accepted by Christians, that Jesus Christ was the Messiah, the Son of God, sent to redeem mankind. Indeed, it has been Judaism's unwillingness to accept this claim, at times even hostility to it, together with the perceived role of Jews in the events leading to the death of Jesus, that has led to much of the Christian hostility toward Jews throughout history. Christianity takes the view that the failure of the Jews to recognize the divinity of Jesus means that they can no longer claim to be the Chosen People, and indeed many have used the term *Chosen People* in pejorative ways to reinforce hostility against the Jews. Judaism, on the other hand, retains the continuity of the Jews as God's Chosen People, and the religion teaches that the Messiah (the anointed Savior) is yet to come.

Islam and Judaism differ from Christianity in other fundamental ways. First, neither religion has a hierarchical clergy as most Christian churches do. Because there are no sacraments, neither the ulema nor the rabbis perform sacerdotal functions as do the Christian clergy, and they do not act as mediators between the people and God. They are learned men who live in the community at large, marry, have families, and act as teachers and guides rather than as priests and bishops. Judaism differs from both Islam and Christianity in one important respect, however. Both Islam and Christianity were militarily and politically successful over the centuries, establishing empires or states in which their respective beliefs and principles were put into practice. Judaism had no such experience from the destruction of the Second Temple in 70 C.E. until the establishment of Israel in 1948.

Judaism is unique in that it is a religion limited to one people, and while not all Jews live by their Judaic traditions, religion is a central element of their history, binding them in a spiritual, as well as a historical, unity. The emphasis of Judaism upon the Jews as the Chosen People links the salvation of the Jewish people and all of mankind through a restoration of the Jews to Palestine. In this book we will examine the two pivotal events in modern Judaism, the Holocaust and the establishment of the state of Israel. Both events have raised the fundamental question of Judaism in the most dramatic way for 2,000 years—namely, the nature of the presence and role of God in history in relation to God's chosen people.

Although in many respects Judaism and Islam are similar, important differences exist that lead to tension between the two religious groups. While Judaism is not a proselytizing religion, and does not seek converts, Islam, with its universalistic implications, divides the world into two groups: the first, where Islamic law and order prevail (*Dar-al-Islam*—the House of Submission); the second, which constitutes the areas that have not yet submitted to Allah (*Dar-al-Harb*—the Abode of War). One of the important duties of Muslims is to extend Islam through all means such as international diplomacy, economic pressure, and war, if necessary. The *Jihad* (The word means to struggle or to strive but is often translated as Holy War) can be interpreted as the duty to fight a defensive rather than an aggressive war, although the term is very flexible and capable of various interpretations—indeed, it has been used to justify initiating war across a wide range of situations. We should not infer, however, that Arabs oppose Israel simply because Jihad is a duty for Muslims, just as we should not infer that because it does not seek converts, Judaism has a live-and-let-live attitude. Arabs and Israelis have other reasons besides religion to oppose each other, as we shall see in the following chapters. The establishment of Israel has not only raised central questions for Judaism; it has also dramatically highlighted a major question facing Islam today. That issue is how to accommodate other political and economic structures on equal terms. The Arab and Muslim response to Israel is, in part at least, a particularly acute example of the difficulty this poses.

A key question in both religions as far as the Arab–Israeli conflict is concerned is: What is the attitude of the religion to the outsider? Both religions are ambiguous and contradictory in relation to this question. They make positive and negative references to others and are both welcoming and exclusive. As in all religions, in both Islam and Judaism, justifications can be found to sanctify the basest as well as the noblest actions. Disturbingly, extremist religious leaders on both sides—imams and rabbis—responding, in part at least, to the perceived failure of secular nationalism to meet people's spiritual and material needs, lend their voices to the cause of violence.

The Task of the Historian

At the outset, we must ask ourselves: Just what is the task of the historian? Is the historian a participant in the events he or she describes, or simply an observer? Does the historian set out to make a political case for one position or another, or to "tell the truth"—letting the chips fall where they may? Determining what we mean by the truth is difficult enough as it is. Does the historian set out to recreate the past as fully as possible? What do we mean by this expression, and how would we set out to recreate the past? What kind of events should the historian look at—political, social, cultural, economic? Should we look at society from the top down, that is, at leaders; or from the bottom up, at those who were the actual hewers of stone and carriers of water?

There are, of course, no easy answers to these questions. It is difficult to tell where the boundaries between these categories begin and end. They are all intellectual constructs, and our perceptions and interpretations are in constant flux. In this book we have tried to relate what we regard as the most important events and to explain how both sides have interpreted the unfolding of these events.

One of the central questions historians investigate is the role of force and violence in history. Force and violence are certainly one of the major aspects of Arab–Jewish relations over the past century. How much could have been avoided? Need violence continue? These are crucial questions. It is essential, we believe, to keep in mind that history is not some sort of seamless web of necessity. There is no law of inevitability in history, however passionately politicians may argue that in such and such a case the use of force was "necessary." History is not a process determining events in which humans are powerless to act and to change things. Human agency is the key to understanding the past, as it is to an understanding of the present and future. Throughout history, there have always been alternatives to the resort to force, especially war, however unpalatable those options might have appeared to leaders at the time. Throughout this text we have tended to assess actions with this thought in mind.

All investigations must begin with an awareness of self and how we define ourselves in relation to others. The distinguishing element in the study of history is to explore how that definition relates to, and changes over, time. Central to how we define ourselves is an understanding of our relationship to the space around us. A knowledge of the environment, or at the very least the landscape, of the Middle East—especially that area embracing Palestine—is crucial to an understanding of the Arab–Israeli conflict. The most important aspect of landscape to the Jews and Arabs of Palestine is the concept of homeland and the meaning they attach to this concept.

The values people attach to such concepts are historically as well as culturally derived. A homeland provides nourishment, permanency, reassurance, and an identification with the soil, and it provides historical ties of identity. Looked at in this way, we can quickly see that Palestine/Israel takes on special significance to the two groups who have been in such bitter conflict for almost a century.

The Landscape of Palestine

Let us now turn to the landscape itself. It is impossible to understand the depth of feeling on both sides without an awareness of the ecological or environmental relationship that exists between the Jews and Arabs who inhabit the region, as well as the historical and cultural ties that link the two peoples to the land. That part of the former Ottoman Empire today thought of as Palestine received its rather arbitrary boundaries between 1920 and 1922 as the result of discussion between the great powers, following the end of World War I.

These boundaries circumscribe a total land area of about 26,320 square kilometers (10,162 square miles), which is about the size of New Jersey. It extends from the Gulf of Eilat (or the Gulf of Aqaba) in the south, to hills just south of the Litani River in Lebanon in the north, and from the Mediterranean Sea and the Sinai on the west to the Jordan River, the Dead Sea and the Arava Valley (Wadi Araba) on the east. Throughout this book, whenever we refer to Palestine, we mean the area administered by the British as a mandated territory between World War I and 1948. It does not include Transjordan, the area beyond the Jordan River, which was administered separately after 1921.

Palestine is a very hot and dry land, especially in the south, which receives little or no rain. The northern half of Palestine receives winter rain and streams run during winter. Springs and wells are to be found in the north. The River Jordan is the only perennial river in Palestine, and it, in fact, marks the border of Palestine with Syria in the north and Jordan further south. The center of the country consists of a central mass of hills running north-south. While these are often steep and rocky, their highest peaks reach an altitude of only 2,400 to 3,000 feet. On either side of the hills lie lowlands—the Maritime plain to the West and the Jordan Valley to the East. On the South sprawls the desert district now commonly known as the Negev. Bisecting the hills in the northern region on a northwest to southeast axis are the contiguous valleys of Esdraelon and Jezreel.

The hills of Palestine cover approximately 2 million acres, of which over a half million are largely uninhabitable wilderness. That area of the hills that is inhabited consists of some scattered valleys of great fertility, but overall the steepness of the hillsides, the numerous rock outcroppings, and the very high limestone content, combined with an unpredictable rainfall, make the area generally very poor agriculturally. Much of it is simply uncultivable. The terracing of hillsides and the exploitation of those springs and streams that do exist has enabled the limited cultivation of grains, olives, vines, and deciduous fruits.

The hills are surrounded by five principal plains. The largest and most important is the Maritime Plain from Rafah on the southern border to Mount Carmel in the north, which includes in its northern section the Plain of Sharon. This plain occupies over 800,000 acres of which two-thirds or more are capable of being irrigated. The mild lowland winters and the light sandy soils make this excellent citrus-growing country. The Plain of Acre covers about 140,000 acres

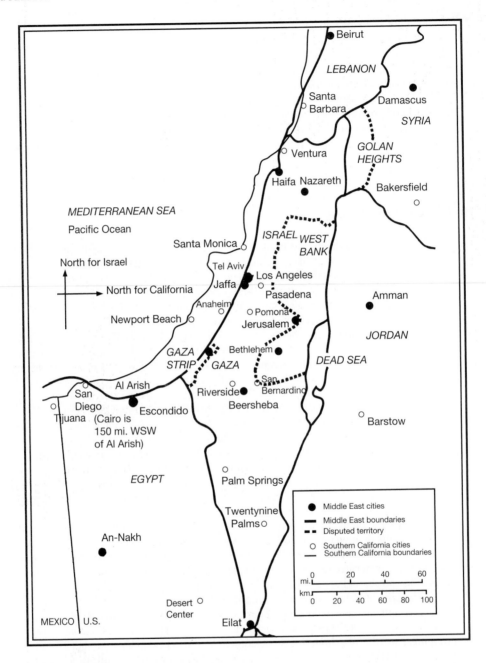

MAP INTRO.–1 Israel Superimposed on Southern California (to scale)

lying along the coast north of Haifa. Here there is plentiful water from springs and streams, and the heavy alluvial soils lead to intensive cultivation of a wide variety of vegetables, fodders, and deciduous fruits. The Plain of Esdraelon, which comprises about 100,000 acres, has traditionally been regarded as the most fertile and productive district in Palestine, and cereals

Jerusalem in the late nineteenth century.

and fruit are grown on its alluvial clays. The Huleh Plain is to be found in the extreme northeast corner of Palestine, and about one-fifth of this plain, the area to the south ending in Lake Huleh, was marshlands before it was reclaimed. Last, there is the valley of the Jordan River, which occupies about 250,000 acres. This region is extremely productive when irrigated with the waters from the Jordan River. Palestine also includes the mostly desert region south of Beersheba (the Negev), which extends over 3,140,000 acres or about 48 percent of the entire locale. Irrigated parts of this district have proven fertile.

Clearly, a very close link has existed and still continues between the landscape and the pattern of settlement in Palestine. Although historically Palestine supported a relatively low population, the various habitation patterns have reinforced, and in turn have been reinforced by, the historical, cultural, and religious experiences we outlined above. It is not surprising, then, that both Israelis and Palestinians hold deeply felt and fundamental attitudes about the landscape and their identification with it as a sacred place and homeland. Both groups have sought once again to give practical expression to these attitudes and aspirations over the past century, and in so doing have revealed vastly different visions. How those visions have led to the bloodshed of the past century will be the subject of our inquiry.

Suggestions for Further Reading

HOBSBAUM, ERIC, *On History*, London, Abacus, 1998.

ESPOSITO, JOHN, *Islam: The Straight Path*, New York, Oxford University Press, 1988.

EPSTEIN, ISIDORE, *Judaism: A Historical Presentation*, Baltimore, Penguin Books, 1959.

GOLDSCHMIDT, ARTHUR, JR., and LAWRENCE DAVIDSON, *A Concise History of the Middle East*, 8th edition, Boulder, Colorado, Westview Press, 2006.

HOURANI, ALBERT, *A History of the Arab Peoples*, Cambridge, Harvard University Press, 1991.

HUMPHREYS, R. STEPHEN, *Between Memory and Desire: The Middle East in a Troubled Age*, Berkeley, University of California Press, 1999.

JACKSON, J. B., *The Interpretation of the Ordinary Landscape*, New York, Oxford University Press, 1979.

SACHAR, HOWARD, M., *A History of Israel*, Vol. 1, 2nd ed., New York, Alfred A. Knopf, 1986.

SAID, EDWARD, *Orientalism*, London, Routledge & Kegan Paul, 1978.

SHIPLER, DAVID, *Arab and Jew: Wounded Spirits in a Promised Land, New York, Times Books*, 1986.

SMITH, CHARLES D., *Palestine and the Arab–Israeli Conflict*, 5th ed., New York, St. Martin's Press, 2004.

TESSLER, MARK A., *A History of the Israeli-Palestinian Conflict*, Bloomington, Indiana University Press, 1994.

See also the *Encyclopedia of Islam* and the *Encyclopedia Judaica*.

O N E

Palestine in the Nineteenth Century

C H R O N O L O G Y

1516–1918	Ottoman rule over Palestine
1791	Pale of Settlement established in Russian Empire
1860–1904	Life of Theodor Herzl
1879	Establishment of Anti-Semitic League
1876–1909	Rule of Sultan Abdul-Hamid II
1881	Assassination of Czar Alexander II of Russia
1882	Beginning of first aliyah
1882	Landing of first *Chibbat Zion* group at Jaffa
1882	Turkish legislation restricting Jewish immigration to Palestine
1892	Railroad between Jerusalem and Jaffa completed
1894	Trial of Alfred Dreyfus in France
1896	Publication of Herzl's *Der Judenstaat*
1897	First Zionist Congress in Basel, Switzerland; formation of World Zionist Organization
1901	Establishment of Jewish National Fund
1904	Second *aliyah* begins
1905	Railroad between Haifa and Deraa completed
1908	Young Turk Revolution
1909	Abdul-Hamid II deposed
1909	Establishment of Tel Aviv

For us to understand what was happening in nineteenth-century Palestine, we must consider the topic from several sides. We need to look at the diplomatic history of the European powers which struggled for influence in the area—notably England, France, and Russia—and the impact these nations left on the local society. We must also examine the political, socioeconomic, and cultural-ideological developments among the local population. These developments include the rise of local leaders and notables, demographic changes and economic conditions, intercommunal relationships, the status of the Jewish population, and the emergence of the Zionist and Arab national movements.

Israelis and Palestinians disagree on almost all of these issues. Throughout the conflict, apologists on both sides have made exaggerated claims about the circumstances of Palestine in the late nineteenth and early twentieth centuries. Thus, Zionist ideologues claim that there were no defined borders of Palestine; that the land was uninhabited and barren—"a land without a people for a people without a land" to quote one slogan; that Zionist settlers made the desert bloom; and that they were met with unremitting hostility by organized bands of Bedouins and had no choice but to defend themselves with arms. On the other hand, Palestinian zealots claim that Zionist settlers arrived determined to ignore or "remove" the settled population; that backed by foreign capital they secretly purchased the best lands at above market prices; and that they abandoned traditional land and labor usages, leading the local populations to assert their rights and identity and forcibly to defend themselves from being driven off their land. As with all such sweeping claims, there are some elements of truth in all these characterizations, but the situation was far more complex.

Palestine Under the Ottoman Empire

Under Ottoman rule, which lasted four centuries (1516–1918), Palestine never formed a political administrative unit of its own. It was divided into several districts, called *sanjaks*, and these were part of larger provinces or administrative units, called *vilayets*. Most of Palestine was part of the vilayet of Syria governed by the pasha of Damascus, but after 1841, following a decade of occupation of the region by Egypt, except for an area east of the Jordan River, which remained part of the vilayet of Syria, it consisted of a northern portion placed in the vilayet of Beirut and a southern portion, the sanjak of Jerusalem. (See Map 1–1.) The Ottoman government in Constantinople did not attach much importance to the Palestine districts until the middle of the nineteenth century; the area raised very little revenue, it had little military or strategic importance, and its borders were not precisely defined. The Muslim sultan did feel a political and religious obligation to protect the Holy Places of Islam, Christianity, and Judaism. His need to maintain cordial relations with the European powers meant that he also had to protect Christian and Jewish pilgrims to Palestine.

The attainment of virtual autonomy from the Ottoman Empire by Egypt in the mid-nineteenth century, as well as Anglo-French strategic rivalry to control the Suez isthmus, meant that the Palestine districts became more strategically and politically important to Constantinople. Accordingly, the Ottomans tightened their control of Syria and Palestine. The sanjak of Jerusalem was given higher status and made directly responsible to Constantinople in an attempt by the imperial government to regain central control over the region and to make the administration more efficient. Palestine had been a poor and neglected part of the Ottoman Empire. Over the previous two centuries, local governors had become independent of Ottoman control, had become corrupt, and had neglected their duties. The result was that there was considerable disorder and insecurity; public works had not been carried out; agriculture and trade had declined; and the majority of the population was impoverished and oppressed.

Much of this oppression had come from local leaders like the rural sheikhs of Nablus, the Judean Hills, and Hebron; Druze emirs in southern Lebanon and northern Palestine; and Bedouin

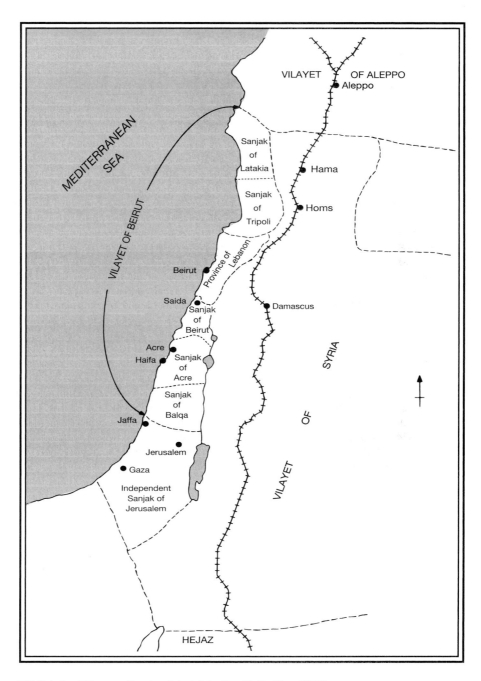

MAP 1–1   Ottoman Empire Administrative Units (Pre-1918)

Source: William R. Polk, David M. Stamler, and Edmund Asfour, *Backdrop to Tragedy* (Boston: Beacon, 1957), p. 53.

chiefs in other areas. Heads of prominent families, called notables, sought to gain political power in order to collect land taxes and security payments from pilgrims. During the second half of the nineteenth century, the Ottomans gradually reestablished central control, Bedouin attacks became less frequent, general security increased, oppression of the urban population diminished somewhat, and the European powers greatly expanded their involvement in Palestine, as in the rest of the Levant. As a result, the area's economy and the conditions of the inhabitants significantly improved. Under Sultan Abdul-Hamid II, who ruled the Ottoman Empire from 1876 to 1909, important changes took place in Palestine. Abdul-Hamid encouraged modernization in communications, education, and the military in order to strengthen his control. When he began his rule, Palestine had no railroad, hardly any carriage roads, and no developed port. There were few medical services, and disease and illiteracy were widespread. Within a few years of Abdul-Hamid's accession, new roads were opened, and European companies completed a railroad between Jerusalem and Jaffa in 1892 and another between Haifa and Deraa, Transjordan, in 1905. In reorganizing the Ottoman Empire and attempting to strengthen central control by using European engineers and investors, the sultans, paradoxically, encouraged the very European penetration of Palestine they were seeking to prevent.

The Arabs of Palestine

The Arab population of Palestine, which numbered about 446,000 in the late nineteenth century, was heterogeneous and divided. In addition to the differences among urban, rural, and nomadic populations, continual rivalries existed within the villages and among the nomads. There was a great gulf between the Palestine gentry and the peasants (*fellahin*). City dwellers had nothing but contempt for the peasants and had almost no contact with them. Much of the land in Palestine was state land (*miri*). Whether state or privately owned, the land was cultivated by fellahin who exercised a kind of communal, as opposed to formal-legal, ownership over it. The fellahin were frequently in debt and did all they could to avoid paying taxes. Peasant reluctance to pay taxes or gain legal title to their land was stimulated in part by their fear of being subject to military recruitment.

The villages of Palestine were small, isolated, and poor. In northern Palestine the vast majority of the fellahin were tenant farmers who lived in villages while working the land owned by absentee landowners, most of whom lived in Beirut or Damascus. By the time Zionist immigration began in the 1880s, the land had, legally at least, passed from the peasants to Palestinian notables, many of whom had gained wealth as tax collectors or as merchants living elsewhere. Consequently, some Arabs of Palestine identified themselves not with Palestine but with Syrian or Lebanese centers. By the last quarter of the century, only 20 percent of the land in Galilee and 50 percent of Judea remained in the hands of the fellahin. Nevertheless, the land they possessed represented two-thirds of the arable land, for much of the land purchased by the notables and absentee landowners was not being tilled. The primary identification and loyalty of the peasants was undoubtedly a kind of "village patriotism," which stemmed from their attachment to the land they worked, regardless of who had legal title to it, and to the village in which they and their families lived.

Villagers supported themselves by growing crops and raising a few sheep or goats. Methods of agriculture had changed very little over the centuries, although demand for Palestinian grain, cotton, and citrus fruits had increased in the last half of the century. Nevertheless, many villagers sought some relief from their poverty by moving into the towns. The social relations of the village were based on kinship; this was because the village was frequently made up of one or more extended families. Thus, what might seem to modern Europeans to be a lack of privacy, or overcrowding, in the village was to the Palestinian peasant a sense of security, continuity, and familial cohesiveness. In southern Palestine most of the population were nomadic pastoralists who made a meager living through raising and selling sheep, camels, and goats.

There were also religious divisions within the Arab population of Palestine. Sunni Muslims, Shiites, and Druze were at odds, and there were constant rivalries between Muslims and Christian Arabs (approximately 16 percent of the population—mostly Greek Orthodox). The Muslims of Palestine were overwhelmingly Sunni, and the local Muslim elites to whom they gave their allegiance gained their political identity and position through loyalty to the sultan. As a result of all the factors mentioned above, there was little sense of Palestinian nationalism among the Muslim Arabs during this period. Gradually, however, Christian Arabs were influenced by their European Christian contacts, both in the Middle East and in Europe, and a sense of nationalism began to emerge. Christian Arabs participated in a literary and cultural movement in the late nineteenth century that led to the rediscovery of the glorious heritage of the Arabs and reawakened a sense of ethnic identity. Initially, these Arab nationalists were concerned about parity between Arabs and Turks and between Arab Muslims and Arab Christians within the Ottoman Empire. (See Document 1–1.)

Further significant changes occurred in the first fifteen years of the twentieth century. The Young Turk revolution of 1908 brought to the forefront Turkish nationalists who intended to preserve the Ottoman Empire through ruthless policies of centralization and Islamization. The seeds of Arab nationalism sprouted from the soil of Turkish nationalism, as historian Zeine N. Zeine has noted. Some recent scholars have even suggested that Arab nationalism was "invented" by disenchanted Syrian Arab notables who lost their local administrative positions as a result of the Young Turk rejection of notions of decentralization and autonomy for non-Turkish ethnic groups. (See Document 1–2.) In any event, groups now formed that were dedicated to achieving political independence as Arabs from the Ottoman Empire. As time passed, nationalist sentiment among Arabs in Palestine also grew, partly in response to the strong nationalist feelings of Jews toward Palestine, or *Eretz Yisrael* (the Land of Israel).

Jews in Nineteenth-Century Palestine

The Jewish population of Palestine and Syria at the beginning of the nineteenth century totaled about 25,000. Most were Sephardim, that is, descendants of Spanish Jewry and ancient local families, and they were Ottoman subjects. The rest were Ashkenazim, that is, Jews of European origin who had come to the Holy Land throughout the centuries, and they retained their former citizenships. The Jews lived mostly in cities; about half of them lived in the four towns in Palestine particularly holy to Jews—Jerusalem, Hebron, Safed, and Tiberias—and half in the Syrian cities of Aleppo, Damascus, Beirut, and Tripoli. The Muslim-Ottoman state was organized on a system of self-governing groups (*millets*), and the Jewish communities were given a considerable degree of autonomy and self-government in matters of religious worship, education, and other areas. Overall, however, the position of Jews was precarious. The Ottoman state was based on the principle of Muslim superiority, and the Jews, along with the Christians, were regarded as infidels and second-class citizens (Dhimmis) and had to pay a special poll tax (jizyah) for the protection of the state and as a sign of their inferior status.

Jews were subject to a number of discriminatory regulations. For example, their testimony against Muslims in a court of law was not accepted; they were normally not eligible for appointment to the highest administrative offices; they were forbidden to carry arms or to serve in the army; and they were often subjected to oppression, extortion, or violence by both the local authorities and the Muslim population. During the 1840s and 1850s, the position of Jews in Palestine improved, however. This significant change in their religious, economic, and political conditions led to a considerable increase in the numbers of Palestinian Jews through immigration from Europe.

The improvement in the situation of Jews in Palestine coincided with the end of the decade of Egyptian rule of Palestine and Syria, which occurred between 1831 and 1840. The change was brought about partly because of reforms within the Ottoman Empire itself (the *Tanzimat* reform), which aimed at political and religious equality for all Ottoman subjects, and partly because of increasing indirect European involvement and intervention in the affairs of the empire. Consular reports from the 1850s indicate, for example, that Jews obtained more redress from the local governors in Palestine and that the oppression of the Turkish governors almost completely ceased. Jews observed their religion without opposition, and they gradually obtained better treatment and more justice in the courts. Some European consulates, particularly the British, and to a lesser extent the Russian, Austrian, and Prussian, also intervened more actively on behalf of the Jews of *their* nationalities.

The British government in particular began showing an interest in the Jews of Palestine. This interest was both humanitarian and political. Even at this early stage, Viscount Palmerston, the British foreign secretary, perceived an emerging Jewish national feeling for Palestine, and he hoped that he could gain the support of the Jewish community for British aims in the Middle East in return for British protection. During the 1850s the Russian government also assisted Russian and Polish Jews in Palestine and even allowed Jewish emigrants to travel cheaply in Russian ships that were sailing from Odessa to Palestine. Not surprisingly, the number of Jews emigrating from Europe, and especially from Russia, dramatically increased during these decades. Thus, the Jewish population of Jerusalem increased from around 5,000 in 1839 to about 10,000 by the late 1850s. Of course, European protection of Jews was not comprehensive because most Jews in Palestine were Ottoman subjects, and sometimes foreign protection was a liability rather than an asset, because such Jews were regarded as collaborating with foreign powers.

In the final analysis, the welfare of local Jews was dependent upon the attitudes of the local Ottoman authorities and the Muslim population, and during the second half of the nineteenth century the attitudes of both these groups toward Jews underwent a gradual improvement because of the new generation of more liberal pashas. The Jews of Palestine also made an effort to live independently of assistance from Europe, making their living as artisans, craftsmen, and agricultural workers. At the same time, Western European Jews were becoming increasingly aware of the depressed condition of their brethren in Eastern Europe and increased the level of their aid. The improved Muslim-Jewish relations provided the Jews of Palestine the opportunity to consolidate their position, to advance socially and economically, and, perhaps even more important, to increase considerably in number through emigration from Europe and thus become an important element in the country.

The Birth of Modern Zionism

The History of the Jews in Europe

Like Arab nationalism, Jewish nationalism remained a religious and cultural phenomenon until the nineteenth century, when the idea of creating a Jewish state in Eretz Yisrael assumed the character of a political ideology. It was a product of the European environment and was influenced by Western ideologies like rationalism, secular nationalism, and imperialism. The situation of the Jews in Europe had taken a different course from that of the Jews who lived under Islam, and it is necessary to look briefly at that history if we are to understand the strength of Jewish feeling toward establishing a Jewish state in Palestine.

The history of Jews in Christian Europe reflects very little credit on European Christianity. It is a story of almost uninterrupted oppression and persecution of Jews throughout all the countries of Europe. And it culminated in the horrific genocide of Hitler's "final solution," known as the Holocaust. Historians have offered several reasons for the shocking ways Jews were treated in Europe, especially during and after the Middle Ages, and it is difficult to escape the conclusion that it was based largely on irrational and ill-informed religious prejudice. This has led most interpretations of Jewish history to concentrate on the religious and ideological aspects of anti-Semitism and Jewish responses to it, to the exclusion of social and economic factors present. We believe that this emphasis distorts our understanding of Jewish history. The traditional view tends to stress the image of Jews as victims and emphasizes the importance of Zionism as an ideology in modern Jewish history. Recent historians, however, while acknowledging the importance of religious identification as a factor in shaping both Christian and Muslim attitudes and behavior toward Jews, have drawn a more complete picture of Jewish history.

By placing more importance on the socioeconomic elements in the story, recent historical interpretations have restored dignity and pride to Jews. Throughout European history Jews made significant contributions in all walks of life; something quite inconsistent with the picture of a small religious, passive minority suffering unmitigated persecution and oppression. There is no doubt that Jews suffered persecution because of their religion at various times in European history, but that is far from the whole story. The Jewish people have maintained their ethnic, religious, and linguistic characteristics through the centuries primarily because they have been an ethnic minority that has fulfilled a distinct socioeconomic role in the societies in which they have lived. Jews migrated from Palestine voluntarily in the Classical period, forming merchant classes around the Mediterranean basin. In the Roman Empire, Jews played an important role in the economy as traders, financiers, goldsmiths, jewelers, and craftsmen, and, in doing so, they preserved their ethnic identity and separateness. The destruction of the Second Temple by the Romans in the year 70 C.E. led to a considerable increase in the number of the Jewish Diaspora, as those Jews who lived outside Palestine were called, and they were gradually transformed into a mercantile class.

After the Christianization of the Roman Empire in the fourth century, and during the Middle Ages, although Jews were permitted communal autonomy and self-government, religious antagonism against them led to Jews being gradually deprived of their rights as citizens, and they were increasingly limited to certain professions. In the High Middle Ages, in England, e.g., the Jews functioned primarily as moneylenders and were dependent upon the rulers for protection. When Italian and other bankers began to take over their limited economic functions, the Jews were expelled in 1290. They were expelled from France by the end of the next century, and from Spain by 1492. Where Jews remained in Europe, they were forced into prescribed areas that we know as *ghettos*. The first ghetto appeared in northern Italy in the sixteenth century. Many Jews left Western Europe for the Ottoman Empire and Eastern Europe—particularly Greater Lithuania (which included much of what is today western Russia and the Ukraine) and Poland—where they were initially welcomed because of their commercial skills. The Jewish community of greater Poland became the largest in the world, with impressive political and cultural institutions, but economic rivalry and religious antagonism eventually impoverished and threatened that community as well.

The growth of industrial capitalism more or less altered the economic function of Jews in Western Europe, and Jews gradually integrated into the capitalist and professional classes. The rationalism of the eighteenth-century Enlightenment had also benefited Jews and paved the way for their "emancipation" after the French Revolution. The ideals of the French Revolution nurtured the ideology of secular nationalism, so that by the end of the nineteenth century Jews had widely assimilated into the population of most Western European countries.

In Eastern Europe, however, the slow rate of industrialization and the hostile political and religious conditions led to the dislocation of Jews there, forcing them to seek new social and geographical horizons. As for the Russian Empire, ever since 1791 the Jews had been restricted to a region between the Black Sea and the Baltic known as the Pale of Settlement, where they lived in poverty in small towns called *shtetls*. Much of the Pale was formerly Poland (in the late eighteenth century Poland was partitioned among Russia, Prussia, and Austria), and about three-quarters of a million of the inhabitants of the Pale were former Polish Jews. Jews were excluded from the larger Russian cities and other parts of the country. In Czarist Russia, the ideas of the French Revolution were anathema, and Jews continued to be a scapegoat of the Russian people and Orthodox Church. Throughout the century Russian Jews were subjected to numerous restrictions and state-sponsored persecutions (*pogroms*). By 1850, there were about 2.3 million Jews in Russia, and despite massive emigration, forced conscription into the Russian Army, and deportations, this figure was 5 million by the end of the century. In the 1880s, under the impact of successive savage pogroms in Russia and discriminatory legislation, many Eastern European Jews fled to the United States and, to a far lesser extent, to Palestine.

Toward the end of the century, building on popular fear and suspicion of the Jews, an unknown author working for the Russian secret police concocted an infamous forgery that came to be known as the "Protocols of the Learned Elders of Zion." The Protocols, which were purportedly the records of an alleged conference of leaders of world Jewry bent on world domination, were eventually translated into all major languages. They contributed to hatred of the Jews in both Western and Eastern Europe especially in the twentieth century, and they have been used by enemies of Israel in the Arab–Israeli conflict. Even today, the Protocols are widely available in the Arab countries, and they were reportedly a favorite gift of the Saudi kings to their visitors.

The Russian government sponsored massacres, restrictions, and persecutions of Jews, following the assassination of Czar Alexander II of Russia in 1881 in which one of the plotters was found to be a young Jewess. The restrictions enforced within the Pale and in other Russian areas led to a mass migration in the next twenty years. Over a million people fled to the United States between 1880 and 1900, and this figure was to reach over 2.6 million by 1914. Others stayed and tried to revolutionize the system—but few chose this course. Those who did joined a radical socialist organization called the *Bund*, the *Allgemeine Yiddisher Arbeiterbund*, or General Union of Jewish Workers of Lithuania, Poland, and Russia, which was founded in Vilna in 1897. Although it represented only a minority of the Jewish population, it constituted a dynamic faction within the Russian revolutionary intelligentsia. The Bund, which united Jewish workers against the Czarist regime, advocated secular Yiddish culture as a way of maintaining Jewish identity.

Another solution to the plight of the Jews in Russia and Europe was the reaffirmation of Jewish identity in a secular, socialist form through a movement whose goal was an autonomous Jewish nation-state. This was advocated by Leo Pinsker in his book, *Auto-Emancipation*, written in 1882, following the 1881 pogroms. Pinsker argued that Jews would never be accepted as equals in Europe unless they made the effort to become a nation among the nations. He was eventually persuaded that Eretz Yisrael was the most suitable place for a Jewish state. However, the movement that would come to be known as Zionism received its greatest impetus from events that occurred in France in the 1890s, as we shall see.

Theodor Herzl and the Emergence of Political Zionism

Theodor Herzl, more than any other person, has become identified with the emergence of modern Zionism. His life (1860–1904) has acquired legendary proportions, and his portrait, one of the trademarks of Zionism, has become a powerful symbol for Zionists. In many ways this is strange, because few of Herzl's ideas were new or original. He had no financial backing and no political support; indeed, many Jewish leaders saw him as an eccentric, irresponsible egotist. He was not a political extremist; in fact, his politics were conservative and reflected his middle-class background. But Herzl was incredibly successful in bringing ideas that were known only in Jewish communities to the attention of the world and into the general

Theodor Herzl.

consciousness of the age. He transformed one solution to the plight of Jews into a major issue in world politics.

Herzl was born in Budapest where his father was a well-to-do merchant. When he was young, his family moved to Vienna where he graduated in law and became one of the most popular journalists of the liberal Viennese newspaper, the *Neue Freie Presse*. Herzl was a typical product of the emancipation of European Jewry, and as a journalist in Vienna, and from 1891 in Paris, he worried about the increasing ambiguity of the position of Jews in Europe and the anti-Semitism that was so dramatically illustrated by the notorious Dreyfus Affair.

Alfred Dreyfus was a Jewish officer of the French General Staff who in 1894 was convicted of treason and sentenced to a life term on Devil's Island. Herzl was one of many who believed that Dreyfus had been framed and the trial rigged. That this was the case emerged later with the confession in 1899 of one of the French officers involved, and the lifting of Dreyfus's sentence, following a second retrial, in 1906. But Herzl, who covered the trial and public disgrace of Dreyfus for the *Neue Freie Presse*, was shocked by the anti-Semitism the trial unleashed in France, the land of Liberty, Equality, and Fraternity. The Dreyfus Affair became the symbol of Jewish inequality and anti-Semitism in Europe and confirmed in Herzl's mind the belief that anti-Semitism was an incurable Gentile pathology. The only solution was for Jews to have a nation-state of their own. Herzl set out this proposition in his book *Der Judenstaat* (*The Jews' State*), published in 1896. (See Document 1–3.)

An early theoretician of Zionism had been Moses Hess, a German Jew who in his youth was associated with Karl Marx and Friedrich Engels. Hess, unlike Marx, maintained his Judaism and kept up the Yiddish he learned as a child. Hess wrote two works outlining his ideas for Jewish return to Palestine: *Rome and Jerusalem* (published in 1862) and *Plan for the Colonization of the Holy Land* (1867). However, Hess's books, which advocated the colonization of

Palestine as a solution to the Jewish problem, were not considered seriously, as Western Jews felt settled in the countries in which they had lived for hundreds of years, and Eastern Jews were yet to experience the pogroms of twenty years later. Herzl, as noted above, had also been foreshadowed by Leo Pinsker. The word Zionism itself was probably first used in an article published in 1886 by Nathan Birnbaum. The term has come to mean the movement to reestablish a Jewish nation in Palestine, although for many years the more vague phrase *national home* was used.

The turning point in the history of Zionism came with the first Zionist Congress, which met in Basel (Switzerland) on August 29, 1897, with 204 delegates from all over the world. (Interestingly, as we noted above, this was the same year as the founding of the Bundist movement in Russia.) The assembly defined the objective of Zionism: "to create for the Jewish people a home in Palestine secured by public law." To achieve this goal, the assembly resolved to promote systematically the settlement of Palestine with Jewish agriculturalists, artisans, and craftsmen; to organize all Jews and strengthen the national consciousness of Jews; and to seek the approval of whatever governments were necessary to achieve the goals of Zionism. (See Document 1–4.)

What is important to recognize about these goals is their vagueness or open-endedness. We must keep this in mind when we consider the response of Herzl and later Zionist leaders to offers that were made to them by various governments in subsequent years. Herzl was quite prepared, for example, to consider the British offer made in 1902 of the el-Arish region in the Sinai Peninsula, and the offer in the following year of a territory in Kenya (the so-called Uganda Plan), although Russian Jews were not happy with these schemes. Cyprus had also been considered briefly in 1899. Nevertheless, however vague Herzl's Zionist vision, dependence upon a European power was prophetic of what later happened.

Although Herzl left open the specific location of the Jewish homeland, he had a clear idea of how to implement the plan. A Jewish company would be formed to purchase land and to organize the settlers, rather like the Rhodesian experience. Following the Basel Congress, the newly formed World Zionist Organization set out to build the financial and economic instruments and political structure to achieve these aims. In 1901, the Jewish National Fund was established for the purchase of land; and in 1908, the Palestine Land Development Company, linked to the Jewish National Fund, was also created to assist in the colonization. Herzl continued his efforts to gain international support for the plan, but he was unsuccessful in his negotiations with the Sultan Abdul-Hamid, with the German kaiser, and, in October 1902, with British Colonial Secretary Joseph Chamberlain. Although a persuasive speaker and a striking figure of a man, Herzl was unable to gain the support he needed from Europe's political leaders, or, indeed, within the Zionist organization he had done so much to create.

Herzl's political goals, for example, were not supported by all Zionist leaders. Asher Ginsberg, a Russian intellectual better known by his pen name Achad Ha-Am ("One of the People"), one of the most influential voices in the Zionist movement, feared the consequences of a purely political entity. He saw Zionism as a spiritual-cultural phenomenon, and he envisaged the gradual building up of Palestine by only those committed to the task. His practical Zionism was aimed at both colonization and cultural activity that would heighten the sense of belonging to the Jewish people. But Achad Ha-Am's sense of Jewish ethics led him to reject the view of those Zionist leaders who saw Palestine as a "land without people for a people without land." He recognized the Arab presence in Palestine, and in an 1891 essay again attacking the "mere" political Zionism of Herzl, he warned against neglecting the Arab question. Throughout the subsequent history of the Zionist movement, many individuals and groups supported his attitude. Zionism is attacked by opponents as an imperialistic movement because of its approach to the Arab population of Palestine, but it must be remembered that in the late nineteenth century most European nations expressed identical attitudes toward indigenous non-European peoples.

The First Zionists Arrive in Palestine

The emancipation of the Jews in Western Europe aroused powerful anti-Semitic reflexes among the middle classes. Racial anti-Semitism—which defined and attacked Jews in terms of race rather than religion—emerged in both Germany and France from the 1840s on. Racial anti-Semitism relied on pseudoscientific Social-Darwinian theories to "prove" the superiority of the Aryan race over the inferior Semitic race, and it was largely in response to this outbreak of anti-Semitism that modern Zionism emerged as presenting a viable alternative. It became clear to some that complete emancipation and equality of Jews was unobtainable even in advanced and enlightened Western Europe. Their solution was an autonomous Jewish nation-state.

This aspiration tapped into another trend among the traditionalist Jews of Eastern Europe—that of preserving Judaism and the Jewish tradition through the reestablishment of a religiously based Jewish culture located in the traditional Jewish homeland Eretz Yisrael. The coming together of these two aspirations—one secular, the other religious—led to the birth of modern Zionism as a political ideology and organizational tool, and it contributed to the settlements that became the foundation of the economic, social, and cultural rebirth of the Jewish nation. Small groups of Jewish youths (mainly students) met in Russia and other parts of Eastern Europe and planned the kind of settlements they would set up in Eretz Yisrael.

The first small group of the new movement, known as *Chibbat*—or *Chovevei-Zion* (Lovers of Zion)—numbering fourteen and including one woman, landed at Jaffa on July 7, 1882. This was the beginning of the first modern wave of Jewish immigrants to Palestine, which lasted from 1881 to 1903 and is known to Zionists as the first *aliyah*, which means "going up" to the Land of Israel. By 1903 about twenty new agricultural villages had been founded, about 90,000 acres of land had been purchased, and some 10,000 Jews had settled in the country, about half of them on the soil. Hebrew was spoken and taught in a few schools, but by and large the settlers were not accustomed to farm work; they had insufficient funds, and had it not been for the generous support of Baron Edmond de Rothschild, who assisted the newcomers, the entire venture could have failed. As it was, the scheme had come to a standstill by 1903.

The French philanthropist Baron Edmond de Rothschild was not a Zionist, but he was interested in sponsoring Jewish settlement in Palestine as an investment and as an act of piety. He bought land from the Arab *effendis* (landowners), now and then using bribes to do so, and drove the fellahin off the land. They were then replaced by Jewish settlers. By 1900, he had subsidized over 350 families and 19 Jewish settlements and had established a Jewish agricultural school; altogether there was a population of around 5,000 and over 68,000 acres. Until he transferred the venture to the Jewish Colonization Association, led by Baron Maurice de Hirsch in 1900, Rothschild maintained strict control over his settlements, and several Jewish settlers soon took to employing Arabs as peasant farmers, in some cases treating them with hostility and cruelty, rather than working the land themselves.

By 1904, these early Jewish settlements were Jewish in name only, as almost all the labor was performed by Arab peasant workers. One observer noted that for every few dozen Jews, there appeared to be hundreds of Arabs. We should note that Rothschild was not the only wealthy Jew the Ottoman sultan had allowed to purchase land for Jewish settlement in Palestine. Sir Moses Montefiore, a British Jew, was permitted to buy land as early as 1856, and the Belgian railroad magnate Baron Maurice de Hirsch, an associate of Rothschild, was another who poured millions of francs into Palestinian settlement schemes.

Socialist and Zionist Jews in Palestine

The second wave of Jewish immigration, which began in 1904, was made up of many young Russian pioneers who were committed to a return to the land. Dismayed at the course that Zionist colonization had been taking, they attempted to reintroduce the idea of Jewish labor. They differed from the earlier settlers also in that the land they worked was purchased by the Jewish National Fund, established in 1901, and was deemed to be inalienable Jewish national property and thus protected from property speculation and the kinds of contracts imposed on the settlers by Rothschild. The new pioneers were also strongly influenced by socialist ideas, and many belonged to the *Poalei-Zion* (Socialist or Labor Zionist) party that was formed between 1903 and 1906. Among the leaders of this group were David Ben-Gurion and Izhak Ben-Zvi, and they introduced a spirit of enterprise in the settlements and also in the towns. This aliyah, for example, established the garden suburb of Tel Aviv on the outskirts of Jaffa in 1909. By 1914, it had a population of 2,000. In 1909, the first collective settlement, or *kibbutz*, Deganiah— the birthplace of Moshe Dayan—was established, and, in 1921, the first *moshav*, or cooperative village—an outgrowth of the kibbutz—was established.

Of the approximately 40,000 new immigrants who arrived between 1904 and the outbreak of World War I, a very large number left the country because of the inhospitable climate and conditions. Some estimate the figure of emigrants as high as 90 percent. By 1914, there were about forty Jewish settlements in Palestine, owning about 100,000 acres, but only about 4 percent of this land was owned by the Jewish National Fund. According to Justin McCarthy, in his study of the population of Palestine, the total population at that time was approximately 722,000, of whom approximately 60,000 were Jews. Of these, about 12,000 belonged to kibbutzim and moshavim.

Many Zionists have explained the increase in Jewish settlement in Palestine as a reflection of the growing appeal and strength of Zionism. The difficulty with this explanation is that, despite the deep feeling of attachment to the land of Israel, which is such a distinctive feature of Jewish self-identity, the simple reality is that most Jews did *not* move to the land of Zion—the land they prayed to be delivered to three times a day. This is the paradox of Zionism. Only about 1 percent of the almost 3 million Jews who emigrated from Russia in the thirty-five years following 1880 went to Palestine, and very few emigrated from Western Europe. Zionism, with its assertion that Palestine was the only legitimate home for the Jewish people, was not the answer to the "Jewish question" for the great majority of Jews. This is largely because Zionism was not seen as a solution to the traditional Jewish problems of economic, political, social, religious, and racial oppression in Europe. Indeed, the Jewish experience in the United States, where so many settled, has proven a viable alternative to resettlement in Palestine. And despite the exceptions, in the period between 1815 and 1914, Jews had moved from the periphery to the center of European society; they had been great beneficiaries of the Enlightenment, Emancipation, and Industrial Revolution. From any conceivable point of view, the nineteenth century was the best century Jews had ever experienced, collectively and individually. The European Jewish population increased from 2 million at the end of the eighteenth century to 7.5 million in 1880 and 13 million by 1914. This was twice the rate of population increase of non-Jews. The Jewish problem by the end of the nineteenth century was a new one: How could Jews and Christians define themselves in an emancipated and liberal secular environment where none of the traditional religious barriers existed?

The nineteenth century saw the emergence of the modern, secular liberal state in Europe, and increasingly Christians began to identify themselves in these secular and ethnic terms. Zionism was the Jewish answer to establishing this secular identity—a national state for Jews. It is sometimes called "secular messianism." It was this nationalist dimension that transformed the passive, quietistic, and pious hope of the Return to Zion into an effective social force. Zionism, then, was not simply an assertion of the links of Jews to Palestine; nor was it just a reaction of a people to persecution. It was a quest for self-determination and liberation in a modern, secular, and liberal age. Zionism was also a recognition that it was futile, impossible, and pointless to try to fight anti-Semitism; Zionism was an escape from it. Looking back, especially at events in Nazi Germany, Zionist fears seem to have been reinforced beyond all measure. At the same time we must be careful not to accept the assumption of some Zionist proponents that the subsequent establishment of Israel was an inevitable culmination of Jewish history. As we shall see in a later chapters, European anti-Semitism and the Holocaust did as much as Zionism to secure a Jewish state in Palestine.

The Jewish and Arab Communities of Palestine on the Eve of World War I

As noted above, by the outbreak of World War I, the Jewish community, called the *Yishuv*, numbered about 60,000 people, or slightly less than 10 percent of the total population of Palestine. This represented a higher proportion of Jews than in any other country, and in some major centers, like Jerusalem, they represented a majority of the population. The Jewish community presented a strange paradox, however. It constituted the center of traditional Judaism and of the Jewish national movement, but at the same time it was the most divided Jewish community in the world. Not only did it fail to establish an organization uniting the Jewish population of the country as a whole, but it also had great difficulty in unifying individual local communities.

Internal divisions before 1914 were so deeply entrenched in the social character of the Yishuv that even "practical" Zionists, those determined to establish a modern title to Palestine through Jewish economic enterprise and colonization, were unable to achieve much success. Events in the Ottoman Empire after 1908 set in motion a process that did lead to the overall organization and unification of the Yishuv, but, by 1914, this outcome had not been achieved. Even the millet framework of the Ottoman Empire, which, following the millet law of 1865, granted fairly wide judicial powers to the rabbinical authorities, did not unite the Jews of Palestine—again because it applied only to Ottoman subjects. The great majority of Jews who migrated to Palestine up until the 1880s retained their previous nationalities, and the division between the Sephardic (non-European) Jews and the Ashkenazic (European) Jews kept them apart organizationally, ethnically, liturgically, and linguistically. Attachment to a particular ethnic or national community was stronger for most Jews than attachment to the Yishuv as a whole.

The new settlements of the early 1880s—the "new" Yishuv—carried with them the idea of national unity, but they lacked cohesion from the very beginning. They were not the result of a comprehensive organization or program but were founded by various associations and individuals who lacked a practical economic plan. Nor did they consider the relationships that should exist among the new settlements and the existing Jewish communities, the local population, or the government. Indeed, the early groups did little beyond purchasing land and setting up newly formed settlements. They did not seek Ottoman citizenship but, as in the case of one of the first such settlements, Rosh Pina, instead sought to establish separate Jewish settlements adjacent to existing Arab communities under the protection of the European consuls.

While there was contact between the existing Jewish community and the new settlers, there was little sign of communal unity before 1908, although some young intellectuals, merchants, and professionals did form groups such as *Bnei Israel* and *Bnei Yehuda* to overcome communal divisions. The Chibbat Zion movement attempted unsuccessfully to unite the various national communities. The conflict was based on ideological and practical differences between the old and new Yishuv. The new settlers regarded the existing Jewish community as nonproductive, living off *halukkah* (donations from Jews abroad). The older community, which comprised a large number of artisans, unskilled laborers, small shopkeepers, and Talmudic scholars, did live a rather precarious life. Nevertheless, they resisted attempts to change their traditional ways. Some of the new Yishuv also moved into the cities, but where they did so, in towns like Jaffa and Haifa, they took up trades and commerce so as to be independent of overseas support. The Young Turk revolution in 1908 highlighted the divisions between the old and new Yishuvim. The older Sephardic intelligentsia and leadership saw the revolution as leading to Jewish development within the Ottoman Empire. The new Yishuv and "practical" Zionists, on the other hand, believed that little could be achieved through negotiations with Constantinople and stressed the importance of strengthening the Yishuv in Palestine independently of Constantinople.

As for the Arab population, there was little unified opposition to Jewish immigration and land purchases in the late nineteenth and early twentieth centuries. Ottoman officials and large landowners in the north seemed willing to ignore regulations restricting Jewish immigration and land sales. Local authorities frequently allowed Jewish land purchases in return for financial

Tel Aviv in 1921 with the Arab city of Jaffa in the background.

Jewish settlers in early twentieth-century Palestine.

favors. Initial Arab peasant opposition subsided when the peasants realized that Jewish landowners would maintain the tradition of permitting them to work the land and keep their income. The number of Jewish settlers was too small to have any serious impact upon Arab agriculture, especially in the hill country. Interestingly, public opposition to Zionist settlement was led by the Greek Orthodox Christians of Palestine. The editors of the two newspapers most vociferous in their hostility to Jewish settlement and exclusiveness, *al-Karmil* (established in 1908) and *Filastin* (1911), were both Greek Orthodox.

Palestinian Arab life at the outbreak of World War I was very different than it had been only a century earlier. The notable families especially had benefited from the economic links with and technologies imported from Europe. They sent their children to private schools (sometimes in Europe), and the gulf between the rich and poor became increasingly evident. The fellahin were impoverished by taxes to pay for the improvements the coastal townspeople enjoyed.

Palestine was at a critical juncture as far as relations between Palestinian Arabs and Jews were concerned. There was, on the one hand, a rapidly increasing Jewish population with very different attitudes and aspirations from the traditional Jewish population both with regard to the future of the land itself and the existing Arab population. And, on the other hand, there was an Arab population experiencing dramatic changes as the result of the actions of their own leaders, as well as those of the Jewish arrivals and their supporters overseas. Not only was some of the Arab land they worked on being sold to Jewish settlers, but Palestine was being slowly but surely integrated into the European world economy. This was bringing with it changes in the traditional methods of agriculture and in the government and administration of their lives. Finally, the region was being drawn into the diplomatic vortex of the world powers, and following World War I Palestine was to change in ways no one could have foreseen in 1914.

Suggestions for Further Reading

ANTONIUS, GEORGE, *The Arab Awakening: The Story of the Arab Nationalist Movement*, Simon Publications, 2001.

HAIM, SYLVIA, Ed., *Arab Nationalism: An Anthology*, Berkeley, University of California Press, 1964.

HERTZBERG, ARTHUR, Ed., *The Zionist Idea*, New York, Atheneum, 1969.

HOURANI, ALBERT, *Arabic Thought in the Liberal, Age, 1978–1939*. Cambridge University Press, 1983.

KHALIDI, RASHID, Ed., *The Origins of Arab Nationalism*, New York, Columbia University Press, 1991.

————, *Palestinian Indentity: The Construction of Modern National Consciousness*, New York, Columbia University Press, 1997.

KHALIDI, WALID, *Before Their Diaspora: A Photographic History of the Palestinians, 1876–1948*, Washington, D.C., Institute for Palestinian Studies, 1984.

LAQUEUR, WALTER, *A History of Zionism*, New York, Weidenfeld & Nicholson, 1974.

MANDEL, NEVILLE, *The Arabs and Zionism Before World War I*, Berkeley, University of California Press, 1976.

MA'OZ, MOSHE, Ed., *Studies on Palestine During the Ottoman Period*, Jerusalem, Magnes Press, 1975.

MCCARTHY, JUSTIN, *The Population of Palestine: Population, History and Statistics of the Late Ottoman Period and the Mandate*, New York, Columbia University Press, 1990.

MENDES-FLOHR, PAUL, AND JEHUDA REINHARZ, Eds., *The Jew in the Modern World: A Documentary History,* 2nd ed., New York, Oxford University Press, 1995.

MUSLIH, MUHAMMAD Y., *The Origins of Palestinian Nationalism*, New York, Columbia University Press, 1988.

PAWEL, ERNST, *The Labyrinth of Exile: A Life of Theodor Herzl*, New York, Farrar, Straus & Giroux, 1989.

SHAFIR, GERSHON, *Land, Labor and the Origins of the Israeli-Palestinian Conflict 1882–1914*, New York, Cambridge University Press, 1989.

DOCUMENT 1-1

Program of the League of the Arab Fatherland: Negib Azoury

There is nothing more liberal than the league's program.

The league wants, before anything else, to separate the civil and the religious power, in the interest of Islam and the Arab nation, and to form an Arab empire stretching from the Tigris and the Euphrates to the Suez Isthmus, and from the Mediterranean to the Arabian Sea.

The mode of government will be a constitutional sultanate based on the freedom of all the religions and the equality of all the citizens before the law. It will respect the interests of Europe, all the concessions and all the privileges which had been granted to her up to now by the Turks. It will also respect the autonomy of the Lebanon, and the independence of the principalities of Yemen, Nejd, and Iraq.

The league offers the throne of the Arab Empire to that prince of the Khedivial family of Egypt who will openly declare himself in its favor and who will devote his energy and his resources to this end.

It rejects the idea of unifying Egypt and the Arab Empire under the same monarchy, because the Egyptians do not belong to the Arab race; they are of the African Berber family and the language which they spoke before Islam bears no similarity to Arabic. There exists, moreover, between Egypt and the Arab Empire a natural frontier which must be respected in order to avoid the introduction, in the new state, of the germs of discord and destruction. Never, as a matter of fact, have the ancient Arab caliphs succeeded for any length of time in controlling the two countries at the same time.

The Arab fatherland also offers the universal religious caliphate over the whole of Islam to that sherif (descendant of the Prophet) who will sincerely embrace its cause and devote himself to this work. The religious caliph will have as a completely independent political state the whole of the actual vilayet of Hijaz, with the town and the territory of Medina, as far as Aqaba. He will enjoy the honors of a sovereign and will hold a real moral authority over all the Muslims of the world.

Le Réveil de la Nation Arabe dans l'Asie Turque en Présence des Intéréts et des Rivalités des Puissances Étrangères, de la Curie Romaine et du Patriarcat Oecuménique (Paris, 1905), pp. 245–247, 248. (S. G. H.)

Source: Sylvia Haim, *Arab Nationalism: An Anthology* (Berkeley: University of California Press, 1964), pp. 81–82.

DOCUMENT 1-2

Announcement to the Arabs, Sons of Qahtan

*See how on the day of battle we fill
the universe with flame and fire*

O Sons of Qahtan! O Descendants of Adnan! Are you asleep? And how long will you remain asleep? How can you remain deep in your slumber when the voices of the nations around you have deafened everyone? Do you not hear the commotion all around you? Do you not know that you live in a period when he who sleeps dies, and he who dies is gone forever? When will you open your eyes and see the glitter of the bayonets which are directed at you, and the lightning of the swords which are drawn over your heads? When will you realize the truth? When will you know that your country has been sold to the foreigner? See how your natural resources have been alienated from you and have come into the possession of England, France, and Germany. Have you no right to these resources? You have become humiliated slaves in the hands of the usurping tyrant; the foreigner unjustly dispossesses you of the fruit of your work and labor and leaves you to suffer the pangs of hunger. How long will it be before you understand that you have become a plaything in the hand of him who has no religion but to kill the Arabs and forcibly to seize their possessions? The Country is yours, and they say that rule belongs to the people, but those who exercise rule over you in the name of the Constitution do not consider you part of the people, for they inflict on you all kinds of suffering, tyranny, and persecution. How, then, can they concede to you any political rights? In their eyes you are but a flock of sheep whose wool is to be clipped, whose milk is to be drunk, and whose meat is to be eaten. Your country they consider a plantation which they inherited from their fathers, a country the inhabitants of which are their humble slaves. Where is your Qahtanic honor? Where your Adnanian pride?

. . .

Arise, O ye Arabs! Unsheathe the sword from the scabbard, ye sons of Qahtan! Do not allow an oppressive tyrant who has only disdain for you to remain in your country; cleanse your country from those who show their enmity to you, to your race and to your language.

O ye Arabs! Warn the people of the Yemen, of Asir, of Nejd, and of Iraq against the intrigues of your enemies. Be united, in the Syrian and Iraqi provinces, with the members of your race and fatherland. Let the Muslims, the Christians, and the Jews be as one in working for the interest of the nation and of the country. You all dwell in one land, you speak one language, so be also one nation and one hand. Do not become divided against yourselves according to the designs and purposes of the troublemakers who feign Islam, while Islam is really innocent of their misdeeds. . . .

Unite then and help one another, and do not say, O ye Muslims: This is a Christian, and this is a Jew, for you are all God's dependents, and religion is for God alone. God has commanded us, in his precious Arabic Book and at the hand of his Arab Adnanian Prophet, to follow justice and equality, to deal faithfully with him who does not fight us, even though his religion is different, and to fight him who uses us tyrannously. . . .

Know, all ye Arabs, that a *fada'i* society has been formed which will kill all those who fight the Arabs and oppose the reform of Arab lands. The reform of which we speak is not on the principle of decentralization coupled with allegiance to the minions of Constantinople, but on the principle of complete independence and the formation of a decentralized Arab state which will revive our ancient glories and rule the country on autonomous lines, according to the needs of each province. This state will begin by liquidating some flattering foxes among the Arabs who are, and have always been, the means whereby these murderous minions have trampled on our rights, as the world will see when they proceed to bring about the disasters they have in store for us.

Manifesto of Arab Nationalists disseminated from Cairo at beginning of World War I, printed by Ahmed Izzat al-A'zami, The Arab Question, vol. IV (Baghdad, 1932), pp. 108–117.

Source: Haim, *Arab Nationalism: An Anthology*, pp. 83–84.

 DOCUMENT 1–3

Theodor Herzl, *Der Judenstaat* (*The Jews' State*), published in 1896 [Excerpts]

. . . The Jewish question still exists. It would be foolish to deny it. It is a remnant of the Middle Ages, which civilized nations do not even yet seem able to shake off, try as they will. They certainly showed a generous desire to do so when they emancipated us. The Jewish question exists wherever Jews live in perceptible numbers. Where it does not exist, it is carried by Jews in the course of their migrations. We naturally move to those places where we are not persecuted, and there our presence produces persecution. This is the case in every country, and will remain so, even in those highly civilized—for instance, France—until the Jewish question finds a solution on a political basis. The unfortunate Jews are now carrying the seeds of Anti-Semitism into England; they have already introduced it into America.

I believe that I understand Anti-Semitism, which is really a highly complex movement. I consider it from a Jewish standpoint, yet without fear or hatred. I believe that I can see what elements there are in it of vulgar sport, of common trade jealousy, of inherited prejudice, of religious intolerance, and also of pretended self-defence. I think the Jewish question is no more a social than a religious one, notwithstanding that it sometimes takes these and other forms. It is a national question, which can only be solved by making it a political world-question to be discussed and settled by the civilized nations of the world in council.

We are a people—one people.

. . .

Oppression and persecution cannot exterminate us. No nation on earth has survived such struggles and sufferings as we have gone through. . . .

No one can deny the gravity of the situation of the Jews. Wherever they live in perceptible numbers they are more or less persecuted. Their equality before the law, granted by statute, has become practically a dead letter. They are debarred from filling even moderately high positions, either in the army, or in any public or private capacity. And attempts are made to thrust them out of business also: "Don't buy from Jews!". . . .

Everything tends, in fact, to one and the same conclusion, which is clearly enunciated in that classic Berlin phrase: "*Juden Raus!*" (Out with the Jews!)

I shall now put the Question in the briefest possible form: Are we to "get out" now and where to?

Or, may we yet remain? And, how long?

Let us first settle the point of staying where we are. Can we hope for better days, can we possess our souls in patience, can we wait in pious resignation till the princes and peoples of this earth are more mercifully disposed towards us? I say that we cannot hope for a change in the current of feeling. And why not? Even if we were as near to the hearts of princes as are their other subjects, they could not protect us. They would only feel popular hatred by showing us too much favor. By "too much," I really mean less than is claimed as a right by every ordinary citizen, or by every race. The nations in whose midst Jews live are all either covertly or openly Anti-Semitic.

. . .

THE PLAN

The whole plan is in its essence perfectly simple, as it must necessarily be if it is to come within the comprehension of all.

Let the sovereignty be granted us over a portion of the globe large enough to satisfy the rightful requirements of a nation; the rest we shall manage for ourselves.

The creation of a new State is neither ridiculous nor impossible. We have in our day witnessed the process in connection with nations which were not largely members of the middle class, but poorer, less educated, and consequently weaker than ourselves. The Governments of all countries scourged by Anti-Semitism will be keenly interested in assisting us to obtain the sovereignty we want.

The plan, simple in design, but complicated in execution, will be carried out by two agencies: The Society of Jews and the Jewish Company.

The Society of Jews will do the preparatory work in the domains of science and politics, which the Jewish Company will afterwards apply practically.

The Jewish Company will be the liquidating agent of the business interests of departing Jews, and will organize commerce and trade in the new country.

We must not imagine the departure of the Jews to be a sudden one. It will be gradual, continuous, and will cover many decades. The poorest will go first to cultivate the soil. In accordance with a preconceived plan, they will construct roads, bridges, railways and telegraph installations; regulate rivers; and build their own dwellings; their labor will create trade, trade will create markets and markets will attract new settlers, for every man will go voluntarily, at his own expense and his own risk. The labor expended on the land will enhance its value, and the Jews will soon perceive that a new and permanent sphere of operation is opening here for that spirit of enterprise which has heretofore met only with hatred and obloquy.

This pamphlet will open a general discussion on the Jewish Question, but that does not mean that there will be any voting on it. Such a result would ruin the cause from the outset, and dissidents must remember that allegiance or opposition is entirely voluntary. He who will not come with us should remain behind.

Source: Walter Laqueur and Barry Rubin, eds., *The Israel–Arab Reader: A Documentary History of the Middle East Conflict,* 4th ed. (New York: Penguin Books, 1984), pp. 6–11.

DOCUMENT 1–4

The Basel Declaration

This official statement of Zionist purpose was adopted by the first Zionist Congress in Basel in August 1897.

The aim of Zionism is to create for the Jewish people a home in Palestine secured by public law.

The Congress contemplates the following means to the attainment of this end:

1. The promotion, on suitable lines, of the colonization of Palestine by Jewish agricultural and industrial workers.
2. The organization and binding together of the whole of Jewry by means of appropriate institutions, local and international, in accordance with the laws of each country.
3. The strengthening and fostering of Jewish national sentiment and consciousness.
4. Preparatory steps toward obtaining government consent, where necessary, to the attainment of the aim of Zionism.

Source: Laqueur and Rubin, *Israel–Arab Reader,* pp. 11–12.

TWO

Palestine During the Mandate

CHRONOLOGY

Aug. 1914	World War I begins
Nov. 1914	Ottoman Empire enters war on side of Germany
May 1915	The Damascus Protocol
July 1915– Mar. 1916	Hussein-McMahon correspondence
May 1916	Sykes–Picot Agreement
June 1916	Arab revolt begins
Nov. 1917	Balfour Declaration
Dec. 1917	Allenby captures Jerusalem
June 1918	Declaration to the Arab Seven
1918–1919	Meetings between Feisal and Weizmann
Aug. 1919	King–Crane commission report
Mar. 1920	Arab nationalist congress proclaims Feisal king of Greater Syria
Apr. 1920	San Remo conference assigns mandate for Palestine to Great Britain
July 1920	Feisal expelled from Syria by French; established as king of Iraq by British
Aug. 1920	Treaty of Sèrres
1920–1921	Arab attacks on Jewish areas of Jerusalem and Jaffa
1921	Haganah formed
Mar. 1921	Churchill suggests Transjordan be administered separately within Palestine Mandate; Abdullah established as emir, or prince
Apr. 1921	Hajj Amin al-Husseini appointed mufti of Jerusalem and head of Supreme Moslem Council by high commissioner, Sir Herbert Samuel

Spring 1921	Haycraft investigation
June 1922	British White Paper reaffirms Balfour Declaration; limits Jewish immigration to economic absorptive capacity of country
July 1922	Palestine Mandate ratified by League of Nations. Includes Balfour Declaration; provides for separate development of Transjordan
Sept. 1922	Transjordan exempted from provisions of Balfour Declaration
June 1925	Hebrew University opens
Aug. 1929	Riots at Western (Wailing) Wall and massacre of Jews in Jerusalem, Safed, and Hebron
Mar. 1930	Shaw commission report
Oct. 1930	Hope-Simpson report and Passfield White Paper halt Jewish immigration and land sales
Feb. 1931	MacDonald letter negates White Paper provisions
Apr. 1936	Arab Higher Committee formed
1936–1939	Arab rebellion in Palestine
July 1937	Peel Commission report
July 1938	Evian-les-Bains Refugee Conference
May 1939	White Paper restricts Jewish land purchases and immigration
Sept. 1, 1939	World War II begins
May 1942	Biltmore Declaration calls for Jewish state in all of Palestine
Nov. 1942	Allied victory at el-Alamein

This chapter examines the deepening of the conflict between the Arabs and Jews of Palestine between the two World Wars. During those years Palestine was ruled by Great Britain as a mandated territory. Fierce battles had taken place in Palestine during the Great War, and parts of the country were devastated and badly in need of reconstruction. The population had declined to around 560,000—500,000 Arabs and 60,000 Jews—in 1918. Not surprisingly, the British government's primary concern was preserving and extending British strategic and economic interests in the Middle East and India. Palestine occupied a relatively minor role in the British imperial scheme of things. Also not surprisingly, the policies pursued and actions taken by British government representatives, both in Palestine and in London, created considerable resentment among the inhabitants of Palestine, both Jews and Arabs. Initially, the Arabs and Jews of Palestine had reason to believe that Britain would favor their clearly different national aspirations. However, within a few years, as events unfolded and violence between them intensified, both sides felt betrayed by Britain, and they turned their forces against the mandatory power in an effort to throw off the colonial yoke. This caused irreparable damage to the Arab cause. The Zionist cause, however, benefitted greatly as a result.

At the outbreak of war in 1914, Palestine was the southern part of what was known as geographical Syria. This area, situated between the Suez Canal to the west and the Persian Gulf and India to the east, was of strategic importance especially for the British and was considered vital to their geopolitical and economic interests. When the Ottoman Empire, the "sick man of Europe," joined Germany against the Allied powers of England, France, and Russia, Britain took the opportunity to secure allies and influence in the region by appealing to the aspirations of the empire's subject peoples. Many of these groups were eager to achieve self-determination. The British, quick to see the advantages of the situation, held discussions with Arabs and Jews about support for Allied war aims in return for pledges to support the goals of both communities in the region after the war. The trouble for Britain was that both Arabs and Jews had equally persuasive claims to the same piece of territory. In 1914, that territory was under the control of a third party, the Turks. During the war, and after, the great powers manipulated the situation primarily in their own interests.

The British had to coordinate policy with their allies, and planned the partition of the Ottoman Empire with France, Russia, and Italy even while the war was in progress. During and immediately following the hostilities, secret agreements were signed and public declarations were made resulting in misunderstandings and confusions that have plagued the Middle East ever since. With regard to the Fertile Crescent area generally, and to Palestine in particular, three such sets of agreements and statements enormously complicated the postwar situation, as they appeared to contain contradictory or conflicting promises. These were the Hussein-McMahon Correspondence of 1915–1916; the Sykes-Picot Agreement of 1916; and the Balfour Declaration of 1917.

The Hussein-McMahon Correspondence

Sherif Hussein of Mecca, ruler of the Hejaz, was perhaps the Arab figure at that time with the greatest prestige and potential power. As a Hashemite, and therefore a member of the Prophet Muhammad's house, and as guardian of the Holy Places of Islam, he was the natural spokesperson for the Arabs. After the war broke out, Sherif Hussein and the British high commissioner in Egypt, Sir Henry McMahon, exchanged a series of letters that discussed the conditions for an Arab uprising against the Turks in return for the independence of the Arabs and perhaps the reestablishment of an Arab Caliphate under Hussein, a pressing concern of the sherif. In the letters, the British expressed sympathy for Arab claims to the Arabic-speaking parts of the western Asian provinces of the Ottoman Empire, excluding Egypt and Aden, which Hussein recognized as areas of British hegemony. (See Documents 2–1 through 2–3.) McMahon also excluded from consideration the southern parts of Iraq from Basra to Baghdad, in which he asked the Arabs to recognize Britain's "established position and interest," and the vilayets of Aleppo and Beirut, because of the connection of Britain's ally France with the predominantly Maronite Christian population in those areas and its territorial claims in Syria-Lebanon. Further, he excepted from any proposed Arab states or states the districts of Mersin and Alexandretta in northern Syria, because of their sizable Turkish populations, and "portions of Syria lying to the west of the districts of Damascus, Homs, Hama and Aleppo," which, he added, "cannot be said to be purely Arab."

For the purposes of our discussion, the central question is whether the Hussein-McMahon correspondence viewed Palestine as part of an Arab state or states. "Palestine" in the nineteenth century was not an Ottoman province, and its boundaries would not be defined precisely until after World War I. What we now think of as Palestine consisted of the sanjak of Jerusalem and part of the vilayet of Beirut. The correspondence between Hussein and McMahon, the full text of which was not published until 1939, was in Arabic. Subsequently, disagreement arose over the meaning of the word *vilayet* (Arabic: *wilayah*), which Hussein and McMahon had used interchangeably to refer generally to a *district* and to an Ottoman administrative unit. The British later claimed that in excluding certain parts of the Levant, they had meant the area west of the districts of the three towns of Aleppo, Hama, and Homs, and of the Ottoman administrative division of Syria (of which Damascus was the capital), in which case Palestine would have been excluded. (See Map 1–1 in Chapter 1.) The Arabs later argued that they had understood British use of the word *vilayet* to mean the districts of the four towns mentioned and that Palestine, therefore, was to have been included in an Arab state. The Arab interpretation, in the opinion of most observers, appeared more credible.

Looking closely at their correspondence, it can be seen that Hussein wrote McMahon that although he was prepared to await a definite decision until an Allied victory was assured, he considered all the territory of the eastern Mediterranean to be purely Arab and was opposed to its being surrendered to France or any other power. It should also be noted that while care was taken to name various Ottoman administrative divisions, including the vilayet of Beirut, which included part of northern Palestine, nowhere in the Hussein-McMahon letters did McMahon mention the sanjak of Jerusalem, in which lay most of the rest of Palestine. Therefore, the Arabs later argued, Palestine was never specifically excluded from the territory to be granted Arab independence.

The Hussein-McMahon correspondence was not a formal agreement, but Hussein and those Arab notables who had been made privy to it assumed that the British would honor their wartime promises and would support Arab claims to independence after the war. In June 1916, therefore, the Arab Revolt began, led by Feisal, son of Sherif Hussein, and eventually aided by the colorful British colonel T. E. Lawrence (Lawrence of Arabia), whose involvement was subsequently publicized by the American broadcaster Lowell Thomas and chronicled in Lawrence's own books, *Seven Pillars of Wisdom* and *Revolt in the Desert*, its popular abridgement.

The Arab Revolt, fueled by British gold, aided the Allied effort by diverting and harassing the Turkish forces, both in Arabia and later in Syria. It began in western Arabia and succeeded by September 1916 in capturing the principal towns of the Hejaz with the important exception of Medina. While one group of Arabs remained in Arabia to lay siege to Medina, another column under Feisal marched north to aid British general Allenby's main expeditionary force heading east and north out of Egypt. As Allenby pushed up the Mediterranean coast, capturing Gaza and then marching inland to take Jerusalem by December 1917, Feisal proceeded on a parallel course east of the Jordan River. Before launching the final offensive against the Turks by an attack on Damascus and northern Syria, Allenby planned to sever vital Turkish communications between Damascus and the south. The Arabs cooperated with the British by blowing up part of the Hejaz railroad linking Damascus and the holy places of Mecca and Medina, first between Deraa and Amman, and then at points to the north and west of Deraa. The way was clear for a sweep to Damascus, which the Arab armies reached just ahead of an Australian force at the beginning of October 1918. By the end of October, Aleppo and the rest of Syria had been occupied, with the

Arabs playing a considerable role in the advance from Damascus through Homs and Hama to Aleppo. On October 30, 1918, the Ottoman Empire signed the Mudros Armistice.

Although significant, the Arab Revolt did not involve large numbers of men; the majority of the Arabs of the Ottoman Empire remained loyal subjects of the Ottoman sultan, who had in the nineteenth century revived and appropriated the title of caliph in order to appeal to his Muslim subjects. Furthermore, the sultan had co-opted many Arabs by appointing them to high positions. The British later claimed that Hussein and his sons were acting in their own behalf in their negotiations with the British. However, there was an Arab nationalist movement in Syria, with which Feisal had made contact even before the initiation of the Hussein-McMahon correspondence.

Al-Fatat and *al-Ahd* were two secret societies that had been formed before the war to work for Arab independence from the Ottomans. Founded in 1911 in Paris by seven young Arabs, al-Fatat was basically a civilian group. It shifted its activities to the Middle East in 1914, and its numbers grew to around 200. Al-Ahd was an association of army officers whose program at first called for a kind of dual monarchy. In early 1914, its leader was arrested and tried by the Turkish authorities on a number of unrelated and trumped-up charges, which infuriated his supporters and encouraged the members of al-Ahd to broaden their goals. In May 1915, al-Fatat and al-Ahd established contact and produced a document called the Damascus Protocol, which outlined their own conditions for cooperation with the British and an Arab revolt against the Turks. The provisions of the Damascus Protocol were remarkably similar to those presented by Hussein later that summer to the British and indicated an Arab nationalist sentiment that was quite real, even if limited in its constituency.

To buttress their arguments that the British intended to satisfy their aspirations, the Arabs also pointed to a later public statement issued in June 1918, when the British Foreign Office replied to seven Arab notables who had asked for a clarification of British policy. The "Declaration to the Seven" stated that with regard to the future government of territories liberated by the Allies, the principle of the consent of the governed should apply. In a Fourth of July speech that same year, President Woodrow Wilson of the United States enunciated his famous Fourteen Points, one of which was the principle that a postwar settlement must be acceptable to the people immediately concerned. The twelfth point explicitly mentioned the Ottoman Empire. These British and American statements may have helped allay Arab doubts and fears raised in the meantime by two other documents that had become known to them. These documents, containing provisions that appeared to contradict pledges made to the Arabs, were the Sykes-Picot Agreement and the Balfour Declaration.

The Sykes-Picot Agreement

At the same time that Hussein and McMahon were exchanging letters, the British were also holding secret discussions with their allies about the future partition of the Ottoman Empire. With regard to Palestine, the relevant document is the Sykes-Picot Agreement, named after the chief negotiators, Sir Mark Sykes, an Arabist and member of Parliament, for the British, and diplomat Charles François George-Picot for the French. In this agreement the two powers divided the Levant and Iraq areas into zones in which they would exercise either direct or indirect influence. (See Map 2–1.) In the areas of indirect British or French control, semi-independent Arab states or a state might be established. Regarding Palestine, the territory west of the Jordan River and including Jerusalem but excluding the Negev would be placed under international administration. Interestingly, British and French discussions referred obliquely to the Hussein-McMahon correspondence, with the British indicating that in return for cooperating with the Allies, the Arabs would obtain the towns of Homs, Hama, Damascus, and Aleppo, but under French

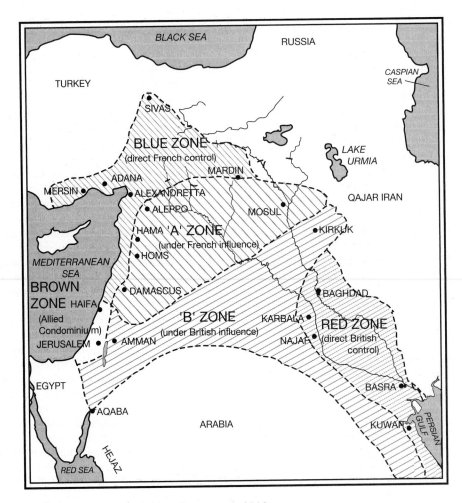

MAP 2–1   The Sykes-Picot Agreement, 1916

Source: Arthur Goldschmidt, Jr., *A Concise History of the Middle East*, Copyright © 1999 by Westview Press. Reprinted by permission of Westview Press, a member of Perseus Books, L.L.C.

supervision. Russia approved the Sykes-Picot Agreement in return for recognition by Britain and France of Russian rights to control parts of eastern Anatolia from Trebizond to the Caucasus. The Russians had previously gained Allied support of their claim on the Bosphorus and Dardanelles straits. Initialed in May 1916, the Sykes-Picot Agreement contained provisions that to some later interpreters contradicted the terms of the Hussein-McMahon correspondence that had preceded it.

The Balfour Declaration

A third document dealing specifically with Palestine further complicated the situation and lends credence to the saying that Palestine was "the much promised land." The Balfour Declaration, issued on November 2, 1917, was a public statement of the British government in the form of a letter from the foreign secretary, Arthur J. Balfour, to Lord Rothschild, head of the

British Zionist Organization. (See Document 2–4.) The declaration stated first that the British government "viewed with favor" the establishment in Palestine of a national home for the Jewish people. It then declared that in facilitating this objective, nothing should be done that might prejudice the "civil and religious rights of existing non-Jewish communities" in Palestine, or the rights and political status enjoyed by Jews in other countries.

A number of drafts were prepared, and the final version was attenuated and ambiguous. This was due primarily to opposition in the British cabinet of, ironically, its one Jewish member, Sir Edwin Montagu, who feared that an endorsement of Jewish nationality would lead to a charge of dual loyalty. (See Document 2–5.) The phrases "in Palestine" and "a national home" left the proposed entity vague and without defined borders. Moreover, the section relating to the civil and religious rights of the existing non-Jewish communities, while accurately reflecting the profusion of religious groups and the predominantly religious and cultural basis of identity among the Arabs at that time, mentioned nothing about their economic, political, and national rights. The last part of the declaration clearly attempted to emphasize that Jews could be and were patriotic citizens of countries in which they already resided, and that their rights and political status should not be harmed by the enthusiasm of Zionist co-religionists.

Perhaps the most intriguing aspect surrounding the declaration is why it was issued at all. Certainly, it made Britain's administration of the postwar mandate immensely more complicated and burdensome, and British postwar aims in the region would have been realized with far less difficulty had no such statement been made. Yet there were several cogent reasons why the British government was prepared to issue the Balfour Declaration. The most important involved the immediate progress of the war and Britain's domestic politics.

The immediate wartime situation pushed British policymakers to endorse Zionist goals. For one thing, issuing such a declaration might well persuade the new revolutionary leaders of Russia, many of whom were Jews, not to leave the war. It might also influence American Jews to press the U.S. government, which had just entered the war, to prosecute it with greater vigor. The British also wished to forestall a similar declaration by either the German or the Ottoman government, which might appeal to Jews to help achieve a similar purpose. Furthermore, supporting a Jewish national home in Palestine might strengthen British efforts to establish a protectorate or at least continue to exert influence in a strategic area on the eastern flank of the Suez Canal after the war. Palestine was a vital link on the land routes to India. The growing importance of oil and of air transport also necessitated the continuance of British hegemony over the important communications lanes of the Middle East.

Jews generally supported the Allied war effort. In Palestine, a Jewish spy ring known as *NILI (Netzach Yisrael Lo Y'shaker—The Strength of Israel Will Not Deceive)* operated between 1916 and September 1917 when it was uncovered by the Turks. It supplied the British with vital information that greatly aided the Allied effort and facilitated Allenby's successful march to Jerusalem.

Chaim Weizmann, a Russian-born chemist at the University of Manchester who made an important contribution to the British war effort, was a link between the Zionist cause and British pro-Zionist sympathizers. Weizmann was called to London to devise a process for synthesizing acetone, a chemical needed to produce the explosive cordite. An avid Zionist, and then president of the World Zionist Organization, Weizmann took the opportunity to make contact with many British leaders whom he swayed to the Zionist cause. Some, influenced already by a romantic, back-to-the-Bible, strain in English literature of the previous century, or by the idea that the Second Coming of Christ would be hastened by the restoration of the Jews in the land of Israel, needed little urging to support the idea of a Jewish national home. Others were compelled by Weizmann's brilliant mind, dignified bearing, and personal charm and charisma. Thus, David Lloyd George, who would become British prime minister in 1916, Winston Churchill, who would become colonial secretary, Henry Wickham Steed, editor of the London *Times*, C. P. Scott, editor of the *Manchester Guardian*, Mark Sykes, chief secretary of the War Cabinet, Colonel Richard

Meinertzhagen, who had served to the Near East, Balfour himself, and many others were willing to lend a sympathetic ear to those ideas that resulted in issuance of the Balfour Declaration.

Some also thought a Jewish national home in Palestine would attract Jewish immigrants, especially from Eastern Europe, who were not always welcomed with open arms in the British Isles. Balfour himself, as prime minister, had introduced a bill in 1905 to limit Jewish immigration into Britain. A Jewish homeland, as Herzl had recognized, could serve the needs of Jews and anti-Semites alike.

Postwar Settlement

Once the war ended and the peace conference got underway in Paris, problems regarding the postwar settlement of Palestine rapidly surfaced. The Arabs in particular were confused about British policy, especially since the new government in Russia had published the wartime secret arrangements, including the Sykes-Picot Agreement. Contradictions were apparent between British commitments to the Jews in the Balfour Declaration and the Arab interpretation of British pledges in the Hussein-McMahon correspondence, as well as in public statements like the "Declaration to the Seven." Meanwhile, France, because of its commercial interests and traditional religious connection with the Maronite Christians in the region, was laying claim to most of the Levant coast, which would surely restrict Arab independence elsewhere in the area. Hussein and Feisal, inexperienced in dealing with the European powers, seemed to be even more wary of French ambitions in the Levant than of the British and the Zionists. Because the British and the French distrusted each other, they encouraged these Arab concerns. Although the British seemed to be firm in their support of the Balfour Declaration, they also indicated their readiness, albeit vaguely, to honor Arab aspirations. Therefore, at the suggestion of the British, Feisal and Weizmann met, first at Aqaba in the spring of 1918 and later in the year in London, to discuss matters of mutual concern.

In January 1919, Feisal made a provisional agreement with Weizmann in which they alluded to the common ancestry of the two groups and the hope that they could work together in the Near East. (See Document 2–6.) They agreed that, provided the rights of the Arab peasant and tenant farmers were protected and that there were no restrictions on religious freedom, the Arabs would work with the Jews to implement the Balfour Declaration. The document clearly envisaged a Jewish state in Palestine alongside an Arab state and spoke about Jewish help in surveying the economic possibilities of the Arab state and assisting in its development. However, in 1919, the fate of both Arab and Jewish nationalists was in the hands of the victorious Allies. Feisal, therefore, appended a proviso that he would not honor the agreement with Weizmann in any way unless the Arabs received their independence. Nevertheless, Feisal seemed clear in his own mind. A few months later he wrote Felix Frankfurter, the American Zionist leader, that it was a "happy coincidence" that Arabs and Jews who are "cousins in race" were taking the first steps toward the attainment of their national ideals together, and that there was room in "Syria" for both national movements. (See Document 2–7.)

Both the British and the Zionists ignored or failed to appreciate the views of the indigenous Arab population. This was due not only to the fact that they were concerned primarily with their own interests, but also to the fact that there were few Arabs except Feisal in a position to speak authoritatively on behalf of the Arab people, and that there were internal divisions and rivalries among the Arabs themselves. However, Feisal was not as much a free agent as he had believed, nor were the Arabs altogether mute. Feisal's right to represent "the Arab people" was open to question, and an Arab congress at Damascus repudiated his dealings with the Zionists. This action reflected growing local opposition to the Balfour Declaration and fear of unlimited Jewish immigration, with its probable economic, cultural, and political consequences. This negative attitude was observed by the King-Crane Commission, dispatched to Syria and

Chaim Weizmann and Emir Feisal near Aqaba, June 4, 1918.

Palestine by President Wilson during the peace conference to gauge the sentiment of the local population regarding the future of the region. (See Document 2–8.) The commission confirmed the Arab rejection of Zionist goals, as well as Arab opposition to the possible imposition of French rule. If independence were unattainable, and if they had to accept a form of temporary outside control, then the Arabs preferred American or, secondarily, British supervision. Nobody, however, took any serious notice of the King-Crane report. In any event, the British and French were unwilling to let the Arabs rule themselves. The United States under the ailing President Wilson withdrew from the peace negotiations, and the postwar settlement regarding the Middle East was left in the hands of the British and French.

It is not surprising, therefore, that the actual postwar settlement in the Levant area came close to the provisions of the Sykes-Picot Agreement. The arrangements were agreed upon at San Remo in April 1920. They were incorporated into the Treaty of Sèvres of August 1920 and were ratified by the League of Nations in 1922. Instead of zones of British or French direct or indirect influence and internationalized areas, as the British and French had proposed, the League of Nations divided the territory into new entities, called *mandates*. The mandates would be administered like trusts by the British and French, under supervision of the League, until such time as the inhabitants were believed by League members to be ready for independence and self-government. The mandate idea was a kind of compromise between the principle of self-determination stressed in Wilson's Fourteen Points, and the desire of the colonial powers to maintain control in the region at the same time that they attempted to neutralize each other's potential power. Wartime pledges and promises to Arabs and Jews alike were postponed, if not altogether negated, by these arrangements.

The Mandates

The mandate territories were Syria and Lebanon, awarded to France; Iraq, awarded to Britain; and a new entity called Palestine, which was also placed under British control. Palestine, as defined for the first time in modern history at San Remo, included the land on both sides of the Jordan River and encompassed the present-day countries of Israel and Jordan. However, boundary changes were soon made. As the British and French moved in to assume their new responsibilities, Arab nationalists rebelled in Iraq and Syria. Feisal, who in March 1920 had been proclaimed king of Greater Syria by a nationalist congress in Damascus, was summarily expelled from Syria by the French, who ruled it virtually as a colony until 1943. Abdullah, Feisal's brother, appeared east of the Jordan at Ma'an and was said to be recruiting a force to reclaim Syria for Feisal. In order to protect British interests, Winston Churchill, then British colonial secretary, convened a conference of British officials and soldiers in Cairo in March 1921. There, the British decided to install Feisal as constitutional monarch in Iraq and to carve out of the Palestine mandate a new entity east of the Jordan River. This would be administered as a separate emirate ruled over by Abdullah as *emir*, or prince.

Transjordan, as the new territory came to be known, consisted in 1921 of about 300,000 inhabitants, mostly Bedouin, and was heavily fractionated by tribe and clan loyalties. It is significant that most Palestinian notables had thrown in their lot with Feisal after the war. Now, however, with Feisal king of Iraq, politically inclined Palestinians began to focus on Palestine as a discrete political entity, although some continued to dream of Palestine within a reconstituted, independent Greater Syria.

In July 1922, the League of Nations ratified the mandate arrangements, including the changes that had been made since 1920. (See Map 2–2.) The preamble of the Palestine mandate included the Balfour Declaration, thus elevating it to the status of international law. It recognized "the historical connection of the Jewish people with Palestine" and referred to their justification for "reconstituting their national home in that country." Article 4 suggested that the British recognize the Zionist Organization as a Jewish agency to cooperate with the mandatory government in establishing the national home and to represent the interests of the Jewish population. Article 6 instructed the British to "facilitate Jewish immigration under suitable conditions" and to encourage "close settlement by the Jews on the land" while ensuring "that the rights and position of other sections of the population are not prejudiced." Presumably, the latter statement referred to the Arabs, then 85 to 90 percent of the population. The mandate instrument never mentioned the Arabs by name, however, and members of the League of Nations were evidently thinking of the various religious communities that then existed in Palestine rather than a national group as such other than the Jews.

Only in Article 25, which referred to "the territories lying between the Jordan and the eastern boundary of Palestine as ultimately determined" (that is, Transjordan), were there statements about the possibility of postponing or withholding implementation of the provisions of the mandate should they be "inapplicable to the existing local conditions." In September 1922, because of disturbances caused by continuing Arab nationalist frustration and growing hostility to Jewish immigration into Palestine, the British officially stated that the Balfour Declaration would not apply to Transjordan, which would be closed to Jewish immigration. With regard to Jewish hopes, it was therefore clear that if there were to be a Jewish homeland in Palestine, it would emerge somewhere west of the Jordan River. This book will now call only the land west of the river (Cisjordan) "Palestine," keeping in mind that Transjordan, the area east of the Jordan River, was still technically part of Britain's mandatory obligations.

But what kind of state would emerge if and when the mandate ended? Did a national home for the Jews imply eventual political sovereignty? Would Palestine, even if restricted to land west of the Jordan River, become a Jewish state? And how were the provisions of the Balfour Declaration consistent with the rights of the existing non-Jewish communities; that is, the majority Arab population? What would the relationship be between Arabs and Jews in Palestine during the mandate? Both communities realized, of course, that the eventual outcome would be determined by numbers and ownership of land. Therefore, the issues of immigration and land purchase became crucial in the mandate period, with the Jews attempting to increase both, and the Arabs trying to slow down or halt Jewish immigration and land purchases.

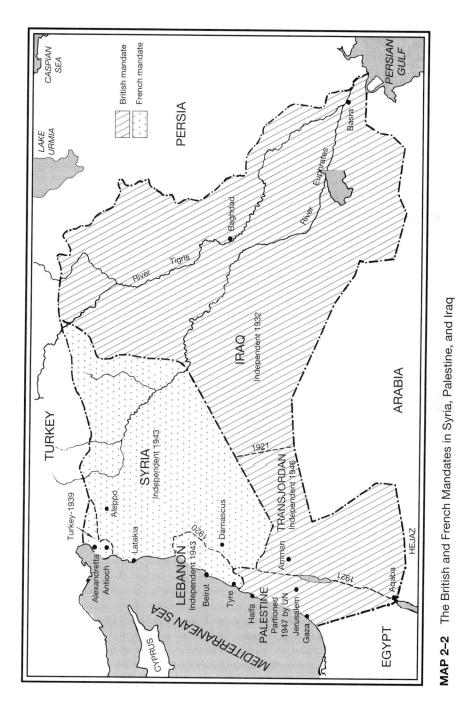

MAP 2-2 The British and French Mandates in Syria, Palestine, and Iraq

Source: Reprinted by permission of the Putnam Publishing Group from *The Arab Awakening* by George Antonius. Copyright © 1939 by G. P. Putnam's Sons.

Very often these issues spawned violence, and the British were forced to respond, a lesson not lost on either community. When we examine the mandate period in Palestine, therefore, it must be from three different perspectives: the Jewish, the Arab, and the British.

The Jews and the Mandate

At the beginning of the mandate period, the Jews of Palestine thought it served their best interests to work closely with the British. This was facilitated greatly by that provision of the mandate instrument suggesting that a Jewish agency be established to take care of the needs of the population and to cooperate with the mandatory administration. The World Zionist Organization (WZO) was recognized as the Jewish Agency, but its president, Chaim Weizmann, remained in London to be close to British centers of power. David Ben-Gurion headed the standing executive committee of the WZO in Palestine. Being on the spot, the executive committee, for all intents and purposes, became the Jewish Agency and, for the most part, accommodated itself to the mandate arrangements and to cooperation with the British.

The Jewish community in Palestine, or Yishuv, elected its own assembly, the *Vaad Leumi*, which contained political parties representing all viewpoints on the Zionist spectrum. The *Histadrut*, an originally apolitical federation of labor and trade union organizations, established a system of universal medical coverage, set up an extensive network of schools, and controlled several industries. Because of Arab attacks on Jewish settlements, the Jews also formed a clandestine defense organization called the *Haganah* in 1921. As for education, the Haifa Technion had been operating since 1912, and in 1925 the Hebrew University opened on Mount Scopus, capping a Jewish school system that produced high literacy rates among the Jewish population. The Yishuv had its own courts and tax collection, and the kibbutzim and moshavim, as well as growing urban and industrial enterprises, provided an economic base. There was a high degree of organization and cooperation within the Jewish community, which was creating the institutions of national life.

This does not mean, however, that the Jewish community was united internally. Serious differences existed among the myriad groups over ideology, relations with the Arabs, and the degree of cooperation with the authorities. The majority of the Labor Zionists who controlled the Jewish Agency were socialists who ardently desired good relations with the Arabs and myopically believed that Zionism was good for the Arabs as well as the Jews. Many of them hearkened back to the ideals of Achad Ha-Am. Although all the activities of the Jewish Agency were geared to the development of an eventual state, this political goal remained unarticulated throughout most of the mandate period.

On the other hand, the Revisionist Zionists, founded in 1925 and led by Vladimir Jabotinsky, never accepted what they called the first partition of Palestine in 1921 and explicitly demanded a Jewish state, not merely a homeland, on both sides of the Jordan River. They sought a political entity with an army and all the other trappings of national life, and they viewed the leaders of the Jewish Agency as accommodationist, weak willed, and cowardly. The Revisionists fully realized that their goals were inconsistent with those of the Arabs, but for Jabotinsky (and especially later, when the situation of the Jews in Europe became desperate) the moral claim of the Jews to Palestine outweighed that of the Arabs. In 1937, in testimony before the Palestine Royal Commission, Jabotinsky stated that given the fact the Arabs already had several states and the Jews had such great need for just one safe refuge, Arab claims on Palestine were like the claims of appetite versus the claims of starvation. Although the Revisionists were a minority representing particularly urban, nonsocialist, property-owning Jews, they were a vocal and ideologically consistent group throughout the mandate period. In 1931, they formed their own military arm, called at first Haganah Bet, later renamed the *Irgun Zvai Leumi (ETZEL)*, or national military group, which actively retaliated against Arab marauders. During World War II, and with the death of Jabotinsky in 1940, the Irgun ceased its activities. In 1942, however, the Irgun was revitalized when a deserter from General Anders' refugee-recruited Polish army-in-exile arrived in Palestine. This was Menachem Begin, who later led the maximalist Herut party and became prime minister of Israel as head of the Likud coalition between 1977 and 1983. Many members of the Likud continue to espouse elements of Revisionist ideology that deny Palestinian sovereignty in any part of Eretz Yisrael.

At the other end of the Zionist spectrum were individuals and groups who perceived the incompatibility of Jewish and Arab goals and who cared about the relationship between Jews and Arabs in Palestine. *Brit Shalom* was one such group that advocated a binational state in Palestine. Judah Magnes, an American-born Reform rabbi who became chancellor of Hebrew University in 1925, as well as important intellectuals like Martin Buber, advocated this kind of solution. A more politically active group was *HaShomer HaZair*, or "Young Guard," a left-wing party that advocated equality between the Jewish and Arab working classes in a binational state.

The Yishuv, despite its internal differences, however, was creating the institutions of statehood while building up the national home. Moreover, ideological discussions became academic as World War II broke out and as details of the Holocaust in Europe became known. In 1942, at the Biltmore Hotel in New York, the World Zionist Organization for the first time unequivocally called for a Jewish state in all of Palestine that was under mandate.

The Arabs and the Mandate

For the most part, the roughly 500,000-strong Arab community within Palestine remained opposed to the mandate and to Zionism. They saw the Balfour Declaration as encouraging the Jews to establish a politically sovereign state in Palestine, which they were determined to resist. They were hampered throughout the mandate period, however, by their lack of organization and by the maximalist position that many of their leaders adopted. This often prevented them from reacting in ways that could have achieved their aims and thwarted those of the Zionists.

There was no Arab agency like the Jewish one, although the British proposed such a body in 1923. The Arabs believed that since the mandate instrument specifically mentioned a Jewish agency to cooperate with the British in facilitating Zionist objectives, it would signal their acquiescence to the Balfour Declaration and to Zionism were they to cooperate in any way with the British. Therefore, the Arab community failed to form a representative body.

Moreover, the British retained the previous Ottoman millet system, which recognized the division of the population into fairly self-governing autonomous confessional units. This tended to reinforce religious, cultural, and economic differences between Muslims and Christians. Educationally, too, although the mandate did provide some funds for public education, for the most part the various religious groups ran their own schools. Thus, while literacy among the Arabs (especially Christians) rose overall during the mandate period, public schools did not suffice to serve the Arab population, and their literacy lagged behind that of the Jews. A certain, although declining, proportion of the Arab population also remained nomadic.

Politically, the Arabs were also divided. Disagreements were particularly acute between the two most influential Jerusalemite Arab Muslim families, the Husseinis and the Nashashibis. In 1921, the British high commissioner, Sir Herbert Samuel, named Hajj Amin al-Husseini grand mufti of Jerusalem and appointed him head of the Supreme Muslim Council, which controlled the Muslim courts and schools and much of the revenue generated by religious charitable endowments. The mufti was supposed to be chosen from three candidates who received the greatest number of votes from a convocation of Islamic scholars and notables. Samuel appointed Hajj Amin despite the fact that he had received fewer votes than the top three candidates. Although a lower-ranking British civil servant evidently pushed the idea of co-opting a strong Arab nationalist, it is sometimes argued that Samuel, a Jew himself, bent over backward to illustrate his impartiality by choosing the violently anti-Zionist Hajj Amin as mufti. Because the

Hajj Amin al-Husseini, grand mufti of Jerusalem.

high commissioner was committed to facilitating Jewish immigration in accordance with British mandatory obligations, it is possible that he appointed Hajj Amin to placate the Arabs. Unfortunately, the mufti and the Husseinis remained implacably opposed to the mandate, the British, and the Jews. The Nashashibis were also opposed to Zionism but were somewhat more inclined to cooperate with the British to achieve Arab aims. The two groups fought against and sometimes murdered each other in their jockeying for power and influence.

The Arabs were constrained not only by their maximalist position but also by lack of organization. An Arab executive existed between 1920 and 1934. Headed by Musa Kazem al-Husseini, a relative of the mufti, it presented Arab views to the high commissioner, called political strikes, and convened Palestine Arab congresses. When it dissolved after the death of Musa Kazem in 1934, several political "parties" appeared, usually organized around a powerful personality and representing family or parochial interests. In 1936, leaders of five of the six parties (that of the Nashashibi family remained aloof) formed a body called the Arab Higher Committee, with Hajj Amin al-Husseini as its president. This move had been catalyzed largely by independently organized "national committees," which had begun a general strike (discussed later in the chapter). Escalating violence and political murders led the British to ban the Arab Higher Committee and to issue a warrant for the arrest of Hajj Amin. He escaped, however, and orchestrated Arab resistance to the British and the Jews from various capitals, including Berlin, during World War II.

Economically, there were many advances in the Arab sector during the mandate, especially in construction, agriculture, and citriculture. However, in terms of services, industrial growth, and the development of agricultural land, there was never enough capital to support the Arab population, which doubled during the mandate period. Owing largely to efforts by the British, the Arab death rate declined, infant mortality decreased, and thousands of Arabs immigrated into Palestine. These newcomers, it seems, were attracted by the generally higher living standard than in the surrounding areas and by opportunities opened up by developments in the Jewish sector. Nevertheless, the Arabs remained hostile to Zionism, and their hostility manifested itself over issues of land purchase and immigration, as we shall see. It was abundantly clear that the more land the Jews purchased and the more Jews who arrived, the more chance the Arabs would one day find themselves in the minority.

The British during the Mandate

British colonial rule was in general conscientious, efficient, and responsible. In India and Iraq, for example, the British attracted capable people who did a creditable job in training lower-echelon administrators and providing some opportunities for local populations to gain experience in self-government. The British had a good record in Palestine, too, in terms of developing administrative institutions, municipal services, public works, and communications. The mandate government laid water pipelines, extended railroad lines, and completed port facilities at Haifa. An electric power grid was begun by a Russian Jewish engineer, Pinchas Rutenberg, who obtained a concession from the mandate government. But Palestine was a special case, and the British were caught in a web of their own making by the contradictions inherent in the mandate instrument and the conflicting claims of Arabs and Jews. Policy was shaped by a series of "white papers" issued usually in response to outbreaks of violence over land or immigration issues. As many observers have noted, the British seemed to be muddling through, while trying to keep the peace.

The aims and aspirations of the three protagonists appeared incompatible. The Arabs feared, and especially after the rise of Nazism in Germany, that continuing Jewish immigration would result in a Jewish majority that would claim all of Palestine. The Jews sought to build a viable base, both in numbers and in land, that would make feasible a national home. The British wished to retain their influence and keep the peace, while, in accordance with the obligations imposed upon them by the mandate, they tried simultaneously to implement the Balfour Declaration, safeguard the civil and religious rights of all the inhabitants, and develop self-governing institutions. Lacking a clear policy on how to proceed, the British responded to the sporadic violence by dispatching commissions of inquiry and then issuing white papers based on the findings of the commissions.

Land, Immigration, and White Papers

In 1920, the British reopened the Land Registry, which had been closed since 1918 because of the war and the dissolution of the Ottoman Empire. Jews immediately began to buy land, some from the British, who had taken over the former state lands of the Ottoman Empire, but mostly from Arab landowners. Zionist purchases from Arabs were facilitated by the fact that the Ottoman system of land registration had been fairly chaotic, and that most land had not been registered by the peasants working it, but by wealthy city merchants or absentee landowners willing to sell it at vastly inflated prices. Zionist agencies like the Jewish National Fund (JNF) utilized contributions of Jews all over the world to purchase land on behalf of the Jewish people and to coordinate its development. In 1917, the JNF possessed only about 160,000 dunams (1 dunam equals approximately ¼ acre) in Palestine. The first major purchase after the war was of about 80,000 dunams, containing some twenty-two villages, in the Jezreel Valley. The land was purchased in 1921 from the Sursuk family of Lebanon for £726,000. (Sursuk himself had purchased the land from the Ottoman government in 1872 for about £20,000.)

Because of the predominantly socialist ideology of the Yishuv, and the preponderance of Labor Zionists in important leadership positions both in Palestine and in the World Zionist Organization, land acquired during the mandate was usually made into kibbutzim or moshavim. The Jews hoped to avoid the creation of a Jewish landlord class exploiting a landless Arab peasantry, but land purchases often led to the eviction of Arab peasants. This occurred in the

British authorities quelling Arab riot at Jaffa Gate, Jerusalem, in October 1927.

Jezreel Valley, where about twenty collective settlements were founded on the principle of Jews performing their own labor. It is important to remember that all the land purchased in the mandate period was legally purchased, and much of it was swamp or marshland or was otherwise uninhabited. Nevertheless, some Arabs lost land that they had worked and that had been in the hands of their families for centuries. Moreover, socialist idealism notwithstanding, the almost total lack of contact and exchange between Jews and Arabs engaged in agriculture resulted in lost opportunities for Jewish and Arab cooperation on the land.

While land purchases continued in the 1920s, there were also spurts of Jewish immigration, although the number of Jews leaving Palestine exceeded the number entering for many years of the decade. Not surprisingly, Jewish immigration was viewed with suspicion by the Arabs. As the mandate arrangements were being worked out in 1920 and 1921, Arab sentiment became inflamed against the British and the incoming Jews.

The White Paper of 1922

In 1920, Palestinian Arabs attacked Tel Chai and other Jewish settlements in the Galilee region, and anti-Jewish riots broke out in Jerusalem. In 1921, Jaffa was subjected to violence, which spread to Petach Tikvah, Hadera, and other Jewish communities. Forty-seven Jews were killed and 140 wounded. Forty-eight Arabs were killed and scores were wounded, mostly by British troops trying to keep the peace.

The chief justice of Palestine, Sir Thomas Haycraft, headed a commission of inquiry into the disturbances. He concluded that, whereas the Arabs had been responsible for the violence, Arab resentment had a legitimate basis in the Arab fear of economic danger posed by Jewish immigrants and the perceived political influence of the Jews on the mandatory government. In a pattern that repeated itself throughout the mandate period, immigration was temporarily suspended and then resumed, as the colonial secretary, Winston Churchill, attempted to clarify his government's policy. The Churchill White Paper reaffirmed Britain's commitment to the Balfour Declaration and stated that the Jews were in Palestine "by right and not on sufferance," but that all citizens of Palestine were Palestinians. (See Document 2–9.) It went on to say that the document meant what it said—there would be a Jewish home in Palestine—and that Jewish immigration should not exceed the economic absorptive capacity of the country, a principle extrapolated from the mandate instrument and enunciated at the time of the first immigration ordinance in 1920. The explicit reference to economic absorptive capacity in the 1922 White Paper, however, highlighted this consideration and raised new questions and doubts about its meaning.

What, in fact, did "economic absorptive capacity" mean? The 1922 White Paper provided no definition, but the Jews interpreted the phrase as an incentive for further economic development. In their view, economic growth and opportunities would justify continued Jewish immigration. Indeed, there was general economic growth in Palestine, in both the Arab and the Jewish sectors, most notably in agriculture and citriculture. The mandatory authorities were responsible for great strides in basic administration, public works, and expansion of infrastructure. Compared to the surrounding Arab areas, the economic situation of Palestine was sufficiently favorable, and the living standard notably enough higher, to attract Arabs from outside Palestine, particularly to the cities and urban areas.

Historians have debated whether changes in the Arab economy and increases in the Arab population were due to developments in the Jewish sector. The third wave of Jewish immigration, or aliyah, between 1919 and 1923 brought into Palestine about 35,000 young Jews primarily from Russia and Eastern Europe who had already attended agricultural training programs and were enthusiastic and experienced "pioneers" on the land. The fourth aliyah (1924–1928) of 78,000 consisted mainly of middle-class shopkeepers and artisans fleeing from economic depression and anti-Semitic outbreaks in Poland. These arrivals tended to settle in the towns and cities. The fifth aliyah (1932–1938) brought many well-educated German immigrants who also settled mainly in urban areas and who arrived with capital that contributed greatly to growth in construction and industry as well as agriculture. Zionist proponents stress that development in the Jewish sector created new and attractive work opportunities for Arabs as well as Jews, and that the rapid growth of the Arab population owing to natural increase resulted from the introduction by the Jews of improved health and sanitary conditions. Arab population changes within the country caused a relative decrease of the rural population and an increase of Arabs in cities and areas where there were large numbers of Jews. This urbanization of the Arabs, some observers claim, resulted from increased opportunities caused by Jewish development.

Others point out, however, that the economy grew not only because of Jewish development but also because of efforts by the mandatory government and changes in the Arab sector. The British established a framework through administrative institutions and infrastructure. The awareness of the Arab population of Palestine was stimulated not only by developments within Palestine but also by strides being made by Arabs in the surrounding countries. These historians point out, too, that while there may have been mutual influence and interchange between Jews and Arabs in the urban centers, the effect, positively or negatively, was still limited because the two groups seldom interacted. Rural populations, especially peasants and farmers, almost never had contact with each other. The resources of Palestine were limited, and although there was general economic growth, Jews and Arabs were basically in conflict in the economic sphere.

The Political Situation

Politically, Palestine took a very different course from the other mandate areas. In Iraq, Syria, and Lebanon, even after delays and false starts, constituent assemblies, parliaments, constitutions, and other institutions of self-government that were supposed to be modeled on those of the Western democracies eventually emerged. In Palestine, the Jewish and Arab communities rarely cooperated, except at the local and sometimes municipal level. In order to encourage the development of self-governing institutions at a "national" level, in 1922, and again in 1923, the high commissioner attempted to establish a legislative council, which would have reflected the Arab majority. The Arabs rejected the idea of a council, however, partly because they suspected British manipulation, but largely because to join such a council would mean to acquiesce in the imposition of the mandate and the Balfour Declaration. The Arabs did not wish to legitimize a situation that they rejected in principle.

The White Paper of 1930

Personal relationships between Jews and Arabs could be friendly at times, even if they competed economically and politically at the national level. This was especially true in the 1920s as Jewish immigration leveled off and indeed fell below emigration in some years. In 1929, however, as a result of the worldwide economic depression and anti-Semitic outbreaks in Europe, Jewish immigration to Palestine began to rise once again, engendering fear and anger among the Arabs. An incident around the Western (or Wailing) Wall in August 1929 inflamed Arab mobs and set off riots that resulted in the death of Arabs and Jews in Jerusalem, Safed, and Hebron. The riots left nearly 250 Arabs and Jews dead with more than 500 wounded. The massacre of more than sixty Jews in Hebron was especially traumatic; Hebron was the burial place of the Patriarchs, and Jews had lived there from the time of Abraham.

 The British responded by sending an investigative commission, headed by Sir Walter Shaw, which conducted hearings and issued a report on March 31, 1930. While blaming the Arabs for the violence, it went on to say that the disappointment of Arab political and national aspirations and fear for their economic future were the fundamental causes of the disturbances. It further recommended that a study be made of land and immigration issues. Sir John Hope-Simpson was dispatched to conduct this inquiry, and Jewish immigration was temporarily suspended. On the basis of Hope-Simpson's report in 1930, the British issued another statement, the Passfield White Paper, which called for a halt to Jewish immigration. It recommended that government land be sold only to landless Arabs, and that determination of "economic absorptive capacity" be based on levels of Arab as well as Jewish unemployment. The outcry from Palestine Jews and Zionists in London and throughout the world caused Prime Minister Ramsey MacDonald to issue an explanatory letter the following year that in effect nullified the provisions of the Passfield White Paper. The Arabs referred to MacDonald's statement as the Black Letter, and various Arab groups began to boycott government activities and to subvert its functioning whenever possible.

 By this time, the early 1930s, events in Europe once again began to influence the situation in Palestine. Government-sponsored anti-Semitism led to Jewish emigration from Poland, Hungary, and Romania. The rise to power in Germany of Adolf Hitler, the Nuremberg racial laws, and subsequent legislation directed against the Jews, and the deliberate encouragement of Jews to leave the country, led to new waves of Jewish immigration into Palestine. Between 1933 and 1936 approximately 165,000 Jews entered Palestine, and by 1936 the Jewish population of Palestine stood at almost 400,000 or 30 percent of the total. For the first time, there seemed a real possibility that the Jews might eventually outnumber the Arabs. There were serious outbreaks of violence against Jews in 1933 and again in 1935 in reaction to these new waves of immigration.

 At the end of 1935, the British broached the idea of a Palestinian constitution and a legislative council, but both the Arabs and the Jews rejected the proposal. The Arabs would have had a majority on the council, but the British would have maintained control through their selection of nonelected representatives and a provision that no legislation could abrogate or supersede the authority of the mandatory government. The mufti and his followers rejected the proposal anyway, because the Jews would have been represented. The Jews rejected it because they were still a minority and because the British proposed restrictions on land purchases. In Britain the program was attacked for one reason or another by both houses of Parliament. It was in this situation of tension that the great Arab rebellion began, reflecting an Arab nationalist sentiment that had grown along with, and partly in response to, Jewish nationalism. This rebellion persisted for three years until 1939 and the outbreak of World War II.

Arab Rebellion, 1936–1939

The Arab rebellion of 1936–1939 began with rather spontaneous acts of violence by a religiously and nationalistically motivated group inspired by Sheikh Izz ad-Din al-Qassam, a preacher in a Haifa mosque, who urged his several hundred followers to take up arms against the British. Before he could do much, however, he was killed by the British in 1935. Qassamite groups had already achieved some notoriety in the previous few years, but their robbery and murder of three Jews in April 1936, followed by retaliation against two Arabs, quickly degenerated into widespread chaos. Arab groups in Jaffa and Nablus initiated a general strike. This was taken up by "national committees" in other towns, and the first stage of the rebellion was under way. It was at this point that five of the Arab political parties put aside their differences to form the Arab Higher Committee, under the leadership of the mufti. The Arab Higher Committee loosely coordinated various Arab organizations, sports clubs, Boy Scouts, women's committees, a labor organization, the Jaffa Boatmen's Association, and others participating in the strike. The committee held a congress that called for civil disobedience, nonpayment of taxes, and shutting down the municipal governments. Thousands of Arabs mobilized in towns and villages across the country. Violence continued against the British military and, in some instances, against Jews. The British poured in 20,000 troops to contain the upheaval. Arabs reluctant to participate were intimidated and sometimes even murdered by the mufti's followers.

Peel Commission Report

Another Royal Commission, this one headed by Lord Robert Peel, was sent to investigate. The Peel Commission Report, issued in 1937, was significant in that it proposed for the first time that the territory be partitioned into separate Jewish and Arab states. It recommended a small Jewish state of approximately 5,000 square kilometers and an Arab state that would be merged with Transjordan under Emir Abdullah. (See Document 2–10 and Map 2–3.) The idea of a link between a Palestinian Arab state and Transjordan, which Abdullah had nursed since the beginning of the mandate as part of his desire for a Greater Syrian state, persisted through the subsequent decades.

Arson, bombings, and assassinations continued, and in 1937 the strike moved into a second more violent stage. The murder, in September 1937, of the British district commissioner for the Galilee led the British to dissolve the Arab Higher Committee and the Supreme Muslim Council. Most of the members of the Higher Committee were arrested and deported to the Seychelles, thus depriving the Arabs of their leadership. Hajj Amin, however, escaped to Lebanon and eventually made his way, via Iraq, Iran, and Turkey, to Rome and eventually to Berlin.

Far from defusing the Arab national movement, however, the British acts seemed to inflame it, and by 1938 they seemed unable to control much of the Arab rural population. Arabs inside Palestine were aided by those outside. Fawzi al-Qawuqji, a guerrilla leader in Syria, for example, entered Palestine and with Syrians, Iraqis, and Palestinian Arabs attacked British installations in the northern part of the country. There was, however, little centralized control of the Arab resistance. By the end of the rebellion in 1939, it is estimated that around 5000 Arabs had been killed, 15,000 wounded, and 5,600 arrested and detained. An indication of the disunity and lack of control among the Arab population can be seen by the fact that as many as one quarter of the casualties were inflicted by other Arabs. By 1939, the British garrison had been increased to nearly 25,000 men.

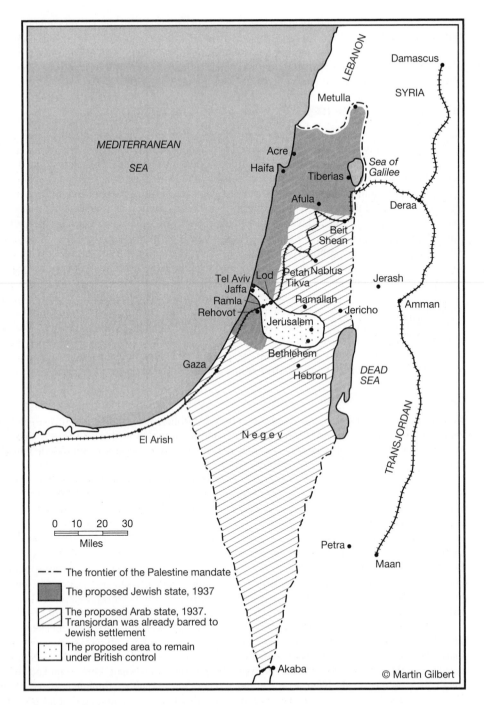

MAP 2–3   The Peel Commission Partition Plan, July 1937

Source: Atlas of the Arab–Israeli Conflict, 6th ed., Martin Gilbert, 1993, © New York: Oxford University Press, p. 22. Reproduced by permission of Taylor & Francis Books UK.

One result of the Arab Revolt was a temporary collaboration between the British and Jews against the Arabs to suppress the rebellion. The British recognized the Haganah for the first time as a legitimate Jewish defense force and agreed to its receiving arms and training legally. The principle of *Havlagah*, or restraint—that is, defending the Jewish community without retaliation, which the Haganah had adopted largely in order to maintain the goodwill of the British—now gave way to the "active defense" concept of Yitzhak Sadeh, the Haganah field commander. Haganah members were trained as uniformed auxiliary guards authorized by the British; by the end of the Arab rebellion nearly 15,000 Jews were under arms. An important figure in their training was Orde Wingate, another colorful British personality like T. E. Lawrence. Wingate, a fundamentalist Christian, believed the Jews must be in Palestine in order for the biblical prophecies to be fulfilled, and he became a passionate Zionist. Placing an emphasis on night patrols and mobile units to counter the Arab guerrilla tactics, Wingate developed Jewish special night squads and provided invaluable training for a whole generation of later leaders of Israel's army, including Moshe Dayan and Yigal Allon. In 1937, the Irgun, a Revisionist, military force, had also taken up arms and began terrorist operations against Arabs with little British opposition.

At the same time, all the parties were debating partition. Arabs continued to insist that Palestine was indissolubly Arab. Jews, however, tended to regard the idea more favorably and reluctantly accepted the Peel plan. An international conference on refugees at Evian-les-Bains, France, in 1938 made dramatically clear the increasingly perilous position of the Jews in Europe. Only one of the thirty-one countries represented at Evian, the Dominican Republic, was prepared to lift or alter immigration quotas. Jews who could still leave Germany in 1938, to say nothing of those who managed to escape the Nazi net once the war started, were severely restricted in the number of places they could go. To the Jewish Agency, therefore, a partitioned Palestine became increasingly acceptable as a possible asylum for the beleaguered Jews of Europe.

In 1938, the British established yet another commission of inquiry under the chairmanship of Sir John Woodhead to determine whether or not partition was practical and, if so, what the boundaries of the two states should be. Woodhead's report concluded that the Peel partition plan was not feasible and suggested boundaries that enraged the Jewish leaders, since many Jewish settlements and developed areas were excluded from the proposed Jewish entity. The arrangement was also absolutely unacceptable to the Arabs; they rejected all attempts to give any part of Palestine over to Jewish sovereignty.

As it happened, the British themselves were not prepared to implement the scheme. Shortly after Woodhead's report was issued, the British government rejected any partition of Palestine as impractical. To dampen the conflict, the British resumed the curtailing of Jewish immigration and land purchases, even rejecting a request in 1938 for the admission of 10,000 Jewish children from Central Europe, although the government eventually admitted the children into Great Britain.

Still attempting to find a solution acceptable to both parties, the British government announced it would convene a meeting in London of representatives of the Zionists, Palestinian Arabs, and Arabs from the surrounding countries to try to work out an agreement. If this attempt failed, the British government stated it would make a policy decision itself. Significantly, the British accepted the request of the mufti, at this time still in Lebanon, that members of the Arab Higher Committee interned in the Seychelles be released and allowed to represent the Palestine Arabs. Other Arab delegates included Emir Abdullah of Transjordan, Nuri al-Said of Iraq, Prince Feisal of Saudi Arabia, and representatives from Egypt and Yemen. The Jewish delegation included Chaim Weizmann, David Ben-Gurion, the American Zionist Rabbi Stephen Wise, and others. Except for one session, the talks, which began in February 1939, were conducted by the British with the Jews and the Arabs separately, since the Arabs would not sit in the same room with the Jews. It was obviously not going to be possible to achieve an agreement acceptable to both groups at the "Roundtable Conference"; therefore, the colonial secretary, Malcolm MacDonald, proposed a new formula, which was embodied in an official White Paper on Palestine in May 1939. (See Document 2–11.)

The 1939 White Paper

The 1939 White Paper declared that Palestine would become an independent state allied to the British Empire within ten years. This would obviously be an Arab state, since Jewish immigration was limited to 75,000 over the next five years, with Arab consent being necessary thereafter. Land sales to Jews were severely reduced by being prohibited or restricted to certain parts of the territory at the discretion of the high commissioner. This new White Paper in essence repudiated the Balfour Declaration and reversed British policy in Palestine of the previous twenty years. By 1939, as a global conflict again appeared imminent, the British were concerned about having reliable bases in the Middle East and could not afford to risk alienating the Arabs or their Muslim co-religionists in India. The Arabs, however, with their leadership destroyed, were in no position to act on the recommendations of the White Paper.

The Yishuv was shocked and enraged by the 1939 White Paper, coming as it did at a desperate time for European Jewry, and the Jewish community refused to cooperate further with the mandate authorities. Ben-Gurion later declared: "We shall fight the war as if there were no White Paper; we shall fight the White Paper as if there were no war!" Both Jews and Arabs for the most part supported the British war effort against the Germans. Once the immediate threat to the British receded after the Allied success at el-Alamein in 1942, however, both communities resumed the war in Palestine, and the British position became increasingly untenable, as we shall see in the next chapter.

Suggestions for Further Reading

ABU-LUGHOD, IBRAHIM, Ed., *The Transformation of Palestine: Essays on the Origin and Development of the Arab–Israeli Conflict*, Evanston, Ill., Northwestern University Press, 1971.

ANTONIUS, GEORGE, *The Arab Awakening*, London, Hamish Hamilton, 1938; New York, Capricorn Books, 1965.

BETHELL, NICHOLAS, *The Palestine Triangle, 1935–1946*, London, Andre Deutsch, 1979.

ESCO FOUNDATION FOR PALESTINE, INC., *Palestine: A Study of Jewish, Arab and British Policies*, 2 vols., New Haven, Conn., 1947; Kraus Reprint.

FRIEDMAN, ISAIAH, *The Question of Palestine, 1914–1918: British-Jewish-Arab Relations*, 2nd expanded ed., New Brunswick, N.J., Transaction Books, 1992.

FROMKIN, DAVID, *A Peace to End All Peace: Creating the Modern Middle East, 1914–1922*, New York, Henry Holt & Company, 1989.

HUREWITZ, J. C., *The Struggle for Palestine*, New York, W. W. Norton., 1950; 1968 Reprint, Greenwood Press, Westport, Conn.

KEDOURIE, ELIE, *In the Anglo-Arab Labyrinth: The McMahon-Hussein Correspondence and Its Interpretation, 1914–1939*, Cambridge, Cambridge University Press, 1976.

KHALIDI, WALID, ed., *From Haven to Conquest: Readings in Zionism and the Palestine Problem until 1948*, 2nd ed., Washington, D.C., Institute for Palestine Studies, 1987.

LESCH, ANN M., *Arab Politics in Palestine 1917–1939: The Frustration of a Nationalist Movement*, Ithaca, N.Y., Cornell University Press, 1979.

MATTAR, PHILLIP, *Mufti of Jerusalem: Muhammad Amin al-Husayni and the Palestinian Question*, New York, Columbia University Press, 1988.

NASHASHIBI, NASSER EDDIN, *Jerusalem's Other Voice: Ragheb Nashashibi and Moderation in Palestinian Politics, 1920–1948*, Exeter, England, Ithaqa Press, 1990.

POLK, W. R., STAMLER, D., AND ASFOUR, E., *Backdrop to Tragedy: The Struggle for Palestine*, Boston, Little Brown, 1957.

SAID, EDWARD, *The Question of Palestine*, New York, Times Books, 1979.

SANDERS, RONALD, *The High Walls of Jerusalem: A History of the Balfour Declaration and the Birth of the British Mandate for Palestine*, New York, Holt, Rinehart & Winston, 1983.

SEGEV, TOM, *One Palestine, Complete*, trans. by Haim Watzman, New York, Metropolitan Books, 2000.

STEIN, KENNETH, *The Land Question in Palestine, 1917–1939*, Chapel Hill and London, University of North Carolina Press, 1984.

SYKES, CHRISTOPHER, *Crossroads to Israel: Palestine from Balfour to Bevin*, London, New English Library, 1969; Cleveland and New York, World Publishing Company, 1965.

WEIZMANN, CHAIM, *Trial and Error*, Westport, Conn., Greenwood Press, 1971.

 **DOCUMENT 2–1**

Sir Henry McMahon's Second Note to the Sharif Husain

Cairo, October 24, 1915.

Complimentary titles.

I have, with gratification and pleasure, received your note of the 29th Shawwal, 1333, and its tokens of sincere friendship have filled me with satisfaction and contentment.

I regret to find that you inferred from my last note that my attitude towards the question of frontiers and boundaries was one of hesitancy and lukewarmth. Such was in no wise the intention of my note. All I meant was that I considered that the time had not yet come in which that question could be discussed in a conclusive manner.

But, having realised from your last note that you considered the question important, vital and urgent, I hastened to communicate to the Government of Great Britain the purport of your note. It gives me the greatest pleasure to convey to you, on their behalf, the following declarations which, I have no doubt, you will receive with satisfaction and acceptance.

The districts of Mersin and Alexandretta, and portions of Syria lying to the west of the districts of Damascus, Homs, Hama and Aleppo, cannot be said to be purely Arab, and must on that account be excepted from the proposed delimitation.

Subject to that modification, and without prejudice to the treaties concluded between us and certain Arab Chiefs, we accept that delimitation.

As for the regions lying within the proposed frontiers, in which Great Britain is free to act without detriment to the interests of her ally France, I am authorised to give you the following pledges on behalf of the Government of Great Britain, and to reply as follows to your note:

1. That, subject to the modifications stated above, Great Britain is prepared to recognise and uphold the independence of the Arabs in all the regions lying within the frontiers proposed by the Sharif of Mecca;

2. That Great Britain will guarantee the Holy Places against all external aggression, and will recognise the obligation of preserving them from aggression;

3. That, when circumstances permit, Great Britain will help the Arabs with her advice and assist them in the establishment of governments to suit those diverse regions;

4. That it is understood that the Arabs have already decided to seek the counsels and advice of Great Britain exclusively; and that such European advisers and officials as may be needed to establish a sound system of administration shall be British;

5. That, as regards the two vilayets of Baghdad and of Basra, the Arabs recognise that the fact of Great Britain's established position and interests there will call for the setting up of special administrative arrangements to protect those regions from foreign aggression, to promote the welfare of their inhabitants, and to safeguard our mutual economic interests.

I am confident that this declaration will convince you, beyond all doubt, of Great Britain's sympathy with the aspirations of her friends the Arabs; and that it will result in a lasting and solid alliance with them, of which one of the immediate consequences will be the expulsion of the

Turks from the Arab countries and the liberation of the Arab peoples from the Turkish yoke which has weighed on them all these long years. . . .

Compliments.

Source: George Antonius, *The Arab Awakening* (New York: Capricorn Books, 1965), pp. 419–420. Reprinted by permission of The Putnam Publishing Group. Copyright © 1939 by G. P. Putnam's Sons.

 DOCUMENT 2-2

The Sharif Husain's Third Note to Sir Henry McMahon

Mecca, Zul-Hejja 27, 1333.
[November 5, 1915.]

Complimentary titles.

With great gratification have we received your note of the 15th Zul-Hejja [October 24] to which we would reply as follows.

First, in order to facilitate agreement and serve the cause of Islam by the removal of possible sources of hardship and tribulation, and in earnest of the particular esteem in which we hold Great Britain, we no longer insist on the inclusion of the districts of Mersin and Adana in the Arab Kingdom. As for the vilayets of Aleppo and Bairut and their western maritime coasts, these are purely Arab provinces in which the Moslem is indistinguishable from the Christian, for they are both the descendants of one forefather. And we Moslems intend, in those provinces, to follow the precepts laid down by the Commander of the Faithful, 'Umar ibn al-Khattab (God have mercy upon him!), and the caliphs who came after him, when he enjoined upon the Moslems to treat the Christians on a footing with themselves, saying: they are to enjoy the same rights and bear the same obligations as ourselves. They will have, moreover, their denominational privileges, as far as the public interest allows. . . .

The Arabs firmly believe that, after the War, the German-ridden Turks will try to give them constant provocation, in religious as well as temporal matters, and to wreak the utmost vengeance upon them. On their side, the Arabs have resolved and vowed to fight the Turks and continue fighting them until not one of them (save for women and children) remains in any of the Arab countries. Our present deliberation is on account of the considerations stated above. . . .

Source: Antonius, *Arab Awakening*, pp. 421–422.

 DOCUMENT 2-3

Sir Henry McMahon's Third Note to the Sharif Husain

Cairo, December 13, 1915.

Complimentary titles.

Your note of the 27th Zul-Hejja, 1333, has reached me, and I was glad to find that you consent to the exclusion of the vilayets of Mersin and Adana from the boundaries of the Arab countries. . . .

As for the vilayets of Aleppo and Bairut, the Government of Great Britain have fully understood your statement in that respect and noted it with the greatest care. But as the interests of their ally France are involved in those two provinces, the question calls for careful consideration. We shall communicate again with you on this subject, at the appropriate time. . . .

In token of our good faith, and as a contribution to your endeavours in our joint cause, I am sending the sum of £20,000 with your trusted messenger.

Compliments.

Source: Antonius, *Arab Awakening*, pp. 423–424.

 DOCUMENT 2–4

Letter by Arthur James Balfour to Lord Rothschild (The Balfour Declaration)

Foreign Office
November 2nd, 1917.
Dear Lord Rothschild,

I have much pleasure in conveying to you, on behalf of His Majesty's Government, the following declaration of sympathy with Jewish Zionist aspirations which has been submitted to, and approved by, the Cabinet.

"His Majesty's Government view with favour the establishment in Palestine of a national home for the Jewish people, and will use their best endeavours to facilitate the achievement of this object, it being clearly understood that nothing shall be done which may prejudice the civil and religious rights of existing non-Jewish communities in Palestine, or the rights and political status enjoyed by Jews in any other country."

I should be grateful if you would bring this declaration to the knowledge of the Zionist Federation.

Yours sincerely,
ARTHUR JAMES BALFOUR.

Source: Walter Z. Laqueur and Barry Rubin, eds., *The Israel–Arab Reader: A Documentary History of The Middle East Conflict*, 4th ed. (New York: Penguin Books, 1984), p. 18.

 DOCUMENT 2–5

British Cabinet Discussion on Support for Zionism, October 4, 1917 [Excerpt]

Mr. Montagu urged strong objections to any declaration in which it was stated that Palestine was the "national home" of the Jewish people. He regarded the Jews as a religious community and himself as a Jewish Englishman. He based his argument on the prejudicial effect on the status of Jewish Britons of a statement that His Majesty's Government regarded Palestine as the national home of Jewish people. Whatever safeguarding words might be used in the formula, the civil rights of Jews as nations in the country in which they were born might be endangered. How could he negotiate with the peoples of India on behalf of His Majesty's

Government if the world had just been told that His Majesty's Government regarded his national home as being in Turkish territory? He specially urged that the only trial of strength between Zionists and anti-Zionists in England had resulted in a very narrow majority for the Zionists, namely, 56 to 51, of the representatives of Anglo-Jewry on the Conjoint Committee. He also pointed out that most English-born Jews were opposed to Zionism, while it was supported by foreign-born Jews, such as Dr. Caster and Dr. Herz, the two Grand Rabbis, who had been born in Roumania and Austria respectively, and Dr. Weizmann, President of the English Zionist Federation, who was born in Russia. He submitted that the Cabinet's first duty was to English Jews, and that Colonel House had declared that President Wilson is opposed to a declaration now.

Lord Curzon urged strong objections upon practical grounds. He stated, from his recollection of Palestine, that the country was, for the most part, barren and desolate; there being but sparse cultivation on the terraced slopes, the valleys and streams being few, and large centres of population scarce, a less propitious seat for the future Jewish race could not be imagined. How was it proposed to get rid of the existing majority of Mussulman inhabitants and to introduce the Jews in their place? How many would be willing to return and on what pursuits would they engage?

To secure for the Jews already in Palestine equal civil and religious rights seemed to him a better policy than to aim at repatriation on a large scale. He regarded the latter as sentimental idealism, which would never be realized, and that His Majesty's Government should have nothing to do with it.

War Cabinet 245 CAB 23/24

Source: T. G. Fraser, *The Middle East, 1914–1979* (New York: St. Martin's Press, 1980), pp. 15–16.

 DOCUMENT 2-6

Text of the Faisal-Weizmann Agreement

His Royal Highness the Amir FAISAL, representing and acting on behalf of the Arab Kingdom of HEJAZ, and Dr. CHAIM WEIZMANN, representing and acting on behalf of the Zionist Organisation, mindful of the racial kinship and ancient bonds existing between the Arabs and the Jewish people, and realising that the surest means of working out the consummation of their national aspirations, is through the closest possible collaboration in the development of the Arab State and Palestine, and being desirous further of confirming the good understanding which exists between them, have agreed upon the following Articles:

ARTICLE I

The Arab State and Palestine in all their relations and undertakings shall be controlled by the most cordial goodwill and understanding and to this end Arab and Jewish duly accredited agents shall be established and maintained in their respective territories.

ARTICLE II

Immediately following the completion of the deliberations of the Peace Conference, the definite boundaries between the Arab State and Palestine shall be determined by a Commission to be agreed upon by the parties hereto.

ARTICLE III

In the establishment of the Constitution and Administration of Palestine all such measures shall be adopted as will afford the fullest guarantees for carrying into effect the British Government's Declaration of the 2nd of November, 1917.

ARTICLE IV

All necessary measures shall be taken to encourage and stimulate immigration of Jews into Palestine on a large scale, and as quickly as possible to settle Jewish immigrants upon the land through closer settlement and intensive cultivation of the soil. In taking such measures the Arab peasant and tenant farmers shall be protected in their rights, and shall be assisted in forwarding their economic development.

ARTICLE V

No regulation nor law shall be made prohibiting or interfering in any way with the free exercise of religion; and further the free exercise and enjoyment of religious profession and worship without discrimination or preference shall for ever be allowed. No religious test shall ever be required for the exercise of civil or political rights.

ARTICLE VI

The Mohammedan Holy Places shall be under Mohammedan control.

ARTICLE VII

The Zionist Organisation proposes to send to Palestine a Commission of experts to make a survey of the economic possibilities of the country, and to report upon the best means for its development. The Zionist Organisation will place the aforementioned Commission at the disposal of the Arab State for the purpose of a survey of the economic possibilities of the Arab State and to report upon the best means for its development. The Zionist Organisation will use its best efforts to assist the Arab State in providing the means for developing the natural resources and economic possibilities thereof.

ARTICLE VIII

The parties hereto agree to act in complete accord and harmony in all matters embraced herein before the Peace Congress.

ARTICLE IX

Any matters of dispute which may arise between the contracting parties shall be referred to the British Government for arbitration.

Given under our hand at LONDON, ENGLAND, the THIRD day of JANUARY, ONE THOUSAND NINE HUNDRED AND NINETEEN.

[*Translation*]

Provided the Arabs obtain their independence as demanded in my Memorandum dated the 4th of January, 1919, to the Foreign Office of the Government of Great Britain, I shall concur in the above articles. But if the slightest modification or departure were to be made [*sc.* in relation to the demands in the Memorandum] I shall not then be bound by a single word of the present Agreement which shall be deemed void and of no account or validity, and I shall not be answerable in any way whatsoever.

FAISAL IBN HUSAIN (in Arabic)
CHAIM WEIZMANN

Source: Antonius, *Arab Awakening*, pp. 437–439.

 DOCUMENT 2-7

Feisal-Frankfurter Correspondence

DELEGATION HEDJAZIENNE, Paris, March 3, 1919.
DEAR MR. FRANKFURTER: I want to take this opportunity of my first contact with American Zionists to tell you what I have often been able to say to Dr. Weizmann in Arabia and Europe.

We feel that the Arabs and Jews are cousins in race, having suffered similar oppressions at the hands of powers stronger than themselves, and by a happy coincidence have been able to take the first step towards the attainment of their national ideals together.

We Arabs, especially the educated among us, look with the deepest sympathy on the Zionist movement. Our deputation here in Paris is fully acquainted with the proposals submitted yesterday by the Zionist Organization to the Peace Conference, and we regard them as moderate and proper. We will do our best, in so far as we are concerned, to help them through: we will wish the Jews a most hearty welcome home.

With the chiefs of your movement, especially with Dr. Weizmann, we have had and continue to have the closest relations. He has been a great helper of our cause, and I hope the Arabs may soon be in a position to make the Jews some return for their kindness. We are working together for a reformed and revived Near East, and our two movements complete one another. The Jewish movement is national and not imperialist. Our movement is national and not imperialist, and there is room in Syria for us both. Indeed I think that neither can be a real success without the other.

People less informed and less responsible than our leaders and yours, ignoring the need for cooperation of the Arabs and Zionists have been trying to exploit the local difficulties that must necessarily arise in Palestine in the early stages of our movements. Some of them have, I am afraid, misrepresented your aims to the Arab peasantry, and our aims to the Jewish peasantry, with the result that interested parties have been able to make capital out of what they call our differences.

I wish to give you my firm conviction that these differences are not on questions of principle, but on matters of detail such as must inevitably occur in every contact of neighbouring peoples, and as are easily adjusted by mutual goodwill. Indeed nearly all of them will disappear with fuller knowledge.

I look forward, and my people with me look forward, to a future in which we will help you and you will help us, so that the countries in which we are mutually interested may once again take their places in the community of civilised peoples of the world.

Believe me,
Yours sincerely,

(*Sgd.*) FEISAL.
5th March, 1919.

Source: Laqueur and Rubin, *Israel–Arab Reader*, pp. 21–22.

DOCUMENT 2-8

Recommendations of the King-Crane Commission, August 28, 1919 [Excerpt]

5. We recommend, in the fifth place, serious modification of the extreme Zionist program for Palestine of unlimited immigration of Jews, looking finally to making Palestine distinctly a Jewish State.

   (1) The Commissioners began their study of Zionism with minds predisposed in its favor, but the actual facts in Palestine, coupled with the force of the general principles proclaimed by the Allies and accepted by the Syrians have driven them to the recommendation here made.

   (2) The Commission was abundantly supplied with literature on the Zionist program by the Zionist Commission to Palestine; heard in conferences much concerning the Zionist colonies and their claims and personally saw something of what had been accomplished. They found much to approve in the aspirations and plans of the Zionists, and had warm appreciation for the devotion of many of the colonists, and for their success, by modern methods, in overcoming great natural obstacles.

   (3) The Commission recognized also that definite encouragement had been given to the Zionists by the Allies in Mr. Balfour's often quoted statement in its approval by other representatives of the Allies. If, however, the strict terms of the Balfour Statement are adhered to—favoring "the establishment in Palestine of a national home for the Jewish people," "it being clearly understood that nothing shall be done which may prejudice the civil and religious rights of existing non-Jewish communities in Palestine"—it can hardly be doubted that the extreme Zionist Program must be greatly modified. For "a national home for the Jewish people" is not equivalent to making Palestine into a Jewish State: nor can the erection of such a Jewish State be accomplished without the gravest trespass upon the "civil and religious rights of existing non-Jewish communities in Palestine." The fact came out repeatedly in the Commission's conference with Jewish representatives, that the Zionists looked forward to a practically complete dispossession of the present non-Jewish inhabitants of Palestine, by various forms of purchase.

   In his address of July 4, 1918, President Wilson laid down the following principle as one of the four great "ends for which the associated peoples of the world were fighting": "The settlement of every question, whether of territory, of sovereignty, of economic arrangement, or of political relationship upon the basis of the free acceptance of that settlement by the people immediately concerned, and not upon the basis of the material interest or advantage of any other nation or people which may desire a different settlement for the sake of its own exterior influence or mastery." If that principle is to rule, and so the wishes of Palestine's population are to be decisive as to what is to be done with Palestine, then it is to be remembered that the non-Jewish population of Palestine—nearly nine-tenths of the whole—are emphatically against the entire Zionist program. The tables show that there was no one thing upon which the population of Palestine were more agreed than upon this. To subject a people so minded to unlimited Jewish immigration, and to steady financial and social pressure to surrender the land, would be a gross violation of the principle just quoted, and of the peoples' rights, though it kept within the forms of law.

   It is to be noted also that the feeling against the Zionist program is not confined to Palestine, but shared very generally by the people throughout Syria, as our conferences clearly showed. More than 72 per cent—1350 in all—of all the petitions in the whole of Syria were directed against the Zionist program. Only two requests—those for a united Syria and for independence—had a larger support. This general feeling was only voiced by the "General Syrian Congress," in the seventh, eighth and tenth resolutions of their statement.

The Peace Conference should not shut its eyes to the fact that the anti-Zionist feeling in Palestine and Syria is intense and not lightly to be flouted.

_____

Source: Laqueur and Rubin, *Israel–Arab Reader*, pp. 28–29.

DOCUMENT 2-9

The Churchill White Paper, 1922 [Excerpt]

The tension which has prevailed from time to time in Palestine is mainly due to apprehensions, which are entertained both by sections of the Arab and by sections of the Jewish population. These apprehensions, so far as the Arabs are concerned, are partly based upon exaggerated interpretations of the meaning of the Declaration favouring the establishment of a Jewish National Home in Palestine, made on behalf of His Majesty's Government on 2nd November, 1917. Unauthorized statements have been made to the effect that the purpose in view is to create a wholly Jewish Palestine. Phrases have been used such as that Palestine is to become "as Jewish as England is English." His Majesty's Government regard any such expectation as impracticable and have no such aim in view. Nor have they at any time contemplated, as appears to be feared by the Arab Delegation, the disappearance or the subordination of the Arabic population, language, or culture in Palestine. They would draw attention to the fact that the terms of the Declaration referred to do not contemplate that Palestine as a whole should be converted into a Jewish National Home, but that such a Home should be founded *in Palestine*. . . .

So far as the Jewish population of Palestine are concerned it appears that some among them are apprehensive that His Majesty's Government may depart from the policy embodied in the Declaration of 1917. It is necessary, therefore, once more to affirm that these fears are unfounded, and that that Declaration, re-affirmed by the Conference of the Principal Allied Powers at San Remo and again in the Treaty of Sèvres, is not susceptible of change. . . .

When it is asked what is meant by the development of the Jewish National Home in Palestine, it may be answered that it is not the imposition of a Jewish nationality upon the inhabitants of Palestine as a whole, but the further development of the existing Jewish community, with the assistance of Jews in other parts of the world, in order that it may become a centre in which the Jewish people as a whole may take, on grounds of religion and race, an interest and a pride. But in order that this community should have the best prospect of free development and provide a full opportunity for the Jewish people to display its capacities, it is essential that it should know that it is in Palestine as of right and not on sufferance. That is the reason why it is necessary that the existence of a Jewish National Home in Palestine should be internationally guaranteed, and that it should be formally recognized to rest upon ancient historic connection.

This, then, is the interpretation which His Majesty's Government place upon the Declaration of 1917, and, so understood, the Secretary of State is of opinion that it does not contain or imply anything which need cause either alarm to the Arab population of Palestine or disappointment to the Jews.

For the fulfilment of this policy it is necessary that the Jewish community in Palestine should be able to increase its numbers by immigration. This immigration cannot be so great in volume as to exceed whatever may be the economic capacity of the country at the time to absorb new arrivals. It is essential to ensure that the immigrants should not be a burden upon the people of Palestine as a whole, and that they should not deprive any section of the present population of their employment.

Source: Laqueur and Rubin, *Israel–Arab Reader*, pp. 45–48.

DOCUMENT 2-10

The Peel Commission's Justification for Proposing Partition for Palestine, 1937

An irrepressible conflict has arisen between two national communities within the narrow bounds of one small country. About 1,000,000 Arabs are in strife, open or latent, with some 400,000 Jews. There is no common ground between them. The Arab community is predominantly Asiatic in character, the Jewish community predominantly European. They differ in religion and in language. Their cultural and social life, their ways of thought and conduct, are as incompatible as their national aspirations. These last are the greatest bar to peace. Arabs and Jews might possibly learn to live and work together in Palestine if they would make a genuine effort to reconcile and combine their national ideals and so build up in time a joint or dual nationality. But this they cannot do. The War and its sequel have inspired all Arabs with the hope of reviving in a free and united Arab world the traditions of the Arab golden age. The Jews similarly are inspired by their historic past. They mean to show what the Jewish nation can achieve when restored to the land of its birth. National assimilation between Arabs and Jews is thus ruled out. In the Arab picture the Jews could only occupy the place they occupied in Arab Egypt or Arab Spain. The Arabs would be as much outside the Jewish picture as the Canaanites in the old land of Israel. The National Home, as we have said before, cannot be half-national. In these circumstances to maintain that Palestinian citizenship has any moral meaning is a mischievous pretence. Neither Arab nor Jew has any sense of service to a single State.

Palestine Royal Commission Report,
(Cmd. 5479, 1937)

Source: Fraser, *The Middle East*, pp. 22–23.

DOCUMENT 2-11

The 1939 White Paper on Palestine [Excerpt]

In the light of these considerations His Majesty's Government make the following declaration of their intentions regarding the future government of Palestine:

(1) The objective of His Majesty's Government is the establishment within ten years of an independent Palestine State in such treaty relations with the United Kingdom as will provide satisfactorily for the commercial and strategic requirements of both countries in the future.

The proposal for the establishment of the independent State would involve consultation with the Council of the League of Nations with a view to the termination of the Mandate.

(2) The independent State should be one in which Arabs and Jews share in government in such a way as to ensure that the essential interests of each community are safeguarded.

. . .

14. It has been urged that all further Jewish immigration into Palestine should be stopped forthwith. His Majesty's Government cannot accept such a proposal. It would damage the whole of the financial and economic system of Palestine and thus affect adversely the interests of Arabs and Jews alike. Moreover, in the view of His Majesty's Government, abruptly to stop further immigration would be unjust to the Jewish National Home. But, above all, His Majesty's Government are conscious of the present unhappy plight of large numbers of Jews who seek a refuge from certain European countries, and they believe that Palestine can and should make a further contribution to the solution of this pressing world problem. In all these circumstances, they believe that they will be acting consistently with their Mandatory obligations to both Arabs and Jews, and in the manner best calculated to serve the interests of the whole people of Palestine, by adopting the following proposals regarding immigration:

(1) Jewish immigration during the next five years will be at a rate which, if economic absorptive capacity permits, will bring the Jewish population up to approximately one-third of the total population of the country. Taking into account the expected natural increase of the Arab and Jewish populations, and the number of illegal Jewish immigrants now in the country, this would allow of the admission, as from the beginning of April this year, of some 75,000 immigrants over the next five years. . . .

(2) The existing machinery for ascertaining economic absorptive capacity will be retained, and the High Commissioner will have the ultimate responsibility for deciding the limits of economic capacity. Before each periodic decision is taken, Jewish and Arab representatives will be consulted.

(3) After the period of five years no further Jewish immigration will be permitted unless the Arabs of Palestine are prepared to acquiesce in it.

(4) His Majesty's Government are determined to check illegal immigration, and further preventive measures are being adopted. The numbers of any Jewish illegal immigrants who, despite these measures, may succeed in coming into the country and cannot be deported will be deducted from the yearly quotas.

15. His Majesty's Government are satisfied that, when the immigration over five years which is now contemplated has taken place, they will not be justified in facilitating, nor will they be under any obligation to facilitate, the further development of the Jewish National Home by immigration regardless of the wishes of the Arab population.

Palestine: Statement of Policy (Cmd. 6019, 1939)

Source: Fraser, *The Middle East*, pp. 23–24.

T H R E E

World War II,
Jewish Displaced Persons,
and the Partition of Palestine

C H R O N O L O G Y

Jan. 30, 1933	Adolf Hitler assumes power in Germany
Sept.–Nov., 1935	Nuremberg Laws against Jews passed
April, 1936	Formation of Arab Higher Committee
July, 1937	Evian Refugee Conference
July, 1938	MacDonald White Paper
Dec., 1941	Death camps put into operation
May, 1942	Zionist Conference at Biltmore Hotel in New York City
Nov. 4, 1944	Churchill makes promise to Weizmann
Nov. 6, 1944	Lord Moyne assassinated in Cairo
Feb., 1945	President Roosevelt meets with King Ibn Saud of Saudi Arabia
March 22, 1945	Arab League founded in Cairo
Apr. 12, 1945	Death of FDR; Harry S Truman becomes U.S. president
May 8, 1945	Germany surrenders
Nov. 13, 1945	Anglo-American Committee of Inquiry into Jewish refugee question announced
May 1, 1946	Anglo-American Committee report issued
July 22, 1946	British headquarters in King David Hotel in Jerusalem bombed
Aug. 5, 1946	Jewish agency meeting in Paris indicates willingness to accept partition of Palestine west of the Jordan River
Oct. 4, 1946	Truman announces support for partition of Palestine into Jewish and Arab states
Jan., 1947	British Cabinet decides to refer Palestine question to United Nations
Apr. 28, 1947	Opening of special session of U.N. General Assembly on Palestine issue
May 13, 1947	U.N. General Assembly establishes a Special Committee on Palestine (UNSCOP)
Aug. 31, 1947	UNSCOP report presented to General Assembly
Nov. 29, 1947	U.N. General Assembly votes to partition Palestine
Jan., 1948	Arab Liberation Army enters Palestine
Mar. 18, 1948	Weizmann sees Truman
Mar. 19, 1948	U.S. proposes U.N. Trusteeship in Palestine
Apr. 9, 1948	Jewish attack on Deir Yassin
Apr. 13, 1948	Arab attack on bus convoy to Mt. Scopus
Apr 22, 1948	Haganah captures Haifa
May 14, 1948	Israel established; U.S. extends de facto recognition

World War II was a pivotal point in the history of twentieth-century Palestine, as well as the dominant event of twentieth-century Europe. Within three years of war's end in Europe, British forces withdrew from Palestine and David Ben-Gurion, head of the Jewish Agency in Palestine, immediately proclaimed the existence of the state of Israel. Palestine, as constituted under the mandate, ceased to exist, and a new era began as the struggle between the Arabs and Jews of Palestine now became part of a general Arab–Israeli conflict.

In this chapter we shall trace the events leading to the decision of the UN General Assembly on November 29, 1947, recommending the partition of Palestine into a Jewish state and an Arab state with economic union, and we will weigh the arguments of both sides about the significance of World War II and the Holocaust on the history of Palestine.

When reviewing the period preceding the establishment of Israel, the majority of Zionist historians stress the importance of the Allied victory, the Holocaust, and the plight of its survivors in shaping the events that led the newly formed United Nations to opt for the partition of Palestine into a Jewish state and an Arab state, which provided the legal framework for the Jewish Agency to makes its proclamation. Pro-Palestinian and revisionist Zionist historians, on the other hand, while not entirely ignoring the destruction of the European Jews and efforts to find a safe homeland for the "remnants" following the war, emphasize the Yishuv's use of "gun-Zionism" in Palestine itself and the effective use of terror and guerrilla tactics in ousting the British from Palestine and later defeating the Palestinian Arabs and their supporters. Interestingly, both groups of historians agree that American Jews played an important role in influencing Washington to adopt a policy of support for the partition of Palestine, and that the United States was significant in persuading the United Nations General Assembly to vote for partition.

What is noteworthy about British policy during and immediately after World War II, especially in the light of the Holocaust, is just how closely it preserved the intent of the White Paper of 1939, issued before Hitler embarked upon the "final solution." Considering what Britain and its allies later learned about the fate of European Jewry in all its horrific detail and the continued tragedy of the survivors following Germany's defeat, the British government's adherence to its stated 1939 policy concerning the admission of Jewish refugees into Palestine is quite extraordinary. It does, however, add weight to the argument that if World War II was important in the establishment of Israel, it was not because the Christian nations felt an obligation to the survivors of the Holocaust to provide them with a homeland. British policy, at least in this respect, tends rather to support the view that the war was important because it forced the Yishuv to realize that if Jews wanted a state, they would have to win it with deeds as well as words.

In fact, during the war the British government did reconsider its postwar policy toward Palestine. Recognizing that the end of the mandate was inevitable, in December 1943, a cabinet committee on Palestine backed by Churchill recommended British support for the partition of Palestine—the plan first proposed by the 1937 Peel Commission. Chaim Weizmann and the Jewish Agency knew of this decision. The assassination in Cairo on November 6, 1944, of Lord Moyne, deputy minister of state for Middle East affairs and a close personal friend of Churchill's, by the Jewish terrorist group *LEHI* ("Fighters for the Freedom of Israel"—also known as the Stern Gang, after its founder Abraham Stern), prevented this recommendation from becoming official British policy.

Had there been no war in Europe, the Jews of Palestine in their resort to arms would, presumably, have met the same fate at the hands of the British army as had the Arabs of Palestine in the 1936–1939 uprising. In this context, it is perhaps also worth considering what would have happened to the Jews of Palestine had General Erwin Rommel of Germany won his North African campaign. Clearly the history of Palestine and the Middle East would have been entirely different; under an agreement signed by the mufti of Jerusalem, Hajj Amin al-Husseini and the Italian dictator Benito Mussolini in October 1941, the Jews of Palestine would have been exterminated by the Germans, with the help of the Arabs.

Both Arabs and Jews objected to British policy in 1939. The Arabs felt cheated; their hoped-for independence had once again been deferred, and Jewish immigration was going to continue for five more years. Zionists had to face the unacceptable idea that the British felt that the existing Jewish population and their institutions were such that they had fulfilled their promise of establishing a Jewish national home in Palestine. Although most people see the two statements of British policy as mutually contradictory, the 1939 White Paper may be compared with the previous major document of British policy toward Palestine—the Balfour Declaration. Both documents appear to make contradictory promises; both appear to be the result of compromises that failed to satisfy fully either Jews or Arabs; and while Jews accepted the Balfour Declaration, both Jews and Arabs rejected the 1939 White Paper.

During World War II, Zionists supported the Allies against Germany. They had no alternative. Hajj Amin al-Husseini, the most influential leader of Palestinian Arabs, supported Germany, and many Arab leaders, including Anwar Sadat, for example, joined German front organizations. But far more important was the Nazi policy of extermination of Jews both in Europe and, if they had been victorious, in Palestine.

Although the Holocaust may be viewed by many as the catalyst in the establishment of Israel after World War II, the internal forces of Jewish history striving toward independent statehood had been set in motion long before and were reinforced by institutions established in Palestine during the mandate. Zionist leaders did not learn the facts of the Holocaust until the summer of 1942, following the Biltmore conference held in New York City. Even then they did not grasp its scale and extent. It was deeply shocking that such events could happen in the twentieth century. While for the world's Jews—and doubtless also for the majority of Christians in Britain and the United States—the Holocaust created an irresistible sense that something should be done in Palestine to atone for the Holocaust and to compensate the remnants of European Jewry, this attitude did not prevail over all other concerns among British and American policymakers. The Holocaust clearly did not influence Ernest Bevin, the British foreign secretary in the new Labor government, who resisted efforts to admit Jewish displaced persons into Palestine between 1946 and 1948. Nor did it figure in the minds of American State Department officials, including Secretary of State George Marshall, whose prime concern was European security and the future interests of American oil firms in the Middle East. Harry Truman, the grandson of Southerners forced to become refugees after the Civil War, was an exception, but even he had many other reasons for his attempt to persuade the British to admit 100,000 Jewish displaced persons into Palestine. And the Holocaust certainly did not figure in the minds of Palestinian Arabs. They took the understandable view that they did not perpetrate the Holocaust, and if Europeans felt, rightly, that they should make amends, they should not do so at the expense of the Arabs.

The Holocaust

There are a number of observations we should make about the Holocaust before we continue. In the first place we must be very clear what we mean when we speak of the Holocaust. Was it just a greater version of previous Jewish persecutions, or an extended pogrom? The Holocaust does not simply mean that Jews suffered more death and destruction than other groups in Europe, such as the Russians or Poles, or others, such as the Cambodians or Rwandans, who have been massacred by the millions since that time. There are many examples in history of mass murder; for example, the Armenians by the Turks during World War I. We should remember also that 29 million non-Jews perished in World War II in addition to the approximately 6 million Jews. But the Holocaust differs from these events in one basic way: The Holocaust was the attempt to *annihilate*—indeed, totally exterminate—all the Jews of Europe. None of the other massacres—with the possible exception of that of the Armenians—however horrifying, had as their basic aim the total elimination of a people. And none were conducted on the scale of the Holocaust.

Second, we should note that while the Holocaust was and remains a Jewish tragedy, it was carried out by Gentiles, and so it raises fundamental questions for non-Jews as well as for Jews. The Holocaust had a profound effect on surviving Jews worldwide, and it also had a profound effect on non-Jews. It forced Europeans to ask themselves just what did European civilization stand for; what levels of bestiality was it capable of? Nor was it the Holocaust *per se* that most influenced subsequent events in Palestine; the future of Palestine was shaped more by the question of the future of the survivors of the Holocaust. We cannot overemphasize the effect of the Holocaust on the European survivors and especially the Yishuv. The Holocaust created the determination that "Never Again" would Jews be victims, that "Never Again" would Jews be found wanting in the capacity to defend themselves. This almost fanatical but understandable resolve has been the driving force of all Israeli policies relating to the security and future of the Jewish state in its dealing with the Palestinians and the Arab states.

Third, we must also understand the equally strong sense of bitterness and betrayal among the Palestinian Arab population in relation to the Holocaust. Their sense of resentment and hatred is not directed so much against Jews as it is against Western Europeans. Palestinians did not initiate or participate in the Holocaust, but they feel they have been made to pay the price for the actions of Europeans, both during and after the Holocaust. First, because the European powers did so little to intervene to prevent or lessen the Holocaust and second, because following the end of the war, Palestine was seen as the appropriate location for the survivors, thereby depriving the Arabs of their homes and land. Thus, they too feel they are victims of the Holocaust. Eric Hobsbawm has claimed that the Holocaust has given superiority to Jewish assertions of the right to the land, and he quotes Israeli writer Amos Elon as arguing that the genocide of the Jews by Hitler has been turned into a legitimizing myth for the existence of the state of Israel.

The Holocaust differed quantitatively and qualitatively from previous European anti-Semitism. Hitler's "final solution" was the logical conclusion of neo-Darwinian views: Aryans were superior to Jews (and Gypsies and Slavs as well), who were polluters of civilization and culture. Jews should, therefore, be eliminated. In addition, Hitler believed that Jews were part of a Jewish-Communist conspiracy that, in his mind, was responsible for Germany's defeat in World War I. Beginning in 1942, extermination of Jews ranked high in priority among the Nazis' activities. At the beginning of World War II, there were approximately 18.5 million Jews in the world; by the end of the war, 6 million had been murdered. Only 1 million of Europe's 7 million Jews survived the Holocaust.

The German government had not embarked on mass murder of Jews at the outset; the "final solution" was reached by stages. The first step was to define Jews in terms of race. The Nuremberg Laws of 1935 prohibited marriage and sexual relations between Aryans (the designations "Aryan" and "non-Aryan" were introduced in 1933) and Jews in an attempt to isolate and identify Jews. Nazi regulations became more and more repressive; soon, Jews were required to register with the state and to wear the Jewish badge—a large yellow six-pointed star worn on the back and on the chest.

With the events of *Kristallnacht* in November 1938, when roving Nazi gangs destroyed Jewish homes, property, and synagogues throughout Germany, Nazi policy approached that of inciting a pogrom. Jews were "encouraged" by threats of internment in concentration camps to leave Germany and to abandon their possessions. The majority did not leave, of course, because they either felt assimilated, believed that the danger would pass, or had nowhere else to go. Remember, most European nations had their own problems at that time—it was still the period of world depression—and non-European Western countries like the United States, Australia, South Africa, and nations in South America had restrictions (usually economic and/or racial) upon the number and type of immigrants they would admit. These restrictions barred most of Europe's

Jews. The depressed economic conditions most nations were experiencing during the late 1930s probably made it easier for most statesmen to believe Hitler would not carry out his stated policies toward Jews, even though it was becoming clearer, day by day, that he would indeed attempt to exterminate them.

Some belated steps were taken, however—although it was pretty much a case of too little, too late. In July 1938, President Franklin Delano Roosevelt had convened an international conference at Evian, on the French shore of Lake Geneva, to discuss ways of rescuing Jewish refugees from Germany. It was a failure. Most countries would take very few if any Jews. Moreover, leaders of world Zionism did not really want the Jews to go to lands other than Palestine. The British, as we noted earlier, would not allow increased Jewish entry into Palestine, but they did try to find alternative locations for some Jewish refugees, such as Guyana and, later, Australia.

After the Germans marched into Poland in 1939, Jews were rounded up and concentrated in ghettos. Nazi leaders decided on mass murder as the "final solution" to the "problem" of European Jewry after the invasion of the Soviet Union in 1941. Several methods were used. At first, the *Einsatzgruppen*, killing squads of the S.S. (*Schutzstaffel*) who were especially selected and trained, followed front-line troops, and, after rounding up suspected Jews, shot them *en masse* and buried them in huge graves that they had forced their victims to dig. The S.S., formed in 1925, became the elite organization of the Nazi party and carried out the central tasks in the "final solution." Hitler placed Adolf Eichmann in charge of ridding Germany and German-occupied Europe of all Jews and gave him practically unlimited powers. Heinrich Himmler, head of the S.S., became the chief executor of the "final solution." Gassing in sealed trucks became the preferred method of killing as early as December 1941, and eventually special camps, or extermination centers, were created for the purpose of mass murder. It is impossible to convey the brutal, sadistic, and terrifying nature of these camps by merely describing them. All we can say is that the use of death camps by the Nazis was a horrifying example of how humanity can debase itself. (See Document 3–1.)

Jewish Resistance to the Holocaust

Prompted by the stupefying immensity and brutality of the Holocaust, people continue today to ask questions about the Jewish response to these events. How much Jewish resistance was there? What did the Allies do? What could they have done? A popular notion was that the Jews somehow contributed to the magnitude of their own destruction because they went without resistance "like lambs to the slaughter." In a sense, the murdered victims have become the defendants. The absurdity of this view can be seen when we recall that the German Army swept through most of Europe in less than a year. France surrendered in the Blitzkrieg without a major battle, and the Baltic and Balkan states, many of whose people were deported for slave labor and never returned, capitulated with little defense or defiance. In addition, the Nazi policy of persecuting Jews, if not actively supported, certainly was not opposed by large sections of the non-Jewish populations of Germany and Eastern Europe, especially in Poland. Some Gentiles, to be sure, did attempt to help individual Jews, but the number was small. The best-known "Righteous Gentile" was Raoul Wallenberg, a Swedish diplomat who was instrumental in saving the lives of thousands of Hungarian Jews before his capture and imprisonment by the Russians in 1945. Even the Roman Catholic Church was ambivalent in its response to Jewish persecution at the hands of the Nazis. Finally, the entire operation of the death camps was shrouded in secrecy.

What is surprising about Jewish resistance when we consider these facts is not that there was so little resistance, but that there was so much. Despite the lack of arms or the means to buy them, there are countless stories of active Jewish resistance to the Nazis, both inside and outside the death camps. The Warsaw Ghetto uprising in April 1943 is the most dramatic example. The Allied war planners contented themselves with the belief that the most effective method of assisting Jews was victory over Germany.

Jewish resistance to the Holocaust also included Jewish Agency efforts to rescue Jews from Europe and transport them to Palestine, and offers to form Jewish fighting units with the British against the Germans in North Africa. Both these activities formed part of the broader Zionist goal of circumventing the Malcolm MacDonald White Paper and securing ultimate Jewish statehood. And both were opposed by the British, who were anxious not to anger the Arabs, whose support they would need for their own postwar interests. The conflict between Jewish efforts to spirit Jewish refugees to Palestine and British determination to stop them from reaching their destination was dramatically highlighted with the sinking of two ships, the *Patria* and the *Struma*, filled with refugees. In November 1940, the *Patria*, with over 1,700 "illegal" refugees whom British authorities were deporting to Mauritius, was sabotaged by the Haganah and sank in Haifa Bay with the loss of more than 200 lives. In February 1942, 770 refugees were lost when the *Struma* sank in the Black Sea after being delayed by British pressure on Turkey to prevent its passage to Palestine. There was one survivor.

Meanwhile, Chaim Weizmann, the Jewish Agency, and the Haganah sought to gain British approval for the formation of a Jewish unit, either a brigade or a division, to fight under the Zionist flag alongside British troops. There were several reasons for this proposal. One was for the Haganah to gain greater military training, experience, and access to arms; another was to strengthen Jewish claims on British gratitude in the negotiations over Palestine that would take place after the war. Finally, of course, was the desire to defeat the Nazis. Winston Churchill supported the idea, but it was not until late 1944 that a Jewish infantry brigade was formed that fought as a separate unit in Europe (in Italy), although many Jews fought in regular British units. Altogether, some 26,000 Palestinian Jews had joined British forces by the end of the war.

Some Zionist goals were realized. A considerable number of arms were stored by the Haganah. Several underground paramilitary groups had been formed: the Irgun, led by a young Polish soldier, Menachem Begin, and LEHI (the Stern Gang), among whose members was Yitzhak Shamir, organized along militaristic lines. The function of the Irgun and LEHI was to strengthen the armed capabilities of the Yishuv for what they regarded as the inevitable war with the Arabs, as well as with the British. This was done by building up the supply of weapons (mainly stolen from the British), conducting guerrilla—or terrorist—attacks on the local British forces and police, and by arranging the illegal entry of refugees from Europe on ships secretly purchased or leased for this purpose by the Jewish Agency. Communication networks were established for the movement of refugees from Europe to Palestine. These networks later became especially useful to the *Bricha*, meaning "flight," the organized underground network of Jewish fighters and Zionist leaders from Palestine, who helped many thousands of Holocaust survivors break the British blockade to reach Palestine between 1945 and 1948. The function of Bricha was essentially that of getting the refugees to the point of embarkation in Europe.

The United States, American Jews, and Palestine to 1945

As the dimensions of the Holocaust became clearer, Jewish communities everywhere became increasingly anxious and united, and support for Zionist aspirations dramatically grew in strength. This was particularly true of the 4.5 million Jews in the United States. Many claims have been made about the persuasiveness of Zionist pressure groups in influencing American policy; indeed, it has been argued by some that Jewish control of the mass media meant that Zionists were able to manipulate American public opinion at large. These claims are mostly exaggerations, based either on ignorance of the situation of Jews in America or on hostility to Zionism, which stems often from opposition to policies pursued by Israel in its relations with its Arab neighbors and with the Palestinian refugees who were displaced by the establishment of the Jewish state. However, it should also be said that these claims are also made by pro-Zionists attempting to emphasize the importance of Zionism in the United States. Thus, this view that Jews are far more significant in American politics than their numbers suggest is very widespread. There is some truth in this, as in all such exaggerations, but as we shall see when we look at the events between 1942 and 1948, there were also many other factors at work in shaping American policy toward the Middle East. Only where there was a coincidence of Jewish (or Zionist) and non-Jewish aspirations did the Zionists achieve their goals.

Given the importance that historians have attached to American Jewry in influencing U.S. policy toward supporting a Jewish state in Palestine, we should say something about the political activities of American Jews during and after the war. The Jews of the United States, some 1.5 million of whom had migrated from Russia and Eastern Europe in the first decade of the twentieth century, were a highly assimilated group by the 1930s, although they were hardly as well-off or as educated as Jews are today. There were still visible signs of anti-Semitism in those years, and Jews were excluded from joining certain organizations and clubs. In particular, America's restrictive immigration laws were based on a quota system, which discriminated against people of Eastern European origin, thereby limiting the number of Jews admitted. If Jewish immigrants—refugees—were to be admitted, it would be at the expense of nationals of predominantly Catholic, or possibly even Protestant, countries. Neither Catholics nor Protestants, inside or outside of Congress, desired this. Nor, it must be said, did some Zionist leaders desire this. They believed that if refugees could be resettled anywhere, including the United States, it would weaken their claim on Palestine as the only homeland for Jews. In addition, many feared that additional Jewish immigrants would inflame anti-Semitism and cost money to absorb.

The Jewish population of the United States was heavily concentrated in the urban states of New York, New Jersey, Pennsylvania, Illinois, and California. For a number of reasons—mostly to do with the policies of the Democratic administration of Franklin Delano Roosevelt during the Great Depression, the role of many Jews in the New Deal, and FDR's opposition to Nazi Germany even before the outbreak of the war—Jews identified with the Democratic party and supported it with their votes and campaign funds. Before the war, the Zionist movement in the United States was opposed by most of the religious establishments and Jewish organizations. Orthodox rabbis objected to Zionism for upsetting the messianic idea, and Reform rabbis objected to its parochial nationalist emphasis rather than the universal sense they attached to Judaism. Some Jewish organizations rejected the notion that Jews everywhere constituted one nation and were unassimilable as casting doubt on their loyalty to the United States. They feared such views would only fuel anti-Semitism throughout the country.

Zionist leaders, on the other hand, believed that the war in Europe and the Holocaust made it essential that they enlist American Jewry in an attempt to get U.S. government support for a Jewish state. To Zionists, the Holocaust proved beyond all doubt that security was a vain dream. They argued that neither emancipation nor assimilation had stayed the hands that throughout history had been raised against the Jews. The survivors would find security and peace only in a national home in Palestine.

Prior to World War II, the American government had regarded Palestine as a British responsibility. The oil resources of the Middle East, and the strategic importance of Palestine in relation to containing Soviet expansion into the region, did not emerge as major considerations until the postwar years. The United States had officially endorsed the Balfour Declaration in 1922, but beyond sending an American delegation—which included Senator Warren Austin (later to be the U.S. ambassador to the United Nations at the time of the partition resolution)—to Palestine in 1936 at the time of the Arab Rebellion, the United States had not shown much interest. The war was to change that situation. By March 1943, the U.S. State Department was concerned about American production of oil for the war and the supply of oil for postwar Europe. In May 1943, alarmed over the security of the Middle East and its oil supplies, the State Department advised President Roosevelt that he should reassure the Arab world of American friendship. In early 1945, returning from the Yalta conference shortly before his death, Roosevelt met with the king of Saudi Arabia, Abdul-Aziz Ibn Saud, and promised him that no decision would be made concerning the future of Palestine without full consultation with both Arabs and Jews.

Meanwhile, in May 1942, an Extraordinary Conference was called by the Emergency Committee for Zionist Affairs in the United States and held at the Biltmore Hotel in New York City. At this conference, Zionist leaders finally called unequivocally for the establishment of Palestine as a Jewish Commonwealth (that is, a Jewish state). (See Document 3–2.) This now became the policy of the World Zionist Organization. Shortly after the Biltmore conference, Chaim Weizmann was replaced as Zionist leader by David Ben-Gurion. Weizmann, longtime president of the World Zionist Organization, had advocated a policy of gradualism, which meant using diplomacy and working with the political leaders of Britain and the United States. Ben-Gurion, at the time leader of the Mapai (Labor) party in Palestine and chairman of the Jewish Agency Executive in Palestine, was an activist. He advocated achieving immediate statehood by the use of force if necessary, and he backed a policy of pressuring the United States into supporting a revolutionary change in Palestine to which the British would then have to agree. The conflict over the role of diplomacy, or the role of force, as a means of achieving their goals has remained a major source of division among Zionists.

By the end of 1943, to Jews throughout the world, the situation seemed hopeless. Groups sympathetic to Zionism, such as the Christian American Palestine Committee, formed in 1941 and chaired by New York senator Robert Wagner, a Roman Catholic, joined with the newly formed American Zionist Emergency Council, jointly chaired by two rabbis, Stephen S. Wise and Abba Hillel Silver, in lobbying Congress and the White House to support a Jewish state in Palestine and unrestricted immigration of Jews into Palestine. Early in 1944, the American Palestine Committee was able to have resolutions introduced into the Congress calling on the United States to urge Britain to permit unrestricted Jewish immigration into Palestine. Both Secretary of State Cordell Hull and Chief of Staff George C. Marshall strongly opposed these resolutions, on the grounds that American troops might very well be involved in maintaining oil supplies to the Allies were the Arabs to carry out their threats to resist unrestricted Jewish immigration with force. Thus, the resolutions were dropped. At this stage, as throughout, national interest defined in military and strategic terms by the State Department won out over moral and humanitarian considerations. The only significant step taken in this direction by the U.S. government was the establishment, in January 1944, of the War Refugee Board to bring help to the persecuted Jews and other minorities in Europe, but by then it was too late to save most of the victims.

Both the British and U.S. governments opposed Zionist policies because they realized that the Arabs would not support the Allies if it meant that Palestine would then be handed over to the Jews. Prime Minister Churchill was sympathetic to the Zionist cause, and on November 4, 1944, he promised Chaim Weizmann unreservedly to find an acceptable solution. He told Weizmann of his government's plans for the immediate immigration of 100,000 Jewish orphans, settlement of 1.5 million refugees over a ten-year period, and the partition of Palestine. On the other hand, the Foreign Office under Anthony Eden was unsympathetic. As with the U.S. State Department, the British Foreign Office did not wish to antagonize Arab leaders. Britain's oil interests and its preeminent influence in the Middle East would be endangered, it was argued, by the establishment of a Jewish state. Furthermore, there was increasing violence from the Jewish extremists in Palestine. On November 6, 1944, just two days after Churchill's promises to Weizmann, the British resident ambassador in the Middle East, Lord Moyne—who had in fact supported the partition of Palestine—was murdered in Cairo by the Stern Gang. The Jewish Agency attempted to curb terrorist activity, but the damage had been done; the British were not prepared to consider a change in their Palestine policy under these circumstances.

Palestine After World War II

At the end of the war in Europe, no one knew what would happen in Palestine. The British government wanted an end to the mounting violence perpetrated by the Yishuv, and it wanted to retain its predominance in the Middle East. In particular, the British wanted to keep control of the strategic oil port of Haifa. The U.S. government wanted to increase its share of the oil resources in the Middle East. It did not, however, want to send in troops in the event of a Soviet intrusion or a possible conflict between Arabs and Jews over the future of Palestine. The U.S. government was prepared to let the British have that responsibility. The Palestinian Arabs wanted an end to Jewish immigration and an independent Arab state, while Palestinian Jews wanted a Jewish state, probably achieved by partition of the mandated area, although the Revisionists always envisaged having a Jewish state on both sides of the Jordan River. The other factor pervading all the discussions on the future of Palestine was the question of the fate of the survivors of the Holocaust. Between May 1946 and November 1947, events moved in the direction of partition and the establishment of a Jewish state.

The most important factors leading to the formation of Israel in this postwar period were, first, the success of the Yishuv in creating a situation that forced the British to take the issue to the United Nations, and second, activities related to Europe's Jewish displaced persons. During the war, the Jewish Agency and its military arm, the Haganah, had greatly strengthened the position of the Yishuv in Palestine. The Haganah had operated on several fronts, in line with Ben-Gurion's motto to fight the British as if there were no war and to fight the war as if there were no White Paper. The Yishuv, fired by shame, agony, and hatred caused by the Holocaust, merged into a cohesive and determined national community. It was, in reality, far stronger than Cairo, Damascus, London, or Washington believed.

The Displaced Persons and Palestine

After Germany's surrender in May 1945, the Allied forces faced the staggering problems of repatriating about 7 million dislocated and displaced persons (DPs). By September 1945, 1.5 million refused to, or could not, return to their former homes. Of these, 50,000 to 100,000 DPs were Jews who had been liberated by the Allied armies. By 1946, this number had swelled to 250,000 with the arrival of refugees from Eastern Europe. The story of the Jews in the DP camps, and the emigration of the survivors over the next three years, is the last chapter in the Nazi persecution of the Jews. We should note several aspects of this story.

First, various Jewish and non-Jewish philanthropic organizations such as the American-based Joint Distribution Committee and the UN Relief and Rehabilitation Agency (established in November 1943), together with the Allied armies, provided for the immediate physical and material needs of the DPs. Second, Zionist groups worked in Europe to assist Jews to get to Palestine or to DP camps in the American Zone of Germany and Austria. Third, the Jewish Agency and Zionist organizations in Britain, and especially in the United States, tried to influence their respective governments to solve the problem of admitting the Jewish DPs to Palestine. Fourth, the British and American governments moved slowly in deciding the fate of the DPs and accepting the viability of a Jewish state in Palestine. And finally, the Yishuv and the Haganah used all the means at their disposal to win a Jewish state. All these factors can be seen in the web of events leading to the UN General Assembly resolution to partition Palestine into a Jewish and an Arab state.

The Allied forces, especially Supreme Commander General Dwight D. Eisenhower, were shocked by the discovery of the concentration camps and the condition of the prisoners. Nothing had prepared the officers or troops for what they found, and they worked feverishly to restore some level of health, nutrition, decency, and self-esteem to the survivors. Despite their best efforts, however, conditions remained far from desirable. The United States had trouble feeding and clothing the DPs, and many remained billeted in the camps where they had been prisoners, wearing the same striped uniforms the Nazis had required them to wear. And after the initial shock, many American GIs began to regard the Jewish DPs as a nuisance. Officers complained that the Jews wanted special consideration and did not seem very grateful to their liberators. Nor were Jewish philanthropic organizations much able to alleviate the situation.

In fact, Jewish survivors from Germany and Austria could not return because their homes were either destroyed or occupied, and there was no legal mechanism for recovery or compensation from the governments of those countries. The Jewish communities, synagogues, and schools were virtually nonexistent, and survivors could not bear to return to such devastated places. In other countries like Poland, the anti-Semitism was still so strong that returning Jews risked their lives. In July 1946, in Kielce, Poland, over 130 returning refugees were killed by the local inhabitants. Not surprisingly, thousands of Eastern European Jews made their way to the American Zone in Germany for protection. Bricha set up an underground railroad to get their fellow Jews to safety. The Jewish Agency encouraged this process in the hope that if enough Jews congregated in the American Zone, the U.S. government would pressure the British government to allow 100,000 Jews into Palestine.

The Allied nations had not planned much beyond the immediate locating of Jewish DPs into camps at the end of the fighting, as they hoped that most would return to their former homelands. When it became apparent, as it had by June–July 1945, that 50,000 to 100,000 Jews were either stateless or homeless, the Allies did not know what to do. The British government wanted the survivors to stay and rebuild their lives in Europe, and it was unwilling to

April 12, 1945, Gotha, Germany. General Eisenhower and other Allied generals tour a concentration camp.

allow further immigration into Palestine. Its opposition was strengthened by the increase in Jewish terrorist activity against the British in Palestine and by attempts to embarrass London by the highly publicized voyages of ships packed with refugees trying to run the British blockade that was enforcing the restrictions.

Perhaps the best-publicized venture was that of the ship *Exodus*, which in 1947 arrived in Haifa with 4,500 refugees but which was forced to return to Europe. Another dramatic humiliation for the British was the bombing of the King David Hotel in Jerusalem in July 1946. The hotel was the main British military and civilian headquarters in Palestine and was heavily fortified. Irgun leader Menachem Begin planned the bombing, and on July 22 the wing of the hotel housing the military headquarters was blown up, killing approximately ninety people, many of them Arabs and Jews. Begin and others claimed that the British had been warned of the impending explosion in time to evacuate the hotel, but the evidence is conflicting, and not everyone has accepted Begin's version.

The United States government wanted to resolve the situation of the DPs for several reasons. The DP camps could not remain in existence indefinitely—conditions there were not acceptable, and the United States felt an obligation to care for the survivors. Also, the camps were expensive to maintain. The new American president, Harry Truman (FDR, exhausted by the war, had died on April 12, 1945), prompted by Jewish complaints, sent Earl G. Harrison, who was experienced in assisting refugees, to report on the condition of the camps in July 1945. Among his many observations, Harrison noted that the majority of the DPs wanted to go to Palestine, and he recommended that 100,000 be allowed to do so as soon as possible.

Truman was appalled by the conditions Harrison described. He immediately ordered General Eisenhower to place the Jews in separate camps and to move them into towns and villages, and he wrote to British prime minister Clement Attlee (the Labor party had defeated Churchill and the Conservatives in the British elections in July) urging him to admit 100,000 Jews into Palestine without delay. Americans might have felt an obligation to rehabilitate the survivors of the German death camps, but they were not, it seems, willing to admit them to the United States—although it must be said that Truman did try to get Congress to enact legislation that would allow for this. Despite the fact that some estimates suggested that almost half the DPs would have preferred to come to the United States or some other European nation, Congress allowed only 20,000 Jewish survivors into the country.

Postwar British and American Policy

The new Labor government once again assessed Britain's situation in the Middle East. Foreign Secretary Ernest Bevin worried about Britain's ability to defend the Middle East oil fields and pipelines from the designs of the Soviet Union. And the Soviet Union seemed to the British and the United States very interested indeed in establishing itself in the Middle East and was causing great anxiety by its presence in Iran and its pressure on an unstable Greece and Turkey. It seemed to Bevin more urgent than ever to foster Arab goodwill. Accordingly, he pursued two policies.

First, he opposed large-scale Jewish immigration to Palestine. Second, he tried to involve the United States not only in solving the refugee crisis but also in securing the Middle East for the West. These policies antagonized Zionists everywhere, and Bevin was bitterly attacked as anti-Semitic. This was not altogether fair since Bevin had supported the Zionists in the early 1930s, and he was not opposed to a Jewish state in Palestine as such. He was, however, very blunt in his manner, and he may have shared many of the vulgar anti-Jewish prejudices of his working-class background, a background he had not forgotten. Furthermore, he was undoubtedly the strongman of the British Labor party. He could not be threatened or intimidated, and he resented what he regarded as undue Zionist pressure. In addition, he was to some extent in the hands of his Foreign Office officials. Nevertheless, Bevin also believed in conciliation, and he did not want to get involved in a major conflict over Palestine; thus, he tried to get the United States to share the responsibility.

Both the U.S. State Department and President Truman shared Bevin's reluctance to get involved in a shooting war in the Middle East. The Joint Chiefs of Staff told Truman that it would take 100,000 troops to keep the peace in the event of hostilities in Palestine, and while Truman was ready to do what he could to help get Jewish DPs to Palestine, he was not prepared to send American soldiers. We must keep in mind that everyone, except the Jewish Agency and the Haganah, believed at that time that if hostilities did break out in Palestine, the Yishuv, which at that time numbered only about 608,000 while the Arab population of Palestine was approximately 1.2 million, would be convincingly defeated, even massacred, by the Arab armies opposing them. (For population and land ownership, see Maps 3–1 and 3–2.)

The Anglo-American Committee of Enquiry

On November 4, 1945, Bevin proposed an Anglo-American Committee of Enquiry into the refugee problem. Truman agreed. The committee, consisting of six Britons and six Americans, held hearings and heard proposals from spokespersons for both Jews and Arabs in Washington, London, Palestine, and Europe where the committee visited the DP camps. (See Documents 3–3 and 3–4.) In its report, issued on May 1, 1946, the committee unanimously recommended that 100,000 Jews be immediately admitted into Palestine, but on the future of the area they could not reach agreement. As a result, the report rejected either a Jewish or an Arab state and recommended a vague kind of unitary state to which Jews could be allowed to immigrate, but in which they would not constitute a majority. Until this was established, the mandate should continue. Despite his assurance that he would support a unanimous report, Bevin flatly rejected the proposal to admit 100,000 refugees into Palestine.

Looking back, we can say that Bevin's refusal to admit the suggested number of DPs at this point was a serious error of judgment. It would have taken much of the force out of the Zionist arguments and would probably have avoided much of the subsequent bloodshed. Nevertheless, he followed the advice of his military planners, who informed him that such a step would require eight divisions of troops and over £40 million, neither of which Britain in 1946 could afford. Truman, on the other hand, supported the proposal. Prime Minister Clement Attlee cabled Truman on May 26 that if the United States helped with costs and troops he would go ahead. Further talks were scheduled.

These developments produced considerable friction and hostility between the United States and Britain. The future of Palestine, coupled as it was with the fate of the Jewish DPs and the many other strategic and economic considerations already mentioned, was a highly emotional issue. All those involved—Jews, Arabs, British, and American leaders—were deeply committed to finding a solution. The only problem was they all believed they had the right or only solution. Truman wanted the British to resolve the problem by allowing DPs into Palestine, a stand that angered Attlee and Bevin. Bevin accused Truman of bowing to domestic political pressure from Jews, and he accused the Americans of favoring Jewish migration to Palestine because they did not want the Jews admitted into the United States.

British frustration was understandable. Between May 1945 and September 1946, the United States had admitted fewer than 6,000 Jewish refugees. The British, on the other hand, had 80,000 troops in Palestine by the end of 1945, and Jewish terrorist activity was increasing. Between November 1945 and July 1946, approximately 20 British army personnel had been killed and over 100 wounded, and the police had about the same number of casualties at

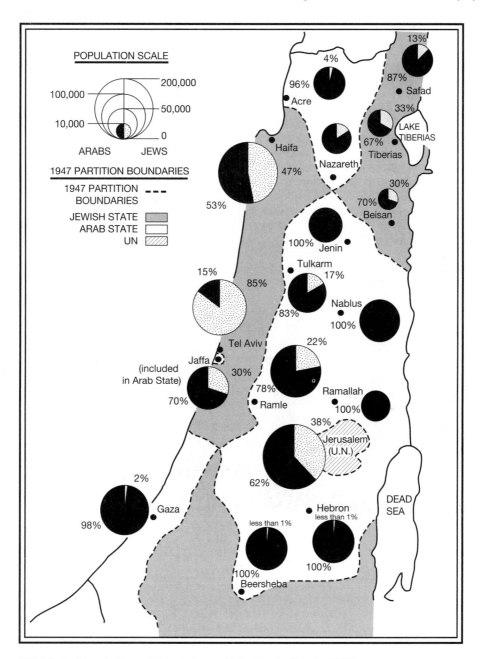

MAP 3–1   Distribution of Population in Palestine (estimate 1945)

Source: Statistics from UN Map No. 93(b), August 1950, and the Columbia Lippincott Gazetteer, 1952.

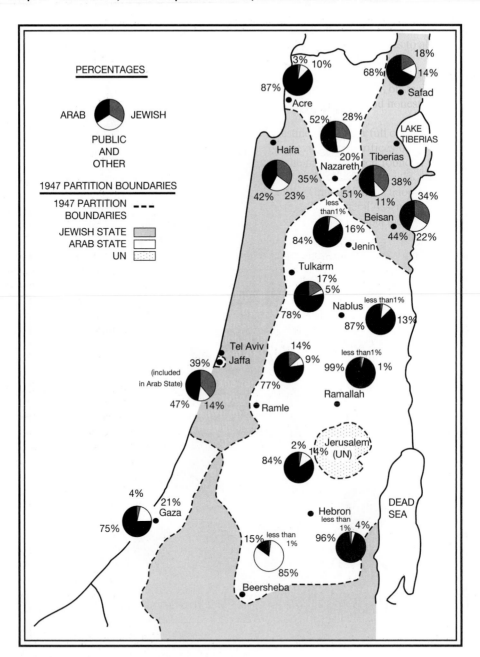

MAP 3–2   Land Ownership in Palestine, 1945

Source: Statistics from UN Map No. 94(b), August 1950.

the hands of the Irgun or Stern groups. Railway installations and airfields were also targets of sabotage, which caused damage estimated at around £4 million. In return, the British, already laden with heavy military commitments elsewhere, sought out arms caches and carried out raids on the Jewish Agency and Haganah headquarters, arresting suspected ringleaders. Attitudes on both sides hardened.

Several solutions were considered in the next few months. At the end of June 1946, the U.S. War Department agreed to provide the transportation necessary to move 100,000 Jews to Palestine. In July, Bevin suggested that an Arab province that included part of Transjordan and Lebanon could be formed and an independent Jewish state created. Truman indicated that he would ask Congress to admit 50,000 Jewish refugees into the United States. A second Anglo-American Committee (the Morrison-Grady Committee) recommended setting up separate and autonomous Jewish and Arab provinces, with Britain retaining final authority for the time being, and with the right of the 100,000 Jewish refugees to enter Palestine conditional upon the adoption of the plan. It was a solution that satisfied no one.

The failure to reach a satisfactory solution was due largely to the fact that many Zionist activities were counterproductive, and that Arab opposition to the establishment of a Jewish state in Palestine remained, not surprisingly, inflexible. American Zionists and the Jewish Agency in Palestine were frustrated and angry by the turn of events. It was at about this same time that Polish and Eastern European Jews were learning how much anti-Semitism remained in their homelands. Between July and September 1946, 90,000 of them fled to the safety of the American zones in Germany and Austria. By the end of the year, more than 250,000 Jews crowded the DP camps of West Germany.

This situation alarmed the Americans. Many in the State Department and the military in Europe thought that it was a deliberately organized mass movement planned by Zionists to force a decision in favor of their migration to Palestine. It should be said that many of Ben-Gurion's remarks as head of the Jewish Agency, and the creation of the underground railroad moving Jews around Europe, lent credence to this point of view. Ben-Gurion had told the Anglo-American Committee of Enquiry in relation to the DPs, for example: "We are not going to renounce our independence, even if we have to pay the supreme price, and there are hundreds of thousands of Jews. . . both in the country and abroad who will give up their lives, if necessary, for Jewish independence—for Zion." From this time on, as noted earlier, Haganah harassment of the British and illegal Jewish immigration increased. The violence between the British and the Jewish military organizations in Palestine increased, not only in terms of the number of clashes, but also in cruelty and vindictiveness. Bevin, in particular, resented the fact that Jews were killing English soldiers who, in his view, had fought the battles of the Jews against the Nazis.

Let us cite just one example of the process of brutalization that was taking place. A sixteen-year-old convicted Zionist terrorist, too young to be hanged, was sentenced in December 1946 to eighteen years' imprisonment and given eighteen lashes with a cane. This humiliation outraged Menachem Begin, and his Irgun kidnapped four British officers and flogged them, giving each eighteen cuts with rawhide whips. The act and the reprisal did not reflect well on either side.

The Arabs told the British in October 1946 that they wanted a unitary Arab state in which they would be the permanent majority. They feared that a Jewish state would transform the region economically as well as demographically. By now, Bevin had begun to think seriously about handing the entire problem over to the United Nations. In this, he was helped by events in the United States.

The Zionist leader, Nahum Goldman, had indicated in August 1946 that the Jewish Agency in Palestine would accept partition, and Truman believed that if this could be achieved peacefully, it was a solution that would not involve the United States directly. American oil interests in the Middle East would, therefore, not be threatened. At the same time, it would enable the American president to satisfy Jewish voters in the forthcoming congressional elections, thereby retaining their support for the Democratic party. Thus, on October 4, on the eve of the Jewish Day of Atonement, Truman announced that he believed partition would "command the support of public opinion in the United States."

Truman's Day of Atonement statement accomplished few, if any, of the things he had hoped for. The Saudi king, Ibn Saud, not to mention the Arab League, was angry that Truman favored admitting 100,000 Jewish refugees to Palestine. At home, the Republicans won a majority in both houses of Congress in the 1946 congressional elections despite Truman's words. Furthermore, Truman was becoming very annoyed with the threats of political retaliation by American Zionist leaders if he did not pursue a pro-Zionist line. Truman indicated to Britain that the United States would take responsibility for the protection of Greece and Turkey from Russian aggression but hinted that this might depend on the British finding a peaceful settlement to the Palestine question. This was a halfhearted threat, for, as with the emergence of the Cold War, the security of Greece, Turkey, and Iran was far too important to the United States to be jeopardized by the situation in Palestine.

Palestine Before the United Nations

In January 1947, the British government decided that if no settlement could be reached the matter would have to go to the new United Nations organization, and, on February 14, the British took that course without recommending any preferred solution. The future of Palestine was among the first questions addressed by the new world body and was a crucial test case. In place of war, public debate and private bargaining were to resolve international conflicts. Not wanting to give up this strategically valuable area, the British, at first, had hoped that the United Nations General Assembly might not be able to find an acceptable formula and would turn the matter back to them. However, the British had gone through a cold winter in 1946–1947, with fuel shortages, exhausted credit reserves, and growing Communist pressure in Greece and Turkey, all of which made the maintenance of a garrison in Palestine unpalatable. Moreover, the British were finding it increasingly difficult to keep the peace.

The United States hoped to use the United Nations as a tool to contain Communist influence and Soviet expansion. As it happened, there was no real issue between the United States and the Soviet Union over partition and the founding of a Jewish state in Palestine. The Soviets welcomed the idea of a Jewish state as a way of extending their influence into the Middle East; they believed that the predominantly Socialist ideology of the Jewish leaders would gain them an ally in the region. It would also mean the departure of Britain from at least one area of the region. In fact, one of the worries that the American intelligence community (the OSS, now the CIA) had about the establishment of Israel was the number of Communists from Soviet satellites who might take up residence in the new nation.

The UN General Assembly met in April 1947 and agreed to a British request for a Special Session to consider the problem. This Special Session, the first such, immediately set up a Special Committee on Palestine (UNSCOP) of eleven "neutral" nations to investigate and draw up recommendations. The nations comprising UNSCOP were Australia, Canada, Czechoslovakia, Guatemala, India, Iran, the Netherlands, Peru, Sweden, Uruguay, and Yugoslavia. It was a reasonably balanced group, and it was given the task of investigating all aspects of the Palestine question, including the plight of the displaced persons. The committee's hearings included five weeks in the Middle East gathering evidence from the Jewish Agency and nations of the recently formed Arab League. The Arab League had been established in Cairo in 1945 and was endorsed by Great Britain as a possible way of continuing to exert influence and provide a sounding board and outlet for ideas of Arab nationalism. Despite the tension and disorder in Palestine created in part by the Haganah's hostility to the British, the Jewish Agency cooperated fully with the committee. On August 5, 1946, in Paris, the Jewish Agency, in a retreat from the maximalist position espoused at the Biltmore Conference, had accepted partition of Palestine west of the Jordan River, on more or less the principles set out in the Peel Commission Report. The Palestine Arab Higher Committee, on the other hand, boycotted the proceedings and treated the committee with defiance, asserting that Arab rights were self-evident, and that the committee's membership was weighted in favor of the Zionists. Delegates from some states of the Arab League did meet with UNSCOP in Lebanon, however, to present the Arab case. On August 31, 1947, UNSCOP presented its report to the General Assembly at its second regular session. (See Document 3–5.)

The members unanimously recommended termination of the mandate, the granting of independence to Palestine, provision of a transitional period before independence, and they agreed on a number of other related issues. On the vital question of the future shape of Palestine, a majority of seven (Canada, Czechoslovakia, Guatemala, the Netherlands, Peru, Sweden, and Uruguay) recommended partition into an Arab state, a Jewish state, the internationalization of Jerusalem, and economic union between the two states. Britain was to administer the mandate during a two-year interim period under UN auspices and admit 150,000 refugees into the proposed Jewish state. The minority (India, Iran, and Yugoslavia) proposed an independent federal state. Australia abstained.

UNSCOP Majority Report

In the majority proposal, of the 10,000 square miles comprising Palestine, the Arabs were to retain 4,300 square miles (approximately 43 percent). The Jews, who at that time made up roughly one-half of the population (the population of Palestine at the end of 1946 was estimated at around 1,269,000 Arabs and about 608,000 Jews), were allotted 5,700 square miles (approximately 56 percent). At this time Jews owned 6 to 8 percent of the total land area, representing approximately 20 percent of the arable land. The Arab territory was to be the less fertile hill country of central Palestine and northern Galilee. The Jewish territory was to be the more fertile coastal plain from a line south of Acre to a line south of Jaffa. Jaffa, almost totally Arab, was included in the Jewish state. The Jewish state also would include most of the Negev Desert. Strangely, the Jews were denied those places such as Jerusalem and Hebron to which they were most sentimentally attached. Demographically, the Jewish state would face the problem of a built-in hostile fifth column. As envisaged, it was to contain almost as many Arabs (approximately 407,000) as Jews (approximately 498,000) at least until the immigrants arrived. And the boundaries of the Jewish state seemed to make it virtually indefensible in the event of hostilities with the Arabs. The Arab state would have 725,000 Arabs and 10,000 Jews. An international enclave of Jerusalem and its environs would contain approximately 100,000 Jews and 105,000 non-Jews.

Despite its shortcomings from their point of view, the Jewish Agency welcomed the majority report of UNSCOP. It was preferable to the minority report, and it did offer two essential requirements: sovereignty and uninterrupted immigration. The Arabs rejected both reports outright. The reports, by legitimizing the Balfour Declaration and the mandate, in essence stated that the claims of the Jews, the majority of whom had been in Palestine less than thirty years, were equal to those of the Arabs, many of whose ancestors had lived there for hundreds of years. The Arabs were so angered by the UNSCOP reports that the Arab League threatened war if the United Nations approved either report. There was no room for negotiation between the two positions. The British stated that they would accept the recommendation to end the mandate but would remain neutral on the outcome for Palestine; the General Assembly would have to decide the future of the region. The British did not want to be seen in the eyes of the

Arabs—especially the Egyptians with whom they were negotiating the future of their Suez Canal bases—as participating in something as objectionable to the Arabs as a Jewish state.

The British, too, were determined to get out of Palestine as soon as possible; they had had enough and were bitter toward the Zionists. During the months of the UNSCOP investigations, the attacks on British soldiers and police, especially by the Irgun, reached new levels of ferocity and barbarism. One particularly horrifying incident had occurred in July 1947. Two British Army sergeants were hanged in retaliation for the execution of Zionist terrorists. British and American outrage was triggered not so much by the hanging of two innocent men as by the fact that a mine had been left in the vicinity of the corpses. Menachem Begin boasted: "We repaid our enemy in kind," but many Americans as well as British wondered about the sanity of the terrorist mentality that lurked behind such outrages. It was this event, as much as any other, that led British foreign secretary Ernest Bevin to refuse to allow the 4,500 illegal DPs aboard the *Exodus* to land in Palestine. Britain could no longer support the financial and human drain of maintaining troops in Palestine. In 1947, about 80,000 troops and 16,000 British and local police tried to preserve the peace in Palestine, and the British had spent £50 million since the Labor party had come to power. In September 1947, the British government decided to end the mandate by May 1948, and Bevin made this public the following month. By announcing in advance of the UN General Assembly's (UNGA) decision that it would surrender the mandate, and that it would not participate in enforcing any UNGA decision, it could be argued that Britain was sabotaging the United Nations' solution. Britain's stance—together with the pro-Zionist positions taken by the United States and the Soviet Union—strengthened the views of both Arabs and Zionists that they could achieve their objectives without compromise.

The United States and the Partition Proposal

The United States supported the UNSCOP majority plan. President Truman had indicated in November 1946 that he favored partition. Many historians have explained the president's support for a Jewish state as the result of domestic political considerations. They argue that Truman and the Democratic party needed the strategically important Jewish vote for electoral success, and consequently American policy was shaped in ways demanded by Zionist pressure groups. They further argue that the president's policy was not in the nation's interest and was opposed by the State Department. Truman, in his memoirs, adds credence to this point of view. He expressed his displeasure at "the striped-pants boys" in the State Department, and he resented the patronizing attitude of pro-Arab foreign service officers.

Referring to Zionist pressure, Truman wrote that he had never had so much pressure on him as he had on the question of Palestine. And he certainly did have pressure placed on him. The Zionist Organization of America under the aggressive and dynamic leadership of Rabbi Abba Hillel Silver, and other organizations like the American Christian Palestine Committee, constantly sent letters of advice, comment, and threats of political retaliation to the White House, and many meetings were held between the president and Jewish leaders. But Truman was not a man who gave way to threats; his record as president suggests a strong, independent, even stubborn Missourian. All chief executives are subject to domestic political pressure in reaching their decisions. The mere existence or even the amount of that pressure does not mean that it is effective.

Zionist pressure was often counterproductive since it made Truman angry. In reality, Truman felt strongly that something had to be done for the Jewish refugees, and largely because of his fundamentalist Protestant background he believed that the Jews should be allowed to return to their ancient homeland. If he was influenced by domestic political considerations, it was not because of the letters and pressure from Zionist groups, but because of the advice of his

White House political consultants, David Niles, himself a Jew and a Zionist, and Clark Clifford—who was later to become secretary of defense in the Johnson administration. Certainly, Truman did not go nearly as far in his support for partition as American Zionist leaders wanted. Indeed, in the 1948 presidential election—despite Truman's apparent giving way to Zionist pressure—the president did not carry the heavily Jewish state of New York.

There were many factors influencing Truman in addition to domestic political considerations. Truman shared the concern of the State Department over the postwar spread of Soviet influence especially in the increasingly important and unstable Middle East. The degree of conflict between the president and Foggy Bottom has been overstated; Truman and Secretary Marshall had an unusually close working relationship. In addition to its own oil interests in Saudi Arabia, the United States was concerned about Europe's access to the region's oil for postwar reconstruction. By 1947, American oil companies owned about 42 percent of Middle Eastern supplies. The Middle Eastern desk of the State Department argued, wrongly as it turned out, that American support for partition would drive the Arabs into the waiting arms of the Soviet Union. Some even believed that the new Jewish state would be a Communist regime.

The Joint Chiefs of Staff believed that in the event of Soviet penetration of the Middle East the United States would have to fight a war without the oil resources of the region. There was also the possibility that the United States might have to send troops to the area once the British had withdrawn. Truman was more convinced by the Zionists' argument that the new Jewish state would be a bastion of democracy in the Middle East, and that supporting Israel would be a clear indication of the world leadership role America was to assume. These arguments, whether used by Zionists as propaganda pressure on the White House or not, influenced Truman much more than those suggesting the political expediency of gaining Jewish votes.

UNGA Approves the Partition of Palestine

Two days after receiving the UNSCOP report, in September 1947, the General Assembly designated itself an Ad Hoc Committee to consider the two UNSCOP proposals. All members of the United Nations were represented on this Ad Hoc Committee. Between September 25 and November 25, the committee held thirty-four meetings. Both the Jewish Agency and the Arab Higher Committee—who had by now grasped their error of not cooperating with UNSCOP—made presentations. On November 25, 1947, the Ad Hoc Committee passed what was essentially an amended version of the UNSCOP majority partition proposal for consideration by the General Assembly. The amendments slightly altered the boundaries and the populations of the two proposed states. Jaffa was to be an Arab enclave in the Jewish state, and the Arab population of the Jewish state was to be reduced. The final outcome was as follows: The Arab state was to occupy 4,500 square miles and contain approximately 800,000 Arabs and 10,000 Jews. The Jewish state was to be an area of 5,500 square miles and contain 538,000 Jews and 397,000 Arabs. (See Map 3–3.)

On November 29, 1947, the General Assembly in UN Resolution 181 voted in favor of the partition of Palestine by a vote of 33 to 13 with 10 abstentions. The Muslim countries (together with India, Yugoslavia, and Greece) voted against partition. The United States and the Soviet bloc (together with several other nations, including France and Australia) supported partition. Great Britain abstained. Considerable controversy abounds over the role of the United States in securing a favorable outcome.

In the few days prior to the vote, American Zionists exerted unprecedented pressure on the White House to influence the delegates of other nations to vote for partition. President Truman, however, refused, but in some cases private American citizens did make strenuous efforts to secure votes. The pressure that was exerted on delegates who appeared hesitant—for example, those

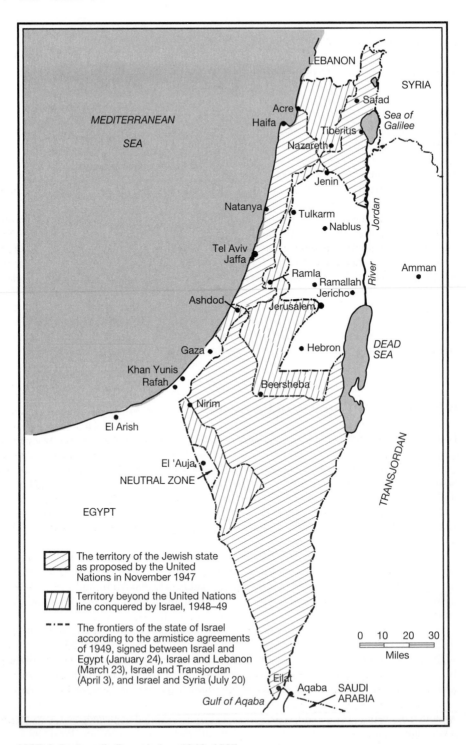

MAP 3–3   Israel's Boundaries, 1949–1967

from Haiti, the Philippines, Liberia, Greece, and China—was primarily exerted by Jewish Agency representatives. Not all of this pressure was effective; Greece and Turkey, for example, which were so dependent upon American aid, did not vote for partition. At the same time, Arab spokespersons, in their attempts to influence the outcome, warned that a bloodbath would erupt and retaliation would ensue against Western oil interests if partition were approved. In any event, partition was construed by most as an American plan.

In the final analysis, partition was successful probably because the Jews were perceived as Western as opposed to the Eastern Arabs. And to a United Nations that consisted mostly of Western nations at the time, the Jewish argument was strengthened by the West's sense of guilt for its inaction, which was partly responsible for the Jews' present plight. This time the West would do something. In addition, a major push for adoption of the partition resolution came from Latin American and European nations, in part because Catholics liked the special international status planned for Jerusalem, a plan that the United Nations found it could not enforce.

Passage of the partition resolution in November 1947 virtually assured a Jewish state in Palestine. The resolution liquidated the mandate, defined a legal framework in which the Yishuv could establish a state, and gave to the Haganah a definite goal around which it could rally its forces. Passage of the resolution was, however, merely the acceptance of a principle; it was not a specific blueprint. This must be kept in mind when considering the events of the next six months, especially when reflecting on American policy.

Arab and Jewish Response to the UN Partition Resolution

These months were full of uncertainty and confusion as to the future of Palestine. Efforts by moderate Palestinian leaders to prevent bloodshed failed. Arab leadership was divided. World War II had led to the dispersion of the Husseini family; the mufti, Hajj Amin, had been exiled following his escape late in 1937, and his nephew, Jamal, was interned in Rhodesia during the war. This provided an opportunity for their rivals, the Nashashibis, to seek leadership of Palestinian politics. Two other groups also sought successfully to extend their power: the Palestine Arab party under the leadership of a Greek Orthodox, Emile al-Ghuri, and the popular and widely supported party Istiqlal (meaning Independence). At the end of the war, the Palestine Arab party was the most powerful Arab voice opposing a Jewish state and calling for an Arab government to control the entire mandate area. Nevertheless, by 1947–1948, using their local kin leaders and village heads, the urban-based notable family of the Husseinis had again reasserted its traditional leadership among the Palestinian Arabs.

Both the Zionists and Abdullah, who became king in 1946 when Britain recognized Transjordan's independence, were concerned that the partition resolution would result in a Palestinian state headed by the mufti, Hajj Amin al-Husseini. Both had a common interest in preventing such an outcome. Abdullah, as noted in Chapter 2, had long sought to control Arab Palestine, and there had been contacts over the years with officials of the Jewish Agency about their mutual interests.

Shortly before the UN partition resolution, in early November 1947, Abdullah met with representatives of the Jewish Agency, including Golda Meir, acting head of the agency's Political Department. An understanding was reached in which the Jewish Agency agreed to Abdullah's annexation of Arab Palestine; in return, Abdullah promised not to attack the Jews or stand in the way of the establishment of a Jewish state. Another meeting was to have followed the vote on partition, but owing to the tumult in Palestine, it did not take place. As the months passed, Abdullah was unable to avoid the pressures on him to join the Arab states in their determination to fight the Jews.

There was one last meeting between Golda Meir and the king just before the partition plan was to take effect, but by then, the constraints on the king were simply too great. Moreover, the outbreak of hostilities would provide him with an opportunity to cross the Jordan and annex central Palestine whether or not a Jewish state came into being.

In January 1948, the volunteer "Arab Liberation Army" (ALA), formed in December 1947 and organized, trained, and armed by Syria for the Arab League states, began entering Palestine. By the end of March, 5,000 men, mainly Arab irregulars from Iraq, Syria, and Lebanon, had infiltrated the territory. Surprisingly few Palestinian Arabs joined the ALA. Many Palestinian Arabs were suspicious of the other Arab states. They feared, for one thing, that their neighbors had designs of their own for the future of Palestine, which did not include an independent Palestinian state. For that reason, many Palestinians favored partition and indicated a willingness to live in peace alongside a Jewish state. The ALA was also billeted in various Arab villages and in the major Arab towns where their presence was often a source of local resentment. The strategy of the ALA was to dominate the roads, thus controlling the lines of communication. It hoped in this way to isolate the outlying villages from the main centers of Jewish population in Jerusalem, Haifa, and Tel Aviv. At first, the ALA had considerable success; the Haganah was forced on the defensive, and the Yishuv was completely demoralized by Arab successes by the end of January 1948. By March, Jerusalem was virtually in the hands of the Arabs, and Jewish hopes appeared slight without outside assistance. It was with the knowledge of these circumstances that Truman stated that he was prepared to send troops to Palestine to assist in enforcing a UN trusteeship.

During April, the balance swung in favor of the Haganah. Armed with a shipment of arms that arrived from Communist-controlled Czechoslovakia at the end of March 1948, the Haganah took the offensive. Its most significant victory was the capture of Haifa on April 22, 1948. By early May, the Haganah also had control of Jaffa and most of eastern Galilee. But eastern Jerusalem remained in Arab hands. The most surprising aspect of the Haganah offensive was the complete evacuation of the Arabs from their towns and villages as the Jews advanced, the cause of which remains a subject of heated debate even today. Both sides resorted to terrorist atrocities against each other, especially in the major cities, with little regard for noncombatants or women and children. In one series of attacks and retaliation, Jewish terrorists (Irgun or LEHI members) threw bombs at a group of Arab oil refinery workers in Haifa, killing six and wounding forty-two. The Arabs then rioted and killed forty-one Jews and wounded forty-eight more before being quieted by British troops.

Two days later, Haganah members disguised as Arabs entered a village close to Haifa and killed approximately sixty people, including a number of women and children, to avenge the Jewish deaths in Haifa. Later we will discuss the well-known incidents at Deir Yassin and Mount Scopus, which occurred at this time. British forces, who were withdrawing, found it increasingly difficult to be evenhanded. They assisted Jewish settlers against a Syrian terrorist attack, and they arranged a truce for the withdrawal of about 10,000 Arabs from Haifa. Both sides accused the British of favoring the other. By May 2, the Haganah had carved out for itself a state roughly equivalent to that approved by the United Nations earlier in November 1947. The Jews went ahead with plans to announce an independent state as soon as the British left. The United Nations let events take their course.

Partition in Doubt

With Palestine in chaos by early 1948, members of the UN Security Council concluded that an international police force would be required to put partition into effect. America's representative to the UN, Warren Austin, told the Security Council that the United States doubted the ability of the UN to carry out partition. Ambassador Austin did not formally present any specific American alternatives for consideration, but his comments, made on February 25, reflected President

Truman's dilemma. The United States, Austin said, was not prepared to impose partition by force, but it would join any UN effort to safeguard international peace and security. Truman made another final appeal to the Arabs for peace, but it was summarily rejected. As March of 1948 drew to a close, there were signs that the Arabs were planning massive military action.

Faced with this prospect, President Truman agreed to Secretary of State Marshall's suggestion that Palestine be placed under a temporary United Nations trusteeship. He had little choice. If he stood by and did nothing, it seemed certain that the Jews would be driven into the sea. It was essential to the success of the Yishuv, however, with the British withdrawal now set for May 15, that the United Nations not abandon partition. Partition was, in fact, already crystallizing in Palestine. Both Jews and Arabs were, to a large degree, obedient to their own institutions. The central British administration was in a state of virtual collapse. The Jewish Agency intended to proclaim the state of Israel when the British left, but without continued American support for partition this seemed almost impossible.

Early in March 1948, as American policy appeared to waver, Chaim Weizmann had sailed from Palestine to put the Zionist case before President Truman, but by this time Truman was refusing to see anyone. Jewish leaders realized that this might be the turning point. At this juncture, the president of the B'nai B'rith, Frank Goldman, turned to the president's old friend and former partner in a Kansas City haberdashery, Eddie Jacobson, who agreed to intercede for Weizmann. Jacobson decided to visit the White House personally and was given an appointment with Truman. According to Jacobson, Truman angrily refused to see Weizmann. Jacobson then appealed to Truman by using an analogy to Truman's hero, Andrew Jackson. Weizmann, Jacobson said, was his hero just as Jackson was Truman's hero. Jacobson voiced surprise that the president refused to see Weizmann simply because of the treatment the president had received at the hands of some of America's Jewish leaders. Truman relented, and a meeting was arranged.

Truman saw Weizmann on March 18, 1948. The Zionist leader stressed that abandonment of partition at a time when Palestine was threatened by outside Arab aggression and internal warfare would be disastrous. He also argued that there was no reason to think that the Arabs would accept, or assist in setting up, trusteeship any more than they would partition. Truman was convinced, and he told Weizmann that the United States would not abandon partition. However, on the following day, March 19, in the Security Council, Ambassador Austin called for a suspension of all efforts aimed at partition and asked for a special meeting of the General Assembly to approve United Nations' trusteeship.

Austin's announcement, coming as it did the day after the president's assurance to Weizmann, considerably embarrassed Truman, who was bitterly condemned by all sections of Jewish opinion for "betraying" the Jews and was criticized in non-Jewish quarters for "brutally reversing" American policy. If the president was seeking political advantage in his Palestine policy, he was very inept in going about it. In fact, Truman had approved Ambassador Austin's statement *prior* to his meeting with the Zionist leader, but he had not known when it was to be made.

The U.S. trusteeship proposal was not, in fact, an abandonment, reversal, or substitute for the partition plan. Truman was concerned that there would be no public authority in Palestine capable of preserving law and order when the mandate terminated. Trusteeship was the only solution. Secretary of State Marshall explained American thinking to the Senate Foreign Relations Committee a few days later. If partition had to be implemented by the use of UN forces, this would involve Soviet troops. They, Marshall said, had shown a tendency to remain in the areas they occupied. The Soviets would again press down on Greece, Turkey, and the Arabian oil fields, which were vital for the entire European recovery program. The fact that the Soviets were looking for a warm-water port also added to the danger of Soviet troops in the area. The only solution, Marshall argued, was to turn the matter over to the UN Trusteeship Council. The Soviet Union was not represented on the council, so the danger of Soviet military intervention could be avoided.

The second Special Session of the General Assembly met briefly to discuss Palestine on April 1 and resumed on April 16 to discuss the American proposal. It soon became clear that the

General Alan Cunningham, British high commissioner, saluting the colors
as he leaves Government House, Jerusalem, May 14, 1948.

discussion would be drawn out and that trusteeship, like partition, could not be enforced without an adequately armed neutral force. Britain was determined not to remain longer than May 15,
1948, a fact only then being fully realized by the United States and both protagonists in Palestine. On the morning of May 14, 1948, the Union Jack was hauled down from Government
House in Jerusalem for the last time, and as the British high commissioner, Sir Alan Gordon
Cunningham, sailed out of Haifa at 11:30 P.M. that night, the British mandate came to an end.

Suggestions for Further Reading

BAUER, YEHUDAH, *A History of the Holocaust*, New York, Franklin Watts, 1973.
CLENDINNEN, INGA, *Reading the Holocaust*, Cambridge, Cambridge University Press, 1999.
COHEN, MICHAEL J., *Palestine and the Great Powers, 1945–1948*, Princeton, Princeton University Press,
    1982.
———, *Palestine, Retreat from the Mandate: The Making of British Policy, 1936–1945*, New York,
    Holmes and Meier, 1978.

HILBERG, RAUL, *The Destruction of the European Jews*, revised and definitive edition, New York, Holmes and Meier, 1985.

LOUIS, W. ROGER, AND STOOKEY, ROBERT, *The End of the Palestine Mandate*, Austin, University of Texas Press, 1986.

SHLAIM, AVI, *Collusion Across the Jordan: King Abdullah, the Zionist Movement, and the Partition of Palestine*, Oxford, Clarendon Press, 1988.

WASSERSTEIN, BERNARD, *Britain and the Jews of Europe 1939–1945*, New York, Oxford University Press, 1988.

WYMAN, DAVID, *The Abandonment of the Jews*, New York, Pantheon, 1985.

 DOCUMENT 3–1

Rudolf Hoess on the Methods of the "Final Solution"

The "final solution" of the Jewish question meant the complete extermination of all Jews in Europe. I was ordered to establish extermination facilities at Auschwitz in June 1941. At that time there were already in the general government three other extermination camps: Belzek, Treblinka and Wolzek. These camps were under the Einsatzkommando of the Security Police and SD. I visited Treblinka to find out how they carried out their extermination. The Camp Commandant at Treblinka told me he had liquidated 80,000 in the course of one-half year. He was principally concerned with liquidating all the Jews from the Warsaw ghetto. He used monoxide gas and I did not think that his methods were very efficient. So when I set up the extermination building at Auschwitz, I used Cyclon B, which was a crystallized prussic acid which we dropped into the death chamber from a small opening. It took from 3 to 15 minutes to kill the people in the death chamber depending upon climatic conditions. We knew when the people were dead because their screaming stopped. We usually waited about one-half hour before we opened the doors and removed the bodies. After the bodies were removed our special commandos took off the rings and extracted the gold from the teeth of the corpses.

Nazi Conspiracy and Aggression, vol. VI, document 3868-PS.

Source: T. G. Fraser, *The Middle East, 1914–1979* (New York: St. Martin's Press, 1980), pp. 25–26.

 DOCUMENT 3–2

Declaration Adopted by the Extraordinary Zionist Conference, Biltmore Hotel, New York City, May 11, 1942

1. American Zionists assembled in this Extraordinary Conference reaffirm their unequivocal devotion to the cause of democratic freedom and international justice to which the people of the United States, allied with the other United Nations, have dedicated themselves, and give expression to their faith in the ultimate victory of humanity and justice over lawlessness and brute force.

2. This Conference offers a message of hope and encouragement to their fellow Jews in the Ghettos and concentration camps of Hitler-dominated Europe and prays that their hour of liberation may not be far distant. . . .

3. In our generation, and in particular in the course of the past twenty years, the Jewish people have awakened and transformed their ancient homeland; from 50,000 at the end of the last war their numbers have increased to more than 500,000. They have made the waste places to bear fruit and the desert to blossom. Their pioneering achievements in agriculture and in industry, embodying new patterns of cooperative endeavor, have written a notable page in the history of colonization.

4. In the new values thus created, their Arab neighbors in Palestine have shared. The Jewish people in its own work of national redemption welcomes the economic, agricultural and national development of the Arab peoples and states. The Conference reaffirms the stand previously adopted at Congresses of the World Zionist Organization, expressing the readiness and the desire of the Jewish people for full cooperation with their Arab neighbors.

5. The Conference calls for the fulfillment of the original purpose of the Balfour Declaration and the Mandate which "*recognizing the historical connection of the Jewish people with Palestine*" was to afford them the opportunity, as stated by President Wilson, to found there a Jewish Commonwealth.

The Conference affirms its unalterable rejection of the White Paper of May 1939 and denies its moral or legal validity. The White Paper seeks to limit, and in fact to nullify Jewish rights to immigration and settlement in Palestine, and, as stated by Mr. Winston Churchill in the House of Commons in May 1939, constitutes "a breach and repudiation of the Balfour Declaration." The policy of the White Paper is cruel and indefensible in its denial of sanctuary to Jews fleeing from Nazi persecution; and at a time when Palestine has become a focal point in the war front of the United Nations, and Palestine Jewry must provide all available manpower for farm and factory and camp, it is in direct conflict with the interests of the allied war effort.

6. In the struggle against the forces of aggression and tyranny, of which Jews were the earliest victims, and which now menace the Jewish National Home, recognition must be given to the right of the Jews of Palestine to play their full part in the war effort and in the defense of their country, through a Jewish military force fighting under its own flag and under the high command of the United Nations.

7. The Conference declares that the new world order that will follow victory cannot be established on foundations of peace, justice and equality, unless the problem of Jewish homelessness is finally solved.

The Conference urges that the gates of Palestine be opened; that the Jewish Agency be vested with control of immigration into Palestine and with the necessary authority for up-building the country, including the development of its unoccupied and uncultivated lands; and that Palestine be established as a Jewish Commonwealth integrated in the structure of the new democratic world.

Then and only then will the age-old wrong to the Jewish people be righted.

Source: Walter Laqueur and Barry Rubin, eds., *The Israel–Arab Reader: A Documentary History of the Middle East Conflict,* 4th ed. (New York: Penguin Books, 1984), pp. 77–79.

 DOCUMENT 3-3

The Zionist Case: Golda Meir, Testimony Before the Anglo-American Committee of Enquiry, Jerusalem, March 25, 1946

This generation decided that the senseless living and senseless dying of Jews must end. It was they who understood the essence of Zionism—its protest against such a debased existence.

The pioneers chose to come to Palestine. Other countries in the world were open to Jews, but they came to Palestine because they believed then, as they believe now, as millions of Jews believe, that the only solution for the senselessness of Jewish life and Jewish death lay in the creation of an independent Jewish life in the Jewish homeland.

The pioneer generation had still another purpose in coming here. They had two goals which inevitably shaped themselves into one. Their second aim was the creation of a new society built on the bases of equality, justice, and cooperation. When they arrived here, they were faced with tough realities. Their mission was to conquer not their fellowmen, but a harsh natural environment, marshes, deserts, the malaria-bearing mosquito. They had also to conquer themselves for these young people were not accustomed to physical labor. They had no experience of a society based on principles of cooperation. They had to overcome much within themselves in order to devote themselves to physical labor, to agriculture, and to the making of a cooperative society.

From the outset they sought to achieve these goals in complete friendship and cooperation with the Arab population and with Arab laborers. It is significant that the first organization of Arab labor in this country was founded by the Jewish workers who came at that time.

As I have said, we came to Palestine to do away with the helplessness of the Jewish people through our own endeavors. Therefore, you will realize what it meant for us to watch from here millions of Jews being slaughtered during these years of war. You have seen Hitler's slaughterhouses, and I will say nothing about them. But you can imagine what it meant to us to sit here with the curse of helplessness again upon us; we could not save them. We were prepared to do so. There was nothing that we were not ready to share with Hitler's victims.

I don't know, gentlemen, whether you who have the good fortune to belong to the two great democratic nations, the British and the American, can, with the best of will to understand our problems, realize what it means to be the member of a people whose very right to exist is constantly being questioned: our right to be Jews such as we are, no better, but no worse than others in this world, with our own language, our culture, with the right of self-determination and with a readiness to dwell in friendship and cooperation with those near us and those far away. Together with the young and the old survivors in the DP camps, the Jewish workers in this country have decided to do away with this helplessness and dependence upon others within our generation. We Jews only want that which is given naturally to all peoples of the world to be masters of our own fate—only of our fate, not of the destiny of others; to live as of right and not on sufferance, to have the chance to bring the surviving Jewish children, of whom not so many are now left in the world, to this country so that they may grow up like our youngsters who were born here, free of fear, with heads high. Our children here don't understand why the very existence of the Jewish people as such is questioned. For them, at last, it is natural to be a Jew.

We are certain that given an opportunity of bringing in large masses of Jews into this country, of opening the doors of Palestine to all Jews who wish to come here, we can go on building upon the foundation laid by the labor movement and create a free Jewish society built on the basis of cooperation, equality, and mutual aid. We wish to build such a society not only within the Jewish community, but especially together with those living with us in this country and with all our neighbors. We claim to be no better but surely no worse than other peoples. We hope that with the efforts we have already made in Palestine and will continue to make we, too, will contribute to the welfare of the world and to the creation of that better social order which we all undoubtedly seek.

Source: Golda Meir, *A Land of Our Own: An Oral Autobiography* (New York: G. P. Putnam's Sons, 1973), pp. 53–55.

DOCUMENT 3-4

The Palestine Arab Case: Jamal Bey Husseini, Arab Higher Committee, Before the *Ad Hoc* Committee on the Palestinian Question on Palestinian Arab Reactions to the UNSCOP Proposals, September 29, 1947

The case of the Arabs of Palestine was based on the principles of international justice; it was that of a people which desired to live in undisturbed possession of the country where Providence and history had placed it. The Arabs of Palestine could not understand why their right to live in freedom and peace, and to develop their country in accordance with their traditions, should be questioned and constantly submitted to investigation.

One thing was clear; it was the sacred duty of the Arabs of Palestine to defend their country against all aggression. The Zionists were conducting an aggressive campaign with the object of securing by force a country which was not theirs by birthright. Thus there was self-defence on one side and, on the other, aggression. The *raison d'être* of the United Nations was to assist self-defence against aggression.

The rights and patrimony of the Arabs in Palestine had been the subject of no less than eighteen investigations within twenty-five years, and all to no purpose. Such commissions of inquiry had made recommendations that had either reduced the national and legal rights of the Palestine Arabs or glossed them over. The few recommendations favorable to the Arabs had been ignored by the Mandatory Power. It was hardly strange, therefore, that they should have been unwilling to take part in a nineteenth investigation. It was for that, and for other reasons already communicated to the United Nations, that they had refused to appear before the United Nations Special Committee on Palestine. Mr. Husseini assured the Committee, however, of the respect felt by the Arab Higher Committee for the United Nations and emphasized that his Committee looked to it for justice and equity.

The struggle of the Arabs in Palestine had nothing in common with anti-Semitism. The Arab world had been one of the rare havens of refuge for the Jews until the atmosphere of neighbourliness had been poisoned by the Balfour Declaration and the aggressive spirit the latter had engendered in the Jewish community.

The claims of the Zionists had no legal or moral basis. The case was based on the association of the Jews with Palestine over two thousand years before. On that basis, the Arabs would have better claims to those territories in other parts of the world such as Spain or parts of France, Turkey, Russia or Afghanistan, which they had inhabited in the past.

Mr. Husseini disputed three claims of world Jewry. The claim to Palestine based on historical association was a movement on the part of the Ashkenazim, whose forefathers had no connexion with Palestine. The Sephardim, the main descendants of Israel, had mostly denounced Zionism. Secondly, the religious connexion of the Zionists with Palestine, which he noted was shared by Moslems and Christians, gave them no secular claim to the country. Freedom of access to the Holy Places was universally accepted. Thirdly, the Zionists claimed the establishment of a Jewish National Home by virtue of the Balfour Declaration. But the British Government had had no right to dispose of Palestine which it had occupied in the name of the Allies as a liberator and not as a conqueror. The Balfour Declaration was in contradiction with the Covenant of the League of Nations and was an immoral, unjust and illegal promise.

The solution lay in the Charter of the United Nations, in accordance with which the Arabs of Palestine, who constituted the majority, were entitled to a free and independent State. Mr. Husseini welcomed the recent declaration of the representative of the United Kingdom that the Mandate should be terminated and its termination followed by independence and expressed the hope that the British Government would not on that occasion, as in the past, reverse its decision under Zionist pressure.

Regarding the manner and form of independence for Palestine, it was the view of the Arab Higher Committee that that was a matter for the rightful owners of Palestine to decide. Once Palestine was found to be entitled to independence, the United Nations was not legally competent to decide or to impose the constitutional organization of Palestine, since such action would amount to interference with an internal matter of an independent nation.

The future constitutional organization of Palestine should be based on the following principles: first, establishment on democratic lines of an Arab State comprising all Palestine; secondly, observance of the said Arab State of Palestine of human rights, fundamental freedoms and equality of all persons before the law; thirdly, protection by the Arab State of the legitimate rights and interests of all the minorities; fourthly, guarantee to all of freedom of worship and access to the Holy Places.

In conclusion, Mr. Husseini said that he had not commented on the Special Committee's report because the Arab Higher Committee considered that it could not be a basis for discussion. Both schemes proposed in the report were inconsistent with the United Nations Charter and with the Covenant (sic) League of Nations. The Arabs of Palestine were solidly determined to oppose with all the means at their command any scheme which provided for the dissection, segregation or partition of their country or which gave to a minority special and preferential rights or status. Although they fully realized that big Powers could crush such opposition by brute force, the Arabs nevertheless would not be deterred, but would lawfully defend with their life-blood every inch of the soil of their beloved country.

UNO Ad Hoc Committee on the
Palestinian Question, Third Meeting

Source: Fraser, *The Middle East*, pp. 49–51.

DOCUMENT 3-5

UNSCOP's Plan of Partition with Economic Union

1. The basic premise underlying the partition proposal is that the claims to Palestine of the Arabs and Jews, both possessing validity, are irreconcilable, and that among all the solutions advanced, partition will provide the most realistic and practicable settlement, and is the most likely to afford a workable basis for meeting in part the claims and national aspirations of both parties.

2. It is a fact that both of these peoples have their historic roots in Palestine, and that both make vital contributions to the economic and cultural life of the country. The partition solution takes these considerations fully into account.

3. The basic conflict in Palestine is a clash of two intense nationalisms. Regardless of the historical origins of the conflict, the rights and wrongs of the promises and counter-promises, and the international intervention incident to the Mandate, there are now in Palestine some 650,000 Jews and 1,200,000 Arabs who are dissimilar in their ways of living and, for the time being, separated by political interests which render difficult full and effective political cooperation.

4. Only by means of partition can these conflicting national aspirations find substantial expression and qualify both peoples to take their places as independent nations in the international community and in the United Nations.

5. The partition solution provides that finality which is a most urgent need in the solution. Every other proposed solution would tend to induce the two parties to seek modification in their favor by means of persistent pressure. The grant of independence to both States, however, would remove the basis for such efforts.

6. Partition is based on a realistic appraisal of the actual Arab-Jewish relations in Palestine. Full political cooperation would be indispensable to the effective functioning of any single-State scheme, such as the federal State proposal, except in those cases which frankly envisage either an Arab or a Jewish-dominated State.

7. Partition is the only means available by which political and economic responsibility can be placed equally on both Arabs and Jews, with the prospective result that, confronted with responsibility for bearing fully the consequences of their own actions, a new and important element of political amelioration would be introduced. In the proposed federal-State solution, this factor would be lacking.

8. Jewish immigration is the central issue in Palestine today and is the one factor, above all others, that rules out the necessary cooperation between the Arab and Jewish communities in a single State. The creation of a Jewish State under a partition scheme is the only hope of removing this issue from the arena of conflict.

9. It is recognized that partition has been strongly opposed by Arabs, but it is felt that opposition would be lessened by a solution which definitively fixes the extent of territory to be allotted to the Jews with its implicit limitation on immigration. The fact that the solution carries the sanction of the United Nations involves a finality which should allay Arab fears of further expansion of the Jewish State.

10. In view of the limited area and resources of Palestine, it is essential that, to the extent feasible, and consistent with the creation of two independent States, the economic unity of the country should be preserved. The partition proposal, therefore, is a qualified partition, subject to such measures and limitations as are considered essential to the further economic and social well-being of both States. Since the economic self-interest of each State would be vitally involved, it is believed that the minimum measure of economic unity is possible, where that of political unity is not.

11. Such economic unity requires the creation of an economic association by means of a treaty between the two States. The essential objectives of this association would be a common customs system, a common currency and the maintenance of a country-wide system of transport and communications.

12. The maintenance of existing standards of social services in all parts of Palestine depends partly upon the preservation of economic unity, and this is a main consideration underlying the provisions for an economic union as part of the partition scheme. Partition, however, necessarily changes to some extent the fiscal situation in such a manner that, at any rate during the early years of its existence, a partitioned Arab State in Palestine would have some difficulty in raising sufficient revenue to keep up its present standards of public services.

One of the aims of the economic union, therefore, is to distribute surplus revenue to support such standards. It is recommended that the division of the surplus revenue, after certain charges and percentage of surplus to be paid to the City of Jerusalem are met, should be in equal proportion to the two States. This is an arbitrary proportion but it is considered that it would be acceptable, that it has the merit of simplicity and that, being fixed in this manner, it would be less likely to become a matter of immediate controversy. Provisions are suggested whereby this formula is to be reviewed.

13. This division of customs revenue is justified on three grounds: (1) The Jews will have the more economically developed part of the country embracing practically the whole of the citrus-producing area which includes a large number of Arab producers: (2) the Jewish State

would, through the customs union, be guaranteed a larger free-trade area for the sale of the products of its industry: (3) it would be to the disadvantage of the Jewish State if the Arab State should be in a financially precarious and poor economic condition.

14. As the Arab State will not be in a position to undertake considerable development expenditure, sympathetic consideration should be given to its claims for assistance from international institutions in the way of loans for expansion of education, public health and other vital social services of a non-self-supporting nature.

15. International financial assistance would also be required for any comprehensive immigration schemes in the interest of both States, and it is to be hoped that constructive work by the Joint Economic Board will be made possible by means of international loans on favourable terms.

RECOMMENDATIONS.
A. PARTITION AND INDEPENDENCE.

1. Palestine within its present borders, following a transitional period of two years from 1 September 1947, shall be constituted into an independent Arab State, an independent Jewish State, and the City of Jerusalem, the boundaries of which are respectively described in Parts II and III below.

   UNSCOP Report, vol. 1, chapter VI, part I, Plan of partition with economic union.

Source: T. G. Fraser, *The Middle East, 1914–1979* (New York: St. Martin's Press, 1980), pp. 45–47.

FOUR 4

The Proclamation of Israel and First Arab–Israeli War

CHRONOLOGY

May 15, 1948	Arab armies invade Israel
May 17, 1948	Soviet Union extends full recognition to Israel
Sept. 17, 1948	Count Bernadotte assassinated
Jan. 6, 1949	Israel and Egypt announce cease-fire
Jan. 25, 1949	Great Britain extends de facto recognition to Israel
Jan. 31, 1949	United States extends full recognition to Israel and Transjordan
Feb. 24, 1949	Israel and Egypt sign armistice agreement at Rhodes
Mar. 11, 1949	Israel and Transjordan sign cease-fire
May 11, 1950	Israel admitted to the United Nations
July 27, 1950	U.N. mediator Ralph Bunche reports end of military conflict in Palestine
Apr. 24, 1950	King Abdullah issues official statement on annexation of East Jerusalem and Arab Palestine held by Arab Legion; Transjordan to be called the Hashemite Kingdom of Jordan

Israel Declared and the War of 1948

At 4:00 P.M. in the afternoon of May 14, 1948, as the British made final preparations to depart from Haifa, David Ben-Gurion, standing under a portrait of Theodor Herzl in a museum in Tel Aviv, proclaimed the state of Israel. (See Document 4–1.) The United States extended de facto recognition to the new state 11 minutes later, and the Soviet Union followed shortly after with de jure recognition. On May 15, various Arab armies entered Palestine: The Arab Legion went into the area allocated to the Arabs in Judea and Samaria; the Egyptian army moved through Gaza and Beersheba; the Lebanese went into Arab Galilee; the Iraqis moved alongside the Arab Legion; the Syrians remained at the border. The first Arab–Israel war—the Israeli War of Independence—was under way. In this chapter we shall describe these events and explore some of the immediate consequences.

The course of the war can be outlined very briefly. On May 14, the General Assembly had passed a resolution providing for a UN mediator in Palestine. The mediator, Count Folke Bernadotte, was to work with the Truce Commission established by the Security Council to promote a peaceful settlement. Count Bernadotte succeeded in arranging a month-long truce in mid-June. The Israelis used the truce to build up their supply of arms from Czechoslovakia and other countries, and when fighting resumed they embarked on a series of offensives that succeeded in stalling the Arabs and securing Tel Aviv. Control of Jerusalem was a key goal for both sides. On September 16, Bernadotte recommended to the United Nations that Jerusalem become an international city under UN control as envisaged in the partition resolution; that the Negev be allocated to the Arabs and Galilee to Israel; and that Arab refugees be allowed to return home. The following day, Bernadotte was assassinated by members of the Stern Gang. Ben-Gurion ordered the dissolution of the Irgun and Stern groups and over 200 people were arrested, but no one was ever brought to trial for Bernadotte's murder, and Ben-Gurion never denounced terrorism as a weapon. While Stern Gang extremists doubtless regarded the UN mediator's recommendations as hostile to the Jewish state, it should be noted that Bernadotte had played a central role in rescuing over 5,000 Jews from concentration camps in March and April of 1945. Following Bernadotte's death, fighting broke out again, but on December 1, King Abdullah of Transjordan agreed to a cease-fire with Israel.

By January 1949, Egypt's army in the Gaza and Negev was in disarray, and on February 24, Egypt signed an armistice agreement with Israel at Rhodes. Ralph Bunche, an American who had been appointed by the United Nations as mediator to take Bernadotte's place, skillfully handled the difficult truce negotiations. As the result of these, and later armistice agreements with Lebanon, Syria, and Transjordan, Israel increased its land area by about 20 percent (some 2,500 square miles). In fact, by the end of fighting, Israel covered almost 75 percent of the area of the former Palestine mandate west of the Jordan. Transjordan occupied and later annexed the thickly populated hill country of Judea and Samaria (later called the "West Bank") and East Jerusalem. Abdullah renamed his kingdom the Hashemite Kingdom of Jordan, a move recognized only by Great Britain and Pakistan. Egypt retained and administered the Gaza Strip. The armistice agreements were not regarded as permanent border arrangements, but, despite constant violations, they did remain the boundaries between Israel and her neighbors until the Six-Day War of 1967.

There is disagreement among historians on almost every aspect of the first Arab–Israeli war. Claims and counterclaims have been made by both sides, so that it is virtually impossible to reach conclusions that are not disputed. Of the many questions raised by the first Arab–Israeli war, there are two that merit our attention. The first is: How did 600,000 Jews manage to defeat the armies of 40 million Arabs they claimed were ranged against them? The second is: How did the war result in 725,000 or more Palestinian Arab refugees? The short answer to the first question is, of course, that the Jews of Palestine did not defeat millions of Arabs. The number engaged in the fighting is hard to calculate exactly, but according to some estimates, in April 1948,

On May 14, 1948, in Tel Aviv Museum, David Ben-Gurion, the country's first prime minister, declared the independence of Israel. The following day, the new state was attacked by five neighboring Arab nations.

the Zionists had about 30,000 armed men and women (about 15,000 were "on line" troops), with 10,000 for local defense and another 25,000 as a kind of home guard. There were, in addition, about 2,000 Irgun terrorists and about 800 in the Stern Gang. However, they had few heavy weapons and no artillery, armored vehicles, or planes. The combined Arab forces amounted to 40,000, of whom 10,000 (about 4,500 were battle ready) were in the British-trained Arab Legion. Many in the Arab armies were irregulars. The main strength of the Arab armies was their possession of armor, although they did not use it as effectively as they might have had they known the full extent of Jewish weakness.

The Arabs' major difficulties were logistical and organizational. The distance from Baghdad to Haifa is 700 miles, and the Egyptians had a 250-mile line of supply across the desert. Perhaps more important, the Arab forces had no unified command, nor did they have agreed-upon goals. Despite his previous understanding with the Jewish Agency, on May 14, King Abdullah of Transjordan declared himself commander-in-chief, but it was a meaningless gesture; he had no control of the other Arab troops or their specific objectives. The Arabs remained divided along traditional rivalries. King Farouk of Egypt would rather not have fought at all, but his fear of domestic unrest and the increase in influence his rivals in the Arab world—the Hashemite kings of Transjordan and Iraq—would gain if they fought and he did not drove him to enter the conflict. In addition, Arab League secretary general Abd al-Rahman Azzam and others played upon the king's vanity, and this was crucial in his decision to enter the war. Syria wanted the Arab areas of Palestine, and neither Syria nor Egypt wanted them to fall into the hands of Transjordan.

King Abdullah, as we have seen, would never have accepted an Arab Palestine under the control of either the mufti (Hajj Amin al-Husseini) or Syria. He entered the war to gain control of the Arab area of Palestine, especially Jerusalem, for Transjordan, and he too would have preferred not to fight. The mufti envisaged an Arab Palestine ruled by himself and in 1948 declared the All Palestine Government in Gaza. Hajj Amin's forces were led by his nephew, Abd al-Qadir al-Husseini, son of a former mayor of Jerusalem, and the mufti wanted control of all Arab funding to ensure his control over future Palestinian Arab affairs. The Arab League, however, refused to recognize Abd al-Qadir as leader of the Palestinian government-in-exile and funded his rival, Fawzi al-Qawuqji, who led a group of non-Palestinian Arab volunteers. Egypt supported the mufti as a way of preventing Abdullah—who was supported by the Nashashibi faction within the Palestinians—from gaining control of central Palestine and Jerusalem. All of these divisions among the Arab leadership meant that the war was fought with no unity of command or goals. It was largely localized as far as each Arab group was concerned, and this greatly assisted the centralized and unified Haganah. Nevertheless, the 608,000 Jews of Israel suffered the loss of 6,000 killed in the war—roughly 1 percent of their population. The Arab armies were far from untrained, undisciplined mobs. The Arab Legion, in particular, won notable victories, and the majority of fighters were efficient and effective. Among these was Abd al-Qadir al-Husseini, killed in action in April 1948. Like Izz ad-Din al-Qassam, he became a Palestinian national hero.

For the Yishuv, the first Arab–Israeli war was, in some ways, an extension of the military operation the Haganah had conducted against the British; this time it was directed against the Arab enemy. Many factors contributed to the Israeli victory. The Jewish forces had a unified command, and they fought with fierce determination, using weapons obtained from Czechoslovakia during the truce period. The war also set a pattern for terrorism, a tactic that had long been a part of Palestine's history, and one that both Jews and Arabs often employed in their future dealings with each other.

One of the most dramatic examples of this tactic took place on April 9, 1948, at Deir Yassin, a small village on the outskirts of Jerusalem, eighteen miles outside the boundaries of the Jewish state outlined in the partition plan. On the morning of April 9, a group of 132 of Begin's Irgun and the Stern Gang attacked the sleeping village, which had, until then, avoided being involved in the fighting. The village was captured and two-thirds of the villagers, some estimate as many as 254 men, women, and children, were murdered. Many, including young girls and old women, were allegedly raped, and in some cases the dead were mutilated and their bodies thrown down a well. Although the Haganah high command condemned the massacre, the officers in charge of the attack were not punished.

The Arabs believed that Deir Yassin was part of a campaign of terrorism by the Haganah and the Jewish Agency to "encourage" the Arab population to leave their villages and homes. Begin, in *The Revolt*, defended the "heroic" actions of his men (four were killed in overcoming the "fierce resistance" put up by the villagers) and asserted, as he did in relation to the King David Hotel bombing, that warnings were given for women and children to leave the village before the attack began. It is hard to describe Deir Yassin as a retaliation or reprisal raid. It took place outside the area assigned to the Jewish state in the partition plan, and, of course, it occurred before the Jewish state came into existence. Furthermore, the village had apparently entered into a "nonaggression" pact with the Haganah. It was, in fact, an integral part of Plan Dalet, a plan to acquire at least those areas of Palestine allocated to Israel in the partition resolution by clearing out hostile forces. This scheme—which involved the collaboration of the Irgun, the Haganah, and the elite commando force, the Palmach—was to undermine the morale of the Arab population through the use of terror and to "cleanse" the area of the Arab inhabitants. It also required the establishing of a corridor connecting Tel Aviv with Jerusalem. Twenty villages had to be destroyed and evacuated. Deir Yassin was one of them.

In their own defense, Zionist historians point out that Iraqi troops and Palestinian irregulars had been using Deir Yassin as a base for snipers against Jewish occupants of Jerusalem and that the attackers had allowed over 200 residents to leave the village unharmed. They call attention to a number of premeditated Arab atrocities prior to Deir Yassin; in mid-January 1948, for example, thirty-five members of the Palmach had been ambushed and their bodies mutilated by Arab soldiers. Deir Yassin was an unduly bloody incident, and while it cannot be condoned, it should be borne in mind that the incident took place in the context of the general violence that occurred in April and May of 1948.

Some Zionists have argued that guerrilla reprisal tactics and the use of terror against Arab civilians was the only way Israelis could win the war—any war—against the overwhelming number of Arabs opposing them. And terrorism was certainly not confined to the Israelis; the British and the Arabs had utilized terror in their campaigns against the Zionists. Needless to say, the Arabs retaliated for Deir Yassin. On April 13, they besieged a convoy of mainly Jewish doctors and nurses on the road to the Hadassah Hospital just outside Jerusalem on Mount Scopus, and they killed seventy-seven of them.

The Palestinian Refugees

The first Arab–Israeli war, in addition to securing the state of Israel, created about three-quarters of a million homeless Palestinian Arabs. As noted in the previous chapter, hundreds of thousands of Palestinian Arabs fled from their homes, or were expelled, during the Jewish War of Independence. At the end of hostilities early in 1949, the United Nations estimated that there were 726,000 Arab refugees from Israeli-controlled territories, about 70 percent of the Arab population of Palestine. The exact number is difficult to determine because it is impossible to know the true number of Arab illegals living in Palestine when the war broke out and the number of Bedouin who had become refugees. A figure of about 600,000 to 760,000 is probably more accurate. (See Map 4–1.)

Why did the refugees leave their homes and where did they go? Israelis long contended that during the Israeli War of Independence the Palestinian Arabs abandoned their homes and villages of their own free will. Not only that, they did so at the urging of the Arab leadership, who, the argument goes, told the Palestinians to leave until the Jewish state was destroyed and then they could return. The evidence, however, is inconclusive. According to some sources, the Arab League and the mufti ordered the Palestinians to remain where they were.

Israeli revisionist historians now maintain that as part of the campaign to evacuate Arabs from the Jewish state, the Haganah deliberately destroyed Arab houses and villages, broadcast false stories in Arabic of the spread of cholera and typhus epidemics, and urged the population to escape the bloodbath while there was still time. On the other hand, some efforts were made to reassure the Arabs, and in some instances, as in Haifa, Arabs were encouraged by the Jews to stay put, but by the first truce in mid-June 1948, over 250,000 Palestinians had fled, and this exodus had reached 300,000 by July. Arab Palestinians fled in some cases of their own free will, in some cases through terror; in other cases they were expelled.

There were several additional reasons for the Arab exodus. Among the more important was the damage done to the Palestinian political and economic infrastructure by the British during their suppression of the Arab revolt of 1936–1939. Thus, Palestinian leadership was absent just at the time when it was needed most. Further collapse occurred during 1947–1949, as many of the local mayors, judges, communal and religious officials fled. Palestinian society, as noted in earlier chapters, was semifeudal in character, and once the landlords and other leaders had made good their own escape—as they did from Haifa, Jaffa, Safed, and elsewhere—the Arab townspeople, villagers, and peasants were left helpless. The Palestinians themselves refer

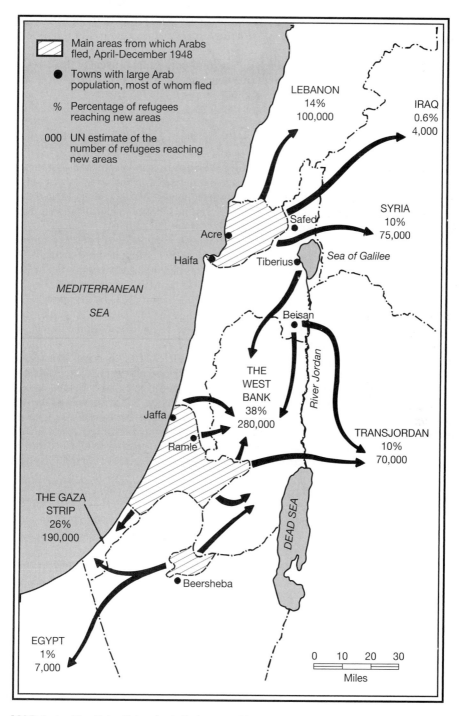

MAP 4–1   The Palestinian Arab Refugees, 1948

Source: Martin Gilbert, *Atlas of the Arab–Israeli Conflict* (New York: Macmillan, 1974), p. 49.

to this episode in their history as *al-Nakba*, "the catastrophe." Their sense of helplessness and fear was greatly intensified by some of the savage attacks carried out by the victorious Jewish forces.

Nevertheless, Israel insisted it had no moral responsibility or legal obligation to restore the Arab refugees to their property, or even compensate them for their losses. There was some flexibility on all this, at least until the summer of 1949. The Israelis then took the stand that all these matters were negotiable only within the framework of direct peace negotiations, which, by that time, the Arabs refused.

In any event, the truth was far from Chaim Weizmann's description of events as the "miraculous clearing of the land: the miraculous simplification of Israel's task." The Zionists had come a long way in the thirty years since Weizmann, who became the first president of Israel, had assured the Arabs of Jaffa that it was not the Zionists' intention "to turn anyone out of his property." It should be remembered, however, that Zionist leaders had stated they were prepared to accept the proposed Arab state in Palestine and the internationalization of Jerusalem, although evidently the other Arab governments were not.

Where did the refugees go? Again, exact figures are not possible, but according to Benny Morris, in his study of the Palestinian refugees, the British estimated in February 1949 that about 320,000 Palestinians moved into, or already resided in, the eastern portion of Palestine, which was controlled by the Arab Legion, and into Transjordan. Approximately 210,000 were in camps in the Gaza region, 100,000 went into Lebanon, and 75,000 to Syria. A few went to Egypt and others to Iraq. Some 150,000 remained within the Jewish state. Although most were displaced, 4 out of every 5 Palestinians remained within the boundaries of the former mandate. The Israeli government was not prepared to allow the refugees to return; indeed, Ben-Gurion had told the Israeli cabinet on June 16, 1948, that Israel should "prevent their return." The future of the Palestinians has remained a major issue between Israel and the Arab states. No one in 1948 viewed the refugee problem in long-range terms. Neither Israel nor the Arabs, at least for many years, did very much toward finding a solution. In the years after the establishment of Israel, it suited both Israel and the Arab states to do little. Nor was there a great deal that either the United States or the United Nations, working through its relief agency—the United Nations Relief and Works Agency (UNRWA)—could do other than try to alleviate the refugees' immediate situation. On December 11, 1948, UN General Assembly passed Resolution 194 establishing a Palestine Conciliation Commission comprised of representatives from the United States, France, and Turkey. One of the PCC's main tasks was to facilitate the repatriation or compensation of the Palestinian Arab refugees. (See Document 4–2.) However, Israel linked the whole refugee issue to comprehensive and direct peace negotiations with the Arab states.

Israel: A Jewish State

One of the first tasks for the new nation of Israel was the formation of a system of government. Israel was ruled by a Provisional Council of State from May 1948 until the first constitutional government was installed on March 10, 1949, following elections held in January 1949. The Israeli form of government is a modified British system. The parliament—called the *Knesset*—consists of a unicameral (one chamber) legislature of 120 members elected by a system of proportional representation. All Israeli citizens above the age of eighteen are eligible to vote without distinction of race, creed, or sex. Twenty-one political parties put up candidates in the first election of January 25, 1949. Until the 1990s, electors voted for the party list, decided by party caucus, rather than individuals standing as endorsed candidates. In the 1990s, however, some parties moved toward national primaries, and for the first time in 1996, there were direct elections for the prime minister, although this electoral change was rescinded in 2001.

Parties must receive 2 percent of the vote before they are entitled to seat representatives. In the first election, the Labor parties were awarded fifty-seven seats, the Center-Right parties thirty-one, and the Religious parties sixteen. Following the election, Chaim Weizmann, who had been elected Israel's first president by the provisional government, asked David Ben-Gurion, leader of the moderate left Labor party (Mapai), to form the state's first regular government.

The Knesset elects its own speaker, draft bills go through three readings before becoming law, and much of the work of the Knesset is done through permanent standing committees. One of the results of the system of proportional representation is that throughout Israel's political history there have always been a large number of parties, many with very few representatives, and most governments have been coalition governments. Consequently, government in Israel has been largely conducted by the cabinet and the prime minister rather than by the legislature. Despite early factional divisions, which reflected differences within the Zionist movement, continuity was maintained until 1977; the predominant party was Ben-Gurion's. It should be mentioned that Israel has no written constitution like that of the United States; instead, Israel has Fundamental or Basic Laws that govern the conduct of the country. The Israelis intended to draft a constitution but could not achieve consensus between secular and religious Jews.

The establishment of Israel had ramifications beyond Palestine and its borders, of course. In the first place, it cleared the way for Jewish DPs in Europe to migrate to Palestine. Between September 1948 and August 1949, fifty-two European DP centers were closed. By the end of 1948, 100,000 DPs had arrived in Israel, and they were followed by Jews from Czechoslovakia, Bulgaria, Yugoslavia, Poland, Romania, and Hungary. By 1950, the population of Israel was 1,174,000. There were also demographic changes in Africa and the Middle East. By 1957, over half a million Jews had left or been expelled from Muslim countries in North Africa and the Middle East and had settled in Israel. Within the first five or six years of Israel's existence, approximately 47,000 immigrants came from Yemen, 113,000 from Iraq, 14,000 from Lebanon and Syria, and 39,000 from Iran. By the end of 1951, over 680,000 immigrants had arrived in Israel—one-third more than arrived in the sixty years prior to the establishment of the nation. They were divided almost equally between European Jews (Ashkenazim) on the one hand and non-European Jews (Sephardim and Oriental Jews) on the other. Before 1948, almost 90 percent had arrived from Europe. This coming together in Israel of the Ashkenazim from Eastern and Central Europe, who had played such a central role in building up the national home, with the non-European Jews, who were so different in language, customs, and culture, created great problems for Israel. In 1948, the Jews of Europe made up 75 percent of Israel's Jews; by 1961, they represented only 55 percent. There was a danger that two Israels would be created—one consisting mainly of Ashkenazi leaders who held power and understood the state because they helped create it, and the other mostly of underemployed, undereducated, and underprivileged Sephardic and Oriental Jews.

Life was not easy for the new arrivals. There was no housing and rather chaotic government administration and bureaucracy. Many had to live in temporary reception centers, later called transit camps (by the end of 1951, about 250,000 were still in transit camps), while new self-supporting autonomous village settlements were established. Between 1948 and 1951, 345 villages were established; many were built on the sites of "abandoned" Arab villages and tracts of land. Some were kibbutzim, but the majority were moshavim, a cooperative system in which each family was responsible for its own holding. The villages were located mainly in the coastal plain, but also in areas where only isolated settlements had existed previously: Upper Galilee, the Judean Hills, and the arid Negev. One of the first tasks was land improvement and forestation. In 1948, the land cultivated by Jews totaled 1.6 million dunams; by 1958, it was 3.9 million dunams (a dunam equals one-quarter acre). Fifty percent of the immigrants were unskilled. Despite the fact that, by 1958, about one-third of the newcomers who had settled in collective settlements had moved into the cities of Tel Aviv, Haifa, and Jerusalem, at the end of its first decade of existence, Israel was feeding itself in the key staples of dairy products, poultry, vegetables, and fruit.

Mass immigration, while essential to provide military manpower and to preempt vulnerable empty spaces, also created economic difficulties for Israel. Productivity was low, and capital costs for housing, health, and development were high; thus, taxes were high and rationing was introduced. In the years following the destructive War of Independence, Israel had no exports to speak of; trade with the Arab states ceased because of an Arab economic boycott; the Haifa oil refinery closed; and citrus production was down. Israel depended upon outside assistance. That assistance came in the form of a $100 million loan from the Export-Import Bank in January 1949 and a series of Grants-in-Aid from the U.S. government. Diaspora Jews, especially those in the United States, also provided funds through various fund-raising campaigns such as the United Jewish Appeal. Private aid from the United States amounted to between $60 million and $100 million annually. Further assistance was provided by the Federal Republic of Germany (West Germany). Following an emotional and heated national controversy in Israel, an agreement was signed (in 1953) whereby West Germany was to pay Israel DM 3 billion ($715 million), most of it in machinery and goods over the next twelve years as partial reparations for material losses incurred by the Jews during the Nazi regime. In addition to the German reparations were restitution payments to individual Israeli Jews.

Slowly the state began to take shape. Compulsory education acts and labor laws (including equal rights for women in the workforce in 1951) were passed. El Al, the Israeli national airline, and a merchant marine were established; roads, hospitals, and schools were built and compulsory military service introduced. Despite the progress, the economic hardship the new state was experiencing led to a drastic reduction in immigration; 24,000 immigrants arrived in 1952 and only 11,000 in 1953.

To see Israel strictly as just another nation-state, or even to see it in the immediate terms of the triumph of modern Zionism, is, as one observer, Melvin Urofsky, has noted, "to miss the deeper meaning of Israel in the collective consciousness of the Jewish people." Zionism has been the only modern successful national movement based on the idea of a people's *return*,

President Chaim Weizmann presents a Torah to President Harry S. Truman.

an expression that has been part of Jewish experience for nearly 2,000 years. Some black Americans tried to return to Africa, especially to Liberia and Sierra Leone, but Zionism is clearly the greater success thus far. Eretz Yisrael (the Land of Israel) not only was an ideal earthly dwelling place but also reflected and supported the ideals and customs of Judaism. Now Jews were once again in their own land. But for Jews of the Diaspora, especially in Europe and the United States, the creation of Israel was not just the fulfillment of a long-cherished dream; it was a time of reckoning.

The Hebrew prophets had assumed that all Jews would live together. Dispersal, or exile, had been a temporary condition. The question for Jews around the world now became: How do I remain a Jew and not live in Israel? It remains a central question for Jews to this day. Ultra-orthodox Jews rejected Israel as an abomination; only God, not man, could cause the coming of the Messiah and thus redeem the Jewish people. Ultra-assimilationist Jews feared that a Jewish state would accentuate anti-Semitic hostility by questioning the loyalty of Jews to the countries in which they lived. They wanted to be regarded as, for example, Americans of the Jewish faith. The issue of emigration to Israel was, naturally, an important one. It had been widely assumed, in Europe at least, that given a choice between a homeland of their own and anti-Semitism in exile, Jews would naturally emigrate. This attitude was not shared by Jews in the United States. Most Diaspora Jews resolved the issue, whether or not simply, by staying where they were.

David Ben-Gurion was determined that if the answer of Diaspora Jews was to stay where they were, they would make a substantial contribution, if not spiritually, then financially, to help the new state establish itself economically. In 1951, Ben-Gurion led a campaign for the "ingathering of the exiles." The Israeli position clearly and simply divided the Jewish world into *Moledet* and *Galut* (Homeland and Exile). All Jews, especially Zionists, should make *aliyah* (or immigrate) as soon as possible. Israelis found it hard to accept the permanence of the Jewish Diaspora, once the state was established. To Israelis, it was incomprehensible that all Jews would not wish to live in the security and normalcy of a reborn Jewish nation. To facilitate the process of aliyah, one of the first acts of the Israeli Knesset was the Law of Return, which stated that Jews immigrating to Israel were entitled to citizenship automatically—that is, without undergoing a naturalization process.

If the vast majority of Diaspora Jews did not migrate to the Jewish nation, Israel nevertheless had a profound impact on Jews throughout the world. In the first place, it made the memory of the Holocaust bearable. It was a kind of partial compensation for the memories of disaster that haunted the Jewish subconscious. Second, it provided dignity and pride, a model for the new, free, victorious Jew whose motto is "Never Again!" And it reinforced the idea of the continuity and vitality of the Jewish people. Israel and the Diaspora both exist as part of the larger *Klal Yisrael* (the Jewish people). For most of the world's Jews, then, Israel does not exist for itself alone; it exists, as Melvin Urofsky has observed, for the Jewish people everywhere; it is "the lamp of Jewish life and culture in the world today." This is why the issue of Israel's apparent indifference to the suffering of the Palestinian refugees is so important to new generations of Jews.

The Arabs of Palestine: 1948

For the Palestinian Arabs, May 1948 meant that Palestine no longer existed. Three-quarters of the land of Palestine was now part of Israel, and the rest (the West Bank) was absorbed by the Kingdom of Transjordan. Jerusalem became a divided city. More than half of the Arabs of Palestine became refugees; the community was destroyed. More than 60 percent of Israel's total land area, excluding the Negev, was land formerly occupied by Palestinians. Furthermore, entire cities and towns were taken over by Israel. Jaffa, Acre, Lydda, Ramle, Beit Shean, and Majdal were among these 388 towns and villages. Large parts of 94 other towns were also seized by the new state. In all, a quarter of all buildings in Israel (100,000 dwellings and 10,000 shops, businesses, and stores) formerly belonged to Palestinian Arabs.

Those Palestinians with skills—intellectuals, businessmen, and professionals—went to cities such as Beirut, Damascus, and Amman; but the vast majority—about four-fifths—were unskilled workers and dispossessed peasants, and they went to refugee camps where they remained. The refugee camps were set up with the help of the United Nations Relief and Works Agency for Palestine Refugees in the Middle East (UNRWA) in the vicinity of the neighboring Arab capital cities or on old unused British or French army campsites. Conditions were appalling; there was little sanitation, no sewage, and only basic medical facilities. Gradually, tents were replaced with small huts, and electricity and communal running water were supplied in the 1950s. The camps were organized according to where the refugees came from, so that adjoining villages in Palestine found themselves neighbors in the camps. Nevertheless, the camps were places of desperation, degradation, and insecurity—and they remain so today. The situation was not helped by the refusal of the refugees to cooperate in making the camps more attractive places, or to consider UNRWA resettlement schemes, as they wanted to emphasize the temporary nature of the camps and their hope of someday returning home. The Palestinians did take advantage of the education and training programs provided by UNRWA. In the meantime, little work was available for the refugees, and this demoralized them even more.

Opportunities differed depending upon where the refugees were. Palestinians in Jordan were allowed to become citizens of the Hashemite Kingdom—the only Arab country to extend them citizenship. They were granted full political rights and opportunities for advancement. Many entered business and the professions, and some have served in the government; however, they have for the most part been excluded from the more sensitive areas of the Jordanian establishment. In Syria, Palestinians could join the army and civil service and acquired most rights except for citizenship. Many also left the refugee camps and were integrated into the general society. The Palestinians have fared worst in Lebanon. Although some Palestinians, mainly Christians or those having family connections, were able to acquire citizenship in the 1950s and 1960s, the majority have no civil rights in Lebanon and most professions are forbidden to them. They have been marginalized, and their rights to work, travel, and engage in political activities have been severely circumscribed. Lebanon, with its delicate confessional balance, has always kept their status a temporary one, and since the majority in the camps are Sunni Muslims, they have often conflicted with both the Christian and the Shia groups in Lebanon. About

Beach Camp for Palestine refugees, Gaza Strip, 1949.

Beach Camp, 1986.

60 percent live at the poverty level and UNRWA estimates put the unemployment level in the camps at about 40 percent. Some Palestinians also moved to Saudi Arabia and the Persian Gulf countries where many prospered but few were granted nationality. It is possible to trace the dynamics of the Palestinian diaspora. Over a period of forty years, the sons and daughters of illiterate subsistence peasants who were turned into refugees obtained training or education, worked hard, saved money, and moved into the middle class and intelligentsia of other Arab countries, although very few have been able to acquire full citizenship in those countries.

At the time of the 1949 armistice agreements, as we have noted, there were around 150,000 Arabs residing in Israel, most of them in the north in Galilee. Once again, Israeli and Palestinian spokespersons differ in their interpretation of the condition of the Arab population of Israel. Israeli supporters point to a number of areas in which Arabs were treated well. They note that the Nationality Law of 1951, for example, was extended to all inhabitants of the state. Arabs were allowed to vote, run for office, and, on paper, enjoy equal rights with Jews, the notable exception being army duty (except for Druze and Circassians, who do serve in the army). Arab women in Israel were the first Arab women anywhere to have the right to vote.

Palestinian advocates, on the other hand, describe the measures often employed by Israel as oppressive. The Palestinian Arabs in Israel at first were placed under military rule and forbidden to move outside their areas without permits. They were forbidden to form their own political parties. Under the Defense (Emergency) Regulations imposed, which were not lifted until 1966, military governors had extensive powers over the Palestinians. Arabs could be exiled or arrested and detained without reason; villages and land could be expropriated by declaring an area a "security zone."

The Arabs of Israel also believe they were discriminated against in terms of educational and employment opportunities. They cite the history of Nazareth to illustrate the situation of the Palestinians. Nazareth has become the largest Arab town in Israel, and it has been neglected by the Israeli government; factories were closed, and very little was spent on housing despite the dramatically increasing population. At the same time, during the 1950s, Arab land was expropriated to build an exclusively Jewish town on the hill overlooking Nazareth. Although

Upper Nazareth was only one-third the population of Nazareth, it received more assistance from the state than did the Arab town, and it also had several factories. Despite the fact that accommodations are available in Upper Nazareth, Arabs are discouraged from buying or renting property there.

Arabs see the story of the Arab population in the Negev and Galilee as a similar case of denial of civil rights. The 10,000 Bedouin remaining in the Negev lost nearly all their cultivable land and pasture and were transferred to an area northeast of Beersheba from which they were prevented from moving. In the "triangle" in the Galilee, originally under the partition plan to be located in the Arab state, some villagers were separated from their land, which was then expropriated as "absentee" property. In these ways, Arabs claim their agricultural economy was disrupted in the decade following Israel's establishment.

The situation of the Israeli Arabs was made even more difficult by their being a minority in a state that was at war with the neighboring Arab countries. They were bound to be regarded with suspicion and fear; they recognized this. Many accepted the Jewish state and cooperated with it; others totally rejected it. And the majority, perhaps, remained ambivalent. The response of Israeli Arabs to Israel varied and depended largely upon their personal circumstances. The reason most frequently given for what was seen as the harsh and discriminatory treatment of the Arabs in Israel was Prime Minister Ben-Gurion's hostile or reactionary attitude to Arabs. Ben-Gurion's view was shared by many Israeli leaders, including Golda Meir. Israelis were also obsessed by the idea of national vulnerability, and their hostility and prejudice toward the Arabs stemmed from their largely unjustified fear that Israeli Arabs would act as a fifth column against them.

Conclusion

The armistices of early 1949 did not finalize any of the issues surrounding the proclamation of the new state. Arab neighbors still resolutely opposed its existence. The future of the Palestinian refugees was still to be resolved. The United States and the United Nations tried unsuccessfully to get cooperation between Israel and the Arab states on such development schemes as the sharing of the Jordan River waters for irrigation. The United States, Britain, and France also attempted to limit further warfare in the region by a tripartite agreement in 1950 that restricted the sale of arms to either side. The allies worried about their future influence and strategic interests. Gradually, these issues got out of control, just as they did in the events leading to the formation of Israel. The history of the first decade of Israel's existence, in addition to being the story of how the new Jewish state consolidated its internal structure, is also very much the story of just how the Western powers lost control of events in the region.

Suggestions for Further Reading

ABDULLAH, KING, *My Memoirs Completed: Al-Takmilah*, London, Longman, 1978.

BEN-GURION, DAVID, *Israel: Years of Challenge*, New York, Holt, Rinehart & Winston, 1963.

COLLINS, LARRY, AND LAPIERRE, DOMINIQUE, *O Jerusalem!*, New York, Simon & Schuster, 1972.

GLUBB, JOHN BAGOT, *A Soldier with the Arabs*, New York, Harper & Row, 1957.

HAZONY, YORAM, *The Jewish State: The Struggle for Israel's Soul*, New York, Basic Books, 2000.

HERZOG, CHAIM, *The Arab–Israeli Wars, War and Peace in the Middle East*, New York, Random House, 1982.

KARSH, EFRAIM, *Fabricating Israeli History: The "New Historians,"* London, Frank Cass, 2000.

LOUIS, W. ROGER, *The British Empire in the Middle East, 1945–1951*, Oxford, Oxford University Press, 1984.

MEIR, GOLDA, *My Life*, New York, Putnam, 1975.

MORRIS, BENNY, *The Birth of the Palestinian Refugee Problem, 1947–49*, Cambridge, Cambridge University Press, 1987.

———, *The Birth of the Palestinian Refugee Problem Revisted*, Cambridge University Press, 2003.

———, *Righteous Victims: A History of the Zionist–Arab Conflict*, New York, Alfred A. Knopf, 1999.

SAYIGH, ROSEMARY, *Palestinians: From Peasants to Revolutionaries*, London, Zed Books, 1979.

SILBERSTEIN, LAURENCE J., *Postzionism Debates: Knowledge and Power in Israeli Culture*, New York, Routledge, 1999.

STERNHELL, ZEEV, *The Founding Myths of Israel: Nationalism, Socialism and the Making of the Jewish State*, Trans. by David Maisel, Princeton, N.J., Princeton University Press, 1999.

TURKI, FAWAZ, *The Disinherited: Journal of a Palestinian Exile*, New York, Monthly Review Press, 1972.

UROFSKY, MELVIN I., *American Zionism from Herzl to the Holocaust*, Garden City, N.Y., Anchor Press, 1975.

WILSON, MARY C., *King Abdullah, Britain and the Making of Jordan*, Cambridge, Cambridge University Press, 1987.

 DOCUMENT 4-1

State of Israel Proclamation of Independence

The Proclamation of Independence was published by the Provisional State Council in Tel Aviv on May 14, 1948. The Provisional State Council was the forerunner of the Knesset, the Israeli parliament. The British Mandate was terminated the following day.

The Land of Israel was the birthplace of the Jewish people. Here their spiritual, religious and national identity was formed. Here they achieved independence and created a culture of national and universal significance. Here they wrote and gave the Bible to the world.

Exiled from the Land of Israel the Jewish people remained faithful to it in all the countries of their dispersion, never ceasing to pray and hope for their return and the restoration of their national freedom.

Impelled by this historic association, Jews strove throughout the centuries to go back to the land of their fathers and regain their statehood. In recent decades they returned in their masses. They reclaimed the wilderness, revived their language, built cities and villages, and established a vigorous and ever-growing community, with its own economic and cultural life. They sought peace, yet were prepared to defend themselves. They brought the blessings of progress to all inhabitants of the country and looked forward to sovereign independence.

In the year 1897 the First Zionist Congress, inspired by Theodor Herzl's vision of the Jewish State, proclaimed the right of the Jewish people to national revival in their own country.

This right was acknowledged by the Balfour Declaration of November 2, 1917, and re-affirmed by the Mandate of the League of Nations, which gave explicit international recognition to the historic connection of the Jewish people with Palestine and their right to reconstitute their National Home.

The recent holocaust, which engulfed millions of Jews in Europe, proved anew the need to solve the problem of the homelessness and lack of independence of the Jewish people by means of the re-establishment of the Jewish State, which would open the gates to all Jews and endow the Jewish people with equality of status among the family of nations.

The survivors of the disastrous slaughter in Europe, and also Jews from other lands, have not desisted from their efforts to reach Eretz-Yisrael, in face of difficulties, obstacles and perils; and have not ceased to urge their right to a life of dignity, freedom and honest toil in their ancestral land.

In the Second World War the Jewish people in Palestine made their full contribution to the struggle of the freedom-loving nations against the Nazi evil. The sacrifices of their soldiers and their war effort gained them the right to rank with the nations which founded the United Nations.

On November 29, 1947, the General Assembly of the United Nations adopted a Resolution requiring the establishment of a Jewish State in Palestine. The General Assembly called upon the inhabitants of the country to take all the necessary steps on their part to put the plan into effect. This recognition by the United Nations of the right of the Jewish people to establish their independent State is unassailable.

It is the natural right of the Jewish people to lead, as do all other nations, an independent existence in its sovereign State.

ACCORDINGLY WE, the members of the National Council, representing the Jewish people in Palestine and the World Zionist Movement, are met together in solemn assembly today, the day of termination of the British Mandate for Palestine; and by virtue of the natural and historic right of the Jewish people and of the Resolution of the General Assembly of the United Nations.

WE HEREBY PROCLAIM the establishment of the Jewish State in Palestine, to be called Medinath Yisrael (The State of Israel).

WE HEREBY DECLARE that, as from the termination of the Mandate at midnight, the 14th–15th May, 1948, and pending the setting up of the duly elected bodies of the State in accordance with a Constitution, to be drawn up by the Constituent Assembly not later than the 1st October, 1948, the National Council shall act as the Provisional State Council, and that the National Administration shall constitute the Provisional Government of the Jewish State, which shall be known as Israel.

THE STATE OF ISRAEL will be open to the immigration of Jews from all countries of their dispersion; will promote the development of the country for the benefit of all its inhabitants; will be based on the principles of liberty, justice and peace as conceived by the Prophets of Israel; will uphold the full social and political equality of all its citizens, without distinction of religion, race, or sex; will guarantee freedom of religion, conscience, education and culture; will safeguard the Holy Places of all religions; and will loyally uphold the principles of the United Nations Charter.

THE STATE OF ISRAEL will be ready to co-operate with the organs and representatives of the United Nations in the implementation of the Resolution of the Assembly of November 29, 1947, and will take steps to bring about the Economic Union over the whole of Palestine.

We appeal to the United Nations to assist the Jewish people in the building of its State and to admit Israel into the family of nations.

In the midst of wanton aggression, we yet call upon the Arab inhabitants of the State of Israel to preserve the ways of peace and play their part in the development of the State, on the basis of full and equal citizenship and due representation in all its bodies and institutions— provisional and permanent.

We extend our hand in peace and neighbourliness to all the neighbouring states and their peoples, and invite them to co-operate with the independent Jewish nation for the common good of all. The State of Israel is prepared to make its contribution to the progress of the Middle East as a whole.

Our call goes out to the Jewish people all over the world to rally to our side in the task of immigration and development, and to stand by us in the great struggle for the fulfillment of the dream of generations for the redemption of Israel.

With trust in the Rock of Israel, we set our hand to this Declaration, at this Session of the Provisional State Council, on the soil of the Homeland, in the city of Tel-Aviv, on this Sabbath eve, the fifth of Iyar, 5708, the fourteenth of May, 1948.

Source: Walter Laqueur and Barry Rubin, eds., *The Israel–Arab Reader: A Documentary History of the Middle East Conflict*, 4th ed. (New York: Penguin Books, 1984), pp. 125–128.

 DOCUMENT 4–2

UN General Assembly Resolution 194 (III) Adopted on December 11, 1948 [Excerpts]

THE GENERAL ASSEMBLY,

HAVING CONSIDERED FURTHER the situation in Palestine, . . .

ESTABLISHES a Conciliation Commission consisting of three States Members of the United Nations which shall have the following functions: . . .

INSTRUCTS the Conciliation Commission to take steps to assist the Governments and authorities concerned to achieve a final settlement of all questions outstanding between them; . . .

INSTRUCTS the Conciliation Commission to present to the fourth regular session of the General Assembly detailed proposals for a permanent international regime for the Jerusalem area which will provide for the maximum local autonomy for distinctive groups consistent with the special international status of the Jerusalem area; . . .

RESOLVES that the refugees wishing to return to their homes and live at peace with their neighbors should be permitted to do so at the earliest practicable date, and that compensation should be paid for the property of those choosing not to return and for loss of or damage to property which, under principles of international law or in equity, should be made good by the Governments or authorities responsible; . . .

INSTRUCTS the Conciliation Commission to facilitate the repatriation, resettlement and economic and social rehabilitation of the refugees and the payment of compensation, and to maintain close relations with the Director of the United Nations Relief for Palestine Refugees and, through him, with the appropriate organs and agencies of the United Nations. . . .

FIVE

The Conflict Widens: Suez, 1956

CHRONOLOGY

1869	Suez Canal opens
1875	Britain becomes largest single shareholder in the Suez Canal Company
1876	Anglo-French debt commission arrives in Egypt
1881	Colonel Arabi leads nationalist uprising in Egypt
1882	Britain occupies Egypt
1888	Constantinople Treaty provides for international transit of Suez Canal
1914	Egypt declared a British protectorate
1922	Britain gives Egypt internal independence
1936	Farouk becomes king of Egypt
1936	Anglo-Egyptian Treaty provides for end to British occupation of Egypt and limiting of troops to Canal Zone and Sinai
Sept. 1, 1939	Outbreak of World War II
Feb. 4, 1942	Britain forces Farouk to accept Wafd cabinet
Feb. 1949	Egypt signs armistice with Israel
Apr. 24, 1950	Jordanian parliament ratifies annexation of "West Bank" and East Jerusalem
Apr. 27, 1950	Great Britain recognizes annexation of "West Bank" and East Jerusalem (Pakistan only other country to do so)
May 25, 1950	Tripartite agreement among United States, France, and Britain
July 20, 1951	Assassination of King Abdullah
Oct. 27, 1951	Wafd parliament unilaterally abrogates 1936 treaty
July 23, 1952	Free Officers' coup; Muhammad Naguib emerges as leader; Farouk abdicates on July 26, 1952
Feb. 12, 1953	Agreement with Britain on the Sudan issue
May 2, 1953	Hussein becomes king of Jordan
June 18, 1953	Republic of Egypt declared
Apr. 18, 1954	Gamal Abdul Nasser replaces Naguib; emerges as real leader of revolution
July 1954	Lavon affair
July 27, 1954	Anglo-Egyptian agreement to complete withdrawal of all British forces from Egypt; ratified in October
Feb. 28, 1955	Israel attacks Gaza
Apr. 1955	Nasser attends Bandung conference
Fall 1955	Baghdad Pact in place
Sept. 27, 1955	Nasser announces Soviet-bloc arms deal
Mar. 1, 1956	King Hussein dismisses British General Glubb
May 1956	Nasser recognizes Communist China
July 19, 1956	John Foster Dulles withdraws American offer to help finance Aswan High Dam
July 26, 1956	Nasser nationalizes Suez Canal Company
Oct. 1956	Hungarian revolt begins
Oct. 29, 1956	Israel invades Sinai
Oct. 31, 1956	Britain and France bomb Egyptian airfields
Nov. 5, 1956	Britain and France invade Egypt
Nov. 6–7, 1956	Britain, France, and Israel agree to cease-fire
Jan. 9, 1957	Anthony Eden resigns as British prime minister
Mar. 1, 1957	Israel agrees to withdraw from Sinai; Egypt agrees to deployment of UN emergency force on border between Gaza Strip and Israel and at-Sharm al-Sheikh

The Uncertain Years, 1949–1956

The years following the establishment of Israel were years of uncertainty, anxiety, and turmoil for all concerned. No permanent peace was achieved. No state in the region gave diplomatic or legal recognition to Israel. Israel, even as it sought to put in place the economic, political, social, and diplomatic infrastructure essential to run an independent nation, feared the intentions of the bordering Arab states, and hostility between Israel and the Arab states soon embroiled the Middle East in the broader realm of international politics. The kingdom of Jordan, now including the West Bank, which Transjordan annexed in 1950, grappled with a new and potentially disruptive Palestinian population. The regimes in Syria and Lebanon were also shaken by the influx of Palestinian refugees, who became a new factor in the politics of both countries. The Egyptians threw off a decadent and inefficient old order, and their new military leaders, by and large indifferent to the fate of Palestine and the Palestinians, defied former colonial rulers Britain and France by seizing the Suez Canal, thereby setting in motion a chain of events that brought about a second war with Israel in 1956. This chapter explores these turbulent years.

Israel and the Palestinians

In December, 1948, UN General Assembly Resolution 194 established the Palestine Conciliation Commission (PCC). The Commission's task was to work toward a peace settlement between Israel and the Arab states, to facilitate the repatriation, resettlement, and economic and social well-being of the Palestine refugees, and to determine the status of Jerusalem. The PCC, however, failed to achieve any of its goals, and in fact these issues remained points of contention for the next fifty or so years. Both Israel and the Arabs rejected the UN position that Jerusalem should become an international city. The Jordanians and the Israelis came to a working arrangement by dividing the city between them, essentially disregarding the views of other nations. Israel later proclaimed Jerusalem its capital and gradually transferred government departments to the city.

Recommendations by the United Nations regarding the Palestinian refugees were also unacceptable to both sides. Israel insisted that any repatriation of refugees was dependent upon recognition of its existence and directly negotiated peace treaties with the Arab governments. For their part, the Arabs were unwilling to accept resettlement schemes without acknowledgment of the refugees' right to return. Meanwhile, the Arab states also used the pitiful conditions of the Palestinian refugees as a political weapon. They argued that the camps were visible evidence to the world of the harmful results of Zionist success. They hoped in this way to call upon world opinion to force Israel to make concessions. Some observers have suggested that the Arab governments' cynical manipulation of the Palestinian refugees was a lesson learned only too well from Zionist exploitation of the Jewish refugee issue after World War II. The Arab states also encouraged the Palestinians in Jordan, the Gaza Strip, and the demilitarized zones to cross the borders to reclaim possessions and to harass the Israelis.

The 1949 Rhodes armistice agreements established four such demilitarized zones (DMZs). One of these was in the north along the former Palestine-Syrian border; another surrounded the Hebrew University and Hadassah Hospital on Mount Scopus outside Jerusalem; a third consisted of the high commissioner's former palace; and a fourth was around al-Auja on the Egyptian border. The armistice talks also resulted in the drawing of temporary boundaries between Israel and its neighbors. They did not, however, lead to peace treaties between the new state of Israel and the Arabs. Iraq, in fact, refused to conclude even an armistice agreement.

Except for the border with Lebanon, which was for the most part quiet, raids into Israel by individuals and unorganized groups of Palestinian refugees from Jordan, Syria, and the Gaza Strip were frequent after the cessation of hostilities in 1949. These incursions reflected, among other things, the artificiality or uncertainty of the armistice lines, which, although considered temporary, had often divided Arab villages or cut off villagers from their fields or wells. Thus, Palestinians crossed over into Israel to reclaim possessions, harvest their crops, steal, smuggle, and sometimes to kill Israelis. The Rhodes agreements had set up Mixed Armistice Commissions (MACs), consisting of an equal number of Arab and Israeli delegates. They were intended to help resolve border disputes peacefully under the supervision of the UN Truce Supervisory Organization (UNTSO), but they were ineffective in preventing Arab raids.

Although at first most of the incidents were relatively minor and both Israel and the Arab governments took measures to prevent them, violence escalated on all the borders, and a cycle of raids and reprisals began. While both sides argued about the facts and the rights and wrongs of events, raids, counterraids, shootings back and forth, commando attacks, foraging expeditions, and day-to-day incidents continued. The MACs were kept busy sorting out claims and counterclaims, censuring and making recommendations, while being powerless to stop the activity.

The Israeli response to what it considered acts of provocation and murder was retaliation, often massive, by regular army units. The first major retaliatory raid, carried out by the newly formed "Unit 101," commanded by Ariel Sharon, took place in October 1953 against the Jordanian village of Qibya, and it destroyed fifty houses and killed more than sixty Jordanians, including women and children. Israel was condemned for this attack in the United Nations. Nevertheless, another large attack against the Jordanian village of Nahhalin occurred in early 1954 to avenge the Arab ambush of an Israeli bus and murder of eleven Israelis at Scorpion's Pass in the eastern Negev. A third major raid against Jordan prior to the Suez war took place in early October 1956, when Israel killed more than twenty-five Arabs at Qalqilya.

It should be noted that the Jordanian government actually tried to prevent this kind of terrorist activity because it was particularly susceptible to Israeli retaliation. Moreover, given the large percentage of the Jordanian population that was Palestinian, there was fear that Palestinian guerrilla groups, given too much leeway, would turn against the Hashemite king. Despite Jordan's annexation of the West Bank of the Jordan River and extension of citizenship to Palestinian refugees, many Palestinians regarded the Jordanians as "Bedouin," and the Jordanians were skeptical about Palestinian loyalty to the royal family. Many Arabs believe that Palestinian guerrilla activities from Jordan were also checked because Englishman John Bagot Glubb continued to command the Arab Legion.

On the Syrian border, there were several crises arising in the DMZ, many of which were the result of conflicting views about the legal status of the DMZ. (See Map 5–1.) The Israelis claimed that the armistice arrangements allowed them complete sovereignty and freedom of movement in the DMZ. Israel, therefore, took over Arab land, extended Israeli cultivation, and began to drain Lake Huleh over Arab objections. The Syrians and the United Nations argued that the question of sovereignty had not been settled by the armistice agreement, that neither party had a free hand, and that it was the responsibility of the Mixed Armistice Commission to interpret the provisions of the agreement. A particular source of tension involved fishing rights in Lake Tiberias (the Sea of Galilee). Syrian gun positions overlooking the lake fired on Israeli fishing boats and killed Israeli fishermen, while Israel employed armed patrol boats not only to protect the fishermen but also to prevent Syrian use of the lake. In December 1955, Israel attacked the Syrian gun positions and nearby Syrian settlements and was censured in the Security Council, partly because of the scale of the attack, and partly because Israel had chosen to bypass the UN peacekeeping machinery. It should be noted, however, that when

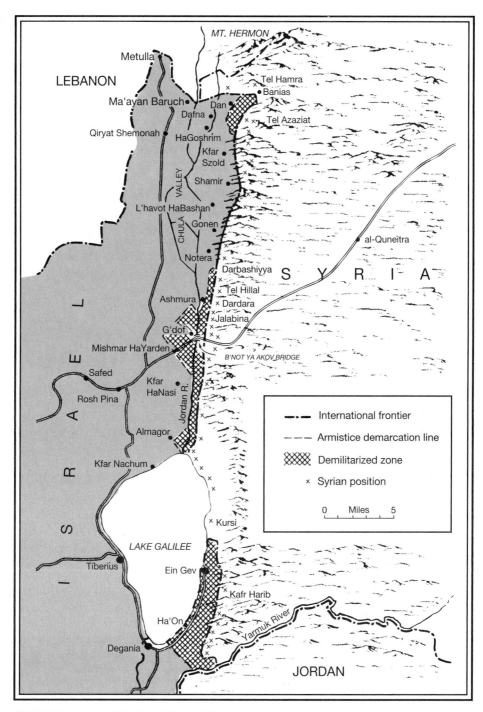

MAP 5–1   Israel–Syria Demilitarized Zones

Source: Howard M. Sachar, *A History of Israel: From the Rise of Zionism to Our Time*, vol. I, p. 448. Map by Jean Paul Tremblay. Copyright © 1976 by Howard M. Sachar. Reprinted by permission of Alfred A, Knopf Inc.

Israel took a case to the United Nations, the Soviet Union vetoed resolutions introduced on Israel's behalf.

On the Egyptian border, Palestinian and Egyptian infiltrators mined roads, blew up pipelines and bridges, murdered Israeli civilians, and carried out deep penetration raids into Israeli territory. Initially, the Israelis did not retaliate on a large scale. In February 1955, however, Israeli forces launched a massive attack against an Egyptian military post in Gaza, killing thirty-eight and wounding thirty-one. Egyptian President Gamal Abdul Nasser claimed that the Israeli Gaza raid impelled him to set up commando training camps for the refugees. These fighters, called *fedayeen* (those who sacrifice themselves), equipped and encouraged by the Egyptian government, were sent across the borders, beginning in August 1955, to spy, commit acts of sabotage, and murder Israelis. The fedayeen raids became an extension of other anti-Israel policies like the Arab economic boycott and Nasser's closing of the Suez Canal and Gulf of Aqaba to Israeli or Israeli-bound shipping. Between September and November of 1955, Israel drove Egyptian units from the demilitarized zone at al-Auja and took over complete control. The Gaza raid in particular, however, had already convinced Nasser that Egyptian arms were not sufficient to retaliate in kind and provided a catalyst for him to seek arms wherever he could acquire them. Before going any further at this point, however, we should look at developments in the Middle East taking place between 1948 and the end of 1955.

Israel and the Arab States

Much of the explanation of Israel's attitude toward the Arab states can be understood by looking again at Map 3–3 of the area after the conclusion of the armistice agreements, paying particular attention to the borders. Israel had over 600 miles of land borders, and 75 percent of its population lived in the coastal plain from Haifa to Tel Aviv and the corridor to Jerusalem. Many of Israel's cities were within 18 miles of an Arab border, and at its "waist," Israel was less than 10 miles wide from Jordan to the Mediterranean Sea. Not only was the population of the Arab states forty times that of Israel, but the Arab standing armies also outnumbered Israel eight to one. This situation, and the conviction that the Arabs were committed to the destruction of Israel as an independent state, had a profound effect on the thinking of Israeli leaders.

In fact, however, the Arab states were wracked by internal upheaval. The Arabs could do little except utilize economic weapons against Israel. They imposed an economic boycott in January 1950, which was strengthened by the closure of the Suez Canal to Israeli shipping and the removal to Tripoli, Lebanon, of the Haifa refinery by the Iraq Petroleum Company. Having been defeated by Israel confirmed the view of the younger generation of Arab nationalists that the old leadership must be overthrown and the Arab states modernized. Thus, upheavals occurred throughout the Arab world in the next decade. The army led the first of many coups in Syria in March 1949. In Jordan, a Palestinian refugee assassinated King Abdullah in July 1951, and in 1953, his grandson, the eighteen-year-old Hussein, assumed power. In July 1952, a group of army officers led by Muhammad Naguib deposed King Farouk in Egypt, and in October 1954, the charismatic Gamal Abdul Nasser took over as president of Egypt. One of Nasser's primary goals was the removal of Western influence from the Middle East. He also became a symbol of pan-Arabism and its determination to eradicate Israel. The continuing Arab–Israeli conflict, however, provided another arena for the rivalries of outside powers, especially the United States and the Soviet Union, as the Cold War extended into the region. In the absence of peace, tensions remained high, and in 1956 the Suez-Sinai war broke out. The background to this war begins with a discussion of Britain's influence in Egypt in the previous century.

Background to the 1956 War

Egypt and Britain

Egypt had been a focus of European colonialism and imperialism ever since the beginning of the nineteenth century. In 1854, the Khedives, whom the Ottomans recognized as semi-autonomous rulers of the country, gave a preliminary concession to the Frenchman Ferdinand de Lesseps to cut a canal between the Red Sea and the Mediterranean. The Suez Canal, built by the unpaid labor of some 20,000 Egyptians and financed by various schemes that milked the Egyptian treasury, opened to great fanfare in 1869. It was operated by a commercial company, the Compagnie Universelle du Canal Maritime de Suez, and the company's concession was to run until 1968.

The Suez Canal had revolutionary effects on Egypt, as that country, like others in Africa and Asia, became the focus of European imperialist interests. In 1875, the British became the largest single shareholder when they bought the Khedive Ismail's 44 percent of the stock to help him defray interest payments on the many loans he had contracted.

Ismail could not avoid bankruptcy, however, and in 1876, a British and French debt commission arrived to supervise Egyptian finances. This engendered much xenophobia, and a nationalist uprising in 1881, led by an Egyptian colonel, Ahmad Arabi, resulted in the British occupying Egypt in 1882 to protect the European creditors and to preserve British interests in the region. The British were particularly concerned about the Suez Canal, which was assuming increasing importance militarily and strategically and which was their gateway to India. Other maritime nations were also concerned to protect their interests, and at an international conference in Constantinope in 1888, nine European countries signed an agreement providing for free passage to ships of all flags. The British signed with reservations and managed to circumvent the Constantinople Convention during both world wars.

At the outbreak of World War I, the British declared Egypt a protectorate and used the country as a base of operations. Egyptians were transported to Gallipoli to aid the Allies; the country's economy was geared to the war effort; and several hundred thousand English and Australian troops were stationed in Egypt, contributing to inflationary pressures on the economy. Nationalist sentiment ran high immediately after the war, and although the British would not give up their hold on Egypt, they did alter their relationship with the Egyptians by concluding a formal treaty in 1922. This treaty gave the Egyptians some internal independence under a constitutional monarch, while reserving important matters like foreign affairs and national defense to the British. The "reserved" areas also included the protection of foreign interests and minorities in Egypt, control over the Anglo-Egyptian Sudan, and the protection of the Suez Canal, considered by now to be the most vital link in the communications network of the British Empire.

In 1936, a revised treaty was initialed. Its provisions included the abolition of the high commissioner's office, withdrawal of British troops except in the Canal Zone, greater Egyptian control over the judicial system, and membership of Egypt in the League of Nations. It gave the Egyptians a somewhat more visible role in the operation of the Suez Canal and a larger share of the profits. The treaty provided for the right of Britain to return to Egypt in case of emergency, however, an eventuality that the impending world war soon provided.

The conditions of World War I practically repeated themselves in Egypt during World War II, including the resentment of much of the population against the massive presence and obvious influence of the British, who at one point gave the young king Farouk a choice of accepting a pro-British prime minister or abdicating. Egyptian army officers were humiliated by their inability to defend the throne and by their helplessness in the war situation, but they remained loyal to the king. Later, however, stung by their defeat in the first Arab–Israeli war in 1948–1949, and by reports of corruption and a defective arms scandal involving even the palace, they turned against the monarchy and indeed began to discuss ways of supplanting it.

In 1951, with the British still in Egypt and the Canal Zone, a defiant Egyptian parliament unilaterally (and ineffectually) nullified the 1936 treaty. Disturbances resulted, and confidence in the king, who had also lost respect because of his personal vulgarity and excesses, waned. Events were set in motion that led to the "free officers" coup the night of July 22–23, 1952 and the proclamation of the Republic of Egypt. Although Muhammad Naguib emerged as the front man, he was ousted in 1954 by the real leader of the revolution, Gamal Abdul Nasser. One of the primary goals of the revolution, and certainly of Nasser, was to remove the last vestiges of foreign control from Egyptian soil. In Nasser's book *The Philosophy of the Revolution*, it is clear that regaining Egypt for the Egyptians, and not challenging Israel, was the most important objective. Indeed, Nasser expressed admiration for the Jewish effort to eject the British from Palestine. At this point, Egypt under Nasser was Egypt-centered, and that meant removing the British from the Nile Valley and the Canal Zone.

Nasser and Britain

Great Britain had emerged after World War II as the only European power of any importance in the Arab world, having influence and a large measure of control in Egypt, Iraq, and Jordan, and important oil concessions in Iraq. The British were war-weary, however, and financially exhausted; they were inclined to come to terms with Nasser, as long as they retained control over the Suez Canal and the right of free passage for their ships. By the time of the 1952 coup in Egypt, Britain had already given up Palestine, granted independence to India and Pakistan, and was in the throes of a crisis in Iran, where Mohammed Mossadeq led a movement against the Anglo-Iranian Oil Company in an attempt to nationalize Iranian oil.

In 1954, Egypt and Britain negotiated over the evacuation of British troops from the Canal Zone, and the British agreed in October 1954 to abrogate the 1936 treaty and to evacuate their troops within twenty months. An important clause in the agreement, however, said that in case of attack on a member of the Arab League or on Turkey, Britain or its allies could reoccupy the Canal Zone. This pretext was used to justify the Anglo-French invasion in 1956. As the British presence in the postwar Middle East diminished, the United States became the most important Western player on the scene.

Nasser and the United States

Up to 1945 the United States had not been very much involved in the Middle East, except for Christian missions, educational efforts, and oil interests. World War II brought with it various forms of economic and military involvement and a growing concern about and dependence on Middle East oil, but the United States would probably have been satisfied to leave diplomacy and policy initiatives to the British. The perceived Soviet threat, however, coupled with the decline in British influence, led to a postwar policy of "containment" of communism. The first manifestation in the Middle East of American determination to check the spread of communism was the Truman Doctrine of 1947, which extended economic and military aid to Greece and Turkey. In the next year, Iran also received a small economic and military allocation.

As Communist pressures mounted in the postwar period, with the victory of the Chinese Communists in 1949, the Berlin blockade in 1948–1949, and the invasion of Korea in 1950, the policy of containment was extended to the Arab states of the Middle East as well, now considered of vital geostrategic importance to the free world, especially since the region contained two-thirds of the free world's oil reserves.

Additionally, and in order to maintain stability and the free flow of oil, the United States sought to neutralize the Arab–Israeli conflict and, if possible, to convince Arabs and Israelis to make common cause with the West against the threat of Soviet encroachment. In May 1950, the United States, Britain, and France signed a Tripartite Declaration outlining their commitment to peace and stability in the area and their opposition to the use or threat of force. They pledged to take action within and outside the United Nations to prevent violations of the frontiers or armistice lines. Further, they reiterated their opposition to the development of an arms race. The three powers recognized, however, that the Arab states and Israel needed to maintain a certain level of armed force for purposes of internal security and legitimate self-defense, and they declared that they would consider arms requests in light of these principles—including requests that would permit the countries to "play their part in the defense of the area as a whole." An important but somewhat unenforceable clause of the Tripartite Agreement also stressed that the three powers would only sell arms with an assurance that the purchasing nations would not use them for acts of aggression against other nations.

On October 13, 1951, the United States, Britain, France, and Turkey proposed that Egypt, considered to be the strategic center of the Middle East, join in the formation of a Middle East Command (MECOM or MEC) against communism. At that time, MEC proposals provided for the withdrawal of British troops from Egypt except for those assigned to an Allied command. Not surprisingly, the Egyptian government, which just five days earlier had unilaterally abrogated the 1936 treaty, rejected the MEC idea, which it saw as a continuation of British and colonial interference in a new guise.

When the Egyptian revolution toppled King Farouk in 1952, American interests were in a state of flux. The change of regime in Egypt coincided roughly with the transition in the United States from the Truman to the Eisenhower administration. Relations between the two countries were cordial initially, as Egypt solicited American help in its negotiations with the British for evacuation of the Suez Canal Zone. The United States did intervene in Egypt's

U.S. Secretary of State John Foster Dulles in Cairo, May 1953, with Gamal Abdul Nasser (left) and Muhammad Naguib (right).

behalf, helping secure Britain's agreement to withdraw from the Sudan and to evacuate the Canal Zone bases. The United States, meanwhile, had been providing Egypt with technical aid through the Point IV program. This program, proposed by President Truman in January 1949 during his second inaugural address, was an attempt to help underdeveloped nations help themselves through technical assistance. Now, this aid was supplemented with further economic assistance, and the United States held open the promise of military aid as well.

America had its own agenda for the Middle East, of course, and still hoped for an alliance that would help secure reliable air bases in the region. To try to implement what the Eisenhower administration called its "New Look" foreign policy, Secretary of State John Foster Dulles made a trip to the Middle East in 1953. He concluded that it was not at that time realistic to attempt to create a Middle East version of NATO. The Arab states did not share U.S. concerns about communism. Having just gotten rid of Western entanglements in the previous few years, they had no desire to let the West in through a different door. The Arabs already had a collective security pact, signed in June 1950, which Egypt wanted Iraq to uphold, and Nasser believed that Israel was a greater military threat to the Arabs than was the Soviet Union. Washington began to focus on what Dulles called the "northern tier" nations bordering the Soviet Union, which he had found much more receptive to American proposals.

The Baghdad Pact, 1955

By 1954, the United States, through a series of treaties and military assistance agreements involving Greece, Turkey, Iran, and Pakistan, had what it believed to be a defense line from Europe to the Far East, and along the entire length of the southern border of the Soviet Union. It now sought to bring Iraq into this scheme, as another country that was on the southern flank of Russia and perhaps as a first step in encouraging other Arab countries to reconsider a collective security pact. The pro-British Hashemite monarchy and especially the prime minister and strongman of the country, Nuri al-Said, were amenable. Nuri hated communism and feared the Soviet threat, and he was eager for the benefits that an alliance with the West would bring.

In April 1954, the United States extended military assistance to Iraq, and in early 1955, Turkey and Iraq signed a mutual cooperation pact open to all members of the Arab League. Britain joined this alliance in April 1955. By the fall of 1955, Iran and Pakistan had also become members, and the Baghdad Pact was born. For a variety of reasons, the United States did not join as a full member. The United States did not want to offend the Saudis, and there was still at this point some hope that America could establish a relationship with Nasser. Nevertheless, Nasser, who was becoming recognized as a dominant leader among the Arabs, felt threatened by the pact. Based in Baghdad, it bypassed the Arab League and seemed a slap in the face to him. He responded angrily against Nuri al-Said, the British, and the United States, which, despite its lack of formal adherence, was a member in every way but name, attending the meetings of the pact, participating in its subcommittees, and supporting it financially and militarily.

The Baghdad Pact had implications not only for great-power rivalries and inter-Arab antagonisms but also for the Arab–Israeli conflict. Both Egypt and Israel had reason to be fearful of the other, and both also had reason to resent the Western powers and their patronage of Iraq. Indeed, there had been a basic contradiction all along between the avowed intention of the Tripartite Agreement to limit the amount of arms in the area and maintain an arms balance between the Arabs and the Israelis, on the one hand, and the almost simultaneous efforts to induce the Arabs to join Western defense arrangements to contain communism on the other.

American support for the Baghdad Pact was a tactical mistake in the light of subsequent events. It polarized the Arab world between Iraq and Egypt, led to destabilization in many countries in the region, and was indirectly responsible for bringing the Soviet Union into the heart of the Middle East.

By this time, Washington had decided against selling military equipment to Nasser. In November 1954, President Eisenhower had offered Nasser $13 million in economic aid and $27 million in military aid in return for Egyptian concessions in the British withdrawal arrangements. The American ambassador to Egypt, Henry A. Byroade, persuaded by Nasser's argument after Israel's Gaza raid that Egypt had to secure arms in order to deal with Israel as an equal, recommended that Eisenhower make good on his pledge. But American military aid never materialized, for several reasons. One was Eisenhower's sensitivity to British objections, but others were Nasser's rejection of Western-inspired collective security pacts and his support of "liberation" movements in various countries. In April 1955, Nasser attended the first conference of nonaligned nations at Bandung, Indonesia. Israel had been excluded, and resolutions were passed endorsing the Arab position on Palestine. At Bandung, Nasser met India's Nehru, Indonesia's Sukarno, China's Chou-en Lai, and others, and he embraced the idea of "positive neutralism." This concept seemed to mean avoiding entanglements with the West while remaining free to accept aid from any source prepared to offer it without strings attached. Nasser believed that the Arab world had to become self-reliant and completely emancipated from foreign control and influence; that the defense of the Arab countries had to rest upon the Arabs themselves, not their association with any European power; and that it was legitimate to encourage the masses in countries still under foreign control to topple the regimes in power. When Nasser requested arms from the West, therefore, the British sent some tanks but no ammunition; the French refused even to consider the idea unless Nasser stopped supporting the Algerian rebels; and the United States would not supply arms except in token amounts—for cash in dollars—without the strings of a collective security pact attached.

Nasser turned to the Soviet bloc. In September 1955, Nasser announced an arms purchase agreement with Czechoslovakia, to be paid for primarily with Egyptian cotton. The weapons were Russian and worth approximately $400 million. Tanks, artillery, MiG jets and other aircraft, two destroyers, two submarines, minesweepers, rifles, and guns were part of the arms package Egypt acquired. In one stroke, the Soviets were able to leap over the "northern tier" and emerge for the first time as an important and powerful influence in the area. The Cold War was thus extended into the Middle East, despite policies of containment or new looks.

Nasser entered the arms deal with the Soviets in 1955 in part because of the worsening situation on the border between Egypt and Israel described above. Israel was convinced that Egypt sought arms to attack her, but Nasser said he needed arms both to defend Egypt and to offset those that Iraq was receiving through the Baghdad Pact.

From the Soviet point of view, a foothold in the Arab world was a convenient way to embarrass and challenge the West and to outflank NATO. The Russians wanted to effect a shift in the international balance of power. Initially, the Soviet Union had been an early supporter of Israel. The socialist ideology of the Yishuv had led Russian leaders to believe that Israel would commit itself to Soviet goals. (Interestingly, those who opposed a Jewish state in U.S. policy-making circles held the same view.) The Soviet Union supported the UN partition resolution, which was also seen as a way to get the British out of Palestine; and Soviet arms, via Czechoslovakia, helped Israel win its war of independence. The Soviet Union was the first country to extend the full de jure recognition to the new Jewish state. Although the United States had been the first country to recognize Israel, it had done so only de facto and did not extend full recognition until early 1949.

Israel sought to remain neutral in the developing Cold War. However, Israel's reliance on American economic aid, both private and governmental, and its denunciation of North Korea at the time of the Korean War, helped sour its relationship with the Soviet Union. One also cannot dismiss traditional Russian anti-Semitism and the fear within Russia of an important minority with ties abroad. In 1952, through trials of "economic criminals," and in 1953, with charges against a "conspiracy" of doctors, most of whom were Jewish, the Soviets embarked upon an anti-Jewish and anti-Israel campaign. The die was cast when Israel explored the possibility of a bilateral defense treaty with the United States. As Soviet relations with Israel worsened, Nasser's situation and outlook provided the Soviets with an opportunity to undercut the West and undermine the Baghdad Pact.

The Suez Crisis

Background

Nasser's arms deal with the Soviet bloc and the enthusiastic reception he received at the conference of nonaligned nations in Bandung propelled him into the role of a leader of Arab unity and a symbol of resistance in the Middle East to "colonialism, imperialism, and Zionism." Syria made its own arms deal with the Soviet bloc in 1956, and Jordan was subjected to intense "pan-Arab" pressure emanating from Egypt and Radio Cairo. Iraq was isolated; obstacles to a combined effort against Israel seemed to have been removed.

Partly in an effort to recoup influence after the Egyptian-Soviet arms deal, and partly out of a continuing desire to maintain good relations with the Arab states, Washington indicated it would provide economic assistance to Egypt to help build a dam at Aswan on the Nile River. Nasser considered this project essential to his plans to combat the effects of poverty and a soaring population and to develop Egypt economically. Nasser did not immediately accept Washington's offer, and lobbying efforts by American cotton interests in the South, by Zionists, and by supporters of Nationalist China began to influence American policymakers against the loan. American opinion about Nasser was changing, and Secretary of State Dulles was beginning to detest him. Dulles and others had little patience with Arab nationalism and were increasingly frustrated, disappointed, and angry at Nasser's "neutralism" and unwillingness to follow the American game plan for the region. The last straw for Dulles was Nasser's recognition of Communist China on May 4, 1956. In a meeting on July 19, 1956 with the Egyptian ambassador to the United States, Dulles abruptly withdrew the loan offer and rebuffed the ambassador. Official U.S. statements questioned Egypt's ability to assure the success of the project or ever repay any debt that would be incurred, since the country's economy was being mortgaged to pay for Soviet arms.

On the heels of the American renege on the Aswan High Dam, an angry Nasser in an emotional speech on July 26 declared that in order to pay for the costs of building the dam, Egypt would nationalize the Suez Canal. (See Document 5–1.) In this dramatic gesture, Nasser also struck at the remaining large symbol of Western imperialism operating on Egyptian soil. He thus set in motion the events that would lead to war in October 1956, when Britain, France, and Israel operated in concert to try to topple him.

The Role of the British and the French

Nasser's abrupt nationalization of the canal infuriated British prime minister Anthony Eden and others who were reluctant to abdicate Britain's imperial interests. The Suez Canal was still seen as the gateway to the Far East and of strategic importance to British oil interests in the Persian Gulf. Not only was there concern that the Egyptians would not be able to run the canal themselves, but Eden also believed that Nasser was an upstart whose ambitions had to be checked. The spectre of Munich was never far from Eden's mind, and he was determined not to be another Neville Chamberlain. The British were also concerned about what they considered Nasser's destabilizing activities in other areas of the Middle East like Jordan, where the British had maintained influence and a military presence in the form of the Arab Legion. (See Documents 5–2[a] and 5–2[b].) In March 1956, in a gesture of support for the ideas of pan-Arabism emanating from Cairo, King Hussein of Jordan abruptly dismissed Glubb, the British commander of the Arab Legion and the most visible symbol of British and Western influence in Jordan. By the fall of 1956, Eden was convinced that the time had come to deal decisively with Nasser.

The French had their own reasons for wanting to get rid of Nasser. France had continued to hold on to former colonies longer than Britain and was attempting to deal with a volatile situation in North Africa. Morocco, Tunisia, and Algeria would eventually become independent, but in the mid-1950s, the French had a serious rebellion on their hands in Algeria. Nasser actively supported the Algerian rebels through anti-French Radio Cairo broadcasts and through the shipment of arms. There was also sympathy for Israel in France at this time. There had been scientific cooperation between the two countries after World War II, and support for Israel existed in both the military and political establishments. French and Israeli socialists shared common ideals, and many Jews had fought in the French Resistance. France was the first Western power to supply up-to-date arms to Israel, beginning in 1954. Like Britain's Anthony Eden, Prime Minister Guy Mollet of France also saw the removal of Nasser as the best way to protect and uphold French interests in the Middle East.

The Israeli Role

Israel was prepared to go to war against Nasser for several reasons. Israel believed an imbalance of arms unfavorable to the Jewish state had arisen because of arms shipments to Iraq as a member of the Baghdad Pact and to Egypt from the Soviet arms deal. Additionally, border raids were becoming more severe and more destructive of life and property, and there was a desire to deal decisively with the fedayeen problem. The Arab economic boycott and continued closing of the Suez Canal and the Gulf of Aqaba to Israeli shipping impeded Israel's economic growth. The strategic thinking of Israeli "hawks," especially those who agreed with Ben-Gurion's policy against the Arabs, was also part of Israel's decision to go to war.

After a very shaky and unpromising start, Israel had begun to make progress economically, but this would not have been possible without outside assistance, especially from the United States in the form of grants, loans, technical assistance, and support for Export-Import Bank appropriations. American aid totaled about 35 percent of all imports into Israel by 1953. Charitable contributions, funds from the various Israel appeal campaigns all over the world, and the sale of Israel bonds also became important sources of external funding. German reparations for the first several years of Israel's existence were also substantial. With this money, Israel was able to absorb new immigrants, especially from the Arab countries, improve the living standard, and build up her defenses, spending about 7.2 percent of her gross national product (GNP) annually on military expenditures. The Israel Defense Forces (IDF) were shaped into an effective and vigorous army, especially under the leadership of Moshe Dayan, who was appointed chief of staff in 1953.

Modern arms, however, were difficult to obtain. By the mid-1950s, with Egypt and Syria being supplied by the Communist bloc, and Iraq by Western powers, the Israelis felt at a distinct disadvantage. The United States had not invited Israel to join MEC (later MEDO, or Middle East Defense Organization) and had rebuffed Israeli suggestions that Israel be considered for admission into NATO, or that the United States and Israel establish a bilateral mutual defense treaty. The United States would not match the Czech weapons that Egypt was receiving; indeed, Secretary of State John Foster Dulles told the Senate Foreign Relations Committee that Israel would be better off depending for its security on measures other than the acquisition of arms,

Moshe Dayan and General E. L. M. Burns (UN) studying map of Sinai,
December 6, 1956.

especially since Israel, with its much smaller size and population, could not possibly win an arms
race against Soviet-supplied Arabs.

France approved the sale of twelve Ouragan jet fighters to Israel in December 1954, as Paris
became increasingly concerned about and angered at Nasser's support of the Algerian rebels.
When David Ben-Gurion returned to the Defense Ministry in February 1955, after twenty-two
months of retirement at his desert home in Sde Boker, he accepted the contention of Shimon
Peres, the Ministry's director general, that the French connection should be pursued. During the
1950s, Peres created a military-industrial complex for Israel. By the fall of 1955, after Soviet
weapons began flowing in great quantities into Egypt, arrangements were made for fourteen additional Ouragan fighters and twelve Mystere-4 jet fighter-bombers to be sent to Israel. These
arrived in the spring of 1956. By this time, as the United States became increasingly disenchanted with Nasser, there was American encouragement for the French arms shipments to
Israel, and the United States even requested Canada to provide Israel with American-licensed
jets. From then on, until 1967, the French were the major suppliers of Israel's military needs.

The British, meanwhile, were evacuating troops from the Suez Canal Zone in accordance
with the treaty negotiated in 1954. The departure of the British troops removed an important
potential buffer between Israel and Egypt. In October 1955, Egypt and Syria agreed to a joint
military command. The Israelis interpreted this alliance as an Arab preparation for war. Israeli
fears were heightened by verbal attacks from Radio Cairo, as well as the continued closure of
the Suez Canal to Israeli shipping and blockade of the Gulf of Aqaba. Unceasing and punishing Arab raids into Israeli territory did not help calm Israeli apprehension.

Fedayeen incursions into Israel had increased in intensity and destructiveness, especially
after the Gaza raid, when Nasser used them deliberately as a weapon against Israel. In 1955, over
twenty-five Israeli civilians were killed or wounded by the fedayeen. The policy of retaliation
Israel adopted, however, did not seem to provide any satisfactory solution, at least to Israeli
moderates like Moshe Sharett, who had become prime minister in November 1953. These moderates believed that repeated censure in the United Nations, no matter how one-sided it seemed

to Israel, and American disapproval were counterproductive and only encouraged the cycle of violence. They noted that retaliation did not necessarily discourage fedayeen raids, and they argued further that Israel's policies were creating a situation in which it would be impossible for the Arabs even to consider making peace. They were overruled, however, by the "activists," led by David Ben-Gurion, Golda Meir, and Moshe Dayan.

These Israeli leaders argued that the best defense was a good offense, that Israel within its unacceptable and insecure borders could not afford to dismiss lightly or ignore Arab threats or intimidation, and that murderous raids and constant harassment were just another form of Arab warfare against Israel. They insisted that retaliation was never on a one-to-one basis but after an accumulation of incidents.

Ben-Gurion replaced Sharett as Israeli prime minister in November 1955, temporarily retaining the Defense portfolio as well. Ben-Gurion's detractors insist that his was an activist, aggressive policy, designed to prove Israel's superiority and to persuade the Arab states that they were no match, and that he was determined to undertake a preemptive war against Nasser. They point not only to the often out-of-proportion retaliatory raids launched by Israel but also to the Lavon affair (see below) and to the eventual taking over of the al-Auja DMZ as a launching pad for invasion.

Ben-Gurion did seem to believe that the Arabs would only understand the use of force, that Israel must operate from a position of strength, and that only an appreciation of Israel's military superiority would convince the Arabs to accept the reality of the Jewish state. He believed that it was not in the interest of Israel, or the West, or the United States, to favor the Arabs at Israel's expense. Therefore, in 1954, when the United States indicated it might be sympathetic to Egypt's military and economic needs as the British prepared to withdraw, and when the possibility still existed of attracting Egypt into some kind of defense arrangement, Israel used agents in Egypt to sabotage American and British installations in the hope that Egypt would be blamed and a wedge created between Egypt and the United States.

This was the so-called Lavon affair, associated with then Defense Minister Pinhas Lavon, who always insisted that the operation had taken place without his authorization, and that Dayan and Chief of Army Intelligence Benjamin Gibli gave the orders behind his back. (It was when Sharett upheld the version given by Dayan and Shimon Peres, director general of the Foreign Ministry, that Lavon resigned and Ben-Gurion returned to office as defense minister.) In any event, with Ben-Gurion on the scene, it was almost a certainty that Israel, if possible, would try to seize the advantage. By July 1956, the same month that Nasser nationalized the Suez Canal, Ben-Gurion instructed his general staff to draw up contingency plans for war and to concentrate initially on opening the Strait of Tiran at the entrance of the Gulf of Aqaba. Thus, the stage was set for the collusion that later occurred with Britain and France and that led to the 1956 Suez-Sinai war.

British, French, and Israeli Collusion

By 1956, primarily as a result of the nationalization of the Suez Canal, Britain, France, and Israel felt that cooperation among the three countries was feasible and even necessary. The British, as the principal shareholders and primary users of the Suez Canal, had been furious at Nasser's action. The French, realizing that Nasser was not about to accommodate them by desisting from his efforts to aid the Algerian rebels, to whom he was sending the obsolete weapons that he no longer needed, were more inclined than ever to aid Israel militarily. As the British and the French began to hold discussions about possible military action against Egypt, they hatched a plan that soon provided a role for Israel. Israel was favorable to the idea, since it had already begun preparations for a possible attack on Egypt to secure passage through the Strait of Tiran. A larger military operation would remove Soviet arms from Egypt, destroy the fedayeen threat, and, with any luck, get rid of the archenemy, Gamal Abdul Nasser. It is interesting to speculate what Israel believed the political outcome would be in Egypt had Nasser been defeated.

There were attempts to defuse the crisis through diplomacy and negotiations. In early October, the UN Security Council debated the issue, but the resolution eventually drafted was unacceptable to one or another of the parties concerned. Clearly, the canal had become a symbolic issue for both the Egyptians and the Europeans. Egypt, insisting on its "sovereign rights" and, supported by the Soviet Union, steadfastly refused to accept the idea of an international authority to run the canal—and Britain and France, unwilling to recognize Egypt's sovereignty over the canal, were determined to undertake the war they had been planning and into which they now brought in the Israelis.

By September 1, 1956, Israel's military attaché in Paris had informed Dayan that there was an Anglo-French plan against the canal and that the French were considering inviting Israel to participate. Six days later, an initial meeting took place between Israeli and French military representatives, while Shimon Peres, now Israel's defense minister, had talks in Paris with his counterpart. At the end of September, an Israeli mission consisting of Foreign Minister Golda Meir, Defense Minister Peres, and Chief of Staff Dayan met with a French mission that included the foreign and defense ministers. Then, on October 21, Prime Minister Ben-Gurion, Peres, and Dayan flew to France for joint talks with the British and French missions.

The timing of the attack was planned to coincide with the upcoming presidential election in the United States, when it was hoped that the American administration would be preoccupied. The Russians were also distracted in Eastern Europe by restiveness in Poland and Hungary that would soon erupt into revolution in Hungary. In order to draw attention away from their mobilization and retain an element of surprise, the Israelis created the impression that they intended to retaliate against Jordan for a fedayeen raid that had occurred on October 10. In that same month, Jordan had joined the Syrian-Egyptian military pact. Israel did attack an Arab League police fort at Qalqilya on October 11, and as the situation on that border heated up, the impression was that Israel was mobilizing to undertake a military offensive against Jordan.

Instead, on October 29, 1956, Israel made a paratroop drop deep into central Sinai and completely surprised the Egyptians who, at first, may have believed that the Israelis were simply making a retaliatory raid. This was a calculated effect, to give Israel the opportunity to halt the operation if the British and French did not follow through. (See Document 5–3.) The Egyptians responded, however, and a full-scale war erupted in the Sinai. The British reminded Egypt of the British right to intervene if Egypt were attacked by a third power. They announced that a combined British and French force would land to secure uninterrupted navigation of the Suez Canal. Through clever use of the reserve clause in the 1954 treaty, the British and French on October 30 delivered an ultimatum calling for a halt to hostilities and a warning to Egypt to withdraw ten miles from the canal. For Egypt, of course, that would mean a retreat from the canal, and Egypt refused. Nasser replied to the ultimatum on November 1, 1956. (See Document 5–4.)

Meanwhile, British and French planes attacked Egyptian air bases. An allied landing, originally scheduled for November 1, which might have quickly secured the desired results, almost never took place at all and was largely ineffective when it did. The allied task force did not even set sail until November 1, but as it made its way slowly across the Mediterranean, threats from the Russians and diplomatic pressure from the United States in the United Nations grew. So did political limitations internally, especially in Britain, and there was a great deal of hesitation about proceeding further on the part of the political leadership. Britain and France vetoed efforts by the UN Security Council for a cease-fire, and the Anglo-French force eventually arrived at Port Said on November 5 and attempted, albeit with some confusion, to secure the area. The French wanted to proceed until concrete military results were achieved, but before more operations could be undertaken, the British agreed to a cease-fire on the night of November 6–7. The French reluctantly followed. Israel, which meanwhile had conquered the

Israeli tanks ten miles from the Suez Canal, November 1956.

entire Sinai all the way to the Suez Canal and had taken control of the Egyptian positions at Sharm al-Sheikh overlooking the Strait of Tiran, also agreed to the cease-fire.

Outcome

Britain and France were completely discredited by the war, and their prestige and influence plummeted throughout the Arab world. In some respects this situation tended to thrust the United States even more definitively into the role formerly played by its allies in the region. American policymakers, however, had no greater love for Nasser than before, and the United States was associated in the popular mind with Western interests and with Israel. Therefore, the United States became more and more closely identified with Israel, as the Soviet Union took advantage of the situation to reinforce its relations with the Arabs and particularly to consolidate its position in Egypt. Soviet arms were quickly replaced, and Soviet aid also arrived for the building of the Aswan High Dam, which became a Russian showpiece in the Middle East.

International, especially American, pressure forced Israel to withdraw from the Gaza Strip and the Sinai in March 1957, in return for what the Israelis believed were American and United Nations guarantees of freedom of passage through the Gulf of Aqaba. In addition, the United Nations agreed to station an emergency force (UNEF) in Egyptian territory at Sharm al-Sheikh and between Israel and Egypt in Gaza. This removed the fedayeen problem from the Egyptian border. Although navigating the Gulf of Aqaba was primarily a symbolic issue for Israel, the Israeli town of Eilat became an important port on the gulf, and shipping through the Strait of Tiran allowed Israel to receive oil from Iran (under the table). The gulf provided a window on Africa and Asia, which became markets for Israeli goods, influence, and expertise. Israel developed good relations with many African and Asian countries that lasted until the Arab oil embargo of 1973.

Although defeated militarily, Gamal Abdul Nasser and the Egyptians were the big winners politically. Nasser emerged as the hero of the hour and as the symbol of pan-Arabism and its valiant stand against imperialism, colonialism, and Zionism. It was a role he appeared to relish. In the next decade, Arab nationalism would be an important factor in the domestic politics of most Arab countries, and the idea of Arab unity under Nasser became a compelling goal. The state of Israel, however, was a constant irritant and continued to block the fulfillment of pan-Arabism. The Suez war only deepened the Arab desire for revenge. In the absence of peace, the Middle East remained a powder keg.

Suggestions for Further Reading

ALTERAS, ISAAC, *United States–Israel Relations, 1953–1960*, Gainesville, Fla., University Press of Florida, 1995.

CHILDERS, ERSKINE, *The Road to Suez: A Study in Western-Arab Relations*, London, Macgibbon & Kee, 1962.

COOPER, CHESTER L., *The Lion's Last Roar, 1956,* New York, Harper & Row, 1978.

DAYAN, MOSHE, *Diary of the Sinai Campaign*, New York, Harper & Row, 1966.

EDEN, ANTHONY, *Full Circle*, London, Cassell, 1960.

FINER, HERMAN, *Dulles over Suez*, Chicago, Quadrangle, 1964.

GOLDSCHMIDT, ARTHUR, JR., *Modern Egypt: The Formation of a Nation-State*, Boulder, Colo., Westview Press, 1988.

HEIKAL, MOHAMED, *Nasser: The Cairo Documents*, New York, Doubleday, 1973.

———, *Cutting the Lion's Tail: Suez Through Egyptian Eyes*, New York, William Morrow & Company, Arbor House Imprint, 1987.

LOVE, KENNETT, *Suez: The Twice-Fought War*, New York, McGraw-Hill, 1969.

MORRIS, BENNY, *Israel's Border Wars, 1949–56: Arab Infiltration, Israeli Retaliation, and the Countdown to the Suez War*, Oxford, Clarendon Press, 1993.

NEFF, DONALD, *Warriors at Suez*, New York, The Linden Press, Simon & Schuster, 1981.

NUTTING, ANTHONY, *No End of a Lesson: The Story of Suez*, London, Constable, 1967.

RABINOVICH, ITAMAR, *The Road Not Taken: Early Arab–Israeli Negotiations*, New York, Oxford Universtiy Press, 1991.

STOCK, ERNEST, *Israel on the Road to Sinai, 1949–56*, Ithaca, N.Y., Cornell University Press, 1967.

THOMAS, HUGH, *Suez*, New York and Evanston, Ill., Harper & Row, 1966.

 DOCUMENT 5–1

Speech by President Nasser Justifying Nationalization of the Suez Canal Company, July 28, 1956 [Excerpts]

The uproar which we anticipated has been taking place in London and Paris. This tremendous uproar is not supported by reason or logic. It is backed only by imperialist methods, by the habits of blood-sucking and of usurping rights, and by interference in the affairs of other countries. An unjustified uproar arose in London, and yesterday Britain submitted a protest to Egypt. I wonder what was the basis of this protest by Britain to Egypt? The Suez Canal Company is an Egyptian company, subject to Egyptian sovereignty. When we nationalized the Suez Canal Company, we only nationalized an Egyptian limited company, and by doing so we exercised a right which stems from the very core of Egyptian sovereignty. What right has Britain to interfere in our internal affairs? What right has Britain to interfere in our affairs and our questions? When we nationalized the Suez Canal Company, we only performed an act stemming from the very heart of our sovereignty. The Suez Canal Company is a limited company, awarded a concession by the Egyptian Government in 1865 to carry out its tasks. Today we withdraw the concession in order to do the job ourselves.

Although we have withdrawn this concession, we shall compensate shareholders of the company, despite the fact that they usurped our rights. Britain usurped 44 per cent of the shares free of charge. Today we shall pay her for her 44 per cent of the shares. We do not treat her as she treated us. We are not usurping the 44 per cent as she did. We do not tell Britain that we shall usurp her right as she usurped ours, but we tell her that we shall compensate her and forget the past.

The Suez Canal would have been restored to us in 12 years. What would have happened in 12 years' time? Would an uproar have been raised? What has happened now has disclosed hidden intentions and has unmasked Britain. If the canal was to fall to us in 12 years, why should it not be restored to us now? Why should it cause an uproar? We understand by this that they had no intention of fulfilling this pledge 12 years from now. What difference is it if the canal is restored to us now or in 12 years' time? Why should Britain say this will affect shipping in the canal? Would it have affected shipping 12 years hence?

· · ·

Shipping in the Suez Canal has been normal for the past 48 hours from the time of nationalization until now. Shipping continued and is normal. We nationalized the company. We have not interfered with shipping, and we are facilitating shipping matters. However, I emphatically warn the imperialist countries that their tricks, provocations and interference will be the reason for any hindrance to shipping. I place full responsibility on Britain and France for any curtailment of shipping in the Suez Canal when I state that Egypt will maintain freedom of shipping in the Suez Canal, and that since Egypt nationalized the Suez Canal Company shipping has been normal. Even before that we maintained freedom of shipping in the canal. Who has protected the canal? The canal has been under Egyptian protection because it is part of Egypt and we are the ones who should ensure freedom of shipping. We protect it today, we protected it a month ago, and we protected it for years because it is our territory and a part of our territory. Today we shall continue to protect the canal. But, because of the tricks they are playing, I hold Britain and France responsible for any consequences which may affect shipping.

· · ·

Compatriots, we shall maintain our independence and sovereignty. The Suez Canal Company has become our property, and the Egyptian flag flies over it. We shall hold it with our blood and strength, and we shall meet aggression with aggression and evil with evil. We shall proceed towards achieving dignity and prestige for Egypt and building a sound national economy and true freedom. Peace be with you.

SWB, Part IV, Daily Series, no. 6, 30 July 1956

Source: T. G. Fraser, *The Middle East, 1914–1979* (New York: St. Martin's Press, 1980), pp. 88–89.

DOCUMENT 5-2

Anthony Eden's Views of Gamal Abdul Nasser
(a) In His Memoirs
(b) In a Letter to Eisenhower, September 6, 1956

(a) It is important to reduce the stature of the megalomaniacal dictator at an early stage. A check to Hitler when he moved to reoccupy the Rhineland would not have destroyed him, but it would have made him pause. The world would then have had time to assess the truth, and the

Germans occasion to question themselves. This process would have been altogether salutary. "Though your enemy be an ant," runs the Turkish proverb, "imagine that he is an elephant." Nowadays it is considered immoral to recognize an enemy. Some say that Nasser is no Hitler or Mussolini. Allowing for a difference in scale, I am not so sure. He has followed Hitler's pattern, even to concentration camps and the propagation of *Mein Kampf* among his officers. He has understood and used the Goebbels pattern of propaganda in all its lying ruthlessness. Egypt's strategic position increases the threat to others from any aggressive militant dictatorship there.

If any dictatorial government has it in mind to pursue an aggressive policy, it will do well to label itself "Socialist" from the start. Hitler was the first to understand the value of this camouflage. Despite the world's experience of German National Socialism, there is still a tendency to regard even a Government like Nasser's as Socialist and therefore as having a left-wing colouring. I have observed with amazement how national leaders in other countries, who hold left-wing views, have thought that they had more affinity with, for example, Colonel Nasser in Egypt than with Nuri es-Said in Iraq. The administration of Iraq under Nuri was infinitely more progressive and mindful of its people's welfare than the Egyptian. Three-quarters of Iraq's revenues from oil were devoted to public works, irrigation, electrification and improved living conditions. Only Kuwait, in a much smaller area, has attempted anything comparable. The poverty of the Egyptians further deepened when Colonel Nasser forced out General Neguib: arms before bread.

Source: Anthony Eden, *Full Circle: The Memoirs of Anthony Eden* (Boston: Houghton Mifflin, 1960), p. 481.

(b) . . . the seizure of the Suez Canal is, we are convinced, the opening gambit in a planned campaign designed by Nasser to expel all Western influence and interests from Arab countries. . . .

In short we are convinced that if Nasser is allowed to defy the eighteen nations it will be a matter of months before revolution breaks out in the oil-bearing countries and the West is wholly deprived of Middle Eastern oil. In this belief we are fortified by the advice of friendly leaders in the Middle East. . . .

You may feel that even if we are right it would be better to wait until Nasser has unmistakably unveiled his intentions. But this was the argument which prevailed in 1936 and which we both rejected in 1948. Admittedly there are risks in the use of force against Egypt now. It is, however, clear that military intervention designed to reverse Nasser's revolution in the whole continent would be a much more costly and difficult undertaking. I am very troubled, as it is, that if we do not reach a conclusion either way about the canal very soon one or other of these Eastern lands may be toppled at any moment by Nasser's revolutionary movements.

Source: Eden, *Full Circle*, pp. 519–521.

DOCUMENT 5-3

Speech to the Security Council by Abba Eban, Israel, on his Country's Offensive in Sinai, October 30, 1956 [Excerpt]

33. At this morning's meeting I defined the objective of the security measures which the Israel defence forces have felt bound to take in the Sinai Peninsula in the exercise of our country's inherent right of self-defence. The object of the operations is to eliminate the Egyptian

fedayeen1 bases from which armed Egyptian units, under the special care and authority of Mr. Nasser, invade Israel territory for purposes of murder, sabotage and the creation of permanent insecurity to peaceful life.

34. World opinion is naturally asking itself what these *fedayeen* units are, what their activities imply for Israel's security, whether their actions in the past and their plans for the future are really full of peril for Israel, and whether this peril is so acute that Israel may reasonably regard elimination of the danger as a primary condition of its security and indeed of its existence.

35. The Government of Israel is the representative of a people endowed with a mature understanding of international facts. We are not unaware of the limitations of our strength. We fully understand how certain measures might at first sight evoke a lack of comprehension even in friendly minds. Being a democracy, we work under the natural restraints of a public opinion which compels us to weigh drastic choices with care and without undue precipitation. It is therefore a Government which governs its actions by its single exclusive aim of securing life, security and opportunities of self-development for the people whom it represents, whilst also safeguarding the honour and trust of millions linked to it by the strongest ties of fraternity.

36. In recent months and days the Government of Israel has had to face a tormenting question: Do its obligations under the United Nations Charter require us to resign ourselves to the existence of uninterrupted activity to the south and north and east of our country, of armed bands practising open warfare against us and working from their bases in the Sinai Peninsula and elsewhere for the maintenance of carefully regulated invasions of our homes, or lands and our very lives, or, on the other hand, are we acting in accordance with an inherent right of self-defence when having found no other remedy for over two years, we cross the frontier against those who have no scruple or hesitation in crossing the frontier against us?

UNO SCOR, Eleventh Year, 749th meeting

Source: Fraser, *The Middle East*, pp. 90–91.

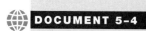 **DOCUMENT 5–4**

President Nasser's Response to the Anglo-French Ultimatum, November 1, 1956

Today, we face these plots as one, one heart, one man. These plots began with the conspiracy of Britain, France and Israel. Israel suddenly on Monday 29 October began an offensive, for no other reason except Britain's rancour. Our armed forces rose and did their duty with rare gallantry. Our air force did its duty with eternal courage, in the history of the homeland. When Israel attacked, Britain announced that she would not seize the opportunity. But when it appeared that Egypt was able to dominate the battle, an Anglo-French ultimatum was presented.

This ultimatum asked for a halt to the fighting—while the Israeli forces were inside Egyptian territory—the aggressor Israeli forces. It asked Egypt and Israel to withdraw 10 km (sic) from the Suez Canal. It then asked Egypt and also Israel to agree to the occupation of Port Said, Ismailia and Suez by the Anglo-French forces, for the protection of shipping in the Canal. This happened at a time when navigation was in progress and was not threatened. This happened while the Egyptian forces were concentrating to face the aggressor Israeli forces, and the Egyptian forces were repelling the Israeli forces.

In her ultimatum Britain said that if a reply was not received within 12 hours she would act to execute the ultimatum. Do we agree to the occupation by Britain and France of part of

Egyptian territory? Do we willingly agree to such occupation? Or do we fight for the freedom of our homeland, for the safety of our territory, for honour and for dignity? After this ultimatum Egypt decided upon her attitude. It was this: It is impossible for her to permit, it is impossible for her to accept, and it is impossible for her to agree to the occupation of Port Said, Ismailia and Suez by foreign forces—Anglo-French—and declared that this was a violation of her freedom—the freedom, sovereignty and dignity of the Egyptian people.

SWB, Part IV, Daily Series, no. 88,
3 Nov. 1956

Source: Fraser, *The Middle East*, pp. 91–92.

SIX

The Turning Point: June 1967

CHRONOLOGY

Mar. 5, 1957	Congress approves Eisenhower Doctrine
Feb. 1, 1958	Egypt and Syria unite to form United Arab Republic (UAR)
July 14, 1958	Monarchy overthrown in Iraq
July 1958	Civil war in Lebanon; U.S. Marines called in July 15
July 17, 1958	British troops to Jordan
Oct. 1958	Moscow announces financing for first stage of Aswan High Dam
Sept. 29, 1961	Syria withdraws from UAR
Sept. 1962	Civil war breaks out in Yemen
Sept. 1962	United States announces first direct sale of American weapons (Hawk missiles) to Israel
Late 1962–Dec. 1967	Egypt involved in civil war in Yemen
Jan. 1964	First Arab summit; Arab governments broach idea of a Palestine Liberation Organization under Ahmad Shuqayri
May 1964	Founding conference of the PLO
Jan. 1, 1965	Al-Fatah undertakes first guerrilla raid against Israel
Jan. 1966	King Feisal of Saudi Arabia first proposes Islamic summit
Feb. 25, 1966	Salah Jadid takes power in Syria
Apr. 1966	Clashes between Syria and Israel
Nov. 4, 1966	Egypt and Syria sign defense pact
Nov. 13, 1966	As-Samu raid by Israel against Jordan
Spring 1967	Syrian–Israeli clashes
May 22, 1967	Nasser demands withdrawal of UNEF troops; Gulf of Aqaba closed to Israeli shipping
May 30, 1967	Egypt and Jordan sign defense pact; Arabs and Israel mobilize for war
June 5, 1967	Israel attacks Egypt; Six-Day War begins
June 10, 1967	Cease-fire; Israel in possession of East Jerusalem, West Bank, the Gaza Strip, Sinai, and the Golan Heights
Aug.–Sept. 1967	Khartoum conference
Nov. 22, 1967	UN Security Council passes Resolution 242

The decade following the Suez-Sinai war was the longest period in the Arab–Israeli conflict without a major confrontation or war. In Israel, the years between 1956 and 1967 saw a consolidation of previous gains and impressive growth economically, militarily, politically, and culturally. For Palestinians the decade was one of dispersal and disillusion, political impotence, ineffectual leadership, and futile attempts to retrieve some of what they had lost. In the wider Arab world, pan-Arabism reached its zenith in the late 1950s, with Egyptian president Nasser as its symbol. Syria, and to some extent Iraq, after the coup against the monarchy in 1958, followed Nasser's lead in embracing radical social and economic change and rejecting foreign commitments, although they accepted aid from the Soviet Union. Israel viewed these developments with considerable alarm. However, not all Arab states followed the lead of Egypt, and a kind of Arab "Cold War" developed. Countries still led by conservative monarchs like Jordan and Saudi Arabia, and to a lesser degree Lebanon, approached change in a more evolutionary way and were linked financially and ideologically to the West.

After Suez, Britain and France were almost totally discredited. As a result, the region could not escape entanglement in the Cold War Soviet–American rivalry. Increasingly, the ties between the Soviets and their allies, and between the United States and its Arab friends and Israel, assumed the model of a patron-client relationship. In turn, the Arab states and Israel used the superpowers to engage in an arms race, which in turn became an important factor leading to the next Arab–Israeli war in 1967. In this chapter we trace the developments leading to that war.

Israel After 1956

Israel made significant progress in both domestic and foreign affairs after 1956. The Israelis were forced to relinquish all territorial gains and to withdraw to the 1949 armistice lines, but the fedayeen threat was mitigated by the presence of the UNEF in the Gaza Strip. Passage of Israeli ships and cargo through the Gulf of Aqaba was assured (or so it was assumed) by the presence of the UNEF at Sharm al-Sheikh overlooking the Strait of Tiran at the entrance to the gulf. The U.S. government also seemed to guarantee Israel's right to use the waterway in an Aide Memoire stating that the United States would be prepared to exercise the right of free and innocent passage and would join other nations to secure the general recognition of such a right. For two years between 1957 and 1959, Israeli cargo on ships licensed elsewhere transited the Suez Canal as well, until Nasser forbade this traffic to continue.

The Aqaba outlet was of greater importance to Israel than the Suez Canal, however, and the Israeli seaport of Eilat soon grew from a sleepy little town to a bustling, busy city. Israel now had a window on Africa and Asia, new markets, and new friends. Trade flourished, as did contacts and friendly relations with scores of nations in the developing world, from Ethiopia and Ghana to Burma and Nepal. Useful diplomatic connections were made that helped buttress Israel's position in an increasingly hostile United Nations. And the new outlet enabled Israel to obtain oil from Iran, which maintained a de facto relationship with the Jewish state, rather than from suppliers as far away as Venezuela.

The industrial, commercial, and agricultural development of the Negev Desert was further encouraged by the completion of a national water carrier in 1964. The United States had unsuccessfully proposed a joint irrigation scheme to Israel and the Arabs in 1953, based on sharing the Jordan River waters. President Eisenhower's envoy Eric Johnston attempted to sell this plan in five trips to the Middle East. In 1955, after temporary agreement had been reached, the Arab League decided to "postpone" a decision, thereby in effect rejecting the plan. According to Arab sources, the postponement was the result of Israel's raid on Gaza and the Arabs' assertion that Israel refused UN supervision. Israelis maintain that the Arabs were again unwilling to cooperate in any venture that would imply recognition of the Jewish state.

Water for irrigation, however, was absolutely crucial for Israel's continuing development, and even during the mandate period irrigation possibilities had been studied and plans outlined, especially by Dr. Walter Lowdermilk, an American soil conservationist. Based on his and subsequent appraisals, the Israel Water Planning Authority developed a blueprint for utilization of the Jordan waters it claimed was within the limits established by the Johnston plan. Water was taken from the Sea of Galilee, into which the Jordan emptied, and used to replenish the water table along the coast and to supply water to the northern Negev. Completion of the national water carrier opened up the possibility of industrial and agricultural growth, especially in the northern Negev, which by 1967 was self-sufficient in vegetables, dairy products, and fruit. In this way, the Israelis "made the desert bloom" and also provided incentives for the development of new communities and the opportunity for settlement of new immigrants.

Immigration from the Iron Curtain countries increased in the wake of the Hungarian revolution, as it did from Egypt following the Suez war when Nasser imposed certain restrictions against foreigners and Jews. Others came from North Africa, where the establishment of independent governments posed hard choices for those who were not Arabs or Muslims. The new immigrants contributed certain skills and lent their diversified talents to Israel, as well as providing more manpower. Immigration from non-European countries also inaugurated a slow change in the demographic composition of Israel. This would have significant repercussions politically, socially, culturally, and economically in the years to come, as the Sephardim and Oriental Jews came to outnumber the European Jews, or Ashkenazim, who had been the founders and "veterans" of the young state and who continued to lead it.

Meanwhile, if the Israelis were winning new friends in Africa and Asia, they were also mending fences with old enemies. German reparations were already an important part of the Israeli economy, and economic aid was extended by an agreement in 1960 for German loans. A secret weapons agreement had been made after the Suez war, and German weapons, although not as significant to Israel as those from France, began to flow into Israel as early as 1959. Obsolete American equipment was also transshipped via Germany beginning in 1964. Finally, in 1965, formal diplomatic relations were initiated between Bonn and Jerusalem.

Interestingly, the relationship with France, Israel's staunchest ally during and immediately after Suez, slowly began to change. France helped Israel build its nuclear reactor at Dimona, and the Israeli air force was almost entirely French equipped. Nevertheless, in the mid-1960s, with the Algerian war no longer a consideration, the French sought ways to reestablish ties and influence in the Arab and Islamic countries, which meant a lessening of its ties with Israel. Just how significantly the relationship had changed was illustrated graphically in the events preceding the 1967 war when France under Charles de Gaulle stopped the flow of French arms to Israel. By that time, however, Israel had diversified its sources of weapons, and the United States had begun to sell arms directly to Israel, more or less committing itself to maintaining a balance of arms between Israel and the Arab "radicals" (Egypt, Syria, Iraq), who were being supplied with massive amounts of Soviet equipment. The Kennedy administration had agreed to sell Hawk ground-to-air missiles and tanks to Israel, as well as to give further military assistance to Jordan and Saudi Arabia. By 1967, Israel emerged as a major American client in the region.

The unprecedented growth in Israel leveled off by the mid-1960s as the economy began to be plagued by a growing trade deficit, inflationary pressures caused in part by rapid growth, and the continual rise in military expenditures. The government imposed a policy of "restraint" in 1965, partly in order to curb inflation, but the recession and unemployment that followed led to emigration from the country. For the Israeli government, incessant Syrian attacks on the northern borders and by guerrilla raids emanating from the Jordanian-controlled West Bank and the Syrian-held Golan Heights exacerbated the economic crisis. These were inspired by two Palestinian movements, the PLO and al-Fatah, which played an important role in the events leading to the Six-Day War.

The Arab States After 1956

There were many changes in the Arab world after 1956, owing partly to the rise in Nasser's stature as the leader of pan-Arabism and symbol of resistance to "colonialism, imperialism, and Zionism." The appeal of Arab nationalism, whether promoted by Nasser or by the ideology of the Arab Renaissance, or *Baath*, party, became almost irresistible. The Baath party, formed in Syria in the mid-1950s, combined the idea of Arab unity with that of revolutionary socialism, and its slogan became "Arab freedom, Arab socialism, and Arab unity." Described as being "post-Communistic," it rejected Marxist internationalism and allowed for some private ownership in the economic sphere. The party established branches in Lebanon, Jordan, and Iraq. It eventually seized power in Syria and Iraq, although a bitter rivalry marked the relations of the two groups.

For a few heady years after Suez, however, the idea of Arab unity focused on Nasser. The high point for him personally, and for pan-Arabism, was achieved in 1958 when Syria joined Egypt in creating the United Arab Republic (UAR). Yemen, under a hereditary monarch, became a federated member of the UAR. In that same year, the pro-Western monarchy in Iraq was toppled, and one of the first acts of the new military regime was to withdraw from the Baghdad Pact, known henceforth as Cento and headquartered in Ankara, Turkey. Meanwhile, a civil war had erupted in Lebanon, precipitated in part by the waves rippling out from Egypt. The Christian Lebanese president, Camille Chamoun, concerned about the effect in Lebanon of the coup in Iraq, called in the U.S. Marines on July 15. There was also instability in Jordan, where King Hussein in 1957 had dismissed his parliament, alleging a Communist plot against him inspired by Nasser. On July 17, Hussein requested the landing of British troops to help stabilize the monarchy.

In Syria, the Baath party had assumed increasing power in the mid-1950s and had initiated economic and social changes. Supplied with Soviet arms and equipment but coming under Soviet influence internally as well as externally, and fearful of a Communist takeover within Syria, the Baath party leaders precipitated the union with Egypt in 1958. Baath ideology, however, was inconsistent with the goal of international communism, and it was also incompatible with the kind of authoritarian, one-man rule personified by Nasser. Moreover, Syria's economy, which had been built up after the war largely by a vigorous middle class, and which, despite Arab socialism, remained more freewheeling than that of Egypt, was sacrificed to Egyptian needs.

The UAR was a complete merger of the two countries rather than a confederation of equals, and Egypt was the dominant partner. In 1961, after Nasser announced drastic nationalization decrees affecting almost 90 percent of industry, manufacturing, and trade, Syria withdrew from the UAR. As the Arabs debated the implications of unity, civilian control was temporarily restored in Syria, only to be replaced by a Baath military coup in 1963, and yet another in 1966, which brought to the fore General Salah Jadid, the most radical leader till then in the Arab world. Jadid was critical of other Arab leaders whom he accused of passivity, and he openly threatened Israel. Committed to the idea of guerrilla warfare, he sponsored the activities of Palestinian groups against Israel. The escalating situation on the Israeli–Syrian border, as we shall see, provided the catalyst for the 1967 hostilities.

Despite the prestige that Nasser continued to enjoy with the masses and the role he filled as an all-Arab leader, the internal economic situation in Egypt deteriorated. By the mid-1960s, Egypt was in serious financial straits. The costs of intervention elsewhere were very high, especially in Yemen, where Egypt became embroiled after 1962 in a civil war that drained its manpower and money (to the tune of about $1 million per day). A determined but largely frustrated effort to industrialize exhausted Egypt's foreign-currency reserves. Egypt was simply unable to keep up with population growth, unemployment, and inflation. Nasser had changed Egypt's economy from a basically free-enterprise system to one in which the state predominated, but nationalization had been undertaken largely for political reasons. Although Egypt did make industrial progress, politics continued to impinge on economic planning. Meager resources and bureaucratic inefficiency also hampered development. Therefore, although Nasser personally, and as the symbol of pan-Arabism, may have wanted to destroy the Jewish state, his actual policy, as opposed to his bombastic rhetoric, was cautious and restrained, at least until 1967. The change then, and the brinksmanship that followed, has much to do with the involvement of the superpowers in the region, to which we now turn.

U.S.–Soviet Involvement: The Cold War and the Arms Race

The U.S. Role

The United States played a prominent role in the United Nations in separating the combatants and ending the hostilities in 1956. As we noted in the previous chapter, this was hardly because the American administration was sympathetic to Nasser's plight or to Arab nationalism. The Americans felt deeply embarrassed and compromised by their allies, Britain and France, who had acted without consulting them—and right on the eve of a presidential election at that. The American public expressed concern about upholding the principles of the UN Charter, and President Eisenhower displayed a sense of moral outrage that they had been violated. Although this stand scored points in the short run, subsequent U.S. actions tended to erode Arab goodwill. American refusal to supply medical help for the victims of allied bombing at Port Said, and the cessation of the CARE program in Egypt, which had provided free lunches to Egyptian schoolchildren, spoke louder than pious platitudes. Indeed, the United States adhered to a Western economic boycott of Egypt, refusing to sell surplus wheat and oil. In this way, the United States exhibited its continued friendship for its European allies and its disdain for Nasser. At the same time, this attitude enabled and encouraged the Soviet Union and its satellites to extend their influence. Economic and technical assistance on an increasingly large scale were evident after 1957, capped in Egypt by the Soviet agreement in October 1958 to help build the Aswan High Dam. The worth of Soviet arms to Egypt would eventually total about $2 billion. This compared to American economic and technical aid to Israel of about $850 million between 1949 and 1965.

Because Britain and France had been so completely discredited in the region, however, the United States found itself in the position of defending Western interests and resisting the expansion of Soviet influence in those countries that had not followed Nasser's lead. The new instrument of American policy became the Eisenhower Doctrine, approved by Congress in March 1957. By its terms, the president was authorized to extend economic and military assistance, including troops, to any Middle Eastern nation that requested it against the threat of international communism. No Arab country, with the exception of Libya and Lebanon, was eager to embrace the doctrine. Zionism, not communism, was considered the enemy. Moreover, the United States was seen as attempting to weaken Arab unity by insisting that the Arab countries line up on one side or the other in the Cold War. Although the United States continued to maintain an important airbase at Dhahran (until 1961), and the Saudis were considered to be "allies," the Saudi king did not endorse the Eisenhower Doctrine. Nor did King Hussein, even though the United States extended $10 million in financial assistance to Jordan when the king quashed a Nasser-supported Communist plot against the monarchy in 1957.

The one Arab country enthusiastic about the Eisenhower Doctrine was Lebanon, especially under its Christian president, Camille Chamoun. Chamoun despised Nasser and was disturbed about growing Egyptian and Soviet influence, especially in neighboring Syria. Closer adherence to the West through formal adherence to the Eisenhower Doctrine, however, seemed to violate the spirit of Lebanon's "national pact," through which a balance of interests had been maintained among Lebanon's many religious and family groups. Moreover, Chamoun's overt identification with Western interests alienated other Lebanese political leaders and a large part of the Muslim population whose sympathies were with Nasser and Arab nationalism. Chamoun attempted to secure a second term as president in violation of the constitution. Anti-Chamoun and pro-Nasserist groups in Lebanon, supplied with funds, weapons, and propaganda from the newly formed United Arab Republic, saw this as an opportunity to gain power, and this set off a brief civil war in 1958.

At the same time, in July 1958, in Iraq the pro-Western monarchy was overthrown. Fearing that a Communist takeover in the region was imminent, and worried about his own safety, Chamoun asked for American help. Largely because of the situation in Iraq, Eisenhower responded promptly. American troops landed on the beaches of Lebanon, as British troops rushed to the aid of King Hussein to stabilize his regime. Chamoun, who had helped precipitate the crisis by hinting that he would not give up the presidency, wisely left office in September at the end of his term. A more neutral government was formed in Lebanon, and the U.S. Marines departed, indicating, among other things, that the United States would not directly interfere with the Lebanese political process. The new Lebanese government repudiated the Eisenhower Doctrine, which left the next American administration with the task of reevaluating U.S. foreign policy in the region.

In Washington, the Arab–Israeli conflict continued to be placed within the context of basic American interests in the area. These included uninterrupted communications facilities and access to oil; the maintenance of general stability; and the protection of strategic interests against the threat of Soviet expansionism. In the Kennedy administration, however, a new approach to the Arab–Israeli conflict evolved, which John Badeau, Kennedy's ambassador to Egypt, later called the "icebox" device: deal with those issues on which Middle Easterners and Americans can agree, and put the others in cold storage for the time being. One such issue was the Palestinian refugee problem, which the United States unsuccessfully took a stab at in the fall of 1961. Kennedy sent Dr. Joseph Johnson, president of the Carnegie Foundation, to consult the Israelis and Arabs about ways to deal with the situation. Johnson's own plan was to offer the refugees, under the active supervision of the United Nations, the choice of return or compensation for settlement outside Israel. Johnson had no luck on his first or on a subsequent trip the next spring in moving the different parties from their respective positions. The Arabs continued to insist on the right of return of all refugees, the Israelis on recognition and direct negotiation of all outstanding issues, including that of the refugees.

The United States assured Israel that it upheld the principle of the territorial integrity of all countries in the region and would defend Israel against aggression. There seemed during the Kennedy years, however, a somewhat greater appreciation of the dynamics and complexities of the Arab world. American policymakers began to realize that the achievement of American objectives did not require a specific form of political or economic system. Indeed, many believed that America could aid constructive change in Middle Eastern countries through non-military aid and cultural exchange, to the mutual benefit of the Arabs and the United States. Economic and technical aid was therefore offered to Egypt, especially through Public Law 480, which enabled recipient countries to purchase surplus wheat and other commodities with local currency that remained in the country to generate development projects. In the early 1960s, for example, the United States supplied about $150 million a year in wheat surpluses, which was more than half the grain consumed in Egypt.

Meanwhile, quantities of Soviet arms were pouring into Egypt, Syria, and Iraq. Israel used Nasser's involvement in the Yemen civil war, as well as his hiring of German technicians to help develop surface-to-surface missiles and jet fighters, as arguments to persuade the United States to sell Israel weapons directly for the first time. The Kennedy administration agreed to sell Israel Hawk ground-to-air missiles and tanks at the end of September 1962, and shipments of American arms went to Saudi Arabia and Jordan. In this way, the United States attempted to maintain a balance between Israel and the Arabs, and between the "radical" Arab countries supplied by the Soviet Union and those supplied by the United States.

The administration of Lyndon Johnson continued the basic approach of an arms balance and upholding the territorial integrity of all Middle Eastern countries including Israel, but with a different style and far less consistency. The different style arose to some extent because of personal antipathy between Nasser and Johnson. Nasser took an almost instant dislike to the American president and mentioned in his letters how he was put off by photographs of Johnson showing reporters the scar from his recent gallbladder operation and with his feet up on his desk. Nasser also feared that the United States might move to oust him, as it had Mossadeq in Iran and Ngo Dinh Diem in South Vietnam. He suspected, too, that the United States had been involved in removing such leaders as Ahmed Ben Bella, Ahmed Sukarno, and Kwame Nkrumah. Johnson himself was not attuned to the sensibilities of foreign leaders, and he had little patience with Nasser. The conduct of American foreign relations in the Middle East was further complicated after 1964 by difficulties on the domestic scene and by the escalating war in Vietnam.

When the United States expressed its displeasure over Nasser's aid to rebels in the Belgian Congo, Nasser told the United States at the end of 1964 to forget its aid and go drink seawater. With less surplus wheat available to dispose of anyway, American economic aid to Egypt was discontinued shortly thereafter, causing severe repercussions in the Egyptian economy. This seemed to end any hope of a rapprochement between the two countries and to signal that Egypt would not break out of the Soviet orbit. The Soviet Union greatly enhanced its role in the Middle East in the 1960s. Still, the United States believed that, by maintaining Israel's military strength and aiding friendly Arab countries like Jordan and Saudi Arabia, its basic goals— maintaining stability in the region and thus diminishing the prospect of an Arab–Israeli war that could lead to superpower confrontation—had been preserved.

The Soviet Role

Like the United States, the Soviet Union had its successes and failures in the Middle East. While the Soviet leaders would like to have seen the victory of communism in the area and were constantly reminded by the Chinese not to forget ideological imperatives, Soviet policy was of necessity based on realpolitik. Soviet goals included outflanking NATO, neutralizing the United States in the Middle East, and working to achieve preeminence in an area the Russians considered as almost their own backyard. After loosening their ties with socialist Israel in the 1950s and unequivocally adopting the Arab and Palestinian causes, the Soviets imitated the West in extending economic and military aid to their allies in the region. Under Nikita Khrushchev, between 1955 and 1959, the Soviets established a diplomatic presence in the area, made extensive arms deals, trained local armies, offered economic and technical assistance, and energetically supported anti-Western regimes.

The Soviet leap over the so-called northern tier, however, had brought it right into the tangled web of inter-Arab affairs and created unavoidable dilemmas, similar to those experienced by the United States. As America had discovered, the Soviet Union found it difficult to have its cake and eat it too. The events surrounding the Iraqi coup in 1958, when Abdul Karim Qasim came to power supported by local Communists, illustrated the problem. Moscow was delighted by the revolution in Iraq but alienated Nasser by its support of Qasim, who had very different ideas about Arab unity and who in fact put down a pro-Nasser movement in Iraq. (This climate had, of course, made it easier for the United States to effect its own rapprochement with Nasser in the late 1950s and early 1960s.) Within two years, however, Qasim had also rejected local Communist support and refused recognition to the Iraq Communist party. This was a bitter disappointment to the Soviets.

Nevertheless, the Soviet Union continued economic and especially military aid to regimes that were anti-West, at a high cost to its own economy. Thus, the Russians pledged support to Egypt to help build the second stage of the Aswan High Dam at the same time that the United States was providing Egypt with the bulk of its grain; and the arms flow to Egypt, Syria, and Iraq continued, albeit with a temporary halt in Iraq when Qasim was toppled by a Baath coup in 1963 that purged local Communists. In the meantime, the stakes had also been raised. It was one thing to embarrass the West, but another to challenge it. The Soviets began to realize the danger of local outbreaks that could eventually spark a wider conflagration. Moreover, the Russians found themselves in the position of sometimes seeing arms they had supplied being used in ways over which they had little control, or which involved their own warring clients (Nasser versus competitive regimes in Baghdad or Damascus, Baghdad versus the Kurds, etc.).

In particular, the Soviet Union was ambivalent about Nasser, applauding and supporting his actions when they hurt the West but being less sanguine when they threatened other Soviet clients. In the mid-1960s, the Soviets themselves decided that their ultimate ideological objectives might be reached by a continuation of aid and a policy of encouraging local Communists to work with the various governments in return for being left alone. This approach may or may not have encouraged the radicalization of the regimes in Egypt, Syria, and Iraq. However, as it became more apparent that circumstances for the achievement of both ideological and Cold War objectives were increasingly favorable, particularly in Syria after 1966, the Russians found themselves in the position of wanting and needing to preserve and extend their gains. The closer involvement in Middle East affairs, however, brought them right into the arena of the Arab–Israeli conflict, a fact illustrated dramatically in the events that precipitated the Six-Day War.

Syria, the Palestinians, and the War of 1967

In order to understand the events immediately preceding the outbreak of war in June 1967, it is necessary to examine somewhat more closely the situation in Syria and among the Palestinian groups that had emerged by this time.

As noted above, there were Baath military coups in Syria, first by General Amin al-Hafez (1963–1966), and then by General Salah Jadid (1966–1970), the first Alawite (a minority Shiite sect considered heretical by the Sunni mainstream) to become Syrian strongman. The Baathists, whose political ideology combined leftist social and economic ideas with pan-Arabism, instituted radical domestic policies and were more openly hostile to the West and to Israel than any previous regime. In the mid-1960s, for example, Syria tried to prevent Israel pumping water from the Sea of Galilee by constructing canals to divert the headwaters of the Jordan River arising in her territory. Israeli artillery and planes made this too hazardous to continue, and Nasser refused to help Syria because of the anticipated Israeli reaction. The Syrians abandoned the project, but there was increasing tension on the Syrian-Israeli border. (See Map 5–1.) Along the DMZ in the north, Syrian gun posts on the Golan Heights fired on Israeli settlements and farmers below, and Israel retaliated. There were also disputes in the central and southern sectors over cultivation rights, with both sides arguing that the other was violating the DMZ provisions.

Under Salah Jadid, Syria established a much closer relationship with the Soviet Union and Maoist China and identified itself with "liberation" movements everywhere from Vietnam to Latin America. Jadid supported Syrian Communists and even appointed two Communist ministers, thus gratifying Syria's Soviet sponsors and providing justification for their continuing protection of the regime, which, it was hoped, would turn Syria into the Arab world's first Communist state. However, the government did not enjoy widespread domestic support. Although the Baath dealt a blow to "feudalism" on the land and improved the lot of the peasant farmers and small villagers, the majority Sunnis, drawing strength from the merchant and middle classes, resented Alawi preeminence. Moreover, economically, the long tradition of laissez-faire and free enterprise was hard for them to relinquish. The one issue that united all classes and sects, however, was hostility to Israel, which tended to push Jadid toward ever greater militancy. His admiration of guerrilla-type warfare led him to active sponsorship of Palestinian groups that had been organized over the years, especially the Palestine Liberation Organization (PLO) and al-Fatah.

The PLO was a product of the first Arab summit meeting held at the Arab League headquarters in Cairo in January 1964 to discuss Israel's planned diversion of the Jordan River waters. Unwilling or unable to challenge Israel militarily, League members informed the Palestinians that they themselves must assume the responsibility of "liberating" Palestine. Five months later in May 1964, King Hussein convened a Palestine National Council of about 400 Palestinians in Jerusalem. This meeting established the Palestine Liberation Organization and provided for the formation of a Palestine Liberation Army (PLA). The purpose of the organization was to liberate Palestine from its colonialist oppressors, the Zionists, and "armed struggle" was to be the method adopted to achieve this end. Ahmad Shuqayri, a former influential lawyer from Acre, and spokesperson in the service, respectively, of Syria, Saudi Arabia, and Egypt, was elected as chairman of the PLO. Troops for the PLA were recruited from among Palestinians scattered through the Arab world. At this point, however, the PLO was primarily an instrument of the Arab governments, especially Egypt, and was dependent on budgetary support and direction from outside its ranks. PLO leadership appeared as disinterested in alleviating the appalling conditions of the many thousands of Palestinians, who remained in crowded refugee camps, as did the Arab states themselves.

It was not the PLO, however, but al-Fatah, which emerged as the primary Palestinian organization before the war of 1967. *Fatah*, meaning "conquest," was an acronym whose letters in reverse stand for *Harakat al-Tahrir al-Falastini*, or "Movement for the Liberation of Palestine." It had been founded in the late 1950s by a group of Palestinian students in Cairo, including Yasser Arafat, a member of the family of Hajj Amin al-Husseini, from whom he evidently inherited some of his Palestinian patriotism and anti-Zionist zeal. Being connected to one of the notable families of Palestine gave Arafat a motive to claim the family's prestige and preeminence as well as providing credibility and a built-in following for his cause. Members of al-Fatah and other Palestinians undoubtedly participated in fedayeen raids before the Suez-Sinai war. After that, with UN Emergency Forces (UNEF) on the borders between Egypt and Israel, al-Fatah tended to languish, and Arafat, trained as an engineer, moved to Kuwait, where he became a successful contractor. In the 1960s, al-Fatah began to gravitate into the orbit of Syria, which saw it as a useful adjunct for its own agenda against Israel. In January 1965, Fatah members carried out their first significant raid against Israel from Syrian territory. After Jadid took power in 1966, he substantially increased weapons and support for Fatah. While the Syrian army fired down on Israeli farmers from the Golan Heights, Fatah guerrillas struck at Israeli patrols and conducted numerous raids, particularly in the Almagor area.

Toward the end of 1966, in a departure from previous policy, PLO leader Shuqayri signed an agreement with the Syrian government providing for full coordination between the PLO and al-Fatah. He did this despite Egypt's reservations about the latter organization and Nasser's unwillingness to allow guerrilla bases in Egypt and Gaza. The reasons for Shuqayri's rapprochement with Fatah included his fear that the growing popularity of Fatah's exploits would leave him exposed as ineffective. Additionally, the relationship between the PLO and King Hussein had been worsening, and this made an agreement with Fatah an attractive front against

Unit of Palestinian soldiers during a December 1966 rally in Rafah, Gaza Strip.

the Jordanians. Shuqayri had established a headquarters in the Old City of Jerusalem, imposed taxes on the Palestinian refugees, and set up training camps. King Hussein believed that the PLO was building up a state within a state (which would indeed be the case fifteen years later), and he therefore arrested many PLO members and shut down PLO operations.

Hussein's action, which was also a blow against Egyptian and Syrian sponsorship of the Palestinian organizations, intensified the split between the "radicals" and the "reactionaries" in the Arab Cold War. Nasser had labeled Feisal—the Saudi king who had been promoting the idea of an Islamic pact against Nasserism, and who was the chief supporter of the royalists in Yemen—the "Pope of Islam." He cast aspersions against King Hussein, who received his military equipment and financial aid from the United States, as the "dwarf from Amman" and the "Hashemite harlot." The Jordanians and Saudis countered by attacking Nasser, accusing him of cowardice, fear of Israel, and unwillingness to live up to his promises to the other Arabs when they were challenged by Israel. The situation on the borders between Syria and Israel and between Jordan and Israel, exacerbated by Palestinian guerrilla activity, brought many of these inter-Arab tensions to the surface, as well as contributing to the outbreak of full-scale war between Israel and the Arab states in 1967.

Prelude to War

As noted above, al-Fatah's first raids into Israel were from Syrian territory. However, although based in Syria, Palestinians most often launched attacks from Jordanian territory, since the longer border was easier and safer to cross. As in the past, the Israeli government adopted the policy of retaliation by regular army units and held to account the country from which the raid emanated, even though both the Jordanian and Lebanese governments made serious attempts to prevent such incursions from their territory.

Meanwhile, raids from Syria had also continued, and these led in mid-August 1966 to a major clash between Israel and Syria. Both sides eventually agreed to UN requests for a cease-fire, but subsequent guerrilla operations against Israel resulted in Security Council debates in which Western nations called upon Syria to prevent Fatah operations from her territory and the Eastern bloc chastised Israel for her aggressive intentions against Syria.

Nevertheless, the Russians were concerned that the general instability of the Salah Jadid regime in Syria and the volatility of the border situation might lead to massive Israeli retaliation against their client. Their fear that Jadid might be overthrown and/or that a wider conflagration involving the superpowers might be sparked brought the Soviets more directly into the picture in 1966–1967. They called on the Syrian leader to contain the guerrillas and to restrain his bellicose rhetoric against Israel. Moreover, the Soviets encouraged a joint defense pact between Egypt and Syria, signed in early November 1966, either because they hoped it would restrain the Syrians and hold them in check, or because they believed Egyptian adherence would provide a deterrent to Israeli retaliation.

Shortly thereafter, on November 13, 1966, Israel undertook a major military assault against as-Samu and neighboring Jordanian towns, killing eighteen, including three civilians. Fifty-four were wounded, and a clinic, school, and over a hundred houses were destroyed. The Israeli position was that this raid was in retaliation for several guerrilla attacks launched from Jordan over the previous six months, some of which had resulted in death or injury to Israelis. The as-Samu raid, however, was condemned by the world community both within and outside the United Nations. The United States supported the Security Council resolution condemning Israel, not only because of the scale of the attack, but also because it undercut and embarrassed King Hussein. The as-Samu incursion compromised the king in the eyes of the Palestinians and provided the Arab "radicals" and their patron, the Soviet Union, with a further excuse to try to undermine his regime.

There was wide speculation that Israel had struck at Jordan rather than Syria, which unlike Jordan had actively aided and abetted the Palestinian groups, because Israel did not want to provoke Egypt in light of the recently signed Egypt–Syria defense pact. There is no indication, however, that Egypt would have responded to an attack on Syria, if, as we shall see, the events of April 1967 are any proof. Indeed, the escalation that led finally to war in June 1967 appears to have been precipitated by Russian miscalculation.

The Road to War

In 1958, Gamal Abdul Nasser was the leading figure in the Arab world. By 1961, however, Syria had seceded from the UAR, and Qasim's regime in Iraq was forging its own destiny, which would continue to diverge from that of Egypt with successive military coups. Internally, as noted above, Egypt's economy was in poor shape. Moreover, Nasser's friends from the Bandung conference and in the third world, leaders like Nehru, Sukarno, Ben Bella, and others, were no longer in power.

Nasser had determined after 1956 that he would not become involved in a major confrontation with Israel unless he could win; that is, unless he were fully prepared militarily and the international circumstances were right. He recognized Israel's growing economic and military strength and the international support Israel enjoyed in the West and among many of the developing nations. Because of Arab unpreparedness and Israel's policy of retaliation, Nasser did not lend support for Syrian efforts to halt Israel's water-diversion scheme. Nor did he react, despite Jordanian taunts, to Israel's attack against as-Samu, except to insist to King Hussein that responsibility for repulsing Israel reprisal raids rested with the individual countries. Nasser retreated to this position again in April 1967, when, after several months of violent incidents in the north, an air battle erupted between Israel and Syria in which Israel violated Syrian airspace, shot down six MiGs, and buzzed Damascus. Nasser remained aloof.

To the Russians, however, it seemed absolutely crucial to prod the Egyptians into living up to the commitment implied in the joint defense pact. The unstable Jadid regime in Syria had raised the stakes in the north without much apparent success and had embarked on a course that promised the counterproductive effect of massive Israeli retaliation. The achievement of Soviet objectives in Syria seemed to be in jeopardy. Only by the device of Nasser restraining Jadid and/or causing Israel to pause before retaliating for Syrian raids, because of the possibility of Egyptian action in the south, could some Soviet control be exerted over this situation. In early May 1967, therefore, the Russians passed on to the Egyptians information about heavy Israeli troop concentrations on the Syrian border and an Israeli contingency plan for an attack on Syria.

The Soviets, and probably Nasser himself, knew that information about massive Israeli troop concentrations was false. Indeed, the UN Truce Supervision Organization (UNTSO), U.S. intelligence, and Egyptian observers on the spot failed to detect any Israeli moves. Nasser, however, decided to become involved and to take some action for several reasons. He was convinced that the United States was trying to get at him indirectly by urging Israel to hit Syria, but he believed the Russians would now stand behind him whatever action he took. Nasser had a false estimation of Egyptian strength based on the great amounts of military hardware he had amassed. His poor economic situation called for some outlet for the frustration that had been building among the Egyptian people. And he certainly hoped that assuming an active role against Israel would quiet his critics and restore his position of leadership in the Arab world.

Thus, on May 14, 1967, Cairo announced that Egyptian armed forces were in a state of maximum alert, and combat units crossed the Suez into Sinai. On May 16, Egypt requested the UNEF to be concentrated in the Gaza Strip; and on May 18, the Egyptian foreign minister demanded that UN Secretary General U Thant recall all troops of the UNEF stationed in the Gaza Strip and on UAR soil. This was a step Nasser had every legal right to take, but instead of procrastinating in order to defuse the growing crisis, U Thant complied almost immediately. Egyptian troops and tanks began to rumble across the Sinai and to take over UN positions. Syria also began to mobilize, as did Jordan and Iraq. On May 22, with Egyptian troops at Sharm al-Sheikh, Nasser announced the closing of the Gulf of Aqaba to Israeli vessels or any vessels carrying goods to Israel. Prime Minister Levi Eshkol replied the next day that Israel would consider any interference with freedom of shipping as an act of aggression against Israel. Bellicose speeches continued to emanate from Cairo, however, and during the next week, Nasser on several occasions stated that Palestine must be liberated and Israel destroyed. (See Document 6–1.)

As the crisis escalated, the Security Council met in emergency session, but its discussions were fruitless and hampered by the Soviet veto. Israeli foreign minister Abba Eban flew to Paris, London, and the United States, as the Western countries groped for some way to defuse the situation. Although President Johnson publicly denounced Nasser's closing of the waterway and promised that the United States would try to get other maritime nations to join in testing the blockade, the American Aide Memoire of 1957 was obviously a worthless scrap of paper. Privately, Johnson warned Israel against a preemptive strike, and Israeli moderates hesitated to act unilaterally. Nasser appeared to have Israel in a bind; the prolonged general mobilization in Israel was beginning to have a dire psychological as well as economic effect. To the Arabs, what had perhaps started as some limited action began to take on the possibility of a potentially successful military operation, as Nasser, believing he had the support of the Russians, went to the brink. On May 30, 1967, King Hussein of Jordan flew to Egypt to sign a defense pact with Egypt. He agreed to allow Iraqi troops to enter Jordanian territory in the event of hostilities and to place his troops under Egyptian military authority. PLO leader Shuqayri, although no friend of Hussein, was present at the signing ceremony and flew back to Jordan with the king.

The situation was extremely difficult for Israel. (See Document 6–2.) There were Arab armies poised on all its borders; mobilization was taking a toll economically, as normal life came to a standstill; and politically, there was a crisis situation, as Eshkol's government seemed incapable of making a decision about what course of action to take. All armies have contingency plans, and as early as 1964 Israel had worked out such a plan for an attack against Egypt if necessary. Israel had on several occasions threatened reprisals against Syria and undoubtedly had various alternatives on the drawing board. Given Israel's borders, the idea of the preemptive strike (or what some Israeli military leaders like Yigal Allon called the "preemptive counterstrike") had come to be accepted, since Israel within its present borders was not in a position to absorb a first blow and survive. Because of Israel's policies of massive retaliation and offensive warfare as the best defense, some historians and writers see all the Arab–Israeli wars as the result of Israeli aggressiveness and expansionism, which they attribute to an inherent dynamic and master plan of Zionism. In their view, while Nasser may have shown antipathy to Israel, and with good reason, he was not a warmonger—in contrast to Ben-Gurion and a coterie of younger Israeli "hawks" who had been planning another strike against Nasser for a decade.

Other historians argue that despite the existence of military contingency plans, there is no evidence that Israel would have launched a full-scale war against Egypt had Nasser not taken the provocative actions he did. They contend, on the contrary, that the failure of Israel to retaliate for the closing of the Gulf of Aqaba, retaliation that was expected among both the Arabs and the superpowers, and the hesitation and indecisiveness evident in Israel as diplomatic solutions were floated, fed Nasser's megalomania and encouraged King Hussein of Jordan to put aside past differences and climb on the bandwagon. They maintain that no matter how pragmatic Nasser could be, the defeat of 1948, and the drubbing of 1956, had only nourished Arab hatred of Israel and the desire for revenge. In any event, the Egyptian-Jordanian defense pact seems to have galvanized the Israelis, who put together a government of national unity (which included Menachem Begin, the leader of the opposition for all the years since statehood), in which Moshe Dayan was named minister of defense.

With Dayan in the cabinet, and with the Israeli belief that the existence of the entire nation was indeed in jeopardy, it was almost a certainty that Israel would strike the first blow. According to apologists for Israel, this is precisely what Nasser wanted. Were he to initiate hostilities, the issue would not be about shipping in the Gulf of Aqaba but about the continued existence of the Jewish state, which the United States was pledged to uphold. In this view, Nasser believed that Israel, in striking a first blow, would be diplomatically isolated, especially from the United States, and that the Americans would hesitate to intervene on Israel's side. Wiser leaders than Eshkol and Nasser, however, might have averted conflict.

The Six-Day War broke out on the morning of June 5, 1967, as Israeli planes destroyed most of Egypt's air force on the ground. Details of the war itself have been told in countless books and will not be repeated here, but the importance of air power, and the cohesiveness of Israel's citizen army, should be mentioned as significant factors in Israel's success. The outcome was even more dramatic, since the Arabs seemed to be superior in almost every weapons category. (See Tables 6–1 and 6–2.) After the initial Israeli air strike, Israeli ground troops defeated the Egyptian army, seizing the Gaza Strip and the entire Sinai Peninsula. In a still-disputed incident on June 8, the Israelis attacked an American intelligence-gathering ship, the USS *Liberty*, sailing off the Egyptian coast. Thirty-four sailors were killed and 164 wounded. Some writers insist that this was a deliberate and premeditated attack; Israel continues to maintain that the attack on the *Liberty* was a case of mistaken identity and an accident. Israel apologized and later paid $3 million in reparations for the families of the victims to the U.S. government, which accepted Israel's explanation and apology.

Israel asked King Hussein to stay out of the war and assured him it would not attack him first. Hussein, however, was badly misled by the Egyptians, who intimated that they were being successful against Israel on the southern front. Jordanian guns began to fire from across the borders in Jerusalem while Jordanian troops seized the UN headquarters in no-man's land. This was all the excuse the Israelis needed to take the Old City of Jerusalem and the entire

TABLE 6-1   Approximate Land and Air Force Strengths, 1967 War

	Israel	Arabs	Egypt	Jordan	Syria	Iraq
Mobilized Operational Manpower[1]	250,000	328,000	210,000	55,000	63,000	—
Brigades	25	42	22	10	12	—
Artillery Pieces	200	960	575	263	315	—
Tanks	1,000[2]	2,330	1,300[5]	288[7]	750	—
APCs	1,500[3]	1,845	1,050	210	585	—
SAMs	50	160	160	0	0	0
AA Guns	550	2,000+	950	143	1,000	—
Combat Aircraft	286[4]	682	431[6]	18	127[8]	106[9]

[1]On the Arab side includes forces available for commitment.
[2]200 M48s, 250 Centurions, 150 AMX-13s, 400 Shermans and Super-Shermans.
[3]M3 Halftracks.
[4]Includes 92 Mirages, 24 Super-Mystères, 82 Mystères, 55 Ouragans, 24 light bombers.
[5]Includes 400+ T-34s, 450+ T-54/55s, 100+ Su-100s, 100+ JS-3s.
[6]Includes 55 Su-6s, 163 MiG-21s, 40 MiG-19s, 100 MiG-15/17s, 30 Tu-16s, 43 Il-28s; only 350 pilots.
[7]Includes about 200 M48s, about 90 Centurions.
[8]Includes 40 MiG-21/19s, 68 MiG-15/17s, 15 Tu-16s, 4 Il-28s.
[9]About 45 committed.

TABLE 6-2   Estimated Naval Strengths, 1967 War

	Israel	Egypt	Syria
Manpower	4,000	13,000	1,000
Patrol and Torpedo Boats	9	44	17
Guided Missile Boats	0	18[1]	4[2]
Destroyers and Frigates	3	7	0
Submarines	3	12	0
Amphibious Craft	0	5	0
Small Craft	?	?	?
Vessel Totals	15+	86+	21+

[1]Includes 8 *Komar* class and 10 Osa class.
[2]Komar class, just received; not ready for combat.

Source: Trevor N. Dupuy, *Elusive Victory: The Arab–Israeli Wars, 1947–1974* (New York: Harper & Row, 1978), p. 337. Reprinted by permission of Hero Books.

West Bank. Israel then turned toward Syria, which had been attacking Israel's northern settlements by air and with artillery. Although the United Nations called for a cease-fire, the Israelis did not stop until they had captured the Golan Heights in some of the fiercest fighting of the war. By June 10, 1967, six days later, the war was over. (See Table 6–3.)

Results

The results of Israel's stunning and spectacular victory were far-reaching and of crucial importance in the years since 1967. A new map of the Middle East came into being, with Israel three times larger than it was in 1949. (See Map 6–1.) Israel's occupation of the Sinai Peninsula, the Golan

TABLE 6-3   Losses, 1967 War

	Killed	Wounded	Captured/ Missing	Total Casualties	Tanks Lost	Aircraft Lost
Israel	983	4,517	15	5,515	394[1]	40
(vs. Egypt)	303	1,450	11	1,764	122	—
(vs. Jordan)	553	2,442	0	2,995	112	—
(vs. Syria)	127	625	4	756	160	—
Arabs	4,296	6,121	7,550	17,967	965[2]	444
(Egypt)	3,000	5,000	4,980	12,980	700	356[3]
(Jordan)[4]	696	421	2,000[5]	3,117	179	18
(Syria)	600	700	570	1,870	86	55
(Iraq)	—	—	—	—	—	15

[1]At least half of these were repaired and returned to full operational status.
[2]About 150 captured T-54/55s were modified by the Israelis and put into their postwar inventory, thus largely offsetting unrepairable losses during the war.
[3]Of these, 322 were lost the first day.
[4]Recent figures, official except for estimate of missing; 20% factor added to killed and wounded to allow for these losses among missing.
[5]Of these, 530 were prisoners of war.

Source: Dupuy, *Elusive Victory*, p. 333. Reprinted by permission of Hero Books.

Heights, the West Bank, the Gaza Strip, and East Jerusalem brought new opportunities and new problems. Certainly the conquest of all this territory provided Israel with "strategic depth," presumably more defensible borders, and some breathing room. However, we shall see that the continued occupation of the territories and Jewish settlements on the West Bank and in Gaza did not bring Israel any closer to the peace it desired. On the contrary, with 1.3 million Palestinians under Israeli control in Gaza and on the West Bank, the Palestinian problem became Israel's problem. If Palestinian nationalism was nascent or held in check before 1967 when the Palestinians lived under Arab governments, it grew into an authentic manifestation of the desire of Palestinian Arabs for self-determination as the years passed. Many Palestinian groups representing Palestinian interests came into being. They differed on strategy and tactics and the order in which their various enemies—reactionary Arab regimes and Israel—should be overcome, but the significant growth of Palestinian national aspirations and the world recognition that was gained for a variety of reasons, especially by a reorganized PLO led after 1968 by Yasser Arafat, are undeniable.

For Israel, a new image of strength and power replaced the previous one of the threatened underdog, the gallant little country surrounded by enemies who wished to exterminate it. Israel's victory had a profound effect on Jews everywhere, engendering self-confidence, pride, and assertiveness. In the Soviet Union, where Jewish religious and national identity had been submerged since the Bolshevik Revolution, a new Jewish self-consciousness began to emerge that would have significant repercussions. Israelis themselves were euphoric that their army and people had been able to stand up to the combined Arab armies and win a war without help from any other nation even though, in their initial disbelief and humiliation, Nasser and Hussein had fabricated a story that the United States had participated in and been responsible for Israel's victory. The image of the Israel Defense Forces as one of the best armies in the world was heady stuff, and, as we shall see, an exaggerated sense of power resulted, as well as an arrogance toward the enemy that led later to serious miscalculations on Israel's part. The results of the Six-Day War on Egypt and Syria will be examined in the next chapter.

The Soviet Union and several East-bloc countries severed diplomatic ties with Israel in the aftermath of the war, which hurt the Soviets more than Israel in the region, since the Russians

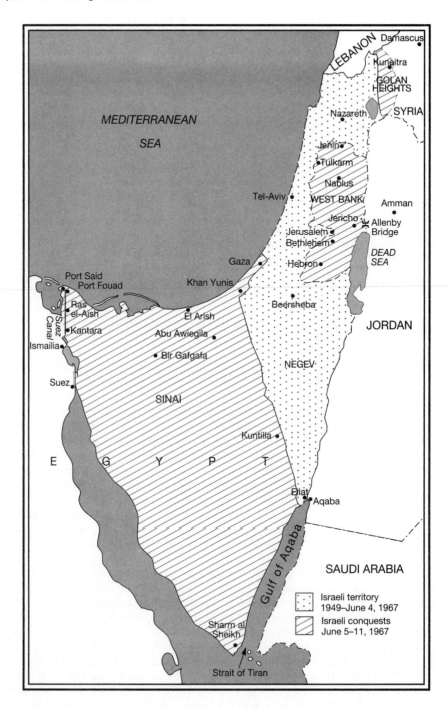

MAP 6–1   Israeli Conquests, 1967

Source: Atlas of the Arab–Israeli Conflict, 6th ed., Martin Gilbert, © 1974, New York: Macmillan, p. 70. Reproduced by permission of Taylor & Francis Books UK.

lost their leverage with both sides. Egypt, Syria, Iraq, Sudan, Algeria, and Yemen severed diplomatic ties with the United States, and American relations with the Arabs in general deteriorated as a result of the war. Nevertheless, the United States still retained important ties with Saudi Arabia and Jordan, while at the same time becoming the guarantor of Israel's survival. France under Charles de Gaulle, anxious to recoup in the Arab world, declined to supply Israel's military needs any longer, and Britain was beginning to withdraw from her installations east of Suez. The United States and Israel were thrown closer together, therefore, although this was a situation that both nations might have wished to avoid. A strong Israel was increasingly seen in the United States as a strategic ally, and the identification of interests became closer on both sides.

The diplomatic solution to the 1967 hostilities was UN Resolution 242, a masterpiece of diplomatic ambiguity that became the key document in all attempts to arrive at a peaceful solution to the conflict. (See Document 6–3.) While insisting on the inadmissibility of the acquisition of territory by war, a rather new and startling international principle, UN Resolution 242 proposed (in so many words) the idea of peace in return for territory—without specifying which should come first. In the first article of Resolution 242, which the Security Council passed in November 1967, Israel was called upon to return occupied territories (but not "the" territories). A second article recognized the right of all states in the region to live in peace within secure and recognized borders. Other important points included freedom of passage through international waterways and a just solution to the "refugee" problem. Resolution 242 was accepted by Israel, Egypt, and Jordan (but not by Syria) and was a notable milestone in its implicit acknowledgment by these Arab states of Israel's existence and its expectation of a negotiated settlement. There was no machinery to implement the resolution, however, except through the good offices of a special UN mediator, Dr. Gunnar Jarring, whose task was to try to facilitate talks among the parties. The Israelis held the view that explicit recognition through direct negotiations should come before withdrawal, and that they were not required to withdraw from

Israeli soldier on watch at Suez Canal, January 23, 1968.

all the occupied territory. The Arabs insisted on Israel's withdrawal from all the occupied territory, including East Jerusalem, which the Israelis annexed shortly after the conclusion of hostilities. Nor did the resolution address the escalating arms race. Even more significant in both the short and long run was the absence of any specific reference to the Palestinians, except for the provision that there should be a just solution to the refugee problem. The Eshkol government continued to reiterate its desire for direct peace negotiations (see Document 6–4); but in late August–early September 1967, even before passage of Resolution 242, an Arab summit in Khartoum, Sudan, proclaimed that there would be "no peace, no recognition, and no negotiations" with Israel. (See Document 6–5.) These were three "no's" that Israel took seriously and that continued to influence Israeli policymakers.

Recapitulation

The long-range causes of the 1967 war were the continued inability of the Arabs to recognize and accept the political sovereignty of the Jews in Israel; the antagonism and desire for revenge that had been fueled by defeats and humiliation in the previous wars, as well as by Israel's excessive retaliations; Arab fear of Israeli aggressiveness and expansionism; and Israeli "hawkishness" and the determination to maintain military superiority. The inability to find a solution for the plight of the Palestinian refugees, because of intransigence on both sides, provided the *raison d'être* and rallying point for the Arab crusade against Israel. The short-term and more proximate causes were the arms buildup on both sides in the previous decade; superpower interference and especially Soviet meddling; the volatile situation in Syria; Nasser's brinksmanship; the defense pacts that linked together Egypt, Syria, and Jordan; and the failure of the international community to prevent war through diplomacy. All sides thus must share the blame for the outbreak of hostilities and for the consequences that followed.

Suggestions for Further Reading

ABU-LUGHOD, IBRAHIM, ed., *The Arab–Israeli Confrontation of 1967: An Arab Perspective*, Evanston, Ill., Northwestern University Press, 1970.

CONFINO, MICHAEL, AND SHAMIR, SHIMON, eds., *The U.S.S.R. and the Middle East*, Jerusalem, Israel Universities Press, 1973.

DUPUY, COL. T. N., *Elusive Victory, The Arab–Israeli Wars, 1947–74*, New York, Harper & Row, 1978.

HEIKAL, MOHAMED, *The Sphinx and the Commissar: The Rise and Fall of Soviet Influence in the Middle East*, New York, Harper & Row, 1978.

KERR, MALCOLM, *The Arab Cold War: Gamal Abdul Nasir and His Rivals, 1958–1970*, 3rd ed., Oxford, Oxford University Press, 1971.

KIMMERLING, BARUCH, AND MIGDAL, JOEL, *Palestinians: The Making of a People*, New York, The Free Press, 1993.

LAQUEUR, WALTER, *The Road to Jerusalem: The Origins of the Arab–Israeli Conflict, 1967*, New York, Macmillan, 1968.

O'BALLANCE, EDGAR, *The Third Arab–Israeli War*, London, Faber and Faber, 1972.

OREN, MICHAEL, *Six Days of War: June, 1967 and the Making of the Modern Middle East*, Presidio Press, 2003.

QUANDT, WILLIAM, JABBER, FUAD, AND LESCH, ANN MOSELY, *The Politics of Palestinian Nationalism*, Berkeley, University of California Press, 1973.

SAFRAN, NADAV, *Israel: The Embattled Ally*, Cambridge, Harvard University Press, 1978.

SEALE, PATRICK, *The Struggle for Syria: A Study of Post-War Arab Politics, 1945–1958*, 2nd ed., New Haven, Yale University Press, 1987.

TILLMAN, SETH P., *The United States and the Middle East*, Bloomington, Indiana University Press, 1982.

DOCUMENT 6–1

Nasser's Speech to Egyptian National Assembly Members, May 29, 1967

Israel used to boast a great deal, and the Western powers, headed by the United States and Britain, used to ignore and even despise us and consider us of no value. But now that the time has come—and I have already said in the past that we will decide the time and place and not allow them to decide—we must be ready for triumph and not for a recurrence of the 1948 comedies. We shall triumph, God willing.

Preparations have already been made. We are now ready to confront Israel. They have claimed many things about the 1956 Suez war, but no one believed them after the secrets of the 1956 collusion were uncovered—that mean collusion in which Israel took part. Now we are ready for the confrontation. We are now ready to deal with the entire Palestine question.

The issue now at hand is not the Gulf of Aqabah, the Straits of Tiran, or the withdrawal of the UNEF, but the rights of the Palestine people. It is the aggression which took place in Palestine in 1948 with the collaboration of Britain and the United States. It is the expulsion of the Arabs from Palestine, the usurpation of their rights, and the plunder of their property. It is the disavowal of all the UN resolutions in favour of the Palestinian people.

The issue is far more serious than they say. They want to confine the issue to the Straits of Tiran, the UNEF and the right of passage. We demand the full rights of the Palestinian people. We say this out of our belief that Arab rights cannot be squandered because the Arabs throughout the Arab world are demanding these Arab rights.

We are not afraid of the United States and its threats, of Britain and her threats, or of the entire Western world and its partiality to Israel. The United States and Britain are partial to Israel and give no consideration to the Arabs, to the entire Arab nation. Why? Because we have made them believe that we cannot distinguish between friend and foe. We must make them know that we know who our foes are and who our friends are and treat them accordingly.

If the United States and Britain are partial to Israel, we must say that our enemy is not only Israel but also the United States and Britain and treat them as such. If the Western Powers disavow our rights and ridicule and despise us, we Arabs must teach them to respect us and take us seriously. Otherwise all our talk about Palestine, the Palestinian people, and Palestinian rights will be null and void and of no consequence. We must treat enemies as enemies and friends as friends.

Source: Walter Laqueur and Barry Rubin, eds., *The Israel–Arab Reader: A Documentary History of the Middle East Conflict*, 4th ed. (New York: Penguin Books, 1984), pp. 187–188.

DOCUMENT 6–2

Speech by Abba Eban, Israeli Foreign Minister, to the Security Council on Israel's Reasons for Going to War, June 6, 1967

I thank you, Mr. President, for giving me this opportunity to address the Council. I have just come from Jerusalem to tell the Security Council that Israel, by its independent action and sacrifice, has passed from serious danger to successful resistance.

Two days ago, Israel's condition caused much concern across the humane and friendly world. Israel had reached a sombre hour. Let me try to evoke the point at which our fortunes stood.

An army, greater than any force ever assembled in history in Sinai, had massed against Israel's southern frontier. Egypt had dismissed the United Nations forces which symbolized the international interest in the maintenance of peace in our region. Nasser had provocatively brought five infantry divisions and two armoured divisions up to our very gates; 80,000 men and 900 tanks were poised to move.

A special striking force, comprising an armoured division with at least 200 tanks, was concentrated against Elath at the Negev's southern tip. Here was a clear design to cut the southern Negev off from the main body of our State. For Egypt had openly proclaimed that Elath did not form part of Israel and had predicted that Israel itself would soon expire. The proclamation was empty; the prediction now lies in ruins. While the main brunt of the hostile threat was focused on the southern front, an alarming plan of encirclement was under way. With Egypt's initiative and guidance, Israel was already being strangled in its maritime approaches to the whole eastern half of the world. For sixteen years, Israel had been illicitly denied passage in the Suez Canal, despite this Security Council's resolution of 1 September 1951. And now the creative enterprise of the patient years which had opened an international route across the Strait of Tiran and the Gulf of Aqaba had been suddenly and arbitrarily choked. Israel was and is breathing with only a single lung.

Jordan had been intimidated, against its better interest, into joining a defence pact. It is not a defence pact at all: it is an aggressive pact, of which I saw the consequences with my own eyes yesterday in the shells falling upon institutions of health and culture in the City of Jerusalem. Every house and street in Jerusalem now came into the range of fire as a result of Jordan's adherence to this pact; so also did the crowded, and pathetically narrow coastal strip in which so much of Israel's life and population is concentrated.

Iraqi troops reinforced Jordanian units in areas immediately facing vital and vulnerable Israeli communication centres. Expeditionary forces from Algeria and Kuwait had reached Egyptian territory. Nearly all the Egyptian forces which had been attempting the conquest of the Yemen had been transferred to the coming assault upon Israel. Syrian units, including artillery, overlooked Israeli villages in the Jordan Valley. Terrorist groups came regularly into our territory to kill, plunder and set off explosives, the most recent occasion was five days ago.

In short, there was peril for Israel wherever it looked. Its manpower had been hastily mobilized. Its economy and commerce were beating with feeble pulses. Its streets were dark and empty. There was an apocalypse air of approaching peril. And Israel faced this danger alone.

We were buoyed up by an unforgettable surge of public sympathy across the world. The friendly Governments expressed the rather ominous hope that Israel would manage to live, but the dominant theme of our condition was danger and solitude.

Now there could be doubt what was intended for us. I heard President Nasser's speech on 26 May. He said:

"We intend to open a general assault against Israel. This will be total war. Our basic aim is the destruction of Israel."

On 2 June, the Egyptian Commander-in-Chief in Sinai, General Murtagi, published his order of the day, calling on his troops to wage a war of destruction against Israel. Here, then, was a systematic, overt, proclaimed design at politicide, the murder of a State.

The policy, the arms, the men had all been brought together, and the State thus threatened with collective assault was itself the last sanctuary of a people which had seen six million of its sons exterminated by a more powerful dictator two decades before.

UNO SCOR, S/PV, 1348

Source: T. G Fraser, *The Middle East, 1914–1979* (New York: St. Martin's Press, 1980), pp. 107–109.

DOCUMENT 6-3

UN Security Council Resolution 242, November 22, 1967

The Security Council

Expressing its continuing concern with the grave situation in the Middle East.

Emphasizing the inadmissibility of the acquisition of territory by war and the need to work for a just and lasting peace in which every State in the area can live in security.

Emphasizing further that all Member States in their acceptance of the Charter of the United Nations have undertaken a commitment to act in accordance with Article 2 of the Charter.

1. *Affirms* that the fulfillment of Charter principles requires the establishment of a just and lasting peace in the Middle East which should include the application of both the following principles:

    (i) Withdrawal of Israeli armed forces from territories occupied in the recent conflict;

    (ii) Termination of all claims or states of belligerency and respect for and acknowledgement of the sovereignty, territorial integrity and political independence of every State in the area and their right to live in peace within secure and recognized boundaries free from threats or acts of force;

2. *Affirms further the necessity*

    (a) For guaranteeing freedom of navigation through international waterways in the area;

    (b) For achieving a just settlement of the refugee problem;

    (c) For guaranteeing the territorial inviolability and political independence of every State in the area, through measures including the establishment of demilitarized zones;

3. *Requests* the Secretary-General to designate a Special Representative to proceed to the Middle East to establish and maintain contacts with the States concerned in order to promote agreement and assist efforts to achieve a peaceful and accepted settlement in accordance with the provisions and principles in this resolution;

4. *Requests* the Secretary-General to report to the Security Council on the progress of the efforts of the Special Representative as soon as possible.

Source: The Middle East, 7th ed. (Washington, D.C.: Congressional Quarterly, Inc., 1990), p. 301.

DOCUMENT 6-4

Principles Guiding Israel's Policy in the Aftermath of the June 1967 War as Outlined by Prime Minister Eshkol, Jerusalem, August 9, 1967 [Excerpts]

(a) The Government of Israel will endeavour to achieve peace with the neighbouring Arab countries. We shall never permit a return to a situation of constant threat to Israel's security, of blockade and of aggression.

(b) The Government of Israel is prepared for direct negotiations with all the Arab States together, or with any Arab State separately.

(c) The State of Israel strives for economic cooperation and regional planning with all States in the Middle East.

(d) Israel will cooperate fully in the solution of the refugee problem . . . within the framework of an international and regional plan.

(e) The Government endeavours to maintain fair and equitable relations with the population in the new areas, while maintaining order and security.

After our military victory, we confront a fateful dilemma; immigration or stagnation. . . . By the end of the century, we must have five million Jews in Israel. We must work hard so that Israel may be able to maintain decent human, cultural, technical and economic standards. This is the test of Israel's existence as a Jewish State in the Middle East.

Source: Yehuda Lukacs, *Documents on the Israeli–Palestinian Conflict, 1967–1983* (Cambridge: Cambridge University Press, 1984), p. 79.

 DOCUMENT 6–5

Resolutions of the Khartoum Conference, September 1, 1967

1. The conference has affirmed the unity of Arab ranks, the unity of joint action and the need for coordination and for the elimination of all differences. The Kings, Presidents and representatives of the other Arab Heads of State at the conference have affirmed their countries' stand by and implementation of the Arab Solidarity Charter which was signed at the third Arab summit conference at Casablanca.
2. The conference has agreed on the need to consolidate all efforts to eliminate the effects of the aggression on the basis that the occupied lands are Arab lands and that the burden of regaining these lands falls on the Arab States.
3. The Arab Heads of State have agreed to unite their political efforts at the international and diplomatic level to eliminate the effects of the aggression and to ensure the withdrawal of the aggressive Israeli forces from the Arab lands which have been occupied since the aggression of 5 June. This will be done within the framework of the main principles by which the Arab States abide, namely, no peace with Israel, no recognition of Israel, no negotiations with it, and insistence on the rights of the Palestinian people in their own country.
4. The conference of Arab Ministers of Finance, Economy and Oil recommended that suspension of oil pumping be used as a weapon in the battle. However, . . . the summit conference has come to the conclusion that the pumping of oil can itself be used as a positive weapon, since oil is an Arab resource which can be used to strengthen the economy of the Arab States directly affected by the aggression. . . . The conference has, therefore, decided to resume the pumping of oil, since oil is a positive Arab resource that can be used in the service of Arab goals.

Source: Fraser, *The Middle East*, pp. 115–116.

SEVEN

Holy Days and Holy War: October 1973

CHRONOLOGY

Dec. 1967–1968	First Jarring mission
Dec. 1967	Shuqayri resigns as PLO chairman
Mar. 21, 1968	Battle of Karameh
July 10–17, 1968	Palestine National Council Meeting: PLO covenant revised
July 23, 1968	First PLO airplane hijacking
Jan. 1969	Israel begins construction of Bar-Lev line
Jan. 20, 1969	Nixon administration begins in United States
Feb. 1969	Yasser Arafat recognized as head of PLO at fifth PNC meeting
Mar. 1969	Nasser announces "liberation phase" of War of Attrition along Suez Canal
Mar. 15, 1969	Bar-Lev line completed
June 25, 1970	Rogers Plan announced
Aug. 7, 1970	Cease-fire along Suez Canal
Sept. 16–25, 1970	Showdown between King Hussein and Palestinians
Sept. 28, 1970	Nasser dies; Anwar al-Sadat becomes Egyptian president
Nov. 13, 1970	Hafez al-Assad assumes power in Syria; becomes president March 13, 1971
Early May 1971	Secretary of State Rogers visits Cairo
May 27, 1971	Soviet-Egyptian Treaty of Friendship
Nov. 28, 1971	Black September assassinates Jordanian prime minister Wasfi Tell in Cairo
Mar. 15, 1972	King Hussein proposes federal-type solution for West Bank
May 1972	Nixon visits Moscow
July 18, 1972	Sadat expels Russian advisors
Sept. 5, 1972	Israeli athletes murdered at Munich Olympics by Black September terrorists
June 1973	U.S.–Soviet summit meeting
Oct. 6, 1973	Egypt and Syria attack Israel; Yom Kippur, or Ramadan, War begins
Oct. 17, 1973	OAPEC imposes oil embargo
Oct. 22, 1973	Cease-fire; UN Security Council Resolution 338 calls for direct negotiations based on Resolution 242
Dec. 21, 1973	Geneva conference
Oct. 28, 1974	Arab League summit meeting at Rabat recognizes PLO as sole, legitimate representative of Palestinian people

As noted in the previous chapter, the military defeat of 1967 was a terrible blow for the Arabs. The absence of a negotiated settlement, however, made another round in the Arab–Israeli conflict almost a certainty, especially when the injury done to Arab honor, pride, and self-respect was added to the loss of territory. In this chapter we shall examine the events leading to the next war, that of 1973, and its consequences.

The Israelis were jubilant after their astonishing victory. In less than a week, they had increased their territory by 28,000 square miles and had achieved, they believed, strategic depth and defensible borders. The Western (or Wailing) Wall of the Second Temple was again under Jewish control, and the barriers separating the two halves of Jerusalem were torn down. Israel annexed the Old City and East Jerusalem at the end of June 1967 and declared that the city would never again be divided. Developed and undeveloped oil fields in the Sinai Peninsula came into Israeli hands, and Israelis could now visit Mount Sinai where Moses had received the Ten Commandments. There was a sense of having "arrived" as a truly independent member of the family of nations. Most Israelis believed that their incredible victory could lead to a negotiated settlement with the Arabs.

Moshe Dayan declared that he was simply waiting for a telephone call from King Hussein, and he indicated that everything was negotiable in return for peace. Israel considered the occupied territories its trump card for peace, especially with Jordan, but the telephone call never came. Hussein and the Israelis, in fact, had many secret meetings, but the king evidently feared the kind of public dealings that had resulted in the assassination of his grandfather, King Abdullah, before his very eyes. Hussein was also constrained by the Arab interpretation of UN Resolution 242 and consensus against direct and separate negotiations, and by the Palestinian dimension of the situation as it developed. As time passed, the fluid situation immediately after the 1967 war hardened into a new reality, as did the official positions of all the governments concerned.

At their summit meeting in Khartoum in late August–early September 1967, the Arab states had declared that with regard to Israel there would be no peace, no recognition, and no negotiations, and that action should be taken to safeguard the right of the Palestinian people to their homeland. Some historians explain away these statements as necessary to appease the Arab masses. They point to Egypt's and Jordan's acceptance of UN Security Council Resolution 242 as proof of the willingness of Nasser and King Hussein to work for a political and diplomatic solution. Nevertheless, Nasser's public resolve was that what had been taken by force would be recovered by force.

In Egypt, President Nasser had immediately attempted to resign from office, but popular opinion forced his reconsideration. Still a charismatic figure and the leading spokesperson in the Arab world, he never again exercised the actual power that he had exhibited before the debacle of the Six-Day War of 1967. Moreover, his health, already bad, steadily deteriorated, and in September 1970, while mediating a civil war in Jordan between King Hussein and the Palestinian resistance movements, Nasser died of a heart attack. He was succeeded by Anwar al-Sadat.

The Soviets were quick to resupply the Egyptians, although the marriage between the two countries was always one of convenience. Russian advisors arrived, along with Russian equipment, and many areas of Egypt were declared off-limits to the Egyptians themselves. The Soviet Union began to establish an impressive navy and naval support facilities in the eastern Mediterranean. As early as 1968, once the new Russian military equipment was in place, the Egyptians began to harass the Israelis dug in on the other side of the Suez Canal, and these operations soon developed into what would come to be known as the War of Attrition between 1969 and 1970. The War of Attrition certainly had the object, if possible, not only of forcing a political solution but of recovering territory by force if necessary.

Both Israel and the Arab states continued to be on a war footing, military expenditures increased, and the inventory of weapons became ever more destructive. Egypt extricated itself from Yemen and settled its differences with the Saudis. The Arab oil-producing nations gave both Egypt and Jordan a yearly subsidy to help compensate for the loss of revenue caused by the closing of the Suez Canal and a decline in tourism because of Israel's capture of the Sinai Peninsula, East Jerusalem, and other important sites. The Arab–Israeli conflict remained as a powder keg of superpower rivalry, both diplomatically and militarily, although a certain thaw between the United States and the Soviet Union and a period of détente did have some important implications for the actors in the Middle East. However, it has been said with some truth that the superpowers supplied their various clients in order to test new weapons under battlefield conditions, and détente or not, arms shipments to both Israel and the Arabs continued unabated.

While waiting for the telephone call from King Hussein, Israel missed opportunities to deal with a situation in the occupied territories whose evolution very few in Israel or elsewhere could have foreseen in the weeks and months right after June 1967. Israel's continued occupation of the West Bank and the Gaza Strip would instill among the Palestinians a growing sense of separateness and emancipation from the Arab governments. This went unrecognized by the Israelis, however, who failed to foster an indigenous leadership acceptable to the Palestinians. Instead, Israel worked through traditional elites and functionaries and expelled nationalist leaders, thereby assisting, in part at least, the growing influence and success of the PLO not only in the occupied territories but on the world stage.

The Palestinians and the PLO After 1967

Among the most notable features of the Arab–Israeli conflict after 1967 was a growing sense of Palestinian identity and nationalism. With it came increased activity on the part of the Palestinian guerrilla organizations. The approximately 500,000 Palestinians in Sinai and the Gaza Strip, as well as the approximately 800,000 Palestinians on the West Bank under Israeli occupation, could now envisage an alternate future that they might be able to help shape themselves should there be a settlement and Israeli withdrawal from the conquered territories. Prior to the 1967 war, the prospects of the Palestinians had not been bright. In 1948, for example, Hajj Amin al-Husseini had declared an all-Palestine government in Gaza, but it had come to nothing. The Egyptians had severely restricted the movement of Palestinians in Gaza, and King Hussein had done his best to efface the separate identity of Palestinians in the West Bank. Most Palestinians could look forward only to the possibility of remaining under Egyptian, Jordanian, Lebanese, or Syrian control. Israeli occupation, however, encouraged the evolution of Palestinian nationalism and the emergence of new leaders not associated with the Arab governments and Arab armies that had so dismally failed the Palestinians in 1967.

For a decade after 1949, primarily because Arab Palestine as envisaged by the partition resolution did not come into being, the plight of the displaced Palestinian Arabs was considered by all parties concerned as a humanitarian issue to be resolved within the context of the relationship between Israel and the existing Arab states. Arab leaders certainly did not see the Palestinians as a separate political/national group, nor did most of the refugees define themselves in such terms. Egypt kept a tight rein on the Gaza Strip, and Jordan annexed the Old City of Jerusalem and the West Bank of the Jordan River. No manifestations of Palestinian nationalism were allowed. The Jordanian king was the only ruler in the Arab world to extend citizenship to Palestinians who desired to become Jordanian citizens, but this was less out of altruism than a desire to legitimize the annexation of Arab Palestine and to utilize the talents of many of the Palestinian Arabs in a kingdom that had consisted until then largely of Bedouin and peasant farmers. The Christian government of Lebanon did not wish to tip the confessional balance of its population in favor of Muslims, and the Syrian government refused to integrate the Palestinians, as this would be a form of recognition of Israel.

The Palestinians themselves, up to June 1967, for the most part tended to rely on the Arab governments and to believe that Arab unity was the key to the liberation of Palestine from the Zionists. There were, as we have seen, fedayeen attacks against Israel from across the various borders, and, indeed, unorganized guerrilla groups undertook raids in order to encourage a renewal of the conflict between the Arab states and Israel. It was precisely to avoid being drawn into hostilities at a time and place not of their own choosing that the Arab governments had attempted to control the guerrillas through the formation of the Palestine Liberation Organization (PLO) and the Palestine Liberation Army (PLA) in 1964. Popular armed struggle was not part of their plan, and the PLA had been the instrument of the sponsoring Arab governments, to be used only as a conventional army. Moreover, Ahmad Shuqayri's chief activity had been to pontificate about how the Arabs were going to push the Jews into the sea. Needless to say, among the Palestinians, the old PLO under Shuqayri was entirely discredited in 1967, along with the Arab governments that had sponsored it; and a new type of guerrilla organization appeared, one not tied to any Arab government but committed to the tactic of armed struggle.

The PLO Covenant and Armed Struggle

Israel's control of the Gaza Strip and the West Bank, its destruction of commando bases and houses of those suspected of harboring or aiding fedayeen, and its expulsion of suspected troublemakers presented problems for the Palestinian movements, of course. Nevertheless, Palestinian resistance achieved enormous popularity among the masses and became an important factor in the Arab–Israeli equation through highly publicized attacks from across the borders. The incident at Karameh in March 1968 was particularly important in this regard. Karameh was a Palestinian camp and guerrilla base in Jordan where Palestinian fighters aided by elements of the Jordanian army fiercely resisted an Israeli assault and inflicted heavy casualties (twenty-six killed and seventy wounded) on the enemy.

In July 1968, at a meeting of the Palestine National Council (PNC) in Cairo, the original PLO covenant—drafted when the PLO was formed in 1964—was amended. Both old and new articles negated Israel's right to exist and included the principle of armed struggle in the liberation of Palestine. (See Document 7–1.) In Article 10 of the new document, the fedayeen were named as the nucleus of the armed struggle. As we shall see, this statement had implications for Jordan as well as Israel. In resolutions adopted in the same period, the PNC suggested that Israel be replaced by a "democratic, secular" state. As Palestinians themselves admitted, this was a euphemism for propaganda purposes to dismantle Israel and was intended to replace the admittedly ineffective slogan of "driving the Jews into the sea." Israel insisted that the covenant be disavowed or changed before it would even consider dealing with the PLO. Ahmad Shuqayri had resigned as chairman of the old PLO in December 1967, but the PLO continued to serve as an umbrella organization for the various guerrilla groups. (See Chart 7–1.) Within two years after the war, al-Fatah had emerged as the most important group within the PLO; and in 1969, the PNC elected its leader, Yasser Arafat (Abu Ammar), chairman of the executive committee, a position he retained until his death in 2004. Although the PLO has a centralized structure on paper (see Chart 7–2), and the PNC met at regular intervals, all important decisions continued to be made by Arafat himself in consultation with his closest associates in al-Fatah.

Fatah became the largest and most popular Palestinian organization for several reasons. One was its desire and ability, for the most part, to avoid too close an identification with any one Arab country, thus enabling it to stay clear of inter-Arab quarrels. With diverse sources of support, it was not required to follow a particular political line. Indeed, Fatah's very lack of

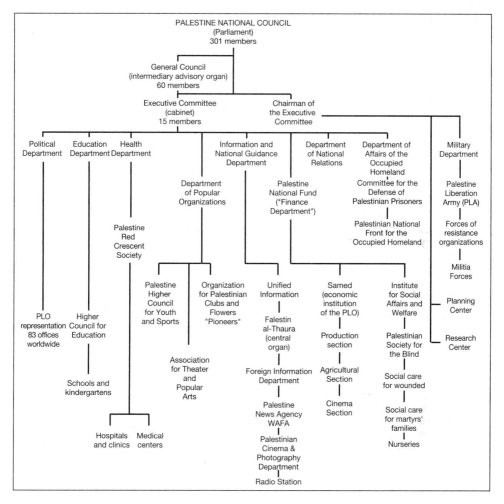

CHART 7–1   Structure of the PLO in the Mid 1980s.

Source: Shaul Mishal, *The Plo Under Arafat: Between Gun and Olive Branch* (New Haven, Conn.: Yale University Press, 1986), Appendix 1.

specific ideology and doctrinal vagueness also enabled it to attract followers, unlike some of the smaller groups that often put ideology ahead of the national struggle. Fatah at the start also had an appeal to some Muslim activists, who equated the religious cause with the national cause and who desired in the name of Islam to liberate Palestine from the Jews. Not surprisingly, all the PLO factions rejected the West, which they equated with Zionism and imperialism, and all were willing to accept aid and support from the Soviet Union. Some, however, like the Popular Front for the Liberation for Palestine (PFLP), led by Dr. George Habash, a Greek Orthodox Christian born in Lydda (now Lod, Israel), and the Democratic Front for the Liberation of Palestine (DFLP), led by Nayef Hawatmeh, a Jordanian Christian, became overtly Marxist-Leninist in ideology. These groups believed that there had to be fundamental social and economic changes in the Arab world itself, and especially that there had to be revolutionary change

PLO MAINSTREAM

Al Fatah

Yasir Arafat: PLO chairman, leader of Al Fatah... believed to have been born in 1929 in Cairo or Gaza, though Mr. Arafat said he came from Jerusalem, the home of his mother's family... in early 1950s, a student leader in Cairo among Palestinians and in the Muslim Brotherhood... in 1957 moved to Kuwait... founding member of Al Fatah in 1959... became chairman of PLO executive in 1969... moved to Lebanon in 1970, after Jordan fought and then expelled Palestinian guerrillas... moved to Tunis after 1982 Israeli invasion ousted PLO from Lebanon... returned to Gaza in 1994... elected President of Palestinian Authority in 1996. Died in November, 2004.

Saleh Khalef: Was Al Fatah's No. 2 leader... born in 1933 in Jaffa... friend of Mr. Arafat from their Cairo-Kuwait days and founding member of Al Fatah... viewed as more radical than Mr. Arafat... in early 1970s, was associated with Black September terror group... identified by British journalist Alan Hart as mastermind of 1972 seizure of Israeli athletes at Munich Olympics... Nom de guerre: Abu Iyad. Assassinated 1991 at hands of Abu Nidal.

Khalil al-Wazir: Close friend of Arafat since student days in Cairo and founding member of Al Fatah... a favorite of Arafat, he was mastermind of many large terrorist operations... in 1980s coordinated terrorist attacks in Israel and in the occupied territories... PLO political liaison to the Intifada. ... Nom de guerre: Abu Jihad. Assassinated by Israeli hit team in 1988 in Tunis.

PLO RADICALS

Popular Front for the Liberation of Palestine

George Habash: Born in Lydda (now Lod, Israel) in 1926 to a Greek Orthodox Christian family... studied medicine at American University of Beirut... in 1968, helped found Popular Front, now second-biggest group in PLO... moved to Beirut, then Damascus... one-time advocate of hijackings and other acts of terrorism... a Marxist revolutionary implacably opposed to recognizing Israel's right to exist... opposed decision to accept United Nations resolutions envisioning Israeli withdrawal from occupied land in exchange for peace.

Democratic Front for the Liberation of Palestine

Nayef Hawatmeh: Born in Salt, Jordan, in 1935 to Greek Catholic parents... degree in social psychology from Arab University in Beirut... helped found Popular Front, but broke away to create Democratic Front, which considers itself more pragmatic... in 1974, was first PLO figure to advocate a "mini-state" in occupied territories.

Arab Liberation Front

Abdul Rahim Ahmed: His movement formed as Iraqi response to Syrian support of other Palestinian groups.

Palestine Liberation Front

Mohammed Abu Abbas: Known as Abul Abbas... masterminded 1985 hijacking of cruise ship Achille Lauro... captured by U.S. forces in Iraq, April, 2003; died in prison in March 2004 of natural causes.

PARTIES OPPOSED TO PLO

Popular Front for the Liberation of Palestine-General Command

Ahmad Jibril: Born in Jaffa in 1928... broke with Popular Front over its emphasis on class conflict... closely aligned with Syria... some in group linked to technologically sophisticated acts of terrorism, such as barometrically triggered bombs, like that which blew up Pan Am 103 over Lockerbie, Scotland in 1988.

Popular Struggle Front

Samir Gosheh: Broke with Mr. Habash in 1960s... leads splinter group committed to Arab nationalism... thought to display greater independence from Syria than Mr. Jibril.

Fatah dissidents

Saed Musa: Broke with Mr. Arafat in 1983 in Syrian-sponsored revolt... widely known as Abu Musa... had been regarded as a military hero because of actions in Lebanon during its civil war and 1982 Israeli invasion.

Saiqa

Considered an integral part of Syrian military machine with only nominal Palestinian identity.

Fatah Revolutionary Council

Abu Nidal: Believed to have been born in Jaffa in 1937... real name Sabry al-Banna... came from rich merchant family, later lived in a refugee camp tent... studied engineering at Cairo University... PLO representative in Baghdad but broke with PLO in 1974... expelled from Iraq in 1983 and moved to Syria—engaged in numerous terrorist attacks against both Arab and Jewish targets—expelled from Syria in 1987 and moved to Libya—moved to Egypt in 1998... expelled from Egypt later that year... died in Iraq, 2002.

Source: Adapted from *The New York Times*, January 22, 1989, Section E, p. 5. Copyright © 1989 by The New York Times Co. Reprinted with permission.

CHART 7–2 Brief Description of Important PLO Groups and Leaders

Palestinian terrorist or heroine: airplane hijacker Leila Khaled.

in the conservative Arab states like Jordan and Saudi Arabia even before the liberation of Palestine.

The PFLP, DFLP, and other splinter groups like the PFLP–General Command, led by Ahmad Jibril, began the tactic of hijacking airplanes in 1968 and initiated other terrorist attacks against civilians outside the Middle East in order to draw attention to the Palestinian cause. Terrorism was condemned by the world community, which seemed powerless or unwilling to do much about it, but it served the Palestinian cause by encouraging the passage of resolutions in the UN General Assembly and other forums that recognize as legitimate the aspirations of the Palestinian people and their right to self-determination. Although there was always diversity and fragmentation over questions of ideology and tactics within the PLO, Yasser Arafat was unable, and perhaps unwilling, to eliminate his more extreme rivals. While using the extremists as a convenient excuse to retain freedom of action, Arafat became their hostage as well, at least until recent years.

The PLO and the Arab States

As for the Arab states, Egypt prevented the Palestinians from operating within or from its territory. Syria and Iraq, however, sponsored their own commando units. These had to follow the political ideology and goals of the host government and were kept on a short leash. The fragmented government of Lebanon was much more vulnerable both to PLO activities within its borders and to punitive reprisals by Israel for terrorist actions against Israel that emanated from Lebanon. In Jordan, the PLO became a serious threat to political stability. It prevented King Hussein from considering any negotiated settlement with Israel that did not include the PLO; it invited Israeli retaliation for its activities; and both indirectly and directly it undermined the monarchy through the PLO covenant's avowed intention to liberate all of mandatory Palestine and the leftists' death threats against the U.S.-supported king. In 1966, Shuqayri had declared: "We must liberate Amman before we liberate Tel Aviv." Palestinian anger intensified when Hussein seemed receptive to a plan of U.S. Secretary of State William Rogers in June 1970 that called for Israeli withdrawal from the occupied territories in return for recognition of the Jewish state.

The PLO became so much like a state within a state in Jordan that eventually there was a showdown with Hussein. This occurred after Palestinians hijacked three airplanes to Amman (Jordan's capital) in September 1970 and subsequently blew them up on the ground, making the king appear impotent. After bloody confrontations between the Jordanian army and Palestinian commandos, in which around 3,000 Palestinian fedayeen were killed, and the Jordanians turned back Syrian tanks, Hussein reasserted his control. He could not have succeeded, however, without the support of Israel, which, at the request of the United States, had threatened to intervene to prevent Syrian success. At that time, the Syrian Air Force commander was Hafez al-Assad, later Syria's president, who was afraid of Israeli–U.S. intervention and refused to provide air cover for the Syrian tanks. By July 1971, Hussein had expelled PLO terrorists and fighters from Jordanian territory. This crisis provides another example of the underlying common interest between King Hussein and Israel. It also demonstrated to the United States that Israel could be a reliable, effective American ally in the region.

Another important result of these events was the spawning of a new terrorist group, called Black September, an arm of al-Fatah. Its first act was the murder of the Jordanian prime minister, Wasfi Tell, in Cairo in November 1971. The next year, at the 1972 Olympic Games in Munich, Black September was responsible for the deaths of eleven Israeli athletes. Another result of the showdown in Jordan was the removal of the PLO to Lebanon, where their military and political activities were a significant factor in the Lebanese civil war that began in 1975 and in the unraveling of that fractured country.

For many reasons—some of which were adroit public relations efforts, terrorist exploits, sympathy for and popularity of "liberation movements" all over the world, and perceived Israeli intransigence—the Palestinian cause was soon being described as the "crux" of the issue in the Arab–Israeli dispute. Not only in the United Nations but in the capitals of the world, as well as in the deliberations of regional and international conferences, the right of the Palestinian people to self-determination was recognized. Israeli prime minister Golda Meir in the late 1960s remarked that there was no such thing as a Palestinian people as a distinct national group within the Arab nation. This statement may have been technically correct when it was uttered, but Palestinian nationalism certainly became a reality. This was especially true after 1967 for several reasons: the absence of a negotiated settlement between the Arab states and Israel; the failure of the Palestinians to achieve repatriation or resettlement (except in Jordan) within the Arab world; the circumstances of continued occupation, first by the Arabs, and then by Israel; and finally the success of their self-generated resistance, given the opportunity to seize the initiative after 1967. This situation fostered and nurtured the feeling of a separate identity among the Palestinian people, and what was originally perceived by many as a refugee problem did indeed become the problem of Palestinian nationalism.

Whether Palestinian nationalism or the inability of the Arabs to accept the reality and legitimacy of Israel's existence was the "crux" of the conflict is a moot question. In any event, the Palestinian question added urgency to the Arab–Israeli dispute after 1967 and made the search for a settlement even more complicated than it already was. Supporters of Israel insisted that the fundamental problem in the Arab–Israeli conflict was the inability of the Arabs to accept the sovereignty of the Jewish state. All Arabs, whether sympathetic or not to the plight of their Palestinian brothers, could unite behind the Palestinian cause so as to force concessions from Israel to relinquish territory in what Israelis saw as the first step toward the eventual dismantling of the Jewish nation. Nevertheless, the Palestinian issue took on a life of its own.

Eventually, Palestinians in Gaza and the West Bank lived under Israeli occupation longer than they had been under Arab control; their destiny clearly diverged from that of their Arab brothers; and the Arab world eventually acquiesced in the designation of the PLO, rather than any Arab government, as the sole, legitimate representative of the Palestinian people.

Diplomacy, the War of Attrition, and the Rogers Plan

Security Council Resolution 242 of 1967 had provided for a UN special mediator to help achieve a settlement following the 1967 war. Gunnar Jarring of Sweden was appointed and began his mission in late December 1967. He made little headway in his meetings with the various governments, meetings that lasted throughout 1968; the Israelis wanted direct negotiations with the Arab states, and the Arabs insisted on indirect negotiations and the withdrawal of Israel from all the occupied territories. The diplomatic effort stalled, although bilateral talks between Egypt and the United States took place in the last few months of the Johnson presidency in an attempt to keep the Jarring mission alive. When Richard Nixon became U.S. president in January 1969, he sought ways both to improve relations with Egypt and Syria, which had broken off diplomatic relations after 1967, and to keep Israel militarily at an advantage. Nixon believed these policies would offset Russian influence and prevent another conflict. The United States also opted initially to work through the United Nations and in concert with the Big Four powers—the United States, Britain, France, and the Soviet Union—to try to find ways out of the diplomatic impasse, but with no immediate result.

Meanwhile, the Soviets had resupplied the Egyptians and Syrians with ammunition, tanks, and planes. Egypt launched commando attacks and shelled Israeli positions across the Suez Canal, and in October 1968, an Egyptian missile boat sank an Israeli destroyer off the coast of Sinai. The Israelis responded with retaliatory raids, sometimes penetrating deep into Egyptian territory. As Egyptian artillery barrages increased, however, the Israelis began construction of the Bar-Lev line of fortifications (named for the then Israeli chief of staff) along the length of the Suez Canal. The Egyptians bombarded the fortifications repeatedly in an effort to destroy them, and Egyptian commando units continued to cross the Suez Canal to sabotage and harass. In the spring of 1969, Nasser announced that the cease-fire of June 1967 was null and void, and the "War of Attrition" was officially launched. This war was costly to both sides. Although the Egyptians did not release casualty figures, they lost many men, and the economy was again sacrificed to the exigencies of combat. Israel, with over 200 dead, suffered more casualties than in the Six-Day War. Evidently, Nasser believed that he could inflict such a heavy toll that the Israelis would retreat back into the Sinai, and/or that they would become more amenable to a political solution on Egypt's terms.

Egyptian success, however, led Israel to commit its air power, and in mid-1969, Israel began to bomb Egyptian gun emplacements on the west bank of the Suez Canal and to undertake deep-penetration raids into Egyptian territory. The situation began to escalate, and another full-scale war became more likely. In January 1970, Nasser made a secret trip to Moscow to request more sophisticated weapons, including planes capable of offensive strikes against Israel. The Russians believed advanced aircraft would increase the likelihood of war and would encourage the United States to step up arms deliveries to Israel. Although the Soviets would not supply the planes, it did agree to participate more actively in the air defense of Egypt and to send Egypt surface-to-air missiles (SAMs) along with Russian crews to man them. By the end of June 1970, Soviet pilots were flying patrols all along the Canal Zone, Soviet military advisors and technicians were supervising Egypt's armed forces, and the Soviets were dramatically increasing their presence in the eastern Mediterranean, building up a naval fleet and an infrastructure to handle and repair Soviet ships. To America, the eastern Mediterranean began to look more and more like a Soviet lake.

Gamal Abdul Nasser in his last official act on September 27, 1970, mediating between PLO chief Yasser Arafat and King Hussein of Jordan.

The United States, watching these developments and concerned about Britain's intention to pull out of bases and installations east of Suez by 1971, attempted to improve relations with the Arab world and thereby prevent further Soviet encroachment. The United States continued to support Israel militarily and diplomatically (casting its veto in the Security Council when there were anti-Israel resolutions, for example). However, Secretary of State William Rogers, in a December 1969 statement, proclaimed that U.S. policy henceforth would be more "even-handed." In June 1970, the Rogers Plan was announced. It enunciated the principle of Israeli withdrawal from the occupied territories in return for recognition, provided for a ninety-day cease-fire at the Suez Canal, and called for a renewal of the Jarring mission. Nasser announced Egypt's intention to accept the proposal after a frustrating and prolonged visit (for medical treatment) to Moscow in late June and July. Israel also accepted, albeit with misgivings about Nasser's intentions.

The cease-fire along the canal came into effect in August 1970. Unfortunately for the negotiating process, however, its provisions were violated almost immediately by Egypt, which used the occasion of the military standstill to move the Soviet SAM missiles into the Canal Zone. With the missiles in forward positions, Egypt increased its ability to cross the canal, since the missiles would cover the Israel side on the east bank and neutralize the Israeli air force. Egypt and Jordan accepted the renewed Jarring mission, but Israel refused until Egypt stopped the movement of the missiles. The talks resumed in December, after the United States promised to give Israel increased economic and military aid. Gunnar Jarring made an attempt in the next few months to bring the two sides together, but nothing came of his efforts.

Some observers believe there were missed opportunities in the months that followed and lay the blame on Israel, insisting that the Arab states had modified their position by 1970. Anwar Sadat, who became Egyptian president on Nasser's death in September 1970, and Hafez al-Assad, who had assumed power in Syria in 1970, were much more pragmatic men than their predecessors, these critics argue, and Sadat was much more concerned with Egypt than with pan-Arab interests. Even King Hussein, they note, was inclined to be more flexible after his successful showdown with the Palestinians.

Critics further point out that Israel, under the leadership of Golda Meir, who had become prime minister in March 1969, distrusted the Arabs, felt secure in its military superiority, and preferred the status quo unless or until it could secure a peace on its own terms; namely, prior recognition by the Arabs of Israel's right to exist, direct peace negotiations, and the retention of territory deemed necessary to its security and survival. With Meir's tacit encouragement, and the more vocal assertiveness of Defense Minister Moshe Dayan, who was responsible for the administration of the conquered territories, Israel had begun a policy of "creeping annexation" (or "creating facts," in Dayan's terms). Jewish settlements began to appear in militarily strategic places in the Jordan Valley, the Golan Heights, the Gaza Strip, and the Sinai Peninsula.

This picture of Israeli intransigence is countered by other observers who point to public statements by Israeli leaders indicating flexibility and a desire to compromise, and they emphasize Israel's stated position that, in the context of face-to-face peace talks, every issue would be open to negotiation. They cite the fact that within Israel itself, debate existed from the very beginning on the question of the territories. At one extreme were supporters of the Land of Israel movement, who believed in the retention of the West Bank of the Jordan River on religious-historical grounds. Judea and Samaria, as they called the area, had been part of biblical and historical Israel. Dayan and others wanted to integrate the conquered territories on pragmatic grounds of security. Plans were proposed for the partial retention of territory, the most well-known being that proposed by Yigal Allon, the deputy prime minister, who wanted to retain a string of security outposts along the Jordan River and relinquish the rest. Other Israelis were vehement about the need to return the territories; they envisioned many of the practical and moral problems that confronted Israel as an occupier over the ensuing years. With so much difference of opinion internally, Meir's inclination in terms of any policy decision was to procrastinate. Therefore, in the absence of peace negotiations, the Israeli occupation continued as new realities in the territories emerged.

Détente and the Role of the Superpowers

Diplomatic efforts always have to be seen in context, of course, and between 1968 and 1973 not only was an actual, if unofficial, war going on between Egypt and Israel, but the Palestinians were also creating their own "facts" through guerrilla warfare, airplane hijackings, and other terrorist acts (such as the massacre of tourists at Israel's Lod airport and the murder of Israeli athletes at the Munich Olympics). Another factor in this period was the new era of détente between the United States and the Soviet Union, which brings us again to the role of the superpowers in the Middle East.

Détente, or the relaxation of tensions between the United States and the Soviet Union, had the effect, with regard to superpower involvement in the Middle East, of putting the Arab–Israeli conflict on the back burner. When President Richard Nixon first visited Moscow in May 1972, he and Soviet premier Leonid Brezhnev agreed to try to achieve a "military relaxation" in the Middle East, to be followed by a freezing of the situation. Neither superpower wanted to be dragged into a war on behalf of one of its clients, and there was a certain degree of cooperation in attempting to dampen the fires in the Middle East. This had the temporary effect, in terms of Soviet military aid to Egypt, of the Russians holding up or refusing advanced offensive weapons requested by the Egyptians, as we have seen. Such weapons would have enabled the Egyptians to continue the War of Attrition—and perhaps even launch a military offensive to recover lost territory.

To the Israelis, the present situation was quite satisfactory. They believed that they had secure and defensible borders, and that they were in a strong enough position to be able to force the Arabs eventually to make peace on their terms. They also felt confident in American support for their military requirements. No war was a plus, and no peace could be lived with. For the Arabs, no war and no peace was intolerable. This was especially true of the Palestinians. Ignored as they were by Resolution 242, the lack of any movement, either diplomatic or military, diminished any prospects they entertained of achieving self-determination. PLO groups did everything possible to hold the attention of the world, including the continuation of spectacular airline hijackings and terrorist activities.

Egypt Prepares for War

The existing situation was particularly problematic for Egypt, however. The war in Yemen had been exceedingly costly, as had the price of Egypt's defeat in 1967. The Egyptian economy was suffering greatly because of the loss of tourism and Suez Canal revenues, and because offshore and Sinai oil fields were in the hands of the Israelis. Egyptian socialism had taken on a Marxist tinge, with individual initiative stifled and the populace increasingly dependent on the state to satisfy all economic needs. No substantial outside economic aid alleviated the burden, and by the early 1970s, the Egyptian treasury was empty and the country almost bankrupt. Anwar Sadat was not able to get the arms he wanted from the Soviet Union, and the Egyptian army was restive. The Egyptian people had followed the charismatic Nasser almost sheepishly, but they were becoming more painfully aware after his death how he had mortgaged the social and economic development of Egypt to his political and military objectives. Sadat, lacking Nasser's charisma, faced mounting internal unrest and unease.

Sadat wrote in his autobiography that he believed the key to Egypt's political, military, and economic well-being was to redress the situation ensuing from the 1967 debacle—that the basic task was to wipe out the disgrace and humiliation of 1967 in order to regain self-confidence at home and the respect of the world community. If diplomacy failed, then Egypt should resort to war. Indeed, he embarked on a two-pronged approach, declaring 1971 to be the "year of decision" and also sending out diplomatic feelers. Sadat had extended the Rogers Plan in November; but in February 1971, after the second ninety-day cease-fire had expired, he said he would extend it again for one month only while Israel and the world had the chance to consider a new "initiative" that he proposed. If Israel were to withdraw to the Mitla and Gidi passes in the Sinai Peninsula, Sadat offered to reopen the Suez Canal, extend the Rogers Plan six months, officially declare a cease-fire, restore diplomatic relations with the United States, and sign a peace agreement with Israel contingent upon the fulfillment of the provisions of Resolution 242.

The political leadership of Egypt, which Sadat had inherited from Nasser, and which included several pro-Soviet ministers, was totally against this proposal. Since Egypt continued to insist that Resolution 242 committed Israel to withdraw completely from all occupied territory, Israel was loathe to accept a proposal such as Sadat's in advance of direct peace negotiations. Moshe Dayan had floated his own proposal for a mutual interim withdrawal, but the basic positions of Israel and Egypt were incompatible in the long run, and nothing came of his idea either. Gunnar Jarring was a persistent but not forceful mediator, and one wonders what would have happened had he been prepared to exert some pressure when opportunities such as those described here arose.

Meanwhile, in early March 1971, Sadat made the first of what would be four trips to Moscow. He wanted to secure replacement ammunition for the vast quantities lost in the War of Attrition. He also wanted to acquire deterrent weapons. The Soviets agreed to send missile-equipped aircraft and to train Egyptian crews—but only on the condition that the planes be used with prior Soviet permission, a condition Sadat angrily rejected. Shortly after his return to Cairo, having received no response to his "initiative," Sadat allowed the cease-fire to expire. The Soviets did send Egypt SAM missile batteries in April 1971, but they did not send any aircraft and replaced only part of the ammunition Sadat requested. Therefore, Sadat was not able to resume the War of Attrition, let alone embark on any decisive offensive. When the "year of decision" came and went without any military action, most observers decided that Arab rhetoric was at work again and that Egyptian threats were hollow.

The United States had taken the opportunity of Nasser's death to initiate contacts with Egypt and had noted Sadat's relative diplomatic flexibility compared with Nasser's. Rogers visited Egypt in early May 1971, the first visit by an American secretary of state in many years, but he was unsuccessful in attempts to get Egypt and Israel to work for an interim agreement. Sadat's "initiative," and flirtation with the United States, spurred the pro-Soviet cabal in Egypt to step up its activity against him. Sadat acted first, however, dismissing several key figures in the government in mid-May 1971. This action was followed shortly by a visit to Egypt by Soviet president Nikolai Podgorny, who pressed Egypt to sign a Treaty of Friendship and Cooperation. Sadat signed the agreement in late May 1971. Although the United States was deeply suspicious of this move, and indeed tended to view it as a confirmation of the worst fears about Sadat's intentions, the Egyptian president saw the treaty as the only way to allay Soviet fears and to get the arms he wanted.

The Soviets subsequently sent Egypt arms, but not the ones the Egyptians had requested. Sadat made three more trips to Moscow, in October 1971 and in February and April of 1972. Convinced that the Russians would always constrain him, he became angry and disillusioned. Moreover, in July 1972, after Richard Nixon's visit to Moscow, and in the spirit of détente, the United States and the Soviet Union issued a joint communique that hardly mentioned the Middle East and did not refer at all to Resolution 242. Sadat determined that the superpowers had agreed to freeze the situation, which would perpetuate Egypt's military disadvantage.

Yet Sadat had always meant what he said about retaining a military option. He was determined to recover the lost territory either by diplomacy or by force. He reasoned that even a limited war would help him achieve his aims by at least forcing the international community to turn its attention once again to the Middle East. Clearly, his first priority was Egypt; Palestinian goals had little to do with Egyptian military planning. Sadat first removed the 15,000 or so Soviet military technicians and military personnel in Egypt, in order to have the freedom of action to go to war. Accordingly, he dismissed the Russian advisors in July 1972. This move was completely misinterpreted in the West and in Israel. In the United States and in Israel, it was widely assumed that Sadat was making some gesture of conciliation toward the West and that he could not go to war without active Soviet involvement. Yet that is precisely what he intended to do.

Sadat and the Egyptians were disenchanted with the Russians. The Soviet advisors had been resented for their high-handedness, patronizing attitude, and tendency to look down upon the Egyptians. Sadat also saw the United States as the only power capable of bringing about a solution, because only the United States could exert pressure on the Israelis. He wanted and needed direct U.S. involvement for political and diplomatic reasons at the same time that he needed the Soviet Union for arms and military supplies. There was little interaction with the United States after the Rogers visit in May 1971, largely because of Sadat's treaty with the Russians. Rogers had left office in 1972 and was replaced as secretary of state by Henry Kissinger, who had previously been Nixon's national security advisor. Kissinger would eventually be a key player, but 1972 was not only a year of détente but also an American presidential election year, when U.S. foreign policy initiatives are usually on hold. In early February 1973, following Nixon's reelection victory, Hafez Ismail, Sadat's representative, met in Washington with Kissinger, who, in effect, told him that although the United States could exert pressure on Israel, it could not impose its will, and that the Egyptians would have to offer something in exchange for Israeli withdrawal from the occupied territories.

Despite the strained relationship between Egypt and the Soviet Union, therefore, the official ties remained. The Soviets were also more amenable to Egyptian arms requirements by the spring of 1973. Earlier, in January, the United States had decided to ship arms to Saudi Arabia and Kuwait and, after Golda Meir's visit to Washington in March, had agreed to sell Israel Phantom F-4E fighter-bombers and other military hardware. The Soviets responded by shipping Egypt SCUD surface-to-surface missiles as a deterrent. The shipment of the SCUDs seems to have been a turning point in Sadat's decision to go to war. Moreover, by 1973, the Egyptian military and intelligence services had been completely overhauled, and a sophisticated battle plan had been conceived.

Part of the Egyptian plan was for a two-front attack against Israel, which meant that the Syrians would have to play a role. President Assad was more than amenable. He believed not only in the cause but also in the use of conventional force to achieve it, unlike his mercurial predecessor, Salah Jadid, who had relied so heavily on guerrilla operations. Syria wanted to regain the Golan Heights and its strategic advantage—and, if possible, to carry the war into Israel. It will be recalled that Syria did not accept Resolution 242; and Syria continued to reject, even implicitly, Israel's right to exist. Sadat also had general discussions with King Feisal of Saudi Arabia about the possible use of oil as a weapon in any future hostilities, and this tactic was generally approved by May 1973. Feelers were put out to King Hussein, who was not made privy to all the details of the impending operation but who was glad once again to be on the side of the Arab consensus. Egypt had severed diplomatic relations with Jordan after Hussein, in March 1972, had proposed a federal-type plan for the west and east banks of the Jordan that implied the recognition of Israel.

While talks were going on among the Arabs, the United States and the Soviet Union were discussing détente at the second summit meeting that took place in June 1973. Almost simultaneously with discussions about détente, however, came massive infusions of Soviet weapons into Egypt (including the SCUD missiles) and into Syria, where the Soviets supplied a surface-to-air missile system and FROG surface-to-surface missiles. The Soviets acted in a pragmatic manner throughout; having built up an impressive war machine, they were not simply going to abandon Egypt.

Many analysts have noted that Israel did not believe, even at this late date, and in the face of clear evidence and public declarations by Sadat, that Egypt would go to war. The Israeli intelligence services had all the information they needed, but they failed to evaluate it properly. Their thinking was colored in large part by the notion that Israel had defensible borders, was militarily superior, and that the Arabs would not strike a first blow. Israeli thinking was also shaped by the belief that the Arabs would be deterred by their nuclear option. Even when war was imminent, on the morning of October 6, the total mobilization (including the reserves) requested by Chief of Staff David Elazar was opposed by Defense Minister Dayan as superfluous. (A later meeting in the prime minister's office resulted in a compromise call-up of 100,000 Israeli troops.) When it became clear that hostilities were about to commence, the Israeli military was constrained from making a preemptive attack by the government's own assessment, and by the warning of Secretary of State Henry Kissinger, that to do so would be to forfeit the goodwill and assistance of the United States.

The 1973 War and its Aftermath

On October 6, 1973, Egypt and Syria attacked Israel in what the Israelis call the Yom Kippur War. This is because the conflict broke out on the Jewish Day of Atonement. To the Arabs, it was the Ramadan war since Muslims were in the midst of the holy month of Ramadan. The Egyptian code name for the war was "Operation Badr," referring to the site of the Prophet Muhammad's first victory over the pagan Arabs in Arabia. Again, we shall leave the details of the military

Golda Meir, Israeli prime minister during the October 1973 war.

operations to the military historians, although weapons never before used in combat were employed and there were many noteworthy operations, from the Egyptian crossing of the Suez Canal, to the recrossing of the canal by the Israelis, to the furious and deadly tank battles on the Golan Heights—the largest since World War II.

The October 1973 war destroyed many myths. It proved, for example, that the Arabs could cooperate and that they could keep their intentions a secret. It demonstrated that they were capable of sophisticated intelligence gathering and analysis and of a brilliant operational plan to cross the Suez Canal and demolish the Bar-Lev line. It showed that Arab soldiers could fight bravely and well when properly trained and motivated and that they could handle the most technologically advanced weapons. It proved that Israel was not invincible. Israel turned the tide, but only with difficulty, and not without having come perilously close to running out of ammunition until an American airlift began to arrive on October 14. Indeed, although Secretary of State Kissinger had been kept informed of Israeli losses of planes, tanks, and ammunition in the first week of the war, he withheld American aid in the hope that Israel would accept a cease-fire in place. This, he believed, would preserve the sense of Arab victory and honor and perhaps break the diplomatic stalemate of the Arab–Israeli conflict.

However, by October 11, it was clear that a massive Soviet airlift was under way to both Egypt and Syria. Kissinger (having been given pretty much a free hand by President Nixon, who was mired in the Watergate scandal) decided, in the face of this Soviet challenge, that the military balance had to be restored in Israel's favor in order for the United States to retain influence and leverage in the region. With a massive infusion of material from the United States, Israel captured Mount Hermon and advanced to within 40 kilometers of Damascus in the north. In the south, an Israeli army unit led by Ariel Sharon recrossed the Suez Canal and commanded the approaches to Cairo. A Soviet–American cease-fire proposal was approved by the United Nations on October 22, but violations by both sides resulted in the continuation of hostilities and in the surrounding and trapping of the Egyptian Third Army in the western Sinai. After Soviet threats to intercede, and an American military alert—just short of a nuclear alert—a second cease-fire was accepted by both parties on October 24, with Israel the obvious military victor.

TABLE 7-1   **Estimated Losses, October War, 1973**

	Israel	Arab Total	Egypt	Syria	Jordan	Iraq	Other Arabs
Personnel							
Killed	2,838*	8,528	5,000	3,100	28	218	100
Wounded	8,800*	19,549	12,000	6,000	49	600	300
Prisoners or Missing	508	8,551	8,031	500		20	?
Tanks**	840	2,554	1,100	1,200	54	200	?
APCs	400	850+	450	400		?	?
Artillery Pieces	?	550+	300	250		?	?
SAM Batteries		47	44	3			?
Aircraft	103	392	223	118		21	30
Helicopters	6	55	42	13		?	?
Naval Vessels		1	15	10	5		

*About 10% has been added to officially reported Israeli casualties to represent approximately the wounded who died of their injuries, and the fact that official Israeli figures apparently do not include those wounded not evacuated from aid stations and field hospitals.

**Tanks destroyed or put out of action for one or more days. For instance, the Israelis seem to have repaired and returned to operation about 400 of the tank losses shown here. They also recovered about 300 repairable Arab tanks.

Source: Trevor N. Dupuy, *Elusive Victory: The Arab–Israeli Wars, 1947–1974* (New York: Harper & Row, 1978), p. 609. Reprinted by permission of Hero Books.

But it was a war that Israel had come very close to losing, and it had lasting effects in that country. Israel suffered over 2,800 dead and 8,500 wounded (see Table 7–1), and the direct monetary costs were $4 billion. The war was an emotional and psychological shock that exposed some serious problems. One was Israel's overconfidence that had prevented accurate intelligence assessments. Others were a lack of appreciation for Arab abilities; a static defense line that proved to be a liability; and a generally erroneous concept of defensible borders that were not as defensible as had been thought. The war also indicated to the Israelis that the military, economic, and diplomatic balance was shifting in the direction of the Arab states, and in any future conflict the task of defending Israel would be correspondingly greater. Furthermore, Israel was increasingly to feel a sense of diplomatic isolation in the world community.

Israel became more and more dependent on the United States, not only for military but also for economic aid, since the war cost Israel about one-third of its yearly budget for 1973. The Arab oil embargo and the resulting skyrocketing price of energy, which was another feature of this war, also hurt Israel. The war weakened the Labor government, which had led Israel since 1948, and virtually ended the political careers of Golda Meir and Moshe Dayan. In a few short years, the Likud coalition, headed by Menachem Begin, would be voted into office. This occurred in 1977, and it reflected the polarity that had developed in Israel after the 1973 war on a number of issues, including the disposition of the occupied territories. The disengagement agreements between Egypt and Israel that heralded some movement toward the exchange of territory in the Sinai in return for recognition tended to encourage Israeli hardliners to dig in their heels on the issue of the West Bank. The Labor government itself, in the face of political challenges and new developments concerning King Hussein and the PLO, gave the go-ahead to civilian, as opposed to military/security, settlements on the West Bank. This issue and other matters affecting and complicating negotiations will be discussed in the next chapter.

The Arabs lost the October war militarily; more than 8,500 Arab lives were lost and over 19,500 were wounded. As Table 7–1 indicates, Egypt especially suffered. The Arabs, however, won an important psychological victory, and, even more crucial, they won the war diplomatically. The war did indeed jolt the attention of the world back to the Arab–Israeli conflict and provided the impetus for Kissinger and for American diplomacy to mediate the dispute. UN Security Council Resolution 338 secured the cease-fire, but it was a cease-fire worked out by Kissinger in Moscow. (See Document 7–2.) Resolution 338 was extremely important because it called for direct negotiations between the parties concerned under appropriate auspices to implement Resolution 242 in all its parts. After one meeting of a peace conference, convened in Geneva in December 1973, however, a comprehensive approach was scuttled in favor of Kissinger's "step-by-step" diplomacy. The United States became the primary superpower player in the region, a role capped by the part it played in an eventual peace treaty between Egypt and Israel in 1979.

Conversely, the Russians lost ground in the Middle East. They had had no diplomatic relations with Israel since 1967 and had lost their influence and base in Egypt. Syria, therefore, became the keystone of the Soviets' Middle East policy, and they continued to press for comprehensive negotiations as a way of playing a role in the region.

As for the Palestinians, the PLO emerged stronger as a result of the war. The Arab League, meeting at Rabat in 1974, recognized the PLO as the "sole, legitimate representative of the Palestinian people," undermining the role of King Hussein and his ability to speak for the Palestinians as envisaged by UN resolutions. (See Documents 7–3 and 7–4.) King Hussein agreed to honor the PLO's claim to negotiate for the Palestinians (and was rewarded with an annual $300-million grant for four years from the Arab League). He further stated that it was "totally inconceivable" that Jordan and a Palestinian entity could form a federation—a suggestion he had floated earlier. Perhaps the real significance of the Rabat summit was that this decision meant that Hussein was forced to acknowledge Palestinian rights to what he had lost physically to the Israelis in 1967. It was a diplomatic triumph for the PLO that repaid the defeat of Black September in 1970. The Rabat decision also weakened the American position. Kissinger agreed with the Israelis that it was preferable to negotiate with Hussein rather than with the PLO.

The mainstream PLO groups scaled down their demands. Statements in 1974 suggest that the PLO was willing to forgo a "secular, democratic state" in all of Palestine and to settle for a state in any territory evacuated by Israel. Continuing PLO terrorism, however, and attempts to sabotage the Kissinger shuttle missions and the diplomatic process altogether worked against any moderation of the PLO position.

The Arab Embargo and the Oil Weapon

The Arab oil embargo was probably one of the most significant features of the 1973 hostilities. During the war, on October 17, OAPEC, the Organization of Arab Oil-Producing Countries, including Saudi Arabia, a traditional friend of the United States, imposed a total embargo on oil exports to America. The oil cartel also placed embargoes of varying degrees on other countries, depending upon the extent of their support for Israel, and announced monthly production cuts. Two months later, on December 23, 1973, the Organization of Petroleum Exporting Countries (OPEC), of which the Arab oil states were members, announced a fourfold increase in the posted price of oil to $11.65 per barrel.

Until this time, OPEC, which had been formed in 1960, had achieved only moderate success in its goal of bringing about higher oil prices and profits and a greater share in oil production. During the 1960s, however, OPEC members began increasingly to cooperate, and in 1971, inspired by the success of Libya's Muammar al-Qaddafi, who had come to power in 1969 and who had gotten higher oil prices and more revenue from higher taxes on profits, they won important pricing concessions from the oil companies. By 1973, several OPEC countries

(Algeria, Libya, Iraq, and Iran) had nationalized their oil and taken over full production. It was the October 1973 war, however, that enabled the Arab countries in OPEC for the first time to utilize oil as a weapon.

The effect of the oil embargo on the economies of the European countries—and their subsequent change of attitude toward Israel in the United Nations—was even more dramatic than the Arabs had hoped for. In 1973, the Arab states produced 37 percent of the oil consumed by the non-Communist world, and the participation in the embargo by Saudi Arabia, which produced over 7.5 million barrels per day (approximately 40 percent of Arab production and the third largest producer in the world), ensured the success of the embargo. American production, on the other hand, had decreased during the three previous years. The nations totally boycotted, in addition to the United States, included the Netherlands (the Dutch port of Rotterdam was the largest refinery and transshipment center in Europe), Canada, Portugal, Rhodesia, and South Africa. Britain, France, and Spain were exempted. According to a 1974 Department of Energy report, the embargo, which lasted five months, until March 1974, cost the United States 500,000 jobs and a $10 billion to $20 billion loss in its gross national product.

Politically, the impact was equally effective. On November 6, 1973, the European Economic Community (EEC) meeting in Brussels called on Israel and Egypt to return to the October 22 cease-fire lines (before Israel had completed the encirclement of the Egyptian Third Army). More significantly, the EEC urged Israel to end its occupation of the territory seized in 1967 and stated that the "legitimates rights" of the Palestinians must be taken into account in any settlement. In December, Japan also urged Israel to withdraw totally from occupied Arab territory. The Arabs rewarded these movements toward their position by exempting Japan and Europe from cuts in oil supplies. The embargo against the United States ended only after America had strenuously exerted itself in mediation efforts that resulted in a disengagement agreement between Israel and Egypt in 1974 and the resumption of U.S.–Egyptian diplomatic relations.

Some mention should be made at this point of the use and limitations of the so-called oil weapon. There is a widespread perception that the oil-producing nations can use their oil policies to favor those who cooperate with them and to punish those who do not. For entirely opposite reasons, it is in the interests of both the Arab states and Israel to encourage this perception. There is no denying that the OAPEC cartel benefited from this fear of an oil weapon. For example, France agreed to sell Iraq equipment to help develop a nuclear capability in exchange for oil. Similarly, Saudi Arabia threatened a cutback in oil production if Congress refused to sell it American AWAC radar aircraft. Many commentators believe that the UN General Assembly resolution of November 1975, which described Israel as a racist regime in occupied Palestine, and which equated Zionism with racism, underscored the effectiveness of oil as an Arab weapon against Israel. The Senate Energy Committee concluded in 1980 that oil was not merely an economic commodity but was also "a source of enormous political leverage in the hands of the oil-producing nations." The Persian Gulf region would increase dramatically in importance over the next twenty years, and this had a significant effect on the geopolitical balance in the Middle East. The oil of this region was, and still is, critically important to the world economy (Europe imports 85 percent and Japan 90 percent of their oil needs from the Persian Gulf states).

Not all commentators agree with this assessment, however. Some argue, for example, that Arab oil producers will act in their own economic interests, and that as long as so many OPEC countries are dependent on oil revenues exclusively to fuel their own economies, there is no need to fear the oil weapon. They point out that OPEC decisions to limit production and raise prices were goals that predated the 1973 war. Moreover, efforts by the industrialized nations to conserve energy and to discover and exploit alternate sources of fuel, the oil glut of the 1980s, and the unwillingness of some of the OPEC countries to keep to their agreed quotas and prices also lend weight to the argument that the "oil weapon" can be blunted.

We should also note that price increases and cutbacks hurt friends as well as enemies. The economies of pro-Arab countries, especially in the developing world, were seriously hurt by OPEC actions in the 1970s. The damage caused to poor and highly oil-dependent nations threatened to create an anti-Arab political backlash. Indeed, many African countries that broke relations with Israel in 1973 have now resumed ties.

Nevertheless, at that time, the ramifications of the oil embargo of 1973 were numerous, and for a while it caused a disruption of the world economy and recession that many associated with the October 1973 war. As destructive as the conflict was, however, it did set in motion events that would later lead to a peace treaty between Egypt and Israel. That process will be discussed in the next chapter.

Suggestions for Further Reading

BAR-SIMAN-TOV, YAACOV, *The Israeli-Egyptian War of Attrition, 1969–70*, New York, Columbia University Press, 1980.

COBBAN, HELENA, *The Palestinian Liberation Organization: People, Power, and Politics*, Cambridge, Cambridge University Press, 1984.

HARKABI, YEHOSHAFAT, *The Palestinian Covenant and Its Meaning*, London, Vallentin Mitchell, 1979.

HART, ALAN, *Arafat: A Political Biography*, Bloomington, Indiana University Press, 1984.

HEIKAL, MOHAMED, *The Road to Ramadan*, New York, Quadrangle, 1975.

HERZOG, CHAIM, *The War of Atonement*, Boston, Little, Brown, 1974.

Journal of Palestine Studies, "The October War and Its Aftermath," Institute of Palestine Studies, Beirut and Kuwait University, Vol. III, No. 2, 1974.

KHOURI, FRED J., *The Arab–Israeli Dilemma*, 3rd ed., Syracuse, N.Y., Syracuse University Press, 1985.

RABINOVICH, ABRAHAM, *The Yom Kippur War: The Epic Encounter That Transformed the Middle East*, Schocken Brooks, 2005.

SHWADRAN, BENJAMIN, *Middle Eastern Oil Crises since 1973*, Boulder, Colo., Westview Press, 1986.

"Sunday Times" Insight Team, *The Yom Kippur War*, London, Andre Deutsch, 1975.

WALLACH, JANET, and WALLACH, JOHN, *Arafat: In the Eyes of the Beholder*, New York, Carol Publishing Group, 1990.

YERGIN, DANIEL, *The Prize: The Epic Quest for Oil, Money, and Power*, New York, Simon & Schuster, 1991.

 DOCUMENT 7–1

The Palestinian National Covenant, 1968 [Excerpts]

This Covenant will be called The Palestinian National Covenant (*al-mithaq al-watani al-filastini*).

Article 1: Palestine is the homeland of the Palestinian Arab people and an integral part of the great Arab homeland, and the people of Palestine is a part of the Arab nation.

Article 2: Palestine with its boundaries that existed at the time of the British mandate is an integral regional unit.

Article 3: The Palestinian Arab people possesses the legal right to its homeland, and when the liberation of its homeland is completed it will exercise self-determination solely according to its own will and choice.

Article 4: The Palestinian personality is an innate, persistent characteristic that does not disappear, and it is transferred from fathers to sons. The Zionist occupation, and the dispersal of the Palestinian Arab people as a result of the disasters which came over it, do not deprive it of its Palestinian personality and affiliation and do not nullify them.

Article 5: The Palestinians are the Arab citizens who were living permanently in Palestine until 1947, whether they were expelled from there or remained. Whoever is born to a Palestinian Arab father after this date, within Palestine or outside it, is a Palestinian.

Article 6: Jews who were living permanently in Palestine until the beginning of the Zionist invasion will be considered Palestinians. [For the dating of the Zionist invasion, considered to have begun in 1917.]

Article 7: The Palestinian affiliation and the material, spiritual and historical tie with Palestine are permanent realities. The upbringing of the Palestinian individual in an Arab and revolutionary fashion, the undertaking of all means of forging consciousness and training the Palestinian, in order to acquaint him profoundly with his homeland, spiritually and materially, and preparing him for the conflict and the armed struggle, as well as for the sacrifice of his property and his life to restore his homeland, until the liberation of all this is a national duty.

Article 8: The phase in which the people of Palestine is living is that of national (*watani*) struggle for the liberation of Palestine. Therefore, the contradictions among the Palestinian national forces are of secondary order which must be suspended in the interest of the fundamental contradiction between Zionism and colonialism on the one side and the Palestinian Arab people on the other. On this basis, the Palestinian masses, whether in the homeland or in places of exile (*mahajir*), organizations and individuals, comprise one national front which acts to restore Palestine and liberate it through armed struggle.

Article 9: Armed struggle is the only way to liberate Palestine and is therefore a strategy and not tactics. The Palestinian Arab people affirms its absolute resolution and abiding determination to pursue the armed struggle and to march forward towards the armed popular revolution, to liberate its homeland and return to it [to maintain] its right to a natural life in it, and to exercise its right of self-determination in it and sovereignty over it.

Article 10: Fedayeen action forms the nucleus of the popular Palestinian war of liberation. This demands its promotion, extension and protection, and the mobilization of all the masses and scientific capacities of the Palestinians, their organization and involvement in the armed Palestinian revolution and cohesion in the national (*watani*) struggle among the various groups of the people of Palestine, and between them and the Arab masses, to guarantee the continuation of the revolution, its advancement and victory. . . .

Article 13: Arab unity and the liberation of Palestine are two complementary aims. Each one paves the way for realization of the other. Arab unity leads to the liberation of Palestine, and the liberation of Palestine leads to Arab unity. Working for both goes hand in hand. . . .

Article 15: The liberation of Palestine, from an Arab viewpoint, is a national (*qawmi*) duty to repulse the Zionist, Imperialist invasion from the great Arab homeland and to purge the Zionist presence from Palestine. Its full responsibility falls upon the Arab nation, peoples and governments, with the Palestinian Arab people at their head.

Article 16: The liberation of Palestine, from a spiritual viewpoint, will prepare an atmosphere of tranquility and peace for the Holy Land in the shade of which all the Holy Places will be safeguarded, and freedom of worship and visitation to all will be guaranteed, without distinction or discrimination of race, colour, language or religion. For this reason, the people of Palestine looks to the support of all the spiritual forces in the world.

Article 17: The liberation of Palestine, from a human viewpoint, will restore to the Palestinian man his dignity, glory and freedom. For this, the Palestinian Arab people looks to the support of those in the world who believe in the dignity and freedom of man. . . .

Article 19: The partitioning of Palestine in 1947 and the establishment of Israel is fundamentally null and void, whatever time has elapsed, because it was contrary to the wish of the people of Palestine and its natural right to its homeland, and contradicts the principles embodied in the Charter of the UN, the first of which is the right of self-determination.

Article 20: The Balfour Declaration, the Mandate document, and what has been based upon them are considered null and void. The claim of a historical or spiritual tie between Jews and Palestine does not tally with historical realities nor with the constituents of statehood in their true sense. Judaism, in its character as a religion of revelation, is not a nationality with an independent existence. Likewise, the Jews are not one people with an independent personality. They are rather citizens of the states to which they belong.

Article 21: The Palestinian Arab people, in expressing itself through the armed Palestinian revolution, rejects every solution that is a substitute for a complete liberation of Palestine, and rejects all plans that aim at the settlement of the Palestine issue or its internationalization.

Article 22: Zionism is a political movement organically related to world Imperialism and hostile to all movements of liberation and progress in the world. It is a racist and fanatical movement in its formation: aggressive, expansionist and colonialist in its aims; and fascist and Nazi in its means. Israel is the tool of the Zionist movement and a human and geographical base for world Imperialism. It is a concentration and jumping-off point for Imperialism in the heart of the Arab homeland, to strike at the hopes of the Arab nation for liberation, unity and progress. . . .

Article 24: The Palestinian Arab people believes in the principles of justice, freedom, sovereignty, self-determination, human dignity and the right of people to exercise them. . . .

Article 27: The Palestine Liberation Organization will cooperate with all Arab States, each according to its capacities, and will maintain neutrality in their mutual relations in the light of and on the basis of, the requirements of the battle of liberation and will not interfere in the internal affairs of any Arab State.

Article 28: The Palestinian Arab people insists upon the originality and independence of its national (*wataniyya*) liberation and rejects every manner of interference, guardianship and subordination. . . .

Article 33: This covenant cannot be amended except by a two-thirds majority of all the members of the National Assembly of the Palestine Liberation Organization in a special session called for this purpose.

Source: Yehuda Lukacs, ed., *Documents on the Israel-Palestinian Conflict, 1967–1983* (Cambridge: Cambridge University Press, 1984), pp. 139–143.

 DOCUMENT 7-2

Security Council Resolution 338, October 22, 1973

The Security Council

1. *Calls* upon all parties to the present fighting to cease all firing and terminate all military activity immediately, no later than 12 hours after the moment of the adoption of this decision, in the positions they now occupy;

2. *Calls* upon the parties concerned to start immediately after the cease-fire the implementation of Security Council Resolution 242 (1967) in all of its parts;

3. *Decides* that, immediately and concurrently with the cease-fire, negotiations start between the parties concerned under appropriate auspices aimed at establishing a just and durable peace in the Middle East.

Source: *The Middle East*, 7th ed. (Washington, D.C.: Congressional Quarterly, Inc., 1990), p. 301.

 DOCUMENT 7-3

Arab Heads of State Declaration at Rabat, October 28, 1974

The Conference of the Arab Heads of State:
1. *Affirms* the right of the Palestinian people to return to their homeland and to self-determination.
2. *Affirms* the right of the Palestinian people to establish an independent national authority, under the leadership of the PLO in its capacity as the sole legitimate representative of the Palestine people, over all liberated territory. The Arab States are pledged to uphold this authority, when it is established, in all spheres and at all levels.
3. *Supports* the PLO in the exercise of its national and international responsibilities, within the context of the principle of Arab solidarity.
4. *Invites* the kingdoms of Jordan, Syria and Egypt to formalize their relations in light of these decisions and in order that they be implemented.
5. *Affirms* the obligation of all Arab States to preserve Palestinian unity and not to interfere in Palestinian internal affairs.

Source: *The Middle East*, 7th ed., Congressional Quarterly, p. 302.

 DOCUMENT 7-4

Israel Knesset Statement, Prime Minister, Yitzhak Rabin, Following the Rabat Conference, November 5, 1974 [Excerpt]

The meaning of [the Rabat] Resolutions is clear. The Rabat Conference decided to charge the organizations of murderers with the establishment of a Palestinian State, and the Arab countries gave the organizations a free hand to decide on their mode of operations. The Arab countries themselves will refrain, as stated in the Resolution, from intervening in the "internal affairs" of this action.

We are not fully aware of the significance of the fourth Resolution, which refers to "outlining a formula" for the coordination of relations between Jordan, Syria, Egypt and the PLO. It is by no means impossible that it also intended to bring about closer military relations between them.

The significance of these Resolutions is extremely grave. The aim of the terrorist organizations is well known and clear. The Palestine National Covenant speaks bluntly and openly about the liquidation of the State of Israel by means of armed struggle, and the Arab States committed themselves at Rabat to support this struggle. Any attempt to implement them will be accompanied by at least attempts to carry out terrorist operations on a large scale with the support of the Arab countries.

The decisions of the Rabat Conference are merely a continuation of the resolutions adopted at Khartoum. Only, further to the "no's" of Khartoum, the roof organization of the terrorists has attained the status conferred upon it by the presidents and kings at Rabat. Throughout this conference not a voice was raised expressing readiness for peace. The recurring theme of this conference was the aspiration to destroy a member-state of the United Nations. The content of this gathering has nothing whatsoever in common with social progress or the advancement of humanity among the Arab nations or in the relations with the peoples in the region and throughout the world.

There is no indication of any deviation from the goal and policy of the terrorist organizations, so let us not delude ourselves on this score. The terrorist organizations had no success in the administered territories, but the successes they achieved at the U.N. General Assembly and at Rabat are encouraging them to believe that the targets they had so confidently set themselves are now within reach.

The policy laid down at Khartoum and Rabat shall not be executed. We have the power to prevent its implementation. The positions of the government of Israel in the face of these resolutions of the Rabat Conference is unequivocal:

A. The government of Israel categorically rejects the conclusions of the Rabat Conference, which are designed to disrupt any progress towards peace, to encourage the terrorist elements, and to foil any step which might lead to peaceful coexistence with Israel.

B. In accordance with the Knesset's resolutions, the government of Israel will not negotiate with terrorist organizations whose avowed policy is to strive for Israel's destruction and whose method is terrorist violence.

C. We warn the Arab leaders against making the mistake of thinking that threats or even the active employment of the weapon of violence or of military force will lead to a political solution. This is a dangerous illusion. The aims of the Palestinian National Charter will not be achieved, either by terrorist acts or by limited or total warfare.

Source: Lukacs, *Documents*, pp. 96–97.

EIGHT

The Search for Peace, 1973–1979

CHRONOLOGY

Nov. 11, 1973	Israel–Egypt cease-fire signed at Kilometer 101	July 16, 1977	Egyptian president Anwar Sadat announces willingness to accept Israel after signing of a peace treaty
Dec. 21, 1973	First Geneva Peace Conference convenes	Nov. 9, 1977	Sadat states he is prepared to speak to Israeli Knesset if necessary to obtain peace
Jan. 18, 1974	Israel and Egypt sign first disengagement accord		
Feb. 28, 1974	United States and Egypt resume full diplomatic relations	Nov. 19, 1977	Sadat addresses Israeli Knesset
		Dec. 25, 1977	Begin and Sadat meet in Ismailia, Egypt
May 31, 1974	Israeli–Syrian disengagement accord		
June 12–17, 1974	Nixon visits Middle East	Mar. 14, 1978	Israel occupies Lebanese territory in "Operation Litani"
June 16, 1974	United States and Syria resume diplomatic relations	June 13, 1978	Israel completes withdrawal from Lebanon
Oct. 28, 1974	Arab League summit meeting at Rabat recognizes PLO as sole, legitimate representative of the Palestinian people	Sept. 17, 1978	Camp David peace accords signed
		Dec. 10, 1978	Nobel Peace Prize awarded jointly to Sadat and Begin
		Jan. 16, 1979	Mohammed Reza Shah Pahlavi leaves Iran
Nov. 13, 1974	PLO chairman Yasser Arafat addresses UN General Assembly	Feb. 1, 1979	Ayatollah Khomeini returns to Iran
June 5, 1975	Suez Canal reopens after eight years	Mar. 8–13, 1979	Carter visits Middle East
Sept. 4, 1975	Israel and Egypt sign second disengagement accord		
Nov. 10, 1975	UN General Assembly passes resolution equating Zionism with racism	Mar. 26, 1979	Peace treaty between Egypt and Israel signed in Washington, D.C.
		Apr. 1, 1979	Khomeini proclaims an Islamic Republic—"A Government of God"
Dec. 4, 1975	UN Security Council allows PLO to participate in debate on Arab–Israeli question		
July 4, 1976	Israeli commandos raid airport at Entebbe, Uganda, freeing hostages of hijacked jetliner	Mar. 31, 1979	Egypt expelled from Arab League, which moves headquarters to Tunis. League and PLO break diplomatic relations with Egypt and impose boycotts
Nov. 2, 1976	Jimmy Carter elected president of the United States		
		Apr. 30, 1979	First Israeli freighter since independence passes through Suez Canal
Mar. 16, 1977	Carter endorses a Palestinian "homeland" in address at Clinton, Massachusetts		
		May 9, 1979	Egypt expelled from Islamic conference
May 17, 1977	Menachem Begin and Likud coalition win Israeli general elections	May 25, 1979	Israel begins withdrawal from Sinai Peninsula
May 19, 1977	Begin calls for new Jewish settlements in occupied territories	Nov. 4, 1979	American hostages seized at U.S. Embassy in Tehran

The Peace Process, 1973–1979

Anwar Sadat used the 1973 war to try to end the struggle with Israel within the broad context of lessening Egyptian dependence upon the Soviet Union. Buoyed by the psychological "victory" of 1973 and concerned about Egypt's deteriorating economy as a result of the Nasser era, Sadat saw the necessity of peace with Israel, and he called upon the rest of the Arab world to unite with him. He wanted Syria, Jordan, and the Palestinians to join Egypt in Geneva to negotiate a peace settlement with Israel. He hoped for Arab recognition of Israel as an independent state and the formal renunciation of the "liberation" of Palestine as an Arab national aim, in return for which Israel would surrender all the occupied territories, including the Old City of Jerusalem.

Egypt was in a better position to seek peace with Israel than were any of the other Arab states. Because Egyptians feel a deep identification with their own past and cultural heritage and have always seen themselves as Egyptians as well as Muslims or Arabs, Sadat could consider peace with Israel outside of the Arab context. Moreover, although the plight of Palestinians moved him, the establishment of an independent Palestinian homeland did not have any particular urgency for Sadat. Thus, following lengthy negotiations, Anwar Sadat succeeded in reaching a bilateral peace accord with Menachem Begin on September 17, 1978, at Camp David, the presidential retreat in the United States. This was confirmed as a formal peace treaty between Egypt and Israel signed in Washington, D.C., on March 26, 1979. For various reasons, however, this was not the first step toward the hoped-for comprehensive peace settlement between Israel and the Arabs.

The "peace process," which in the first instance led to the Camp David accords, had begun in Washington, D.C. At the conclusion of the war in October 1973, Secretary of State Henry Kissinger, realizing the United States had greater bargaining power with Israel and Egypt, and concerned about the effects of the Arab oil embargo imposed on October 17, determined to seek an American solution in the Middle East. The war had indicated, he now believed, that peace in the Middle East could not be maintained through Israeli military strength. Peace would necessitate Israel making some territorial concessions. Since Sadat had expelled his Russian advisors, Kissinger seized the advantage of the Soviet absence in Egypt.

Kissinger's Shuttle Diplomacy

Kissinger acted quickly, visiting the Middle East in November 1973, and securing, on November 11, a cease-fire agreement between Israel and Egypt that resulted in a return to the cease-fire lines of October 22 and the relief of the Egyptian Third Army. This accord (signed in a tent 101 kilometers from Cairo) was the first bilateral agreement signed by the two parties since the 1949 armistice at the end of the first Arab–Israeli war. In early December, Kissinger persuaded the Egyptians and the Jordanians (the Syrians refused) to negotiate with the Israelis—even to sit in the same room—through a UN-sponsored peace conference to be convened in Geneva, Switzerland, in accordance with the provisions of UN Resolution 338. Israel agreed to participate on condition that the negotiations were "face to face" and that no member of the PLO would be present. This conference was held on December 21 with Egypt, Jordan, Israel, the United States, and the Soviet Union present. It collapsed after one day, although there was an agreement to begin talks on separating Egyptian and Israeli forces along the Suez Canal.

This provided the opportunity for Kissinger to bypass the United Nations and Soviet Union, while appearing to keep within the parameters of UN Resolution 338, which called for all the parties to implement Resolution 242 in its entirety. Although initially believing he could secure a comprehensive peace settlement and supremely confident in his negotiating skills,

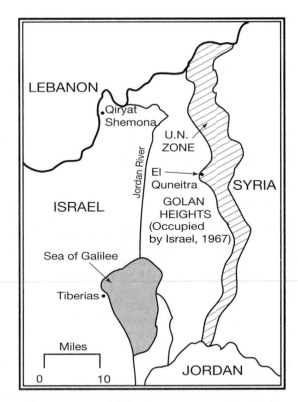

MAP 8–1   Golan Heights Disengagement Accord,
May 1974

Source: The Middle East, 6th ed. (Washington, D.C.:
Congressional Quarterly, Inc., 1986), p. 45.

persuasiveness, and energy, Kissinger soon realized (just like his predecessors in "shuttle diplomacy," Ralph Bunche and Gunnar Jarring) that peace would be achieved only through a "step-by-step" approach.

In January 1974, on another round of shuttle diplomacy, Kissinger persuaded Egypt and Israel to sign a disengagement accord, whereby Israel withdrew from the western bank of the Suez Canal, to about twenty miles from the east bank of the canal. Egypt agreed to a major reduction of troops east of Suez, the establishment of a UN-patrolled buffer zone, defensive missile emplacements only west of Suez, and the allowing of nonmilitary Israeli shipping through the canal (though not in Israeli vessels). In late February 1974, the United States and Egypt renewed full diplomatic relations after a seven-year hiatus. In May 1974, Kissinger also achieved a disengagement accord between Israel and Syria regarding the Golan Heights. Israel agreed to withdraw from some occupied territory in the Heights in return for the establishment of a UN buffer zone and defensive Arab missile placements. (See Map 8–1.) President Hafez al-Assad of Syria also agreed in a private memorandum to prevent any Palestinian terrorist groups from launching attacks from Syria. In return, the United States resumed diplomatic relations with Syria.

Divisions within Israel

Kissinger was very successful in these early stages. American prestige was high, all the Arab states involved regarded Kissinger as a mediator, and President Richard Nixon was well received during a tour of the Middle East in June 1974. But there was a long way to go before any peace treaty could be agreed upon. Kissinger was, in fact, making contradictory and unrealistic promises to both parties. He promised the Israelis that disengagement accords would reduce American demands for concessions and lessen criticism of Israel. He told Egypt the opposite, namely that accords would set the peace process in motion and increase the pressure on Israel for further concessions. Israel was not particularly happy with Kissinger's efforts.

In December 1973, Israel had held elections and was undergoing a political reappraisal following the findings of the official report on the war. The ruling Labor party led by Golda Meir and Moshe Dayan won the election with a significantly reduced plurality in the Knesset: down to 39 percent (51 seats) from 46 percent (56 seats). The main challenge had come from the newly formed Likud party led by Menachem Begin. The Likud was a coalition of the Herut party, the Liberal party, and other parties of the political right, engineered by the hero of the 1973 campaign in Egypt, former general Ariel Sharon. The Likud, which opposed returning any territory to Egypt, won 30 percent of the vote and 39 seats in the Knesset.

A disillusioned Golda Meir resigned in April 1974, and the Labor party elected Yitzhak Rabin, chief of staff during the Six-Day War and former ambassador to the United States, as prime minister. Policymaking was further complicated by internal strife within the Labor party. The ambitious Shimon Peres, who became defense minister, wanted the top job and sought to undermine Rabin's authority. He and Deputy Prime Minister Yigal Allon frequently disagreed with their nominal leader. In March 1975, Kissinger began a new round of shuttle diplomacy seeking further disengagement accords in the Sinai. Rabin resisted an Israeli pullback from the Sinai Peninsula. He insisted upon retaining the important oil fields of Abu Rudeis, the two strategic passes in the area (Mitla and Gidi), and the post-1967 Israeli settlements in the Sinai. Egypt regarded these conditions as unacceptable. Negotiations stalled. President Gerald Ford threatened a total reassessment of American Middle East policy and suspended arms deliveries to Israel. Sadat met with Ford in Salzburg, Austria, on June 2; on June 5 the Suez Canal was reopened to commercial shipping after an eight-year closure.

A week later, Rabin met with Ford and Kissinger in Washington and agreed to renew efforts to negotiate another Sinai peace accord. In August 1975, Kissinger once again visited the Middle East, and Rabin reluctantly accepted his package deal. The agreement, signed by Israel and Egypt on September 4, 1975, involved Israeli withdrawal from the oil fields and the passes, a new UN–monitored buffer zone, and the stationing of American personnel manning early warning systems in the Sinai. (See Map 8–2.) The United States was committed to the security of both countries and promised large sums of aid to both. Each side agreed to avoid "the threat or use of force or military blockade against each other." Kissinger also assured Israeli leaders that the United States would not pressure them into a treaty with Jordan, or demand that they make major territorial concessions in future negotiations with Syria. Finally, in a commitment that was to become more important as the years passed, the United States assured Israel that it would not talk to the PLO, unless the PLO specifically recognized Israel's right to exist and accepted UN Resolution 242. Later, the United States added the rider that the PLO must also renounce terrorism.

The Response of the Arab States

Despite all his skill, Kissinger failed to achieve any further progress in his personal diplomacy. There seemed little likelihood that Egypt, much less any other Arab state, would recognize

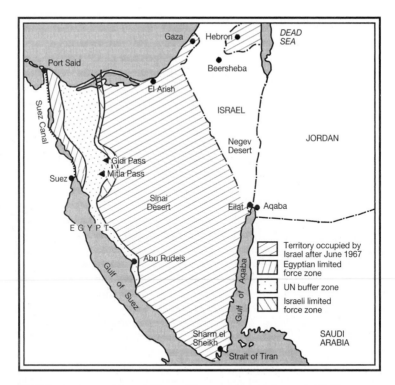

MAP 8–2   Second Israel–Egypt Disengagement Accord, 1975

Source: T. G. Fraser, *The Middle East, 1914–1979* (New York: St. Martin's Press, 1980), p. xviii.

Israel's right to exist or formally end the state of war. Several developments slowed the momentum of diplomacy and the possibility that the disengagement agreements would lead to a more general settlement. Among the more important of these developments was the emergence of Islamic extremists* in the 1970s and 1980s. Revivalist groups like the Muslim Brotherhood had existed in the Middle East since the 1920s, but the rise of religious "fanaticism" is now usually associated with the Iranian revolution of 1979, when the charismatic religious preacher Ayatollah Ruhollah Khomeini emerged into the spotlight. Subsequent events such as the seizure of over fifty hostages at the American Embassy in Tehran in the fall of 1979 and the Iran–Iraq war, which began in September 1980, added considerably to the instability and volatility of the entire Middle East. And the outbreak of a second civil war in Lebanon in the Spring of 1975 created uncertainty on Israel's northern border. These changes did have one important outcome, however. It led some Arab states, especially Egypt, to regard the Arab–Israeli conflict as less threatening to them than the threat of religious fanaticism and Soviet subversion.

Anger and disagreement among the Arabs followed the disengagement treaties between Israel and Egypt. Egypt's negotiations with Kissinger and indirectly through him with the Israelis (although the negotiations at Kilometer 101 were face to face) increasingly isolated

---

*The term *fundamentalist* has overtones of Christian Protestantism. In this book, we shall be using the term *extremist* rather than *fundamentalist* to describe the kind of revivalist, activist, militant Islam that today, by whatever means, including violence, seeks to establish an Islamic polity.

Egypt from the other Arab states. The question of unity among Israel's antagonists was a major problem for Arab diplomacy—and a crucial issue in Israeli foreign policy. It was widely believed at this time that agreement among the Arab states at war with Israel was necessary for an enduring peace. If any one leader negotiated terms with Israel unacceptable to elements of that nation's population, he could only guarantee domestic security (as well as his own) if the negotiations were part of a larger package involving the other frontline Arab states.

In particular, King Hussein of Jordan and President Assad of Syria felt that Sadat had acted purely in his own interests. Hussein had hoped that as a result of diplomatic efforts after the October 1973 war he would recover the West Bank of the Jordan; he wanted it as part of Jordan and to keep the Palestinians from claiming it as their own. He also wanted to regain the holy places of East Jerusalem. Israel, however, rejected a proposal that Hussein put to Kissinger in January 1974, for Israeli withdrawal from the West Bank.

President Hafez al-Assad, too, felt that Sadat had left Syria out in the cold, especially after the second disengagement agreement in 1975. Assad wanted all the Golan Heights back. He may have thought briefly, in 1974, that the U.S. government would somehow pry the Heights from Israeli hands. Syria could not make war without Egypt, but on the other hand, Egypt could not make peace without Syria. Rather than fall into line with Egypt, Syria chose to support the PLO. Yasser Arafat and the PLO were now able to take center stage in the proceedings. As we noted in the previous chapter, the PLO was a loose conglomerate of groups with quite different attitudes toward Israel and the policies they should pursue to achieve their goals. Formally and constitutionally, the PLO remained committed to its covenant as revised in 1968, which called for the dissolution (destruction) of Israel, but in reality the membership was divided over how to achieve this end.

PLO Policy

PLO policy as stated in the Palestinian National Covenant asserted that "armed struggle is the only way to liberate Palestine," and later Palestinian National Council resolutions called for the establishment of a secular democratic state to replace Israel. In terms that must have troubled King Hussein as much as Israel, the covenant stated that "Palestine, with the boundaries it had during the British Mandate, is an indivisible territorial unit." Leftist Palestinian groups like the Popular Front for the Liberation of Palestine (PFLP), led by George Habash, and the Democratic Front for the Liberation of Palestine (DFLP), led by Nayef Hawatmeh, called for the overthrow of King Hussein as part of the liberation of all Palestine. In fact, prior to 1975, these groups argued that before Palestine could be freed, all reactionary Arab governments would have to be reformed or overthrown.

By 1974, however, the PLO had modified its position on the liberation of Palestine, and, at the twelfth Palestine National Council (PNC) meeting in June–July 1974, it indicated through the term *national authority* a willingness to consider the establishment of a Palestinian Arab state in the West Bank and Gaza. Israeli analysts insisted that the modification in policy was only to substitute a two-stage for a one-stage process in the destruction of Israel, and that a so-called national authority would be a launching pad for the achievement of that aim.

The approach of claiming to be a national authority within the confines of the West Bank and Gaza was seen by the PLO as a way of combining both Israeli and Jordanian claims to the occupied territories. Elements within the Palestinian cause, like the PFLP and DFLP, as well as Habash's former associate, Ahmad Jibril, who formed his own splinter group backed by Syria, opposed this approach. They believed it not only gave Israel an opportunity to reject the claim but also weakened the Arab revolutionary struggle to regain all of Palestine. Arafat himself and the majority of West Bank Palestinians preferred the option of the limited goal of regaining the West Bank and Gaza, but Arafat felt his leadership of the PLO was not secure enough for him to speak out against the factions calling for the liberation of all of Palestine. The diverse approaches within the Palestinian cause led to many years of ambiguity and confusion as to what the PLO meant by the term *national authority*. The situation was compounded by the fact that the PLO would not accept UN Resolution 242. The United States demanded PLO acceptance of Resolution 242 recognizing Israel as a precondition to negotiations; the PLO objected to Resolution 242 because it referred only to Arab refugees and did not recognize Palestinian rights of self-determination.

In April and May 1974, in an attempt to derail U.S. efforts to mediate the Syrian–Israeli disengagement accords signed in Geneva on May 31, groups within the PLO mounted a series of spectacular terrorist missions: one in April in the northern Israeli town of Qiryat Shemona in which the three terrorists (members of the PFLP) and eighteen Israelis—eight of them children—were killed; and another in May in Galilee, in the village of Ma'alot, where DFLP terrorists and twenty of the ninety children they were holding hostage were killed. The Israeli government's response to these acts of terrorism was to harden its resolve against the Palestinians, despite the increasingly unrealistic nature of continuing to deny the existence of a Palestinian people. Arafat's unwillingness or inability to control the extremists in his organization not only weakened the credibility of the moderates within the PLO but also seemed to add weight to the argument that the PLO was a terrorist organization that should not be negotiated with. At this point of stalemate, the UN General Assembly once again stepped in. It called for a full debate on the "Question of Palestine" and invited the PLO as representative of the Palestinian people to take part in it. This was a far greater triumph for the PLO, and for the more moderate elements in that organization, than any achieved by the extremists and their terrorist acts. And it was a complete rejection of the Israeli position. (See Document 8–1.)

Palestine/Israel had come full circle in the United Nations. In 1947, the General Assembly was a smaller, more Western-oriented body that was sympathetic to the cause of the Jewish survivors of the Holocaust and the Zionist argument for a Jewish homeland. In 1974, in a larger General Assembly, the votes of newly formed third-world states—many of them Muslim—and countries fearful of economic repercussions because of their dependence upon Arab oil, reflected sympathy for the Palestinian cause. In 1969, the General Assembly had affirmed for the first time the right of "the people of Palestine" to "self-determination" and had restated and extended that view in 1970 and again in 1973. On November 13, 1974, Arafat himself spoke before the General Assembly, the first representative of a nonstate ever invited to do so. After setting out the PLO position calling for a democratic, secular state in Palestine—which did not include a recognition or acceptance of Israel—Arafat concluded his speech with this appeal: "I have come bearing an olive branch and a freedom fighter's gun. Do not let the olive branch fall from my hand." (See Document 8–2.)

The majority of Israelis saw only Arafat's gun. (See Document 8–3.) The Israeli government believed a Palestinian state would be merely a platform for renewing warfare against an Israel reduced to its earlier, more vulnerable size. Strategic considerations precluded even the Israeli doves from disagreeing with their government's policy. Israel repeated the position it held throughout the 1970s that Jordan was Palestine, since a majority of the Jordanian population were Palestinians. King Hussein, despite the 1974 Rabat decision, maintained that he had the right to speak for Palestinians on both sides of the Jordan River. In 1974, the majority of the PLO were vehemently against the negotiation process with Israel. On the other hand, a minority of Palestinians saw Arafat's olive branch, and they began to believe that if a Palestinian state were to be established, diplomacy could achieve more than force.

The West Bank and Gaza

Nevertheless, the situation in the West Bank and Gaza was becoming increasingly more problematic for Israel. When the Israelis captured the West Bank and the Gaza Strip in the Six-Day

After terrorist attack on Maalot Kibbutz, the nursery, May 1974.

War, more than a million Arabs came under Israeli control. The military occupation raised some fundamental questions for Israel. One was the so-called demographic time bomb. If Israel were to retain and annex the occupied territories, the higher birthrate of the Arab population might eventually endanger the Jewish character of Israel. Becoming a minority in their own land was unthinkable to Israel's Jews. On the other hand, if Arabs were to be denied their rights, the democratic nature of Israel would be compromised. Other options, such as the annexation of the occupied territories and the expulsion of the Arab population, or returning the areas to their former—Jordanian—status, seemed equally unacceptable to various parties. The option of a Palestinian "entity" alongside Israel was not seriously considered by anybody on either side at that time. Meanwhile, the continuing occupation was bound to create conditions of oppression and further moral and practical dilemmas for Israel.

Not surprisingly, Palestinian and Israeli spokespersons disagreed over the conditions of the Palestinians under Israeli occupation. Supporters of Israel argued that the material prosperity of the Palestinian Arabs occupying the West Bank increased dramatically under Israeli rule. They pointed out that under Jordanian control, between 1948 and 1967, the Palestinians had been kept politically and socially divided in an effort to limit the growth of Palestinian, as opposed to Jordanian, nationalism. Israel continued this policy to prevent the growth of a collective Palestinian identity. The West Bank economy and labor force were incorporated into the Israeli economy. Traditional large landowners suffered as a result of this as they were forbidden to grow crops that competed with those grown in Israel; but their workers, who then became unskilled workers in the Israeli economy (primarily in the construction industry), gained in terms of real wages and living conditions.

Israel and the West Bank and Gaza initially benefited economically from this arrangement. A very high level of employment—approximately 98 percent—existed among the Arabs, and many Jews within Israel experienced upward mobility, leaving the menial and unskilled jobs to be performed now by the Palestinians. At the same time, it must be noted that, as the occupation continued, the cost to Israel of defending the territories increased enormously. This in turn contributed significantly to the high rate of inflation—a record 130 percent in the early 1980s. Furthermore, the dilemma of occupying lands inhabited by a people who did not want to live under Israeli rule caused a breakdown in the sense of national purpose and political consensus in Israel that had not been questioned between 1948 and 1967. Some Israelis even began to call for the expulsion of the Palestinians from the occupied territories.

Of the many options open to it following the 1967 war, Israel soon set out on the path of deliberately establishing Jewish settlements in the Gaza Strip, the Jordan Valley, and in the Golan Heights. At first these were military settlements, and most of them were outside the main centers of Arab population in the so-called Allon Belt, which ran along the Jordan Valley. They were approved, it was argued, for security reasons. This policy was pursued by the ruling Labor party and its coalition partner, the National Religious party, and a new organization that emerged in 1974, *Gush Emunim* (The Bloc of the Faithful). Gush Emunim and similar groups, evoking religious and historical sentiments, called for the absorption of the West Bank, or, as they termed it, Judea and Samaria, as part of what had been Eretz Yisrael, the biblical term denoting the Promised Land. Within a few years, settlements were established among existing Arab towns, and the government was forced to accept them. Defense Minister Shimon Peres, who saw another opportunity to embarrass his personal rival, Prime Minister Yitzhak Rabin, at this point supported Gush Emunim. The result was that the number of new settlements increased by half in the two years from mid-1975, and, by 1977, approximately eighty-five settlements had been established in the occupied territories. Gush Emunim and its supporters would become an increasingly significant factor over the next two decades.

The Labor party also sought cooperation with elected Arab local officials. Municipal elections were held in April 1976, but these did not have the results the Israeli government expected. Many of the candidates put forward by the West Bank towns were either pro-PLO or

Yasser Arafat, leader of the Palestine Liberation Organization, at the United Nations.

more radical in their opposition to Israeli rule than the government could tolerate, and within a few years, most of the mayors had been deported or forced to step down. As the 1977 Israeli elections approached, economic malaise, political problems (including a scandal involving an illegal U.S. bank account held by Mrs. Rabin), and diplomatic isolation caused Israelis to lose confidence in the Labor party, which had ruled the country ever since its creation. In addition to the changing demographics of Israel, the Labor party had also lost support because of its failure to avert the 1973 war.

The victory of Menachem Begin and his right-wing Likud coalition in the Israeli national elections of May 1977 marked a turning point in the history of Israel and the Arab–Israeli conflict. It brought to an end the dominance the Labor party had exercised in setting the national agenda since Israel's foundation. Sephardic Jews, for example, overwhelmingly supported Begin because they were disenchanted with the previous Socialist governments. Ideologically, Begin's election represented a victory for Revisionist Zionism. He had, after all, taken up Jabotinsky's torch and had been leader of the Irgun, and he and his supporters, including Yitzhak Shamir, a former member of the Stern Gang, had no intention of relinquishing the territory Israel had acquired in 1967, especially "Judea and Samaria" (the West Bank) and East Jerusalem. Ultra-nationalists and the ultra-religious agreed with Begin's policy of retaining the territories. Many Begin supporters opposed trading "land for peace" because, believing they knew the Arab mentality, they did not trust the Palestinians. These attitudes gave new ideological impetus to the settlement movement. Menachem Begin approved twenty-one more settlements between 1980 and 1981. This brought the number of Jewish settlers in the occupied territories to about 110,000. Jews controlled more than one-third of the land and 90 percent of the water in the region.

Water and the Arab–Israeli Conflict

In the Introduction, we mentioned the importance of the landscape in the Arab–Israeli conflict. Of all the characteristics of the landscape, perhaps none is more important than the presence or absence of that most fundamental of all human needs—water. Because of the arid nature of much of Israel and the surrounding region, water is a highly prized and valuable resource, and much of the conflict has been focused on that scarce vital commodity.

There are two natural sources of water in the immediate vicinity: rivers and aquifers. (See Map 9–2.) The Jordan and the Yarmuk with their tributaries are the major rivers. Aquifers, underground layers of porous rock or sediment that can store large quantities of water, are to be found under much of Israel and Jordan. Shallow aquifers can be replenished with winter rain, but deep aquifers cannot, because their waters accumulated in an earlier geologic age when higher rainfall occurred. Fresh water can also be obtained through desalination of sea water, although this is a very expensive process. According to Israeli estimates, Israel obtains two-thirds of its 1.8 billion cubic meters (one cubic meter or m^3 equals 264 gallons) annual water consumption from the Jordan and one-third from aquifers; Jordan, two-thirds of its annual consumption of 500 million m^3 from the Yarmuk and one-third from aquifers; while the territories occupied by Israel in 1967 obtain almost all their water (135 million m^3 for the West Bank and 92 million m^3 for the Gaza Strip) from aquifers. This translates into 380 m^3 per capita for Israelis, 140 m^3 per capita for Jordanians, 130 m^3 per capita for the Gaza, and 90 m^3 per capita for the West Bank. Most of the water used is for agricultural purposes. It should also be added that Israel and Jordan are both consuming water faster than nature can replenish it.

From the outset of Zionist settlement in Palestine, water became a source of conflict, and rhetorical as well as physical battle lines were soon drawn up. Zionists claimed that their foresight, use of technology, and good management enabled them to secure and utilize new sources of water in Palestine. Israelis, as evidence of their good planning, point to the draining of the swamps of Huleh, the building of the complex dams, pipelines, and pumping stations that make up the National Water Carrier, and the irrigation schemes and desalination plants that enable Israel to survive. The Arabs describe Israel's disproportionate use of water as virtual theft.

Water use was one of the first sources of disagreement between the newly established state of Israel and Jordan, Syria, and even the United States. The difficulties for Israel stemmed from the fact that virtually none of the water it consumed originated in Israel itself. The Dan River is the only source of the Jordan River originating in Israel. The other two sources—the Banias and Hasbani—rise in Syria and Lebanon, respectively. This is not unusual in the Middle East. More than half of all the water consumed in the area originates in another sovereign state; Egypt and Iraq are two of the most notable cases. More than 75 percent of Syria's water originates in another country's territory, flowing from Turkey in the Euphrates and from Lebanon in the Orontes rivers, respectively.

Israel's attempts to dam and utilize the waters of the Jordan in the early 1950s were hotly contested by Jordan and Syria, and although the Eisenhower administration negotiated an agreement of water allocation among Israel, Jordan, Syria, and Lebanon in 1953 (the Johnston Plan), it was never ratified by all the parties. Syria and Israel engaged in limited military engagements in the demilitarized zone during the 1950s when Israel built its water carrier, because it drew water from the Sea of Galilee and reduced the flow downstream to Jordan. When Israel captured the Golan Heights and the West Bank in the 1967 war, it gained control of not only the headwaters of the Jordan but also the aquifers under the West Bank. Over 10 percent of Israel's water comes from sources on the Golan Heights, and nearly one-third of its waters come from aquifers replenished by rainfall in the occupied territories.

Behind the religious and political rhetoric of the Arab–Israeli conflict, we can see that the need to control water sources and use underlies many of the policies of the parties to the conflict. Agreement on sharing the region's water resources is, as it always has been, essential if peace is to have a chance.

The Camp David Accords

The Role of Jimmy Carter

The changes in administration that took place in 1977 in both the United States (Jimmy Carter became president in January) and Israel produced spectacular results. Menachem Begin, given his strong views and many hawkish statements about the inviolability of the territories occupied since 1967, seemed the most unlikely person to agree to any surrender of territory. Nevertheless, he was willing to make a deal for Sinai in exchange for a free hand in the West Bank. He was correct in thinking that Sadat was so determined to regain Egyptian sovereignty over all the Sinai Peninsula that he would agree to overlook the demands of the PLO for an independent Palestine on the West Bank of the Jordan River. Nevertheless, if the Egyptian leader were to sign an agreement, it would have to satisfy (or at least be capable of interpretation that it did) some of the aspirations of the Palestinian Arabs.

Jimmy Carter came to the presidency with strong Baptist convictions and considerable idealism. He sought a comprehensive settlement and believed that if everyone would sit down around a negotiating table this could be reached. Carter had great faith in his mediating abilities. During 1977, Carter and Sadat sent many signals that they believed fruitful negotiations toward normalization of relations between Egypt and Israel could succeed. The chronology of events during the year can be summarized as follows. In March 1977, Carter, at a town meeting in Clinton, Massachusetts, endorsed the idea of a "Palestinian homeland." In April, during a visit to Washington, D.C., Sadat indicated to Carter that he believed relations with Israel could be "normalized." In May, Carter once again called for a Palestinian homeland. This proposal was met with such opposition from Israel and the American Jewish community that Carter reconsidered his position. On July 12, he said that the Palestinian "entity" should be tied in with Jordan and not be "independent." Sadat, in a Cairo radio broadcast four days later, stated he would accept Israel as a Middle East nation following the signing of a peace treaty. Israel is said to have secretly warned Sadat of an assassination plot by Libya against him in July, and that may have been a possible factor contributing to his peace initiative. In September, King Hassan of Morocco assisted Sadat in initiating secret high-level talks between Egyptian and Israeli officials to reach informal agreement with Israel before the Geneva Peace Conference reconvened. In view of the secret back-channel negotiations that preceded the Israel–PLO accord in 1993, it is interesting to note that on that earlier occasion, the Israeli official was Yitzhak Rabin, then prime minister, who traveled to Morocco in disguise, with thick glasses and a shaggy mustache.

Unexpectedly, Carter adopted a Soviet suggestion that the United States and the Soviets jointly reconvene the Geneva Peace Conference. On October 1, the two superpowers issued a joint statement calling for a comprehensive settlement of the Arab–Israeli dispute, including an eventual Israeli military withdrawal from the 1967 occupied territories and the guarantee of the "legitimate rights of the Palestinian people." The following day, Israel rejected the American–Soviet statement as "unacceptable," but continued discussions with the American administration to reconvene the Geneva Peace Conference without PLO participation. Sadat, who had expelled thousands of Russian advisors in Egypt in 1972 and had been trying to remove all Russian pressure and influence in his country, was aghast. Nevertheless, he requested that the PLO be specifically included in any Geneva peace talks. Israel opposed this suggestion.

Anwar Sadat then took matters into his own hands. In an address to the Egyptian National Assembly, he declared he was ready to go to the Israeli parliament itself to discuss peace. The surprised Begin could do little but agree, and he extended to Sadat (and to any other Arab leader who so wished) an invitation to come to Israel. Sadat, in an extraordinary move, accepted and arrived in Israel on November 19, 1977. In his address to the Knesset (the Israeli parliament), Sadat told his audience: "I declare to the whole world that we accept to live with you in permanent peace based on justice." In his speech, however, Sadat, no doubt hoping (unrealistically) to placate other Arab heads of state, made a series of demands he knew the Israelis would not meet: Israeli withdrawal from all territories occupied in 1967, and Israeli recognition of the right of the Palestinians to self-determination. Although little came of the private talks between Sadat and Begin, the visit did, as Sadat hoped it would, break down some of the psychological barriers between Israel and Egypt that stood in the way of reaching a settlement. Begin agreed to meet with Sadat in December at Ismailia, Egypt, and there he rejected the idea of a Palestinian state in the West Bank and Gaza. Begin said he would agree only to limited home rule for the Palestinians. He later spelled out that what he meant was "administrative autonomy," in the form of elected municipalities, with the Israeli army maintaining law and order. Begin vowed he would have nothing to do with the PLO. Begin and Sadat were a long way from agreement.

Sadat's initiative had, at first, seemed to bypass both the United States and the Soviet Union, but President Jimmy Carter quickly climbed on the bandwagon, determined to seize the reins. On January 4, 1978, in a speech at Aswan, Egypt, he praised Sadat for his efforts and committed the United States to play an active role in achieving a peace settlement in accordance with UN Resolutions 242 and 338. Egypt and Israel, meanwhile, had formed two committees—one political and one military—to discuss the terms of a peace treaty. Plans were submitted and rejected by both sides, and talks dragged on fruitlessly for the next seven months.

Finally, in August 1978, Carter requested that Begin and Sadat meet with him at Camp David, the presidential retreat in Maryland. Several meetings took place; Carter called this "one of the most frustrating experiences of my life," but eventually, as a result of his persistence and dedicated personal involvement, two accords were signed on September 17, 1978. Begin agreed only after Carter threatened to cut off all aid to Israel, and then promised to increase it.

The Camp David Accords and Egypt–Israel Peace Treaty

The importance of the Camp David accords to later negotiations cannot be overestimated. The accords consisted of two agreements, the first of which, "A Framework for Peace in the Middle East," contained provisions that have formed the basis of all subsequent peace negotiations, including those initiated in Madrid in 1991. It called for negotiations among Egypt, Jordan, Israel, and "representatives of the Palestinian people" to settle the question of the West Bank and the Gaza Strip. A self-governing Arab authority would be set up to replace the Israeli military forces for five years while negotiations were taking place on the "final status of the West Bank and Gaza." (See Document 8–4.) The second accord, "A Framework for the Conclusion of a Peace Treaty Between Egypt and Israel," was a draft proposal for a peace agreement to be negotiated and signed within three months. (See Document 8–5.) This provided for a phased Israeli withdrawal from the Sinai over three years and a full restoration of the area to Egypt. Israeli ships were to be allowed free passage through the Suez Canal. The United Nations would oversee provisions of the accords so as to satisfy both sides. The Camp David accords simply ignored the thorny question of Jerusalem and the future of the Golan Heights.

In reaching these accords, both parties made several concessions. Begin agreed to remove all the Israeli settlements from the Sinai as well as to turn over to Egypt the oil fields and Israeli air bases (to be used for civilian purposes). Sadat agreed, in essence, to a separate peace with Israel, without regard for the other Arab states or the Palestinians. Begin, nevertheless, continued

Sadat and Begin meet with Carter at presidential retreat, Camp David.

to expound his view that the Israeli position on the final status of the territories was autonomy for the people, not for the land; that is, that the end result could never be an independent Palestinian state. (See Document 8–6.) He was willing to compromise to achieve peace with Egypt because in his mind the Sinai had always been negotiable. The ideological and national reasons for retaining the West Bank and Gaza did not apply to the Sinai. Begin was also conscious of the growing belief in Israel that the occupied territories, rather than creating secure and defensible borders, were doing the reverse.

The fact that Israel's occupation of the Sinai had enabled Sadat to launch his surprise attack added force to this argument. Prior to 1967, Egypt could not change from a defensive to offensive posture without mobilizing its tanks and moving them across the desert, thereby alerting the Israelis. Israel also gained freedom from Egyptian attack for three years, and neither Jordan nor Syria would go to war without Egypt. Egypt promised "normal commercial sales" of oil to Israel, a promise backed by American guarantees.

Sadat was prepared to come to terms with Israel in 1978 and 1979 because of his "Egypt first" policy. He wanted to free up resources that had been devoted to waging war in order to reconstruct and widen the Suez Canal and to free Egypt from the Soviet orbit. Sadat had conceived the 1973 war as a political as well as a military operation; he had hoped to provoke superpower intervention to force Israel to give up the Sinai. This had been achieved not only by the military operation against Israel but also by the pressure of OPEC's oil embargo. As a result, Sadat and Kissinger were able to set American–Egyptian relations on a more stable basis. We should remember, also, that Sadat and Kissinger both hoped that Jordan would be drawn into peace negotiations with Israel.

Both sides, but especially the Israelis, were fully aware of the importance of future relations with the United States. It was concern for this relationship perhaps more than any other factor that led Begin reluctantly to agree to the concessions that produced the peace settlements. Both sides received massive American economic and military aid as part of separate agreements accompanying the Camp David accords. Israel was to receive $3 billion in military and financial assistance, approximately $800 million of which was to assist the relocation of Israel's two Sinai air bases to the Negev. Egypt was to receive $2 billion in tanks, planes, and antiaircraft weapons. All this was in addition to the existing 1979 foreign aid allocation for the two countries of $1 billion to Egypt and $1.8 billion to Israel.

Predictably, the PLO rejected the accords since they did not specifically call for a fully independent Palestinian state. Even more of a disappointment for Carter was the fact that Jordan and Saudi Arabia, considered Arab moderates and "friends" of the United States, rejected the Camp David agreements. The more radical Arab states like Syria and Iraq, which immediately emerged as leaders of the "rejectionist front," denounced not only the agreements but also Sadat for what they saw as his treason to the Arab cause.

There was little likelihood, at the time, that the Camp David peace accords signed between Egypt and Israel would lead to a comprehensive Middle East peace settlement. Even negotiating the peace treaty between Egypt and Israel proved difficult. Disagreements broke out almost immediately among Carter, Begin, and Sadat as to exactly what had been agreed upon at Camp David. Begin was determined to go ahead with new settlements on the West Bank and Gaza, and he claimed that the accords permitted him to do so after a three-month moratorium. Carter said that Begin had agreed that no new settlements would be established during the five-year transition period. For his part, Sadat claimed that the treaty was linked to the issue of the occupied territories, and he stated that a peace treaty between Egypt and Israel could be signed only after a timetable for Palestinian self-rule had been finalized. And throughout the period, from the signing of the accords until the signing of the peace treaty, both Sadat and Begin were under intense domestic political pressure not to make concessions. This led to last-minute difficulties over such issues as the terms of Egyptian oil sales from the Sinai fields to Israel and the drawing up of a detailed timetable for Israeli withdrawal from the Sinai. It was not until

Carter himself visited Cairo and Jerusalem, in early March 1979, that the Israeli and Egyptian cabinets approved compromises suggested by President Carter. The formal signing of the treaty, which amplified the general provisions of the framework agreement, took place at the White House on March 26, 1979.

The Arab Response to Camp David

For the Camp David accords and the Egyptian–Israeli peace treaty to have led to a further and more comprehensive peace settlement in the Middle East, as we noted above, there would have to have been general agreement among the Arab states on the two "Frameworks" cited earlier, as well as Israeli goodwill concerning the West Bank and Gaza. It is difficult to see how the other major Arab states could have supported the Egyptian–Israeli accords. In the first place, the accords did not mention Jerusalem. The king of Saudi Arabia—a country in which Islam pervades social customs, dominates the political structure, and legitimizes the regime—could not have endorsed an agreement that did not even mention the third holiest city of Islam after Mecca and Medina, namely Jerusalem, a city that houses the Dome of the Rock from which the Qur'an says Muhammad ascended into heaven. It was also unlikely that Saddam Hussein of Iraq, who claimed to be the champion of Arab nationalism, would have been party to accords that omitted any reference to the recovery of all of Palestine. Syria would certainly not agree to any negotiations that omitted an indication that Israel was willing to withdraw from the Golan Heights.

Similarly, King Hussein of Jordan, with his Palestinian subjects, could not have signed an accord that was unacceptable to the majority of his people and his three powerful neighbors. These Arab leaders did not agree to the Camp David accords, therefore, since to have done so would have endangered their own political survival, owing to the ideological and spiritual importance of the issues to their people. They felt threatened by internal instability and external threats. Arab leaders do not rely for their legitimacy and continued role on established political institutions such as parties and parliaments to the extent that Western leaders do. They are much more dependent upon popular support and success in carrying out what is perceived as the popular will. Sadat, as we have noted, was free from these constraints to some extent, and, furthermore, Egypt gained specific benefits. He also demonstrated that a single Arab state could act independently of the rest of the Arab "nation"; Pan-Arabism was no longer—if indeed it ever had been—a straightjacket determining Egyptian policy.

Nevertheless, the reaction of the Arab states to the signing of the peace treaty was far more harsh and swift than anticipated by Egypt or by the United States. Nineteen members of the Arab League immediately met in Baghdad, Iraq, and, on March 31, 1979, issued a communiqué outlining political and economic sanctions against Egypt. (See Document 8–7.) By early May, all the Arab countries except Oman and Sudan, close allies of Sadat, had severed diplomatic relations with Egypt. In addition, Egypt was suspended from the twenty-two member Arab League, expelled from the Islamic Conference, and ousted from a number of Arab financial and economic institutions such as the Federation of Arab Banks and the Organization of Arab Petroleum Exporting Countries (OAPEC).

Some have argued that the Camp David accords hindered the achievement of a comprehensive peace settlement, that the accords radicalized Arab opinion; it was seen by the Arabs as a separate peace "designed to neutralize Egypt from the anti-Zionist struggle." The Arabs saw this as a way of preventing joint Arab action to dislodge Israel from Arab territory and as weakening the legitimate right of the Palestinians for a national home. Overall, the Camp David agreements increased Arab suspicion of Israel and the United States, and the other Arab states refused to be drawn into the process. This hostility, in turn, hardened Israeli attitudes toward the Arabs.

The Significance of the Camp David Accords

The real achievements of the Camp David accords should not be diminished, however. Millions in Israel, Egypt, and throughout the world were thrilled at the sight of Anwar Sadat, the president of Egypt, stepping from his plane at Ben-Gurion Airport, Israel, to a flourish of trumpets. And millions later watched with gratitude and expectation as the television cameras recorded Sadat and Begin, witnessed by Jimmy Carter, signing a peace treaty on the White House lawn on March 26, 1979. In the words of Abba Eban, Israel's foreign minister from 1966 to 1974, Sadat's main achievement "was to separate our future from our past." In an article published in *Foreign Affairs* in 1979, which strongly defended the Camp David negotiations, Eban, who was then one of the leaders of the opposition Labor party in the Knesset, made the telling point that the past was the enemy of the future in the Middle East. He pointed out that nothing in Arab history prepared the Arabs for a Jewish state in the Middle East. Throughout Arab history, Jews had always appeared as subjects, merchants and craftsmen, scholars and doctors, members of a deviant religion, but never as an autonomous political and territorial entity in their own right. He added that Arab difficulties in coming to terms with Israel, in addition to their immediate grievances, should not be taken lightly.

The history of Israel was also one that made conciliation a difficult course to follow. Because they viewed so much of their history as self-defense against implacable enemies, Israelis tended to overreact to any perceived threat to their security. The Camp David agreements simultaneously lessened Arab rejectionism and Israeli suspicion. In this context, the accords could be viewed as a major step forward and, however viewed, must be regarded as a vast improvement on the methods of violence and terror so often employed by both sides.

The future of the West Bank, Gaza, the Golan Heights, and East Jerusalem remained the major unresolved issues of the Camp David accords. In 1978, some 800,000 Arabs inhabited the West Bank and 500,000 more were in Gaza, and they did not regard themselves as part of Israel in any way. (See Document 8–8.) There was a complete separation of language, religion, and culture between the Arabs of the West Bank and the Jews of Israel. Neither of these two worlds sought harmony with the other. Although religious and nationalistic Jews described the region as Judea and Samaria, the inhabitants were Arab in all their loyalties. Israeli "doves" argued that although Israel would be smaller in size if the West Bank and Gaza were returned to Arab sovereignty, a major reason for the Arab world's military, economic, and psychological hostility to Israel would be destroyed, thereby creating a much more secure Israel. Israel would then be freer of the oppressive burden of its military priorities and diplomatic problems and, if peace resulted, would be able to trade and invest in Arab markets to great economic advantage. Although the Camp David accords resulted in a peace treaty between Israel and Egypt, the Palestinians were largely overlooked and ignored as the 1980s began. Instead, events in Lebanon again occupied center stage in the Arab–Israeli conflict. By the end of that decade, however, with the PLO leadership no longer in Beirut but in Tunis, the Palestinians in the territories took their fate into their own hands. We shall be considering these matters in the next chapter.

Suggestions for Further Reading

CARTER, JIMMY, *Keeping Faith*, New York, Bantam, 1982.

DAYAN, MOSHE, *Breakthrough: A Personal Account of the Egypt–Israel Peace Negotiations*, New York, Alfred A. Knopf, 1981.

EISENBERG, LAURA Z. AND CAPLAN, NEIL, *Negotiating Arab–Israeli Peace: Patterns, Problems, Possibilities*, Bloomington, Indiana University Press, 1998.

LOWI, MIRIAM R., Water an Power: *The Politics of a Scarce Resource in the Jordan River Basin*, Cambridge University Press, 1995.

QUANDT, WILLIAM, *Camp David: Peacemaking and Politics*, Washington, D.C., Brookings Institution, 1986.

SACHAR, HOWARD M., *A History of Israel, Vol. II, From the Aftermath of the Yom Kippur War*, New York, Oxford University Press, 1987.

SADAT, ANWAR, *In Search of Identity: An Autobiography*, New York, Harper & Row, 1978.

SHOUKRI, GHALI, *Egypt: Portrait of a President. Sadat's Road to Jerusalem*, London, Zed, 1.

WEIZMAN, EZER, *The Battle for Peace*, New York, Bantam, 1981.

 DOCUMENT 8-1

UN General Assembly Resolution 3236 (XXIX), November 22, 1974

The General Assembly
Having considered the question of Palestine
Having heard the statement of the Palestine Liberation Organization, the representative of the Palestinian people,
Having also heard other statements made during the debate,
Deeply concerned that no just solution to the problem of Palestine has yet been achieved and recognizing that the problem of Palestine continues to endanger international peace and security,
Recognizing that the Palestinian people is entitled to self-determination in accordance with the Charter of the United Nations,
Expressing its grave concern that the Palestinian people has been prevented from enjoying its inalienable rights, in particular its right to self-determination,
Guided by the purposes and principles of the Charter,
Recalling its relevant resolutions which affirm the right of the Palestinian people to self-determination,

1. *Reaffirms* the inalienable rights of the Palestinian people in Palestine, including:
    (a) The right to self-determination without external interference;
    (b) The right to national independence and sovereignty;
2. *Reaffirms also* the inalienable right of the Palestinians to return to their homes and property from which they have been displaced and uprooted, and calls for their return;
3. *Emphasizes* that full respect for and the realization of these inalienable rights of the Palestinian people are indispensable for the solution of the question of Palestine;
4. *Recognizes* that the Palestinian people is a principal party in the establishment of a just and durable peace in the Middle East;
5. *Further recognizes* the right of the Palestinian people to regain its rights by all means in accordance with the purposes and principles of the Charter of the United Nations;
6. *Appeals* to all States and international organizations to extend their support to the Palestinian people in its struggle to restore its rights, in accordance with the Charter;
7. *Requests* the Secretary-General to establish contacts with the Palestine Liberation Organization on all matters concerning with question of Palestine;
8. *Requests* the Secretary-General to report to the General Assembly at its thirtieth session on the implementation of the present resolution;
9. *Decides* to include the item "Question of Palestine" in the provisional agenda of its thirtieth session.

   UNO, doc. BR/74/55/(1974)

Source: T. G. Fraser, *The Middle East, 1914–1979* (New York: St. Martin's Press, 1980), pp. 143–144.

Speech by Yasser Arafat, Palestine Liberation Organization, to the General Assembly, [Excerpts] November 13, 1974

As a result of the collusion between the mandatory Power and the Zionist movement and with the support of some countries, this General Assembly early in its history approved a recommendation to partition our Palestinian homeland. This took place in an atmosphere poisoned with questionable actions and strong pressure. The General Assembly partitioned what it had no right to divide—an indivisible homeland. When we rejected that decision, our position corresponded to that of the natural mother who refused to permit King Solomon to cut her son in two when the unnatural mother claimed the child for herself and agreed to his dismemberment. Furthermore, even though the partition resolution granted the colonialist settlers 54 per cent of the land of Palestine, their dissatisfaction with the decision prompted them to wage a war of terror against the civilian Arab population. They occupied 81 per cent of the total area of Palestine, uprooting a million Arabs. Thus, they occupied 524 Arab towns and villages, of which they destroyed 385, completely obliterating them in the process. Having done so, they built their own settlements and colonies on the ruins of our farms and our groves. The roots of the Palestine question lie here. Its causes do not stem from any conflict between two religions or two nationalisms. Neither is it a border conflict between neighbouring states. It is the cause of people deprived of its homeland, dispersed and uprooted, and living mostly in exile and in refugee camps. . . .

All along, the Palestinian dreamt of return. Neither the Palestinian's allegiance to Palestine nor his determination to return waned; nothing could persuade him to relinquish his Palestinian identity or to forsake his homeland. The passage of time did not make him forget, as some hoped he would. When our people lost faith in the international community which persisted in ignoring its rights and when it became obvious that the Palestinians would not recuperate one inch of Palestine through exclusively political means, our people had no choice but to resort to armed struggle. Into that struggle it poured its material and human resources. We bravely faced the most vicious acts of Israeli terrorism which were aimed at diverting our struggle and arresting it.

In the past ten years of our struggle, thousands of martyrs and twice as many wounded, maimed and imprisoned were offered in sacrifice, all in an effort to resist the imminent threat of liquidation, to regain our right to self-determination and our undisputed right to return to our homeland. With the utmost dignity and the most admirable revolutionary spirit, our Palestinian people has not lost its spirit in Israeli prisons and concentration camps or when faced with all forms of harassment and intimidation. It struggles for sheer existence and it continues to strive to preserve the Arab character of its land. Thus it resists oppression, tyranny and terrorism in their ugliest forms. . . .

The Palestine Liberation Organization has earned its legitimacy because of the sacrifice inherent in its pioneering role, and also because of its dedicated leadership of the struggle. It has also been granted this legitimacy of the Palestinian masses, which in harmony with it have chosen it to lead the struggle according to its directives. The Palestine Liberation Organization has also gained its legitimacy by representing every faction, union or group as well as every Palestinian talent, either in the National Council or in people's institutions. This legitimacy was further strengthened by the support of the entire Arab nation, and it was consecrated during the last Arab Summit Conference, which reiterated the right of the Palestine Liberation Organization, in its capacity as the sole representative of the Palestinian people, to establish an independent national State on all liberated Palestinian territory. . . .

In my formal capacity as Chairman of the Palestine Liberation Organization and leader of the Palestinian revolution I proclaim before you that when we speak of our common hopes for the Palestine of tomorrow we include in our perspective all Jews now living in Palestine who choose to live with us there in peace and without discrimination.

We invite them to emerge from their moral isolation into a more open realm of free choice, far from their present leadership's efforts to implant in them a Masada complex.

We offer them the most generous solution, that we might live together in a framework of just peace in our democratic Palestine.

In my formal capacity as Chairman of the Palestine Liberation Organization, I announce here that we do not wish one drop of either Arab or Jewish (sic) to be shed; neither do we delight in the continuation of killing, which would end once a just peace, based on our people's rights, hopes and aspirations had been finally established.

In my formal capacity as Chairman of the Palestine Liberation Organization and leader of Palestinian revolution I appeal to you to accompany our people in its struggle to attain its right to self-determination. This right is consecrated in the United Nations Charter and has been repeatedly confirmed in resolutions adopted by this august body since the drafting of the Charter. I appeal to you, further, to aid our people's return to its homeland from an involuntary exile imposed upon it by force of arms, by tyranny, by oppression, so that we may regain our property, our land, and thereafter live in our national homeland, free and sovereign, enjoying all the privileges of nationhood. Only then can we pour all our resources into the mainstream of human civilization. Only then can Palestinian creativity be concentrated on the service of humanity. Only then will our Jerusalem resume its historic role as a peaceful shrine for all religions.

I appeal to you to enable our people to establish national independent sovereignty over its own land.

Today I have come bearing an olive branch and a freedom-fighter's gun. Do not let the olive branch fall from my hand. I repeat: do not let the olive branch fall from my hand.

War flares up in Palestine, and yet it is in Palestine that peace will be born.

UNO, GAOR, 29th Session, Two Thousand Two Hundred and Eighty-Second Meeting, A/PV.2282/Corr. 1

Source: Fraser, *The Middle East*, pp. 136–140.

 DOCUMENT 8-3

Speech by Yosef Tekoah, Israel, to the General Assembly, November 13, 1974 [Excerpts]

On 14 October 1974 the General Assembly turned its back on the UN Charter, on law and humanity, and virtually capitulated to a murder organization which aims at the destruction of a State Member of the UN. On 14 October the UN hung out a sign reading "Murderers of children are welcome here."

Today these murderers have come to the General Assembly, certain that it would do their bidding. Today this rostrum was defiled by their chieftain, who proclaimed that the shedding of Jewish blood would end only when the murderers' demands had been accepted and their objectives achieved. . . .

The United Nations is entrusted with the responsibility to guide mankind away from war, away from violence and oppression, toward peace, toward international understanding and the vindication of the rights of peoples and individuals. What remains of that responsibility now that the UN has prostrated itself before the PLO, which stands for premeditated, deliberate murder of innocent civilians, denies to the Jewish people its right to live, and seeks to destroy the Jewish State by armed force? . . .

Are the Arabs of Palestine suffering starvation as are, according to UN statistics, almost 500 million people in Asia, Africa and Latin America? Has the UN left the Palestinian refugees without assistance as it has tens of millions of refugees all over the world, including Jewish refugees in Israel from Arab lands? Are the Palestinian refugees the only ones who cannot be reintegrated as others have been? Have the Palestinian Arabs no State of their own? What is Jordan if not a Palestinian Arab State?

The real reason for the special considerations accorded to questions concerning the Arabs of Palestine has been one and one only—the continuous exploitation of these questions as a weapon of Arab belligerency against Israel. As King Hussein said of the Arab leaders: "They have used the Palestine people for selfish political purposes." This is also the real motivation of the present debate.

In fact, no nation has enjoyed greater fulfillment of its political rights, no nation has been endowed with territory, sovereignty and independence more abundantly than the Arabs. . . .

Now, as a result of centuries of acquisition of territory by war, the Arab nation is represented in the UN by twenty sovereign States. Among them is also the Palestinian Arab State of Jordan.

Geographically and ethnically Jordan is Palestine. Historically both the West and East Banks of the Jordan river are parts of the Land of Israel or Palestine. Both were parts of Palestine under the British Mandate until Jordan and then Israel became independent. The population of Jordan is composed of two elements—the sedentary population and nomads. Both are, of course, Palestinian. The nomad Bedouins constitute a minority of Jordan's population. Moreover, the majority of the sedentary inhabitants, even on the East Bank, are of Palestinian West Bank origin. Without the Palestinians, Jordan is a State without a people. . . .

Indeed, the vast majority of Palestinian refugees never left Palestine, but moved, as a result of the 1948 and 1967 wars, from one part of the country to another. At the same time, an approximately equal number of Jewish refugees fled from Arab countries to Israel.

It is, therefore, false to allege that the Palestinian people has been deprived of a State of its own or that it has been uprooted from its national homeland. Most Palestinians continue to live in Palestine. Most Palestinians continue to live in a Palestinian State. The vast majority of Palestinian Arabs are citizens of that Palestinian State.

The choice before the General Assembly is clear. On the one hand there is the Charter of the UN; on the other there is the PLO, whose sinister objectives, defined in its Covenant, and savage outrages are a desecration of the Charter.

On the one hand, there is Israel's readiness and desire to reach a peaceful settlement with the Palestinian Arab State of Jordan in which the Palestinian national identity would find full expression. On the other hand there is the PLO's denial of Israel's right to independence and of the Jewish people's right to self-determination. . . .

The question is: should there be peace between Israel and its eastern neighbour or should an attempt be made to establish a Palestine Liberation Organization base to the east of Israel from which the terrorist campaign against the Jewish State's existence could be pursued?

On 14 October the General Assembly opted for the PLO, it opted for terrorism, it opted for savagery. Can there be any hope that it might now undo the harm it has already done, by that action, to the cause of peace in the Middle East and to humanity in general? Israel has also made its choice.

The United Nations, whose duty it is to combat terrorism and barbarity may agree to consort with them. Israel will not.

The murderers of athletes in the Olympic Games of Munich, the butchers of children in Ma'alot, the assassins of diplomats in Khartoum do not belong in the international community. They have no place in international diplomatic efforts. Israel shall see to it that they have no place in them.

Israel will pursue the PLO murderers until justice is meted out to them. It will continue to take action against their organization and against their bases until a definitive end is put to their atrocities. The blood of Jewish children will not be shed with impunity.

Israel will not permit the establishment of PLO authority in any part of Palestine. The PLO will not be forced on the Palestinian Arabs. It will not be tolerated by the Jews of Israel.

UNO, GAOR, 29th Session, Two Thousand Two Hundred and Eighty-Second Meeting, A/PV. 2282/Corr. 1

Source: Fraser, *The Middle East*, pp. 140–143.

 DOCUMENT 8-4

Framework for Peace in the Middle East Agreed at Camp David and Signed at the White House, September 17, 1978 [Excerpts]

Preamble.
The search for peace in the Middle East must be guided by the following:

The agreed basis for a peaceful settlement of the conflict between Israel and its neighbors is United Nations Security Council Resolution 242, in all its parts. . . .

To achieve a relationship of peace, in the spirit of Article 2 of the United Nations Charter, future negotiations between Israel and any neighbor prepared to negotiate peace and security with it, are necessary for the purpose of carrying out all the provisions and principles of Resolutions 242 and 338.

Peace requires respect for the sovereignty, territorial integrity and political independence of every state in the area and their right to live in peace within secure and recognized boundaries free from threats or acts of force. Progress toward that goal can accelerate movement toward a new era of reconciliation in the Middle East marked by cooperation in promoting economic development, in maintaining stability, and in assuring security.

Security is enhanced by a relationship of peace and by cooperation between nations which enjoy normal relations. In addition, under the terms of peace treaties, the parties can, on the basis of reciprocity, agree to special security arrangements such as demilitarized zones, limited armaments areas, early warning stations, the presence of international forces, liaison, agreed measures for monitoring, and other arrangements that they agree are useful.

Framework:
Taking these factors into account, the parties are determined to reach a just, comprehensive, and durable settlement of the Middle East conflict through the conclusion of peace treaties based on Security Council Resolutions 242 and 338 in all their parts. Their purpose is to achieve peace and good neighborly relations. They recognize that, for peace to endure, it must involve all those who have been most deeply affected by the conflict. They therefore agree that this fram work is intended by them to constitute a basis for peace not only between Egypt and Israel, but also between Israel and each of its other neighbors which is prepared to negotiate

peace with Israel on this basis. With that objective in mind, they have agreed to proceed as follows:

A. West Bank and Gaza

1. Egypt, Israel, Jordan and the representatives of the Palestinian people should participate in negotiations on the resolution of the Palestinian problem in all its aspects. To achieve that objective, negotiations relating to the West Bank and Gaza should proceed in three stages:

   a) Egypt and Israel agree that, in order to ensure a peaceful and orderly transfer of authority, and taking into account the security concerns of all the parties, there should be transitional arrangements for the West Bank and Gaza for a period not exceeding five years. In order to provide full autonomy to the inhabitants, under these arrangements the Israeli Military Government and its civilian administration will be withdrawn as soon as a self-governing authority has been freely elected by the inhabitants of these areas to replace the existing military government. To negotiate the details of a transitional arrangement, the Government of Jordan will be invited to join the negotiations on the basis of this framework. These new arrangements should give due consideration both to the principle of self-government by the inhabitants of these territories and to the legitimate security concerns of the parties involved.

   b) Egypt, Israel, and Jordan will agree on the modalities for establishing the elected self-governing authority in the West Bank and Gaza. The delegations of Egypt and Jordan may include Palestinians from the West Bank and Gaza or other Palestinians as mutually agreed. The parties will negotiate an agreement which will define the powers and responsibilities of the self-governing authority to be exercised in the West Bank and Gaza. A withdrawal of Israeli armed forces will take place and there will be a redeployment of the remaining Israeli forces into specified security locations. The agreement will also include arrangements for assuring internal and external security and public order. A strong local police force will be established, which may include Jordanian citizens. In addition, Israeli and Jordanian forces will participate in joint patrols and in the manning of control posts to assure the security of the borders.

   c) When the self-governing authority (administrative council) in the West Bank and Gaza is established and inaugurated, the transitional period of five years will begin. As soon as possible, but not later than the third year after the beginning of the transitional period, negotiations will take place to determine the final status of the West Bank and Gaza and its relationship with its neighbors, and to conclude a peace treaty between Israel and Jordan by the end of the transitional period. These negotiations will be conducted among Egypt, Israel, Jordan, and the elected representatives of the inhabitants of the West Bank and Gaza. . . . The negotiations will resolve, among other matters, the location of the boundaries and the nature of the security arrangements. The solution from the negotiations must also recognize the legitimate rights of the Palestinian people and their just requirements. In this way, the Palestinians will participate in the determination of their own future through:

      1. The negotiations among Egypt, Israel, Jordan and the representatives of the inhabitants of the West Bank and Gaza to agree on the final status of the West Bank and Gaza and other outstanding issues by the end of the transitional period.

      2. Submitting their agreement to a vote by the elected representatives of the inhabitants of the West Bank and Gaza.

      3. Providing for the elected representatives of the inhabitants of the West Bank and Gaza to decide how they shall govern themselves consistent with the provisions of their agreement.

4. Participating as stated above in the work of the committee negotiating the peace treaty between Israel and Jordan. . . .

d) Egypt and Israel will work with each other and with other interested parties to establish agreed procedures for a prompt, just and permanent implementation of the resolution of the refugee problem.

B. Egypt-Israel

1. Egypt and Israel undertake not to resort to the threat or the use of force to settle disputes. Any disputes shall be settled by peaceful means in accordance with the provisions of Article 33 of the charter of the United Nations.

2. In order to achieve peace between them, the parties agree to negotiate in good faith with a goal of concluding within three months from the signing of this framework a peace treaty between them, while inviting the other parties to the conflict to proceed simultaneously to negotiate and conclude similar peace treaties with a view to achieving a comprehensive peace in the area. The framework for the conclusions of a peace treaty between Egypt and Israel will govern the peace negotiations between them. The parties will agree on the modalities and the timetable for the implementation of their obligations under the treaty.

C. Associated Principles

1. Egypt and Israel state that the principles and provisions described below should apply to peace treaties between Israel and each of its neighbors—Egypt, Jordan, Syria and Lebanon.

2. Signatories shall establish among themselves relationships normal to states at peace with one another. To this end, they should undertake to abide by all the provisions of the charter of the United Nations. Steps to be taken in this respect include:

a) Full recognition

b) Abolishing economic boycotts

c) Guaranteeing that under their jurisdiction the citizens of the other parties shall enjoy the protection of the due process of law.

For the Government of the Arab Republic of Egypt: Al-Sadat
For the Government of Israel: M. Begin
Witnessed by: Jimmy Carter, President of the United States of America.

Source: The Middle East, 7th ed. (Washington, D.C.: Congressional Quarterly, Inc., 1990), pp. 302–303.

 DOCUMENT 8-5

Framework for the Conclusion of a Peace Treaty Between Egypt and Israel Signed at the White House on September 17, 1978 [Excerpts]

In order to achieve peace between them, Israel and Egypt agree to negotiate in good faith with a goal of concluding within three months of the signing of this framework a peace treaty between them. . . .

The following matters are agreed between the parties:

A. The full exercise of Egyptian sovereignty up to the internationally recognized border between Egypt and mandated Palestine,

B. The withdrawal of Israeli armed forces from the Sinai,

C. The use of airfields left by the Israelis near El Arish, Rafah, Ras en Naqb, and Sharm el Sheikh for civilian purposes only, including possible commercial use by all nations,

D. The right of free passage by ships of Israel through the Gulf of Suez and the Suez Canal on the basis of the Constantinople Convention of 1888 applying to all nations, the Strait of Tiran and the Gulf of Aqaba are international waterways to be open to all nations for unimpeded and nonsuspendable freedom of navigation and overflight.

E. The construction of a highway between the Sinai and Jordan near Eliat with guaranteed free and peaceful passage by Egypt and Jordan,

F. The stationing of forces listed below.

. . . .

After a peace treaty is signed, and after the interim withdrawal is complete, normal relations will be established between Egypt and Israel, including: Full recognition, including diplomatic, economic and cultural relations, termination of economic boycotts and barriers to the free movement of goods and people, and mutual protection of citizens by the due process of law.

Interim withdrawal:

Between three months and nine months after the signing of the peace treaty, all Israeli forces will withdraw east of a line extending from a point east of El Arish to Ras Muhammad, the exact location of this line to be determined by mutual agreement.

For the Government of the Arab Republic of Egypt: A. Sadat
For the Government of Israel: M. Begin
Witnessed by: Jimmy Carter, President of the United States of America.

Source: *The Middle East*, 7th ed., Congressional Quarterly, pp. 303–304.

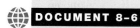

DOCUMENT 8–6

The Likud Response to Camp David: The 1981 Party Platform [Excerpts]

THE RIGHT OF THE JEWISH PEOPLE TO ERETZ ISRAEL

A. The right of the Jewish people to Eretz Israel is an eternal one, which cannot be challenged and is a part of Israel's right to security and peace.

B. The state of Israel has a right to, and demands, sovereignty over Judea, Samaria and the Gaza District. Following the interim period stipulated in the Camp David Accords, Israel will press its demand and take action to realize this right.

C. Any program which entails relinquishing part of Western Eretz Israel to foreign rule, as suggested by the Alignment Party, undermines our right to the land; will inevitably lead to the establishment of a "Palestinian" State; harms the security of the civilian population; endangers the existence of the state of Israel; and frustrates all possibilities for peace. A state in which the cities, towns and villages resided in by the majority of the population would be within firing range of the enemy would serve as a perpetual temptation to aggressors who would again try to destroy it.

D. The autonomy arrangements agreed upon at Camp David are the only guarantee that under no circumstances will a "Palestinian" State be established in part of Western Eretz Israel.

OUR CENTRAL OBJECTIVE—TRUE PEACE AND THE PREVENTION OF WAR

A. The Likud will give the struggle for peace top priority and spare no effort to further peace. The peace treaty between Israel and Egypt is a result of the Likud Government's policies and is a historic turning point for the status of Israel in the Middle East.

B. The government will respect the Camp David Accords.

C. The Likud will act to renew negotiations concerning implementation of the full autonomy agreement for the Arab inhabitants of Judea, Samaria and the Gaza District.

D. The autonomy agreed upon at Camp David does not signify a state, or sovereignty, or self-determination. The Arab nation enjoys self-determination thanks to the existence of twenty-one Arab States.

CONTINUING PROTECTION OF ISRAEL CITIZENS FROM HARM

The terrorist organization which calls itself "PLO" seeks to destroy the state of Israel. There will be no negotiations with this murderous organization, which aims its weapons, supplied by the Soviet Union, against men, women and children. The government will act to protect the civilian population from the terrorists. This will be done by initiating offensive action and preventive attacks against their bases and within them. This policy pursued by the Likud government has proved itself to be the best method for protecting the civilian population.

SETTLEMENTS

Wide-scale settlement activities have been conducted over the past four years in Judea and Samaria: 55 towns were established in Judea and Samaria; 55 posts and towns in the Galilee; five towns in the Golan Heights; six in the Gaza District; five in the Arava; ten in the Besor region; eight on the Negev plateau and the slopes of Mount Hebron. Altogether, 144 towns have been established throughout Eretz Israel in the past four years.

Settlement in the Land of Israel is a right and an integral part of the nation's security. We have observed the rule, and will continue to do so, that Jewish settlement shall not cause the removal of a man from his land, his village or his town. The Likud will act to strengthen the development of, and consolidate its hold over, existing settlements.

Source: Yehuda Lukacs, *Documents on the Israeli-Palestinian Conflict, 1967–1983* (Cambridge, England: Cambridge University Press, 1984), pp. 120–122.

 DOCUMENT 8-7

Arab League Summit Communiqué, Issued in Baghdad, Iraq, March 31, 1979 [Excerpts]

As the Government of the Arab Republic of Egypt has ignored the Arab summit conferences' resolutions, especially those of the sixth and seventh conferences held in Algiers and Rabat; as it has at the same time ignored the ninth Arab summit conference resolutions—especially the call made by the Arab kings, presidents and princes to avoid signing a peace treaty with the Zionist enemy—and signed the peace treaty on 26 March 1979;

It has thus deviated from the Arab ranks and has chosen, in collusion with the United States, to stand by the side of the Zionist enemy in one trench; has behaved unilaterally in the Arab-Zionist struggle affairs; has violated the Arab nation's rights; has exposed the nation's destiny, its struggle and aims to dangers and challenges; has relinquished its pan-Arab duty of liberating the occupied Arab territories, particularly Jerusalem, and of restoring the Palestinian Arab people's inalienable rights, including their right to repatriation, self-determination and establishment of the independent Palestinian state on their national soil.

. . . The Arab League Council, on the level of Arab foreign ministers, has decided the following:

1. (A) To withdraw the ambassadors of the Arab states from Egypt immediately.
   (B) To recommend the severance of political and diplomatic relations with the Egyptian Government. The Arab governments will adopt the necessary measures to apply this recommendation within a maximum period of one month from the date of issuance of this decision, in accordance with the constitutional measures in force in each country.
2. To consider the suspension of the Egyptian Government's membership in the Arab League as operative from the date of the Egyptian Government's signing of the peace treaty with the Zionist enemy. This means depriving it of all rights resulting from this membership.
3. To make the city of Tunis, capital of the Tunisian Republic, the temporary headquarters of the Arab League. . . .

Source: Walter Laqueur and Barry Rubin, eds., *The Israel–Arab Reader: A Documentary History of the Middle East Conflict*, 4th ed. (New York: Penguin Books, 1984), pp. 616–617.

 DOCUMENT 8–8

West Bank Palestinians: Reaction to Camp David, August 30, 1981* [Excerpts]

The Palestinian masses in the occupied West Bank and Gaza Strip continue to reject the declaration made by Sadat and Begin . . . that they had agreed to resume talks concerning so-called "autonomy" for the inhabitants of the West Bank and the Gaza Strip. A large number of Palestinian figures and personalities have commented . . . that the autonomy plan does not concern them in any respect, and that they consider the autonomy plan to be a conspiracy directed against the hopes and aspirations of the Palestinian people who are striving to attain their legitimate rights— which have been established by the international community, as represented by the UN . . . .

Dr. Amin al-Khatib, head of the Federation of Charity Associations in Jerusalem, said: "I do not believe that any plan for a solution to the Palestine problem which does not include the establishment of an independent Palestinian state in the territory of Palestine will be successful, no matter how skillfully its sponsors choose names for it and think up methods of attempting to convince us to accept it. . . .

"We have the following to say to Sadat: 'The Palestinian people, inside the occupied territories, do not wish to have you speak or negotiate in their behalf. Give both yourself and us some peace and do not bother us with this whirlpool which is called "autonomy." ' "

Zalikhah Shihabi, the head of the Jerusalem Women's Federation, said: "Everything concerning autonomy—whether it be the autonomy talks, resumption of such talks, their cessation, or the breaking off of such talks altogether—does not concern us. The reason for this is that we know that it is merely a waste of time, and the objective of those who are calling for autonomy is to decrease the resentment of world public opinion against them, to attempt to outflank

* Excerpts from an article in the Algerian newspaper *Al-Sha'b*.

and encircle the PLO, and to flee from the truth which is shining as brightly as the sun. This truth is that the PLO is the only body authorized to discuss all matters which concern the Palestine question. All of us here agree that there should be an independent Palestinian state. Anything other than that will only meet with rejection and indifference on the part of the Palestinian people."

Mustafa 'Abd al-Nabi al-Natshah, deputy mayor of Hebron: "Autonomy is a continuation of military occupation, only with a mask over it. Autonomy, which is tantamount to local rule, does not contain any of the elements of establishing an independent state. It is a deception utilized in order to impose permanent occupation and would confer permanent legitimacy upon the military occupation. This is something which we totally reject."

Source: Laqueur and Rubin, *Israel–Arab Reader*, pp. 624–626.

NINE

Lebanon and the Intifada

C H R O N O L O G Y

Sept. 22, 1980	Outbreak of Iran–Iraq war
June 7, 1981	Israel bombs Iraqi nuclear reactor at Osirak
Oct. 6, 1981	Anwar Sadat assassinated; Hosni Mubarak becomes president of Egypt
Dec. 14, 1981	Israel annexes Golan Heights
Apr. 25, 1982	Israel returns last portion of Sinai to Egypt
June 6, 1982	Israel invades Lebanon in "Operation Peace for Galilee"
Aug. 21, 1982	PLO begins withdrawal from Beirut. Completed by Sept. 1
Sept. 1, 1982	Reagan peace plan
Sept. 9, 1982	Multinational peacekeeping force arrives in Lebanon
Sept. 1982	Fez peace plan
Sept. 14, 1982	Israelis move into West Beirut
Sept. 18, 1982	Sabra and Shatila massacres
Sept. 20, 1982	Amin Gemayel becomes president of Lebanon after his brother, Bashir, is killed on Sept. 14
Aug. 28, 1983	Menachem Begin resigns
Sept. 12, 1983	Yitzhak Shamir forms government in Israel
Oct. 23, 1983	241 U.S. Marines killed in truck bomb attack in Beirut
Dec. 20, 1983	PLO leaders depart Lebanon to establish headquarters in Tunis
Jan. 19, 1984	Islamic conference readmits Egypt
Feb. 21, 1984	U.S. peacekeeping forces depart Lebanon
July 23, 1984	Israeli elections: Labor-Likud unity government with Shimon Peres as prime minister

Jan. 20, 1985	Israel begins initial withdrawal from Lebanon
Feb. 22, 1985	Jordanian–PLO peace plan
June 10, 1985	Israel completes withdrawal from Lebanon
Oct. 21, 1985	Israeli prime minister Peres calls for Middle East peace conference
Oct. 20, 1986	Yitzhak Shamir takes over as Israeli prime minister
Dec. 9, 1987	Intifada begins
July 31, 1988	King Hussein renounces claims to West Bank
Sept. 29, 1988	Taba given to Egypt by international arbitration panel
Nov. 1, 1988	Israeli general elections; Shamir as prime minister forms coalition government Dec. 17
Nov. 15, 1988	Palestine National Council, in Algiers, proclaims Palestinian state
Dec. 13, 1988	Arafat addresses United Nations in Geneva; says PNC accepts Resolutions 242 and 338; renounces terrorism; United States opens dialogue with PLO
Apr. 6, 1989	Shamir announces election plan for the occupied territories
May 22, 1989	Egypt readmitted to Arab League
Oct. 24, 1989	Lebanese parliament endorses Taif peace plan
Jan.–Feb. 1990	Christian militias battle in Beirut
Mar. 15, 1990	Shamir government falls on no-confidence vote; Shamir forms new Likud government on June 8

As the Egypt–Israel peace treaty formally went into effect the two countries moved to "normalize" relations, and Israel began its withdrawal from the Sinai. The other Arab states rejected Israel's offer of negotiations, and most of them boycotted Egypt. Despite Arab diplomatic and economic sanctions against Egypt, President Anwar Sadat said he would pursue the idea of Palestinian autonomy on the West Bank. Israeli Prime Minister Menachem Begin also publicly upheld the idea of autonomy, but he meant autonomy for the people, not the land. Despite Egyptian, American, and PLO objections, he authorized new Jewish settlements in the territories.

During the Camp David meetings, Israel, for the first time, had agreed that a solution to the Arab–Israeli conflict must acknowledge the "legitimate rights of the Palestinian people and their just demands." Begin had agreed to negotiate with Palestinian representatives over the future of the occupied territories and had specified a limited five-year period of autonomy. As new Jewish settlements continued, however, it became increasingly clear that, if there were ever any negotiations on the "final status" of the territories, the Begin government intended to establish Israel's claim to sovereignty over the land, regardless of any interim arrangements. The Palestinians feared that an interim period of internal autonomy might become a permanent state of affairs and perpetuate the Israeli occupation in a different guise. They were unwilling to recognize the existence of the state of Israel through participation in a negotiating process, and refused to cooperate in any attempt to implement the autonomy provisions of the Camp David accords.

Although the Carter administration wished to continue the momentum of Camp David, the United States was distracted throughout 1979 and 1980 by a number of critical developments in the Persian Gulf region. In Iran, in 1979, the Shah's government collapsed and Ayatollah Ruhollah Khomeini returned from exile. In November of that year, Iranian militants stormed the American Embassy in Tehran and took over fifty hostages. This episode, which lasted for 444 days, preoccupied the American government, led to an abortive rescue attempt in April 1980, and probably contributed to the defeat of Jimmy Carter and the election of Ronald Reagan as president of the United States in November 1980. (The hostages were released Inauguration Day, January 20, 1981.) In addition, war broke out in September 1980 between Iran and Iraq, raising concerns about the continued flow of oil and the future stability of the Persian Gulf region. Additional uncertainty was created in October 1981, when Anwar Sadat was assassinated by Muslim extremists opposed to the Egyptian leader's domestic policies and to the peace treaty with Israel. Sadat's successor was Hosni Mubarak, former commander of the Egyptian air force, a vice president since 1975, and reputedly Sadat's closest advisor. Although Mubarak pledged to uphold the peace treaty with Israel, any further movement toward a comprehensive settlement stalled, as the Reagan administration settled in and as Mubarak attempted to deal with internal economic and political problems. Meanwhile, in Israel, Menachem Begin's mandate was extended in the elections of 1981, and attention turned to the situation on Israel's northern border.

Lebanon

The border with Lebanon had generally been quiet after the cease-fire in 1949. A Mixed Armistice Commission (MAC) had been set up after the first Arab–Israeli war, but as observers liked to point out, the most serious problems the MAC had to deal with involved sheep straying over the frontier. Although opposed to Israel, Lebanon was notable for its virtual non-participation in the 1956, 1967, and 1973 wars. A number of developments in the 1970s, however, brought Lebanon into the forefront of international politics and the Arab–Israeli conflict. A brief background discussion may be necessary to understand how this happened.

As noted earlier in this text, the modern country of Lebanon resulted from the decision after World War I to create French and British mandates out of former Ottoman territory in the Levant area. France was awarded the mandate for Syria and Lebanon, and the boundaries of both countries were drawn in such a way as to facilitate French economic and political control, particularly through a kind of deliberate "balkanization" of the territory and "divide-and-rule" policies between Christians and Muslims. In Lebanon, the French also perpetuated and enshrined the power-sharing formulas among the various religious groups that had begun in the Ottoman period, and that recognized the predominantly Christian character of Lebanon. In general, the French favored, worked through, and recognized the preeminence of the Maronite Christians, namely Catholics who had accepted the authority of the Pope at Rome since the Middle Ages. Many Maronites considered themselves descendants of the ancient Phoenicians and identified with French (and Western) values and ideologies.

In the mid-nineteenth century, the Ottomans had bowed to European pressures to create an autonomous sanjak in Mount Lebanon with a Christian governor, and after the establishment of the mandate, the French worked through a Maronite president. Lebanese political institutions, however, were clearly subordinate to the will of the French high commissioner. Since the French did little to encourage national unity, the major sectarian and ethnic groups of Lebanon—Maronite Christians, Greek Orthodox, Greek Catholics, Sunni and Shiite Muslims, the Druze, and a host of others—continued, in almost tribal fashion, to follow the dictates of their feudal or godfather-type lords (*zaims*) or their individual or confessional leaders.

Lebanon contains a baffling number of mutually exclusive ethnic and religious groups, and by continuing to recognize these divisions in the population, and indeed by encouraging them, the French tried to ensure their own ongoing prominent presence. The mandate of Greater Lebanon was divided geographically and ethnically as follows. To the east was the Bekaa Valley and the anti-Lebanon mountain area, populated largely by a mixed Muslim population that continued to desire close ties with neighboring Syria. These portions were added to Mount Lebanon, traditional home of Maronite Christians, Druze, and Shiites. Large numbers of Sunni Muslims also lived in the coastal areas, along with Maronites, Druze, and Shiites who had migrated in the nineteenth century, especially to Beirut. The south was inhabited largely by Shiite Muslims, the poorest and, until the last few decades, the most quiescent group among the many definable groups in the population.

In addition to the differences among the various sectarian groups, there was tension on a larger scale between the Maronites, most of whom saw Lebanon as a Christian and Western outpost in the Middle East, and those Lebanese, especially Muslims, who espoused the cause of pan-Arab unity, who often looked to Syria, and who identified more with the Arab world and its causes.

Lebanon had fallen under control of the pro-German Vichy government of France between 1940 and 1941. The Free French who "liberated" the country granted the Lebanese their independence in 1941, and elections were held in 1943. The leaders of the major sectarian communities made an unwritten agreement, the so-called National Pact of 1943, to make government possible by a power-sharing formula that provided for a Maronite president, a Sunni prime minister, and a Shiite speaker of the parliament. It was further agreed that in the parliament there would be six Christians for every five Muslims, reflecting the claim, based on the 1932 census, that the Christians were still the numerically superior group in the population.

This internal political "balance" was also reflected in Lebanon's foreign policy. Although Lebanon had joined the Arab League and had declared war on Israel in 1948, its participation in the Arab–Israeli conflict was minimal. Lebanon did not join the Baghdad Pact in 1955 but did not fault the then pro-British government in Iraq for doing so. In 1957, Lebanon was the only Arab country to endorse the Eisenhower Doctrine against communism, but that obvious tilt to the West, as well as too great an assertion of Christian hegemony on the part of the government of President Camille Chamoun, helped create the conditions for a brief civil war in 1958. (At that time, the pan-Arab appeal of Egyptian president Nasser was very strong throughout the region.) That episode encouraged Lebanon to try to restore its previous, if fragile, internal balance and to resume walking the tightrope in its external affairs.

Unfortunately, by the 1970s, a number of changes had occurred that made it impossible to maintain the precarious internal and external balancing act. For one thing, despite the lack of an official census since 1932, it was quite clear that the Muslim population now exceeded that of the Christian, and Muslim demands for greater political parity became more insistent. The Maronite political leaders consistently ignored these demands. Second, greater economic disparities began to be evident throughout the population. Most observers tend to focus on religious differences among the Lebanese, to the exclusion of major and complex non-religious variables, such as locality and economic factors. Class and economic status have created cleavages even within the different confessional groupings. Although Lebanon was lauded as the "Switzerland of the Middle East," there were sections of glittering Beirut that had no electricity or sewage facilities. Southern Lebanon in general was an economically depressed area usually ignored by the central government. There was never a complete correlation between political power and economic status. Nevertheless, in general, the Christian community was wealthier than the Muslim community and had greater economic opportunities. In part, this was because of the economic and educational advantages Christians had enjoyed as a result of their special relationship with the European powers dating back to the nineteenth century. It was also due to a patronage system that reserved certain jobs and positions for Christians.

In the 1970s, as the result of the Arab oil embargo and increased oil revenues in the Arab world, Lebanon both benefitted and suffered. The gross national product grew, but burgeoning inflation caused the economic disparities and discord between the rich and the poor to increase. Perhaps most important for the Arab–Israeli conflict, however, the Palestinian dimension began to intrude into Lebanese politics and into Lebanon's role as a confrontation state.

The Palestinian Factor

Emancipation of the PLO from control by the Arab governments after 1967 and added attention to the Palestinian cause increasingly affected Lebanon's internal situation. With Israel in control of the Golan Heights and the West Bank, PLO guerrilla raids against Israel, launched from Lebanon across Israel's northern border, became more frequent. Israeli retaliation often followed, and in one such series of incidents in 1968, the Israelis undertook a daring commando attack on Beirut International Airport and destroyed thirteen civilian aircraft. PLO raids were greatly resented by the Maronites in particular, who attempted, both through the Arab League and internally, to curb and restrain PLO activity against Israel from Lebanon. In 1969, the Cairo agreement limited PLO guerrillas to certain portions of southern Lebanon, soon called *Fatahland*. However, following the showdown with Jordan's King Hussein in 1970 and 1971, and their expulsion from Jordan, the PLO leaders and many PLO fighters, eventually numbering 15,000, moved to Lebanon, joining the by now 200,000 or more Palestinian refugees already there living in camps. The PLO established bases and began to organize the refugees in the camps. They also began to dominate the Shiite areas of southern Lebanon. Israeli retaliatory strikes against refugee camps and into southern Lebanon began to affect the Shiites in the south, who also came to resent the Palestinian presence. Many of them began to migrate to the north, where they would eventually organize politically and become a significant new political factor in Lebanese politics.

With Lebanon being drawn increasingly into the Palestinian–Israeli situation, tension grew between those attempting to maintain Lebanese "sovereignty" (that is, the existing governmental arrangements, the Western connection, and opposition to the presence of the PLO) and those, especially among the Muslims, who supported the Arab and Palestinian cause against Israel and supported the activities of the PLO. Thus, the Palestinian issue exacerbated already tense economic and political differences. These differences exploded again into civil war in 1975.

Civil War and Its Consequences

In April 1975, civil war broke out in Lebanon between the Maronite militias and those of the Lebanese National Movement (LNM). The LNM represented the Druze and various factions, such as the Syrian Socialist Nationalist party, the Lebanese Communist party, and others, mainly Muslims, who were dissatisfied with the prevailing system. Although holding aloof initially, the PLO soon joined the Muslim belligerents. In this critical situation, the Lebanese army fragmented, and many individual soldiers joined one or another of the competing militias. When it became apparent by March 1976 that the Christian militias were on the defensive, the Syrian army intervened to restore the *status quo ante*. Evidently, Syrian president Hafez al-Assad was afraid of a radical government in Lebanon, in part because it would strengthen the PLO, which would then be capable of operating independently of Syria. Moreover, the Syrians worried that anarchy in Lebanon could lead to an Israeli invasion of Lebanon that could threaten Syria. Syria thus intervened to rescue and to fight for the existing government against the PLO and the Muslim militias. By October 1976, a cease-fire had been worked out by the Arab League, which sanctioned the presence of an Arab Deterrent Force (soon limited to Syrian troops) in Lebanon. The Syrian presence in the form of approximately 35,000 troops remained for the next 29 years, until April, 2005.

The Maronite leaders had no particular love for the Syrians, however; nor were Syrian sympathies necessarily with the Christians. In 1976, a group of Christian leaders had formed the Lebanese Front, a political coalition, whose military arm was the Lebanese Forces. The Lebanese Forces brought together four Christian militias, but the dominant role in both the Lebanese Front and Lebanese Forces was played by the Phalange, a Maronite party founded in the 1930s and led by Pierre Gemayel. Syria did attempt to mediate among the various parties and militias but did not try to disarm them; thus, the level of violence remained high. Moreover, the Syrians allowed the PLO to continue to build up its power south of the so-called red line (generally taken to be the Litani River), where the Israelis said they would not tolerate the presence of Syrian troops. Israel, meanwhile, had been in contact with Pierre Gemayel to discuss matters of common concern. Although both sides had reservations about too close an alliance, by 1978 Israel was supporting the Lebanese Front with arms and training. Israel also helped organize and arm the South Lebanon Army, a predominantly Christian militia in southern Lebanon, led by Major Saad Haddad, a Greek Catholic. Between 1977 and 1982, Israel sold more than $118 million worth of arms to the Lebanese Christians to help prevent what Begin called their "genocide" at the hands of the Muslims.

PLO attacks against Israel from Lebanon had increased during the period of Secretary of State Henry Kissinger's shuttle diplomacy and the disengagement agreements of 1974 and 1975, when it appeared that the United States and the belligerent countries were ignoring the Palestinian cause. Palestinian attacks also increased after Anwar Sadat's trip to Jerusalem in November 1977, and as Israel and Egypt began to negotiate. Lebanon was the usual PLO base. In March 1978, PLO terrorists commandeered a bus on the coastal highway south of Haifa and over thirty people were killed. Israel responded with a major invasion of Lebanon (Operation Litani), designed to destroy the PLO military infrastructure. Although the Israelis withdrew three months later, they established a nine-mile wide "security zone" under Major Haddad's control. In addition, UN troops (UNIFIL, or United Nations Interim Forces in Lebanon) were sent to southern Lebanon. Neither UNIFIL nor Major Haddad, however, was able to prevent the PLO, which was in virtual control of many villages and camps, from developing into a conventional army replete with a growing arsenal that included long-range weapons and rockets.

The Israeli government, especially after the Likud victory in 1977, began to look for ways to crush the PLO and, perhaps at the same time, to deal with the problem of the West Bank. Some Israeli strategists argued that if the PLO were cut off at the head in Lebanon, PLO influence in the occupied territories might also wane, and perhaps Palestinian leaders would emerge who were willing to strike a deal with Israel. They believed PLO funds, patronage, and physical threats—as well as the assassination of those who cooperated with Israeli authorities—had prevented moderate Palestinians from emerging as an alternative to the PLO. Israeli policies in the territories, which included the expulsion or deportation of leaders and others who supported the PLO or publicly espoused the idea of national self-determination, also deprived the Israelis of the opportunity to deal with acknowledged leaders and opinion makers.

"Operation Peace for Galilee"

Israel invaded Lebanon again on June 6, 1982. The pretext was provided by the nearly fatal shooting on June 3 of Shlomo Argov, Israel's ambassador to London. His attackers were not, as claimed, PLO at all, but members of the Abu Nidal group, an anti-Arafat Palestinian faction operating independently of the PLO. Abu Nidal's Fatah Revolutionary Council targeted anyone identified with Israel or the West and is said to have been responsible for the death or wounding of 900 people in twenty countries since breaking away from Arafat in 1974.

In the years prior to 1982, Israel had responded to PLO rocket attacks against its northern border towns with air strikes on Palestinian refugee camps, which often killed innocent civilians. Determined to put a stop to the rocket attacks, in the summer of 1981 Begin ordered the Israeli Air Force to strike PLO targets in Beirut. An American mediator, Philip Habib, secured a cease-fire that held into early 1982. There were no PLO incursions and no Israeli strikes. By the spring of 1982, however, a number of factors led Israel to consider launching another major operation in Lebanon. First, there were several border incidents that heightened tensions. At the same time, Israel was completing its withdrawal from the Sinai in accordance with the provisions of the peace treaty with Egypt. Reasonably sure of noninterference from Egypt, Israel began seriously to consider an invasion of Lebanon. It is also possible that the unpleasant and even at times violent confrontation of the Israeli army with Jewish settlers, who were forced to evacuate their homes when Egypt regained the Sinai, also impelled Prime Minister Begin (who had been handily reelected in June 1981) to exhibit a show of strength against the PLO in Lebanon. Israel also realized that the Arab world was divided over the Iran–Iraq war. Acting from a position of strength, in June 1981, Israel had bombed Iraq's nuclear reactor at Osirak, and in December 1981 had annexed the Israeli-held portions of the Golan Heights.

The official explanation for the 1982 invasion of Lebanon, termed "Operation Peace for Galilee," was that Israel would eliminate the PLO in southern Lebanon and create a secure area up to twenty-five miles (or forty kilometers) north of its border. However, in a plan conceived by Defense Minister Ariel Sharon, a hero of the 1973 war, and Israel's leading hawk, Israeli forces continued to advance, reaching the outskirts of Beirut within four days. On the way, Israel destroyed Syria's surface-to-air missiles in the Bekaa Valley, shot down Syrian fighter planes, and outflanked Syrian ground forces. Confronted with this situation, President Assad of Syria accepted a cease-fire on June 11. During the ensuing siege of Beirut, the PLO withstood Israel's military and political pressures. The Israelis repeatedly bombarded the city, causing thousands of civilian casualties. The idea was to destroy the PLO and to restore the "legitimate" government, preferably in the person of Bashir Gemayel, Pierre Gemayel's son, who now headed the Lebanese Forces. He believed in Christian hegemony in Lebanon and was vehemently opposed to the PLO and to the Syrian presence. For some time previously, he had had contacts with the Israelis, and a personal relationship had developed between him and Ariel Sharon. The Israelis had come to view Bashir as a powerful and potentially successful political leader and as a real ally.

After shelling Beirut for two months, the Israelis entered West Beirut on August 14. On August 21, PLO forces began evacuating Beirut and dispersed to eight different countries. By September 1, the PLO evacuation was virtually complete, and a multinational peacekeeping force (representing the United States, Italy, and France) arrived in Beirut.

Although the PLO forces had left Lebanon, Bashir Gemayel soon backed away from too close an association or public assertion of friendship with Israel, which undoubtedly had helped assure his election as Lebanese president on August 23, 1982. On September 10, the multinational peacekeeping force began to withdraw, but on September 14, Bashir was assassinated at his headquarters, an act attributed to either the Syrians or the Palestinians. The Israelis immediately reentered West Beirut to "keep the peace"; but between September 15 and September 18, in an area controlled by the Israelis, Christian Phalangists, avenging the death of their leader, were permitted by the Israelis to enter the refugee camps of Sabra and Shatila. A fearful massacre of hundreds of Palestinians ensued, for which the Israelis later accepted indirect responsibility, and Ariel Sharon was forced to resign as Israeli defense minister. As a result of this tragedy, President Ronald Reagan agreed to the return and expansion of the multinational peacekeeping force. Amin Gemayel, Bashir's brother, became president. He was less charismatic than his brother but more amenable to pluralism in Lebanon. Seeking to mend fences, he did little but serve as a point around which the multitudinous factions swirled.

The bitter internecine rivalries of the different factions, religious groups, and even families in Lebanon reemerged following the departure of the PLO. Indeed, new groups and militias appeared on the scene. (See Map 9-1.) One of the most important of these was *Amal*. Organized in the mid-1970s by the Imam Musa al-Sadr (who mysteriously disappeared on a trip to Libya in 1978), Amal sought greater recognition and political representation for the Shiite Muslims who had largely been ignored by the Lebanese government. Galvanized by the Iranian revolution, other Shiite groups formed, including *Hizbullah*, an umbrella organization of several Shiite extremist groups inspired, funded, and supplied by Iran. Hizbullah supported that country's Islamic ideology and preached the eradication of Western influence in Lebanon and the Middle East, Holy War against Israel, and the creation of an Islamic state in Lebanon. The Shiites became increasingly aware of the strength of their numbers, and they have now become the largest Muslim group in Lebanon. They also became more radicalized, particularly in the south and in the southern suburbs of Beirut where many had migrated, first because of their enmity toward the PLO and then because of Israel's prolonged occupation after the 1982 invasion.

Not only were Lebanese internal divisions at the time as sharp as ever, but Syrian and now Israeli troops were in Lebanon. Moreover, in mid-1983, President Assad fomented a split in al-Fatah and expelled Arafat from Syria. Assad continued to provide hospitality in Damascus for Arafat rivals like George Habash of the PFLP and Nayef Hawatmeh of the DFLP. The Israelis had been encouraging an accord between themselves and the Phalange in return for their withdrawal, which, in effect, would have made Lebanon the second Arab country to recognize the Jewish state. The American government, and especially Secretary of State George Shultz, supported this idea. Shultz, indeed, brokered such an agreement in May 1983. It called for an end to the state of war between Israel and Lebanon and withdrawal of Israeli troops, if those of Syria also left. President Assad, who had not been consulted, and who vehemently opposed the pact, refused to budge. Two weeks before the initialing of the agreement, on April 18, 1983, a pro-Iranian group bombed the American Embassy in Beirut, killing over sixty people, including many CIA operatives. This attack was a portent of much worse to come.

The United States, in fact, in closely identifying itself with the "legitimate government" of Lebanon—that is, with Christian predominance—was also backing the *status quo* and simply ignoring what the Lebanese themselves had been fighting about since 1975. The Western, and especially American, presence began to be greatly resented by almost all the Lebanese, for their own particular reasons. In October 1983, a terrorist driving a car filled with explosives blew up the U.S. Marine barracks killing 247 men. The French contingent's compound was also bombed. By March 1984, the United States had left Lebanon, and shortly thereafter, Amin Gemayel cancelled the accord with Israel and moved to mend fences with Syria, which continued to occupy the country militarily and to play a role in Lebanese affairs. Western hostages were seized by Lebanese factions, some Westerners were killed, politicians continued their bickering,

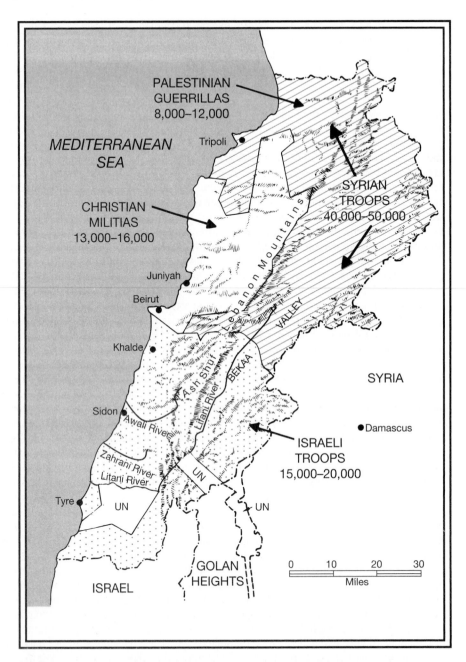

MAP 9–1   Major Factional Military Dispositions in Lebanon, May 1983

the militias became little governments unto themselves, violence and anarchy reigned, and Lebanon slid into economic and political chaos.

The Israeli invasion, then, not only set in motion a train of events that further complicated and worsened the situation in Lebanon but that also failed to achieve its objectives. Many in the PLO returned to Lebanon, including Yasser Arafat. In a showdown with Syrian-supported

PLO rebels, however, he was forced to leave again and to seek refuge in Tunis. Despite President Assad's continuing attempts to undercut Arafat's influence, the PLO leader survived to play a significant role in the further shaping of Israel–Palestinian relations.

Israel Withdraws

By June 1985, Israeli troops had withdrawn from Lebanon. An Israeli presence continued, however, since Israel insisted on maintaining forces in its so-called security zone. Israel had found it much harder to get out of Lebanon than it had expected. The Shiites and southern Lebanese, who had originally welcomed Israeli troops as a means of dislodging the PLO, became unhappy at the disregard for their property, their traditional economic patterns, and at policies that seemed designed to incorporate them into the Israeli economy. Suicide car bombings and sniper attacks against Israeli soldiers escalated, some organized locally, some controlled from Damascus. This led, in turn, to "iron fist" retaliation, in which Israeli squads invaded villages and assassinated suspected leaders of the resistance. Over 500 Israeli troops were killed in Lebanon between 1982 and 1985. These casualties led to enormous internal dissension in Israel and (along with the shock of the death of his wife) to the resignation of Prime Minister Begin in August 1983. Casualties among the occupying troops continued until the withdrawal was completed. The Lebanon adventure exposed weaknesses and divisions within the Israeli armed forces and shocked some of the more moderate Israeli leaders. Begin was succeeded by the even more extreme Yitzhak Shamir, a man who had opposed the Camp David accords.

The Israelis achieved few of their goals by going into Lebanon, as the following developments illustrate. The Lebanese government remained weak and divided, and the civil war continued. The Maronites and the Phalange were unable to reestablish their former control over the country and, in any event, did not seek closer ties with Israel. Israeli and American political influence in Lebanon was commensurately reduced. The Syrian presence was, in fact, strengthened and was backed up by modern Soviet weapons, thus preventing Israel from using Lebanon as a springboard from which to attack Syria. Although PLO leaders were dispersed, and Yasser Arafat correspondingly weakened, even challenged, by Assad-backed factions and other splinter groups, by the late 1980s Arafat had reasserted his control over the PLO. The Palestinians suffered considerable military and civilian casualties during the Israeli invasion, but they also demonstrated a greater capacity for fighting than the Israelis had anticipated. This raised morale and pride among Palestinians everywhere, leading not to greater cooperation in the West Bank and Gaza, as Ariel Sharon had expected, but to an increased determination to resist Israeli rule. Deprived of bases in southern Lebanon, from this time on, the PLO encouraged attacks on Israelis from within the occupied territories. Finally, the large number of casualties among Lebanese and Palestinian civilians, and the widespread destruction that resulted from the Israeli invasion, not only brought worldwide condemnation of Israel but also an upsurge of sympathy and support for the Palestinian cause from all quarters of the globe.

In the Israeli elections of July 1984, the outcome was so close between the Likud and the Labor coalitions that the two groups had to form a "National Unity" government in which both parties shared power and took turns in governing. Thus, Labor's Shimon Peres was prime minister until October 1986 with Likud's Yitzhak Shamir as foreign minister, and then the roles were reversed. It was an uneasy alliance of power between two men whose policies were diametrically opposed. Peres remained committed to his earlier policy of reaching an agreement with Jordan's King Hussein concerning the West Bank, thereby excluding the PLO. The Peres solution involved giving up some territory to Jordan in return for peace and recognition of Israel, although the status of the land to be given up, and the area itself, remained unclear. The Likud's Ariel Sharon (Minister of Commerce and Industry) wanted straight-out Israeli annexation of the occupied land. The ongoing rivalry between Peres and Labor hardliner Yitzhak

Rabin, who was now defense minister and also opposed to negotiations with King Hussein, further blocked any consensus among Israeli politicians on the future of the West Bank.

Increasingly, domestic problems were of greater concern to Israel's leaders. Under Begin, Israel's foreign debt had risen from $11 billion to $21.5 billion; the annual inflation rate from 48 percent to over 150 percent. The basic problem was military expenditure: one-third of the budget went to defense. The Lebanon adventure cost a million dollars a day; the promotion of new West Bank settlements that Begin authorized nearly as much again. Only massive American aid kept Israel afloat. U.S. aid went from $250 million a year after the 1967 war to $1.5 billion after 1973, and to over $3 billion in 1990. (See Table 9–1.)

The American Jewish Lobby and Israel

At this point we should say something about the American Jewish lobby—sometimes called the Israel Lobby—and its role in the Arab–Israeli conflict. Many American commentators and politicians, critical of the close relationship between the United States and Israel, assert that U.S. economic and military assistance to Israel—which they regard as disproportionately high compared with the assistance Washington provides other countries—is the result of the power and influence the Jewish lobby wields in Washington. It is axiomatic to these critics that without such American aid, Israel's economy would falter; that the Jewish state would not be able to sustain the high level of military preparedness and superiority over the Arabs it enjoys; and that therefore, directly or indirectly, the Jewish lobby contributed significantly to the continuation of the Arab–Israeli conflict.

When commentators refer to the Jewish lobby, they usually have three major components in mind: the American Israel Public Affairs Committee (AIPAC), the Conference of Presidents of Major American Jewish Organizations, and a network of Zionist groups. AIPAC, formed in 1954, is perhaps the most visible and successful registered lobbying organization. Based in Washington, it acts as a clearinghouse and coordinating committee for Jewish organizations and groups in the United States seeking to have their views known to Congress and the various executive branches of the federal government. Leaders of most American Jewish organizations sit on the executive committee of AIPAC.

The Conference of Presidents of Major American Jewish Organizations, formed in 1955 and based in New York, also acts as a powerful expression of Jewish opinion. It speaks for about thirty-eight of the main Jewish organizations in the United States. Its major purpose is to try as far as possible to present to Washington officials a consensus of Jewish opinion to ensure a pro-Israeli policy. Zionist groups such as the Zionist Organization of America and Hadassah (the Women's Zionist Organization of America) have also been important in maintaining and building public support for Israel.

The purpose of the Jewish lobby is to strengthen the relationship between the United States and Israel. Its critics describe it as an informal arm of the Israeli government. In addition to the normal lobbying process, the Jewish lobby seeks to limit, or counter, official and press criticism of Israel, to educate officials and the public and thereby gain popular support for pro-Israeli policies, and to act as a kind of go-between interpreting Israel's views to Washington and vice versa.

It is difficult to assess the success of this lobby. While there can be no denying that the United States and Israel have a very "special relationship," it is not clear just what the lobby has contributed to the establishment and maintenance of that relationship. American Jews are very sensitive to accusations of "dual loyalty" and charges that they place Israel's interests ahead of those of the United States. Fear of anti-Semitism has been a powerful weapon in keeping the Jewish lobby within quite limited boundaries. Ironically, AIPAC's apparent success may be its biggest drawback. Although well-funded, staffed, connected, and informed, legislators and public figures know what to expect of the organization and can, if they so wish, find ways of countering the message they receive from AIPAC.

TABLE 9-1 U.S. Assistance to Middle Eastern States, 1946–1988
(U.S. fiscal year—millions of dollars)

	1987	1988	Total Loans and Grants 1946–1988		1987	1988	Total Loans and Grants 1946–1988
EGYPT				Loans	—	—	243.7
Economic	1,015.3	873.4	14,847.3	Grants	0.5	0.4	22.2
Loans	191.7	153.0	5,969.7	Other	—	—	83.2
Grants	823.6	720.4	8,877.6	LIBYA			
Military	1,301.8	1,301.5	12,105.1	Economic	—	—	212.5
Loans	—	—	5,981.2	Loans	—	—	7.0
Grants	1,301.8	1,301.5	6,123.9	Grants	—	—	205.5
Other	—	0.3	471.3	Military	—	—	17.6
IRAN				Grants	—	—	17.6
Economic	—	—	761.8	OMAN			
Loans	—	—	297.6	Economic	14.9	13.0	121.3
Grants	—	—	464.2	Loans	9.9	8.0	77.3
Military	—	—	1,404.8	Grants	5.0	5.0	44.0
Loans	—	—	496.4	Military	—	0.2	167.8
Grants	—	—	908.4	Loans	—	—	167.1
Other	—	—	128.7	Grants	—	0.2	0.7
IRAQ				Other	—	—	—
Economic	—	—	45.5	SAUDI ARABIA			
Loans	—	—	14.4	Economic	—	—	31.8
Grants	—	—	31.1	Loans	—	—	4.3
Military	—	—	50.0	Grants	—	—	27.5
Grants	—	—	50.0	Military	—	—	292.4
Other	—	—	100.5	Loans	—	—	254.2
ISRAEL				Grants	—	—	38.2
Economic	1,200.0	1,200.0	15,025.6	Other	—	—	47.3
Loans	—	—	2,009.9	SUDAN			
Grants	1,200.0	1,200.0	13,015.7	Economic	96.6	63.2	1,379.7
Military	1,800.0	1,800.0	25,826.8	Loans	74.6	40.0	385.3
Loans	—	—	11,204.2	Grants	22.0	23.2	994.4
Grants	1,800.0	1,800.0	14,622.6	Military	6.0	0.9	372.6
Other	—	—	897.4	Loans	—	—	156.3
JORDAN				Grants	6.0	0.9	216.3
Economic	111.1	23.7	1,798.8	Other	—	—	41.7
Loans	2.0	5.2	329.0	SYRIA			
Grants	109.1	18.5	1,469.8	Economic	—	—	353.3
Military	41.9	28.3	1,510.9	Loans	—	—	274.3
Loans	—	—	877.7	Grants	—	—	79.0
Grants	41.9	28.3	633.2	TURKEY			
Other	5.7	28.2	426.5	Economic	103.1	32.4	4,326.8
KUWAIT				Loans	2.4	—	2,035.0
Other	—	—	50.0	Grants	100.7	32.4	2,291.8
LEBANON				Military	493.5	493.5	9,894.6
Economic	22.5	11.9	348.7	Loans	177.9	178.0	4,137.9
Loans	—	—	33.1	Grants	315.6	315.3	5,756.7
Grants	22.5	11.9	315.6	Other	—	—	491.6
Military	0.5	0.4	265.9				

Source: The Middle East, 7th ed. (Washington, D.C.: Congressional Quarterly, Inc., 1990), p. 77.

AIPAC has not always been successful. In 1978, during the Carter administration, it failed to prevent Senate approval of the sale of F15 fighter jets to Saudi Arabia; nor did it succeed in blocking the sale of AWACS aircraft to Saudi Arabia in 1981. Nor has the Conference of Presidents always been successful in maintaining undivided support for Israeli policies within American Jewish ranks. Many influential American Jews, members of the American Jewish Committee, for example, were unhappy with the invasion of Lebanon in 1982, and there were deep divisions within American Jewry over Israel's policies in the occupied territories. Nevertheless, despite their reservations concerning specific Israeli policies, most American Jews have supported continued U.S. aid for Israel.

There are a number of other points we should note in relation to the Jewish lobby. There is nothing new or novel in American political history about an ethnic group involving itself in the political and diplomatic affairs of the nation. Indeed, throughout most of U.S. history, the major issues of American politics have been cultural or ethnic in character. Moreover, the Jewish lobby is not the only lobby trying to influence U.S. policy toward Israel and the Middle East. And the opposition the Jewish lobby faces is formidable. The oil companies, automobile companies, banks, construction companies, and arms manufacturers, and all the related support groups associated with those industries, constitute a reasonably unified block of interests favoring strong ties with the Arab states, and they make the Jewish lobby look like a kindergarten in terms of resources and organization. In addition, Israel, obviously, is only one country in the Middle East with its diplomatic and other representatives in Washington. The Arab states all have their own representation, huge financial resources to spend in Washington compared to Israel, and staunch friends, prepared to use their influence upon Congress, among the groups mentioned above.

Furthermore, the American Arab community has created its own lobbying organization to counter the Jewish lobby. In 1972, the National Association of Arab Americans (NAAA) was formed, modeled on AIPAC. Although not nearly as successful as AIPAC in raising funds or membership, NAAA has nevertheless raised the profile of Arab Americans and the level of support for the Palestinian cause in Washington and among the American people.

While the existence of the so-called Jewish lobby plays some role in the domestic affairs of the United States, it is important to recognize that there is no simple equation whereby its activities can be correlated with American support for Israel. The relationship between the United States and Israel is far more complex and far more deeply rooted in the psyche of the nation than can be explained by the presence of AIPAC and its lobbying activities. The attachment is a commitment to a people and a cause based not only on the bonds of kinship felt by American Jews for the Jewish state, but also on a belief that the survival of Israel is essential if America's sense of its own values and history are to continue.

The Reagan and Other Peace Plans

Despite the very high levels of assistance to Israel, the United States gained surprisingly little influence over Israeli conduct in the Middle East. President Reagan took advantage of the crisis in Lebanon to produce a peace plan in September 1982. This was essentially a return to the Jordanian option already implicit in the Camp David accords. It opposed an independent Palestinian state in the West Bank and Gaza, but also was against Israeli annexation of these areas. Rather, it suggested "self-government by the Palestinians of the West Bank and Gaza in association with Jordan." And, while calling for a freeze on settlements, Reagan assured Israeli Prime Minister Begin that the United States opposed the dismantling of existing Israeli settlements in the occupied areas. For the Palestinians this was unacceptable. The Israelis rejected the initiative out of hand.

In September 1982, at an Arab summit held in Fez, Morocco, Arab leaders responded with their own—the Fez—plan. (See Document 9–1.) The main provisions of the Fez plan called for the complete withdrawal by Israel from all territories occupied in 1967, including East Jerusalem, the dismantling of Israeli settlements in the occupied territories, and a Palestinian state under PLO leadership. In an effort to return to the arena as a major player, on September 15, the Soviets came up with their own—the Brezhnev—peace plan, which essentially mirrored the Fez plan, although it did make specific reference to the future security of Israel, something the Fez plan failed to mention. The Israelis rejected these initiatives as well.

Despite the failure of the Reagan plan, American–Israeli relations remained very close into the second Reagan administration. The United States remained committed to the Jordanian solution essentially and supported the Israeli determination not to negotiate with the PLO. Washington hoped that in so doing it could pressure Israel to make concessions and strengthen its role as an honest broker in the conflict. At the same time, the administration encouraged Israel to talk with selected non-PLO Palestinians from the West Bank and Gaza. Some observers thought that a real chance for peace would come only when the other superpower, the Soviet Union, was also involved, but for most of the Reagan period, the president's staunch anti-Communist stance precluded this possibility. Mikhail Gorbachev's policy of lessening tensions with the West and the subsequent "thaw" in U.S.–Soviet relations held the promise of participation by both superpowers in a settlement of the conflict.

Communal Conflict in Lebanon Continues

Lebanon remained fractured and rent by bloody strife. During 1985 and 1986, Amal attacked Palestinian camps to prevent the return of the PLO, causing heavy civilian casualties. Amal's military actions against the Israelis and the Palestinians were backed by President Assad, who was angry with Yasser Arafat because of his apparent willingness to negotiate with King Hussein of Jordan as a potential partner in negotiations with Israel.

At the end of 1985, an accord was signed in Lebanon under Syrian auspices by the leaders of the Shiites, the Druze, and the Christian leader of the Lebanese Forces. This agreement, which would have reduced the powers of the president and reapportioned parliamentary seats more equitably between Christians and Muslims, was rejected by the Maronite Christian leaders. The cycle of casual violence, bombings, and revenge killings that had ruined Lebanon over the previous ten years continued. The failure in 1988 to select a new president after the expiration of Amin Gemayel's term of office resulted in a divided government, with Muslims following Prime Minister Salim al-Hoss, and the Christians following the commander of the Lebanese Armed Forces, General Michel Aoun, a Maronite Christian trained in France and the United States.

Aoun, backed by Iraq, which became a player on the Lebanese scene after the cease-fire in the Iran–Iraq war in 1987, vowed to drive the Syrians from Lebanon. This resulted in, among other things, the near-total destruction of the already badly bombarded city of Beirut. On October 24, 1989, the Lebanese parliament endorsed an Arab peace plan worked out at Taif, Saudi Arabia. The plan called for a new parliament of 108 members, to be evenly divided between Christians and Muslims, and it reduced the power of the president, by tradition always a Christian. Aoun did not accept the plan, and he condemned it because it did not set a date for a speedy Syrian withdrawal. On November 5, 1989, against the wishes of Aoun, the Lebanese deputies elected Rene Moawad as president, but he was assassinated in a bomb blast after only seventeen days in office. Two days later, on November 24, the Lebanese legislators elected Elias Hrawi president. In early February 1990, particularly fierce and senseless violence broke out between two Maronite rivals, Aoun and warlord Samir Geagea, over control of East Beirut. Geagea, a former medical student at the American University in Beirut, had headed the Phalange Lebanese Forces since 1986. In the fighting that ensued in the first half of 1990, more than 450 Lebanese were killed, and more than 2,000 were wounded. In October 1990, however, while the world's attention was diverted by war in the Persian Gulf, Syria intervened, and Aoun surrendered and subsequently was offered refuge in France. On May 22, 1991, Lebanon signed a Treaty of Cooperation and Brotherhood, which gave Syria de facto control over Lebanon's internal affairs. In September 1991, this was extended to security and foreign affairs as well. For the next decade and a half, Syria remained the real power broker in Lebanon.

The PLO Moves to Tunis

The Palestinians took some time to recover from the setbacks of 1982. The PLO split badly in mutual recriminations after the siege of Beirut. Arafat's opponents within the PLO blamed him for the defeat of the Palestinian fighters and their withdrawal in 1982; they attacked him for his preference for diplomacy rather than the military option for achieving a Palestinian homeland. In November 1983, Amal and the rebel Fatah units under Abu Musa, backed by Syria, drove Arafat from Tripoli in northern Lebanon. He established new PLO headquarters in Tunis. The PLO lost its official status in Lebanon in May 1987 when the Lebanese parliament scrapped the so-called Cairo agreement. However, while the weak Lebanese government sought to establish its own authority, and rival Christian factions fought their own war for control of the country's Christian enclave, the PLO rebuilt its forces in Lebanon. By April 1990, just eight years after Israel had driven the PLO guerrillas out of Lebanon, the organization had regained its military strength. At that time, the PLO had 11,000 trained forces, compared with the 8,000 who were forced out in 1982. Arafat came under pressure from the hardline members of the PLO—Ahmad Jibril of the PFLP-GC and the DFLP—to abandon efforts to negotiate with Israel. The radicals within the PLO asserted that concessions to Israel had achieved nothing, and that a return to force was necessary to realize Palestinian goals. In the meantime, the PLO was seeking formal recognition in any redistribution of political power in Lebanon.

The widespread dispersal of the PLO made united action even more difficult, and despite the fact that he had almost total support within the PLO's governing body, the Palestine National Council, Arafat had to cope with Syrian hostility and President Assad's admittedly unsuccessful attempts to set up a puppet Palestinian organization. In February 1985, King Hussein and Yasser Arafat announced a joint policy. They called for a UN-sponsored international conference, with the PLO representing the Palestinians within a joint Jordanian-PLO delegation, to oversee the following settlement: Israel to withdraw from all the occupied territories, including East Jerusalem, and the establishment of a Palestinian state on the West Bank within the context of a Jordan–Palestine confederation. Although they had different, even competing, goals, Hussein and Arafat viewed this plan as setting in motion the first step toward meeting their immediate needs. Hussein needed the legitimizing support of the PLO if he were to regain the West Bank, and Arafat needed U.S. and international support for PLO participation in negotiations with Israel. Also, the settlement policy that enabled Israel to take even more control over the West Bank and Gaza would be stopped.

Both Israel and the United States opposed an international conference. Both political parties in Israel rejected any negotiations with the PLO over the West Bank. Prime Minister Shimon Peres proposed discussions between Israel and Jordan that would include some non-PLO Palestinians, but the Likud dismissed the idea out of hand. The United States insisted that PLO acceptance of UN Resolution 242 was a precondition for a conference in which the PLO might take part. The United States also opposed an international meeting because it did not want the Soviets to be a party to negotiations at that point. Arafat claimed that by calling for such a conference he had implicitly abandoned the 1968 PLO covenant, with its call for the destruction of Israel. In reality, Arafat did not have the support within the PLO at that time to give the assurances the United States demanded prior to opening negotiations, although he did indicate that he would openly do so as part of the settlement.

Many observers believe that American policy at this point, by its negative response to the Hussein-Arafat initiative, encouraged the extremists within both Israel and the PLO. The extremists within Israel, especially followers of the American-born ultranationalist rabbi and leader of the Kach party, Meir Kahane, not only increased their demands for more Jewish settlements and the annexation of the West Bank (see Map 9–2) but also advocated the forceful removal of the Palestinian Arabs. "Rejectionist Front" elements of the PLO, claiming that moderation would achieve nothing, felt justified in renewing their terrorist activities. On September 25, 1985, three Israeli citizens in Cyprus were assassinated by a PLO extremist group. Israel retaliated by bombing the PLO headquarters in Tunis on October 1. The cycle of violence escalated. Between June and December 1985, there were a series of dramatic terrorist acts of violence that captured world attention. Among the more highly publicized of these episodes were the hijacking of a TWA airliner in the Middle East, the shooting up of the airport passenger lounges in Rome and Vienna, and the hijacking, on October 7, 1985, of the cruise ship *Achille Lauro* by the Palestine National Front headed by Abul Abbas. Extremist voices on both sides prevailed over the advocates of moderation. Israel claimed that PLO terrorism indicated that Arafat could not curb the violent tendencies of the PLO or claim to speak for the Palestinian people. Rejectionist PLO elements and the Saudis refused to give Arafat the green light to continue his diplomatic approach through Jordan. Hussein abandoned the Hussein-Arafat plan and instead began his own discussions with Israel for an international conference. In this situation of stalemate, Yitzhak Shamir and the Likud party took over the government of Israel at the end of 1986.

The Intifada

Violence in the West Bank and Gaza increased throughout 1986 and 1987. By the mid-1980s, an entire generation of Palestinian youth had grown up under Israeli occupation. They had lived with curtailed civil rights and in political limbo. Their economy, although perhaps better than under previous Jordanian or Egyptian rule, was hostage to Israel's economy. They had little faith in the Arab governments, which tended to view them as a nuisance and had done little for them for over twenty years. They were disillusioned with the PLO, which, although a potent symbol of their nationalist feelings, had not succeeded either militarily or diplomatically in securing Palestinian self-determination. Moreover, the Arab summit held in Amman in November 1987, preoccupied with the Iran–Iraq situation, failed to raise the issue of the Palestinians' future. Palestinian rage and frustration began to boil over at the increasing number of Jewish settlements and the often forced land sales and appropriations, while the Israel Defense Forces and Jewish settlers began to react more militantly to Arab resistance. Incidents of violence between Palestinians and Jews became more frequent, a situation Shamir did little to control.

The resistance was unorganized, but Palestinian frustration would soon explode into a full-fledged uprising. On December 9, 1987, an Israeli vehicle plowed into a line of oncoming cars in Gaza, killing four Palestinians and wounding seven others. This tragic accident lit the fuse that resulted in the *Intifada*, or "shaking off," the spontaneous popular uprising in the territories that soon came to dominate the world's attention. During the next year, more than 150 Palestinians were killed and many more arrested; more than 11,500 were wounded (almost two-thirds of whom were under fifteen years of age); universities, colleges, and schools were closed; houses were demolished; and curfews were applied—yet Israel failed to stop the rock-throwing, harassment, and demonstrations.

During the first six weeks of the Intifada, thirty-eight Palestinians were shot and killed by the Israel Defense Forces. Israel's response was deemed by the world to be too harsh, and the Jewish state was widely criticized, even by Jews in the United States. Thirty thousand Israeli demonstrators marched in Tel Aviv, also, to protest the severity of the government's reaction.

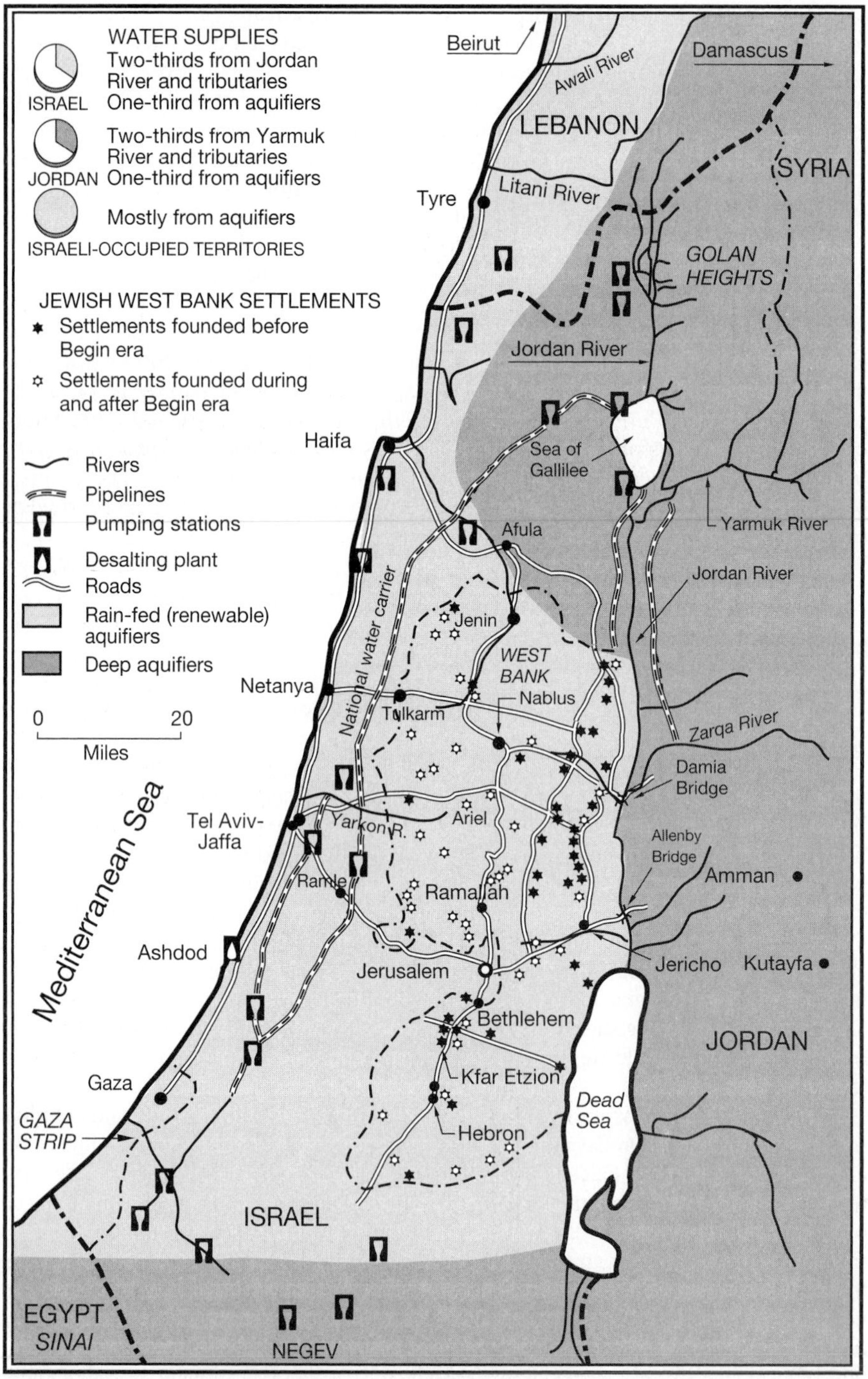

MAP 9–2   West Bank Settlements and Water Resources

Israel's fall 1988 election, which produced another National Unity coalition of the Likud and Labor parties, indicated that opinion within Israel remained divided. While there was no popular mandate for convening an international conference over the future of the territories, or trading land for peace with security (the Labor position), neither was there a clear mandate in support of annexation or a massive Jewish settlement drive in, or retention of, all the territories (the Likud position). During the year, the Peace Now movement, consisting of leftist groups and many of Israel's most senior and respected military leaders, called for an end to the military occupation of the conquered territories, while right-wing extremists, religious zealots, and ultranationalists insisted upon a continued Israeli presence.

The PLO and the Intifada

It took the PLO some time to take control of the Intifada. Although at first the uprising appeared to be spontaneous and the result of individual grievances, Arafat claimed credit for its continuation. In fact, initially the organizing force driving the uprising was a loose confederation of local, primarily leftist, groups that identified themselves as the Unified National Leadership of the Uprising (UNLU). The PLO leader skillfully co-opted these groups under his leadership. Between June and August 1988, he began, through aides, publicly to float ideas outlining what Palestinians would accept in the way of a solution: a Palestinian state in the West Bank and Gaza based on the 1947 UN Partition Plan, and "lasting peace and security" with Israel. King Hussein of Jordan and President Mubarak of Egypt still preferred the land-for-peace solution favored by Shimon Peres, but with Yitzhak Shamir as prime minister that option seemed unlikely. President Hafez al-Assad of Syria wanted neither the Jordanian solution nor an independent Palestinian state; he still dreamed of regaining the Golan Heights and of achieving a "Greater Syria."

In the spring of 1988, U.S. Secretary of State George Shultz, doubtless hoping to achieve a lasting monument for the Reagan administration, placed finding a solution to the Palestinian–Israeli conflict on the front burner, and he launched himself into "shuttle diplomacy," without much visible success.

On July 31, 1988, evidently despairing of success in setting up an international conference, perhaps seeing in the Intifada a threat to his own kingdom, and realizing that, indeed, the Palestinians, especially the younger generation, would never accept him as their spokesperson, King Hussein of Jordan renounced his claim to the West Bank, which in effect reversed the annexation decision made in 1950. (See Document 9–2.) "The independent Palestinian state will be established on the occupied Palestinian land after its liberation, God willing," Hussein stated. Although Jordan continued administration of the daily affairs of the West Bank, the PLO gradually took some responsibility for funding these activities. The Jordanian monarch distanced himself even further from the PLO. On August 7, 1988, he stated that Jordan would not be part of a Jordanian–Palestinian delegation in any peace process.

In the second half of 1988, the harsh Israeli response to the Intifada enabled the PLO to take the diplomatic initiative. Publicizing the Palestinian case on the world stage, the PLO achieved dramatic results. As the PLO increasingly assumed the appearance of a government in exile, the Israeli position hardened. On August 10, 1988, Prime Minister Shamir said that Israel would crush any attempt by the PLO to establish a government in exile. He continued the deportation of Palestinian resistance leaders, a policy adopted the previous January. On August 26, the UN Security Council called on Israel, yet again, to stop the deportations and to allow the return of those already deported (approximately three dozen). The standoff continued.

The Unified National Leadership of the Uprising and HAMAS, an acronym for the Islamic Resistance movement, successfully organized a series of general strikes throughout the West Bank and Gaza. Hamas, meaning "zeal" in Arabic, emerged in the Gaza Strip at the

Young boys and girls
participate in Intifada,
Nablus, April 16, 1988.

beginning of the Intifada as the underground armed wing of the Sunni Muslim Brotherhood in the territories.

The Muslim Brotherhood movement was founded in Egypt in 1928 by Sheikh Hassan al-Banna, and it subsequently spread throughout the Arab world. Opposed to secular and Western influences, its goal was to establish a pan-Islamic state on the basis of the Sharia, or Islamic law. The Muslim Brotherhood supported the Palestinian cause, and its followers among the Palestinian Arabs fought to prevent the establishment of the Jewish state.

There were a number of reasons for the growth and influence of the Brotherhood in the West Bank and Gaza after the Israeli occupation began in 1967. These included financial support from the Gulf states and the Saudi royal family and the relative weakness of competing secular and nationalist groups, especially after the expulsion of the PLO leadership from Jordan in 1971, and its long exile in Tunis after it was forced out of Lebanon in 1982. The Islamic revolution in Iran in 1979 had a powerful effect on the Islamic groups in Palestine, illustrating that it was possible to defeat a ruler associated with the political, cultural, and economic imperialism of the West and establish an Islamic government. The continuing Israeli occupation also aided the growth of the Muslim Brotherhood, partly because the Israelis saw the group as an alternative to Fatah and other PLO groups. Israel did not interfere to any great extent in Brotherhood activities because the group did not at first engage in resistance. The Brotherhood built up an impressive network of religious, charitable, and cultural institutions, and its myriad social services, as well as its message, had widespread appeal to the poor and deprived, especially in Gaza. It spread its ideology through the schools attached to mosques, the number of which doubled on the West Bank and tripled in Gaza between 1967 and the outbreak of the Intifada.

One of the leading members of the Muslim Brotherhood in Gaza was Sheikh Ahmad Yassin, a quadriplegic cleric. When the Intifada started, he was not eager to join. However, as the uprising gained momentum and national sentiment exploded, he did not want the Brotherhood to lose ground to the PLO, or to Islamic Jihad, another offshoot of the original Brotherhood. Islamic Jihad was founded in the territories by Dr. Fathi Shqaqi, who had been inspired by the

Iranian revolution. Shqaqi returned from his studies to Gaza advocating violence to end the Israeli occupation and to establish an Islamic state in the territories and in place of Israel. He was deported by the Israelis in 1988 but continued to direct the activities of his followers from abroad until his assassination by the Israelis in Malta in 1995.

In order to compete with Islamic Jihad, Sheikh Yassin altered the strategy of the Brotherhood. Instead of insisting on a pan-Islamic state as a prerequisite for waging holy war against Israel, he formulated the concept that an Islamic state in Palestine could wage holy war against Israel as the first stage toward the final goal of a pan-Islamic state. Hamas wedded its salvationist platform to the national struggle and rejected as un-Islamic any dealings with Israel and with Jews, "the sons of monkeys and swine." In February 1988, Yassin issued a handbill in the name of the Islamic Resistance movement, and Hamas was launched, emerging as a competitor of the PLO-dominated UNLU. As time passed, its path would diverge even more from that of the PLO.

Hamas quickly resorted to violence, first to execute suspected collaborators, and then to kidnap and kill Israelis. Its military wing, founded in 1990, was called the Qassam Brigades, after Sheikh Izz ad-Din al-Qassam, who was killed by the British in Palestine in 1935. He was revered as the first Muslim leader to unite the ideas of Islam and revolution in armed struggle. In 1991, Sheikh Yassin was arrested by the Israelis and sentenced to life in prison. (He was released and returned to Gaza in 1997.) In mid-October 1988, Arafat, to satisfy American and Israeli objections, modified his position on an independent Palestinian state, stating that the PLO would accept a federation with Jordan. A week later, on October 22, he met with King Hussein and President Mubarak, at Aqaba, to work out the possibilities. Israel seemed unable to convince the United Nations that its methods in containing the Intifada were those of restraint; on November 3, the UN General Assembly, by a vote of 130 to 2 (Israel and the United States

Bus crash, Jerusalem-Tel Aviv highway. A Palestinian extremist forced the bus off the road causing injury and death, July 6, 1989.

voted no) condemned Israeli oppression in the occupied territories and the violations of Palestinian human rights.

Despite the vows of PLO hardliners to derail the PLO chairman's peace initiatives, by the end of the year Arafat appeared to be firmly in control of a more unified PLO. Nevertheless, the PLO was unable, or unwilling, to define its goals or its relationship to Israel in a way that was unambiguous to the Israelis. The first year of the Intifada culminated in the Arab League summit meeting held in Algiers in mid-November 1988. There, on November 15, at the nineteenth meeting of the Palestine National Council (PNC), considered by the PLO to be its parliament in exile, the PNC proclaimed—by a vote of 253 to 46 with 10 abstentions—the establishment of an independent Palestinian state. (See Document 9–3.)

The PLO Declaration of Independence attracted immediate worldwide attention. Within three days, at least twenty-seven nations, mostly Arab and Muslim, extended recognition to the government in exile. On November 18, 1988, the Soviet Union recognized the proclamation of the Palestinian state, and, after initial hesitation, on November 21, Egypt recognized the Palestinian state. Israel denounced the declaration, dismissing it as irrelevant, and the United States rejected the declaration stating that unilateral PLO actions did not satisfy U.S. conditions for determining the future of the occupied territories; it was ambiguous and did not go far enough to warrant opening a dialogue with the PLO. By the mid-1990s, more states recognized the PLO declaration than recognized Israel. As with so many of the public documents crucial to the arguments of each side, almost all aspects of the Palestinian Declaration of Independence were disputed by Israel and Israeli supporters on the one hand, and the PLO and Palestinian supporters on the other. Pro-Palestinians pointed to the declaration's reference to the UN partition resolution—Resolution 181—and "resolution of the United Nations organizations since 1947" as evidence that the PLO implicitly recognized Israel and accepted Resolutions 242 and 338. They also asserted that the PNC had voted specifically to accept Resolutions 242 and 338 on November 14, the day before the declaration was issued. (See Document 9–4.)

Pro-Israelis, in addition to pointing out that there was no authorized English translation of the declaration and no public record of votes taken, searched in vain for clear and unambiguous statements recognizing Israel and accepting Resolutions 242 and 338. Palestinian supporters argued that the declaration, by stating that UN Resolution 181 "provides the conditions of international legitimacy that ensures the right of the Palestinian people to sovereignty," defined the area of the Palestinian state to be the West Bank and the Gaza. Israeli supporters replied that the references to the area the Palestinian state would occupy remained undefined and vague. Palestinians pointed to the affirmation of Palestine as a peace-loving state as evidence of a rejection of terrorism. Israelis dismissed this as deception and pointed to the statements of hardline PLO leaders who contradicted the so-called official policy and called for a continuation of the Intifada.

Most commentators agree that the final weeks of 1988 opened a new chapter in the Arab–Israeli conflict. A group of American Jews met with PLO representative Khalid al-Hassan in Stockholm on November 22 and later, on December 6–7, with Arafat himself and the Swedish foreign minister. They issued a joint statement—quickly dubbed the Stockholm Declaration—stating that the PNC recognized Israel as a state in the region and condemned and rejected terrorism in all its forms, including state terrorism—the PLO's euphemism for Israel's actions. When Arafat was denied a transit visa by the United States to speak to the UN General Assembly, the General Assembly took the unprecedented step of reconvening in Geneva. There, on December 13, 1988, Arafat detailed the proposals agreed to at Algiers. He also outlined his own three-point peace plan, which included the establishment of a UN committee to organize a peace conference, an international conference held under UN auspices with representatives from Israel, Palestine, and their neighbors, and Israeli withdrawal from the West Bank and Gaza, to be replaced by a temporary UN peacekeeping force. Still, Secretary of State George Shultz was not satisfied.

Shamir accused Arafat of a "monumental act of deception." "We are not ready, and will never be ready to talk to the PLO," he fumed. Frantic discussions took place to ensure a positive response from the United States. In addition to Arafat himself, those involved included diplomats from the United States, Egypt, Saudi Arabia, and the Swedish foreign minister. The following day, on December 14, Arafat was more explicit. During a press conference in Geneva, Arafat repeated the PLO's acceptance of UN Resolutions 242 and 338 and fully renounced—not just condemned—terrorism. "Enough is enough. Enough is enough. Enough is enough," he repeated. (See Document 9–5.) Hours later, George Shultz announced that the United States would open a dialogue with the PLO.

The Intifada and Israeli Policy

Israel was crippled by the fact that no government had been formed since the recent elections. Acting Prime Minister Shamir, however, stood by the statement he had made shortly before, that the PLO were "our most extreme enemies. They will never change their position, their philosophy, which is the destruction of Israel," he stated. Arafat lent credence to Shamir's view in early January 1989. American officials claimed that a tape recording of a radio broadcast in which Arafat was speaking about the Intifada revealed that he threatened to kill any Arabs who opposed the uprising. After his government was in place and under U.S. pressure, Shamir presented his own four-point plan as a response to Arafat's November 1988 diplomatic bombshell. (See Document 9–6.)

Rejecting the notion of direct Israeli negotiations with the PLO, Shamir proposed that elections be held in the territories under Israeli supervision to determine who should negotiate with Israel for the Palestinians over the future of the occupied territories.

Shamir's plan was similar to the formula for Palestinian autonomy agreed to at Camp David. President George Bush, who became president on January 20, 1989, supported the proposal, and King Hussein, after a meeting with Secretary of State James Baker, expressed his qualified support. Shamir stated unequivocally that the result would be, at best, Palestinian autonomy. This was seen by the Palestinians as totally out of touch with the new realities created by the Intifada and the 1974 Rabat decision. They believed they should be free to choose their own representatives, whether PLO or not, and that the outcome of any negotiations should not preclude Palestinian self-determination and an independent Palestinian state.

Shamir was under pressure from all sides: On the one hand, the PLO—and the United States to some extent—wanted further Israeli concessions; on the other hand, conservatives within his own Likud party saw Shamir as already having gone too far. On May 9, 1989, following a meeting with French president Mitterand, Arafat declared that the provisions of the PLO charter calling for the destruction of Israel were *caduc*, "null and void." Israeli spokespersons replied with the observation that Arafat could say what he liked, but that the PNC had not issued such a statement. In any event, they added, this could be reversed at any time.

In a further effort to get Israel to accept PLO involvement even indirectly in the election process and peace talks, and to consider some form of territorial compromise, on May 22, 1989, Secretary Baker announced a new American peace plan. Echoing the cry of the Eisenhower administration, Baker called on Israel to "lay aside once and for all the unrealistic vision of a greater Israel" and to "reach out to Palestinians as neighbors who deserve political rights." He called on the Palestinians to amend their covenant and: "Translate the dialogue of violence in the *intifada* into a dialogue of politics and diplomacy. . . . Reach out to Israelis and convince them of your peaceful intentions." Baker's program for peace included Israeli and Egyptian representatives drawing up a list of Palestinians who might take part in Israeli–Palestinian discussions on how to put the Shamir plan into effect. Already under pressure from right-wing elements at home, Shamir immediately rejected Baker's plan.

Nevertheless, variations of the Shamir and Baker plans remained the focus of diplomatic activity for the remainder of 1989. Israel finally agreed to a modified version of the Baker plan, and Egyptian president Hosni Mubarak convinced Arafat to let him act for the PLO in arranging a preliminary dialogue between Israel and the Palestinians. In November, the U.S. State Department began plans to arrange a trilateral meeting among the U.S. secretary of state and the foreign ministers of both Israel and Egypt to discuss the formation of a Palestinian delegation to meet with the Israelis. The PLO, while accepting the Baker plan in principle, insisted that it should have the right to choose its own delegation in any negotiations with the Israelis. It rejected—as it had for the previous fifteen years—the notion that Egypt—or Jordan, with whom Mubarak consulted closely—could speak for the Palestinians. The PLO had been there before.

In November 1989, the Israeli defense ministry revealed that up to that time, the Intifada had cost the Israel Defense Forces (IDF) $500 million. By mid-1990, according to International Red Cross figures, over 800 Palestinians had been killed by Israeli security forces, more than 200 of whom were children under the age of sixteen. Some 16,000 Palestinians were in prison, approximately 1,100 being held under administrative detention. Over 300 Arab homes in the West Bank and in Gaza had been demolished or sealed up. The IDF estimated that an additional 255 Palestinians suspected of collaborating with the Israeli authorities had been killed by fellow Arabs. According to the Associated Press, 47 Israelis had died. Seemingly basing its actions on the principle that the occupied territories were an integral part of Israel, throughout 1986 and 1987, as we have seen, the Israeli government continued its policy of establishing settlements, expropriating property, and encouraging Israeli citizens to move to the occupied territories. By the end of 1987, over 55 percent of the West Bank and 30 percent of the Gaza Strip had been expropriated by Israel. Under the "iron fist" policy Israel adopted toward the Palestinians, the level of despair and hopelessness, violence, and tension in the territories intensified. In 1988 there were 244,416 Palestinian refugees in Gaza Strip camps, and 400,981 Palestinians living outside the camps. The number of Israelis living in the Gaza Strip at the time was 5,000.

Consequences of the Intifada

After December 1987, the question of the future of the Palestinian Arabs acquired special urgency when the Intifada became the center of world attention. The Intifada reordered the political and diplomatic priorities of the Arab–Israeli conflict, bringing the issue of the future of the Palestinian Arabs to the forefront of the conflict.

The Intifada resulted in tragedy for both sides, with young unarmed Palestinian youths confronting Israeli soldiers their own age. Both demonstrating Palestinians and defending Israelis used tactics that put children at risk. The Palestinian organizers of the Intifada were reluctant to weaken the central community–based character of their resistance by making the tactical changes that would help keep children out of harm's way. The Israeli army similarly hesitated to yield its prerogatives as an occupation force and was often unable to enforce the military discipline intended to minimize casualties against a civilian population—a population that had become experienced practitioners of violence without guns. The outcome was that Palestinian children were shot and beaten by Israeli soldiers. The death rate of rock-throwing Palestinians in the first year of the Intifada was six times the annual per capita death rate of American soldiers in Vietnam. The likelihood of either side forgetting the often justified resentment of past wrongs, and of understanding the legitimate grievances and interests of the other, diminished under the growing invective and abuse. Intra-Palestinian violence also took its toll, both in lives and in community cohesion. Frustration among those in the territories and tensions between those in the territories and those in Tunis led to a collapse in internal discipline that resulted in the killing of Palestinians by other Palestinians, either because of suspected collaboration or because of political or religious disputes.

In March 1990, the Knesset passed a vote of no-confidence against Shamir—the first time in Israel's history that a government had fallen through a no-confidence vote. This had occurred because of opposition from factions within his own party led by hardliner Ariel Sharon and because of the defection of Labor's Shimon Peres, Shamir's coalition partner, who advocated adoption of the Baker plan. U.S. Secretary of State Baker had hammered out a compromise plan in February to continue the peace process. His five-point formula called for Israel to accept meetings with Palestinians not active in the PLO although known to have links with the organization. The PLO, in turn, would not insist on direct participation and would drop its demand for prior Israeli agreement to an independent Palestinian state. Under pressure from Likud "hawks," Shamir rejected even this scheme to initiate "talks about talks."

Israel's political stalemate continued through May 1990. Peres failed in his attempt to form a "peace coalition" government, so Shamir once more sought to form a Likud–led government. Encouraged by Peres's failure, Shamir repeated his view that there was no need to hold a dialogue with the Palestinians in the near future. And, in a rebuff to Egyptian president Hosni Mubarak, he stated that once talks began they did not have to take place in Cairo. (Egypt had played a pivotal role in convincing the PLO to support a Palestinian–Israeli dialogue, to be held in Cairo).

Israel's prolonged inability to form a government created a dangerous political vacuum in the Middle East. The "peace process" came to a complete halt. Israel was faced with the issue of creating a government capable of working for a West Bank and Gaza settlement or risking a major break with Washington. Under the impact of the Intifada, relations between the Bush administration and Israel had become strained. By mid-1990, the United States was demanding that Israel stop the beatings and killings (especially of children), harsh detentions, humiliating and inhumane surveillance and curfews (routinely since May 1989, the entire Gaza Strip population had been subjected to dusk-to-dawn curfew), and open the universities that had been closed for over two years.

At a time when Israeli military leaders were predicting that the Intifada was dying or "in retreat," a further outbreak of violence occurred on May 20, 1990, when seven Palestinians were killed in Rishon Lezion south of Tel Aviv in an unprovoked attack by a reportedly deranged former Israeli soldier. Palestinian rage and frustration boiled over into the most violent rioting since the Intifada had begun, and the following day another seven Palestinians were killed and over 600 wounded when the Israeli army attempted to quell the disturbances. A blanket curfew was imposed throughout the Gaza Strip and the major population centers of the West Bank. It took Israeli troops three days to restore order; 17 protesters were killed and over 1,000 wounded. Israeli and Palestinian leaders quickly blamed each other for the renewed outbreak of violence. PLO leader Arafat called on Palestinians to step up protests "in every village, every city and every camp." Even more disturbing to Israeli officials was the open rebellion by Israeli Arabs, the majority of whom joined the general strike called by the heads of the regional Arab councils. The strikes turned violent in many centers, especially cities like Nazareth, Haifa, and other towns with large Arab populations. Within days, a radical element within the PLO, the Palestine Liberation Front (PLF) led by Abul Abbas, attempted a sea-launched reprisal raid against Israeli civilians. Israel naval forces intercepted the raiders, killing four. A beleaguered Acting Prime Minister Shamir immediately went on the diplomatic offensive, claiming that the abortive attack proved that the PLO had not kept Arafat's December 1988 pledge to renounce terrorism and calling on the United States to halt its dialogue with the PLO. Arafat disclaimed any responsibility for the thwarted attack and distanced himself from the Libyan-backed PLF, but he did not condemn the operation. In late June, the United States indeed broke off its dialogue with the PLO.

Following the rioting in May 1990, Egyptian President Mubarak told President Bush that if the peace process remained stalled, more violence would erupt from the Palestinians. The Palestinians had endured extreme economic hardship and deprivation for nearly a quarter of a century without armed revolt, Mubarak told Bush. But, he warned, they would not continue to do so. In something of a turnaround in U.S. policy, Bush called the Palestinian problem a central factor in the Middle East situation that could be resolved only within the framework of a comprehensive settlement. Israel claimed that the core of the conflict was the issue neither of the Palestine Arabs nor of the territories occupied as a result of the 1967 war; it was the fact that the Arab world had not recognized Israel's right to exist. In this context, it is important to keep in mind that in the unfolding Arab–Israeli conflict, a crucial theme in the Palestinian Arabs' struggle for personal identity and national autonomy had been that the Arab world generally had treated them as political pawns for political purposes. Individual Arab states played a dominant—and not particularly positive—role in the Palestinian question from the mid-1930s through the mid-1980s. The superpowers also did not always play a constructive role in seeking a resolution to the conflict.

The Superpowers and the Peace Process

After 1967, the United States advocated a settlement consisting of direct bilateral negotiations between Israel and the existing Arab states, using UN Resolutions 242 and 338 as the basis for a settlement, and proceeding toward a final settlement on a step-by-step basis, separating issues from one another as much as possible. Although the notion of Israel giving up territory in exchange for peace was implicit, there was always doubt as to how much territory would be given up, and to whom. The United States supported Israel's interpretation of Resolution 242—always a problematic document because it altered the status of the West Bank and Gaza from occupied territory to disputed territory that was therefore subject to negotiation. This approach favored Israel in that it allowed Israel undue influence in setting the agenda and the choice of Arab participants in negotiations. Until the end of the Reagan administration, for example, the United States accepted Israel's definition of the Palestinians as terrorists, supported Israel's response to the Intifada, and backed Israeli efforts to exclude the PLO from direct bilateral negotiations.

During the decade of the 1980s, Israel was upgraded from a client to a strategic ally furthering American Cold War aims in the Middle East. Washington opted for the policy of greater reliance on Israel as a means of securing American strategic interest in the region. Israel was given greater access to U.S. military technology, and American aid was increased and converted to outright grants. The United States, anxious to weaken the Soviet-backed regimes in Syria and Iraq and what it regarded as the Soviet-dominated PLO, supported Israel's 1982 invasion of Lebanon as part of a long-term plan to establish closer links with Western-oriented states—Israel, Lebanon, Jordan, Egypt, and Saudi Arabia. As a result of these close American–Israeli ties, Israel was to a large extent protected from international pressure to withdraw from the occupied territories and to negotiate a settlement acceptable to the Palestinians and the Arab countries. American policy assisted Israel in pursuing a hardline approach; indeed, Israel, especially under Likud governments, rejected U.S. peace proposals that called for Israeli withdrawal from any part of the territories. In the meantime, despite American sentiment through several administrations that they were an obstacle to peace, Jewish settlements in the West Bank and Gaza became larger, more numerous, and more entrenched.

The Soviet Union, on the other hand, supported the approach favored by the PLO, the Arab states, and many European and African nations, namely, an international peace conference that would work out a comprehensive peace (also based on UN Resolutions 242 and 338) and set up an international authority to oversee the settlement. The main points of this settlement would be that the Arab states and the Palestinians would recognize the permanence of Israel within its pre-1967 borders, and that Israel would recognize the right of the Palestinians to self-determination.

During the 1960s and 1970s, the Soviet Union had attempted to extend and augment its influence in the Persian Gulf region. The Russians also established a naval base in Ethiopia, where there were 15,000 Cuban troops, sent arms to the northern and southern Yemen Republics, and maintained close ties with Libya and Syria. The Soviets also invaded Afghanistan to support its pro-Soviet government but ended up severely alienating the largely Muslim population in that country.

Preoccupied with internal economic problems, hurt by the Afghanistan debacle, humiliated by Syria's inability (using Russian arms) to contain Israel in Lebanon, and frustrated by the failure to protect the Palestinians in Lebanon, the Soviet Union did not play a significant role in the Arab–Israeli conflict again until the late 1980s, when Soviet president Mikhail Gorbachev signaled a willingness to become an active participant by restoring diplomatic relations with Israel, which had been broken off in 1967, improving Soviet relations with Egypt, and establishing diplomatic ties with conservative Arab Gulf states.

The end of the Cold War, the collapse of the Soviet Union, and the Gulf War of 1991 dramatically altered the dynamics of superpower rivalry in the region. While the United States emerged as the one important superpower on the world stage, the new Russian state was provided with an opportunity to play a different role in the post-Gulf War discussions about regional stability in the Middle East and a resolution of the Arab–Israeli conflict. The Russians would achieve recognition of their continued importance on the world stage and their interest in the Middle East by being a co-sponsor, along with the United States, of the Madrid Peace Conference. The next chapter will explore the consequences of these momentous events for the Arab–Israeli conflict.

Suggestions for Further Reading

ABU-AMR, ZIAD, *Islamic Fundamentalism in the West Bank and Gaza: Muslim Brotherhood and Islamic Jihad*, Bloomington, Indiana University Press, 1994.

AJAMI, FOUAD, *The Vanished Imam: Musa al-Sadr and the Shi'a of Lebanon*, Ithaca, N.Y., Cornell University Press, 1986.

FRIEDMAN, THOMAS, *From Beirut to Jerusalem*, New York, Farrar, Straus & Giroux, 1989.

HELLER, MARK, *A Palestinian State: The Implications for Israel*, Cambridge, Mass., Harvard University Press, 1988.

LESCH, ANN MOSELY, AND TESSLER, MARK, *Israel, Egypt and the Palestinians from Camp David to Intifada*, Bloomington, Indiana University Press, 1989.

MISHAL, SHAUL, AND AHARONI, REUBEN, *Speaking Stones: Communiqués from the Intifada Underground*, New York, Syracuse University Press, 1994.

PERETZ, DON, *The Intifada*, Boulder, Colo., Westview Press, 1989.

RABINOVICH, ITAMAR, *The War for Lebanon, 1970–1983*, Ithaca, N.Y., Cornell University Press, 1984.

RUBIN, BARRY, *Revolution until Victory? The Politics and History of the PLO*, Cambridge, Harvard University Press, 1994.

SCHIFF, ZE'EV, AND YA'ARI, EHUD, *Israel's Lebanon War*, New York, Simon & Schuster, 1984.

———, *Intifada: The Palestinian Uprising: Israel's Third Front*, New York, Simon & Schuster, 1990.

 **DOCUMENT 9–1**

Fez Summit Peace Proposal

An Arab summit was held in Fez, Morocco, in September 1982, in response to the Israeli invasion of Lebanon and President Reagan's September initiative. The following eight-point plan came from that summit.

1. The withdrawal of Israel from all Arab territories occupied in 1967 including Arab Al Qods (East Jerusalem).
2. The dismantling of settlements established by Israel on the Arab territories after 1967.

3. The guarantee of freedom of worship and practice of religious rites for all religions in the holy shrine.
4. The reaffirmation of the Palestinian people's right to self-determination and the exercise of its imprescriptible and inalienable national rights under the leadership of the Palestine Liberation Organization (PLO), its sole and legitimate representative, and the indemnification of all those who do not desire to return.
5. Placing the West Bank and Gaza Strip under the control of the United Nations for a transitory period not exceeding a few months.
6. The establishment of an independent Palestinian state with Al Qods as its capital.
7. The Security Council guarantees peace among all states of the region including the independent Palestinian state.
8. The Security Council guarantees the respect of these principles.

Source: The Middle East, 7th ed. (Washington, D.C.: Congressional Quarterly, Inc., 1990), p. 306.

  DOCUMENT 9-2

Hussein's Renunciation of Claim to the West Bank [Excerpts]

In a July 31, 1988, speech, King Hussein of Jordan renounced his nation's claims to the West Bank and severed all legal and administrative links with it.

In the name of God, the compassionate, the merciful and peace be upon his faithful Arab messenger

Brother citizens . . . . [W]e have initiated, after seeking God's assistance, and in light of a thorough and extensive study, a series of measures with the aim of enhancing the Palestinian national orientation, and highlighting the Palestinian identity. Our objective is the benefit of the Palestinian cause and the Arab Palestinian people.

Our decision, as you know, comes after thirty-eight years of the unity of the two banks, and fourteen years after the Rabat Summit Resolution, designating the Palestine Liberation Organization (PLO) as the sole legitimate representative of the Palestinian people. It also comes six years after the Fez [Morocco] Summit Resolution of an independent Palestinian state in the occupied West Bank and the Gaza Strip. . . .

The considerations leading to the search to identify the relationship between the West Bank and the Hashemite Kingdom of Jordan, against the background of the PLO's call for the establishment of an independent Palestinian state, are twofold:

I. The principle of Arab unity, this being a national objective to which all the Arab peoples aspire, and which they all seek to realize.

II. The political reality of the scope of benefit to the Palestinian struggle that accrues from maintaining the legal relationship between the two banks of the kingdom . . . .

. . . We respect the wish of the PLO, the sole legitimate representative of the Palestinian people, to secede from us in an independent Palestinian state. We say this in all understanding. Nevertheless, Jordan will remain the proud bearer of the message of the great Arab revolt; faithful to its principles; believing in the common Arab destiny; and committed to joint Arab action.

Regarding the political factor, it has been our belief, since the Israeli aggression of June 1967, that our first priority should be to liberate the land and holy places from Israeli occupation.

Accordingly, as is well known, we have concentrated all our efforts during the twenty-one years since the occupation towards this goal. We have never imagined that the preservation of the legal and administrative links between the two banks could constitute an obstacle to the liberation of the occupied Palestinian land . . . .

Lately, it has transpired that there is a general Palestinian and Arab orientation towards highlighting the Palestinian identity in a complete manner. . . . It is also viewed that these [Jordanian-West Bank] links hamper the Palestinian struggle to gain international support for the Palestinian cause, as the national cause of a people struggling against foreign occupation . . . .

. . . At the Rabbat Summit of 1974 we responded to the Arab leaders' appeal to us to continue our interaction with the occupied West Bank through the Jordanian institutions, to support the steadfastness of our brothers there. Today we respond to the wish of the Palestine Liberation Organization, the sole legitimate representative of the Palestinian people, and to the Arab orientation to affirm the Palestinian identity in all its aspects . . . .

Brother citizens. . . . We cannot continue in this state of suspension, which can neither serve Jordan nor the Palestinian cause. We had to leave the labyrinth of fears and doubts, towards clearer horizons where mutual trust, understanding, and cooperation can prevail, to the benefit of the Palestinian cause and Arab unity. This unity will remain a goal which all the Arab people cherish and seek to realize.

At the same time, it has to be understood in all clarity, and without any ambiguity or equivocation, that our measures regarding the West Bank concern only the occupied Palestinian land and its people. They naturally do not relate in any way to the Jordanian citizens of Palestinian origin in the Hashemite Kingdom of Jordan. They all have the full rights of citizenship and all its obligations, the same as any other citizen irrespective of his origin. They are an integral part of the Jordanian state. They belong to it, they live on its land, and they participate in its life and all its activities. Jordan is not Palestine; and the independent Palestinian state will be established on the occupied Palestinian land after its liberation, God willing. There the Palestinian identity will be embodied, and there the Palestinian struggle shall come to fruition, as confirmed by the glorious uprising of the Palestinian people under occupation.

. . . Citizens, Palestinian brothers in the occupied Palestinian lands, to dispel any doubts that may arise out of our measures, we assure you that these measures do not mean the abandonment of our national duty, either towards the Arab-Israeli conflict, or towards the Palestinian cause. . . . Jordan will continue its support for the steadfastness of the Palestinian people, and their courageous uprising in the occupied Palestinian land, within its capabilities.

. . . No one outside Palestine has had, nor can have, an attachment to Palestine, or its cause, firmer than that of Jordan or of my family. Moreover, Jordan is a confrontation state, whose borders with Israel are longer than those of any other Arab state, longer even than the combined borders of the West Bank and Gaza with Israel.

In addition, Jordan will not give up its commitment to take part in the peace process. We have contributed to the peace process until it reached the stage of a consensus to convene an international peace conference on the Middle East. The purpose of the conference would be to achieve a just and comprehensive peace settlement to the Arab-Israeli conflict, and the settlement of the Palestinian problem in all its aspects . . . .

Jordan, dear brothers, is a principal party to the Arab-Israeli conflict, and to the peace process. It shoulders its national responsibilities on that basis.

I thank you and salute you, and reiterate my heartfelt wishes to you, praying God the almighty to grant us assistance and guidance, and to grant our Palestinian brothers victory and success.

May God's peace, mercy, and blessings be upon you.

Source: The Middle East, 7th ed., Congressional Quarterly, p. 309.

DOCUMENT 9-3

Palestine National Council, "Palestinian Declaration of Independence," Algiers, November 15, 1988

Below is the official translation of the Declaration of Independence as carried by WAFA from Algiers, 17 November 1988.

In the name of God, the Compassionate, the Merciful.

Palestine, the land of the three monotheistic faiths, is where the Palestinian Arab people was born, on which it grew, developed, and excelled. The Palestinian people was never separated from or diminished in its integral bonds with Palestine. Thus the Palestinian Arab people ensured for itself an everlasting union between itself, its land, and its history . . . .

Despite the historical injustice inflicted on the Palestinian Arab people resulting in their dispersion and depriving them of their right to self-determination, following upon UN General Assembly Resolution 181 (1947), which partitioned Palestine into two states, one Arab, one Jewish, yet it is this resolution that still provides those conditions of international legitimacy that ensure the right of the Palestinian Arab people to sovereignty and national independence . . . .

In Palestine and on its perimeters, in exile distant and near, the Palestinian Arab people never faltered and never abandoned its conviction in its rights of return and independence. Occupation, massacres, and dispersion achieved no gain in the unabated Palestinian consciousness of self and political identity, as Palestinians went forward with their destiny, undeterred and unbowed. And from out of the long years of trial in evermounting struggle, the Palestinian political identity emerged further consolidated and confirmed. And the collective Palestinian national will forge itself in a political embodiment, the Palestine Liberation Organization, its sole, legitimate representative, recognized by the world community as a whole, as well as by related regional and international institutions . . . .

The massive national uprising, the *intifadah*, now intensifying in cumulative scope and power on occupied Palestinian territories, as well as the unflinching resistance of the refugee camps outside the homeland, have elevated consciousness of the Palestinian truth and right into still higher realms of comprehension and actuality. Now at last the curtain has been dropped around a whole epoch of prevarication and negation. The Intifadah has set siege to the mind of official Israel, which has for too long relied exclusively upon myth and terror to deny Palestinian existence altogether. Because of the Intifadah and its revolutionary irreversible impulse, the history of Palestine has therefore arrived at a decisive juncture.

Whereas the Palestinian people reaffirms most definitely its inalienable rights in the land of its patrimony:

Now by virtue of natural, historical, and legal rights and the sacrifices of successive generations who gave of themselves in defense of the freedom and independence of their homeland;

In pursuance of resolutions adopted by Arab summit conferences and relying on the authority bestowed by international legitimacy as embodied in the resolutions of the United Nations Organization since 1947;

And in exercise by the Palestinian Arab people of its rights to self-determination, political independence, and sovereignty over its territory;

The Palestine National Council, in the name of God, and in the name of the Palestinian Arab people, hereby proclaims the establishment of the State of Palestine on our Palestinian territory with its capital Jerusalem (Al-Quds Ash-Sharif).

The State of Palestine is the state of Palestinians wherever they may be. The state is for them to enjoy in it their collective national and cultural identity, theirs to pursue in it a complete equality of rights. In it will be safeguarded their political and religious convictions and their human dignity by means of a parliamentary democratic system of governance, itself based on freedom of expression and the freedom to form parties. The rights of minorities will duly be respected by the majority, as minorities must abide by decisions of the majority. Governance will be based on principles of social justice, equality and nondiscrimination in public rights on grounds of race, religion, color, or sex under the aegis of a constitution which ensures the role of law and on independent judiciary. Thus shall these principles allow no departure from Palestine's age-old spiritual and civilizational heritage of tolerance and religious co-existence.

The State of Palestine is an Arab state, an integral and indivisible part of the Arab nation, at one with that nation in heritage and civilization, with it also in its aspiration for liberation, progress, democracy, and unity. The State of Palestine affirms its obligation to abide by the Charter of the League of Arab States, whereby the coordination of the Arab states with each other shall be strengthened. It calls upon Arab compatriots to consolidate and enhance the emergence in reality of our State, to mobilize potential, and to intensify efforts whose goal is to end Israeli occupation.

The State of Palestine proclaims its commitment to the principles and purposes of the United Nations, and to the Universal Declaration of Human Rights. It proclaims its commitment as well to the principles and policies of the Non-Aligned Movement.

It further announces itself to be a peace-loving state, in adherence to the principles of peaceful co-existence. It will join with all states and peoples in order to assure a permanent peace based upon justice and the respect of rights so that humanity's potential for well-being may be assured, an earnest competition for excellence be maintained, and in which confidence in the future will eliminate fear for those who are just and for whom justice is the only recourse.

In the context of its struggle for peace in the land of love and peace, the State of Palestine calls upon the United Nations to bear special responsibility for the Palestinian Arab people and its homeland. It calls upon all peace- and freedom-loving peoples and states to assist it in the attainment of its objectives, to provide it with security, to alleviate the tragedy of its people, and to help to terminate Israel's occupation of the Palestinian territories.

The State of Palestine herewith declares that it believes in the settlement of regional and international disputes by peaceful means, in accordance with the UN Charter and resolutions. Without prejudice to its natural right to defend its territorial integrity and independence, it therefore rejects the threat or use of force, violence, and terrorism against its territorial integrity, or political independence, as it also rejects their use against the territorial integrity of other states.

Therefore, on this day unlike all others, 15 November, 1988, as we stand at the threshold of a new dawn, in all honor and modesty we humbly bow to the sacred spirits of our fallen ones, Palestinian and Arab, by the purity of whose sacrifice for the homeland our sky has been illuminated and our land given life . . . .

Therefore, we call upon our great people to rally to the banner of Palestine, to cherish and defend it, so that it may forever be the symbol of our freedom and dignity in that homeland, which is a homeland for the free, now and always.

In the name of God, the Compassionate, the Merciful.

Source: Journal of Palestine Studies, No. 70, Winter 1988, pp. 213–216.

DOCUMENT 9-4

PLO Acceptance of UN Resolutions 242 and 338

The Palestine National Council affirms the necessity of holding an effective international conference concerning the Middle East issue and its essence, the Palestinian cause, under the auspices of the United Nations and with the participation of the permanent member states of the U.N. Security Council and all the parties to the struggle in the region, including the P.L.O., the sole legitimate representative of the Palestine people, on an equal footing, and by considering that the international conference will be held on the basis of U.N. Security Council Resolutions 242 and 338 and the assurance of the legitimate national rights of the Palestinian people and, first and foremost, their right to self-determination in application of the principles and provisions of the U.N. charter concerning the right of peoples to self-determination and the inadmissibility of seizing the lands of others by force or military invasion, and in accordance with the resolutions of the U.N. regarding the Palestinian and Arab territories that it has occupied since 1967, including Arab Jerusalem.

From an unofficial U.S. translation of resolution, adopted by the Palestine National Council on November 14, 1988.

DOCUMENT 9-5

Arafat Statement on Israel and Terrorism

At a December 14, 1988, press conference in Geneva, Palestine Liberation Organization leader Yasir Arafat explicitly recognized Israel's right to exist, renounced terrorism, and accepted UN Security Council Resolutions 242 and 338. Following is the text of Arafat's statement as recorded by Reuters.

Let me highlight my views before you. Our desire for peace is a strategy and not an interim tactic. We are bent on peace come what may, come what may.

Our statehood provides salvation to the Palestinians and peace to both Palestinians and Israelis.

Self-determination means survival for the Palestinians and our survival does not destroy the survival of the Israelis as their rulers claim.

Yesterday in my speech I made reference to United Nations Resolution 181 as the basis for Palestinian independence. I also made reference to our acceptance of Resolution 242 and 338 as the basis for negotiations with Israel within the framework of the international conference. These three resolutions were endorsed by our Palestine National Council session in Algiers.

In my speech also yesterday, it was clear that we mean our people's right to freedom and national independence, according to Resolution 181, and the right of all parties concerned in the Middle East conflict to exist in peace and security, and, as I have mentioned, including the state of Palestine, Israel and other neighbors, according to Resolution 242 and 338.

As for terrorism, I renounced it yesterday in no uncertain terms, and yet, I repeat for the record. I repeat for the record that we totally and absolutely renounce all forms of terrorism, including individual, group and state terrorism.

Between Geneva and Algiers, we have made our position crystal clear. Any more talk such as "The Palestinians should give more"—you remember this slogan?—or "It is not enough" or "The Palestinians are engaging in propaganda games, and public-relations exercises" will be damaging and counterproductive.

Enough is enough. Enough is enough. Enough is enough. All remaining matters should be discussed around the table and within the international conference.

Let it be absolutely clear that neither Arafat, nor any [one] for that matter, can stop the intifada, the uprising. The intifada will come to an end only when practical and tangible steps have been taken towards the achievement of our national aims and establishment of our independent Palestinian state.

In this context, I expect the E.E.C. to play a more effective role in promoting peace in our region. They have a political responsibility, they have a moral responsibility, and they can deal with it.

Finally, I declare before you and I ask you to kindly quote me on that: We want peace. We want peace. We are committed to peace. We are committed to peace. We want to live in our Palestinian state, and let live. Thank you.

Source: *The Middle East*, 7th ed., Congressional Quarterly, p. 311.

 DOCUMENT 9–6

Shamir's Four-Point Plan

The official Israeli Foreign Ministry formulation of the prime minister's proposal, approved by the government on May 14, 1989. Twenty ministers voted in favor of the plan and six voted against. Voting against were three Likud members—Ariel Sharon, Itzhak Modai, and David Levy—and Mafdal member Avner Shaki. Two labor members—Ezer Weitzmann and Rafi Edri—also voted against, but for opposite reasons: they said the plan hinges on PLO agreement and that therefore there should be direct Israeli–PLO talks.

1. The Camp David Partners—Reconfirmation of the Commitment to Peace

Ten years ago, the peace treaty between Israel and Egypt was concluded on the basis of the Camp David Accords. When the accords were signed, it was expected that more Arab countries would shortly join the circle of peace. This expectation was not realized.

The strength of Israel–Egyptian relations and the cooperation between the three partners to the accords have a decisive influence on the chances for Middle East peace, and the Israeli-Egyptian treaty is the cornerstone to the building of peace in the region.

Therefore, the prime minister has called on the three countries whose leaders affixed their signature to the Camp David Accords—the US, Egypt, and Israel—to renew, 10 years later, their commitment to the agreements and to peace.

2. The Arab Countries—From a State of War to a Process of Peace

The prime minister urged the US and Egypt to call on the other Arab countries to desist from hostility toward Israel and to replace belligerency and boycott with negotiation and cooperation. Of all the Arab countries, only Egypt has recognized Israel and its right to exist. Many of these states actively participated in wars against Israel by direct involvement or indirect assistance. To this day, the Arab countries are partners in an economic boycott against Israel, refuse to recognize it, and refuse to establish diplomatic relations with it.

The solution to the Arab–Israeli conflict and the building of confidence leading to a permanent settlement require a change in the attitude of the Arab countries toward Israel. Israel, therefore, calls on these states to put an end to this historic anomaly and to join direct bilateral negotiations aimed at normalization and peace.

3. A Solution to the Refugee Problem—An International Effort

The prime minister has called for an international effort, led by the US and with the significant participation of Israel, to solve the problem of the Arab refugees. The refugee problem has been perpetuated by the leaders of the Arab countries, while Israel with its meagre resources is absorbing hundreds of thousands of Jewish refugees from Arab countries. Settling the refugees must not wait for a political process or come in its stead.

The matter must be viewed as a humanitarian problem and action must be taken to ease the human distress of the refugees and to ensure for their families appropriate living quarters and self-respect.

Some 300,000 people live in refugee camps in Judea, Samaria and the Gaza District. In the 1970s, Israel unilaterally undertook the rehabilitation of residents of refugee camps in Gaza and erected 10 neighborhoods in which 11,000 families reside. This operation was carried out in partnership with the residents despite PLO objections.

The time has now come to ensure appropriate infrastructure, living quarters and services for the rest of the residents of the camps who, at the same time, are victims of the conflict, hostages to it, and an element which perpetuates its continued existence.

Good will and an international effort to allocate the necessary resources will ensure a satisfactory solution to this humanitarian effort and will help improve the political climate in the region.

4. Free Elections in Judea, Samaria and Gaza on the Road to Negotiations

In order to bring about a process of political negotiations and in order to locate legitimate representatives of the Palestinian population, the prime minister proposes that free elections be held among the Arabs of Judea, Samaria and Gaza—elections that will be free of the intimidation and terror of the PLO.

These elections will permit the development of an authentic representation that is not self-appointed from the outside. This representation will be comprised of people who will be chosen by the population in free elections and who will express, in advance, their willingness to take part in the following diplomatic process.

The aim of the elections is to bring about the establishment of a delegation that will participate in negotiations on an interim settlement, in which a self-governing administration will be set up. The interim period will serve as an essential test of cooperation and coexistence. It will be followed by negotiations on the final settlement, in which Israel will be prepared to discuss any option which will be presented.

The US administration has expressed its support for the idea, and following the prime minister's return, his proposals will be discussed here and the various questions surrounding the holding of elections will be examined. Contacts necessary for the implementation of the proposals will be maintained.

Source: Israel Government Press Release, May 14, 1989.

TEN

The Peace of the Brave

CHRONOLOGY

1990

Aug. 2–4   Iraq invades and annexes Kuwait

Nov. 29   UN Resolution 678 sets Jan 15, 1991 deadline for Iraqi withdrawal from Kuwait

1991

Jan. 16   (U.S. time) U.S.-led coalition launches massive air attack on Baghdad

Feb. 23   Allied ground war begins

Feb. 27   Kuwait liberated after 43-day war

May 22   Lebanon and Syria sign Brotherhood Treaty covering internal affairs in Lebanon; extended to foreign and security affairs in Sept.

Oct. 18   Soviet Union reestablishes diplomatic relations with Israel

Oct. 30   Arab–Israeli peace conference opens in Madrid; bilateral and multilateral talks begin

Dec. 16   United Nations repeals Zionism is racism resolution

Dec. 21   Commonwealth of Independent States formed. Gorbachev resigns Dec. 25; Soviet Union ends

1992

July 13   Yitzhak Rabin (Labor) forms coalition government after Israeli general elections; Shimon Peres named Foreign Minister

Aug. 24– Sept. 24   Sixth round of bilateral talks. Rabin indicates land for peace can also apply to Golan Heights

Nov. 16   50,000–100,000 Jewish settlers and protesters demonstrate in Tel Aviv, opposing possible Israeli withdrawal from the Golan Heights

Dec. 17   Israel deports 415 militant Palestinians and suspected Hamas members to South Lebanon

1993

Jan. 16   Knesset repeals law banning contact of Israelis with PLO members

Jan.–Aug.   Fourteen secret meetings between representatives of PLO and Israel in Norway

Feb. 26   Bombing of World Trade Center in New York City

May   Peres endorses "Gaza first" plan; Arafat expresses interest, includes Jericho as well

July 25–31   Israel carries out "Operation Accountability"

Aug. 20   Foreign Minister Peres attends secret meeting in Oslo. Israeli and PLO representatives initial Declaration of Principles; President Clinton endorses process August 27

Sept. 9   Arafat and Rabin sign letters of mutual recognition

Sept. 10   United States resumes dialogue with PLO

Sept. 13   Israel and PLO sign Declaration of Principles on Palestinian Interim Self-Government in Washington

Sept. 14   Jordan and Israel sign agenda for peace negotiations

Oct. 13   Israeli and PLO negotiators begin talks on ways to implement accords

Dec. 13   Target date passes for beginning of Israeli withdrawal from Gaza and Jericho

Dec. 30   Vatican announces decision to establish diplomatic relations with Israel

The End of the Cold War and the Dissolution of the Soviet Union

The wide-ranging implications of the rapidly accelerating Soviet–American détente of the late 1980s, the revolutions that swept Eastern Europe, the acknowledged end of the Cold War by 1990, and the demise of the Soviet Union (which Gorbachev announced in December 1991) were not lost on either side in the Arab–Israeli conflict. Once again, as had occurred so often in the past century, major changes on the world scene dramatically altered the delicate balance of power and people in the Middle East and the fate of the Zionist enterprise. The superpower rivalry of the Cold War had enabled Israel and the Arab states to arm themselves and maintain their mutual opposition. The end of the Cold War presented new challenges.

Israelis viewed the end of the Cold War and the impact of world power realities in two ways. Some argued that withdrawal of Soviet support for the Arab states made it less likely that the Arabs would make war or fight one to a successful conclusion. These Israelis believed that the new situation enhanced Israel's security situation. Others argued that with the "evil empire" no longer a factor, Israel's value to the United States as a strategic ally would be lessened. Moreover, if the Arab states successfully buried the hatchet of inter-Arab rivalry and faced the world and Israel in a united front, they could form a formidable military threat against Israel. The Israelis considered Iraq, in particular, to be a major threat, especially since the 1988 cease-fire in the Iran–Iraq war. That threat, however, was expressed in quite a different way in the late summer of 1990.

The Gulf War

Iraq's Invasion and Annexation of Kuwait

On August 2, 1990, Iraqi troops suddenly and unexpectedly invaded Kuwait. The Middle East, and indeed most of the world, was thrown into confusion. Kuwait's ruling family, the al-Sabah, fled, and two days later, Iraq's president, Saddam Hussein, formally annexed the Gulf kingdom. The Iraqi leader, deprived of port facilities in the Gulf, and with massive debts as the result of his punishing eight-year war with Iran, had genuine grievances against the policies of the Sabah family in helping keep oil prices low. In addition, Iraq claimed historical territorial rights over Kuwait. But the outright seizure of Kuwait provoked one of the worst global crises in recent memory. Many thousands of foreign nationals were trapped, and there was widespread fear that the Iraqi leader planned to invade Saudi Arabia. The industrial countries, and especially the United States, recoiled at the thought of Saddam Hussein in control of over 40 percent of the world's oil reserves.

The international response was immediate and overwhelming. On August 6, the Security Council unanimously adopted a comprehensive trade embargo against Iraq, and President Bush called for collective action to enforce it. Within weeks, a massive multinational naval task force was in place in the Gulf, effectively blockading Iraq. Over 50,000 American air and ground forces were airlifted to Saudi Arabia. The world watched anxiously as the storm clouds of war gathered over the Middle East.

Saddam Hussein's action was a clear indication that the Cold War was over in the region. Soviet support for UN sanctions and acquiescence in the stationing of extensive U.S. forces in Saudi Arabia illustrated a growing agreement between the United States and the Soviet Union on a variety of issues, including the danger of potentially explosive regional conflicts. Saddam Hussein seriously miscalculated the extent of coincidence of Soviet–U.S. interests in opposing his seizure of Kuwait.

Iraq's action also shattered the myth of pan-Arab unity, as the Arab states broke ranks in the struggle against Iraq, and as Saudi Arabia and Syria, for example, found themselves on the same side as Israel. The other ruling families in the Gulf felt threatened and supported the West and Japan in condemning Saddam Hussein and imposing UN sanctions. They were joined by the traditional Arab enemies of Iraq, especially Egypt. King Hussein of Jordan, torn between his traditional ties with the West and the United States on the one hand, and his economic dependence on neighboring Iraq on the other, trod the impossibly fine line of mediator, advocating an Arab-imposed rather than an American-imposed solution. His situation was made all the more difficult by the spontaneous support Palestinians in Jordan—over 60 percent of his population—gave Saddam Hussein.

Arafat, caught in a dilemma because of Saddam Hussein's support for the Palestinian cause, further damaged his relationship with the United States by calling for Arab solidarity against the West and refusing to condemn Saddam Hussein. He did offer to mediate the conflict, however.

Israel's response to the Gulf crisis was mixed. Iraq's military adventurism seriously alarmed Israel. Although Israel was confident that it could withstand an Iraqi attack, the risk of an immediate war—with the possibility of chemical weapons being used—was dramatically heightened. Israel regarded Saddam Hussein's actions as confirmation of its claim that a solution to the Arab–Israeli conflict was not confined to the question of the future of the Palestinians, but was one that involved all the Arab states. Israel's anxiety was increased by the realization that, as with the end of the Cold War, its claim to be the most important ally of the United States in the region was undermined. Furthermore, there were signs that in the new post–Cold War era the United States would regard Israel's failure to resolve the future of the occupied territories as a liability. On the other hand, the crisis distracted world attention from Israel's handling of the Intifada and focused it on the capriciousness and fragility of Arab leadership.

At the request of the United States, Israel played a very low-key role in the Gulf crisis and subsequent war. President Bush pledged new arms to Saudi Arabia, praised Syria's stand against Iraq, and gave considerable prominence to Egypt's contribution, even suggesting that Congress forgive Egypt's $7 billion debt.

The Gulf War and Its Aftermath

By the end of November, the Bush administration believed that military force would have to be used to dislodge Saddam Hussein from Kuwait. Sanctions would take too long and might ultimately strengthen Saddam rather than weaken his regime. Washington rejected the linkage Iraq sought to create between the liberation of Kuwait and the Palestine question, but on November 23, 1990, President Bush met with Syrian President Hafez al-Assad in Geneva and promised to do his best to find a peace settlement to the Arab–Israeli conflict following the defeat of Saddam Hussein. This was widely interpreted as a response to the demand by Assad and America's Arab allies that the United States place pressure on Israel to give ground on the question of the Palestinians and the occupied territories.

On November 29, the UN Security Council passed Resolution 678, which set January 15, 1991, as a deadline for Iraq to begin withdrawal from Kuwait or face appropriate action from the UN forces. Attempts to arrange talks between the United States and Iraq broke down in mid-December, leaving the prospect of war looming. Secretary of State Baker and Iraqi foreign minister Tariq Aziz met in Geneva on January 9, but no agreement was reached. UN Secretary General Javier Perez de Cuellar failed in a last-ditch attempt to mediate, and on January 16 (January 17, Baghdad time), the U.S.-led coalition launched a massive air attack on Baghdad. (See Documents 10–1 and 10–2 and Map 10–1A and B.)

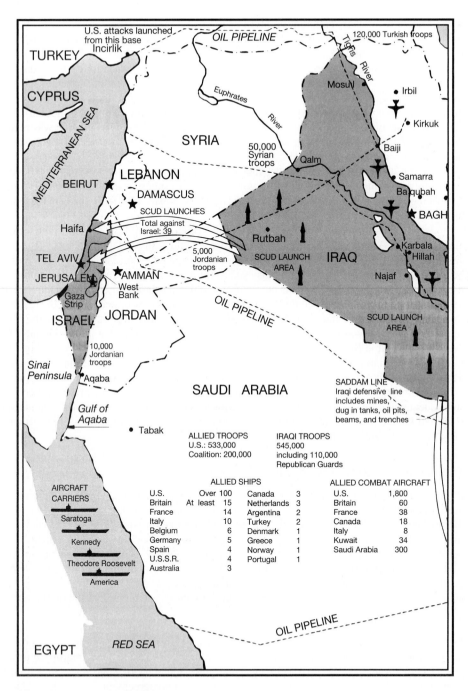

MAP 10–1A   The Gulf War

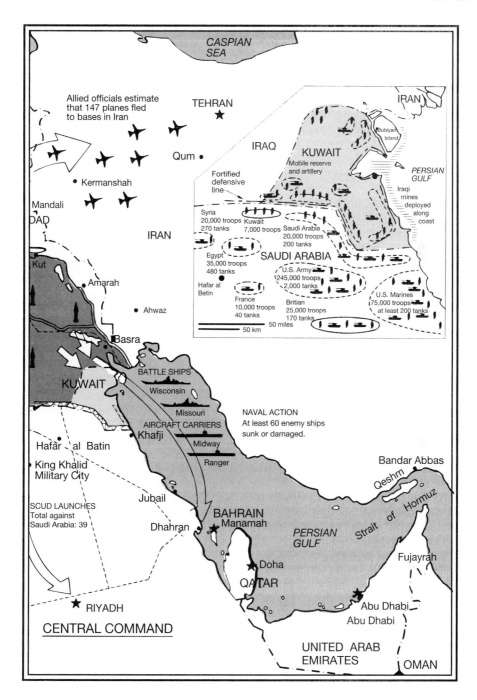

MAP 10–1B The Gulf War

Forty-three days later, following a chilling, unprecedented display of the overwhelming, destructive capabilities of modern air power and an equally unprecedented and brief (100 hours) ground offensive in which the coalition forces met only token resistance from Iraqi forces, "Operation Desert Storm" was over. "The liberation of Kuwait is complete," President Bush announced on February 27, as he ordered a stop to the rout and massacre of the Iraqi army as it fled Kuwait, laden with whatever loot the soldiers could take with them. A formal cease-fire was signed early in April.

We now know more about the Gulf War than we did in the heady days of the allied victory. Casualties were far higher than previously reported in the heavily censored press reports of the war. Less than 7 percent of the weapons used in the Gulf war were "smart." Most were dump bombs, cluster bombs, and napalm B. Seventy percent of the 88,500 tons dropped on Iraq and Kuwait hit both military and civilian targets. The bombing of the Al-Amiriya bunker in February 1991 incinerated more than 300 people, most of them women and children. American armored bulldozers were deployed, burying thousands of Iraqi soldiers in more than 110 kilometers of trenches. Thousands more men, women, and children died, and it is estimated that 1.8 million were made homeless as a direct result of the American-led attack on Iraq. Iraq's electricity, water, sewerage, communications, health, agriculture, and industry infrastructure were substantially destroyed, producing, according to relief agencies, conditions for famine and epidemics. Allied casualties were, as the London *Independent* newspaper reported, "miraculously light."

Meanwhile, the world watched in horror as Saddam Hussein brutally repressed Shiite and Kurdish rebellions within Iraq, which had erupted as the war ended. Hundreds of thousands of Kurdish refugees (by mid-April estimates were as high as 2 million) fought starvation, bitter cold, and disease as they fled Saddam's revenge through the mountains of northern and eastern Iraq to seek safety in Turkey and Iran. In the following months, mounting international concern resulted in the United Nations, backed by Washington, trying to help protect those populations by creating two no-fly zones in Iraq, one north of the 36th parallel and one south of the 32nd parallel, in which Iraqi air force planes were prohibited from flying. The outcome for the Kurds and the Shiites remained by no means clear, however.

Over the next eighteen months, Bush, driven in part by a deep personal hatred of Saddam Hussein, was determined to prevent the Iraqi ruler from rebuilding his military power. The United Nations, backed by threats of American military action if Iraq did not comply, sent several investigative teams to Iraq to ensure that all chemical and potential nuclear weapons and plants were destroyed or dismantled. Indeed, Bush, who was defeated in his reelection bid in November 1992, in the days before departing from the White House, launched a cruise missile attack on Baghdad just to remind Saddam Hussein who was in charge. In the contest to see who would get rid of whom, it has to be said that Saddam won.

The war in the Persian Gulf held the promise that the defeat of Saddam Hussein would not only create a "new world order" but would also enhance regional security in the area. The Bush administration assumed that the war would provide a window of opportunity in which the United States, utilizing its new credibility, would be in a position to shape events in the Middle East—including a peace settlement in the Arab–Israeli conflict. President Bush promised that following the war he would embark on "the difficult task of securing a potentially historic peace." Bush was echoing the hope of almost all post–World War II presidents who had dreamed of a Pax Americana, that he would be the one to find a peaceful solution to regional instability and to the Arab–Israeli conflict.

The Gulf War did not significantly change the way Arabs and Israelis perceived each other, their regional order, and their place in it, but it did alter the balance of power in the Arab–Israeli conflict to some extent. Israel and Syria were relatively strengthened, while Jordan and the Palestine Liberation Organization were weakened, although these changes did little to change the overall situation. In the short term, the reputation and credibility of the PLO were damaged and Yasser Arafat's power base was weakened. It appeared that the Palestinian cause had been undermined and that the Palestinians might end up like the Kurds—stateless and at the mercy of several hostile, even brutal, regimes. On the other hand, Saddam Hussein's invasion and occupation of Kuwait, his attempts to link the cause of the Palestinians with his actions, and the Gulf War did provide an impetus in the war's aftermath to address the questions of the future of the Palestinians and a resolution of the Arab–Israeli conflict.

The Madrid Peace Conference

Background

The end of the Cold War and the Gulf War and its aftermath were significant factors, along with the Intifada, in altering the prospects for a settlement of the outstanding issues of the Arab–Israeli conflict. While the Soviet Union voted with the majority in the United Nations and supported the U.S.-led coalition against Saddam Hussein in 1991, Moscow did not send troops to the Gulf and, even after the war had begun, continued to advocate a negotiated settlement. At that point, Gorbachev needed to retain the support of conservatives and military leaders and wished to demonstrate that the Soviet Union still had a role to play. On the other hand, he desperately needed Western goodwill and financial aid from the United States. To this end, he had already begun to move the Soviet Union away from too close an association with the radical Arab regimes and to make overtures to both the more moderate Arab states and Israel. In response, in November of 1990, Saudi Arabia and the Gulf states offered Moscow several billion dollars in loans and financial aid. Thus, the Soviet Union ceased acting as a patron of radical states like Syria, and this left the United States as the only viable superpower player on the scene. Israelis hoped that the American–Arab alliance would enable the United States to press the Arab states to lessen their hostility to Israel. Israelis wanted pressure taken off them, particularly with regard to the Palestinians, and continued to insist that the core issue was Arab recognition and acceptance of the Jewish state. For their part, the Arabs believed that their cooperation and partnership with the United States would be rewarded by the United States placing greater pressure on Israel to return land for peace and to allow self-determination for the Palestinians in the occupied territories.

Most commentators agreed that Israel, in the short term at least, benefited from the Gulf War. The military capability of its most powerful Arab enemy, Iraq, was seriously damaged, and the Intifada was brought almost to a halt. Furthermore, the Gulf War, and especially Israel's restraint in not responding militarily to Iraqi SCUD attacks, consolidated American support for Israel. Prior to the war, relations between the Bush administration and Israel had been at a low ebb. Direct contact between Washington and Jerusalem had been infrequent, and Secretary of State Baker had been increasing pressure on Prime Minister Shamir to move forward in response to PLO peace initiatives. The war changed the equation, at least temporarily. Israel was subjected to more than forty SCUD attacks, and although few deaths resulted and damage was minimal, Israelis were shocked and outraged. The Bush administration appealed to Israel not to respond with military action, in order to keep the Allied coalition together. Israel reluctantly complied, and as a result the United States indicated it would provide Israel with $13 billion in aid—$3 billion for damages and $10 billion in loan guarantees to assist in the settlement of Soviet Jewish immigrants over the next five years. There was an implicit understanding that the U.S. aid would not be used to settle new immigrants in the occupied territories; nevertheless, Shamir continued to approve the establishing of new Jewish settlements in the territories. Although Bush and Baker repeatedly called new settlements an obstacle to peace, U.S. protests immediately after the Gulf War were muted.

Israel also used the war to crack down even harder on the Intifada. The Palestinians were subjected to an almost total curfew in the West Bank and Gaza during the war, and deportations were stepped up in an attempt to end the Palestinian resistance. The Palestinian economy was virtually crippled as a result of the curfew and the prohibition on Palestinians from the territories entering Israel to work. The discrediting of the PLO and the Palestinians during the Gulf War, however, certainly made them more amenable to compromise as a way of retaining their visibility and viability in an unenviable situation. Moreover, the Arabs and Palestinians also had to face the reality of the declining importance of the Palestine issue on the world scene. The breakup of the former Yugoslavia, which spawned the crisis in Bosnia, and troubles in the former Soviet Union between Armenia and Azerbaijan and in other areas, removed attention from the situation in the occupied territories.

The Road to Madrid

Following the Gulf War, Secretary of State Baker toured the Middle East and continued to press Israel and the Arab states to agree to an international conference to resolve the outstanding issues between them. He made eight visits to the area before achieving his goal of convening a Middle East peace conference, co-sponsored by the United States and the Soviet Union (later Russia), in Madrid, Spain, on October 30, 1991. The Syrians finally agreed to go, having always called for an "international" conference, or the appearance of one, which would allow them to press for the return of the Golan Heights to Syria. Shamir, in agreeing to go to Madrid, reversed the position he had taken in his first major speech to the Knesset after the start of the war, on February 5. In that speech he had categorically ruled out Israeli participation in any postwar international conference on a comprehensive peace settlement. In particular, the Israelis distrusted Syria because of its hold on Lebanon, which was strengthened and consolidated during the Gulf War, and because Assad used the $2 billion provided by the Saudis for Syria's participation

Damage caused by SCUD missiles in Tel Aviv. January 1991

on the side of the Allied coalition to buy tanks and Chinese SCUD "C" missiles. Shamir also remained adamant that there could not be any PLO involvement in negotiations. The PLO, in light of its weakened position after the Gulf War and new realities in the occupied territories, acquiesced in the formation of a joint Jordanian–Palestinian delegation, headed by a venerable Gaza physician, Dr. Haidar Abdul Shafi, which did not officially include PLO members or Palestinians from East Jerusalem. The delegation, however, was accompanied by a group of advisors with ties to Arafat and the PLO, including an articulate Palestinian spokeswoman, Hanan Ashrawi, and an East Jerusalemite, Feisal al-Husseini.

Why did Shamir agree to go to Madrid? "The negotiations have to begin," he was quoted as saying, "because that will signify recognition of Israel's existence by the Arab states." Did Shamir agree because he believed that Syria had signalled it was ready to negotiate directly with Israel after public statements by Israeli officials that even the Golan Heights could be discussed within the framework of peace negotiations? Was it because the Soviet Union reestablished diplomatic relations with the Jewish state on October 18? Was it because of the strong support by the United States in the United Nations for repeal of the 1975 "Zionism is Racism" resolution—carried overwhelmingly on December 16? Was it because he counted on the United States to uphold Israel's official positions with regard to the Palestinian delegation? Was it the result of U.S. pressure?

Hanan Ashrawi, spokesperson for the Palestinian delegation to the Middle East peace talks, addressing the press in December 1991.

Perhaps one reason for Shamir's willingness to negotiate was the confidence instilled by the arrival of a large number of Jews from the Soviet Union. In the first four months of 1990, over 33,000 Soviet Jews had arrived in Israel, and the total number to arrive over the next five years was about 650,000. To Israelis, Soviet Jewish immigration represented a renewal of Israel's purpose. Israelis saw immigration from the Soviet Union as the long-awaited historic wave of aliyah that began in the 1970s with the arrival of over 200,000 Soviet Jews. To them, the questions arising from the immigration centered on the economic, educational, and social status of the immigrants and their impact on Israel's employment and housing situations. Israeli economic planners were, of course, concerned about finding suitable work for the predominantly professional arrivals in a population of about 4 million already severely burdened by unemployment, a long-running recession, and a chronic housing shortage. This situation was aggravated by the airlift of about 15,000 Ethiopian Jews in "Operation Solomon" in May 1991.

To Palestinians and other Arabs, the Soviet influx was a disaster equal to that of the Israeli War of Independence and the 1967 war. While claiming not to oppose Soviet immigration to Israel proper, they believed that the Soviet Jews would be settled in the West Bank and a concerted effort would be made to force the Palestinians across the Jordan River. Shamir's policy of supporting Israeli settlers in the West Bank—and in and around the Old City of Jerusalem—and the sheer value of Jewish West Bank settlements (estimated at several billion dollars) lent weight to Arab fears.

The Palestinians were not alone among those who believed that Jewish immigration from the Soviet Union was a major threat to the future of a Palestinian homeland. In May 1990, the White House had put on hold $400 million voted by Congress for housing loan guarantees for Soviet Jewish immigrants, concerned that Israel would use the funds to settle immigrants in the occupied territories. President Bush had pressured Gorbachev, when they met in the United States in June 1990, and after the meeting the Soviet president suggested that the Soviet Union might delay granting exit visas to Jews if they were to be settled in the territories. Shamir, who had forged a coalition with the minority hardline parties of the Knesset and had formed another Likud-led government by June 8, 1990, had, however, promptly authorized two more Jewish settlements in the occupied territories, asserting that Israeli citizens had the right to live where they pleased.

Although in early fall 1991, Shamir had reminded Washington of its willingness after the Gulf War to extend Israel $10 billion in loan guarantees, this issue had quickly become linked to the impending peace process. The Bush administration threatened to tie its support of the loan guarantees to Israel's willingness to move on the peace process and to place a freeze on West Bank settlements. As the parties moved toward Madrid, the issue of the loan guarantees was put on hold, but American pressure on Israel, to some extent, countered accusations of double standards leveled by Arabs at Washington as the result of American unwillingness to enforce UN resolutions calling for Israeli withdrawal from the occupied territories. The persistence of the Bush administration and of Secretary of State James Baker, in particular, was rewarded when the peace conference began in Madrid on October 30, 1991.

The Madrid Conference

The peace conference opened at the royal palace in Madrid with considerable fanfare in an atmosphere of great excitement and anticipation. It was a significant and important milestone in the effort to reach a solution to the Arab–Israeli conflict; the historical significance of the parties actually conducting face-to-face talks for the first time in the history of the conflict was not lost on anyone. Bush and Gorbachev were co-chairmen, and Israel, Egypt, Syria, Lebanon, and a joint Jordanian–Palestinian delegation were in attendance. Prior to the opening of the conference, the United States provided letters to the Palestinians, Syria, and Israel assuring them that Washington upheld each of their basic positions. The formulas of the "Framework for

Peace in the Middle East" signed at Camp David in 1978 were the starting point for the Madrid negotiations. Three sets of bilateral talks were to follow the opening session: between Israel and Syria, Israel and Lebanon, and Israel and the joint Jordanian–Palestinian delegation. The bilateral talks had as their foundation UN Resolution 242, with its principle of land for peace, and UN Resolution 338, which called for direct negotiations. Among the most important questions the bilateral talks were meant to resolve were the conditions for the signing of peace treaties, the boundaries of Israel, the disposition of the occupied territories, and the future of the Palestinians. The Madrid Conference also set up a series of multilateral working groups to discuss issues affecting the Middle East as a whole.

Despite the promise of the Madrid conference, in the early rounds of bilateral negotiations—there were five rounds of talks preceding the Israeli general elections in June 1992—familiar positions were reiterated, and little progress was achieved. Time and energy were expended determining the credentials of delegates, locations of future meetings, agendas, and other procedural matters. Under the Likud government, the Israeli position regarding the territories and the Palestinians did not move beyond autonomy for the people but not the land; that is, limited self-rule, with Israel retaining full control of security and foreign affairs and of the territories themselves—essentially the 1989 Shamir plan. While the Palestinian delegation was now prepared to accept the idea of "interim" measures, as specified in the Camp David accords (see Document 8–4), they insisted that the end of the process should be self-determination and a Palestinian state. The sides were clearly far apart on this and other outstanding issues. In an effort to pressure Israel to give ground and generate some movement in the talks, Secretary of State Baker announced in February 1992 that the Bush administration would not proceed with the $10 billion loan guarantees unless there was a halt in West Bank settlement activity. Prime Minister Shamir angrily rejected this proposal and withdrew the Israeli request, vowing to continue the settlements. The Israeli–Syrian talks, too, bogged down

Soviet president Mikhail Gorbachev addresses the first meeting of the Mideast Peace Conference, October 30, 1991. Israeli prime minister Yitzhak Shamir sits at the far right. Benjamin Netanyahu sits just behind the sign of the Egyptian delegation.

in endless arguments, and Hizbullah rocket attacks on Israel's "security zone" in southern Lebanon made any progress over Lebanese–Israeli issues almost impossible. Violence continued especially in the Gaza Strip, frequently spilling over to Israel itself. Positions hardened, and the talks appeared to achieve nothing.

Unlike the bilateral talks that focused on Israel and land for peace, the multilateral, or regional, talks were intended to bring together Israel, the Arab states, Turkey, the United States, many European countries, and even China and Japan to discuss more general Middle East issues. The first plenary session was held in Moscow in January 1992, although it was boycotted by the Palestinians because the co-sponsors, the United States and Russia, refused to accredit their delegation, which included Palestinians who lived outside the occupied territories.

In May 1992, regional working groups met to discuss five issues: refugees (in Ottawa); economic development (Brussels); water resources (Vienna); environmental issues (Tokyo); and arms control (Washington). On this occasion, it was Israel's turn temporarily to boycott the talks on economic cooperation and refugees because Palestinian refugees from outside the West Bank and Gaza had insisted on being present. Syria and Lebanon said they would boycott the multilateral talks until there was progress in the bilaterals. With the protagonists behaving in this way, it is not surprising that little agreement was reached on any of the issues. Ironically, while a co-sponsor of meetings to limit an arms buildup in the region, the United States itself remained a major contributor to the proliferation of weapons in the area. Although President Bush called for restraint in the sale of arms, in the nineteen months following Iraq's invasion of Kuwait, the United States delivered roughly $21.4 billion in weapons to the Middle East— primarily to Saudi Arabia ($14.8 billion), Kuwait ($2.85 billion), and Egypt ($2.17 billion). The multilateral talks continued, however, and eventually resulted in productive discussions and studies of the various issues. They also provided room for maneuvering between Israeli and Arab participants who could circumvent the bilateral talks to try to achieve progress.

The Road to Peace

Elections in Israel and New Directions in the Peace Talks

In June 1992, Shamir and the Likud were defeated in general elections held in Israel. The majority of Israelis were clearly ready for a new approach to the peace process. On July 13, Yitzhak Rabin formed a Labor-led coalition government, naming Shimon Peres, his old rival, as foreign minister, and pledging that he would cease all nonstrategic settlement activity and would move quickly on Palestinian autonomy. There is no doubt that Rabin's election breathed new life into the peace process. Although the position of the Israeli government did not change immediately regarding Palestinian autonomy and interim measures, Rabin made several good-will gestures. He freed more than 800 political prisoners, halted most settlement activity, barred private Israeli building permits in the occupied territories, and reiterated the Labor party position of land for peace. Rabin accepted diaspora Palestinians (but not PLO members) at the multilateral talks and said that he would seek repeal of the ban on contacts with the PLO. While disavowing them, he also winked at contacts between the Palestinian delegation and PLO headquarters in Tunis. As a result, in early August, President Bush agreed to send the loan guarantee proposal to Congress, which approved it as part of the general U.S. foreign aid bill in early October 1992.

The Palestinians, however, dismissed most of Rabin's actions as mere "window dressing." At the ongoing peace negotiations, they insisted on a Palestinian Interim Self-Governing Authority (PISGA), which would be a legislative and not just an administrative body, and on a national state as a final outcome. Lack of progress at the talks and increasing frustration in the West Bank and Gaza led to escalating violence, fanned by Hamas and other Islamic extremist groups like Islamic Jihad, as well as by the PFLP and the DFLP, which opposed the peace talks and the PLO's apparent backing of them. It appeared that Arafat's influence was seriously on the wane as Fatah was challenged by rival groups and as the Palestinian negotiators, while acknowledging the PLO as the sole representative of the Palestinian people, sought and gained the spotlight. Moreover, with PLO funding severely diminished because of Arafat's actions during the Gulf War, Hamas and other Muslim groups expanded their influence in the territories through their growing network of economic, social, and educational institutions and seriously eroded the PLO's political base.

In the years preceding the Gulf War, Saudi Arabia, Kuwait, and the Gulf states had provided the PLO with $200–250 million annually, not including the 5 percent tax paid by Palestinian workers in the Gulf and a special fund for the territories. In 1992, no more than $40 million flowed into the territories, compared to $120 million in 1990. Although widespread relief was voiced when it was learned that Arafat had survived the crash of his plane in the Libyan Desert in early April 1992, that sentiment masked serious troubles and tension even within the PLO itself regarding Arafat's style of leadership and control of the purse strings. Further, Arafat, who had always declared that he was married to the Palestinian cause, had surprised almost everyone, including his followers, when it became known early in 1992 that he had married a young Christian woman, Suha Tawil, a year or so before. There was speculation that perhaps he was no longer as dedicated, no longer as fully in control, and that he should step down as leader.

As talks with the Palestinians stalemated, and as Hizbullah, the extremist Shiite Party of God, scored impressive victories in August in the first elections in Lebanon to be held in twenty years, the focus in the bilateral negotiations shifted to Syria and Jordan. In the seventh round, which began in October, Israel and Jordan worked out an agenda of common issues for negotiation toward signing a peace treaty. Rabin also indicated that Israel might withdraw from the Golan Heights in return for full peace with Syria, and the new Israeli negotiator, Itamar Rabinovich, a respected academician and expert on Syria (subsequently also designated Israel's ambassador to Washington), was authorized to work on a document of principles. The pragmatic Assad, heavily and expensively involved in Lebanon, without his Soviet patron to supply arms and diplomatic support, but still on the U.S. list of countries supporting international terrorism—and perhaps also concerned that he might be left out in the cold if a deal were struck between Israel and the Palestinians—had little choice but to keep the discussion open. He was not, however, prepared to say what kind of peace he would offer in return for Israeli withdrawal from the Golan Heights, nor was Rabin in a position to promise full withdrawal.

Talks, however, were suspended until after the U.S. elections. Indeed, there is some indication that President Assad, in his apparent willingness to consider an accommodation with Israel, was gambling that he could get Bush and Baker to put pressure on Israel. He may also have thought that his actions could boost Bush's reelection possibilities. The Arabs certainly believed they would fare better under Bush than his opponent, although editorialists in America questioned whether it was in the U.S. interest in general to be building Assad and Syria up as an alternative to Iraq and Iran. In any event, the November U.S. general elections resulted in a victory for the Democratic party, and Bill Clinton became the new American president. This administration was more openly and unambiguously pro–Israeli than the previous one, and it was expected that the United States and Israel would work closely together.

Bilateral Talks at a Standstill

Although multilateral talks had also been resumed in October 1992, the bilateral talks seemed to be at a standstill. Terrorist incidents continued on the border with Lebanon, and in the territories, the Intifada became increasingly violent and deadly as Palestinians marked its fifth anniversary with more and more assaults on Israelis and the Israelis responded by killing several

Palestinians and wounding scores of others. Attacks on and killings of Israelis both in the occupied territories and in Israel itself, and especially the kidnap and murder of border policeman Nissim Toledano by Hamas terrorists in mid-December 1992, set off shock waves in Israel. Under pressure to do something to deal with the situation, Rabin expelled 415 suspected terrorists to Lebanon. This action was a serious miscalculation, as the Lebanese prime minister, advised by Assad, refused to accept the deportees, and as the world press descended upon the scene to record their plight. The UN passed a resolution calling for their immediate repatriation, Arab countries demanded sanctions against Israel, and the Palestinian negotiators withdrew from the talks that had resumed in December. Israel allowed a few to return for medical or other reasons and permitted UN and other relief efforts, but it was not until February 1993 that a compromise was worked out, largely through the efforts of the new American Secretary of State Warren Christopher during his first visit to Middle Eastern capitals. Israel agreed to let 100 of the deportees return immediately, with the remainder to be repatriated by the end of the year. The deportees and the Palestinian negotiating team rejected this solution, but the UN accepted it and closed the book on this chapter, calling for the resumption of the talks. These were delayed, however, by a worsening situation in the territories.

In March, Prime Minister Rabin visited Washington and secured President Clinton's promise to encourage Congress to maintain the current level of approximately $3 billion in foreign economic and military aid to Israel. His visit was cut short by a series of bloody stabbings and attacks against Israelis in both the territories and Israel proper; fifteen Israelis died—the highest monthly total ever. At the end of March, Rabin sealed off the territories. This gave Israelis a much greater sense of security and provided Rabin with political capital at a time when there was wide suspicion, especially among the settler population, that he was ready to cut a deal on the Golan Heights. For most Israelis, the major exceptions being farmers and contractors who depended on cheap Arab labor, it was a popular move, although the closure did have a negative impact on the Israeli economy. It wreaked particular hardship on the Palestinians, however, especially those who had depended on work in Israel for their livelihood.

The Israeli travel restrictions on Palestinians prevented as many as 120,000 day laborers from going to regular jobs in Israel that were a basic source of income in the territories. Because of its own dwindling resources, the PLO had also cut back drastically on its financial support for Palestinians in Gaza and the West Bank. Millions of dollars from Saudi Arabia, Kuwait, and the Gulf states had stopped flowing to the PLO as a result of Arafat's support for Saddam Hussein, and the PLO's own expenditures and sometimes imprudent investments complicated the problem. Reserves dwindled from $7 billion in the mid-1980s to not more than $2.5 billion by April 1993, and the PLO's annual budget dropped from $245 million to $85 million between 1991 and 1993. The impact of this drastic reduction in revenues was dramatic. Approximately 90,000 families had received monthly payments from the PLO Welfare Department based in Amman, and about 150,000 more individuals received some form of subsidy. In total, approximately 700,000 of the 1.8 million Palestinians in the West Bank and Gaza had been receiving some form of PLO assistance, including the families of "martyrs" and those of Palestinians deported by the Israelis. All these payments were severely reduced or cut. Moreover, PLO monies that had provided millions of dollars a year to hospitals, universities, community centers, and newspapers simply dried up. The result was a loss of jobs, a loss of morale—and a loss of support for the PLO leadership in Tunis.

The Hamas Threat to PLO Leadership

The PLO's dire financial situation (salaries even of PLO officials were slashed or eliminated) doubtless contributed to Arafat's positive response to U.S. calls for a resumption of the peace talks in April 1993. But probably more important to Arafat and the Fatah leadership in keeping the negotiations going was the recognition that Hamas represented a serious threat to PLO leadership of the Palestinians if a breakthrough did not occur. Hamas had greatly strengthened its influence and credibility in the occupied territories during Arafat's long absence in Tunis. It was growing rapidly, especially among younger, more volatile and more radicalized Palestinians. It received its operating funds from Iran—estimated in 1993 at around $20 to $30 million a year—from other sympathetic governments (like Sudan), and from wealthy private individuals, and it was emerging as the most serious alternative to the PLO in the West Bank and especially in Gaza. As we have seen, it had at first also been tolerated by Israel as an alternative to the PLO in the territories. Arafat, by appearing to be cooperative, certainly must have hoped that the United States would try to persuade the Saudis and the Kuwaitis that it was not in their interests any more than that of the PLO to see the further growth of Islamic extremism.

Nevertheless, the threat from religious zealots became more real, not only in the territories, but also regionally, and even internationally. The Sunni Islamic Group in Egypt, for example, had for over a year carried out attacks against tourists, Christian Copts, and Egyptian officials in an effort to undermine the government of Hosni Mubarak and establish an Islamic state in Egypt. One of its leaders, the blind Sheikh Omar Abd al-Rahman, who had been arrested after the assassination of Anwar Sadat but released for lack of evidence, obtained a U.S. visa in the Sudan and preached from the safer confines of New Jersey. In February 1993, Americans were shocked and outraged when the World Trade Center in New York was bombed. Sheikh Omar was widely considered to be the inspiration behind the bombing, as well as behind an aborted plot to blow up the Holland and Lincoln tunnels and the UN building, and to assassinate prominent Americans. In August 1993, he was indicted in a U.S. federal court, and in January 1996, he was found guilty and sentenced to life in prison.

Although Islamic militants and other radical groups in the Middle East continued to oppose the continuation of peace talks, another round, the ninth, opened in Washington on April 27, 1993, after a four-month hiatus. "Too much time has been lost," Warren Christopher said, but he praised the Palestinians for dropping their demand for the return of the deportees and agreeing to resume talks. He pledged that the United States would be a full partner in the negotiating process and in helping the negotiators produce results. It should be noted that Egyptian president Hosni Mubarak, who would continue to be a go-between, had played an important role in the resumption of the talks, working throughout the interval to break the impasse. At the beginning of the month, he had met with both Arafat and Rabin and apparently secured Israel's assent to negotiate with Palestinians from East Jerusalem. As expected, Feisal al-Husseini, a prominent East Jerusalem figure who had attended the Arafat-Mubarak meeting, now became the coordinator of the Palestinian delegation. Israel also agreed to permit the return of thirty Palestinians who had been deported from the territories between 1967 and 1987. Further, Rabin offered to allow 5,000 Palestinian expatriates with families in the occupied territories to remain permanently at the end of their traditional summer visits. Clearly contributing to the concessions on both sides and driving the talks was the fear of Hamas's growing influence. The Rabin-Peres team, for nonideological and basically pragmatic reasons, became increasingly willing to consider the possibility of opening a channel to Arafat and the PLO. As early as January 1993, secret talks were initiated in Oslo, Norway. Over the next seven months, as the official talks dragged on desultorily, at least fourteen meetings were held, at which Israeli and PLO officials, talking directly, agreed on the main points of a framework for peace.

The Issue of Jerusalem Emerges

Meanwhile, the talks in Washington were going nowhere. Syria, which had indicated it would extend full peace to Israel in return for full Israeli withdrawal from the Golan Heights, said it would not define what it meant by peace until Israel agreed to withdraw; and Israel said it would not withdraw until Syria defined what it meant by peace. In early June, Peres commented that only a pen was necessary to sign a final accord with Jordan, no doubt a true statement, but one that was immediately disavowed in Amman, which could not appear to be racing ahead of the other delegations, and especially the Palestinians.

Rifts began to appear increasingly around this time between the Palestinian negotiators and the PLO leadership in Tunis who considered Arafat to be too accommodationist, both with regard to questions of jurisdiction in the West Bank and Gaza and also concerning the future of Jerusalem. Since Feisal al-Husseini had become an official participant in the talks, raising the possibility of a discussion of Jerusalem, it is not surprising that this issue should surface. In an effort to break the logjam of the talks, the United States, in its most direct intervention since Madrid, presented a working paper to the Israeli and Palestinian delegations on June 30, which suggested that the two sides move away from discussion of territorial jurisdiction of an interim self-government to the identification of functions the Palestinians could control, including health, education, and police activities. The U.S. paper also allowed for discussion of the final status of Jerusalem, but only when negotiations began on the permanent status of the occupied territories. In early July an American team, led by Dennis Ross, newly named U.S. special coordinator for the negotiations, met with Rabin, Palestinians, and Egyptian, Syrian, and Jordanian representatives in an attempt to resolve differences, but the delegation returned to Washington empty-handed.

"Operation Accountability"

Midsummer of 1993, however, was notable not for discussions of peace but for the fierce fighting that took place again on Israel's northern border, and for Israel's heavy aerial and artillery bombardment of Lebanon in "Operation Accountability." Since the Madrid conference opened, attacks by Hizbullah on positions in Israel's self-declared security zone in southern Lebanon and retaliation by Israel against guerrilla bases had become fairly routine, especially before each round of talks. Hizbullah was dedicated to getting the Israeli Defense Forces and their ally, the mainly Christian South Lebanon Army, out of the buffer zone. Deliberately trying to provoke a response in order to derail the peace process, and possibly to draw Israel and Syria into open warfare, in July Hizbullah embarked on particularly intense shelling, which included the firing of Katyusha rockets at targets in the buffer zone, resulting in the deaths of seven Israeli soldiers. On July 25, the Hizbullah provocation was answered by a full-scale Israeli bombing of Lebanon north of the buffer zone. (See Map 10–2.)

"Operation Accountability," which aimed at curbing further Hizbullah attacks by undermining its infrastructure in southern Lebanon, was the harshest Israeli attack in more than a decade. More than thirty Shiite villages—suspected Hizbullah strongholds—were targeted, resulting in the deaths of 130 Lebanese, mostly civilians, the injuring of at least 500 by Israeli and South Lebanon Army fire, and the mass exodus of up to 500,000 Lebanese—more than a tenth of Lebanon's population—from their homes and villages. Hizbullah fighters, for their part, unleashed a barrage of at least 250 Katyusha rockets against targets both in southern Lebanon and in northern Israel that sent 100,000 Israelis into bomb shelters. Secretary of State Christopher played an important role in brokering a cease-fire, which came into effect on July 31. In an unwritten cease-fire agreement, Hizbullah pledged not to fire rockets on northern Israel but reserved the right to continue attacks on targets within the buffer zone. And Lebanese Prime Minister Rafik Hariri assured Hizbullah that as long as Israel was in Lebanon, the Lebanese government would not restrict their activities. For its part, Israel agreed to halt its bombardment and assured Beirut that Israeli troops would leave the zone if security arrangements could be made and if the safety of Lebanese in the zone were assured. Despite this agreement, shortly after the cease-fire, nine Israeli soldiers were killed in two separate bombing incidents in the buffer zone.

Christopher began his second shuttle to the Middle East on August 2 in Cairo, where he met with President Mubarak and warned that peace negotiations could deteriorate. A week of frenzied activities followed. Arafat met with the Egyptian foreign minister just before a Christopher-Mubarak meeting, and he met with Mubarak just afterward. Motorcades passed

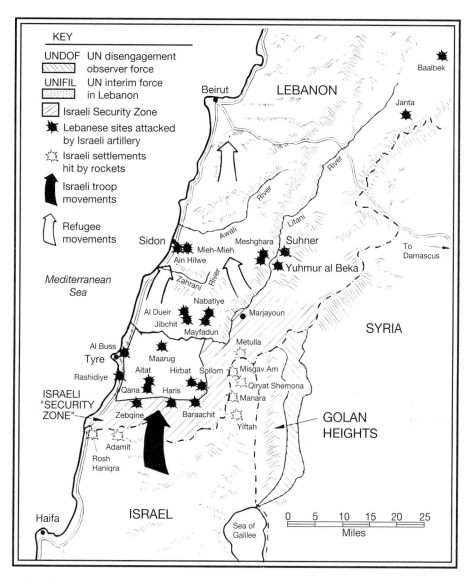

KEY

UNDOF UN disengagement
observer force

UNIFIL UN interim force
in Lebanon

Israeli Security Zone

Lebanese sites attacked
by Israeli artillery

Israeli settlements
hit by rockets

Israeli troop
movements

Refugee
movements

MAP 10–2 "Operation Accountability"

each other almost in comic-book style. Christopher, who became an active intermediary and middleman between Israel, Syria, and, indirectly, Iran, the major supplier of Hizbullah, carried messages back and forth between Rabin and Assad, making two trips in three days to Damascus. Previous to this, Israel and Syria had communicated only through their negotiators in Washington. By cooperating with the United States, Assad was in effect acknowledging Syria's role in allowing Iran to arm and supply Hizbullah, as well as demonstrating his control of southern Lebanon and over the Palestinian terrorist organizations located there. With his assent, Lebanese army units were deployed for the first time in years just to the north of Israel's "security zone," in the vicinity of Tyre in an area controlled by UN forces (UNIFIL), to try to keep the peace and help state agencies and institutions resume normal functions.

The events surrounding "Operation Accountability" raise many questions. Did Israel launch its invasion of Lebanon to eliminate Hizbullah strongholds, or simply to emphasize that it would not tolerate attacks upon its troops in the security zone and on its northern settlements? Or did it do so hoping to increase its bargaining position in the talks with Syria—signalling that in exchange for a guarantee of peace on the Lebanese–Israeli border, Jerusalem would be willing to give up the Golan? Rabin certainly benefited politically. His tough tactics helped to silence critics on the right and build up public support for other concessions, and the cease-fire put an end to a campaign against him from the dovish Meretz party, which might have bolted the coalition had Israel continued the attack against Lebanon. If the purpose of the operation was to prevent the activities of Hizbullah guerrillas, the attack was a failure. Incidents continued to occur in the security zone, and in the spring of 1996, Katyushas again began to fall on northern Israel.

Did Assad cooperate with the United States because Syria wanted to be taken off the State Department's list of countries supporting international terrorism and thereby become eligible for American economic assistance? Or was it because he saw the opportunities for achieving a peace with Israel slipping away? Assad, who was praised by the United States for his cooperation, certainly emerged with enhanced credibility in the West. Was Arafat helpful because he was anxious for the United States to renew its dialogue with the PLO and intercede for him with Saudi Arabia—so he could once again count on financial support from the Arab oil countries? Or was it because he wished to reassert his leadership as a Palestinian statesman seeking peace? For some or all of these reasons, the crisis passed. Christopher believed he had salvaged the peace process and that the way had been cleared for the next round of talks, which were scheduled for August 31, 1993. A new air of optimism replaced the uncertainty of the previous weeks.

Arafat's Role Questioned

Arafat's role during the Christopher shuttle, however, had resulted in further tension and acrimony between him and the Palestinian delegation to the Washington talks. Three senior members of the delegation, the coordinator, Feisal al-Husseini, spokeswoman Hanan Ashrawi, and deputy head of the delegation Saeb Erekat threatened to resign because of sharp differences with Arafat. They were incensed that the PLO leader had agreed to postpone discussion of the status of Jerusalem and seemed prepared to grant concessions to Israel regarding the five-year interim self-rule period. Shimon Peres endorsed a "Gaza first" proposal for Israeli withdrawal gaining currency among many Israelis; Arafat expressed interest but only if Jericho were added as well. The Palestinian delegation, which was demanding total jurisdiction over the territories, including Jerusalem, was not thrilled with this "compromise" either. Haidar Abdul Shafi, the head of the delegation, called on Arafat to expand the Palestinian decision-making process and also to allow hardline factions and independents to participate. After two days of fierce arguments in Tunis, Husseini, Ashrawi, and Erekat withdrew their resignation threat and were appointed along with four others to the PLO Steering Committee. Israel accepted as fact the fiction it had hitherto insisted upon, that somehow the delegates were independent of the PLO, which actually appointed and directed them. Israeli and official PLO representatives would now be able to sit down together for the first time.

The September 1993 Israeli–PLO Accord

Reports had surfaced in July that Israeli officials had met in Washington in June with Nabil Shaath, a senior advisor to Arafat. It later became known that Environment Minister Yossi Sarid of the Meretz party had met with Shaath in July in Cairo, with Rabin's approval. Although the official Israeli position remained that Israel would not negotiate with the PLO unless it amended its charter, and that Israel would never allow the creation of a Palestinian state, the Labor party opened doors to the PLO in a way that would have been inconceivable under a Likud-dominated government. Likud critics indeed insisted that negotiations with acknowledged PLO members would legitimize the objectives of a Palestinian state and the right of return for diaspora Palestinians.

By mid-August, there were published reports that the PLO wanted to develop recent contacts with Israeli officials into a secret but full-fledged channel for direct negotiations, and on August 21, Bassam Abu Sharif, a senior Arafat aide, said he expected direct talks soon between Israel and the PLO. These talks had in fact been going on for several months, and they resulted in perhaps the most surprising, remarkable, and significant breakthrough in the history of the Arab–Israeli conflict.

In late August 1993, newspapers around the world began to report that a series of at least fourteen secret meetings between Israeli and PLO officials had been held in Norway since January. As early as April 1992, at an academic conference in Tel Aviv, Terje Rod Larsen, head of FAFO, a Norwegian institute researching conditions in the territories, offered to put Yossi Beilin, a committed dove who was then a member of the Labor opposition in the Knesset, in touch with senior Palestinian officials. When the Labor party won the Israeli elections and Beilin became deputy foreign minister, Larsen returned to Israel, bringing with him Norway's number two diplomat, Jan Egeland. They met with Beilin and Yair Hirschfeld, a professor of Middle East history at Haifa University, to suggest that Norway could be the bridge between Israel and the PLO. An initial meeting between Hirschfeld and Abu Alaa, better known as Ahmed Khoury (Qurei), head of the PLO finance department, occurred in December 1992, in London.

Subsequent clandestine meetings took place in Norway, with the Norwegian foreign minister Johan Joergan Holst (whose wife just happened to be the author of a FAFO study on the territories) lending support and greatly enhancing the process. In January, the Knesset had repealed the PLO contact ban law, so contacts of individuals with PLO members were now no longer illegal. The Israelis kept in touch with Beilin, who took the information to Peres, and in April, Peres informed Rabin. In April, also, Ahmed Qurei insisted on dealing directly with an Israeli government official, and in May, the director general of the Foreign Ministry, Uri Savir, assisted by Yoel Zinger, a legal counsel for the Foreign Ministry, took charge. From that point until late August, there were eleven more meetings, with Qurei joined by Taher Shah, a PLO legal advisor. The talks in Norway bypassed the major players in Washington, including the United States, and they survived the events in Lebanon in late July. On August 20, while visiting Oslo, Foreign Minister Peres witnessed as Qurei and Savir initialed the Declaration of Principles that had finally been hammered out. This document is now sometimes referred to as the Oslo I accord.

Peres and Holst flew to California on August 27 and briefed the American secretary of state. Christopher telephoned Rabin for details on Israel's position and then talked to President Clinton, who immediately supported the accord. On Tuesday, August 31, the Washington talks resumed but were completely overshadowed by news of the direct talks that had been going on between Israel and the PLO.

On September 1, after a five-hour debate, sixteen members of the Israeli cabinet voted in favor of the draft declaration, with two abstentions. Elyakim Rubinstein, Israel's chief negotiator with the Palestinians, said that the accord enshrined fundamental changes in Israel's position to date, including a readiness to discuss the return to the territories of refugees from the 1967 war. The opposition Likud leader, Benjamin Netanyahu, blasted the accord and said: "It is not just autonomy and it is not just a Palestinian State in the territories but the start of the destruction of Israel in line with the PLO plan." Former Likud prime minister Yitzhak Shamir lamented that the peace plan was the brainchild of deluded Israelis who failed to see the threat still posed by the PLO. "The Old Testament prophets said it then: 'Neither Babylon nor Persia present the danger, but you, the sons of Israel.' I'm beginning to understand the prophets better."

Thousands of Jewish settlers and their supporters chanted "traitor" as they battled police outside Rabin's office. Over the next weekend, after bitter and acrimonious debate, Arafat secured the backing of the Fatah central committee, in a vote of 10 for to 4 against. Critics charged that the agreement offered the Palestinians much less than the Camp David accords, at least initially. Hamas leaders called Arafat a pimp and a traitor, and George Habash said that Arafat could no longer be considered the head of the PLO. Although the Jordanians and Syrians expressed chagrin that they had not been consulted, King Hussein soon voiced his support, and it was expected that if the agreement were indeed signed between Israel and the Palestinians, Jordan, Syria, and Lebanon would eventually hammer out their differences and sign a statement of principles at least. For months, Israel and Jordan had had an agenda containing the framework of a peace agreement, and Peres, appearing on American television, commented that the differences with Syria were paper thin.

Mutual Recognition

As Israel and the PLO were poised to sign statements of mutual recognition and an agreement dealing with the interim peace settlement initialed on August 20, Arafat insisted that there was no going back, and Rabin told the Knesset that "the time has come to take a risk for peace." Peres, who had played a key role in the secret talks that led to the peace agreement, insisted: "We want to live with the Palestinians in peace. They are human beings like us. We don't want to rule over them, we don't want to act towards them disgracefully or disrespectfully. They are not four-legged creatures. We are arriving at the end of 100 years of conflict between us and the Palestinians." As the world watched in wonder, on Thursday, September 9, Norwegian foreign minister Johan Joergan Holst carried a letter from Arafat to Rabin recognizing Israel, renouncing violence, and pledging support for repeal of clauses objectionable to Israel in the PLO charter. Rabin, for his part, signed a letter recognizing the PLO as the representative of the Palestinian people and accepting the PLO as a negotiating partner. (See Documents 10–3 and 10–4.) On Monday, September 13, 1993, in a stunning event on the White House lawn in Washington, the Declaration of Principles on Interim Self-Government for the Palestinians (henceforth referred to as the Israel–PLO peace accord) was signed by Foreign Minister Peres and PLO representative Mahmoud Abbas, with Warren Christopher and Russian Foreign Minister Andrei Kosyrev adding their signatures as witnesses, while President Clinton, Arafat, and Rabin looked on. Clinton was moved to remark: "A peace of the brave is within our reach." (See Documents 10–5, 10–6, 10–7.) In a truly historic moment that seemed almost unbelievable to the millions around the world watching, Arafat then extended his hand to Rabin who, after great hesitation (and perhaps a slight nudge on the back from Clinton), took it and shook it.

In this astonishing turn of events, sworn enemies had agreed to put aside decades of hatred and acrimony, to recognize each other's existence, and to work together for peace. But only time would tell if the accords would be implemented and if the remarkable ceremony on the White House lawn would really lead to a new order in the Middle East.

The Israel–PLO Declaration of Principles on Interim Self-Government Arrangements

The historic Declaration of Principles envisaged a ten-month timetable leading to elections for a Palestinian council to run the West Bank and Gaza Strip for an interim period of five years, during which time Israel and the Palestinians would negotiate a permanent peace settlement. (See Document 10–8.) After signing the accord, Israel and the Palestinians were, within one month, to begin negotiating the details of the withdrawal of Israeli troops from the Gaza Strip and Jericho. This agreement was expected to be reached by December 13, 1993, with the Israelis immediately beginning their withdrawal, to be completed by April 13, 1994, and with Palestinians

President Clinton brings Israeli Prime Minister Yitzhak Rabin (left) and PLO Chairman Yasser Arafat together for a historic handshake after the signing of the Israeli–PLO peace accord at the White House, September 13, 1993.

taking control of all their internal affairs, including taxation and police functions. The five-year interim period of Palestinian self-rule would officially begin with the signing of this agreement. The principle of "early empowerment" would apply to the rest of the West Bank, where authority would be transferred from the Israeli military government and civil administration to "authorized Palestinians" who would take control of health, education and culture, welfare, tourism, and direct taxation. An interim agreement would specify the structure and powers of the Palestinian council that would replace the Israeli administration, and elections for the council were to be held no later than July 13, 1994. Israeli military forces would be redeployed outside populated areas of the West Bank by the eve of the elections but would continue to protect Jewish settlements. Moreover, Israel would retain control of the border crossing from Gaza to Egypt and of the Allenby Bridge linking the West Bank and Jordan. The status of Jerusalem and other outstanding issues would be left to negotiations on the permanent arrangements for the occupied territories. Talks on the final status of the territories would begin no later than December 1995, with the permanent settlement to take effect by December 1998.

For Israel, the "Gaza-Jericho first" option appeared the best shortcut to end the stalemated negotiations in Washington. Israel for some time had been anxious to rid itself of the boiling cauldron of Gaza, and Jericho, close to Jordan and removed from Israeli settlements, had always been relatively quiet. For the embattled Arafat, Gaza and Jericho provided some territory over which to preside right away. In accepting an immediate but partial solution, he gained recognition and resumed a dialogue with the United States on September 10, 1993. Indeed, one of the more awkward aspects of the situation that emerged in September 1993 was the fact that the United States had refused to talk to the PLO since 1990 and had therefore played virtually no role in the events leading up to the signing of the Israel–PLO accord.

The PLO did not gain all that it sought. Although Rabin accommodated PLO aspirations to some extent, Israel retained jurisdiction over foreign affairs, security, and Jewish settlements until final-status arrangements were worked out. The issue of Jerusalem was also postponed until the final stage of negotiations. Israel insisted that the PLO commit firmly to peaceful co-existence, including curbing violence in the occupied territories until the implementation of the limited self-rule agreement, and further required that Arafat pledge his support for removal of articles objectionable to Israel in the PLO charter, pending formal recision by the Palestine National Council.

In reaching the September accord, Israel made significant concessions, however. While Israel may well have wished to rid itself of the troublesome and costly Gaza, the agreement did not preclude a possible future Palestinian state in Judea and Samaria. And the accord may have been too late to counter Islamic extremism, possibly a greater threat in the long run than the demands of the more secular PLO. There is no doubt that the willingness of Rabin and the Labor party to consider seriously land for peace, and the dire straits of Arafat and the PLO helped prepare the way for the breakthrough in August. Equally important, however, was and is the threat of Islamic militancy throughout the Middle East, which had become the major threat not only to Israel but also to secular and moderate Arab governments. It is no accident that President Mubarak, whom Muslim extremists have vowed to overthrow in order to establish an Islamic state in Egypt, played such an active role as an intermediary between Israel and the Palestinians.

On critical points, Israel and the Palestinians were obviously not talking about the same things. Both sides saw the accord as a transition. For Israel, the agreement was only a temporary first step toward Palestinian self-rule or autonomy over the next five years. It was not a commitment that defined the final status of the territories. In fact, Rabin ruled out any form of sovereign statehood for the Palestinians. The Palestinians, however, believed it would lead to some form of nation-state. Both Israel and the PLO talked about some kind of connection of the Palestinian entity with Jordan, but that prospect was not without its own problems for the Hashemite Kingdom. Although the issue of Jerusalem was postponed, Israel made it clear that an undivided Jerusalem would continue to be its capital (the "eternal capital" of the Jewish people, as Rabin stated in his speech in Washington), while the Palestinians made it equally clear that they would claim East Jerusalem as the capital of Palestine. It was not clear if the Jewish settlers would cooperate with the Israeli government and what would happen to the settlements after the five-year period. It was also not clear whether the Palestinian leadership would be able to deal with the many factions within their population. There were grave risks all around, for Israel, for Arafat, and for those supporting the accord, but the general consensus was that a continuation of the status quo was intolerable and that the risks for peace were worth taking.

Suggestions For Further Reading

ASHRAWI, HANAN, *This Side of Peace: A Personal Account*, New York, Simon & Schuster, 1995.

FRANKEL, GLENN, *Beyond the Promised Land*, New York, Simon & Schuster, 1996.

HUNTER, ROBERT, F., *The Palestinian Uprising: A War By Other Means*, 2nd ed., Berkeley, University of California Press, 1993.

KHALIL, SAMIR, *The Republic of Fear: The Inside Story of Saddam Hussein's Iraq*, New York, Pantheon Books, 1989.

MAKOVSKY, DAVID, *Making Peace with the PLO: The Rabin Government's Road to Oslo*, Boulder, Colo., Westview Press, 1996.

MAZEN, ABU (MAHMOUD ABBAS), *Through Secret Channels: The Road to Oslo: Senior PLO Leader Abu Mazen's Revealing Story of the Negotiations with Israel*, Concord: Paul and Company Publishers Consortium, Inc., 1995.

MILLER, JUDITH, AND MYLROIE, LAURIE, *Saddam Hussein and the Crisis in the Gulf*, New York, Times Books, 1990.

NETANYAHU, BENJAMIN, *Fighting Terrorism: How Democracies Can Defeat Domestic and International Terrorism*, New York, Farrar, Straus & Giroux, 1995.

PARKER, RICHARD B., *The Politics of Miscalculation in the Middle East*, Bloomington, Ind., Indiana University Press, 1993.

PERES, SHIMON, *Battling for Peace: A Memoir*, ed. by David Landau, New York, Random House, 1995.

———, *The New Middle East*, New York, Henry Holt, 1993.

RUBIN, BARRY, ed., *From War to Peace: Arab–Israeli Relations, 1973–1993*, New York, New York University Press, 1994.

SAVIR, URI, *The Process: 1,000 Days that Changed the Middle East*, New York Random House, 1998.

DOCUMENT 10–1

President Bush: The Start of Military Action

16 January 1991, Washington time

Just two hours ago, allied air forces began an attack on military targets in Iraq and Kuwait. These attacks continue as I speak. Ground forces are not engaged.

This conflict started August 2 when the dictator of Iraq invaded a small and helpless neighbor. Kuwait, a member of the Arab League, and a member of the United Nations, was crushed, its people brutalized.

Five months ago, Saddam Hussein started this cruel war against Kuwait. Tonight the battle has been joined.

This military action, taken in accord with United Nations resolutions and with the consent of the United States Congress, follows months of constant and virtually endless diplomatic activity on the part of the United Nations, the United States, and many, many other countries.

Arab leaders sought what became known as an Arab solution, only to conclude that Saddam Hussein was unwilling to leave Kuwait. Others travelled to Baghdad in a variety of efforts to restore peace and justice.

Our Secretary of State, James Baker, held an historic meeting in Geneva, only to be totally rebuffed.

This past weekend, in a last-ditch effort, the Secretary General of the United Nations went to the Middle East with peace in his heart—his second such mission. And he came back from Baghdad with no progress at all in getting Saddam Hussein to withdraw from Kuwait.

Now, the twenty-eight countries with forces in the Gulf area have exhausted all reasonable efforts to reach a peaceful resolution, have no choice but to drive Saddam from Kuwait by force. We will not fail.

As I report to you, air attacks are under way against military targets in Iraq. We are determined to knock out Saddam Hussein's nuclear bomb potential. We will also destroy his chemical weapons facilities. Much of Saddam's artillery and tanks will be destroyed. Our operations are designed to best protect the lives of all the coalition forces by targeting Saddam's vast military arsenal.

Initial reports from General (Norman) Schwarzkopf (Commander of the Allied Forces in the Gulf) are that our operations are proceeding according to plan. Our objectives are clear: Saddam Hussein's forces will leave Kuwait, the legitimate government of Kuwait will be restored to its rightful place, and Kuwait will once again be free. . . .

This is an historic moment. We have in this past year made great progress in ending the long era of conflict and cold war. We have before us the opportunity to forge for ourselves and for future generations a new world order, a world where the rule of law, not the law of the jungle, governs the conduct of nations.

When we are successful—and we will be—we have a real chance at this new world order, an order in which a credible United Nations can use its peace-keeping role to fulfill the promise envisioned of the UN's founders. We have no argument with the people of Iraq; indeed, for the innocents caught in this conflict, I pray for their safety. Our goal is not the conquest of Iraq, it is the liberation of Kuwait. It is my hope that somehow the Iraqi people can even now convince their dictator that he must lay down his arms, leave Kuwait and let Iraq itself rejoin the family of peace-loving nations. . . .

Tonight, as our forces fight, they and their families are in our prayers. May God bless each and every one of them, and the coalition forces at our side in the Gulf, and may he continue to bless our nation, the United States of America.

 DOCUMENT 10-2

Saddam Hussein: The Iraqi View

21 February 1991

Excerpts from a speech broadcast on Baghdad Radio discussing the origins of the dispute and a 15 February initiative by the Iraqis offering conditional withdrawal from Kuwait.

O great people; O stalwart men in our valiant armed forces; O faithful, honest Muslims, wherever you may be; O people wherever faith in God has found its way to your hearts, and wherever it found what embodies it in the sincerity of your intentions and deeds; O lovers of humanity, virtue, and fairness, who reject aggressiveness, injustice, and unfairness. In difficult circumstances and their events, some people—more often than not—lose the connection with the beginning and preoccupy themselves with the results—or forget, when there are resemblances—the connection between any result and the reasons that gave rise to those events, and on whose basis those results were based.

Some have either completely forgotten these influential facts in the life of man whether in this or that direction, or the presence of these facts in their minds has become weak. Many facts between causes and effects, or between the prelude to and the results of the circumstances and events that preceded 2 August and what took place 2 August and afterward, have been missed.

This description was in most cases applicable to some Arabs and to many foreigners so that some of them could not remember what Zionism and US imperialism have done against Iraq, beginning with the Iran-gate plot or the Iran-Contra scandal in 1986 until the first months of 1990, when the plot against Iraq reached its dangerous phases; when US and western media began to prepare for the Israeli aggression against us, but which we confronted in the statement of 8 April 1990; when the Americans cut off bread from Iraq and cancelled the grain deal concluded with US companies in the third month of the same year, that is 1990; and when they raised the slogan of an economic, technologic, and scientific boycott of Iraq and worked to make Europe and Japan do the same. . . .

Traitor Fahd, the betrayer of the two mosques, and light-headed Hosni, the ruler with which noble Arab Egypt has been afflicted, stand at the head of the list. Faced with this state of affairs, we found that the enemy media and the enemy policy dropped a heavy screen on every event, stand, or cause that preceded 2 August 1990 that could shed some light on these incidents and explain their true nature. Palestine—whose just cause dates back more than forty years—

as well as its future and the positions on it has been one of the most important pillars of the conspiracy in which the oil rulers have participated as conspirators against Iraq, led by the agent sheiks of Kuwait and the Saudi rulers. . . .

The tendentious media, which have widespread influence and impact, and the suspect politicians and those who seek personal objectives—backed by Zionism everywhere—began to focus on the 2 August events to depict them as having taken place without any basis or background and as though our attention were being devoted only to these events. They even issued orders to silence voices and prevent them from mentioning any historical background that would explain to the foreigner or the Arab what he does not know about the reality of the relationship that exists between Kuwait and Iraq, and that Kuwait is part of Iraq, but was annexed following the partitioning conspiracy to weaken the Arab nation, harm its status and role, and weaken every Arab country that has some kind of leverage. . . .

There is no other course than the one we have chosen, except the course of humiliation and darkness, after which there will be no bright sign in the sky or brilliant light on earth. We have chosen this course. The Iraqis have chosen this course in an era where many characteristics became manifest. They continue to ask and work for what will make them more brilliant, faithful, and lofty. There is no other course. We will protect it with our souls, funds, and hearts. We will proceed on this course, irrespective of the nature of the political efforts which we are exerting and whose formulation and directions Tariq Aziz carried to Moscow, and which, if rejected, will expose all the covers and will only maintain the premeditated intentions of the aggression against us without any cover and without any slogans that will lead to intermingling.

After the 15 February 1991 initiative sprang from its sister initiative of 12 August 1990, what did Bush say, and what did his servant Fahd say? Bush rejected it, and regarded it as a cruel hoax before he understood it. Fahd, who chews his words just as camels chew the grass of their pastures, became an eloquent orator to say the war against Iraq will continue until Iraq does this and that. . . .

It is the entire 15 February initiative, as a new beginning, that will make the Iraqis more determined and more resolved if the initiative is rejected. Their armed forces will become more capable. This will result from the exposure of pretexts and disclosure of the true nature of the premeditated intentions. All this will make them more patient and steadfast and better prepared for the battle which God blesses and which good men support—after which there will be only a glorious conclusion, where a brilliant sun will clear the dust of battle, and where the clouds of battles will be dispelled to make room for a brilliant moon surrounded by a halo, whose size will be commensurate with the sacrifices that are required by the duties and conditions of victory and by the patience that God Almighty expects from the people of holy war.

 DOCUMENT 10–3

Arafat to Rabin Recognizing Israel's Right to Exist

September 9, 1993

Mr. Prime Minister,
The signing of the Declaration of Principles marks a new era in the history of the Middle East. In firm conviction thereof, I would like to confirm the following PLO commitments:

The PLO recognizes the right of the State of Israel to exist in peace and security.
The PLO accepts United Nations Security Council Resolutions 242 and 338.

The PLO commits itself to the Middle East peace process, and to a peaceful resolution of the conflict between the two sides and declares that all outstanding issues relating to permanent status will be resolved through negotiations.

The PLO considers that the signing of the Declaration of Principles constitutes a historic event, inaugurating a new epoch of peaceful coexistence, free from violence and all other acts which endanger peace and stability. Accordingly, the PLO renounces the use of terrorism and other acts of violence and will assume responsibility over all PLO elements and personnel in order to assure their compliance, prevent violations and discipline violators.

In view of the promise of a new era and the signing of the Declaration of Principles and based on Palestinian acceptance of Security Council Resolutions 242 and 338, the PLO affirms that those articles of the Palestinian Covenant which deny Israel's right to exist, and the provisions of the Covenant which are inconsistent with the commitments of this letter are now inoperative and no longer valid. Consequently, the PLO undertakes to submit to the Palestinian National Council for formal approval the necessary changes in regard to the Palestinian Covenant.

    Sincerely,
    Yasser Arafat
    Chairman
    The Palestine Liberation Organization
Yitzhak Rabin
Prime Minister of Israel

 DOCUMENT 10-4

Rabin to Arafat Recognizing the PLO

September 9, 1993

Mr. Chairman,
In response to your letter of September 9, 1993, I wish to confirm to you that, in light of the PLO commitments included in your letter, the Government of Israel has decided to recognize the PLO as the representative of the Palestinian people and commence negotiations with the PLO within the Middle East peace process.

    Sincerely,
    Yitzhak Rabin
    Prime Minister of Israel
Yasser Arafat
Chairman
The Palestinian Liberation Organization

 DOCUMENT 10-5

Clinton Statement at Signing of Israel–PLO Accord

Prime Minister Rabin, Chairman Arafat, Foreign Minister Peres, Mr. Abbas, President Carter, President Bush, distinguished guests, on behalf of the United States and Russia, co-sponsors of the Middle East peace process, welcome to this great occasion of history and hope.

Today we bear witness to an extraordinary act in one of history's defining dramas, a drama that began in a time of our ancestors when the word went forth from a sliver of land between the River Jordan and the Mediterranean Sea. That hallowed piece of earth, and land of life and revelation, is the home to the memories and dreams of Jews, Muslims, and Christians throughout the world.

As we all know, devotion to that land has also been the source of conflict and bloodshed for too long. Throughout this century, bitterness between the Palestinian and Jewish people has robbed the entire region of its resources, its potential, and too many of its sons and daughters. The land has been so drenched in warfare and hatred that conflicting claims of history etched so deeply in the souls of the combatants there that many believe the past would always have the upper hand.

Then, 14 years ago, the past began to give way when at this place and upon this desk three men of great vision signed their names to the Camp David Accord. Today we honor the memories of Menachem Begin and Anwar Sadat, and we salute the wise leadership of President Jimmy Carter.

Then, as now, we heard from those who said that conflict would come again soon. But the peace between Egypt and Israel has endured. Just so, this bold new venture today, this brave gamble that the future can be better than the past, must endure.

Two years ago in Madrid, another president took a major step on the road to peace by bringing Israel and all her neighbors together to launch direct negotiations. Today we also express our deep thanks for the skillful leadership of President George Bush.

Ever since Harry Truman first recognized Israel, every American president, Democrat and Republican, has worked for peace between Israel and her neighbors. Now the efforts of all who have labored before us bring us to this moment, a moment when we dare to pledge what for so long seemed difficult even to imagine: that the security of the Israeli people will be reconciled with the hopes of the Palestinian people, and there will be more security and more hope for all.

Today, the leadership of Israel and the Palestine Liberation Organization will sign a Declaration of Principles on Interim Palestinian Self-Government. It charts a course toward reconciliation between two peoples who have both known the bitterness of exile. Now both pledge to put old sorrows and antagonisms behind them and to work for a shared future, shaped by the values of the Torah, the Koran and the Bible.

Let us salute also today the government of Norway for its remarkable role in nurturing this agreement.

But above all, let us today pay tribute to the leaders who had the courage to lead their people toward peace, away from the scars of battle, the wounds and the losses of the past, toward a brighter tomorrow. The world today thanks Prime Minister Rabin, Foreign Minister Peres and Chairman Arafat. Their tenacity and vision has given us the promise of a new beginning.

What these leaders have done now must be done by others. Their achievement must be a catalyst for progress in all aspects of the peace process, and those of us who support them must be there to help in all aspects, for the peace must render the people who make it more secure.

A peace of the brave is within our reach. Throughout the Middle East, there is a great yearning for the quiet miracle of a normal life. We know a difficult road lies ahead. Every peace has its enemies, those who still prefer the easy habits of hatred to the hard labors of reconciliation.

But Prime Minister Rabin has reminded us that you do not have to make peace with your friends. And the Koran teaches that if the enemy inclines toward peace, do thou also incline toward peace.

Therefore, let us resolve that this new mutual recognition will be a continuing process in which the parties transform the very way they see and understand each other. Let the skeptics of this peace recall what once existed among these people. There was a time when the traffic of ideas and commerce and pilgrims flowed uninterrupted among the cities of the fertile crescent. In Spain, in the Middle East, Muslims and Jews once worked together to write brilliant chapters in the history of literature and science. All this can come to pass again.

Mr. Prime Minister, Mr. Chairman, I pledge the active support of the United States of America to the difficult work that lies ahead. The United States is committed to ensuring that the people who are affected by this agreement will be made more secure by it, and to leading the world in marshalling the resources necessary to implement the difficult details that will make real the principles to which you commit yourselves today.

Together, let us imagine what can be accomplished if all the energy and ability the Israelis and the Palestinians have invested into your struggle can now be channeled into cultivating the land and freshening the waters, into ending the boycotts and creating new industry, into building a land as bountiful and peaceful as it is holy. Above all, let us dedicate ourselves today to your region's next generation. In this entire assembly, no one is more important than the group of Arab and Israeli children who are seated here with us today.

Mr. Prime Minister, Mr. Chairman, this day belongs to you. And because of what you have done, tomorrow belongs to them. We must not leave them prey to the politics of extremism and despair, to those who would derail this process because they cannot overcome the fears and hatreds of the past. We must not betray their future. For too long, the young of the Middle East have been caught in a web of hatred not of their own making. For too long, they have been taught from the chronicles of war. Now, we can give them the chance to know the season of peace.

For them, we must realize the prophecy of Isaiah, that the cry of violence shall no more be heard in your land, nor rack nor ruin within your borders. The children of Abraham, the descendants of Isaac and Ishmael, have embarked together on a bold journey. Together, today, with all our hearts and all our souls, we bid them shalom, salaam, peace.

 DOCUMENT 10-6

Arafat Statement at Signing of Accord

In the name of God, the most merciful, the passionate, Mr. President, ladies and gentlemen, I would like to express our tremendous appreciation to President Clinton and to his administration for sponsoring this historic event which the entire world has been waiting for.

Mr. President, I am taking this opportunity to assure you and to assure the great American people that we share your values for freedom, justice and human rights—values for which my people have been striving.

My people are hoping that this agreement which we are signing today marks the beginning of the end of a chapter of pain and suffering which has lasted throughout this century.

My people are hoping that this agreement which we are signing today will usher in an age of peace, coexistence and equal rights. We are relying on your role, Mr. President, and on the role of all the countries which believe that without peace in the Middle East, peace in the world will not be complete.

Enforcing the agreement and moving toward the final settlement, after two years, to implement all aspects of U.N. resolutions 242 and 338 in all of their aspects, and resolve all the issues of Jerusalem, the settlements, the refugees and the boundaries will be a Palestinian and an Israeli responsibility. It is also the responsibility of the international community in its entirety to help the parties overcome the tremendous difficulties which are still standing in the way of reaching a final and comprehensive settlement.

Now as we stand on the threshold of this new historic era, let me address the people of Israel and their leaders, with whom we are meeting today for the first time, and let me assure them that the difficult decision we reached together was one that required great and exceptional courage.

We will need more courage and determination to continue the course of building coexistence and peace between us. This is possible and it will happen with mutual determination and with the effort that will be made with all parties on all the tracks to establish the foundations of a just and comprehensive peace.

Our people do not consider that exercising the right to self-determination could violate the rights of their neighbors or infringe on their security. Rather, putting an end to their feelings of being wronged and of having suffered an historic injustice is the strongest guarantee to achieve coexistence and openness between our two peoples and future generations. Our two peoples are awaiting today this historic hope, and they want to give peace a real chance.

Such a shift will give us an opportunity to embark upon the process of economic, social and cultural growth and development. And we hope that international participation in that process will be extensive as it can be. This shift will also provide an opportunity for all forms of cooperation on a broad scale and in all fields.

I thank you, Mr. President. We hope that our meeting will be a new beginning for fruitful and effective relations between the American people and the Palestinian people.

I wish to thank the Russian Federation and President Boris Yeltsin. Our thanks also go to Secretary Christopher and Foreign Minister Kozyrev, to the government of Norway and to the Foreign Minister of Norway for the positive part they played in bringing about this major achievement. I extend greetings to all the Arab leaders, our brothers, and to all the world leaders who contributed to this achievement.

Ladies and gentlemen, the battle for peace is the most difficult battle of our lives. It deserves our utmost efforts because the land of peace, the land of peace yearns for a just and comprehensive peace. Thank you.

Mr. President, thank you, thank you, thank you.

 **DOCUMENT 10–7**

Rabin Statement at Signing of Accord

President Clinton, the President of the United States, your excellencies, ladies and gentlemen. This signing of the Israeli–Palestinian declaration of principles here today is not so easy, neither for myself as a soldier in Israel's wars, nor for the people of Israel, nor for the Jewish people in the Diaspora who are watching us now with great hope mixed with apprehension. It is certainly not easy for the families of the victims of the wars, violence, terror, whose pain will never heal, for the many thousands who defended our lives with their own and have even sacrificed their lives for our own. For them, this ceremony has come too late.

Today, on the eve of an opportunity for peace, and perhaps an end to violence and wars, we remember each and every one of them with everlasting love. We have come from Jerusalem, the ancient and eternal capital of the Jewish people. We have come from an anguished and grieving land. We have come from a people, a home, a family that has not known a single year, not a single month, in which mothers have not wept for their sons. We have come to try and put an end to the hostilities so that our children, and our children's children, will no longer experience the painful cost of war, violence and terror. We have come to secure their lives and to ease the sorrow and the painful memories of the past, to hope and pray for peace.

Let me say to you, the Palestinians, we are destined to live together on the same soil in the same land. We, the soldiers who have returned from battles stained with blood; we who have seen our relatives and friends killed before our eyes; we who have attended their funerals and cannot look into the eyes of their parents; we who have come from a land where parents bury their children; we who have fought against you, the Palestinians, we say to you today in a loud and a clear voice, enough of blood and tears. Enough!

We have no desire for revenge. We harbor no hatred towards you. We, like you, are people—people who want to build a home, to plant a tree, to love, live side by side with you in dignity, in affinity, as human beings, as free men. We are today giving peace a chance and saying again to you, "Enough." Let us pray that a day will come when we all will say farewell to arms. We wish to open a new chapter in the sad book of our lives together—a chapter of mutual recognition, of good neighborliness, of mutual respect, of understanding. We hope to embark on a new era in the history of the Middle East.

Today here in Washington at the White House, we will begin a new reckoning in the relations between peoples, between parents tired of war, between children who will not know war. President of the United States, ladies and gentlemen, our inner strength, our higher moral values have been derived for thousands of years from the Book of the Books, in one of which, Koheleth (Ecclesiastes), we read, "To every thing there is a season and a time to every purpose under heaven. A time to be born and time to die, a time to kill and a time to heal. A time to weep and a time to laugh. A time to love and a time to hate, a time of war and a time of peace." Ladies and gentlemen, the time for peace has come.

In two days, the Jewish people will celebrate the beginning of a new year. I believe, I hope, I pray that the new year will bring a message of redemption for all peoples: a good year for you, for all of you; a good year for Israelis and Palestinians; a good year for all the peoples of the Middle East; a good year for our American friends who so want peace and are helping to achieve it. For presidents and members of previous administrations, especially for you, President Clinton, and your staff, for all citizens of the world, may peace come to all your homes.

In the Jewish tradition, it is customary to conclude our prayers with the word "Amen." With your permission, men of peace, I shall conclude with words taken from the prayer recited by Jews daily. I would ask the entire audience to join me in saying "Amen."

May He who makes peace on High, make peace for us and all Israel. Amen.

עושה שלום במרומיו, הוא יעשה שלום עלינו ועל כל ישראל, ואמרו אמן.

DOCUMENT 10-8

The Israel–PLO Declaration of Principles [Excerpts]

Following is the text of "Declaration of Principles on Interim Self-Government Arrangements" signed by Israeli foreign minister Shimon Peres and PLO foreign affairs spokesperson Mahmoud Abbas, in Washington, D.C., on September 13, 1993.

The Government of the State of Israel and the P.L.O. team (in the Jordanian-Palestinian delegation to the Middle East Peace Conference) (the "Palestinian Delegation"), representing the Palestinian people, agree that it is time to put an end to decades of confrontation and conflict, recognize their mutual legitimate and political rights, and strive to live in peaceful coexistence and mutual dignity and security and achieve a just, lasting and comprehensive peace settlement and historic reconciliation through the agreed political process. Accordingly, the two sides agree to the following principles:

ARTICLE I: AIM OF THE NEGOTIATIONS

The aim of the Israeli-Palestinian negotiations within the current Middle East peace process is, among other things, to establish a Palestinian Interim Self-Government Authority, the elected Council (the "Council"), for the Palestinian people in the West Bank and the Gaza Strip, for a transitional period not exceeding five years, leading to a permanent settlement based on Security Council Resolutions 242 and 338.

It is understood that the interim arrangements are an integral part of the whole peace process and that the negotiations on the permanent status will lead to the implementation of Security Council Resolutions 242 and 338. . . .

ARTICLE III: ELECTIONS

1. In order that the Palestinian people in the West Bank and Gaza Strip may govern themselves according to democratic principles, direct, free and general political elections will be held for the Council under agreed supervision and international observation, while the Palestinian people will ensure public order. . . .

ARTICLE IV: JURISDICTION

Jurisdiction of the Council will cover West Bank and Gaza Strip territory, except for issues that will be negotiated in the permanent status negotiations. The two sides view the West Bank and the Gaza Strip as a single territorial unit, whose integrity will be preserved during the interim period.

ARTICLE V: TRANSITIONAL PERIOD AND PERMANENT STATUS NEGOTIATIONS

1. The five-year transitional period will begin upon the withdrawal from the Gaza Strip and Jericho area.
2. Permanent status negotiations will commence as soon as possible, but not later than the beginning of the third year of the interim period, between the Government of Israel and the Palestinian people representatives.
3. It is understood that these negotiations shall cover remaining issues, including: Jerusalem, refugees, settlements, security arrangements, borders, relations and cooperation with other neighbors, and other issues of common interest.
4. The two parties agree that the outcome of the permanent status negotiations should not be prejudiced or preempted by agreements reached for the interim period.

ARTICLE VI: PREPARATORY TRANSFER OF POWERS AND RESPONSIBILITIES

1. Upon the entry into force of this Declaration of Principles and the withdrawal from the Gaza Strip and the Jericho area, a transfer of authority from the Israeli military government and its Civil Administration to the authorised Palestinians for this task, as detailed herein, will commence. This transfer of authority will be of a preparatory nature until the inauguration of the Council.
2. Immediately after the entry into force of this Declaration of Principles and the withdrawal from the Gaza Strip and Jericho area, with the view to promoting economic development in the West Bank and Gaza Strip, authority will be transferred to the Palestinians on the following

spheres: education and culture, health, social welfare, direct taxation, and tourism. The Palestinian side will commence in building the Palestinian police force, as agreed upon. Pending the inauguration of the Council, the two parties may negotiate the transfer of additional powers and responsibilities, as agreed upon. . . .

ARTICLE VIII: PUBLIC ORDER AND SECURITY

In order to guarantee public order and internal security for the Palestinians of the West Bank and the Gaza Strip, the Council will establish a strong police force, while Israel will continue to carry the responsibility for defending against external threats, as well as the responsibility for overall security of Israelis for the purpose of safeguarding their internal security and public order. . . .

ARTICLE XI: ISRAELI-PALESTINIAN COOPERATION IN ECONOMIC FIELDS

Recognizing the mutual benefit of cooperation in promoting the development of the West Bank, the Gaza Strip and Israel, upon the entry into force of this Declaration of Principles, an Israeli-Palestinian Economic Cooperation Committee will be established in order to develop and implement in a cooperative manner the programs identified in the protocols attached as Annex III and Annex IV. . . .

ARTICLE XIII: REDEPLOYMENT OF ISRAELI FORCES

1. After the entry into force of this Declaration of Principles, and not later than the eve of elections for the Council, a redeployment of Israeli military forces in the West Bank and the Gaza Strip will take place, in addition to withdrawal of Israeli forces carried out in accordance with Article XIV.
2. In redeploying its military forces, Israel will be guided by the principle that its military forces should be redeployed outside populated areas.
3. Further redeployments to specified locations will be gradually implemented commensurate with the assumption of responsibility for public order and internal security by the Palestinian police force pursuant to Article VIII above.

ARTICLE XIV: ISRAELI WITHDRAWAL FROM THE GAZA STRIP AND JERICHO AREA

Israel will withdraw from the Gaza Strip and Jericho area, as detailed in the protocol attached as Annex II. . . .

ARTICLE XVI: ISRAELI-PALESTINIAN COOPERATION CONCERNING REGIONAL PROGRAMS

Both parties view the multilateral working groups as an appropriate instrument for promoting a "Marshall Plan," the regional programs and other programs, including special programs for the West Bank and Gaza Strip, as indicated in the protocol attached as Annex IV. . . .

ANNEX I: PROTOCOL ON THE MODE AND CONDITIONS OF ELECTIONS

1. Palestinians of Jerusalem who live there will have the right to participate in the election process, according to an agreement between the two sides.
2. In addition, the election agreement should cover, among other things, the following issues:
   a. the system of elections;
   b. the mode of the agreed supervision and international observation and their personal composition; and
   c. rules and regulations regarding election campaign, including agreed arrangements for the organizing of mass media, and the possibility of licensing a broadcasting and TV station.
3. The future status of displaced Palestinians who were registered on 4th June 1967 will not be prejudiced because they are unable to participate in the election process due to practical reasons.

ANNEX II: PROTOCOL ON WITHDRAWAL OF ISRAELI FORCES
FROM THE GAZA STRIP AND JERICHO AREA

1. The two sides will conclude and sign within two months from the date of entry into force of this Declaration of Principles, an agreement on the withdrawal of Israeli military forces from the Gaza Strip and Jericho area. This agreement will include comprehensive arrangements to apply in the Gaza Strip and the Jericho area subsequent to the Israeli withdrawal.
2. Israel will implement an accelerated and scheduled withdrawal of Israeli military forces from the Gaza Strip and Jericho area, beginning immediately with the signing of the agreement on the Gaza Strip and Jericho area and to be completed within a period not exceeding four months after the signing of this agreement.
3. The above agreement will include, among other things:
   a. Arrangements for a smooth and peaceful transfer of authority from the Israeli military government and its Civil Administration to the Palestinian representatives.
   b. Structure, powers and responsibilities of the Palestinian authority in these areas, except: external security, settlements, Israelis, foreign relations, and other mutually agreed matters.
   c. Arrangements for the assumption of internal security and public order by the Palestinian police force consisting of police officers recruited locally and from abroad (holding Jordanian passports and Palestinian documents issued by Egypt). Those who will participate in the Palestinian police force coming from abroad should be trained as police and police officers.
   d. A temporary international or foreign presence, as agreed upon.
   e. Establishment of a joint Palestinian-Israeli Coordination and Cooperation Committee for mutual security purposes.
   f. An economic development and stabilization program, including the establishment of an Emergency Fund, to encourage foreign investment, and financial and economic support. Both sides will coordinate and cooperate jointly and unilaterally with regional and international parties to support these aims.
   g. Arrangements for a safe passage for persons and transportation between the Gaza Strip and Jericho area.
4. The above agreement will include arrangements for coordination between both parties regarding passages:
   a. Gaza-Egypt; and
   b. Jericho-Jordan.
5. The offices responsible for carrying out the powers and responsibilities of the Palestinian authority under this Annex II and Article VI of the Declaration of Principles will be located in the Gaza Strip and in the Jericho area pending the inauguration of the Council.
6. Other than these agreed arrangements, the status of the Gaza Strip and Jericho area will continue to be an integral part of the West Bank and Gaza Strip, and will not be changed in the interim period.

ANNEX III: PROTOCOL ON ISRAELI-PALESTINIAN COOPERATION ECONOMIC
AND DEVELOPMENT PROGRAMS

The two sides agree to establish an Israeli-Palestinian Continuing Committee for Economic Cooperation, focusing, among other things, on the following:
1. Cooperation in the field of water, including a Water Development Program prepared by experts from both sides, which will also specify the mode of cooperation in the management of water resources in the West Bank and Gaza Strip, and will include proposals for studies and plans on water rights of each party, as well as on the equitable utilization of joint water resources for implementation in and beyond the interim period.

2. Cooperation in the field of electricity, including an Electricity Development Program, which will specify the mode of cooperation for the production, maintenance, purchase and sale of electricity resources.

3. Cooperation in the field of energy, including an Energy Development Program, which will provide for the exploitation of oil and gas for industrial purposes, particularly in the Gaza Strip and in the Negev, and will encourage further joint exploitation of other energy resources. This Program may also provide for the construction of a Petrochemical industrial complex in the Gaza Strip and the construction of oil and gas pipelines.

4. Cooperation in the field of finance, including a Financial Development and Action Program for the encouragement of international investment in the West Bank and the Gaza Strip, and in Israel, as well as the establishment of a Palestinian Development Bank.

5. Cooperation in the field of transport and communications, including a Program, which will define guidelines for the establishment of a Gaza Sea Port Area, and will provide for the establishing of transport and communications lines to and from the West Bank and the Gaza Strip to Israel and to other countries. In addition, this Program will provide for carrying out the necessary construction of roads, railways, communications lines, etc.

6. Cooperation in the field of trade, including studies and Trade Promotion Programs, which will encourage local, regional and inter-regional trade, as well as a feasibility study of creating free trade zones in the Gaza Strip and in Israel, mutual access to these zones, and cooperation in other areas related to trade and commerce.

7. Cooperation in the field of industry, including Industrial Development Programs, which will provide for the establishment of joint Israeli-Palestinian Industrial Research and Development Centers, will promote Palestinian-Israeli joint ventures, and provide guidelines for cooperation in the textile, food, pharmaceutical, electronics, diamonds, computer and science-based industries.

8. A program for cooperation in, and regulation of labor relations and cooperation in social welfare issues.

9. A Human Resources Development and Cooperation Plan, providing for joint Israeli-Palestinian workshops and seminars, and for the establishment of joint vocational training centers, research institutes and data banks.

10. An Environmental Protection Plan, providing for joint and/or coordinated measures in this sphere.

11. A program for developing coordination and cooperation in the field of communication and media.

12. Any other programs of mutual interest.

ANNEX IV: PROTOCOL ON ISRAELI-PALESTINIAN COOPERATION CONCERNING REGIONAL DEVELOPMENT PROGRAMS

1. The two sides will cooperate in the context of the multilateral peace efforts in promoting a Development Program for the region, including the West Bank and the Gaza Strip, to be initiated by the G-7. The parties will request the G-7 to seek the participation in this program of other interested states, such as members of the Organization for Economic Cooperation and Development, regional Arab states and institutions, as well as members of the private sector.

2. The Development Program will consist of two elements:
   a. an Economic Development Program for the West Bank and the Gaza Strip.
   b. a Regional Economic Development Program.

A. The Economic Development Program for the West Bank and the Gaza Strip will consist of the following elements:
   1. A Social Rehabilitation Program, including a Housing and Construction Program.
   2. A Small and Medium Business Development Plan.
   3. An Infrastructure Development Program (water, electricity, transportation and communications, etc.).
   4. A Human Resources Plan.
   5. Other programs.
B. The Regional Economic Development Program may consist of the following elements:
   1. The establishment of a Middle East Development Fund, as a first step, and a Middle East Development Bank, as a second step.
   2. The development of a joint Israeli-Palestinian-Jordanian Plan for coordinated exploitation of the Dead Sea area.
   3. The Mediterranean Sea (Gaza)–Dead Sea Canal.
   4. Regional Desalinization and other water development projects.
   5. A regional plan for agricultural development, including a coordinated regional effort for the prevention of desertification.
   6. Interconnection of electricity grids.
   7. Regional cooperation for the transfer, distribution and industrial exploitation of gas, oil and other energy resources.
   8. A Regional Tourism, Transportation and Telecommunications Development Plan.
   9. Regional cooperation in other spheres.
3. The two sides will encourage the multilateral working groups, and will coordinate towards their success. The two parties will encourage intersessional activities, as well as pre-feasibility and feasibility studies, within the various multilateral working groups. . . .

AGREED MINUTES TO THE DECLARATION OF PRINCIPLES ON INTERIM SELF-GOVERNMENT ARRANGEMENTS. . . . ARTICLE IV

It is understood that:
1. Jurisdiction of the Council will cover West Bank and Gaza Strip territory, except for issues that will be negotiated in the permanent status negotiations: Jerusalem, settlements, military locations, and Israelis.
2. The Council's jurisdiction will apply with regard to the agreed powers, responsibilities, spheres and authorities transferred to it. . . .

ANNEX II

It is understood that, subsequent to the Israeli withdrawal, Israel will continue to be responsible for external security, and for internal security and public order of settlements and Israelis. Israeli military forces and civilians may continue to use roads freely within the Gaza Strip and the Jericho area.

Done at Washington, D.C., this thirteenth day of September, 1993.

E L E V E N

The Peace Progresses

CHRONOLOGY

1994

Feb. 25	Jewish settler massacres twenty-nine Palestinians praying at Ibrahimi Mosque in Hebron
May 4	Gaza-Jericho agreement signed in Cairo
May 13	Israel hands over control of Jericho to PLO; hands over the Gaza strip on May 18
July 1	Arafat arrives in Gaza
July 25	Rabin and King Hussein declare end of state of war between Israel and Jordan
Oct. 1	Gulf states lift secondary economic boycott against Israel
Oct. 26	Formal peace treaty signed between Jordan and Israel
Dec. 10	Rabin, Peres, and Arafat receive Nobel Peace Prize

1995

Jan. 22	Suicide bombing at Beit Lid junction kills twenty-two Israelis
Aug. 27	Israel and Palestinian Authority sign early empowerment agreement for West Bank
Sept. 24	Agreement on Palestinian interim self-rule reached at Taba; the Oslo II, or Taba, accord, is signed in Washington on September 28
Oct. 25	Israel Defense Forces withdraw from Jenin
Oct. 26	Islamic Jihad leader Fathi Shqaqi assassinated in Malta by Israel
Nov. 4	Yitzhak Rabin assassinated by Jewish extremist Yigal Amir
Dec. 7–27	Israel withdraws from remainder of major Arab population centers on West Bank except for Hebron

1996

Jan. 5	Assassination by Israel of Hamas leader Yahya Ayyash, the "engineer"
Jan. 20	Elections held for Palestinian legislative council; Arafat elected president
Feb. 11	Prime Minister Peres calls for early elections in Israel
Feb.–Mar.	Four Hamas suicide bombings in Israel kill fifty-nine Israelis
Mar. 13	"Summit of the Peacemakers" at Sharm al-Sheikh
Apr. 12	Israel launches "Operation Grapes of Wrath" against Lebanon; shells UN compound at Qana on Apr. 18
Apr. 24	Palestine National Council declares it will amend its covenant and cancel clauses calling for the destruction of Israel
Apr. 25	Labor party platform drops opposition to a Palestinian state.
Apr. 27	Cease-fire agreement is reached between Lebanon and Israel
May 29	Israeli elections; Benjamin Netanyahu of the Likud party is elected prime minister
Sept. 4	Netanyahu and Arafat meet for the first time at Erez checkpoint
Sept. 24	Israel opens exit onto Via Dolorosa of Hasmonean tunnel; riots and clashes ensue between Arabs and Jews
Oct. 4	Clinton convenes summit of Netanyahu, Arafat, and King Hussein in Washington

1997

Jan. 15	Agreement on Hebron is reached between Netanyahu and Arafat; Israel redeploys its troops

The Gaza-Jericho Agreement Between Israel and the PLO

The day after the historic handshake in Washington, Jordan and Israel agreed on an agenda for negotiations toward a peace treaty. Israelis hoped that other Arab countries would make peace with the Jewish state and that the Arab economic boycott would be lifted. The Knesset quickly ratified the Israel–PLO accord (by a 61 to 50 vote), and it was also ratified by a majority of the Palestine National Council. The success or failure of Palestinian self-government, and thus the accord, was dependent upon the territories achieving a solid financial footing. The United States moved quickly to convene a conference of donor nations, and by early October, more than forty countries pledged to contribute $2 billion over five years. The European Community pledged $600 million, the United States $500 million, and Israel $75 million. Of the Arab countries, Saudi Arabia and the United Arab Emirates pledged $100 million and $25 million respectively.

On October 13, exactly one month after the ceremony on the White House lawn, Israeli and Palestinian negotiators sat down to try to work out the details of implementing the agreement. Difficulties surfaced almost immediately: What would be the size of the Jericho area? Where would Israeli soldiers be redeployed? What would be the size of the Palestinian police force? How, and by whom, would the border crossings between Gaza and Egypt, and Jericho and the West Bank be controlled? How could violence be warded off on both sides?

As time passed without agreement on the above issues, cynics decried the whole experiment, and, as most observers had predicted, violence by those attempting to sabotage the talks escalated. Palestinians murdered Israelis and assassinated leading Fatah figures in the territories, while Jewish settlers went on rampages against Palestinians. On February 25, 1994, in a fearful massacre at the Ibrahimi Mosque within the Tomb of the Patriarchs in Hebron, Dr. Baruch Goldstein, a Jewish settler and follower of the late Meir Kahane, shot and killed twenty-nine Muslim worshipers. More Arabs died in the panic and melee that followed. With the exception of some of the more extremist settlers, the vast majority of Israelis, including President Ezer Weizman and Prime Minister Rabin, denounced the crime and the criminal. Rabin immediately ordered a top-level investigation and ordered some settlers to be detained, disarmed, or arrested. The Kach party, of which Goldstein was a member, and its offshoot "Kahane Chai" ("Kahane Lives"), were outlawed.

The massacre dramatically drew attention to the whole settler/settlements issue. Initially, the tragedy was explained as the act of a deranged extremist zealot from Brooklyn, but as the special inquiry progressed, wider questions of official responsibility were raised. Palestinians felt great anger and humiliation that the curfew imposed following the killings allowed armed Jewish settlers to travel freely, while punishing the victims by preventing them from leaving their homes. Palestinian negotiators sought to use the incident to rewrite or renegotiate the newly concluded September agreement. They now wanted to include the status of Jerusalem and the issue of the settlements, arguing that these were core issues without whose solution it was pointless to proceed. The Knesset debated removing some of the settlers from the center of Hebron, promised to compensate the families of the massacre victims, and released some 1,000 Palestinian prisoners earlier than agreed, but Israel refused to alter the terms of the Gaza-Jericho agenda. The peace process came to a dead halt.

In April, in revenge for the Hebron killings, members of Hamas carried out two suicide car and bus bombings within Israel, killing at least fifteen Israeli men, women, and children and wounding scores of others. Arafat, in remarks to the Council of Europe, belatedly spoke out against the Hamas actions.

Meanwhile, after five weeks of stalled negotiations, the peace process between Israel and the PLO resumed after Israel agreed to the temporary deployment in Hebron of a small, lightly armed international force to monitor the situation. There appeared to be a determination on both sides to implement the Gaza-Jericho self-rule agreement before political support for Rabin and Arafat eroded further and nullified the Declaration of Principles altogether. The April 13 target date for Israel to leave Gaza and Jericho passed, but Israeli troops did begin preparations for withdrawal.

On May 4, 1994, in Cairo, an agreement detailing the terms of the Israeli withdrawal from Gaza and Jericho was finally signed before an audience of about 2,000, although not without anxious moments. As Arafat examined the various papers, he abruptly refused to initial a map of the Jericho area, and while the speeches continued, diplomats and negotiators huddled. After Rabin and Arafat had walked offstage and Rabin agreed that he would write a letter stating that the map was not necessarily the final word, Arafat signed, appending his own comments. The Israelis agreed to the Jericho area being somewhat larger—twenty-five square miles—than they had first wished, and they agreed that the Palestinian police force would number about 9,000 men. The Palestinians were allowed their own postage stamps and international telephone dialing code, control of exports and imports, and the right to issue travel documents; but they were denied their own currency and the right to station Palestinian police on the Allenby Bridge.

As the first contingents of Palestinian police and administrators began to arrive amid much celebration and jubilation, the Israelis completed their withdrawal from Jericho on May 13 and from Gaza on May 18. On July 1, Arafat entered Gaza in triumph, and on July 5, in Jericho, he swore in members of the Palestine National Authority (PNA, now usually referred to as the Palestinian Authority, or P.A.). There were uncertainties about basic governance and about a steady flow of funds, since Arafat's reluctance to delegate authority to officials of the Palestine Economic Council for Development and Reconstruction (PECDAR) led the World Bank to postpone allocating the $2 billion pledged by the donor countries, which demanded more accountability than Arafat appeared willing to provide. Despite the uncertain future, however, twenty-seven years of Israeli occupation appeared to be coming to an end.

Peace Between Jordan and Israel

As the Palestinian Authority began to take control in Gaza and Jericho, Israel and Jordan moved closer to ending the state of war between the two countries. King Hussein was determined to be a player in the peace process and to consolidate and protect his own interests in the wake of the accord between the PLO and Israel, without waiting for similar progress in Israel's dealings with Syria or other Arab countries. He was also eager for American assistance in rebuilding the Jordanian economy, devastated by the consequences of the Gulf War. According to news reports that were not denied, Israeli Prime Minister Rabin and the king had met secretly in Washington in early June and agreed to reopen bilateral negotiations that had been suspended in February as a result of the Hebron mosque incident.

In mid-July 1994, Israeli and Jordanian negotiators met publicly for the first time in their own region, at Ein Avrona, Israel, in a tent straddling their common desert border. Two days later, Israeli Foreign Minister Peres crossed the border to meet Jordanian Prime Minister Abdul Salam al-Majali and U.S. Secretary of State Warren Christopher. These unprecedented meetings paved the way for a ceremony on July 25 on the White House lawn, where Prime Minister Rabin and King Hussein officially declared an end to the state of war that had existed between Israel and Jordan for forty-six years. The two leaders appeared before a joint session of the U.S. Congress, the first time two world leaders had addressed a joint session, and they pledged to work toward a peace treaty. As a result, on July 29, congressional leaders agreed to speed up relief of the approximately $700 million Jordanian debt by up to $220 million, with future relief dependent on progress toward a final peace agreement, support for ending the Arab economic boycott, and full compliance with international sanctions against Iraq.

The Washington Declaration, as the July 25 declaration was called, paved the way for cooperation between Jordan and Israel on several fronts, including opening direct telephone links and new border crossing points, establishing air service between the two countries, and sharing in water resources. Jordan also agreed to seek an end to the Arab economic boycott against Israel, and Israel agreed to respect Jordan's special role with regard to the Muslim Holy Places in Jerusalem, a move that greatly angered the Palestinians and other Arab leaders.

These developments prompted terrorist incidents. A horrific bombing of a Jewish cultural center in Argentina claimed at least 100 lives, and several bomb attacks occurred in London. Nevertheless, on August 3, the Israeli Knesset overwhelmingly approved the historic agreement with Jordan, and Rabin personally informed King Hussein of the vote as the king, escorted by Israeli Air Force F15s, piloted his jet through Israeli airspace for the first time and circled Jerusalem on his way home to Amman from a trip to London. On October 26, 1994, a formal peace treaty was signed just north of Aqaba in Wadi Arava by Rabin and Jordanian Foreign Minister Majali, with President Clinton as a co-signer. (See Document 11–1.) The two countries established diplomatic relations on November 27, 1994.

As these events unfolded, other Arab countries, with the notable exceptions of Syria, Lebanon, Iraq, and Libya, also moved cautiously toward recognition of the Jewish state. As early as January 1994, Qatar's foreign minister held a secret meeting in London with Israeli officials to discuss a $1 billion gas deal with Israel. In September 1994, Israel and Morocco agreed to establish liaison offices, and, at the beginning of October, the Gulf Cooperation Council countries of Saudi Arabia, Qatar, Kuwait, Oman, the United Arab Emirates, and Bahrain announced a partial lifting of the Arab economic boycott by cancelling the boycott of secondary or tertiary parties doing business with Israel. That same month, Israel and Tunisia announced a low-level exchange of representatives.

King Hussein's plane with Israeli honor guard flying over Jerusalem, August 3, 1994.

The Road to Oslo II

Palestinian Violence Continues

Talks also continued with the PLO on early empowerment for the West Bank; and between August and December 1994, education, social services, tourism, health, and taxation were handed over to the Palestinian Authority.

Along the way, however, and even as it was announced that Arafat, Rabin, and Peres would receive the Nobel Prize in Oslo on December 10, 1994, acts of terror continued by those opposed to the peace process. Attacks by Hamas and Islamic Jihad militants within Israel itself had become more common and more deadly. A suicide bus bomber struck in the heart of Tel Aviv in October, killing twenty-three; and at the Beit Lid junction near Netanya in January 1995, another suicide bombing killed twenty-two, mostly Israeli soldiers and young people, and wounded sixty-one. These attacks now began to give most Israelis pause, as their concern shifted increasingly from border security to personal security. Ezer Weizman, Israel's president, called for a temporary halt in the implementation of the peace accords, and Prime Minister Rabin broached the idea of separation of Israelis and Palestinians, at one point even considering the possibility of a security fence between the two populations. The idea of separation would continue to be a theme even for those Israelis committed to achieving peace with the Palestinians.

De facto separation began to occur in any case, as Israel closed its borders to Palestinian workers for periods of time after terrorist incidents. This caused further distress particularly in Gaza, which was still not experiencing the economic growth and change that had been anticipated with the transfer of authority to the Palestinians themselves. Although economic problems were due primarily to Israeli closures, inadequate funds, which the donor nations hesitated to disburse, added to the problem. There was still not much accountability on Arafat's part, proper procedures were not in place, and the PLO leader had difficulty delegating authority. Arafat found himself in the unenviable position of having to try to satisfy the Israelis that he was doing all he could to control terrorism, at the same time that he had to convince followers of Hamas and Islamic Jihad that he could act as a leader of all segments of the Palestinian population. Indeed, Palestinian dissatisfaction and impatience in Gaza had boiled over in November 1994, when Palestinian police clashed with demonstrators outside the main mosque.

Under intense Israeli pressure, and determined to exert his authority, in February 1995, Arafat arrested some Islamic Jihad members and set up a military court to try suspected assailants in the Beit Lid attack. Rabin then agreed to step up talks on expanding self-rule and eased travel restrictions on Palestinians working in Israel. According to the timetable of the Declaration of Principles, Israel's withdrawal from the major Arab population centers of the West Bank was supposed to have been completed by July 13, 1994, so that Palestinian elections could be held. However, target dates of July 1 and July 15 were deferred as the cycle of violence and closures continued. Some Hamas members now began to acknowledge that violence was hampering progress toward further Palestinian self-government, and in July, Hamas political leaders in the territories met with Arafat and indicated that they would be willing to abandon violence temporarily.

It was apparent that although some Hamas political leaders were willing to forgo violence, its military wing was not. Further suicide bus bombings took place in Ramat Gan in July and Jerusalem in August. Hamas militants claimed that the attacks were part of a new campaign intended to bring down the current Israeli government, and they vowed to continue their activities until the Israeli elections.

West Bank Settlers' Opposition

It was not only militant Islamists who wished to undermine the peace efforts of the Rabin government. The incidents of terrorism greatly eroded support throughout the Israeli population for the peace agenda. Israeli settlers motivated by religious and nationalist ideologies became increasingly angry and disillusioned with Rabin's attitude toward them and toward their objective of retaining all of Eretz Yisrael. Rabin denounced the settlers as a "burden" on the army in its fight against radical Palestinians. "Settlements add nothing, absolutely nothing to Israel's security," he said. "They are a liability rather than an asset." Nervous settlers had begun staking out claims to hilltops and lands they were afraid would be returned to the Palestinians, and they and their supporters blocked Israeli highways to protest the planned expansion of Palestinian self-rule. Ugly protest demonstrations were held in front of the prime minister's home, and posters of Rabin in Nazi garb or wearing a kaffiyeh began to appear. A group of rabbis, called the "refusal" rabbis, issued a ruling that soldiers should disobey any orders to dismantle West Bank army bases. As the Israeli government continued to counter demonstrators, sometimes harshly, the Likud and other right-wing opposition parties stepped up their rhetoric against Rabin and the peace process.

Oslo II, or the Taba Accord

Palestinian and Israeli negotiators, however, continued to meet to try to hammer out the details of implementing the September 1993 accord. On August 27, 1995, the Palestinian Authority and Israel signed an early empowerment agreement in Cairo, transferring administrative power to the P.A. in eight areas—labor, trade and industry, gas and petroleum, insurance, statistics, agriculture, postal services, and local government—and Israeli and Palestinian negotiators continued discussions on the transfer of authority in more than twenty other areas. Previously, key differences had been reached on security and division of control over land, and a compromise was reached on water allocation, with Israel officially recognizing Palestinian rights (in principle) to water sources in the West Bank. Israel agreed that Palestinians in East Jerusalem would be allowed to vote in Palestinian elections. The Palestinians accepted that an IDF presence would remain in Hebron near Jewish areas, and that Israel would continue to be responsible for security at the Tomb of the Patriarchs and for the traffic route between the Jewish settlement of Kiryat Arba and Hebron. Palestinian police would cover the rest of the city. An overall agreement was finally reached at Taba (a Red Sea resort) on September 24, 1995, on the eve of the Jewish new year. It was signed in Washington on September 28, 1995, in a somber ceremony attended by Arafat, Rabin, Peres, Mubarak, and Hussein that was in stark contrast to the celebration that had occurred two years earlier. (See Document 11–2.)

The Israeli–Palestinian Interim Agreement on the West Bank and Gaza Strip, known variously as the Interim agreement, or Oslo II, or the Taba accord, was the second phase of the process that had begun with the establishment of the Palestinian Authority in Gaza and Jericho in May 1994, and it set the stage for the final status talks to begin by May 1996. The agreement established three areas in the West Bank: Area A, which would consist of territory to be placed under direct Palestinian control; Area B, jointly controlled territory, in which the Palestinians would exercise civil and police authority but Israel would retain security responsibility; and Area C, territory in which Israel would have exclusive control. Accordingly, the agreement provided for the Israel Defense Forces to redeploy from the major cities of Jenin, Tulkarm, Qalqilya, Nablus, Bethlehem, Ramallah (to be included in Area A), and from about 450 Palestinian villages and smaller communities (to be included in Area B). Areas A and B, consisting of approximately 3 percent and 24 percent respectively of the West Bank, contained the majority of the Palestinian population. Area C consisted of sparsely or unpopulated areas, Israeli military installations and Jewish settlements. After the Israeli withdrawal from the populated areas, elections would be held for a Palestinian legislative council and the head of the council. In Hebron, the army would redeploy, but special security arrangements would apply. Further redeployments from parts of Area C would occur in three phases at six-month intervals and be completed within eighteen months from the inauguration of the Council. Other provisions concerned prisoner releases, the allocation of water resources, and a commitment by the PLO to amend its covenant within two months after the inauguration of the Palestine council.

Israel began its pullout from some smaller West Bank villages in early October, and, on October 25, the IDF began to withdraw from Jenin, the first large Arab population center named in the agreement. Despite what seemed to be a promising step toward the implementation of peace between Israel and the Palestinians, there were many on both sides who saw the situation in a different light. Palestinian negotiators and much of the ordinary Palestinian population were suspicious of the agreement's provisions for the step-by-step transfer of land and power. They were dismayed that Israel would continue to occupy large parts of the West Bank, while the P.A. would only gradually assume administrative and security functions. They also feared that Israel intended to provide long-term protection for Jewish settlers and would never withdraw fully to allow the creation of a Palestinian state. In attempting to reassure Israelis, Foreign Minister Peres noted that under the accord, Israel would maintain control of 73 percent of the land, 80 percent of the water, and 97 percent of the security arrangements—a statement that only intensified Palestinian anxiety. The Islamic militants were violently opposed to any accommodation with Israel, and their terrorist attacks were directed not only against Israel but against the credibility of Yasser Arafat.

For their part, many ordinary Israelis had misgivings about Arafat, a man who seemed incapable or unwilling to deal decisively with the extremist groups. Moreover, for the right-wing religious and nationalist extremists in Israel, the Oslo II provisions had made the possibility of giving up part of biblical Israel very real, and as Israeli soldiers prepared to turn over villages, towns, and cities on the West Bank to the Palestinian Authority, they increasingly branded Rabin a traitor. There were even some rabbis who called for his death.

The Assassination of Yitzhak Rabin

A Jewish zealot, Yigal Amir, assassinated Israeli Prime Minister Yitzhak Rabin on November 4, 1995. Amir, from the town of Herzliya and a law student at Bar-Ilan university, said that he was acting on God's orders to prevent the land of Israel from being turned over to the Palestinians. Ironically, this murder, the first political assassination of a Jew by a Jew in Israel's modern history, occurred just after Rabin had addressed a huge peace rally in Kings of Israel Square in Tel Aviv, where over 100,000 Israelis had gathered to support the peace process and to sing a song of peace. For the first time anyone could recall, Rabin himself had sung along, and a sheet with the bloodstained words of this song was found later in his jacket pocket.

All of Israel, and much of the world, was stunned. At first, many thought the assailant had acted in revenge for the murder of Fathi Shqaqi, the leader of Islamic Jihad, who had been killed in Malta in late October, probably by agents of the Mossad. When it became clear that Rabin's assassin was a Jew, even most of his political opponents were horrified, and the nation was plunged into grief and soul-searching. For most Israelis, even those who disagreed with the course he had embarked upon, Rabin had brought a credibility to the peace process that no other Israeli leader possessed. His life and career had been concerned with the defense of the state: as a young commander in the elite commando unit, Palmach, during Israel's war for independence; as army chief of staff in 1967; as authorizer of Israel's stunning raid on Entebbe in 1976; and as defense minister during the Intifada. Known as "Mr. Security," it was almost universally believed that he would never jeopardize Israel's security in any kind of territorial compromise. He had outraged Jewish extremists, however, by his "conversion," from defense minister, who had advocated breaking the bones of the young rock-throwers of the Intifada, to prime minister, who came to believe that Israel could not preserve its Jewish and democratic character while continuing to rule over almost 2 million Palestinians who loathed Israeli occupation and sought to determine their own destiny.

An astonishing array of heads of state and other dignitaries, including several from Arab countries, arrived in Jerusalem for Yitzhak Rabin's funeral on Mount Herzl (burial place of Theodor Herzl) on November 6. Obvious affection for Rabin was illustrated by the moving words of President Clinton of the United States and King Hussein of Jordan, who called him his brother. (See Document 11–3.) Mubarak's speech was respectful, if detached; the president of Egypt was making his first trip to Israel since the signing of the Egyptian–Israel peace treaty in Washington in 1979. Although Yasser Arafat did not attend for security reasons, he paid a condolence call to Leah Rabin and her family in Tel Aviv and publicly expressed sorrow over the assassination.

No doubt this incredible gathering of world leaders and the outpouring of condolences from capitals throughout the world reassured Israelis that their state was recognized as a nation among the nations and that Rabin's path to peace was supported by the world community. And yet, even as Shimon Peres pledged to continue the process, there were many questions being asked about the acting prime minister's ability to do so, and about the process itself. Granted, Benjamin Netanyahu and the Likud were on the defensive, at least temporarily, as critics, including Rabin's widow, Leah, excoriated the opposition parties for condoning the

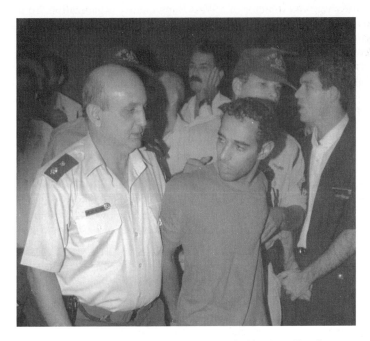

Yigal Amir, who shot Yitzhak Rabin, being led by Israeli police to arraignment in Tel Aviv, November 6, 1995.

rhetoric of hatred, which they blamed for poisoning the atmosphere of civil discourse and leading to Rabin's murder. After Israeli President Weizman asked Peres to form a new government, Netanyahu pledged to support him as prime minister until new elections were held, and polls taken shortly after the assassination showed that 70 percent of Israelis were in support of the peace process. But the political divide appeared to be deep, and it widened in the coming months.

Would Shimon Peres be able to unify the nation and move ahead in implementing the peace accords? Although Peres had been responsible for building up Israel's military-industrial complex and had initiated its nuclear program, he had never served in the military and was perceived as an urbane intellectual, a dreamer and visionary, as different in personality and appeal from the blunt, earthy, soldier-hero Rabin as night and day. Peres is often considered the real architect of the peace process, but he and Rabin eventually came to share the common goal of peace with the Palestinians. Whether he was the person to guide that dream to fruition remained to be seen.

The Election of a Palestinian Legislative Council and Arafat as President

Peres immediately proceeded to implement the Taba accord, and he honored a pledge by Rabin to Arafat to speed up Israel's redeployment from the remaining major Arab population centers on the West Bank. Between December 7 and 27, 1995, the IDF withdrew from Tulkarm, Qalqilya, Nablus, Bethlehem (where Arafat spent Christmas), and Ramallah. Peres indicated that the redeployment from Hebron would be completed by March 1996.

Plans for Palestinian elections could now proceed. Voter registration had begun in November, and elections for the Palestinian legislative council were scheduled for January 20, 1996. Arafat registered as a presidential candidate, his only opponent being Samiha Khalid, a seventy-two-year-old director of a West Bank charity organization. To no one's surprise, Arafat won easily, gaining 88 percent of the vote. What was perhaps more noteworthy was the high turnout of almost 85 percent of those eligible to vote in Gaza, and 73 percent on the West Bank. Israeli security measures and intimidation kept the figures in East Jerusalem to 30 percent. Despite fears that the voting would reinforce clan and local divisions, the Palestinians tended to vote for candidates with credentials in their national struggle. Nearly 700 candidates ran for the 88-seat legislature. Although Hamas and radical PLO secularist groups like the PFLP and DFLP boycotted the elections, some of their members ran as independents and won seats. The elections provided legitimacy for Arafat and the peace process, and, even more important, they provided a basis for Palestinian claims to statehood. Arafat underscored this when he convened the first meeting of the new legislative council in March 1996, declaring: "We are witnessing a new Palestinian struggle for an independent state, with Jerusalem as its capital."

Although there was almost universal consensus that a giant step had been taken toward an eventual Palestinian state, whether that happened or not would depend largely on a continuation of the peace process with Israel and the results of final status talks that were to begin in May 1996.

Arafat and the Islamists

Arafat faced many problems in January 1996. One of the most difficult from an internal, and external, point of view was the issue of containing acts of terror by militant Islamists. The Palestinian Authority had been unable to solve many of the severe economic problems in Gaza especially, and Israel's frequent closure of the territories made the task almost impossible. Many Palestinians, therefore, continued to rely on Hamas institutions for succor. Much of the budget of Hamas (estimated in 1995 at $70 million) went for legitimate religious and charitable purposes. But some of it was used to pay lifetime annuities to families of suicide bombers, and there is no doubt that Hamas institutions were sometimes a cover and recruiting ground for young terrorists. With Sheikh Yassin in prison, the leadership had divided between those inside and outside the territories. From bases abroad, Musa Muhammad Abu Marzouk, head of its Political Bureau, expanded and virtually reinvented Hamas as a well-financed, internationally supported organization. Although the relationship between Hamas's political and military wings was unclear, Marzouk was considered by Israel to be a key policymaker of Hamas, and he was arrested in the United States in July 1995. While Marzouk remained in detention in New York, awaiting possible extradiction to Israel, the activities of the Qassam Brigades, inspired by the suicide bombing exploits of Yahya Ayyash, "the engineer," operating from Gaza, continued greatly to influence the course of Israeli–Palestinan peace efforts.

Arafat had some success in co-opting Hamas civilian figures who tried to build bridges between the more militant leaders and the Palestinian Authority. At a December 1995 meeting in Cairo, they had agreed that although Hamas would not participate in the elections, it would refrain from embarrassing the Palestinian Authority beforehand. In fact, there were no suicide bombings or other Hamas attacks from August 1995 until after the January 1996 assassination by Israel in Gaza of Yahya Ayyash, who was known to have been responsible for most of the incidents within Israel.

It was quite likely that as peace talks moved toward final status negotiations, terrorist activities would resume. The Hamas military wing remained implacably opposed to Israel, to Arafat, and to the peace process. However, Israel also helped precipitate the resumption of deadly acts, by its assassination of Fathi Shqaqi in October 1995, and of Ayyash in January 1996, when his cell phone exploded in his ear as he was talking to his father. This was an operation evidently authorized by Peres, undertaken partly to vindicate the Israeli General Security Services, chafing because of their inability to protect Yitzhak Rabin. Both assassinations, although they removed men responsible for numerous acts of violence, and although some observers believed the terrorist groups would be incapacitated by the elimination of their leaders, were certain to provoke revenge attacks.

Palestinian anger at Ayyash's murder bolstered Hamas's standing, which had eroded somewhat because of rising excitement over elections and self-rule. Although he infuriated the Israelis, Arafat had little choice but to express his condolences to Ayyash's family, calling him a holy martyr and ordering a twenty-one-gun salute. Despite Arafat's hesitance to pursue known terrorists aggressively, or to extradite them to Israel, as one Israeli observer remarked: "He's the only Arafat we've got." Efforts by Arafat to counter Hamas were hampered by family loyalties, by the shared experiences with other Palestinians of battling the Israelis and often sharing common jail cells, and by deep distrust of Arafat's dealings with Israel and disappointment with his administration of the self-rule areas. Hamas, for its part, in an effort to derail the peace process, began to carry out revenge attacks that had dire consequences for the election chances of Shimon Peres and that also weakened Arafat. In late February and early March 1996, in the space of eight days, 59 Israelis were killed and hundreds wounded in four Hamas suicide bombings in the very heart of Israel. On February 25, a suicide bomber blew himself up on the Number 18 bus in Jerusalem, killing 25, including 2 American students engaged to be married. There was a simultaneous attack in the city of Ashkelon. Peres halted the peace negotiations temporarily and maintained the closure of the territories, which had been sealed off during certain periods of Ramadan.

On March 3, the Number 18 bus was attacked again, leaving 19 dead. The next day, as Israelis were celebrating the holiday of Purim and revelers crowded the streets, a suicide bomber blew up himself and 12 others, and wounded more than 100, on Dizengoff Street near Tel Aviv's main shopping mall. Arafat condemned the bombings, and the P.A. sealed off some villages, but Peres called on him to do more to arrest militant Hamas members and especially the known leaders. The terrorist attacks clouded the victory Arafat had hoped to celebrate when he convened the Palestinian legislature for the first time on March 7.

Wreckage of a bus bombing in Jerusalem, February 25, 1996.

With emotions running high, Israel maintained the closure of the borders, postponed the withdrawal from Hebron scheduled for mid-March, and broke off talks with Syria, which had resumed. Although Peres insisted that this was because of the pain of the bombings and was careful not to implicate the Syrians, Assad's support and refuge for terrorists, and his ties with Iran, were certainly a factor.

World leaders condemned these attacks on Israel, and, at the suggestion of President Mubarak, a "summit of the peacemakers" convened at Sharm al-Sheikh on March 13. Twenty-nine countries were represented, and the world leaders included U.S. President Clinton, Russian President Yeltsin, President Demirel of Turkey, President Chirac of France, Britain's Prime Minister Major, and several other heads of state or foreign ministers, including Prince Said al-Faisal of Saudi Arabia. Task forces were set up to address the issue of terrorism, but the conference was basically window dressing and a show of support for Peres and Arafat. Clinton then went to Jerusalem and addressed the Israeli Knesset, promising Israel money and equipment to fight terrorism.

There were a number of indicators in the period from the Oslo I accord to the terrorist incidents in the spring of 1996 that had created a sense of hope and optimism among many observers. One was the growing recognition of Israel among the Arab nations. There were peace treaties with Egypt and Jordan; and Morocco, Tunisia, Mauritania, Qatar, and Oman had opened low-level relations. The multilateral talks, as well as international gatherings, saw Israelis, Palestinians, and other Arabs sitting down with each other. In October 1994, there had been an important economic summit in Casablanca; and in Amman the next October, the largest economic conference ever assembled, called the Middle East–North Africa Economic Summit, had assembled. About 2,000 government officials and business leaders from sixty countries took part in the three-day conference. Syria and Lebanon boycotted the meeting, but it was otherwise

"Summit of the Peacemakers," March 13, 1996.

well-attended, with representatives from Israel, Japan, the United States, many European nations, and most of the Middle East and North African countries. And the many Arab leaders and delegations at Rabin's funeral impressed all who witnessed the coverage of that moment.

All these events, despite the Hamas terrorist attacks, seemed to prove that the "peace of the brave" was succeeding. On Israel's northern border, however, the problem of Hizbullah activity in Israel's "security zone" and against Israel's northern cities continued. Since this situation also involved Syria, the dominant power in Lebanon, we should turn first to a brief look at the course of Syrian–Israeli negotiations.

The Syrian Track

Among the eighty countries represented at Yitzhak Rabin's funeral were Israel's peace partners and other Arab delegations. One voice was notable for its complete silence; although urged to do so by President Clinton, Syrian President Hafez al-Assad uttered no word of regret.

Bilateral negotiations between Syria and Israel had continued after Oslo I but were broken off by Syria in February 1994 at the time of the Hebron mosque massacre. U.S. Secretary of State Christopher tried to keep the Israel–Syrian track viable with countless shuttles between Damascus and Jerusalem. He was in the region in April, May, July, August, October, and December of 1994, and on each occasion he shuttled back and forth between Assad and Rabin, carrying proposals and statements relating in particular to security issues. President Clinton himself stopped over in Damascus following the signing of the Israel–Jordan peace treaty in October. As revealed later, private meetings had also been going on in Washington between the Israeli and Syrian ambassadors, and the Israeli and Syrian chiefs of staff met in December. However, apparently having second thoughts because of what he considered Israeli inflexibility, Assad abruptly cut off the dialogue in Washington. At a two-day summit with Mubarak and King Fahd of Saudi Arabia in late December 1994 in Alexandria, a statement was released calling for full Israeli withdrawal from the Golan and southern Lebanon and the removal of all weapons of mass destruction (read Israel's nuclear arsenal) from the area.

The two sides did not meet again in Washington for direct talks until March 1995, after a week of intense shuttle diplomacy by Christopher. At the end of May 1995, Syria made an important concession by abandoning its insistence that the two countries withdraw their troops an equal distance from the Golan Heights. But the core issues remained: Syria's demand that Israel withdraw from all of the Golan, and Israel's demand for a full peace with diplomatic and trade relations. Other details loomed large, such as a timetable for withdrawal, how far each country would pull back its troops, and whether the border would be the international border or that of June 4, 1967. The last question was a particularly important issue having to do with the waters of the Sea of Galilee and the Jordan River. (See Map 12–2 on p. 319.)

Just when it appeared that there was some positive movement, Rabin stated in June that any peace treaty with Syria would be submitted to a referendum. In July, Assad abruptly cancelled further negotiations because of an Israeli demand that there be ground-based early warning stations on the Golan Heights in the framework of security arrangements.

The impasse persisted until after the assassination of Yitzhak Rabin, when Assad agreed to the resumption of bilateral talks at the Wye plantation in Maryland in late December 1995. There is little doubt that Assad perceived Peres as being more moderate than Rabin. Peres said publicly that he was ready to negotiate on all outstanding issues, he jettisoned Rabin's insistence that talks be held on security between Syrian and Israeli military officials before any other issues could be considered, and he stated that peace with Syria was more important even than winning the next Israeli election. Twelve days of negotiations were conducted in two rounds of meetings at Wye, one in late December and the last ending in late January 1996. However, the talks never moved forward, and although not formally adjourned, they came to a virtual standstill because of Assad's refusal, despite American requests, to condemn the suicide bombings in Israel in late February and early March. The failure of a breakthrough on the Syrian front was one reason for Shimon Peres's announcement of early elections in Israel. As Syrians and Israelis awaited that outcome, however, the situation on Israel's northern border, which led to another Israeli attack against Lebanon, ended any expectation of progress on the Syrian front for the foreseeable future.

"Operation Grapes of Wrath"

On March 20, 1996, an Islamic militant rushed at the lead car of an Israeli army convoy in Israel's "security zone" in southern Lebanon, blowing up himself and an Israeli captain, the sixth Israeli soldier killed in the zone in three weeks. About ninety minutes later, guerrillas detonated a roadside bomb that killed a militiaman of the South Lebanon Army, Israel's ally in southern Lebanon. Hizbullah spokepersons said the bombings were in response to the international antiterrorism conference (the "summit of the peacemakers") held in Egypt the week before. It was the first suicide bombing in southern Lebanon in nearly a year, although in the weeks preceding it Hizbullah had stepped up its attacks in the zone. Many Israelis demanded a vigorous response, but the United States urged restraint on Israel and, indirectly through Syria, on Hizbullah. While the attacks were worrisome, they did not break the unwritten understanding reached following Israel's "Operation Accountability" in 1993 that restricted action against the other side to military targets within the "security zone."

Shortly after the March incidents, however, Hizbullah broke that agreement by firing Katyusha rockets into northern Israel, and in early April, a rocket volley wounded thirty-six civilians and sent several hundred Israelis into bomb shelters or flight. Hizbullah said that the attacks were in retaliation for the killing by Israeli soldiers of civilians outside the buffer zone, which Israel had claimed were accidents. For its part, Israel depicted the rocket attacks as part of a general and deliberate escalation by Hizbullah. After the second Katyusha attack, Prime Minister Peres ordered "surgical strikes" against Hizbullah targets in Lebanon, and, beginning on April 11, Israel sent F16 fighter planes and helicopter gunships deep into Lebanon, including Beirut, the first attack on targets in that city since Israel's 1982 invasion. Suspected military targets, as well as roads, power plants, and reservoirs, were hit. Two hundred Lebanese villagers and noncombatants were killed, with hundreds more wounded, since the guerrillas often operated from cover among their Shiite supporters. Approximately 400,000 Lebanese fled their homes. Infrastructure that the Lebanese had painstakingly begun to build up after the end of the civil war was destroyed, and the damage to property was incalculable.

At first, Israelis applauded this response to Hizbullah, dubbed "Operation Grapes of Wrath," and the United States not only tolerated it but seemed to be giving Israel a green light by its silence. On April 18, however, at least a dozen howitzer shells fell on a UN outpost at Qana, which was sheltering more than 600 civilians displaced by the fighting, and more than 100 of these refugees—men, women, and children—were killed, with many more being wounded. The artillery had been directed at a spot less than 300 yards from the UN post from which Katyushas had been fired, but by the time the IDF aimed their guns, the guerrillas and their launchers were gone. Instead, the shells exploded inside the UN compound. Israel insisted that there had been "a grave error" and that the shelling of Qana was not intentional, although UN and other observers believe that the Israeli action was deliberate. At this point, even President Clinton called for a cessation of hostilities. American, Russian, and French diplomats hurried to find a diplomatic solution.

Although there is no evidence that Peres had approved the operation simply to appear tough on the eve of the Israeli elections, he no doubt hoped to diminish a widespread image of softness by taking steps demanded by the Israeli public. Hizbullah was also a clearer target than Hamas. Some analysts believe the attack was intended to create a situation that would bring unbearable pressure on the Lebanese government to demand that the Syrians rein in Hizbullah and reach an agreement acceptable to Israel.

It is perhaps less clear why Hizbullah escalated its activity when it did, and what Syria was hoping to accomplish. With 35–40,000 troops still in Lebanon, Syria was the real power broker in that country, and Hizbullah could not operate with impunity in Lebanon without Syrian assistance and acquiescence. Were the Katyushas a means of putting pressure on Israel, with Damascus as the address, as one U.S. official put it? Talks with Syria, as noted before, had been suspended in February after the wave of Hamas suicide bombings in Israel. Or did Iran, which funds Hizbullah and supplies its ideology, conclude that Assad was too eager to deal with Israel and encourage Hizbullah in order to delay that process? Or did the attacks mean that Assad himself was not really committed to a negotiated settlement, being concerned

Damage after the Israeli bombardment of Qana in Lebanon, April 18, 1996.

ultimately about the kind of internal threat to his own position in Syria any kind of accommodation with Israel might provoke? Damascus hosts the headquarters of Hamas outside the territories and provides considerable aid to it, and some observers insist that both Hamas and Hizbullah attacks were intended simply to delay or halt the peace process. Assad despised the deal Arafat made with Israel, and some analysts have maintained that Assad's diplomacy was conducted more in the hope of burnishing his own reputation and receiving aid from the West than in a genuine desire to make peace with Israel.

In the end, and after Israeli insistence that only an American solution would be accepted, on April 27, Israel and Lebanon signed an agreement brokered by Christopher. (See Document 11–4.) The agreement did not prohibit actions by anti-Israeli guerrillas from attacking soldiers in the "security zone" but did prohibit attacks by groups in Lebanon, or by Israel and its allied militia groups, from firing at civilian targets on either side of the border. A monitoring committee was set up that included representatives of Lebanon, Syria, Israel, France, and the United States. The importance of this agreement, described as an understanding between the governments of Israel and Lebanon "in consultation with Syria," was that it was a written document, unlike the understanding reached in 1993. Nearly all the negotiating was done with Syria, and Assad was clearly a winner in this confrontation, demonstrating that he was indispensable to stability in the Middle East and that he remained sovereign over Lebanon. Hizbullah was also vindicated in the assertion of its right to fight the Israeli occupation of southern Lebanon, which Israel said it would leave only as part of a negotiated peace. Hizbullah was actually strengthened by the Israeli operation. The antipathy of the Lebanese population toward the Israelis swung even more sympathy and support toward Hizbullah, even if the majority of Lebanese did not subscribe to its Islamic ideology.

For Israel, "Operation Grapes of Wrath," no matter how justified in its inception, ended up severely damaging Israeli relations with moderate Arab regimes and outraging Arab Israelis. The Qana tragedy and Israel's totally inadequate apology, in particular, greatly distressed King Hussein. Israel's retaliation—for rocket attacks in which no Israeli civilians were killed—was so disproportionate, and so devastating for Lebanon, that Israel's integrity was questioned even by its friends. Furthermore, the operation provided additional ammunition for opponents of Israel to continue their campaign against the Jewish state. For Shimon Peres, the debacle did little to inspire confidence in his leadership, and with the Israeli election imminent, it appeared that victory was slipping from his grasp.

The PLO Votes to Amend the Covenant

In the midst of the Israeli attack against Hizbullah in Lebanon and the continued closure of the territories, Arafat convened a meeting of the Palestine National Council, as promised in the Taba accord, to consider amending the PLO covenant to remove those articles calling for the destruction of Israel. The covenant was so symbolic to Israel that Peres allowed some notorious figures to return to Gaza to attend the meeting. Ninety-seven of the 669 member body were absent, including George Habash of the PFLP and Nayef Hawatmeh of the DFLP, but Abul Abbas, mastermind of the 1985 *Achille Lauro* hijacking, Abu Daud Odeh, who is thought to have participated in the 1972 massacre of athletes at the Munich Olympics, and Leila Khaled, who participated in two airplane hijackings, were in attendance. In a resolution adopted on April 24, the PNC declared it would amend the covenant by cancelling clauses that contradicted the letters exchanged between the PLO and the Israeli government in September 1993, and it ordered a new charter to be drafted within six months. The vote was 504 for, 54 against (including Hanan Ashrawi, who said the resolution succumbed to the dictate of the Israelis), and 14 abstentions, well over the two-thirds required, and was a major personal victory for Arafat. After the vote, delegates declared that a new charter would include principles from the 1988

Palestinian Declaration of Independence and would claim East Jerusalem as the Palestinian capital.

The next day, Israel's Labor party, in a landmark vote, abandoned in its platform its long-standing opposition to a Palestinian state. At the same time, it abandoned its position that the Golan Heights were essential to Israel's security. The platform referred only to the political importance of the Heights.

The actions of the PNC and the Labor party now cleared the way for the start of the "final status" talks, which opened in Taba on May 5, 1996. Abu Mazen (Mahmoud Abbas), one of the negotiators at Oslo in 1993, Arafat's most important deputy and now the Palestinian chief negotiator, called for a Palestinian state next to Israel, with East Jerusalem as its capital. Uri Savir, Israel's director general of the Foreign Ministry and Shimon Peres's senior negotiator, described Israel's goal as the separation of the two people while seeking cooperation. He said that Israel's priority was its security, and that it intended to retain Jerusalem as the undivided capital of Israel. It was clear that the most intractable issues would be linked to the question of Palestinian statehood: the status of Jerusalem; the future of the 3 million Palestinian refugees living abroad; the fate of Jewish settlements in Palestinian areas; final borders between Israel and the Palestinians; security arrangements; and vital economic questions like trade and the sharing of water. It was equally clear that real negotiations on these issues would not start until, and would certainly be affected by, the impending Israeli elections.

The Israeli Elections of May 1996

The Victory of Benjamin Netanyahu

Still riding a wave of sympathy after the murder of Yitzhak Rabin, satisfied that peace with the Palestinians was proceeding satisfactorily after the elections in January, and realizing that there would be no immediate breakthrough with the Syrians, in early February 1996, Peres had decided to call early elections in Israel. The date was moved up from October to May 29, 1996.

Almost immediately after the announcement, a wave of Hamas suicide bombings began, and the opposition, led by Benjamin (Binyamin), or "Bibi," Netanyahu, leader of the Likud coalition, relentlessly played on Israeli fears. Up to the period of the Labor party's negotiations with the PLO, Israelis had defined security in terms of secure borders of the state. Now, as a result of terrorist bus-bombers and the political rhetoric of the conservative right wing, security was being defined in terms of personal safety within Israel. Confidence in Peres eroded significantly after the incidents in February and March, despite his closure of the territories and his approval of the air strikes against Lebanon.

New rules governed the Israeli elections of 1996. In 1992, the Knesset had changed the Basic Law on Elections to provide for the direct election of the prime minister. When Israelis went to the polls on May 29, they cast two ballots: one for prime minister and the other for the party of their choice. Twenty-one parties were represented in the competition for seats in the fourteenth Knesset. In party primaries conducted by the two largest parties in March, Shimon Peres was elected to head the Labor list, and Benjamin Netanyahu to head the Likud list. Both candidates promised peace with security, but the nation was deeply divided over different visions of how this should be achieved, and the pace at which negotiations should continue. What risks were worth taking for peace? Could Israel do business with Arafat and perhaps even live side by side with a Palestinian state? Or would a possible Palestinian state run by a leader incapable of controlling terrorists not pose a mortal danger to Israel? Was it conceivable to contemplate giving up the Golan in return for recognition by Syria and a compromise in Lebanon? Would not Assad, supporter of terrorists, again use the Golan as a staging ground for an attack against Israel? And what about Jerusalem? In March, the Israeli press reported that a secret blueprint had been prepared by the Jerusalem Institute for Israel Studies, a leading think tank, outlining options and alternatives for the future of Jerusalem, including a Palestinian state with its capital in a West Bank suburb of the city. (In August 1996, Yossi Beilin, minister without portfolio in the Peres cabinet, and one of the Israeli negotiators who helped shape the document, confirmed secret contacts with Palestinian negotiators and the informal understandings that had been reached.) Were compromise and concession the road to peace, or should Israel depend on its military strength and tough measures to secure the respect and acceptance of its neighbors?

Peres, despite his many accomplishments in a distinguished career in which he served in virtually every cabinet position, and although arguably Israel's best prime minister domestically, had never won an election in his own right. Many Israelis perceived him as being too worldly, too clever, too much the politician, and too much a part of the older generation. And perhaps he was too far ahead of the population in terms of his vision of the future. Peres, in the end, could not convince Israelis that the terrorism, which was his bane, was also an indication of the success of his and Rabin's policies.

The forty-six-year-old Netanyahu had been shaped by the Revisionist Zionism of his family and by his experiences in America, where he spent much of his young adulthood. After a stint in an elite army unit in Israel, he attended college and graduate school at MIT. Greatly affected by the death of his brother Jonathan, commander of Israel's raid on Entebbe and the only Israeli to die in the operation, he returned to Israel to head the Jonathan Institute, which was devoted to a study of terrorism and how to combat it. In his books, he argued forcefully that terrorism is a weapon of states and can be successfully countered. In previous Likud governments, he served as ambassador to the United Nations and as deputy foreign minister. In the 1996 election campaign, Netanyahu played the terrorism card and won.

The race was very close and the outcome unclear until absentee ballots were counted. Netanyahu was declared the winner with a scant 30,000 vote margin. He received 50.4 percent of the vote (but 55 percent of the Jewish vote), and Peres 49.5 percent. A number of blank ballots were cast and did not figure into the final percentages. In the balloting for the Knesset, both major parties lost seats to new and smaller parties, a situation, ironically, that the new electoral law had sought to prevent. Labor won thirty-four seats and Likud only thirty-two. The voters had seen an opportunity to vote for both the leader of their choice and the party of their persuasion. It was widely anticipated that the Arab Israelis would vote in great numbers for Peres. Most in fact did, but many also cast blank ballots, in protest against the Israeli onslaught on Lebanon and what they considered Israeli foot-dragging in the peace negotiations. As expected, the religious groups supported Netanyahu almost unanimously, although they were deeply skeptical of his American veneer, his philandering, and his secularism. Most cast their party vote for one of the religious parties that they knew he would probably have to depend upon to put together a coalition government.

The three religious parties—Shas (the Sephardi Orthodox party), the National Religious party, and United Torah Judaism—in fact, increased their number of seats in the Knesset from sixteen to twenty-three. Another new party that emerged as significant to be considered in Netanyahu's cabinet was "Yisrael B'Aliya" (Israel on the Ascent), headed by former Soviet dissident Natan Sharansky, which was supported by a majority of the approximately 700,000 former Soviet immigrants. Some of the party's demands were specific immigrant demands like more housing and jobs commensurate with their skills, but Sharansky insisted that his political goal was to restore vision to the Jewish state through true integration of all its ethnic and cultural groups.

With Netanyahu's election, the future of Israeli–Arab–Palestinian relations was, at best, uncertain. Would he act as a pragmatist or an ideologue? To what extent would he be constrained by his putative coalition partners, and by his own preelection statements? He insisted he wanted peace, would honor Israel's commitments, and would not reverse any previous agreements. In his campaign speeches, however, he had asserted that Arafat aided and abetted terrorists, that Israel would never accept a Palestinian state on its doorstep, that Jerusalem would remain Israel's undivided capital, that the Golan Heights were essential for Israel's security and could not be returned to Syria, and that Israel reserved the right to enter the Palestinian self-rule areas if necessary. When Netanyahu visited the United States in early July, President Clinton reiterated the friendship of the United States and the close ties between the two countries but was unable to persuade him to moderate his views.

Netanyahu was not an experienced politician, and his leadership capabilities were uncertain and untested. Some clue to his behavior was offered, however, by his yielding to the pressure of his longtime political rival and new foreign minister, David Levy, to bring Ariel Sharon, one of the most outspoken right-wing voices in Israel, into the cabinet. Netanyahu, in fact, created a new Infrastructure Ministry for Sharon that was responsible for roads, railways, ports, water planning, land allocation, energy, and the like. He also controlled the Israel Lands Administration, which was responsible for property in Israel left behind by Arab refugees, and had responsibility for the construction of all bypass roads in the West Bank. In August 1996, Netanyahu announced that the four-year freeze on expansion of settlements would be lifted, although new settlements would have to be approved by the full cabinet. It was also reported that the Israeli Army had drawn up plans to pave at least 300 miles of new roads to link the Jewish settlements. Although some of these roads had already been approved by the Peres government to allow Jewish settlers to bypass the autonomous Palestinian cities, the new plan required the confiscation of more Palestinian land.

The Arab and Palestinian Response

Yasser Arafat's immediate response to the Netanyahu victory was to convene a three-way summit with King Hussein and President Mubarak. A full Arab summit then met between June 21 and June 23, but Arab leaders refused to endorse Syria's proposal to downgrade relations with Israel. Egypt also backed away from Syrian demands for linkage in normalization with Israel to progress in peace negotiations. This stance was also a victory for Jordan, which had lobbied other Arab states to prevent issuing an ultimatum to Israel. Instead, Jordan formed a coalition with Bahrain and Algeria to push summit participants to discuss terrorism emanating from external and internal opponents to their regimes.

Syria was clearly on the defensive at the Arab summit, but Netanyahu, through the summer of 1996, signaled to Syria that he would be willing to resume negotiations without preconditions. The Israelis also worked on a "Lebanon first" approach, suggesting that they would withdraw from southern Lebanon in return for the cessation of Hizbullah attacks and the integration of the South Lebanon Army into the regular Lebanese Army. Assad would not bite, insisting that Netanyahu's statement about never giving up any part of the Golan was indeed a precondition, and that there could be no discussion about Lebanon or about peace until Israel adhered to its previous land for peace position.

Netanyahu visited Egypt and Jordan and attempted to allay the concerns of President Mubarak and King Hussein, but he adamantly refused to meet with Yasser Arafat, sending his advisor, Dore Gold, instead. Netanyahu insisted that he was against separation of the Israeli and Palestinian populations and moved to ease the closure of Israel's borders, although only a small percentage of those Palestinians working in Israel before the terrorist incidents in the spring of 1996 were allowed work permits. What little money filtered into the autonomous Palestinian area from the donor countries went largely to pay salaries and maintain basic infrastructure, and the dire economic situation continued to pose problems for Arafat, not only with the Islamists but also with the Palestinian Legislative Council and members of the Palestine National Council of the PLO. Outspoken critics like Hanan Ashrawi, Haidar Abdul Shafi, and

Edward Said called attention to the human rights abuses of the security services of the Palestinian Authority and the corruption of some of Arafat's closest associates who ran various government monopolies. Tension existed as well between the Palestinian desire for more democratic procedures and Arafat's autocratic tendencies. Arafat was also widely perceived as being under the control of Israel, a quisling, and not much better than Antoine Lahad, head of Israel's proxy, the South Lebanon Army.

The Hasmonean Tunnel Incident

In August 1996, Israeli and Palestinian negotiators met for the first time since the Israeli elections. Both sides accused the other of violations of the Oslo accords. The Palestinians accused Israel of not allowing for a connection between Gaza and the West Bank, not releasing prisoners, and, most important, for not moving to redeploy out of Hebron. The Israelis accused the Palestinian Authority of operating politically out of Orient House in Jerusalem and establishing other Palestinian institutions there, and not doing enough to apprehend terrorists. On September 4, 1996, yielding to pressure both within and outside Israel, Netanyahu finally met with Arafat at the Erez checkpoint near Gaza and the two shook hands, but the act was largely symbolic, since there was no real progress in the continued implementation of the peace accords.

Meanwhile, Israel had secretly completed the excavation of the Hasmonean Tunnel. This tunnel ran alongside the western perimeter of the Temple Mount/Haram al-Sharif compound, and on September 24, a new exit onto the Via Dolorosa was opened. Moslem clerics and others claimed that the tunnel undermined the Dome of the Rock and al-Aqsa Mosque on the Haram al-Sharif, and Arafat called on Palestinians to resist the "Judaization of Jerusalem." Although the tunnel, in fact, did not endanger any of the Moslem holy sites, and although Arafat clearly did not intend his appeal to have the effect it did, Palestinians in Jerusalem and elsewhere on the West Bank and in Gaza rioted and clashed with Israeli police. The situation took an ominous turn when armed Palestinian police shot at Israelis who were shooting at the Palestinian rioters. Several days of ugly confrontations took the lives of fourteen Israelis and at least fifty-eight Palestinians, and the fighting only halted when Arafat and Netanyahu, along with King Hussein, agreed to come to Washington for a hastily arranged "summit" called by President Clinton.

It was the symbolism of the tunnel opening, rather than the tunnel itself, that was the real issue. There does not seem to be any question that Israel was making a statement about Jerusalem as its capital alone, and its absolute rule over the city. Israel's provocative act, however, unleashed Palestinian frustrations after months of waiting for Netanyahu to make some move toward fulfilling Israel's commitments under the Oslo accords. Some cynics even suggested that the tunnel opening was deliberate, that Israel expected the Palestinian reaction, and that Israel would then have an excuse to change or scuttle the terms of the Oslo agreements. In fact, many Israelis immediately called into question the arrangements regarding Hebron and insisted that the terms of Israel's redeployment be changed to guarantee more adequately the security of the approximately 500 Jewish settlers there. Other Israelis, however, were appalled at the deterioration of Israeli–Palestinian relations, the undermining of relations with other Arab countries, including even Jordan, and the condemnation of Israel by much of the world community.

With the American elections a month away, President Clinton attempted to bring the parties together in a neutral setting. Unlike their brief, formal meeting a month earlier, the Washington meetings in early October between Netanyahu and Arafat did seem to bring about a closer relationship and understanding between the two men. Arafat pledged to try to control Palestinian violence, and Netanyahu agreed to resume discussions about Hebron.

Netanyahu and Arafat shaking hands at their first meeting on September 4, 1996.

Agreement on Hebron

On Sunday, October 6, Israeli and Palestinian negotiating teams, assisted by President Clinton's special envoy, Dennis Ross, began discussions on Hebron. The issue of Israel's redeployment soon became linked with the issue of further Israeli withdrawals from the rest of the West Bank, as stipulated in the Oslo accords, and bogged down over this matter, as well as a Palestinian presence at the Tomb of the Patriarchs/Ibrahimi Mosque, and Israel's right of hot pursuit into areas of the city it evacuated.

After three weeks of intense talks without any resolution of key issues, and an apparent deepening of mistrust on both sides, Ross left the area and did not return until December 21, after the American elections. Meanwhile, Netanyahu, having ended the freeze on Israeli settlements, liberalized rules on expanding the existing ones, and offered financial incentives to the settlers, moves criticized by the newly elected Clinton. For his part, and encouraged by President Mubarak, Arafat began to insist on a more rigid timetable for Israel's withdrawal from the rural areas of the West Bank. Netanyahu eventually abandoned Israel's insistence on the right of hot pursuit into areas of Hebron to be evacuated by Israel, and in a gesture of goodwill in mid-December, pledged to allow the reopening of the Islamic University in Hebron, as well as the reopening to Palestinian traffic of a road in Gaza that ran by a small Jewish settlement. With Ross's return to the area, negotiations became more intense, and on several occasions announcements were made that the two sides were on the verge of signing an agreement.

The key breakthrough was secured by King Hussein of Jordan, who flew to Gaza and then to Tel Aviv on January 12, 1997, speaking to both Arafat and Netanyahu and extracting vital concessions from both sides, particularaly relating to further Israeli redeployments from the West Bank. Israel agreed to a timetable, and Arafat accepted a mid-1998, rather than an already delayed September 1997, target date for the completion of Israel's withdrawal.

An agreement on Hebron was finally signed in the early hours of January 15, 1997 by the chief negotiators for both sides, Dan Shomron and Saeb Erekat, at the Erez checkpoint on the Israel–Gaza border. (See Document 11–5.) It was ratified by the PLO cabinet and executive, by the Israeli cabinet (in a vote of 11 to 7) and by the Israeli Knesset by an overwhelming margin of 87 to 17. Israeli forces began their withdrawal from the designated areas of the city immediately, and, on January 19, Arafat returned to the city he had not entered in thirty years.

By the terms of the accord, Israel turned over to the Palestinians control of 80 percent of Hebron, leaving a force of approximately 1,000 Israeli soldiers to guard the approximately 500 Jewish settlers in the center of the city. Whether the accord would resolve or exacerbate the tensions between the settlers and the approximately 160,000 Palestinians of Hebron, including the 20,000 who remained in the Jewish enclave, remained to be seen. A "Note for the Record," which accompanied the accord, specified the reciprocal nature of expectations and obligations and dealt with other unresolved issues. These included the Palestinian desire for Israel's release of their prisoners, a "safe passage" between Gaza and the Palestinian areas of the West Bank, and a Palestinian airport; and on the Israeli side, insistence on the Palestinians handing over suspects wanted for killing Israelis and an explicit revocation of passages in the PLO covenant calling for Israel's destruction. A separate letter from U.S. Secretary of State Christopher reiterated the American view that all three phases of the "further redeployments" should be implemented by mid-1998, but assured Prime Minister Netanyahu that the United States' commitment to Israel's security was "ironclad." (See Document 11–6.)

The stage was now set for the resumption of final status talks and the even more difficult issues of Jerusalem, the future borders of Israel and the Palestinian entity, and the nature of that entity. In early March, the Israeli Cabinet approved a further withdrawal from 9 percent of the rest of the West Bank, but the Palestinian Authority, expecting an Israeli withdrawal of at least 20 percent, rejected this as unacceptable. Partly to placate his right-wing supporters, however, Netanyahu announced plans to proceed with a new 6500-unit housing project for Jews on Har Homa (known to Palestinians as Jabal Abu Ghneim), a hill overlooking East Jerusalem, and on March 18, Israeli bulldozers began work. Widespread rioting and clashes broke out, as Palestinians reacted with fury at what they saw as a preemptive and deliberately provocative act. The Arab League threatened to reinstate their economic boycott, and even King Hussein expressed his disappointment and displeasure at the decision. On March 21, a Hamas terrorist blew up himself and three Israeli women at a cafe in Tel Aviv, and Netanyahu accused Arafat of giving a green light to terrorism by releasing Hamas activists from prison. Arafat instructed the Palestinian security police to cease cooperation with their Israeli counterparts, and tensions increased alarmingly, quieting down somewhat only after both Netanyahu and Arafat met with Clinton in Washington.

Israel's ability to proceed with negotiations was further complicated by release of a police report in April detailing events preceding the January 1997 appointment as Attorney-General of Roni Bar-On, who served briefly before resigning. It was widely speculated that Netanyahu had appointed him at the behest of Aryeh Deri, leader of the Sephardi Orthodox (Shas) party, who expected Bar-On to allow him to plea-bargain on corruption charges. In return, Deri would deliver crucial votes on the Hebron protocol. The police report accused Netanyahu of fraud and betraying the public trust, but he was not indicted. His credibility, integrity, and capacity to lead the nation, however, were seriously compromised.

Although the peace process was imperiled by these events, the Hebron agreement remained of great importance. Its significance lay in the acceptance by Netanyahu of the Oslo formula, the acquiescence by Arafat on the presence of Jewish settlers in Hebron, and the critical role played by the United States in securing the accord. Above all, it appeared that no matter how difficult the journey, a majority on both sides were committed to the peace process and to coexistence.

Suggestions for Further Reading

BEILIN, YOSSI, *Touching Peace: From the Oslo Accord to a Final Settlement*, trans. by Philip Simpson, London, Weidenfeld & Nicolson, 1999.

RABINOVICH, ITAMAR, *Waging Peace: Israel and the Arabs at the End of the Century*, New York, Farrar, Straus and Giroux, 1999.

ROBINSON, GLENN, *Building a Palestinian State: The Incomplete Revolution*, Bloomington, Indiana University Press, 1997.

RUBIN, BARRY, *The Transformation of Palestinian Politics: From Revolution to State-Building*, Cambridge, Harvard University Press, 1999.

DOCUMENT 11-1

Israel-Jordan Peace Treaty, October 1994 [Excerpts]

PREAMBLE

The government of the Hashemite Kingdom of Jordan and the government of the State of Israel:

Bearing in mind the Washington Declaration, signed by them on 25 July 1994 and which they are both committed to honor.

Aiming at the achievement of a just, lasting, and comprehensive peace in the Middle East based on Security Council resolutions 242 and 318 in all their aspects;

Bearing in mind the importance of maintaining and strengthening peace based on freedom, equality, justice, and respect for fundamental and human rights: thereby overcoming psychological barriers and promoting human dignity;

Reaffirming their faith in the purposes and the principles of the Charter of the United Nations and recognizing their right and obligation to live in peace with each other as well as with all states, within secure and recognized boundaries;

Desiring to develop friendly relations and cooperation between them in accordance with the principles of international law governing international relations in times of peace;

Desiring as well to ensure lasting security for both their states and, in particular, to avoid threats and the use of force between them;

Bearing in mind that in their Washington Declaration of 25 July 1994, they declared the termination of the state of belligerency between them;

Deciding to establish peace between them in accordance with this treaty of peace;

Have agreed as follows:

ARTICLE 1—ESTABLISHMENT OF PEACE

Peace is hereby established between the Hashemite Kingdom of Jordan and the State of Israel (the parties) effective from the exchange of the instruments of ratifications of this treaty. . . .

ARTICLE 3—INTERNATIONAL BOUNDARY

a. The international boundary between Israel and Jordan is delimited with reference to the boundary definition under the Mandate. . . .

b. The boundary is the permanent, secure, and recognized international boundary between Israel and Jordan without prejudice to the status of any territories that came under Israeli military government control in 1967. . . .

c. It is agreed that where the boundary follows a river, in the event of natural changes in the course of the flow of the river . . . the boundary shall follow the new course of the flow. In the event of any other changes, the boundary shall not be affected unless otherwise agreed. . . .

d. Taking into account the special circumstances of the Bakura/Naharayim area, which is under Jordanian sovereignty, with Israeli private ownership rights, the parties agreed to apply the provisions set out in Annex I (b). . . .

ARTICLE 5—DIPLOMATIC AND OTHER BILATERAL RELATIONS

1. The parties agree to establish full diplomatic and consular relations and to exchange resident ambassadors within one month of the exchange of the instruments of ratification of this treaty.

2. The parties agree that the normal relationship between them will further include economic and cultural relations.

ARTICLE 6—WATER

With the view to achieving a comprehensive and lasting settlement of all the water problems between them:

1. The parties agree mutually to recognize the rightful allocations of both of them in Jordan River, Yarmuk River waters, and Arab/Arava ground water in accordance with the agreed acceptable principles, quantities, and quality as set out in Annex II, which shall be fully respected and complied with;

2. The parties, recognizing the necessity to find a practical, just, and agreed solution to their water problems and with the view that the subject of water can form the basis for the advancement of cooperation between them, jointly undertake to ensure that the management and development of their water resources do not, in any way, harm the water resources of the other party;

3. The parties recognize that their water resources are not sufficient to meet their needs. More water should be supplied for their use through various methods, including projects of regional and international cooperation;

4. In light of paragraph 2A, with the understanding that the cooperation in water-related subjects would be to the benefit of both parties, and will help alleviate their water shortages, and that water issues along their entire boundary must be dealt with in their totality, including the possibility of trans-boundary water transfers, the parties agreed to search for ways to alleviate water shortages and to cooperate in the following fields:

  (a) Development of existing and new water resources increasing the water availability, including on a regional basis, as appropriate, and minimizing wastage of water resources through the chain of their uses;

  (b) Prevention of contamination of water resources;

  (c) Mutual assistance in the alleviation of water shortages;

  (d) Transfer of information and joint research and development in water-related subjects, and review of the potentials for enhancement of water resources development and use;

5. The implementation of both countries' undertakings under this article is detailed in Annex II. . . .

ARTICLE 9—PLACES OF HISTORICAL AND RELIGIOUS SIGNIFICANCE

1. Each party will provide freedom of access to places of religious and historical significance.

2. In this regard, in accordance with the Washington Declaration Israel respects the present special role of the Hashemite Kingdom of Jordan in Moslem holy shrines in Jerusalem. When negotiations on the permanent status will take place, Israel will give high priority to the Jordanian historic role in these shrines.

3. The parties will act together to promote interfaith relations among the three monotheistic religions, with the aim of working towards religious understanding, moral commitment, freedom of religious tolerance and peace. . . .

Source: Walter Laqueur and Barry Rubin, eds., *The Israel–Arab Reader: A Documentary History*, 5th. ed. (New York, Penguin Books, 1995), pp. 665–671.

 DOCUMENT 11–2

The Taba Accord
The Interim Agreement Between Israel and the PLO, September 28, 1995

MAIN POINTS

Background

. . . To date, preliminary agreements implemented pursuant to the Declaration of Principles include the Gaza-Jericho Agreement of May 4, 1994 which provided for the withdrawal of Israeli forces from the Gaza Strip and the Jericho Area and the transfer of civil powers in these areas to a Palestinian Authority, and subsequent agreements giving the Palestinian Authority limited responsibilities for additional civil spheres throughout the West Bank. All these agreements are superseded by the provisions of the Interim Agreement.

The main object of the Interim Agreement is to broaden Palestinian self-government in the West Bank by means of an elected self-governing authority (the Palestinian Council). This will allow the Palestinians to conduct their own internal affairs, reduce points of friction between Israelis and Palestinians, and open a new era of cooperation and co-existence based on common interest, dignity and mutual respect. At the same time it protects Israel's vital interests, and in particular its security interests, both with regard to external security as well as the personal security of its citizens in the West Bank.

General

The Interim Agreement between Israel and the PLO, including its various annexes, comprises some 400 pages, setting forth the future relations between Israel and the Palestinians. To the main body of the agreement are appended six annexes dealing with: security arrangements, elections, civil affairs (transfer of powers), legal matters, economic relations, and Israeli-Palestinian cooperation.

The agreement states that a Palestinian Council will be elected for an interim period not to exceed five years from the signing of the Gaza-Jericho Agreement (i.e. no later than May 1999). The negotiations on the permanent status arrangements will begin no later than May 1996.

The permanent status negotiations will deal with the remaining issues, including Jerusalem, refugees, settlements, security arrangements, borders, relations and cooperation with neighboring countries, etc.

Elections

The Council is an elected body and, accordingly, the agreement sets out arrangements for democratic elections to the Council by all Palestinians of the West Bank and the Gaza Strip aged 18 or over, who are registered in the population register. The elections will take place 22 days after the conclusion of an IDF redeployment from populated areas in the West Bank. . . .

The Palestinian Council

The Palestinian Council to be established following the elections will assume various powers and responsibilities in security and civil spheres in the West Bank and Gaza, as detailed below. With the establishment of the Council, the Israeli military government will be withdrawn and the Civil Administration dissolved. The Council will assume responsibility for all rights, liabilities, and obligations in the spheres transferred to it. At the same time Israel will retain those powers and responsibilities not transferred to the Council. . . .

Security and Redeployment

The IDF will redeploy in the West Bank according to the timetables set out in the agreement. In the first stage, designed to facilitate the holding of elections, the IDF will withdraw from the populated areas of the West Bank: the six cities—Jenin, Nablus, Tulkarm, Kalkilya, Ramallah and Bethlehem (in the city of Hebron special security arrangements will apply as provided in the agreement)—and 450 towns and villages. At the end of this redeployment, there will be almost no IDF presence in Palestinian population centers.

In general, throughout the West Bank and the Gaza Strip, Israel will have overall responsibility for external security and the security of Israelis and settlements.

With regard to internal security and public order, the agreement establishes different arrangements for three types of area:

—Area "A" comprises the six cities listed above. In these areas, the Palestinian Council will have full responsibility for internal security and public order, as well as full civil responsibilities.

—"B" comprises the Palestinian towns and villages of the West Bank. In these areas, which contain some 68 percent of the Palestinian population, the council will be granted full civil authority, as in Area "A". The Council will be charged with maintaining public order, while Israel will have overall security authority to safeguard its citizens and to combat terrorism. This responsibility shall take precedence over the Palestinian responsibility for public order.

25 Palestinian police stations will be established in specified towns and villages to enable the Palestinian police to exercise its responsibility for public order. The agreement contains provisions requiring that the movement of Palestinian police be coordinated and confirmed with Israel.

—In Area "C", which comprises the unpopulated areas, areas of strategic importance to Israel and the Jewish settlements, Israel will retain full responsibility for security and public order. The council will assume all those civil responsibilities not related to territory, such as economics, health, education, etc.

Further Redeployments

In addition to the redeployment of Israeli military forces described above, the agreement provides that a series of further redeployments are to take place in three phases at six-month intervals following the inauguration of the Council. In the course of these redeployments, additional parts of Area C will be transferred to the territorial jurisdiction of the Council, so that by the completion of the redeployment phases, Palestinian territorial jurisdiction will cover West Bank territory except for the areas where jurisdiction is to be determined under the final status negotiations (settlements, military locations, etc.).

The Revocation of the PLO Covenant

The agreement contains an undertaking to revoke those articles of the Palestinian Covenant calling for the destruction of Israel, within two months of the inauguration of the Council.

The Security Policy for the Prevention of Terrorism and Violence

The agreement provides for the establishment of a strong police force, 12,000 in number, that will constitute the only Palestinian security force. The Security Annex specifies the deployment of the police force, the approved equipment and its modes of action.

The Security Annex specifies the commitment of Israel and the Palestinian Council to cooperate in the fight against terrorism and the prevention of terrorist attacks, according to the following framework:

a. The Palestinian Police is the only Palestinian Security Authority.
b. The Palestinian Police will act systematically against all expressions of violence and terror.
c. The Council will issue permits in order to legalize the possession and carrying of arms by civilians; any illegal arms will be confiscated by the Palestinian Police.
d. The Palestinian Police will arrest and prosecute individuals suspected of perpetrating acts of violence and terror.

Both sides, in accordance with this agreement, will act to insure the immediate, efficient and effective handling of any incident involving the threat, or acts of terrorism, violence or incitement, whether committed by Palestinians or Israelis. To this end they will cooperate in the exchange of information and coordinate policies and activities.

Joint security committees will be established to coordinate between the IDF and the Palestinian police. Regional offices will operate 24 hours a day. Joint patrols will ensure free and secure movement on designated roads in Area "A". Joint Mobile Units will serve as rapid response units in case of incidents and emergencies.

Transfer of Civil Powers and Responsibilities

The agreement sets out the arrangements for the transfer of agreed upon civil powers and responsibilities from the Civil Administration to the Council. In Area "C", powers and responsibilities not relating to territory will be transferred to the Council; powers and responsibilities relating to territory will be gradually transferred along with the redeployments in these areas. The transfer of further civil powers and responsibilities is subject to detailed provisions insuring, among other things, the land rights of Israelis and the continued provision of services (electricity, water, telecommunications, etc.) to the settlements.

Freedom of Movement for Israelis

The IDF and Israelis will continue to move freely on the roads of the West Bank and Gaza. In Area "A" Israeli vehicles will be escorted by joint patrols. Israelis may not in any circumstances be arrested or placed in custody by the Palestinian police, and may only be required to present identity and vehicle documentation. On roads that are jointly patrolled, any request for identification shall only be made by the Israeli side of a joint patrol. . . .

Religious Sites

Responsibility over sites of religious significance in the West Bank and Gaza will be transferred to the Palestinian side. In Area "C" this will be transferred gradually during the "further redeployment phase", except for the issues which will be negotiated during the permanent status negotiations. Both sides shall respect and protect religious rights of Jews, Christians, Moslems and Samaritans to wit:

a. Protecting the holy sites.
b. Allowing free access to the holy sites.
c. Allowing freedom of worship and practice.
   Jewish holy sites are listed in the agreement.

The agreement guarantees freedom of access to and freedom of worship at the holy sites, and defines access arrangements for the holy places located in Areas "A" and "B". With regard to Rachel's Tomb in Bethlehem and Joseph's Tomb in Nablus, special arrangements are set out in the agreement which will also guarantee freedom of access and freedom of worship.

Hebron

In view of the Jewish presence in the heart of Hebron and the sensitive historical and religious aspects involved, special arrangements will apply in this city. These arrangements will enable Palestinian police to exercise responsibilities vis-à-vis Palestinian residents while at the same time Israel will retain the powers and responsibilities necessary to protect Israeli residents living in Hebron and visiting the holy places.

There will be a redeployment of Israeli military forces in Hebron, except for places and roads where arrangements are necessary for the security and protection of Israelis and their movements. This redeployment will be completed no later than six (6) months after the signing of this agreement. Israel will continue to carry the responsibility for overall security of Israelis for the purpose of safeguarding their internal security and public order.

The status quo at the Tomb of the Patriarchs will remain unchanged, for the time being.

There will be a temporary international presence in Hebron. . . .

Water

The agreement contains an undertaking on the part of Israel to increase the amount of water allocated to the Palestinians by 28 million cu.m. Any further addition to either side will be based on an increase in the available water resources to be developed through international funding and channels, among them the tripartite American-Palestinian-Israeli forum which will hold its first meeting after the signing of the Interim Agreement. The agreement provides for the establishment of a joint water committee that will manage water resources and enforce water policies, protecting the interests of both parties by the prevention of uncontrolled drilling and enforcing standards, etc.

Release of Prisoners

In order to foster a positive atmosphere as this agreement is being implemented, and to engender mutual confidence and a basis for cooperation between the two peoples, Israel will release Palestinian prisoners who are in Israeli custody in three (3) stages according to the following format:

Stage 1—Upon the signing of the agreement.

Stage 2—On the eve of elections for the Council.

Stage 3—At a later unspecified date.

Annex VII of the Agreement establishes the criteria which Israel will take into consideration when deciding upon the release. . . .

Source: Information Division, Israel Foreign Ministry, Jerusalem.

 DOCUMENT 11-3

Eulogy for Late Prime Minister and Defense Minister Yitzhak Rabin by His Majesty King Hussein of Jordan, Mount Herzl, Jerusalem, November 6, 1995

My sister, Mrs. Leah Rabin, my friends, I had never thought that the moment would come like this when I would grieve the loss of a brother, a colleague and a friend—a man, a soldier who met us on the opposite side of a divide whom we respected as he respected us. A man I came to know because I realized, as he did, that we have to cross over the divide, establish a dialogue, get to know each other and strive to leave for those who follow us a legacy that is worthy of them. And so we did. And so we became brethren and friends.

I've never been used to standing, except with you next to me, speaking of peace, speaking about dreams and hopes for generations to come that must live in peace, enjoy human dignity, come together, work together, to build a better future which is their right. Never in all my thoughts would it have occurred to me that my first visit to Jerusalem and response to your invitation, the invitation of the Speaker of the Knesset, the invitation of the president of Israel, would be on such an occasion.

You lived as a soldier, you died as a soldier for peace and I believe it is time for all of us to come out, openly, and to speak our piece, but here today, but for all the times to come. We belong to the camp of peace. We believe in peace. We believe that our one God wishes us to live in peace and wishes peace upon us, for these are His teachings to all the followers of the three great monotheistic religions, the children of Abraham.

Let's not keep silent. Let our voices rise high to speak of our commitment to peace for all times to come, and let us tell those who live in darkness who are the enemies of life, and through faith and religion and the teachings of our one God, this is where we stand. This is our camp. May God bless you with the realization that you must join it and we pray that He will, but otherwise we are not ashamed, nor are we afraid, nor are we anything but determined to fulfill the legacy for which my friend fell, as did my grandfather in this very city when I was with him and but a young boy. He was a man of courage, a man of vision and he was endowed with one of the greatest virtues that any man can have. He was endowed with humility. He felt with those around him and in a position of responsibility, he placed himself, as I do and have done, often, in the place of the other partner to achieve a worthy goal. And we achieved peace, an honorable peace and a lasting peace. He had courage, he had vision, and he had a commitment to peace, and standing here, I commit before you, before my people in Jordan, before the world, myself to continue with our utmost, to ensure that we leave a similar legacy. And when my time comes, I hope it will be like my grandfather's and like Yitzhak Rabin's.

May your spirit rise high and may it sense how the people of Jordan, my family, the people of Israel, decent people throughout the world feel today. So many live and so many inevitably die. This is the will of God. This is the way of all, but those who are fortunate and lucky in life, those who are greater, those who leave something behind, and you are such a man, my friend.

The faces in my country amongst the majority of my people and our armed forces and people who once were your enemies are somber today and their hearts are heavy. Let's hope and pray that God will give us all guidance, each in his respective position to do what he can for the better future that Yitzhak Rabin sought with determination and courage. As long as I live, I'll be proud to have known him, to have worked with him, as a brother and as a friend, and as a man, and the relationship of friendship that we had is something unique and I am proud of that.

On behalf of the people of Jordan, my large Jordanian family, my Hashemite family, all those who belong to the camp of peace, to all those who belong to the camp of peace, our deepest sympathies, our deepest condolences as we share together this moment of remembrance and commitment, to continue our struggle for the future of generations to come, as did Yitzhak Rabin, and to fulfill his legacy. Thank you.

Source: Israel Ministry of Foreign Affairs.

 DOCUMENT 11–4

Text of Understanding Between Israel and Lebanon, April 26, 1996

The United States understands that after discussions with the Governments of Israel and Lebanon, and in consultation with Syria, Lebanon and Israel will insure the following:
1. Armed groups in Lebanon will not carry out attacks by Katyusha rockets or by any kind of weapon into Israel.
2. Israel and those cooperating with it will not fire any kind of weapon at civilians or civilian targets in Lebanon.

3. Beyond this, the two parties commit to insuring that under no circumstances will civilians be the target of attack and that civilian populated areas and industrial and electrical installations will not be used as launching grounds for attacks.
4. Without violating this understanding, nothing here shall preclude any party from exercising the right of self-defense.

A Monitoring Group is established consisting of the United States, France, Syria, Lebanon and Israel: Its task will be to monitor the application of the understanding stated above. Complaints will be submitted to the Monitoring Group. In the event of a claimed violation of the understanding, the party submitting the complaint will do so within 24 hours. Procedures for dealing with the complaints will be set by the Monitoring Group.

The United States will also organize a Consultative Group, to consist of France, the European Union, Russia and other interested parties, for the purpose of assisting in the reconstruction needs of Lebanon.

It is recognized that the understanding to bring the current crisis between Lebanon and Israel to an end cannot substitute for a permanent solution. The United States understands the importance of achieving a comprehensive peace in the region. Toward this end, the United States proposes the resumption of negotiations between Syria and Israel and between Lebanon and Israel at a time to be agreed upon, with the objective of reaching comprehensive peace. The United States understands that it is desirable that these negotiations be conducted in a climate of stability and tranquillity.

This understanding will be announced simultaneously at 1800 hours, April 26, 1996, in all countries concerned. The time set for implementation is 0400 hours, April 27, 1996.

Source: New York Times, April 27, 1996.

 **DOCUMENT 11–5**

Protocol Concerning the Redeployment in Hebron and Note for the Record

MAIN POINTS OF THE PROTOCOL

Background
       . . . For the purpose of the redeployment, Hebron is divided into two areas: Area H-1, in which the majority of the Palestinian population reside, and in which the Palestinian police will be responsible for internal security and public order, and Area H-2, a smaller area comprising all the Israeli residents of Hebron together with some 20,000 Palestinians, in which all responsibilities for security and public order will remain with Israel. Civil powers and responsibilities in both areas will be transferred to the Palestinian side. . . .
Security Aspects
       Redeployment: The redeployment of Israeli military forces is to be carried out within 10 days from the signing of the Protocol.
       Security powers and responsibilities: The responsibility for internal security and public order in Area H-1 will be Palestinian; in Area H2 it will be Israeli. In addition, Israel will continue to be responsible for the overall security of Israelis throughout Hebron. The Protocol confirms the applicability to Hebron of the security provisions of the Interim Agreement, which provide that Israel has all the powers to take the steps necessary to meet its security responsibility and enable

Israeli security forces to conduct security activity in areas of Palestinian responsibility (engagement steps) in defined cases.

Joint security measures: The Protocol provides for Joint Mobile Units and Joint Patrols to operate in areas of particular sensitivity. In addition, a Joint Coordination Center, headed by senior officers of both sides, will coordinate all joint security measures.

Special areas: In areas of particular sensitivity located in Area H-1 but close to Area H-2 the Palestinian police will set up checkpoints and prevent the entry of demonstrators or other people threatening security and public order. Any security activity in this area must be notified to the Joint Coordination Center.

Palestinian police: Palestinian police stations and posts shall be located in Area H-1 at the agreed locations shown on the map attached to the Protocol. All policemen will be required to pass a security check in order to verify their suitability for service taking into account the sensitivity of the area. As provided in the Interim Agreement, the Palestinian police will comprise up to 400 policemen with 20 vehicles. The Police will be armed with 200 pistols and 100 rifles. The rifles are for the protection of the police stations only, and may only be used by designated rapid response teams, to handle special security cases. Such teams armed with rifles may only enter the specified areas close to H-2 with the prior approval of the Israeli side in the Joint Coordination Center. . . .

Civil Arrangements

Transfer of civil powers and responsibilities: Civil spheres that have not yet been transferred to Palestinian side in Hebron shall be transferred concurrently with the beginning of the redeployment. In Area H-2, powers and responsibilities relating to Israelis and their property will not be transferred but will continue to be exercised by the Israeli military government. . . .

Source: Israel Foreign Ministry.

NOTE FOR THE RECORD

Mutual Undertakings

The two leaders agreed that the Oslo peace process must move forward to succeed. Both parties to the Interim Agreement have concerns and obligations. Accordingly, the two leaders reaffirmed their commitment to implement the Interim Agreement on the basis of reciprocity and, in this context, conveyed the following undertakings to each other:

Israeli Responsibilities

The Israeli side reaffirms its commitments to the following measures and principles in accordance with the Interim Agreement:

Issues for implementation:

1. Further redeployment phases

The first phase of further redeployments will be carried out during the first week of March.

2. Prisoner release issues

Prisoner release issues will be dealt with in accordance with the Interim Agreement's provisions and procedures, including Annex VII.

Issues for Negotiation:

3. Outstanding Interim Agreement issues

Negotiations on the following outstanding issues from the Interim Agreement will be immediately resumed. Negotiations on these issues will be conducted in parallel:

    a) Safe passage

    b) Gaza airport

    c) Gaza port

    d) Passages

e) Economic, financial, civilian and security issues

f) People-to-people

4. Permanent status negotiations

Permanent status negotiations will be resumed within two months after implementation of the Hebron Protocol.

Palestinian Responsibilities

The Palestinian side reaffirms its commitments to the following measures and principles in accordance with the Interim Agreement:

1. Complete the process of revising the Palestinian National Charter
2. Fighting terror and preventing violence
   a) Strengthening security cooperation
   b) Preventing incitement and hostile propaganda as specified in Article XXII of the Interim Agreement
   c) Combat systematically and effectively terrorist organizations and infrastructure
   d) Apprehension, prosecution and punishment of terrorists
   e) Requests for transfer of suspects and defendants will be acted upon in accordance with Article II (7)(f) of Annex IV to the Interim Agreement
   f) Confiscation of illegal firearms
3. Size of Palestinian Police will be pursuant to the Interim Agreement.
4. Exercise of Palestinian governmental activity, and location of Palestinian governmental offices, will be as specified in the Interim Agreement.

The aforementioned commitments will be dealt with immediately and in parallel.

Other Issues

Either party is free to raise other issues not specified above related to implementation of the Interim Agreement and obligations of both sides arising from the Interim Agreement.

Prepared by Ambassador Dennis Ross at the request of Prime Minister Binyamin Netanyahu and Ra'ees Yasser Arafat.

Source: Israel Foreign Ministry

DOCUMENT 11-6

Letter to Be Provided by U.S. Secretary of State Christopher to Benjamin Netanyahu at the Time of Signing of the Hebron Protocol

Dear Mr. Prime Minister,

I wanted personally to congratulate you on the successful conclusion of the *"Protocol Concerning the Redeployment in Hebron."* It represents an important step forward in the Oslo peace process and reaffirms my conviction that a just and lasting peace will be established between Israelis and Palestinians in the very near future.

In this connection, I can assure you that it remains the policy of the United States to support and promote full implementation of the *Interim Agreement* in all of its parts. We intend to continue our efforts to help ensure that all outstanding commitments are carried out by both parties in a cooperative spirit and on the basis of reciprocity.

As part of this process, I have impressed upon Chairman Arafat the imperative need for the Palestinian Authority to make every effort to ensure public order and internal security within the West Bank and Gaza Strip. I have stressed to him that effectively carrying out this major responsibility will be a critical foundation for completing implementation of the Interim Agreement, as well as the peace process as a whole.

I wanted you to know that, in this context, I have advised Chairman Arafat of U.S. views on Israel's process of redeploying its forces, designating specified military locations and transferring additional powers and responsibilities to the Palestinian Authority. In this regard, I have conveyed our belief, that the first phase of further redeployments should take place as soon as possible, and that all three phases of the further redeployments should be completed within twelve months from the implementation of the first phase of the further redeployments but not later than mid-1998.

Mr. Prime Minister, you can be assured that the United States' commitment to Israel's security is ironclad and constitutes the fundamental cornerstone of our special relationship. The key element in our approach to peace, including the negotiation and implementation of agreements between Israel and its Arab partners, has always been a recognition of Israel's security requirements. Moreover, a hallmark of U.S. policy remains our commitment to work cooperatively to seek to meet the security needs that Israel identifies. Finally, I would like to reiterate our position that Israel is entitled to secure and defensible borders, which should be directly negotiated and agreed with its neighbors.

Source: U.S. Department of State.

TWELVE

Collapse of the Peace Process

CHRONOLOGY

1997

July 30 Two Hamas bombers kill themselves and 14 others, wounding 170, in Mahane Yehuda market in Jerusalem

Oct. 1 Sheikh Yassin released from house arrest in Israel after botched Israeli raid against Hamas operative in Jordan. Goes to Jordan, then returns to Gaza

Nov. 16 Fourth annual regional economic summit convenes in Doha, Qatar

1998

July 7 UN General Assembly votes to upgrade status of PLO delegation

Oct. 15 Wye River plantation talks begin between PLO and Israel

Oct. 23 Wye River Memorandum signed in Washington

Dec. 14 PNC ratifies Arafat letter to Clinton and renounces clauses in PLO charter offensive to Israel

Dec. 21 Knesset votes to dissolve government; calls for new elections

1999

Feb. 7 King Hussein of Jordan dies; succeeded by oldest son Abdullah

Apr. 29 PLO votes to postpone declaration of statehood

May 17 Ehud Barak elected prime minister in Israel; government sworn in July 1

Sept. 4 Sharm al-Sheikh Memorandum signed between Israel and PLO. Sets Feb. 15, 2000 as target date for declaration of principles on outstanding issues and Sept. 2000 as date to reach permanent settlement

Sept. 13 Final status talks begin again

Oct. 5 Agreement on safe passage between Gaza and Tarqumiyya outside Hebron; opens on Oct. 25

Dec. 8 President Clinton announces agreement to resume Syrian–Israeli talks

Dec. 15 Syrian–Israeli talks begin; recessed January 10

2000

Jan. 19 Syrian–Israeli talks scheduled but postponed and not resumed

Mar. 5 Israeli cabinet unanimously decides to withdraw troops unilaterally from South Lebanon by July

Mar. 21–26 Visit of Pope Paul II to Israel and the Palestinian Authority

May 15 Knesset votes to turn over Abu Dis, Al-Azariah and Suwahra to Palestinian control

Mid-May Israel begins turning over outposts in South Lebanon to SLA. SLA challenged by Hizbullah. Israel leaves last outpost on May 24; Hizbullah enters in triumph

June 10 Syrian president Hafez al-Assad dies; son Bashar sworn in as president July 17, after nomination by Baath party, endorsement by parliament, and referendum

July 9 Barak's coalition crumbles

July 10 Barak survives no-confidence vote in Knesset

July 11–25 Clinton Camp David summit

Sept. 10 Palestine Central Council decides to postpone declaration of statehood

Sept. 28 Ariel Sharon visits Temple Mount/Haram al-Sharif; riots begin Sept. 29; demonstrators killed by Israeli police; sets off worst cycle of violence in a decade

Oct. 16–17 Sharm al-Sheikh "summit" tries to halt violence but is ineffective

Oct. 20 UNGA condemns Israel for use of excessive force

Oct. 21–22 Arab summit in Cairo condemns Israel; on Nov. 21, Egypt recalls its ambassador

Nov. 25 Arafat visits Moscow to enlist more active role by Vladimir Putin

Nov. 28 Barak calls for new elections in Israel; resigns on Dec. 10, paving way for elections by February 2001

2001

Jan. 20 George W. Bush sworn in as U.S. president

Feb. 6 Ariel Sharon elected Prime Minister in Israel; assembles national unity government with Shimon Peres as foreign minister

March 7 Knesset votes to do away with direct election of prime minister

This chapter reviews the developments in the conflict from the Hebron accords through the Wye and Sharm al-Sheikh memoranda, to the subsequent collapse of the peace process. The election of Ehud Barak as Israel's prime minister, Israel's precipitous withdrawal from Lebanon, the Clinton Camp David summit, the al-Aqsa "intifada" and virtual war between Israelis and Palestinians, and the election victory of Ariel Sharon were among the dramatic events of this period. Important national leaders who had played a decisive regional role for many years died: King Hassan II of Morocco (1999), King Hussein of Jordan (1999), and President Hafez al-Assad of Syria (2000). It had been hoped that younger, if less experienced, Arab leaders prepared to join the new globalized world, a new prime minister in Israel committed to freeing Israel from the economic and personal burdens of a war footing, an aging and unwell PLO leader determined to complete his life's work, and a lame duck president in the United States anxious to leave a legacy of peace in the Middle East to salvage a sullied personal reputation at home, would breathe life into the peace process. The goal of peace remained elusive, however.

Peace Negotiations Stall

The rioting following Netanyahu's decision to build at Har Homa, and the Hamas suicide bombing in Tel Aviv in March 1997 led to a halt in the peace negotiations. Despite repeated visits to the area, presidential envoy Dennis Ross failed to get the two sides talking to each other. It was unclear whether Netanyahu was indecisive, unwilling to take political chances, or simply content to let the process die on the vine. In June 1997, Washington concluded that the United States would have to move more forcefully to revive the peace effort, and Secretary of State Madeleine Albright considered going to the area herself. However, a terrorist bombing in the Mahane Yehuda market in Jerusalem on July 30, in which 14 people died, again derailed the process.

Repeated Israeli closure of borders and the decision by UNRWA to cut back on services because of lack of funds hurt the Palestinians. Both sides antagonized each other. Arafat, in an attempt to broaden his base of support, called a "national unity" meeting in late August that included Hamas and Islamic Jihad leaders, a move widely criticized by the Israelis. Arafat was equally incensed by Netanyahu's announcement that he would add 300 homes in the West Bank settlement of Efrat and would allow Jewish settlers to occupy a building owned by the American Jewish financier, Irwin Moscowitz, in the Ras al-Amud section of East Jerusalem. Israel was severely rebuked by Albright, who finally made her first visit to Israel in early September.

Netanyahu caused further trouble for Israel by authorizing an assassination attempt against a senior Hamas operative, Khaled Mishal (or Mashaal), in Jordan. The operation failed, and an infuriated King Hussein demanded that Netanyahu release Sheikh Yassin to him, in exchange for the return of the captured Israelis agents. The Sheikh later returned in triumph to Gaza, which would cause potential problems not only for Israel but for Yasser Arafat.

Dennis Ross eventually arranged a face-to-face meeting between Netanyahu and Arafat in October 1997, their first meeting in eight months, but the promised follow-up talks between Foreign Minister Levy and Arafat aide Mahmoud Abbas were postponed. Israeli–Palestinian talks did resume in Washington, and on the eve of a Netanyahu-Albright meeting in early December, Netanyahu's cabinet agreed "in principle" to withdraw from more land but attached tough conditions, and left open the question of "how much" for Netanyahu to present along with his plan for a final settlement. The United States, impatient for results, began to exert pressure. Albright, in fact, gave Netanyahu a kind of ultimatum and a deadline of mid-December to produce a "significant and credible" plan for withdrawal. Two Israeli maps resulted: one, by the Defense Minister Yitzhak Mordechai; the other by Ariel Sharon, the National Infrastructure Minister.

Mordechai's "security interests" map suggested that 42 of 144 Jewish settlements could be excluded from Israel's security zones, which would cover about 52.2 percent of West Bank territory. Under Sharon's proposal, all Jewish settlements would remain under Israeli sovereignty, and Israel would retain about 63 percent of the West Bank.

Netanyahu met Albright in Paris but again did not bring a formal proposal. Albright also met Arafat in Paris and pressed him on the terrorism issue. Both sides seemed to be retreating behind established positions. Israel insisted it could not withdraw without proof the Palestinians would combat terrorism, prevent a "revolving door" release of prisoners, follow through on a nullification of the objectional articles of the PLO charter, and address a detailed Israeli list of violations of the Oslo accords. The Palestinians insisted that Israel was not fulfilling its obligations under the accords, and recriminations between the PLO and Israel continued.

Internal Problems in Israel

Meanwhile, Netanyahu faced increasing problems among members of his ruling coalition and his cabinet. Foreign Minister Levy, upset over Netanyahu's budget proposals, had decided not to attend the December meetings with Albright, indicating serious problems for Netanyahu within his cabinet on domestic issues as well as on the peace process. In a budget crisis in early January 1998, Levy resigned over treatment of his constituents among the Moroccan and other Sephardi communities. With the loss of the five members of Levy's Gesher party, Netanyahu was more dependent than ever before on the religious and right-wing parties and had only a 61–59 vote margin in the Knesset. This occurred at the same time that Dennis Ross was shuttling back and forth, trying to find some kind of formula for a further redeployment, as specified in the interim agreements, and pushing for a 10 percent or more land transfer. Israel continued to maintain that it had fulfilled its obligations under the Oslo II and Hebron agreements, while the Palestinians had not; the Palestinians said Israel was obligated to carry out further *credible* withdrawals; and the reciprocity debate continued.

While the two sides were publicly disagreeing, however, shared Israeli and Palestinian intelligence did result in the discovery of a Hamas arms cache, indicating the possibility of cooperation among the two security services. CIA officers helped to train Palestinians and to develop a program of cooperation among the Palestinian security services, the CIA and Israel's internal security force, the Shin Bet. And some economic relations also continued between Israel and the Palestinians.

Faced with the apparently irreconcilable standoff between the PLO and Israel over the scope of a further Israeli redeployment, however, the United States now came up with its own proposals, and debate over the American figures occupied most of the next year. The American plan called for a 13.1 percent withdrawal over a period of months, in return for specific Palestinian acts to counter terrorism and cooperation with the Israeli security forces. This proposal, however, was not immediately publicized.

Believing that Netanyahu might be willing to compromise between the 9 percent figure he had been publicly insisting upon, and the 13.1 percent proposed by the United States, Clinton again dispatched Ross and his deputy, Aaron Miller, to the Middle East. Netanyahu refused to discuss the geography and "arithmetic" of the U.S. proposal. Israel did not want a referee role for the United States, fearing that the United States would side with the Palestinians in interpreting the accords. Critics of this position noted that Israel wanted to be sole arbiter of Palestinian compliance and could always use some issue to halt a withdrawal. The Palestinians accepted the U.S. proposal, creating something of a dilemma both for Israel and for the United States. There were discussions in Washington about going public with the American plan and the Palestinian acceptance of it, in order to put pressure on Israel. But this was a double-edged sword. While an Israeli refusal would clearly make Israel the recalcitrant party, the public pressure could also "blow up" the peace process, at a time when President Clinton was in the middle of the scandal over his behavior with Monica Lewinsky and was greatly weakened.

Israel could not afford seriously to fall out with America, however. Netanyahu bypassed the White House, appealing directly to American Jews and to Congress. Eighty senators signed a letter urging the Administration not to pressure Israel by formally publishing the U.S. proposal. In Israel, Moledet, an anti-Oslo party, joined Netanyahu's coalition, increasing his parliamentary majority by two votes. Arafat also applied pressure on the United States, reiterating the possibility of a unilateral declaration of a Palestinian state on May 4, 1999, when the five-year timetable envisaged in the Oslo accords ran out. But this would not solve the fundamental problem of defining the area to be encompassed by Palestine. Uri Savir, one of the major participants, noted that Yitzhak Rabin had been willing to cede 50 percent of the West Bank while final status issues were being negotiated, a figure higher than what the Palestinians would have, with or without the current American proposal.

Although the American proposal was never publicly revealed, it was widely leaked, and in early May Albright met with the Israeli and Palestinian leaders in London. A clearly adversarial relationship developed between Netanyahu and the United States, as Washington then proposed a deadline of May 11 for Israeli acceptance of the American plan.

Netanyahu's position was relatively stronger by May, but could he hold out in the end? In January, the Lewinsky scandal had just broken, Clinton was distracted, and Netanyahu had been able to mobilize powerful lobbies in the United States to fend off White House pressure. Netanyahu had received plaudits from the right for standing up to the United States, although it was not clear whether he was holding out for a better deal or, as most suspected, trying to kill the Oslo process altogether. No one knew what his goal was, and he had gotten away with one delay after another. It is, of course, significant that Israel at this juncture seemed to be negotiating not with the Palestinians but with the United States negotiating on behalf of the Palestinians. As Clinton's "deadline" approached, the Republican Speaker of the House of Representatives, Newt Gingrich, said the United States was trying to blackmail Israel by pushing it toward the negotiating table and called Clinton pro-Arafat. A majority (220) of the Houses's 435 members signed a letter saying Israel should not accept the White House's withdrawal plan, which it termed "counterproductive."

Meanwhile, American First Lady Hillary Clinton, speaking by satellite to a youth group holding a meeting in Villars, Switzerland, and responding to a question about Palestinian women, mentioned in passing that the creation of a Palestinian state was very important for the broader goals of peace in the Middle East. Her remarks were immediately disavowed by aides, but there was some speculation that they had been calculated and reflected the views of the Administration.

Netanyahu met with Albright in Washington, but there were no breakthroughs, and the "deadline" was extended. Gingrich, in Israel in early June, denounced Albright as a Palestinian "agent," talked about Jerusalem as the united, eternal capital of Israel, and virtually assured Netanyahu of the support of Congress for his position. On the other hand, Israel's president, Ezer Weizman, in a stunning slap in the face, publicly urged Netanyahu to call early elections because of his indecisive policies.

UN decisions offered encouragement to the Palestinians. In early July, the United Nations General Assembly upgraded the status of the Palestinian delegation. Although not granted voting rights or the authority to nominate candidates for UN offices, the PLO was given unique status for delegates not representing a national government. The delegation would be able to participate in debates, cosponsor resolutions related to the Middle East, and be seated in the General Assembly chamber next to Switzerland and the Vatican, two other states with observer status.

Increasingly isolated at home and abroad, Netanyahu signaled that he was now prepared to cut a deal for an interim Israeli pullback and resume talks with the Palestinians, evoking, as the *Jerusalem Post* noted, "skepticism on the left, despair on the right and hope in the center." Not only did he, for the moment, drop previous demands that the PNC be convened to revoke the offensive clauses in the PLO charter, but he also proposed that perhaps 3 percent of the 13 percent U.S. figure could be a nature reserve, designated as Area D. As a nature reserve, it would be protected from all construction. Another concession was his acceptance of the security memorandum drawn up previously by representatives of the CIA and the Israeli and Palestinian security establishments. If all this worked, then Netanyahu could claim to have achieved a better deal by hard bargaining than Labor might have arrived at. Netanyahu's proposals, however, did little to satisfy his critics.

Negotiations proceeded slowly. Arafat agreed to the Israeli proposal for a portion of the redeployment area to be designated a nature reserve, but he insisted on sharing security in the area, which Israel rejected. Netanyahu now insisted that a full PNC meeting vote on the PLO charter. And on the extradition of terrorists, Israel wanted the P.A. to transfer suspects to Israel; the Palestinians wanted to try them themselves. On questions of reciprocity, Israel was willing to withdraw after the Palestinians fulfilled security commitments; the Palestinians insisted on moves taking place simultaneously.

Dennis Ross returned to the region on September 9, his first trip since April, but left after eleven days without resolution of any of the issues. Later that month, at the opening of the United Nations General Assembly session, Arafat spoke and asked for help in bringing independence to the Palestinians by May 1999. After separate meetings with Clinton, possibly because May 4, 1999, was looming, Netanyahu basically accepted the U.S. plan, and on September 29, it was announced that Netanyahu and Arafat would work together toward reaching a West Bank accord at a mid-October White House summit. Albright then brought the two men together for the first time in a year at the Waldorf Astoria hotel in New York City.

The Wye River Memorandum

Back in the Middle East, Netanyahu and Arafat broke bread together on October 7, 1998, as Netanyahu crossed for the first time to the Palestinian side of the Erez checkpoint near Gaza in an impromptu end to Madeleine Albright's two-day trip to the area. An announcement was also made that talks would begin on October 15, at the Wye River plantation in Maryland, the same location where Israel–Syria talks had been held three years before.

Meanwhile, Arafat had set up three committees—political, economic, and legal—to prepare for a possible declaration of statehood. Israel continued to create facts on the ground by consolidating the settler presence at Tel Rumeida, for example, a small Jewish enclave in Hebron. Settler numbers had continued to rise, and work continued on a ring road around Jerusalem to connect settlements south of the city with those in the north.

Interestingly, Netanyahu named Ariel Sharon as Foreign Minister on October 10, possibly to mollify his right-wing supporters or to provide a broader base of support for concessions he might have to make during the Wye talks. It is not clear why Sharon accepted the position, although he said it was to be in a better position to fight for the Land of Israel. Both Sharon and Netanyahu talked tough before the Wye conference, but it was widely expected that some agreement would be signed.

Talks began at Wye on October 15, 1998, with Netanyahu, Arafat, Albright, and CIA Director George Tenet as full-time participants. President Clinton made it clear that he would not try again if the talks failed. Polls in Israel also indicated that over 80 percent wanted some agreement to be reached at Wye, and 57 percent supported an additional withdrawal. Arafat had to show that he was not simply a pawn of the United States and Israel, and that he could deliver for the Palestinians. Although appearing weak and physically ill, he had the May 4 card in his pocket to play if necessary. Netanyahu had to be able to satisfy his critics that gains in security justified the surrender of more territory. Both leaders ran the risk of alienating their most right-wing opponents: for Netanyahu, the settlers and the parties supporting them; and for Arafat, if he accepted a strict security agreement, elements of Hamas and other rejectionists.

The Wye talks proceeded slowly and in an atmosphere of mutual distrust. Appearances by Clinton and King Hussein of Jordan, who traveled to the conference site two times from the Mayo clinic where he was undergoing treatment for cancer, helped keep the talks moving, but hardliners on both sides condemned the negotiations, and a grenade assault in Beersheba by Hamas militants wounded 67 Israelis. Although the main outlines of an agreement had more or less been a given, the key elements did not fall into place until October 22. Netanyahu demanded and gained an agreement strengthening the U.S. commitment to safeguard Israel's security by enhancing Israel's defensive and deterrent capabilities and upgrading the strategic, military and technical cooperation between the two countries. His last-minute unsuccessful attempt to secure the release of convicted spy Jonathan Pollard, however, almost derailed the proceedings. On October 23, 1998, in a White House ceremony, the Wye River Memorandum was signed. (See Document 12–1.)

At Wye, both sides bowed to the inevitable and accepted what was possible rather than what was desired. The two sides agreed upon an Israeli redeployment plan and a security cooperation plan. The agreement also included a provision for the PNC to eliminate articles in the Charter calling for Israel's destruction. It mandated that the P.A. imprison thirty murder suspects and make sure they remained in prison, and that the P.A. confiscate illegal weapons and reduce the Palestinian police force to the size agreed upon in the Oslo II accords. Following compliance, Israel would carry out in phases the first and second of three additional redeployments called for in previous agreements. A combined 13 percent of the West Bank would be transferred from Area C. Twelve percent would become Area B, of which 3 percent would be designated as a nature reserve, and 1 percent would become part of Area A. In addition, 14.2 percent of Area B would be transferred to Area A. Israel would also release 750 Palestinian prisoners who were not Hamas members and who did not have Jewish or Israeli blood on their hands. Negotiations on a third redeployment would be deferred until a later date. Under these arrangements, Israel retained full military and civilian control of 60 percent of the West Bank (Area C). The Palestinians increased the area of full control from their present 3 percent to about 18.2 percent (Area A) and shared with Israel control of 21.8 percent (Area B).

The by now familiar pattern of extremist opposition greeted the Wye arrangements. In Israel there were demonstrations against Netanyahu and talk of new elections. Not surprisingly, the prime minister found pretexts to stop the implementation of the agreement. Already within a few days of the signing, he persuaded Arafat to agree to a postponement of the start of the deal until the Cabinet and Knesset had ratified it. Finally, after a two-week delay, the Israeli Cabinet in an 8–4 vote, with 5 abstentions, ratified Wye but attached stipulations and threats. It reiterated that the entire PNC should meet to revise the Charter; that in a third redeployment, Israel would withdraw from no more than an additional 1 percent of territory; and that the Cabinet would reconvene to reconsider approval after each phase of the twelve-week implementation period.

It should be noted in passing that the agreement was based on reciprocity and a detailed outline of when commitments were to be fulfilled. If a stage were unfulfilled, the next stage would not be launched. Israel used the reciprocity clauses to delay compliance. Thus, although the United States approved the PLO security plan, which was presented on time, Netanyahu, on the excuse it did not contain a specific timetable for the arrest of thirty "wanted" men over the next twelve weeks, delayed presenting the accord to the Cabinet until November 5. Then a car bomb in Mahane Yehuda market killed the two assailants but wounded several people just in the midst of Cabinet discussions on implementation of Wye.

The PLO faced similar problems. Leaders of radical Palestinian factions in Syria renewed their opposition to canceling articles in the Charter and called for elections of a new Palestinian parliament. The Hizbullah leader in Lebanon, Sheikh Nasrollah, called for Arafat's assassination. Even Iranian President Khatami voiced his opposition to the Wye memorandum. Nevertheless, Palestinian police rounded up an estimated 300 Hamas followers and put Sheikh Yassin under house arrest after a thwarted suicide bombing on an Israeli school bus (he was released in December). There also appeared to be some disagreement between the lead Palestinian negotiator, Mahmoud Abbas, and the head of the Palestinian Security Services in Gaza, Muhammad Dahlan, over the Wye arrangements, signalling a potential post-Arafat leadership struggle. Both men would also have to combat the powerful head of the Palestinian Security Services on the West Bank, Jibril Rajoub, and Hamas elements. Arafat faced a dilemma with Hamas and Islamic Jihad because of the social services, free schools, and clinics provided by those groups, as compared to the minimum services offered by the P.A. The P.A. legislature had enacted 59 laws since being established in 1996, but as of 1999 only a few had received Arafat's necessary signature. Corruption among the ministers also did not help relations with the legislature.

The first Israeli redeployment had been scheduled for November 16 but was delayed because the Knesset had not yet endorsed the Wye agreement. On November 17, the Knesset approved Wye in a 75–19 vote with 9 abstentions; and the Cabinet in a 7–5 vote with 3 abstentions gave the go-ahead to the first stage: transfer of 2 percent from the Jenin area of the West Bank (44 square miles) from sole Israeli control (Area C) to joint Palestinian jurisdiction (Area B); and 7.1 percent (160 square miles) from joint jurisdiction (Area B) to sole Palestinian control (Area A). This redeployment began on November 20 and resulted in the Palestinian-controlled territory growing from 3 to 10.1 percent, and Area B now standing at 18.6 percent. Israel released 250 prisoners, 150 of whom were mostly criminals, not political prisoners.

There was also movement on the economic front. Trade talks commenced for the first time between Israel, Jordan, and the P.A. On November 24, a Palestinian international airport was opened in Gaza. (See Map 12–1.) At a donors' conference at the end of November, 43 nations pledged more than $3 billion dollars to the Palestinians. The EU offered $2 billion over 5 years, and the United States indicated it would increase its contribution by adding $400 million to the $100 million it planned to donate over five years.

Both Clinton and Netanyahu were experiencing serious domestic troubles at this time. Clinton, in fact, flew to the Middle East to oversee the PNC meeting that would discuss the PLO Charter, just as the Judiciary Committee in the House of Representatives was meeting to decide whether to approve articles of impeachment against him. In Israel, the Knesset decided to hold a no-confidence vote against Netanyahu in two weeks' time. On December 7, Israeli lawmakers at the last minute postponed a vote to take a first step toward dissolving parliament and calling new elections, as unrest and demonstrations broke out in the West Bank over the issue of the Palestinian prisoners. President Clinton, whose trip had been written into the Wye memorandum, was clearly sailing into muddy waters. The P.A. and the United States were closer, but some Palestinians, as well as the Israelis, were having problems with that connection because of U.S. bombing attacks not only on Iraq, but also on Sudan and Afghanistan because of their alleged connection with terrorist cells masterminded by Osama Bin Laden, whom the United States held responsible for embassy bombings in Tanzania and Kenya that killed over 200 people. Nevertheless, on December 14, with Clinton in attendance in Gaza, the PNC, in a show of hands, renounced those clauses in the PLO Charter offensive to Israel. The president had flown into Jerusalem on Air Force One, but took a helicopter to Gaza, thus avoiding an official recognition of Palestinian sovereignty, although his appearance in Gaza came very close to doing just that.

Despite the PNC vote, Israel said it would not meet the December 18 timetable for the next pullback, which made Netanyahu appear to stand up to U.S. pressure in a kind of

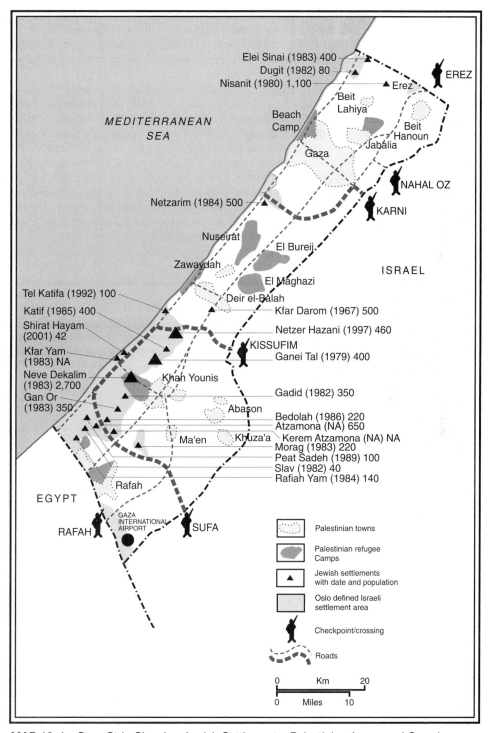

MAP 12–1   Gaza Strip Showing Jewish Settlements, Palestinian Areas, and Crossings

desperate bid to save his coalition. But he was in plenty of trouble anyway. His 1999 budget was stuck, and his finance minister walked out. On December 21, 1998, an overwhelming majority, including the prime minister himself, voted to dissolve the government. May 17, 1999 was later set as the date for new elections. All this, of course, produced a stalemate in the peace process.

By the end of 1998, Netanyahu and the Likud could no longer claim to be upholding the ideology of Greater Israel. As *New York Times* editorialist Thomas Friedman wryly observed, after spending time not crossing the Rubicon so much as swimming laps back and forth in it, Netanyahu finally did cross the Wye River. Unlike the Hebron agreement, which was a left-over Labor legacy, the Wye agreement was his own, although the seeds for this ideological "betrayal" had perhaps been sown in 1978 by another Likud leader, Menachem Begin. Despite his rhetoric to the contrary, Begin had refrained from annexing the occupied territories, pro-posed autonomy for the Palestinians, and signed the Camp David accords. Wye may have expanded the political center in Israel, but it shattered the political right wing. But where else could the right-wing turn? As for the Labor party, now led by Ehud Barak, who had replaced Shimon Peres at its head in 1997, Netanyahu's deal knocked it off its feet.

The Death of King Hussein

The somewhat unexpected and sudden death of King Hussein of Jordan on February 7, 1999, focused the world's attention on the Middle East in quite new ways. Hussein had returned to Amman from the United States in early January declaring that his cancer had been cured, but he soon flew back to the Mayo Clinic after suffering a relapse. He returned to Jordan for the last time in early February and died shortly thereafter. In the interim, however, he had stunned the Jordanians and much of the rest of the world by removing his brother Hassan as regent, a posi-tion he had occupied for thirty-four years, and naming his oldest son Abdullah as the heir-apparent. Hassan was a supporter of the peace treaty with Israel and had otherwise proved himself an adroit ruler in the king's absence.

World leaders in unprecedented numbers gathered in Amman for Hussein's funeral and expressed not only their sorrow at the king's passing but a renewed hope that the Palestinian and Arab conflict with Israel would soon come to an end. Israel's president, Ezer Weizman, in a move that surprised both Arabs and Israelis, shook hands with Nayaf Hawatmeh, the DFLP leader responsible for the 1974 Maalot massacre. Extremist reaction was swift as well as pre-dictable. A coalition of radical Palestinian groups opposed to the peace accords immediately expelled Hawatmeh and his group from their ranks. Arafat, for his part, declared that he still favored creation of a confederation between a future Palestinian state and Jordan, perhaps aim-ing his remarks at those Israelis opposed to an independent Palestinian state on the grounds that it could forge an alliance with Syria, Iraq, or Iran. Netanyahu made a quiet offer to the Palestinians to carry out a few of Israel's obligations under the frozen Wye agreement, such as releasing some petty criminals and opening a safe passage route, but these offers were rejected.

It was not clear whether the inexperienced Abdullah would be able to maintain stabil-ity, given the not-always friendly relations between Jordan and its neighbors, especially Syria, and given the Palestinian majority in the kingdom. The fact that Abdullah had a Palestinian wife, however, was said to be in his favor on that score. And the English-speaking, Western-educated Abdullah also had close ties to the United States. The new Jordanian king, although committed to peace with Israel, did not visit Israel until the next year, however. His first foreign visits were to Syria, Libya, Saudi Arabia, and the United Arab Emirates. He also called for more dialogue with Iraq.

The Election of Ehud Barak

Meanwhile, in Israel, the announcement of the elections had set off a mad scramble of contenders. In mid-January, Netanyahu won the Likud party nomination over Moshe Arens, whom he later appointed to the Defense portfolio. In March, the Labor, Gesher, and Meimad parties joined to form the One Israel party and nominated Ehud Barak, head of the Labor party since 1997, as its leader. The situation demonstrated, among other things, that the electoral system introduced in 1996 clearly did not help solve Israel's chronic political problems. In the old system, with the prime minister representing the party with a plurality of the votes, the parties focused more on national interests and questions. In the new system, one could vote directly for the prime minister of one party and then separately for the party of one's choice, which tended to push ethnic, religious, and sectional concerns to the forefront.

The two "external" issues the campaign focused upon were Lebanon and the Oslo/Wye process. With peace talks stuck, and religious-secular tensions in Israel mounting over the "Who is a Jew?" question, the validity of Reform and Conservative conversions, funds to support schools run by the religious establishment, and other internal matters, both Netanyahu and his major opponents turned their attention to Lebanon. Israel had been mired down in Lebanon in a Vietnam-type situation since 1982. Ehud Barak pledged that if he were elected, he would open negotiations with Syria over the Golan Heights and would "bring the boys home" from Lebanon in a year. The Likud had also suggested pulling the troops out of Lebanon and had, in fact, endorsed UN Resolution 425 on Lebanon the year before. (See Document 12–2.)

Because the target date looming for the completion of the Oslo process and the Israeli elections were both scheduled for May 1999, the two issues became increasingly intertwined. It was widely agreed that the person elected as prime minister would have to move very quickly to establish a new timeline for compliance with the Wye agreement, and that final status talks would have to begin—assuming, of course, that Arafat in the meantime would agree to postpone any declaration of statehood on May 4.

Arafat's dilemma was how to climb down from what he had called the "sacred date" of May 4 without losing face. He had to demonstrate that he was not merely a pawn of the Israelis. Jordan and Egypt, in a joint statement with the Palestinians in mid-March, backed the PNA's right to proclaim a state and urged the world to support this right, but they shied away from saying it should do so on May 4. The PLO leader sought international guarantees he could present to his people and evidence that there would be an eventual payoff (including financial assistance), if he postponed a declaration of statehood. In a tour of Europe that month, Arafat received a declaration of support from the European Union, which issued a statement reaffirming the "unqualified right" of the Palestinians to self-determination, "including the option of a state." The EU urged both sides to agree to an extension of the interim period beyond May 4, but also said that Palestinian self-determination was a right "not subject to any veto" and believed final status negotiations could be concluded within a year. Arafat also met with Clinton at the White House in March, and the president evidently tried to help by promising a more active role in the peace process after the Israeli elections, and by denouncing Israel's continuing expansion of settlements.

There were powerful incentives on both the Palestinian and American sides for not taking any action that would help Netanyahu in his bid for reelection. At least seventeen hillside communities had sprung up on the West Bank since Wye was signed (eventually there would be about forty-two), and Netanyahu moved against Palestinian offices in Jerusalem (a Christian affairs office, a prisoner's advocacy bureau, and a news agency), on the grounds that they were linked to the P.A. and were operating illegally in the city. News of these closures came just after European consuls met with Feisal al-Husseini, the P.A. Minister for Jerusalem Affairs, in Orient House, the P.A.'s unofficial headquarters, to pay their respects on the occasion of the

Muslim Eid al-Adha (Feast of the Sacrifice) holiday marking the end of the Great Pilgrimage to Mecca.

At the March meeting in Washington, Arafat and Clinton came up with the idea of a letter from the president supporting Palestinian statehood. Arafat hoped for a "Balfour Declaration" type of statement. He did not get that, but in the letter issued on the eve of a meeting of the Palestinian Central Council in Gaza, Clinton wrote that he supported the "aspirations of the Palestinian people to determine their own future on their own land," and called Jewish settlements "destructive to the pursuit of peace." Clinton said he supported the goal of Palestinian statehood if it were accomplished through negotiation and reminded Arafat of the trappings of statehood that already existed (a flag, police force, separate telephone country code, etc.) and the international support existing for independence.

Although clearly frustrated, most Palestinians seemed resigned to a delay, and on April 29, at the conclusion of the three-day meeting of the Central Committee, Palestinian leaders decided against a unilateral declaration of statehood on May 4. Arafat had convened the Gaza meeting because he needed a broad consensus for delay after raising peoples' hopes over the previous year. Interestingly, Hamas had been split on whether to attend, but in the end, four leaders did—the first time Hamas had attended a formal gathering of the secular PLO organization. The delegates, led by Sheikh Yassin, and all from Gaza, were given observer status. Hamas members outside Gaza distanced themselves from the decision.

Netanyahu trumpeted the Palestinian decision as a victory for his tough policy, maintaining that Arafat had "backed down." Although uneasy with the spin Netanyahu put on their decision, it was clear that the Palestinians had no desire to help his re-election by a unilateral move. On the eve of the elections, three important candidates for prime minister—Asmi Bishara, Benny Begin, and Yitzhak Mordechai—withdrew, leaving the field to Netanyahu and to Ehud Barak. The election was expected to be too close to call but, surprisingly, Barak won with 57 percent of the vote. His One Israel party, on the other hand, captured only 26 of the 120 Knesset seats.

Netanyahu's ambivalence had alienated almost everyone, including members of his own party and cabinet, who felt betrayed ideologically and politically. He had lost the respect and support of his own cabinet ministers and appeared inept as the head of state. Sara, wife of the thrice-married Netanyahu, was also more of a liability than an asset, as she hired and fired household help and otherwise garnered bad publicity for the couple. Following his defeat, Netanyahu immediately announced that he was stepping down as leader and withdrawing from politics.

In contrast, Barak had a reputation for straight-talking and decisive action. Barak was a classical pianist, fascinated with clocks, a former general, and the most decorated soldier in Israel's history. Many thought of him as a second Yitzhak Rabin, and it was hoped he would lead the nation, which appeared to be going around in circles, in a direct line to tackling and perhaps even resolving some of the most pressing internal and external issues. He made it clear that he wanted to proceed with the Oslo process, that he would be open to serious talks with Syria, and that he would bring the boys home from Lebanon. As the *Jerusalem Report* put it, the blueprint was "that progress on peace would spark the economy, drawing investments, leading to growth and jobs. That would generate revenue for improved health and education sectors creating, in turn, a new climate of optimism in which to address the secular-religious divide."

Barak took his time assembling a government coalition. He first conducted intensive negotiations with Ariel Sharon, acting head of Likud, which had captured 19 seats. It was clear that the Likud would continue to hamper peace efforts, however, and talks broke down. As expected, Barak then turned to Shas, the Sephardi Orthodox party, and was helped in this regard by the resignation of Arye Deri, who had been convicted on corruption charges, as party head. Although opposed by secular and leftist parties like Meretz, which had 10 seats, Shas, with its 17 seats, was a formidable force. Moreover, its spiritual leader Ovadia Yosef was said to consider

Israeli Prime Minister Ehud Barak, July 1999.

the religious imperative even more important than the question of ceding land for peace. The new government was finally announced on June 30 and was sworn in on July 1.

Meanwhile, in a last gesture of defiance, Moshe Arens, the outgoing Defense Minister, had approved plans to enlarge the largest Jewish settlement, Maale Adumim, between Jerusalem and Jericho, by several thousand acres. Barak was silent on the issue, saying only that he would not "dry up" the settlements and would honor decisions taken by the Netanyahu government prior to its dissolution in December, 1998.

The Sharm al-Sheikh Memorandum

Initially, Barak proved no more flexible than Netanyahu. Despite meetings with Mubarak, Arafat, and King Abdullah of Jordan (as well as Turkish President Sulayman Demirel, Jacques Chirac of France, and Tony Blair of England), before flying to Washington for his first meeting with Clinton in mid-July, no progress was made on negotiations with the Palestinians. It should be noted in passing that Clinton had overruled Congress in June and kept the U.S. Embassy in Israel from being relocated from Tel Aviv to Jerusalem, on the grounds that such a move would jeopardize national security.

In his meetings with Clinton, Barak indicated that he would prefer to wrap the Wye agreement into final status issues, which the P.A. was resisting. At most, he wanted to move on implementing Wye gradually and to start final talks before the third phase of Wye was carried out. Although Arafat and the Palestinians wanted full and immediate implementation, in early August, over the objections of his Cabinet, which was opposed to any changes, Arafat accepted Barak's timetable for Wye, with a September starting date.

On September 1, U.S. Secretary of State Albright arrived on the scene and acted as a kind of facilitator between the Israelis and Palestinians. An agreement was signed on September 4, 1999,

Israeli Prime Minister Ehud Barak and Palestinian Chairman Yasser Arafat receive congratulations from Egyptian President Hosni Mubarak (center) after signing the Sharm el-Sheikh memorandum on September 5, 1999, as Jordan's King Abdullah II and U.S. Secretary of State Madeleine Albright look on.

at Sharm al-Sheikh, ending eight months of stalemate. The Sharm al-Sheikh agreement set out a timetable for a permanent peace settlement. A declaration of principles on final status issues was to be reached by February 13, 2000 and a permanent settlement reached by September 13, 2000. Israel accepted the remaining 11 percent redeployment agreed upon at Wye, and Arafat compromised by accepting the release of 350 prisoners, rather than the 400 the Palestinians had requested. On September 9, Israel released 199 Palestinian prisoners, and also approved a further land transfer of 7 percent of the West Bank—about 147 square miles—to the Palestinians. The next day, September 10, with little fanfare, this 7 percent was transferred to the P.A. (See Document 12–3.)

Exactly six years after Oslo, and after two false starts (May 1996 and November 1998), talks began at Erez on September 13 on a final peace accord. The two sides accepted February 13, 2000, as the target date for a framework agreement on the outstanding issues, but the opening positions were far apart. The P.A. wanted a state in all of the West Bank and Gaza, with East Jerusalem as its capital; the repatriation of the 3 to 4 million Palestinian refugees; and the dismantling of Jewish settlements unwilling to remain under Palestinian sovereignty. Israel vowed that it would never relinquish any part of Jerusalem, or allow the return of refugees to areas under its sovereignty, or give up all of the West Bank.

Both leaders faced domestic opposition over all their negotiating positions. This was particularly true of the emotionally charged issue of the future of Israeli settlements in the West Bank. Barak had pledged that he would permit no new settlements, but, at the urging of his housing minister, prominent National Religious party leader Yitzhak Levy, he did authorize new construction and approved nearly 2600 new housing units in the existing West Bank settlements, more than had been authorized annually under Netanyahu. However, in October, a ministerial committee on settlements gave Barak a free hand to close outposts that had sprung up since the Wye agreement. According to the Judge Advocate, thirty of the forty-two that went up after Wye were illegal, many of these established after then Foreign Minister Sharon urged Jewish settlers to grab hilltops and create facts on the ground. The settlers mobilized against the planned evacuation of fifteen West Bank hilltops in response to Barak's announcement that they would be removed and that sixteen others would be barred from continuing construction. This threatened his uneasy pact with a new, more moderate settler leadership.

Palestinian negotiator Saeb Erekat maintained that there was no distinction between state-approved and illegal settlements, that all were illegal under UN resolutions regarding the occupied territory, and that they must be removed. The distressed settlers accepted the voluntary dismantling of twelve of the fifteen outposts, most of which were uninhabited or small. That left 30 intact, as well as the 145 previously existing settlements. The settlers claimed a victory over the deal; Justice Minister Yossi Beilin called attention to the first-time agreement between the government and the settlers; and the Palestinians cried deceit.

Arafat, meanwhile, had attempted to placate Palestinian groups opposed to the whole process. In early August, shortly after his first meeting with Barak, he convened a meeting in Cairo with leaders of factions opposed to the peace process. Although George Habash did not attend, a seven-member delegation of his Syrian-backed PFLP did. The DFLP did not attend, but it was expected that its leader, Hawatmeh, would meet eventually with the PLO chief. It was also becoming increasingly apparent that King Abdullah would, like his father, assume a key role in Mideast talks. In early September, as Albright arrived in the region, the king moved to expel local Hamas leaders, including Khaled Mishal, and closed Hamas offices. Later, Musa Abu Marzouk, who had been released by the United States and returned to Jordan, was also deported. Unlike Hussein, however, Abdullah deferred to Arafat as the sole leader of the Palestinian people, except for those who were Jordanian citizens, and said that the Palestinians should take administrative control of the Muslim holy sites in Jerusalem, still formally under Jordanian control. He rejected the idea of a confederation between Jordan and a Palestinian state, however. While he stood firmly behind the peace process, Abdullah was not followed in this by much of his population. An antinormalization drive continued, and important groups and organizations drew up blacklists of members and acquaintances who had had contact with Israelis.

On October 5, an agreement was reached on a safe passage route for Palestinians traveling between Gaza and Hebron. Israel freed another 151 prisoners, and on October 25, 1999 the 28-mile route from Erez to Tarqumiyya, outside Hebron, was opened. Chief Israeli and Palestinian negotiators Oded Eran and Yasser Abed Rabbo, Palestinian Information Minister, set November 7 as the starting date for further talks on a permanent peace treaty.

Final status talks began again in Ramallah on November 8, but it soon became clear that they would go nowhere. Abed Rabbo set out the Palestinian position that talks must be based on UN Resolutions 242 and 338, including the return of Jerusalem. Israel accepted the UN resolutions as a basis but insisted they were open to interpretation. Eran laid out Israel's interpretation: no return to the pre-1967 borders; Israeli settlements to remain in the West Bank; Israel to continue control over East Jerusalem; and no "foreign army" to deploy west of the Jordan River. To offset this hard line, Barak offered a goodwill gesture: cabinet approval of a troop withdrawal from an additional 5 percent of the West Bank. Remember that at Wye, Israel had pledged to withdraw from 13.1 percent of the territory of the West Bank under their sole control (Area C) in three stages, and that only 2 percent had been returned when the process was frozen by Netanyhu. Seven percent was then transferred from Area C to Palestinian administrative control (Area B) following the Sharm al-Sheikh agreement. The proposed redeployment to be carried out on November 15 was to include 3 percent from Area C to Area B, including an area east of Hebron due to become a nature reserve, as well as 2 percent from Area B to Area A. The November 15 date was not met, however. The Palestinians did not like the map, and Dennis Ross was unable to solve the dispute. Talks between Israel and the Palestinians were put on hold.

The Syrians—and Great Expectations

Israeli–Palestinian negotiations were at a stalemate, but Barak, anxious to be seen doing something in order to regain American goodwill, sought the resumption of negotiations with Syria. Indeed, most observers believed that pursuing the Syrian track was Barak's top priority. Talks with Syria had been broken off in February 1996, and with Netanyahu's election, relations with Syria had remained frozen. The previous talks had halted after twenty or more shuttles between Israel and Damascus by former Secretary of State Warren Christopher, although it was widely believed that clandestine contacts had continued to be maintained. Following a four-day tour of the Middle East by Madeleine Albright that included stopovers in Syria and Israel, President Clinton announced on December 8, 1999, that Israel and Syria would begin top-level peace talks once again.

The time seemed propitious. Following Barak's election, Syrian president Assad, in interviews with Patrick Seale, a British journalist and confidante, had called Barak "strong" and "honest." In a companion piece, Barak said he saw Syria as the "cornerstone" of peace in the Middle East. Later, in Moscow, Assad signaled his willingness to reopen talks with Israel, although it was not until December that the parties got together. It appeared to some commentators that Assad, who despised Arafat and who was always suspicious of Palestinian aspirations, did not want to be left behind. Some thought, too, that the proud but ailing Syrian leader felt that his time was running out. Syria had much to gain by making a deal with Israel. The country was being left behind in the global economy, and the consensus was that, despite the harsh rhetoric, Assad and the Syrian population realized that Israel was not going to go away or be defeated by the Arab states.

In fact, Assad had made a firm strategic decision to seek "normal and peaceful" relations with Israel as early as 1994. He had announced as much in his summit with Clinton in Geneva in January of that year. He had also previously indicated to Seale, in May 1993, that he would agree to a "full peace for a full withdrawal," although the subsequent negotiations, which we traced in the previous chapter, proved fruitless. He repeated these assurances to an Israeli Arab delegation in Damascus in August 1997. By the mid-nineties most Syrians had accepted the reality of peace with Israel. The questions Damascenes were asking themselves apprehensively concerned the nature and implications of the peace.

The positions of the two antagonists had always been pretty clear, the main hurdle being how to get the parties to act simultaneously, since neither would go first. Assad's bottom line was getting Israel to give back all the Golan and return to the June 4, 1967, border between the two countries. Barak, possibly following the lead of Yitzhak Rabin, who put forward the proposal in 1993, insisted as the price of returning the Golan that Syria rein in Hizbullah, which it controlled in Lebanon, and sign a permanent peace treaty normalizing relations between the two countries. The Hizbullah campaign in Lebanon had been Syria's main pressure point on Israel, a tool for efforts to force Israel to renounce its control over the Golan. On the other hand, a unilateral Israeli withdrawal from Lebanon would rob Syria of that particular card.

There was disagreement over the precise border to be returned to. Israel was prepared to withdraw to the international border drawn up in by the British and French in 1923, rather than to the line of confrontation between Israel and Syria on June 4, 1967, the day prior to the outbreak of the 1967 war, as demanded by Syria. Nobody seemed interested in the 1949 armistice line. If Israel withdrew to the 1923 border, it would retain control over a sliver of territory to the east of the Sea of Galilee, thus ensuring access to its water supply. Both sides had security and water concerns whatever boundary was agreed upon. (See Map 12–2.)

The Knesset tepidly endorsed the talks with Syria, voting 47 for, 31 against, and 24 abstaining, and on December 15 and 16, Israel and Syria started meeting again in Washington and agreed to begin intensive negotiations in January. Just after the first of the year 2000, talks resumed at Shepherdstown, West Virginia, with President Clinton often present. The United States presented a draft paper to get things going, without much success. The agenda was in

MAP 12–2   Relief Map of Golan Showing International Boundaries

dispute, and there was disagreement even over what had been agreed to in December. Four working committees were set up to deal with peace terms, security, Israeli withdrawal from the Golan, and water issues, but the talks wound down toward an inclusive recess by January 10. They were scheduled to resume on January 19. During that week, a huge rally took place in

Israel to protest giving up the Golan, but the death blow to the talks occurred when the Israeli newspaper *Haaretz* published a draft of a proposed Israeli–Syrian treaty, which appeared to show that Syria was willing to accept many of the Israeli conditions. Assad was furious, and the talks were postponed. Syria lambasted Israel, and said the talks had stumbled because Israel would not admit that the Golan belonged to Syria. Articles appeared in Syrian newspapers questioning the Holocaust, and Syria showed its muscle by unleashing Hizbullah in Lebanon, creating an ever more problematic situation for Israel. President Clinton, eager to secure some kind of dramatic breakthrough during his last year in office, made a last ditch effort to persuade the Syrians to return to the table when he met Syrian president Assad in Geneva in March, but he was rebuffed.

While talks had been going on at Shepherdstown between Israel and Syria, Israel and the Palestinians broke their deadlock on the transfer of the 5 percent that had been scheduled for November. On January 5, 2000, Israel transferred 3 percent of territory from Area C to Area B (part of the promised 13.1 percent agreed at Wye) and 2 percent from Area B to Area A. The way was cleared for the transfer of a further 6.1 percent to Area A on January 20, as promised at Wye—1 percent from Area C and 5.1 percent from Area B.

Disagreements emerged over the timing and scope of this 6.1 percent. Would Jerusalem suburbs, as demanded by the P.A. be included, for example? On January 17, Barak once again postponed the promised transfer, and although Dennis Ross flew back and forth between the end of January and the first part of February, there was not much progress. No one was surprised when talks were again suspended.

Obviously, the February 13, 2000, target date to achieve a framework agreement came and went without an outcome. Arafat said he would declare a state by September with or without Israel's blessing. Some observers noted that it might be better for Arafat and the P.A. if there were no framework treaty prior to September. Such an agreement, the argument went, would require Arafat to make painful concessions on Jerusalem, refugees, and the other final status issues. In the meantime, in Abu Dis, an Arab suburb of Jerusalem in sight of the Dome of the Rock, the construction of a great hall, widely reported to be the home of a future Palestinian parliament, was well underway. Currently straddling Israel's declared boundary of Jerusalem, Abu Dis had been included in a 1965 Jordanian plan for a greater Jerusalem that was never adopted because of the 1967 war. The town was also part of the international zone for Jerusalem, proposed by the UN in the partition plan of 1947. In the new borders drawn by Israel after 1967, about 10 percent of Abu Dis was in Jerusalem, and the rest was in the West Bank. (See Map 12–3.)

After weeks of deadlock and a two-day "summit" in Ramallah conducted by Dennis Ross, Barak and Arafat, on March 8, agreed to resume negotiations after the four-day feast (Eid al-Fitr) after Ramadan. In a compromise, Barak agreed to the immediate Israeli withdrawal of the 6.1 percent promised for the previous January 20. In return, Arafat accepted that land around Jerusalem would for the time being be excluded, and that an additional Israeli pullback as called for in the interim agreements could wait until after the outline for a final settlement was reached by the new target date of May.

The 6.1 percent redeployment took place on March 21 and included a large area near Hebron and fragments of areas near Bethlehem, Ramallah, Nablus, and Jenin chosen by the P.A. from maps submitted by Israel. The P.A. was now in full or partial control of 42.9 percent of the West Bank, according to their calculations; 39.8 percent, according to Israel's; and about 40 percent, according to the United States. One additional land transfer was to take place in June after the framework agreement was arrived at. (See Map 12–4.) The working delegations headed by Eran and Abed Rabbo again began talks on permanent status issues.

The land transfer, while significant, was largely overshadowed by the first visit to the state of Israel by Pope John Paul II, who also arrived on March 21. The Pope had gone a long way toward mending the bridges between the Vatican and the Jews before his trip to Israel. He was the first Pope to pray for the welfare of the state of Israel in 1984, he declared anti-Semitism "a sin," and he oversaw the establishment of full diplomatic relations between the

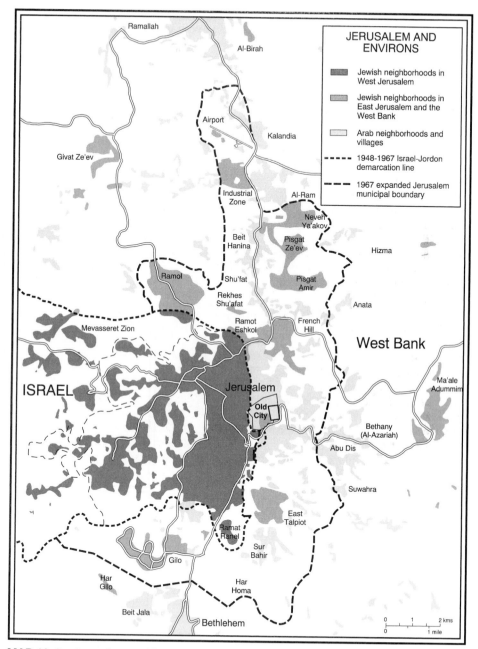

MAP 12–3 Jerusalem and Environs

Vatican and Israel in 1993. In 1994 he acknowledged the historical right of the Jewish people to the land of Israel. On his millennial visit, without specifically mentioning the Holocaust, he apologized to the Jews for the past behavior of adherents of his faith. However, he also referred to the suffering of the Palestinian people and reiterated their right to a homeland. The Vatican had also strengthened relations with the PLO by signing a basic agreement in February 2000,

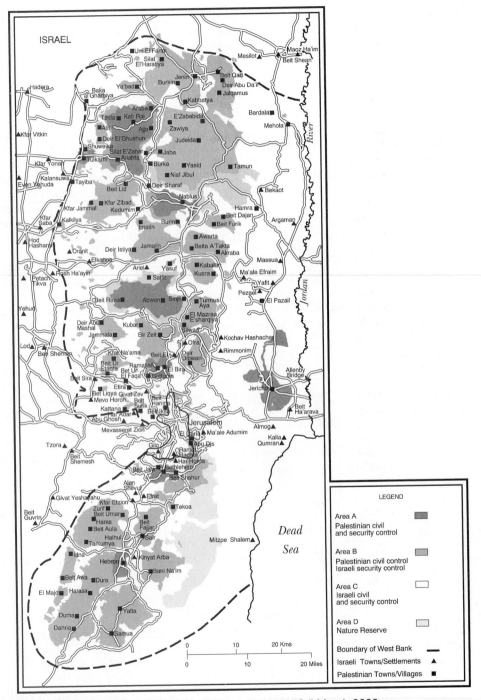

MAP 12–4 West Bank Showing Areas "A," "B," and "C," March 2000

which not only recognized the PLO as the representative of the Palestine National Authority, but continued to state the Vatican's position that Jerusalem should be given a special international status guaranteeing Christians, Jews, and Muslims free access to the city's holy sites.

The Talks Continue

Talks on permanent status issues continued in Washington at Bolling Air Force Base outside Washington in April. A certain air of urgency entered the negotiations as the new May 13 deadline for a framework agreement approached. Meanwhile, there were reports that Barak had all but offered the Palestinians an independent state. Although he continued to refer to a Palestinian entity, not a state, he said he would turn over land for territorial contiguity; and although he tried to reassure Israelis that Jerusalem would remain united under Israeli sovereignty, he indicated that Palestinian suburbs would be handed over, and that Israel would not seek to annex them. On the other hand, most Jewish settlements in the West Bank would be annexed to Israel in a permanent peace treaty. Evidently, in return for the Palestinians giving way on other final status issues, Barak was prepared at that point to see a Palestinian state in as much as 65–80 percent of the West Bank. Not surprisingly, the Palestinians shot down these overtures, repeating their conditions through an Arafat aide that Israel must withdraw from all territory, including Jerusalem, and that they would not give up their demands for repatriation of Palestinian refugees.

Talks resumed in Eilat at the end of April—but on a sour note. Israel had announced its intention to build 174 new homes in Maale Adumim, the largest West Bank settlement. Hawkish cabinet ministers also voiced their displeasure over Barak's apparent willingness to hand over three Jerusalem suburbs, including Abu Dis, to the Palestinians. Many Israelis, on the other hand, seemed resigned to the idea of a Palestinian state, with Abu Dis perhaps as its capital. Haim Ramon, Barak's minister for Jerusalem affairs, responding to a comment by Oded Eran that a Palestinian state might be the outcome of negotiations, said that a de facto state existed, and that negotiations would address, in part, Israel's request to bar it from signing military treaties and acquiring heavy arms. The settlers were disconcerted, however, since it was clear that some would have to be evacuated. Shortly after Barak's election, the settlers had elected a new and more moderate leadership in order to garner public support, and Barak was able to nurture a relationship with them, as seen in the voluntary evacuation of some, but not all, of the hillside settlements that sprang up after Wye. By the spring of 2000, however, a spokesman for the settlers' council declared that "Barak is not everyone's prime minister. . . . He is Arafat's prime minister."

The Israelis seemed to be negotiating among themselves. Bemused Palestinians wondered at Barak's proposing a referendum on a framework agreement, asking "What framework agreement?" And as for Abu Dis and the other villages near Jerusalem, the Palestinians noted that they were already under Palestinian civilian control, and presumably, under the Oslo accords, would eventually fall under their full control anyway.

Dennis Ross again flew to the area to act as a mediator in early May, and interestingly, the Palestinians then said that they would prefer a limited U.S. role, while Israel wanted a more active role, quite a reversal from previous positions. After Ross met with Barak and Arafat separately, the two leaders met at the home of Arafat deputy Mahmoud Abbas in Ramallah, with Abbas and Foreign Minister Levy also participating. On May 15, the Knesset voted 56 to 48 with one abstention to hand over the three villages of Abu Dis, Al-Azariah, and Surahwa as a goodwill gesture. In his own goodwill gesture, Arafat announced the arrest of a key Hamas leader, Muhammad Deif, accused of planning the bus bombings in Tel Aviv in spring 1996, and at the top of Israel's most wanted list.

Meanwhile, Minister of Public Security Shlomo Ben-Ami and Attorney Gilad Sher traveled to Sweden for talks with P.A. officials Ahmed Qurei and Hassan Aspour, who led the

Palestinian delegation to Oslo in the 1990s, and the two teams were authorized to consider permanent status issues and possibly draft a framework agreement. When it became known that back-channel negotiations were being held in Stockholm, Yasser Abed Rabbo, who had not been invited to participate, resigned as Palestinian negotiator, accusing Israel of trying to divide the Palestinians.

The decision on the three villages came in the midst of the worst violence in years in Ramallah, Nablus, Jenin, Bethlehem, and the Jewish settlement of Nitzarim in Gaza, as demonstrations commemorating the "catastrophe," when Israel declared its statehood in May 1948, got out of hand. Israeli intelligence sources blamed Arafat for instigating the demonstrations to put pressure on Barak. Particularly disconcerting to the Israelis was the fact that Palestinian police were also involved in altercations against Israeli soldiers. Four Palestinians were killed, and over three hundred were wounded in the melees. The situation was also inflamed by the prisoner issue, and Israel's reluctance to hand over to the P.A. the approximately 1650 Palestinians still held in Israeli prisons. Nevertheless, in the midst of the fighting, the Israeli Knesset voted to hand over the three villages, indicating a kind of conviction that the situation would not escalate out of control and that both Barak and Arafat would consult each other and take measures to try to defuse the crisis. The situation quieted; however, on May 21 after an Israeli child was badly burned by a molotov cocktail in Jericho, Barak called off the back-channel talks that were going on in Stockholm.

Lebanon

The spring of 2000 had not been good months for Ehud Barak. Internal problems began to become more obvious in Israel. The government faced protests over the Golan, and there were scandals involving pre-election campaign contributions to Barak's One Israel party; monies Israeli President Weizmann had accepted from an American benefactor; and sexual escapades involving Yitzhak Mordechai, the transport minister, who eventually resigned his post. Barak's coalition partners, especially the NRP, Shas, and Yisrael B'Aliyah, had already proved themselves independent in the previous votes on talks with Syria and were becoming even more demanding and recalcitrant. Shas, for example, in return for its votes, continually attempted to squeeze budget concessions from Barak to help fund its school system, infuriating Meretz and other secular parties in the coalition. In March, Barak had survived two no-confidence motions, but there were sure to be more to come.

Externally, the situation in Lebanon had also begun to heat up. In June 1999, the South Lebanon Army had begun a withdrawal south from Jezzine, an enclave that had been in existence for fourteen years, and the deepest point of penetration of Israel's nine-mile deep "security zone" in Lebanon. Hizbullah attacks had hurt the SLA at Jezzine, however, killing over 150 militiamen and 65 civilians. After the pullback, about 200 SLA men stayed behind, taking refuge in a local monastery, whose abbot negotiated with Hizbullah for their lives. The Lebanese government, under Syria's control, refused to send in its army to fill the vacuum, in order not to appear to be agreeing to Israeli conditions. Israel had always insisted that Lebanon provide guarantees that it would control Hizbullah attacks on northern Israeli settlements in return for its possible withdrawal. The Lebanese government insisted on withdrawal with no conditions. Syria supported Hizbullah as the main tool in its efforts to force Israel to renounce control over the Golan. The situation was further complicated by the presence in Lebanon of about 370,000 Palestinians, mostly Sunni Muslims. Lebanon refused to integrate the Palestinians and pressed for their right of return to Israel. As Lebanese president Lahoud noted, many of the Palestinians were armed, and there was concern, expressed by Israel as well, that Syria, whose troops occupied some of the camps, would seek to manipulate the Palestinians and encourage them to follow the Hizbullah model of armed struggle.

With the Shepherdstown talks between Israel and Syria at a standstill by January 2000, it was no coincidence that Hizbullah stepped up its activity and that the highest-ranking SLA leader was assassinated at the end of that month. Secretary of State Albright urged Syria to restrain Hizbullah, and Barak said he would not negotiate with Syria unless it cut off support for Hizbullah, but the violence continued at its highest level in six months. Between 1995 and 1999, 123 Israeli soldiers had been killed in the "security zone," and a series of Hizbullah ambushes and bombings killed seven Israeli soldiers in three weeks in early 2000, prompting Israeli retaliatory missile attacks. Barak's election promise to leave Lebanon within a year had been one of the main reasons for his victory, and although Israel would have preferred to pull out of Lebanon after reaching a peace deal with Syria, there was growing consensus on both sides of the political divide for a unilateral withdrawal. Even Ariel Sharon, one of the architects of Israel's invasion of Lebanon in 1982, and the current Likud chairman, said that the withdrawal should start immediately.

On March 5, 2000, the Israeli cabinet pledged a withdrawal from Lebanon by July. The Israeli decision surprised and alarmed the Arab states, depriving Syria of its main pressure point against Israel and disconcerting the Lebanese government. Having established itself as a Shiite resistance movement against the Israeli presence in South Lebanon, Hizbullah's raison d'etre would be removed. With the Israelis out, and Hizbullah's need for arms reduced, the role of its patrons Syria and Iran would also presumably be diminished. While hailing the Israeli announcement as a victory for the Arabs, Syrian Foreign Minister Farouk al-Shara said that Israel would bear the consequences for pulling out, and "should never use this possibility as a means of pressure against us." However, Israeli officials expressed concern about possible Hizbullah attacks on departing troops and, once again, the vulnerability of the northern settlements. And what about the fate of the 2500 or so SLA militiamen and their families once the Israelis had left? Their chief commander, Antoine Lahad, and many others had been marked out for death sentences, and militiamen and their families, as well as the primarily Christian villagers and townspeople in the buffer zone, feared for their lives and property once the Israelis withdrew. Lahad asked for amnesty for his men if he turned himself over to the Lebanese authorities, but the offer was refused.

The UN resolutions on Lebanon, especially Resolution 425, required the consent of both the Lebanese and Israeli governments for their implementation. By the end of April, Lebanon agreed to UN forces being deployed in the buffer zone when the Israelis withdrew. Earlier, Lebanese President Lahoud set conditions for cooperating with the UN, including UN help in disarming Palestinian and other guerrillas who, it was feared, would move closer to the border and unleash attacks against Israel that would result in Israeli retaliations. Whether or not lightly armed UNIFIL troops would be able to be any more effective along the border than they had been in the areas they were deployed in since 1978 was an open question. Eager to secure international support, however, and upon the suggestion of special UN envoy Terje Roed-Larsen, Israel indicated it would redeploy behind the 1923 international boundary, the deepest possible pullback. Israel and Lebanon, still technically at war, do not have a mutually agreed border, but the 1923 line, drawn by Britain and France, was reaffirmed in the 1949 armistice agreement.

In early May, Hizbullah launched a series of rocket attacks on northern Israeli towns, leading to increased fear that the impending troop withdrawal from South Lebanon and its aftermath would result in violence and instability. Although Israel reacted with massive retaliatory strikes, these were soon called off, with a senior Israeli official saying that Israel had no interest in escalation. Cross-border incidents continued, however, with rocket attacks on Qiryat Shemona and the town of Slomi. In an effort to reassure towns and villages close to the border, Barak also announced a $400-million aid plan to attract more business and residents.

This seemed slight comfort. The United States also reportedly promised $300 million to help with the withdrawal and released $50 million in military aid to bolster security.

Israel had quietly begun moving troops and equipment out of some outposts and hoped to continue the process until the last of its troops was completely out of South Lebanon, a condition required by the UN before it would send in its troops. Eleven countries from Europe and the Americas promised to send peacekeeping troops. Lebanon, however, would not guarantee an end to guerrilla activity as long as there was no formal peace agreement between the two countries, and Hizbullah began stepping up attacks on Israeli troops in Lebanon as they prepared to withdraw.

Israel had hoped to turn over its outposts to the SLA as it withdrew its troops, and to have the time to build new roads, fences, and listening posts on the Israeli side of the border, but a stunning sequence of events ensued. Israel began to turn over military posts to the SLA, but the SLA proved unable or unwilling to hold the line. A "tumble of events" began on Thursday, May 18, when the SLA deserted a small village, and picked up steam on May 21 when Hizbullah hit an outpost on the Israeli side of the border. Hizbullah also chased the SLA from the Taibe outpost in southern Lebanon, which Israel had turned over just a week before, and claimed responsibility for an attack on Har Dov, a listening post at the edge of the Golan Heights. This attack was believed to be the first Hizbullah assault near the Syrian-Lebanese border since 1989. Its purpose was possibly to underscore the idea that the nearby Shebaa farms were also part of Lebanese territory and must be handed over by Israel. The UN, however, concluded that the area was Israeli-occupied Syrian territory, and that this area should be dealt with during negotiations with Syria, not Lebanon.

Events snowballed, catching everyone by surprise. On May 22, Hizbullah guerrillas marched to within a mile of Israel's border with Lebanon, recapturing much of the land Israeli forces had patrolled in southern Lebanon and moving to take over more territory from the SLA. By May 24, about 650 of the 2500-member SLA militia had defected, and hundreds of others fled with their families across the border to Israel. In at least one instance, militia soldiers disappeared so quickly they left tanks with motors running and their rice cooking on stoves.

Before dawn on Wednesday, May 24, six weeks before they planned to shut down the buffer zone, Israeli troops abandoned Beaufort Castle and their few remaining outposts in Lebanon, bringing home their last troops without suffering any casualties. Hizbullah fighters "giddily" rode abandoned Israeli tanks through village after village. Barak declared an end to the "18-year tragedy" and said that he would hold the governments in Beirut and Damascus responsible for any attacks on Israel's northern cities and towns.

All groups and factions hailed the great victory, including Amal, Hizbullah's traditional Shiite rival, the various Palestinian groups, and even many Christian and Muslim villagers in the buffer zone who had supported the SLA, but who now could be reunited with their relatives in the other parts of Lebanon. Hizbullah, through its leader Sheikh Nasrollah, whose eldest son Muhammad Hadi, had been killed in an encounter in the "security zone" in 1997, said that it would not lay down its arms, but he also went out of his way to hail the Hizbullah triumph as a victory for all the Lebanese and even to speak against the backdrop of a Lebanese flag. Hizbullah quickly moved in to offer services that had formerly been provided by the Israelis, sending in doctors, nurses, veterinarians, bulldozers, agronomists, and engineers and operating as a kind of parallel government offering social services, development loans, and reconstruction aid. Its network of social services and institutions had already helped it become one of Lebanon's stongest political forces, and in the impending elections in August, Hizbullah would certainly try to parlay its military success against Israel into electoral votes.

Syria, which had 35,000 or more troops in Lebanon, did not do much except congratulate Hizbullah. Nor did the Lebanese government step in. However, Lebanon's parliament moved to the south on May 31 for a special session in the former Israeli occupied zone—less than two miles from Israel's border. Lawmakers pledged a reconstruction package. The area, with

A crowd of Lebanese walk on the border with Israel in the village of Kfar Kila in South Lebanon, May 25, 2000, a day after the last Israeli soldiers left southern Lebanon after eighteen years of occupation.

about 120,000 people, had been cut off from the rest of the country during the occupation and had been virtually a part of Israel, which provided electricity, water, telephones, hospitals, and jobs.

After several weeks of haggling over the Shebaa farms territory and isolated Israeli military outposts, UN Secretary General Kofi Annan certified that Israel had withdrawn completely from Lebanon, and the Security Council endorsed the pullout. In mid-June, Annan visited the area and even met and shook hands with Sheikh Nasrollah. Annan's special representative in the region, Terje Roed-Larsen, indicated that UNIFIL would be increased to 5600 troops from the 4400 then in Lebanon and tasked with keeping peace along the border. Meanwhile, family reunions took place across the fences, Lebanese flocked for Sunday outings to view Israel, there was some rock throwing back and forth, but business was good for food and souvenir vendors. For some 2200 former SLA members who surrendered to the Lebanese authorities, trials were held in a military court beginning in June 2000. Hundreds were sentenced to prison terms of up to 15 years, and some SLA leaders who escaped were sentenced to death in absentia. About 6000 Lebanese sought refuge in Israel.

Camp David II

Meanwhile, steps were being taken to revive the stalled peace talks on the Israel–Palestinian front, which had been overshadowed by the events in Lebanon. In one development, Israeli and Palestinian negotiators met in Jericho to discuss release of the 1650 Palestinian prisoners. On June 1, after Israel agreed to allow more liberal family visitations, study through Palestinian universities, more telephone privileges, etc., the 500 or so who had been on a liquid diet for a month gave up their hunger strike, thus averting a further round of street protests. There was, however, no immediate resolution of this issue.

On June 5, 2000, Albright began a 3-day Middle East swing that included a meeting with Barak, a conversation with Arafat, and a meeting with Syrian and Egyptian officials in Cairo. Rumors began to fly that Barak was ready to relinquish over 90 percent of the West Bank to the Palestinians, including at least part of the Jordan valley, and to grant them municipal authority over part of Jerusalem. This precipitated a parliamentary crisis in Israel, with a majority of the Knesset members voting for a preliminary bill to dissolve the government and move to new elections. Clearly, Barak was on very shaky ground.

In the midst of this swirl of events came the startling news on June 10, 2000, that President Assad of Syria had died. There had been talk for years about his failing health, and different scenarios had been posed for when the inevitable occurred, but the news still came suddenly and unexpectedly. Perhaps with some kind of premonition, Assad had planned to convene a meeting of the Baath party the next week in order to receive its endorsement of his son Bashar to succeed him. The night of Assad's death, the party's leaders met and unanimously nominated Bashar for the post of president, and the parliament held a special session to amend the constitution, reducing the minimum age for president from 40 to 34 years of age (Bashar's age). Vice President Abdul Halim Khaddam appointed Bashar commander of the armed forces, after promoting him from colonel to lieutenant-general, and at the Baath party congress, the first in 15 years, held as scheduled by Assad the next week, Bashar was unanimously elected the party's secretary-general and nominated formally by the entire membership to be president. He was then endorsed by the 250-member parliament, and on July 10, in a yes or no vote, over 97 percent of the population confirmed him as president.

Bashar Assad is a British-trained eye doctor, who became the heir-apparent after the death in a car accident of his more flamboyant and favored brother, Basil. Bashar became Syria's representative in Lebanon; he also led an anti-corruption drive in Syria that resulted in the dismissal, resignation and, in one case, suicide of former officials. Recent currency and investment laws put in place by presidential decree were widely attributed to him, and he headed a group called the Computer Society, which advocated computer literacy in a country where satellite dishes were forbidden and mobile phones have just recently been permitted. Young and knowledgeable about the West, like his new counterparts in Jordan, Morocco (King Hassan having died in July 1999), Bahrain, and Qatar, it was hoped by some commentators that he would initiate economic and political changes internally in Syria and perhaps even bring Syria back to the negotiating table with Israel. However, given the Old Guard still in powerful positions especially in the Baath party, the challenge posed by Hafezal-Assad's brother Rifaat, who coveted the position himself and publicly expressed his desire to oust Bashar, and the fact that the Assad family are Alawites and represent only 10 to 12 percent of the population (which is mostly Sunni Muslim), it was likely that Bashar would first have to consolidate his power internally. Syria would be removed for some time from Arab–Israeli peace negotiations. This turned attention once again to Israel and the Palestinians.

Throughout June, the United States was actively involved in trying to facilitate final status talks. With Ross in the area, and Albright expected, Barak began to push for a three-way summit to achieve a framework agreement. It was clear that the Palestinians resisted the idea of a summit because they feared the combined pressure upon them of the United States and Israel. Albright arrived on June 27, but after intensive discussions with both sides, she announced that perhaps the time was not yet right for a summit.

Events then began to assume a logic of their own. Frustrated with the lack of progress, Arafat began to renew threats of a unilateral declaration of statehood and to warn that violence could erupt if the September 13 deadline for a final peace agreement were not met. On July 3,

2000, the PLO Central Council, the chief policymaking body of the Palestinians, wrapped up two days of closed-door meetings in Gaza and issued a statement telling the Palestinians to get ready for statehood by September 13 and stating their determination to declare independence by that time, whether or not a permanent peace deal was reached with Israel. It was clear that if a unilateral declaration of statehood were made, Israel might respond by annexing swaths of the West Bank and violence could result.

With these developments, President Clinton, on July 5, said that he would summon Barak and Arafat to Camp David for summit meetings to begin on July 11 to arrive at a framework agreement for a final peace settlement. It was a grave risk for the president, and also for the Palestinians and Israelis. The immediate response in Israel was the defection from Barak's coalition of Sharansky's party, with its 4 seats, the NRP, with its 5 seats, and Shas, with its 17, leaving Barak with a minority government of 42 of 120 members. On the very eve of the summit, Barak narrowly escaped a no-confidence vote in the Knesset. A summit would also put pressure on Arafat, who might be offered and pressured to accept significant concessions on Israel's part that fell short of Palestinian aspirations and declared positions. With the American elections impending, though, failure would mean the end of the whole process for the foreseeable future and unpredictable results should the parties take matters into their own hands.

The Camp David summit opened on July 11, 2000, but after 15 days of intense negotiations that often lasted well into the night, it ended on July 25 with no resolution of the issues. President Clinton was on hand, except for a brief trip to Japan to attend the G8 summit, and took an active role, along with Albright, Sandy Berger, the U.S. National Security Advisor, and Dennis Ross. Despite high hopes, the "red lines" of the two sides as they entered the talks were unbridgeable. On borders, Israel offered to withdraw from over 90 percent of the West Bank, exclusive of Jerusalem and its environs, but wanted to annex those parts of the West Bank and Gaza with major Jewish settlements closest to Israel proper and possibly retain part of the Jordan valley. Presumably, Israeli settlements not annexed by Israel would be evacuated. The Palestinians insisted on Israel withdrawing from all the territory captured in the 1967 war, including all of the West Bank, the Gaza Strip, and East Jerusalem.

On Jerusalem, Israel would turn over Abu Dis and other suburbs of East Jerusalem to the Palestinians for the capital of a Palestinian state. Israel would also give Palestinians municipal autonomy in parts of East Jerusalem as well as the right to fly the Palestinian flag over the Muslim and Christian holy places. But Israel would not surrender sovereignty of East Jerusalem to the Palestinians, as Arafat demanded and on which he would not yield. On the question of refugees, the Palestinians demanded the right of return of all the refugees and their descendants displaced by Israel's creation in 1948 and an admission by Israel of responsibility for their plight. Israel refused to accept moral or legal responsibility for the refugee problem and wanted it solved not by repatriation but by compensation through international aid. Despite the news blackout from Camp David, some "give" was reported on some of the issues, but the talks foundered on the question of Jerusalem. There did not seem to be any way that Israel would share sovereignty over the city or give up parts of East Jerusalem to the Palestinians, and no way that Arafat could accept less than full sovereignty over all of East Jerusalem, which the Palestinians desire as the capital of a Palestinian state.

There were some positive results from the Camp David summit, however. For the first time, the principal players, Arafat and Barak, had met face-to-face to discuss the most intractable issues, including Jerusalem, and there seemed a desire to reach some kind of agreement. President Clinton praised Barak, in particular, for the concessions he appeared willing to make, but both men were the clear losers at Camp David. Clinton did not get the breakthrough agreement he had hoped would cap his presidency, and Barak returned to Israel to face another no-confidence vote, which he survived, but only barely. In another embarrassment, the Knesset elected Moshe Katsav over Shimon Peres as the new president of the state to replace

Ezer Weizman, who had resigned over fraud allegations. Peres, an architect of the Oslo accords, former prime minister and Nobel laureate, was the clear favorite of the Israeli public, but he was tainted with the failures and suspicions of the peace process. Katsav, an Iranian-born Likud legislator, won the victory in a largely political vote in the Knesset. Despite these setbacks, however, because the Knesset began a three-month recess until October, Barak was more free to pursue his own agenda, and perhaps for the Palestinians there was an opportunity to continue negotiating, since under a different, presumably hawkish, Israeli government, they could not count on the same concessions offered by Barak.

Unlike Barak, Arafat returned to Gaza in a blaze of glory, hailed as a new Saladin, who had held his ground and had not given an inch on any of the Palestinian positions. He again reiterated that he would declare a state by September 13 with or without an agreement with Israel. But what kind of state would it be? And of what would it consist? And how would the Palestinians wrest control of the water supplies and other resources now controlled by Israel? And would Israel move in to annex portions of the West Bank? Would violence result? Would the armies of the other Arab states be involved? These were all worrisome questions.

The Al-Aqsa Intifada and Collapse of the Peace Process

In early September, the 129-member Palestinian Central Committee, after a two-day debate, decided to postpone a declaration of statehood on September 13. Palestinian anger and frustration toward Israel, the Palestinian Authority, and the entire Oslo process simmered, however. Palestinians chafed under what they considered continued Israeli control over their daily lives and resented the expansion of Jewish settlements in the West Bank. They also felt betrayed by the Palestinian Authority, which seemed to be in collusion with Israel and which they accused of corruption and fraud; and they were disillusioned by the entire Oslo process, which they had been led to believe would result in the return of all the occupied territory, including East Jerusalem. The impasse at Camp David seemed to bring the whole process to a halt. There were efforts to get the two sides together again, and in late September Arafat traveled to Barak's home at Kochav Yair where the two evidently spent a pleasant evening together. Nothing substantive resulted, however, and a few days later came the spark that ignited the tinderbox situation that had been in the making.

On September 28, Likud leader Ariel Sharon visited the Temple Mount/Haram al-Sharif, accompanied by a phalanx of Israeli police. Although Sharon did not enter the al-Aqsa mosque ("the furthest mosque") or the Dome of the Rock, the Muslim sacred sites built on the Mount, he did make a speech in which he pledged that Israel would never give up the Mount. This provocative act, and the massive police presence, touched off riots the next day, in which Palestinian demonstrators were fired on by Israeli soldiers. The deaths of several young Palestinians in the melee set off a cycle of violence that escalated and that resulted in the next six months in the deaths of close to 500 people and the wounding of more than 8,000, most of them Palestinians. At first called the "al-Aqsa Intifada," this new wave of violence resembled all-out warfare more than the "shaking off" of the original intifada. Rock-throwing Palestinian youths were joined by armed Palestinian police against Israeli soldiers hurling tear gas and firing rubber-coated and sometimes live bullets, backed up by tanks and Blackhawk helicopter gunships. In Gaza, a twelve-year-old Palestinian boy was caught in the crossfire and killed; and in Ramallah, two Israeli reservists were murdered at a Palestinian police outpost, and one was thrown out a window and his body beaten and trampled upon by the crowd. Murders of Israelis were avenged by rockets and bombs hitting Palestinian offices and targets in Gaza and the West Bank. In a disquieting development, Israeli Arabs were also affected, many joining in pro-Palestinian demonstrations within Israel and several being killed. Joseph's Tomb in Nablus, which housed a Yeshiva (Jewish institution

An Israeli security guard holds his hand over the face of opposition leader Ariel Sharon to protect him from rocks being thrown by Palestinians during his visit to the Temple Mount/Haram al-Sharif on September 28, 2000.

of higher learning) of Israeli settlers, was desecrated by Palestinians, and Hizbullah, in a well-planned operation, ambushed and captured three Israeli soldiers at the Lebanese border.

Two weeks into the escalating violence, in mid-October, President Clinton was able to convene a summit at Sharm al-Sheikh, co-hosted by Egyptian President Hosni Mubarak, in which the two sides by unwritten agreement decided to issue public statements calling for an end of violence. However, the cease-fire agreement was never implemented as clashes continued and became even more deadly. As the Palestinian death toll mounted as a result of IDF attacks, the UN passed a resolution condemning Israel for the use of excessive force. In addition to its military response, Israel imposed strict economic sanctions. Border closures, the blocking of roads in the Gaza strip, and the isolation of Palestinian towns behind IDF checkpoints, prevented imports, blocked exports, and completely disrupted the Palestinian economy.

On the Palestinian side, paramilitary organizations linked to Fatah, like the grassroots "Tanzim," with branches in nearly every town, village, and refugee camp in the West Bank and Gaza, cooperated with Hamas and Islamic Jihad in a loose group called the Nationalist and Islamic Movement. Muhammad Dahlan, the head of the Palestinian security forces in Gaza, who until September had worked closely with Israeli security officials and the CIA to thwart terrorist attacks, confirmed that he was part of a tactical alliance among many Palestinian factions, and that he was working closely with Marwan Barghouti, the acknowledged Tanzim leader. The result was sniper attacks and the planting of roadside and car bombs that blew up Israeli busses and shops and killed or injured Israeli children and adults.

An Arab summit in Cairo condemned Israel, and Arab countries with ties to Israel cut those ties. Egypt eventually recalled its ambassador, and the new Jordanian ambassador to Israel delayed presenting his credentials. In early November, at the urging of Leah Rabin, who

Demonstrators walk past a wall with a painting showing 12-year-old Mohammed al-Durra, who was killed October 2, 2000, in crossfire between Israeli troops and Palestinian demonstrators.

An Israeli soldier is thrown from a Palestinian police station window in the West Bank city of Ramallah Thursday, October 12, 2000. He was one of two Israeli soldiers who were killed after they sought shelter in the police station. (Photo from TV.)

died shortly thereafter, Barak reluctantly sent Shimon Peres to meet with Arafat, and the two agreed on a series of steps based on the Sharm al-Sheikh understanding. However, the truce that was to have gone into effect was sabotaged by a bomb in Mahane Yehuda market in Jerusalem. And shortly after Clinton met with Arafat and then Barak in Washington in mid-November, a powerful roadside bomb ripped apart an armored settlers' school bus in Gaza, killing two adults and maiming several children. Arafat attempted to internationalize the conflict. After he unsuccessfully lobbied the Security Council to authorize an international force to keep the peace, he traveled to Moscow to enlist the aid of Vladimir Putin. Putin did intervene, getting Arafat and Barak to agree to some cooperation among their respective security forces, but this cooperation broke down as violent clashes continued to occur all over the West Bank and Gaza on a daily basis.

Meanwhile, the political situation in Israel became even more unstable, creating added uncertainty. Barak, who had failed to bring the Likud into a National Unity government, turned again to Shas, which agreed in October to support Barak for at least a month when the Knesset reconvened, in return for his dropping a plan to initiate a "secular" and "civic" revolution in Israel. His capacity to govern in doubt, however, Barak preempted his opponents and resigned in early December, which meant that elections for a new prime minister would have to be held within 60 days. He may have taken this move to prevent Benjamin Netanyahu, who was not currently a sitting member of the Knesset and was therefore ineligible, from running for office. Nevertheless, Netanyahu, who had been cleared of corruption charges, publicly announced his candidacy for prime minister. Although public opinion polls indicated he would win overwhelmingly, he did not receive enough votes in the Knesset to amend the law to enable him to run. That left Ariel Sharon, the current Likud leader and the Israeli figure most loathed by the Palestinians, to face Barak in elections to be held on February 6, 2001.

In late 2000, with the dissolution of his government, Barak realized that his only hope of re-election depended upon ending the al-Aqsa Intifada and reaching agreement with Arafat. As the election process began, he explored the basis of a possible agreement in which Israel would offer concessions on the Jerusalem issue in exchange for Palestinian flexibility regarding refugee resettlement. Israel would agree to Palestinian sovereignty over the Temple Mount/Haram al-Sharif and its mosques, and Arafat would abandon dreams of attaining recognition for a right of return of the Palestinian refugees. Barak also publicly for the first time said that he would be willing to recognize a Palestinian state.

While these events were occurring, in the United States the November election for president produced no clear winner for weeks, creating a bizarre situation already compromised by the lame-duck status of Bill Clinton that distracted the attention of officials in Washington. Dennis Ross, Clinton's special Middle East envoy, announced that he was stepping down, and, with George W. Bush having been declared president, it was clear that the United States would not be directly involved in the Israeli–Palestinian situation. In December, Clinton, in his last weeks in office, suggested some "bridging proposals." These included Israel's withdrawal from all of the Gaza Strip and 94 to 96 percent of the West Bank. For the 4 to 6 percent retained by Israel, the Palestinians would be compensated from Israeli territory. Obviously, most of the Jewish settlements would be dismantled, except for those in the territory to be annexed to Israel. On Jerusalem, Palestinians would have sovereignty over the Arab neighborhoods and Israel over the Jewish neighborhoods. Various options were proposed for the Old City and the Temple Mount/Haram al-Sharif, including Palestinian control over the platform itself and Israeli control over the Western Wall and the area below. There was even an idea to declare divine sovereignty over the area, with the Palestinians continuing to exercise de facto control over the mosques, as they have since 1967. There would be a "right of return" for the Palestinian refugees, but (except for a few allowed to return to Israel on humanitarian grounds) only to the areas of the West Bank and Gaza that would become the Palestinian state. These "parameters" became the basis for a last-ditch and rather desperate effort to reach a settlement before the Israeli elections. The negotiating teams met at

Taba in mid-January 2001 and reportedly came very close to an agreement, but the talks ultimately foundered on the questions of sovereignty over the Temple Mount/Haram al-Sharif and over the "right of return."

The Election Victory of Ariel Sharon

On February 6, 2001, Ariel Sharon was elected prime minister of Israel, receiving 62.5 percent of the votes to 34.7 percent for Barak. Only 59 percent of the electorate turned out, as most Arab Israelis (12.5 percent of the population) and many Israeli Jews sat out the election, which, in any event, was only for the prime minister. Arab Israelis, who had voted overwhelmingly for Barak in 1999, were protesting the deaths of thirteen of their community during the first days of the al-Aqsa Intifada, and the fact that Barak had not followed through on any of his campaign promises to improve their situation within Israel. Israeli Jews who had voted for Barak previously were disheartened and disillusioned by the recent violence, and the fact that it had occurred so soon after an Israeli leader had offered the Palestinians the most sweeping concessions they could imagine, including a state in most of the West Bank and Gaza, and a shared sovereignty over Jerusalem. In a situation that was reminiscent of Netanyahu's election in 1996, Israelis, deeply pessimistic that peace with the Palestinians was ever possible, or that Arafat was a true partner for peace, voted for security. The collapse of the "center" in Israel boded ill for future peace prospects.

For their part, Palestinians saw the Sharon victory as proof that Israel was not serious about peace, since Sharon was on record as saying that he would never share Jerusalem, and that no more territory would be given up to the Palestinians. He was also adamantly opposed to any "right of return" of Palestinians refugees. Palestinian groups like Hamas and Islamic Jihad, and others opposed to negotiations with the Jewish state on ideological as well as pragmatic grounds, were encouraged by this turn of events. Although Arafat said that he would continue to extend his hand in peace, his own position as leader was in danger of being challenged by younger and more radical elements within the Palestinian population.

After the election, Barak angrily resigned as Labor party chairman, quit his Knesset seat, and put his political and diplomatic activities on hold. With Barak out of the picture, about two-thirds of the Labor party's 1,700-member governing body voted to accept eight ministerial positions in a national unity government. It was by no means clear, however, that a stable coalition would result, or that Sharon would be able to provide the security he had promised, at least not in the short term.

 DOCUMENT 12–1

Wye River Memorandum [Excerpts]

The following are steps to facilitate implementation of the Interim Agreement on the west Bank and Gaza Strip of September 28, 1995 (the "Interim Agreement") and other related agreements including the Note for the Record of January 17, 1997 (hereinafter referred to as "the prior agreements") so that the Israeli and Palestinian sides can more effectively carry out their reciprocal responsibilities, including those relating to further redeployments and security respectively. These steps are to be carried out in a parallel phased approach in accordance with this Memorandum and the attached time line. They are subject to the relevant terms and conditions of the prior agreements and do not supersede their other agreements.

I. Further Redeployments
A. Phase One and Two Further Redeployments

1. Pursuant to the Interim Agreement and subsequent agreements, the Israeli side's implementation of the first and second F.R.D. will consist of the transfer to the Palestinian side of 13 percent from Area C as follows:

1% to Area (A)

12% to Area (B)

The Palestinian side has informed that it will allocate an area/areas amounting to 3% from the above Area (B) to be designated as Green Areas and/or Nature Reserves. The Palestinian side has further informed that they will act according to the established scientific standards, and that therefore there will be no changes in the status of these areas, without prejudice to the rights of the existing inhabitants in these areas including Bedouins; while these standards do not allow new construction in these areas, existing roads and buildings may be maintained.

The Israeli side will retain in these Green Areas/Nature Reserves the overriding security responsibility for the purpose of protecting Israelis and confronting the threat of terrorism. Activities and movements of the Palestinian Police forces may be carried out after coordination and confirmation; the Israeli side will respond to such requests expeditiously.

2. As part of the foregoing implementation of the first and second F.R.D., 14.2% from Area (B) will become Area (A).

. . .

II. Security

In the provisions on security arrangements of the Interim Agreement, the Palestinian side agreed to take all measures necessary in order to prevent acts of terrorism, crime and hostilities directed against the Israeli side, against individuals falling under the Israeli side's authority and against their property, just as the Israeli side agreed to take all measures necessary in order to prevent acts of terrorism, crime and hostilities directed against the Palestinian side, against individuals falling under the Palestinian side's authority and against their property. The two sides also agreed to take legal measures against offenders within their jurisdiction and to prevent incitement against each other by any organizations, groups or individuals within their jurisdiction.

. . .

Pursuant to the prior agreements, the Palestinian side's implementation of its responsibilities for security, security cooperation, and other issues will be as detailed below during the time periods specified in the attached tile line:

A. Security Actions

1. Outlawing and Combating Terrorist Organizations

- The Palestinian side will make known its policy of zero tolerance for terror and violence against both sides.
- A work plan developed by the Palestinian side will be shared with the U.S. and thereafter implementation will begin immediately to ensure the systematic and effective combat of terrorist organizations and their infrastructure.
- In addition to the bilateral Israeli-Palestinian security cooperation, a U.S.-Palestinian committee will meet biweekly to review the steps being taken to eliminate terrorist cells and the support structure that plans, finances, supplies and abets terror. In these meetings, the Palestinian side will inform the U.S. fully of the actions it has taken to outlaw all organizations (or wings of organizations, as appropriate) of a military, terrorist or violent character and their support structure and to prevent them from operating in areas under its jurisdiction.

- The Palestinian side will apprehend the specific individuals suspected of perpetrating acts of violence and terror for the purpose of further investigation, and prosecution and punishment of all persons involved in acts of violence and terror.
- A U.S.-Palestinian committee will meet to review and evaluate information pertinent to the decisions on prosecution, punishment or other legal measures which affect the status of individuals suspected of abetting or perpetrating acts of violence and terror.

2. Prohibiting Illegal Weapons
- The Palestinian side will ensure an effective legal framework is in place to criminalize, in conformity with the prior agreements, any importation, manufacturing or unlicensed sale, acquisition of possession of firearms, ammunition or weapons in areas under Palestinian jurisdiction.
- In addition, the Palestinian side will establish and vigorously and continuously implement a systematic program for the collection and appropriate handling of all such illegal items in accordance with the prior agreements. The U.S. has agreed to assist in carrying out this program.
- A U.S.-Palestinian-Israeli committee will be established to assist and enhance cooperation in preventing the smuggling or other unauthorized introduction of weapons or explosive materials into areas under Palestinian jurisdiction.

3. Preventing Incitement
- Drawing on relevant international practice and pursuant to Article XXII (1) of the Interim Agreement and the Note for the Record, the Palestinian side will issue a decree prohibiting all forms of incitement to violence or terror, and establishing mechanisms for acting systematically against all expressions or threats of violence or terror. This decree will be comparable to the existing Israeli legislation which deals with the same subject.
- A U.S.-Palestinian-Israeli committee will meet on a regular basis to monitor cases of possible incitement to violence or terror and to make recommendations and reports on how to prevent such incitement. The Israeli, Palestinian and U.S. sides will each appoint a media specialist, a law enforcement representative, an educational specialist and a current or former elected official to the committee.

B. *Security Cooperation*

The two sides agree that their security cooperation will be based on a spirit of partnership and will include, among other things, the following steps:

1. Bilateral Cooperation

   There will be full bilateral security cooperation between the two sides which will be continuous, intensive and comprehensive.

2. Forensic Cooperation

   There will be an exchange of forensic expertise, training, and other assistance.

3. Trilateral Committee

   In addition to the bilateral Israeli-Palestinian security cooperation, a high-ranking U.S.-Palestinian–Israeli committee will meet as required and not less than biweekly to assess current threats, deal with any impediments to effective security cooperation and coordination and address the steps being taken to combat terror and terrorist organizations. The committee will also serve as a forum to address the issue of external support for terror.

   In these meetings, the Palestinian side will fully inform the members of the committee of the results of its investigations concerning terrorist suspects already in custody and the participants will exchange additional relevant information. The committee will report regularly to the leaders of the two sides on the status of cooperation, the results of the meetings and its recommendations.

C. Other Issues

1. Palestinian Police Force
   - The Palestinian side will provide a list of its policemen to the Israeli side in conformity with the prior agreements.
   - Should the Palestinian side request technical assistance, the U.S. has indicated its willingness to help meet their needs in cooperation with other donors.
   - The Monitoring and Steering Committee will, as part of its functions, monitor the implementation of this provision and brief the U.S.

2. *PLO Charter*

    The Executive Committee of the Palestine Liberation Organization and the Palestinian Central Council will reaffirm the letter of 22 January 1998 from PLO Chairman Yasir Arafat to President Clinton concerning the nullification of the Palestinian National Charter provisions that are inconsistent with the letters exchanged between the PLO and the Government of Israel on 9/10 September 1993. PLO Chairman Arafat, the Speaker of the Palestine National Council, and the Speaker of the Palestinian Council will invite the members of the PNC, as well as the members of the Central Council, the Council, and the Palestinian Heads of Ministries to a meeting to be addressed by President Clinton to reaffirm their support for the peace process and the aforementioned decisions of the Executive Committee and the Central Council.

. . .

III.   Interim Committees and Economic Issues

1. The Israeli and Palestinian sides reaffirm their commitment to enhancing their relationship and agree on the need to actively promote economic development in the West Bank and Gaza. In this regard, the parties agree to continue or to reactivate all standing committees established by the Interim Agreement, including the Monitoring and Steering Committee, the Joint Economic Committee (JEC), the Civil Affairs Committee (CAV), the Legal Committee, and the Standing Cooperation Committee.
2. The Israeli and Palestinian sides have agreed on arrangements which will permit the timely opening of the Gaza Industrial Estate. They also have concluded a "Protocol Regarding the Establishment and Operation of the International Airport in the Gaza Strip During the Interim Period."
3. Both sides will renew negotiations on Safe Passage immediately. As regards the southern route, the sides will make best efforts to conclude the agreement within a week of the entry into force of this Memorandum. Operation of the southern route will start as soon as possible thereafter. As regards the northern route, negotiations will continue with the goal of reaching agreement as soon as possible. Implementation will take place expeditiously thereafter.
4. The Israeli and Palestinian sides acknowledge the great importance of the Port of Gaza for the development of the Palestinian economy, and the expansion of Palestinian trade. They commit themselves to proceeding without delay to conclude an agreement to allow the construction and operation of the port in accordance with the prior agreements. The Israeli-Palestinian Committee will reactivate its work immediately with a goal of concluding the protocol within sixty days, which will allow commencement of the construction of the port.
5. The two sides recognize that unresolved legal issues adversely affect the relationship between to two peoples. They therefore will accelerate efforts through the Legal Committee to address outstanding legal issues and to implement solutions to these issues in the shortest possible period. The Palestinian side will provide to the Israeli side copies of all of its laws in effect.

6. The Israeli and Palestinian sides also will launch a strategic economic dialogue to enhance their economic relationship. They will establish within the frameword of the JEC an Ad Hoc Committee for this purpose. The committee will review the following four issues:
   1. Israeli purchase taxes;
   2. cooperation in combating vehicle theft;
   3. dealing with unpaid Palestinian debts; and
   4. the impact of Israeli standards as barriers to trade and the expansion of the A1 and A2 lists.
      The committee will submit an interim report within three weeks of the entry into force of this Memorandum, and within six weeks will submit its conclusions and recommendations to be implemented.
7. The two sides agree on the importance of continued international donor assistance to facilitate implementation by both sides of agreements reached. They also recognize the need for enhanced donor support for economic development in the West Bank and Gaza. They agree to jointly approach the donor community to organize a Ministerial Conference before the end of 1998 to seek pledges for enhanced levels of assistance.

IV. Permanent Status Negotiations

The two sides will immediately resume permanent status negotiations on an accelerated basis and will make a determined effort to achieve the mutual goal of reaching an agreement by may 4, 1999. The negotiations will be continuous and without interruption. The U.S. has expressed its willingness to facilitate these negotiations.

V. Unilateral Actions

Recognizing the necessity to create a positive environment for the negotiations, neither side shall initiate or take any step that will change the status of the West Bank and the Gaza Strip in accordance with the Interim Agreement.

Attachment: Time Line

This Memorandum will enter into force ten days from the date of signature.

Done at Washington, D.C. this 23d day of October 1998.

For the Government of the State of Israel:
Benjamin Netanyahu

For the PLO:
Yassir Arafat

Wittnessed by:
William J. Clinton, The United States of America

Source: The Middle East, 9th ed. (Washington, DC: Congressional Quarterly, Inc., 2000), pp. 568–572.

 **DOCUMENT 12-2**

UN Resolution 425 (1978) [On Lebanon]

Adopted by the Security Council at its 2074th meeting on 19 March 1978,

The Security Council,

Taking note of the letters from the Permanent Representative of Lebanon and from the Permanent Representative of Israel, Having heard the statement of the Permanent Representatives of Lebanon and Israel, Gravely concerned at the deterioration of the situation in the Middle East and its consequences to the maintenance of international peace, Convinced that the present situation impedes the achievement of a just peace in the Middle East,

1. Calls for strict respect for the territorial integrity, sovereignty and political independence of Lebanon within its internationally recognized boundaries;

2. Calls upon Israel **immediately** to cease its military action against Lebanese territorial integrity and withdraw forthwith its forces from all Lebanese territory;

3. Decides, in the light of the request of the Government of Lebanon, to establish **immediately** under its authority a United Nations interim force for Southern Lebanon for the purpose of confirming the withdrawal of Israeli forces, restoring international peace and security and assisting the Government of Lebanon in ensuring the return of its effective authority in the area, the Force to be composed of personnel drawn from Member States;

4. Requests the Secretary-General to report to the Council **within twenty-four hours** on the implementation of the present resolution.

 DOCUMENT 12-3

The Sharm el-Sheikh Memorandum

The Sharm el-Sheikh Memorandum on Implementation Timeline of Outstanding Commitments of Agreements Signed and the Resumption of Permanent Status Negotiations

The Government of the State of Israel ("GOI") and the Palestine Liberation Organization ("PLO") commit themselves to full and mutual implementation of the Interim Agreement and all other agreements concluded between them since September 1993 (hereinafter "the prior agreements"), and all outstanding commitments emanating from the prior agreements. Without derogating from the other requirements of the prior agreements, the two Sides have agreed as follows:

1. Permanent Status negotiations:
   a. In the context of the implementation of the prior agreements, the two Sides will resume the Permanent Status negotiations in an accelerated manner and will make a determined effort to achieve their mutual goal of reaching a Permanent Status Agreement based on the agreed agenda i.e. the specific issues reserved for Permanent Status negotiators and other issues of common interest;
   b. The two sides reaffirm their understanding that the negotiations on the Permanent Status will lead to the implementation of Security Council Resolutions 242 and 338;
   c. The two Sides will make a determined effort to conclude a Framework Agreement on all Permanent Status issues in five months from the resumption of the Permanent Status negotiations;
   d. The two Sides will conclude a comprehensive agreement on all Permanent Status issues within one year from the resumption of the Permanent Status negotiations;
   e. Permanent Status negotiations will resume after the implementation of the first stage of release of prisoners and the second stage of the First and Second Further Redeployments and not later than September 13, 1999. In the Wye River Memorandum, the United States has expressed its willingness to facilitate these negotiations.

2. Phase One and Phase Two of the Further Redeployments
   The Israeli Side undertakes the following with regard to Phase One and Phase Two of the Further Redeployments:
   a. On September 5, 1999, to transfer 7% from Area C to Area B;
   b. On November 15, 1999, to transfer 2% from Area B to Area A and 3% from Area C to Area B;

c. On January 20, 2000, to transfer 1% from Area C to Area A, and 5.1% from Area B to Area A.

3. Release of Prisoners
   a. The two Sides shall establish a joint committee that shall follow-up on matters related to release of Palestinian prisoners;
   b. The Government of Israel shall release Palestinian and other prisoners who committed their offences prior to September 13, 1993, and were arrested prior to May 4, 1994. The Joint Committee shall agree on the names of those who will be released in the first two stages. Those lists shall be recommended to the relevant Authorities through the Monitoring and Steering Committee;
   c. The first stage of release of prisoners shall be carried out on September 5, 1999 and shall consist of 200 prisoners. The second stage of release of prisoners shall be carried out on October 8, 1999 and shall consist of 150 prisoners;
   d. The joint committee shall recommend further lists of names to be released to the relevant Authorities through the Monitoring and Steering Committee;
   e. The Israeli side will aim to release Palestinian prisoners before next Ramadan.

4. Committees
   a. The Third Further Redeployment Committee shall commence its activities not later than September 13, 1999;
   b. The Monitoring and Steering Committee, all Interim Committees (i.e. CAC, JEC, JSC, legal committee, people to people), as well as Wye River Memorandum committees shall resume and/or continue their activity, as the case may be, not later than September 13, 1999. The Monitoring and Steering Committee will have on its agenda, inter alia, the Year 2000, Donor/PA projects in Area C, and the issue of industrial estates;
   c. The Continuing Committee on displaced persons shall resume its activity on October 1, 1999 (Article XXVII, Interim Agreement);
   d. Not later than October 30, 1999, the two Sides will implement the recommendations of the Ad-hoc Economic Committee (Article III-6, WRM).

5. Safe Passage
   a. The operation of the Southern Route of the Safe Passage for the movement of persons, vehicles, and goods will start on October 1, 999 (Annex 1, Article X, Interim Agreement) in accordance with the details of operation, which will be provided for in the Safe Passage Protocol that will be concluded by the two Sides not later than September 30, 1999;
   b. The two Sides will agree on the specific location of the crossing point of the Northern Route of the Safe Passage as specified in Annex I, Article X, provision c-4, in the Interim Agreement not later than October 5, 1999;
   c. The Safe Passage Protocol applied to the Southern Route of the Safe Passage shall apply to the Northern Route of the Safe Passage with relevant agreed modifications;
   d. Upon the agreement on the location of the crossing point of the Northern Route of the Safe Passage, construction of the needed facilities and related procedures shall commence and shall be ongoing. At the same time, temporary facilities will be established for the operation of the Northern Route not later than four months from the agreement on the specific location of the crossing-point;
   e. In between the operation of the Southern crossing point of the Save Passage and the Northern crossing point of the Safe Passage, Israel will facilitate arrangements for the movement between the West Bank and the Gaza Strip, using non-Safe Passage routes other than the Southern Route of the Safe Passage;

   f. The location of the crossing points shall be without prejudice to the Permanent Status negotiations (Annex 1, Article X, provision e, Interim Agreement).

6. Gaza Sea Port

     The two Sides have agreed on the following principles to facilitate and enable the construction works of the Gaza Sea Port. The principles shall not prejudice or preempt the outcome of negotiations on the Permanent Status:

   a. The Israeli Side agrees that the Palestinian Side shall commence construction works in and related to the Gaza Sea Port on October 1, 1999;

   b. The two Sides agree that the Gaza Sea Port will not be operated in any way before reaching a joint Sea Port protocol on all aspects of operating the Port, including security;

   c. The Gaza Sea Port is a special case, like the Gaza Airport, being situated in an area under the responsibility of the Palestinian Side and serving as an international passage. Therefore, until the conclusion of a joint Sea Port Protocol, all activities and arrangements relating to the construction of the Port shall be in accordance with the provisions of the Interim Agreement, especially those relating to international passages, as adapted in the Gaza Airport Protocol;

   d. The construction shall ensure adequate provision for effective security and customs inspection of people and goods, as well as the establishment of a designated checking area in the Port;

   e. In this context, the Israeli side will facilitate on an on-going basis the works related to the construciton of the Gaza Sea Port, including the movement in and out of the Port of vessels, equipment, resources, and material required for the construction of the Port;

   f. The two Sides will coordinate such works, including the designs and movement, through a joint mechanism.

7. Hebron Issues

   a. The Shuhada Road in Hebron shall be opened for the movement of Palestinian vehicles in two phases. The first phase has been carried out, and the second phase shall be carried out not later than October 30, 1999;

   b. The wholesale market-Hasbahe will be opened not later than November 1, 1999, in accordance with arrangements which will be agreed upon by the two Sides;

   c. A high level Joint Liaison Committee will convene not later than September 13, 1999 to review the situation in the Tomb of the Patriarchs / Al Haram Al Ibrahimi (Annex I, Article VII, Interim Agreement and as per the January 15, 1998 US Minute of Discussion).

8. Security

   a. The two Sides will, in accordance with the prior agreements, act to ensure the immediate, efficient and effective handling of any incident involving a threat or act of terrorism, violence or incitement, whether committed by Palestinians or Israelis. To this end, they will cooperate in the exchange of information and coordinate policies and activities. Each side shall immediately and effectively respond to the occurrence or anticipated occurrence of an act of terrorism, violence or incitement and shall take all necessary measures to prevent such an occurrence;

   b. Pursuant to the prior agreements, The Palestinian side undertakes to implement its responsibilities for security, security cooperation, on-going abligations and other issues emanating from the prior agreements, including, in particular, the following obligations emanating from the Wye River Memorandum:

     1. continuation of the program for the collection of the illegal weapons, including reports;

     2. apprehension of suspects, including reports;

   3. forwarding of the list of Palestinian policemen to the Israeli Side not later than September 13, 1999;
   4. beginning of the review of the list by the Monitoring and Steering Committee not later than October 15, 9999.
9. The two Sides call upon the international donor community to enhance its commitment and financial support to the Palestinian economic development and the Israeli-Palestinian peace process.
10. Recognizing the necessity to create a positive environment for the negotiations, neither side shall initiate or take any step that will change the status of the West Bank and the Gaza Strip in accordance with the Interim Agreement.
11. Obligations pertaining to dates, which occur on holidays or Saturdays, shall be carried out on the first subsequent working day.

This memorandum will enter into force one week from the date of its signature.[1]

Made and signed in Sharm el-Sheikh, this fourth day of September 1999.

---

[1]It is understood that, for technical reasons, implementation of Article 2-a and the first stage mentioned in Article 3-c will be carried out within a week from the signing of this Memorandum.

Source: Congressional Quarterly, *The Middle East,* 9th ed., pp. 572–574.

THIRTEEN

The Arab–Israeli Conflict in the Post–9/11 World

CHRONOLOGY

2001

June 1 Dolphinarium Disco in Tel Aviv bombed, 21 killed

Sept. 11 Close to 3000 killed in al-Qaeda terrorist attacks in the U.S. that destroyed the World Trade Center towers and a wing of the Pentagon

Oct. 2 U.S. President G. W. Bush endorses idea of Palestinian state. Repeats to UNGA June 24, 2002

Oct. 7 U.S.-led war on Afghanistan launched; Taliban ousted

2002

March 19 Netanya Passover terrorist bombing kills 29 Israelis

March 28 Israel launches "Operation Defensive Shield." Arafat confined to compound in Ramallah. Operation ends April 18

April 3–18 Jenin refugee camp battle. 59 Palestinians and 23 Israeli soldiers killed

June 17 Israel begins building "Security Fence"

Sept. 11 P.A. cabinet resigns; Arafat sets date for Presidential and PLC elections

Oct. 3 "Quartet" "Road Map For Peace" floated. U.S. joins in plan Dec. 20

Oct. 30 Labor quits Israeli government.

2003

Jan. 28 Sharon and Likud re-elected easily in Israeli elections

Mar. 10 Post of Palestinian prime minister created

Mar. 19 U.S.-led war on Iraq launched; Saddam Hussein toppled; Bush declares end of combat operations on May 1

April 29 PLC approves Mahmoud Abbas as prime minister

May 25 Israeli cabinet endorses Road Map with several reservations

June 3 Arab leaders and Abbas endorse Road Map at meeting with Bush in Sharm al-Sheikh; King Abdullah II hosts Bush-Abbas-Sharon summit at Aqaba June 4

June 29 Hamas, Islamic Jihad, and al-Aqsa Brigades agree to 3-month "Hudna"

Aug. 19 Bus bomb in Jerusalem kills 22. Israel kills top Hamas leader in Gaza; militant groups declare end of Hudna on August 24

Sept. 6 Abbas resigns as prime minister; Ahmed Qurei approved prime minister by PLC on Nov. 12

Sept. 11 Israeli security cabinet declares Arafat obstacle to peace; says it will remove him at a time it chooses

Dec. Sharon floats idea of unilateral disengagement, withdrawal from some settlements and new security lines

2004

March 21	Sheikh Ahmad Yassin, Hamas founder, assassinated by Israeli missile; successor Dr. Abdel Aziz Rantisi assassinated April 17
May 18	Israel launches "Operation Rainbow in a Cloud" in Gaza
June 6	Israeli cabinet votes 14 to 7 in principle for the Gaza withdrawal plan
June 30	Israeli Supreme Court rules part of the "Security Fence" be rerouted
July 9	World Court calls the security barrier a breach of international law; July 20 UNGA resolution calls on Israel to dismantle fence
Sept. 30	Israel launches "Operation Days of Penitence" into Gaza Strip
Oct. 25	Knesset approves dismantling all settlements in Gaza and 4 in West Bank
Nov. 11	Yasser Arafat dies; Mahmoud Abbas, new head of PLO, elected President of the P.A. on Jan. 9, 2005
Dec. 23	First Palestinian municipal elections in the West Bank since 1976. Hamas participates

2005

Feb. 8	Sharon and Abbas meet at Sharm al-Sheikh; announce a mutual cease-fire
Feb. 20	Israeli Cabinet approves Gaza pullout and revised route of security fence
June 18	PLC passes new electoral law; elections planned for Jan. 2006
Aug. 15	Israel begins pullout from Gaza; all 21 settlements evacuated by Aug. 22. Last military units leave on Sept. 12. West Bank settlements evacuated by Sept. 20
Nov. 9	Amir Peretz elected leader of Israeli Labor party
Nov. 21	Isereli Knesset disbanded
Nov. 24	Sharon forms new Kadima party. Elections to be held March 28, 2006
Nov. 25	Rafah border crossing between Gaza and Egypt reopens; to be managed by the P.A. with European Union monitors present

2006

Jan. 4	Sharon suffers massive stroke; Ehud Olmert becomes acting prime minister
Jan. 25	Hamas wins victory in Palestinian parliamentary elections

Sharon Forms a New Coalition Government

Violence escalated as Ariel Sharon prepared to take office in March 2001. In presenting his new government to the Knesset, Sharon said that his coalition would be ready for "painful compromises" toward peace with the Palestinians, but, he asserted, not while Palestinian violence and terror continued. The shaky nature of Sharon's eight-party coalition, however, which included the more dovish Labor party, the orthodox Shas party and the far-right National Union party, did not bode well for either internal stability or an ability to deal with external threats. Labor party leader Shimon Peres was appointed foreign minister.

Meanwhile, the U.S. Secretary of State, Colin Powell, outlined the Middle East policy of the incoming Bush administration. In a speech to Congress, he indicated that the Bush team would place the Israeli–Palestinian dispute into the larger context of the Middle East and Persian Gulf region. The first step would be to abolish the post of Middle East envoy to pursue Arab–Israeli negotiations, held most recently by Dennis Ross, and fold the Arab–Israeli conflict into Middle East operations at the State Department. He named William J. Burns, at the time ambassador to Jordan, as Assistant Secretary of State for the Near East.

The Bush administration indicated it would adopt a relatively hands-off approach to the Arab–Israeli conflict, and Bush stated that he would not press Sharon into an early resumption of peace negotiations. The change in emphasis was clear—from active participant to facilitator; or as Bush asserted when Sharon made his first visit to the United States "The U.S. stands ready to assist, not insist." This minimalist approach would hold throughout most of the spring and summer of 2001.

As the Intifada dragged on, the economic situation of Palestinians worsened. Employment opportunities for Palestinians in Israel evaporated and movement within the territories was increasingly restricted. The Persian Gulf sheikhdoms, through the Islamic Development Bank, committed themselves to provide up to $40 million for six months from an "Intifada fund" to help make up for lost revenues. The EU and the United States also promised grants and loans to the Palestinian Authority. Despite lingering resentment of Arafat's support for Iraq in Gulf War I among most major Arab states, especially the Persian Gulf states, the hardships experienced by ordinary Palestinian families in the new Intifada generated intense pro-Palestinian sentiment among Arab populations. Iraqi President Saddam Hussein announced that he would pay $10,000, and later $25,000, to families of Palestinian suicide bombers and those killed in the uprising, and millions of private Saudi dollars went to families of the dead or wounded, through Islamic foundations linked to Hamas and Islamic Jihad, which opposed the P.A. An Arab summit in late March in Amman endorsed the payments to the Intifada fund (although much of the money was never delivered), and at that same meeting, Syrian President Bashar Assad, who used the occasion to label Sharon a "butcher," renewed Syrian relations with Arafat after a ten-year freeze.

While Arab leaders praised the Intifada, tensions mounted as human bombs shook Israel. Sharon, blaming Arafat's inability or unwillingness to control the militants, sent helicopter gunships to rocket Palestinian security forces buildings and suspected training camps in the West Bank and the Gaza Strip. He also parked Israeli tanks 300 yards from Arafat's headquarters in Ramallah. The Israeli prime minister proclaimed that "the days of restraint are over." Although he had received a public mandate to "do something" to stop the terror, Sharon's tactics seemed no more effective than previous attempts, and the bloodshed and retribution continued. Within Sharon's diverse government, a qualitative shift began to be seen in how Arafat was officially regarded and treated, with the majority of members seeing him as little more than a terrorist whom they could never trust.

In this impasse, the Mitchell committee made a five-day visit to Israel and the occupied territories. This was a committee appointed by former U.S. president Bill Clinton during the failed cease-fire summit at Sharm al-Sheikh the previous October to investigate the causes of violence, and to make recommendations as how best to end it and resume negotiations. Headed by former U.S. Senator George Mitchell, who had also brokered a peace agreement in Northern Ireland, the committee included former U.S. Senator Warren Rudman, former Turkish president Sulayman Demirel, the Norwegian Foreign Minister Thorbjoern Jaglond and the EU chief foreign policy coordinator Javier Solana. As the committee went about its business, there were high-level talks between Foreign Minister Peres and Palestinian negotiators Nabil Shaath and Saeb Erekat, and there were also contacts (evidently broken off once publicized) between Arafat and Sharon's son Omri. But there was no real progress, and violence continued.

In early April 2001, Egypt and Jordan presented a joint proposal to President Bush. It called for reciprocal measures: for Israel to lift its siege of Palestinian areas and put a total and immediate freeze on all settlement activity including in East Jerusalem; and for the Palestinian security forces to resume cooperation with their Israeli counterparts. The plan went nowhere, and, in retaliation for mortar fire on Sderot, across the border from Gaza, Sharon rocketed Palestinian security bases in Gaza and temporarily seized some Palestinian-controlled areas. This was the first time there had been a rocket attack on an Israeli town, but the Israeli incursion into Gaza was abruptly terminated after the United States described the retaliation as "excessive and disproportionate."

The Mitchell Report

The Mitchell Committee released a thirty-two page report in April, and it briefly became a touchstone for the resumption of peace negotiations. While the committee investigated the causes of the outbreak of violence in September 2000, it refrained from assigning blame and appeared so balanced and neutral that the *New York Times* called it "toothless." Nevertheless, it insisted that both sides stop the violence immediately and embark upon confidence-building measures that would lead to a resumption of negotiations. The report did not recommend the sending of an international observer force, which the Palestinians had wanted, but it did call for a freeze on Israeli settlement activity. The Palestinian Authority welcomed the report, but Sharon said that he would not reward violence by negotiating under fire, and that the committee "erred in equating settlement activity and terrorism as core catalysts for eroding trust."

Secretary of State Powell also formally endorsed the Mitchell report but ruled out any kind of "shuttle diplomacy." On the heels of the report, Bush instructed William J. Burns to work with both sides in establishing a timeline for measures to resume peace talks. Both Hamas and Islamic Jihad rejected any compromise and made their point clear in a horrific bombing of the Dolphinarium disco in Tel Aviv on June 1, which killed twenty-one, mostly young, Israelis. Before the blast, Arafat had made any cease-fire conditional on Israel publicly endorsing the Mitchell report, but after the bombing, he accepted an unconditional cease-fire. For his part, Sharon showed "restraint," and there was no immediate Israeli retaliation. However, several factions affiliated with the PLO, including the al-Aqsa Martyrs' Brigades, met in Gaza and reaffirmed their commitment to continue the uprising.

The United States in working for a cease-fire, sent CIA chief George Tenet to the area, and after six days of intense mediation by Tenet, both sides reluctantly accepted an American "work plan." The Tenet plan included resuming security cooperation, ending violence, and restoring conditions to the pre-September 2000 situation. Burns remained in the area to try to cement the cease-fire, and Secretary of State Powell, in a trip to the area, announced a seven-week timetable for the sides to end hostilities and move toward political talks. He called for a seven-day period of quiet, followed by a six-week cooling-off period. Even the seven-day period could not be achieved. Palestinian terrorists killed an Israeli motorist, fired mortar shells at

Israeli positions and settlements in Gaza, and the Israelis killed suspected West Bank militants. Israel, in fact, began to adopt a concerted tactic of targeted assassinations, and of going into and out of Palestinian-controlled areas (Area A). Having put himself on the line, it was unlikely that Powell or the U.S. administration would dispatch any more high-profile missions to the area for awhile.

In mid-July, the Israeli army laid siege to Palestinian towns and villages and snatched wanted men. At the end of July, Israel killed Jamal Mansour, a Hamas leader in the West Bank. There were more suicide bombings, though—notably that of the Sbarro pizza parlor in downtown Jerusalem in early August, after which Israel took over nine Palestinian offices in and around East Jerusalem, including Orient House, the symbol of Palestinian hopes of establishing sovereignty in all or parts of East Jerusalem. Israel also swept into Jenin, destroying police stations there before withdrawing. In mid-August, Israel deployed tanks around the largely Christian middle-class town of Beit Jala, after Palestinians fired mortars against the Israeli town of Gilo across the way.

Sharon ignored Washington's half hearted pleas that he exercise restraint and denied that Israeli acts were inflaming the situation. Powell telephoned Sharon about Beit Jala, for example, but the United States was still seen as not being aggressive enough in its efforts to lessen the conflict and too one-sided in support of Israel. Part of this perception stemmed from Bush's reluctance to meet with Arafat, although Sharon had already made several trips to Washington. There seemed little doubt that political power was devolving from the Palestinian Authority to factions among the Palestinians, and that Arafat and Fatah could no longer chart an independent course, as they had during the first Intifada. Arafat as a head of state appeared indecisive and ineffective, and, while he was still the symbol of the national struggle, the core of the "Nationalist and Islamic" forces in the Palestinian territories was moving toward Hamas and Islamic Jihad, although their actual numbers were relatively small. Israel contributed to Arafat's weakness by seeking to marginalize him further, especially after a speech he made at a conference on racism held in Durban, South Africa, at the end of August, in which he attacked Israel as a racist and colonial power. Sharon was even more determined to ignore Arafat when Raed Karmi, the head of the al-Aqsa Martyrs' Brigade affiliated with Fatah, pledged to kill more Jews.

Israel continued its policy of targeted assassinations, and at the end of August, killed Mustafa Zibri (Abu Ali Mustafa), a top-ranking leader of the PFLP, which he had helped to found in 1967. Israel also sent U.S.-made F-15 and F-16 warplanes into action, dropping bombs on police buildings in three Palestinian towns.

September 11, 2001, and the War on Terror

And then came September 11. On a beautiful, cloudless day, four U.S. commercial aircraft were hijacked, two from Boston, one from Dulles International airport in Washington, D.C., and one from Newark. Two flew into the towers of the World Trade Center in New York City, destroying them, one struck and exploded in the Pentagon, and one, probably heading for the White House or the Capitol, crashed into a field in Pennsylvania. The United States was shocked and stunned. In all, close to 3,000 people were killed (including the 19 hijackers) in what President Bush called an act of war against the United States. A hitherto shadowy and relatively unknown organization, *al-Qaeda*, affiliated with the extremist Islamist Taliban rulers of Afghanistan and substantially funded by Osama Bin Laden, a militant dissident Saudi Arabian, was quickly identified as responsible for the attacks.

September 11, 2001, galvanized the Bush administration. In an internationally televised speech to a joint session of Congress, Bush declared a "War on Terrorism." Following desultory attempts to negotiate the handover of Osama Bin Laden to Washington, in November, the United States launched an all-out aerial assault to remove the Taliban regime. Within six weeks, the Taliban leadership fled the capital of Kabul, and the initial military phase of the war was over. Some weeks later, an interim government was installed. Despite attempts to restore law and order and a stable government, Afghanistan remained torn by internal divisions, and outside of Kabul, warlords continued to be powerful.

In forceful language, Bush set out his Manichaean view of the world as a place where good was locked into a war with evil, and placed Arab states on notice that those that tolerated or encouraged a climate that promoted terror were enemies of the United States and would be pursued. During his State of the Union message in January 2002, Bush identified a number of countries (specifically naming Iraq, Iran, and North Korea), as constituting an "axis of evil" and committed the United States to "regime change" in those countries.

The U.S. war to combat terrorism also indirectly refocused attention on the Israeli–Palestinian issue. It was obvious that Washington regarded Hamas, Islamic Jihad, and Hizbullah as terrorist organizations, and that the Palestinian Authority—and Yasser Arafat in particular—were seen as not doing enough to curb terrorist activities. Sharon and Israeli hard-liners were reassured by the strong expressions of support from the Bush administration defending Israel's firm, "legitimate," military actions of "self defense"against the Palestinian terrorist threat. On the other hand, in order to gain support for the global war on terror, including support from the Arab countries, the United States needed to be seen as doing something to defuse the situation in the Middle East.

Although Israel's "war on terror" suddenly seemed to be part of the broader struggle against terrorism, and September 11 had increased sympathy for Israel's predicament, on October 2 Bush told congressional leaders that he affirmed the idea of a Palestinian state, provided it acknowledged Israel's right to exist, becoming the first American president formally to do so. Apparently, even before the World Trade Center attacks, the Bush administration had planned to announce a Middle East diplomatic initiative that included U.S. support for a Palestinian state, in a speech to have been delivered by Secretary of State Powell at the United Nations General Assembly. There had also been talk of Bush meeting Arafat at the UN meeting in New York and possibly shaking his hand, but most of the UNGA session was cancelled after the attacks.

Both Arafat and Sharon seemed to understand that they could not afford to cross the United States in its hour of peril and renewed resolve. In mid-September, Arafat, seeing an opportunity to be brought in from the cold, had again called for a cease-fire in the territories, and Sharon ordered his army to stop offensive actions and to pull back from advanced positions. This was a tactical setback for Sharon, and a hard sell for Arafat, given widespread sympathy for Bin Laden in the Arab and Muslim world and suspicions about U.S. intentions. The German Foreign Minister Joschka Fischer had been trying to set in motion talks between Arafat and Peres, and the two men did meet at the end of September and issued a joint communique reiterating their commitment to the Mitchell and Tenet plans. The Palestinian Cabinet demanded that gunmen stop attacking Israel, and Palestinian police arrested two militants wanted by Israel, one a senior Hamas official, and one a member of Islamic Jihad. But riots against the police resulted, and disputes among the factions surfaced about their ultimate goals, Hamas making clear that it wanted to see the end of Israel altogether. A different voice was that of Sari Nusseibeh, the new political representative of the Palestinians in East Jerusalem. In a speech at the Hebrew University, he criticized the Intifada as hopelessly mired in bloodshed, and said that peace could only come if the Palestinians renounced the right of return and refugees were resettled in a Palestinian state and not in a way that would undermine Israel as a predominantly Jewish state.

Sharon was also experiencing difficulties. Coalition partners were unhappy with his decision to withdraw troops from two Palestinian neighborhoods in Hebron and to ease some travel restrictions on Arabs in Nablus and elsewhere. Two far-right ministers, Avigdor Lieberman, Infrastructure Minister, and Rehavam Ze'evi, Tourism Minister, quit the coalition, taking seven Knesset members with them. But, just as a tentative truce appeared to be taking hold, Ze'evi, a former general who had advocated expelling or killing Arafat and the voluntary "transfer" of Palestinians across the Jordan River, was assassinated at the Hyatt hotel in Jerusalem on October 17. The Popular Front for the Liberation of Palestine (PFLP) claimed responsibility, ostensibly in revenge for the killing of Abu Ali Mustafa in late August. Although Arafat ordered the arrest of some PFLP members, Sharon gave him an ultimatum to hand over the gunmen involved in Ze'evi's murder. The P.A. rejected this demand, and Israeli tanks rolled into the outlying districts of seven towns and villages on the West Bank, including a move into Bethlehem for the first time. Sharon reportedly told his cabinet: "As far as I am concerned, the era of Arafat is over."

Shimon Peres continued to back Arafat, but he was almost alone in the Israeli cabinet in urging continued ties with the Palestinian leader, and other members of the Labor party seriously considered leaving the coalition. More than forty Palestinians were killed in the territories in a week, but Israel rejected U.S. demands to pull back its troops until Arafat turned over Ze'evi's assassins and took measures against the militant groups. As Israel went in and out of the Palestinian areas, some speculated that Sharon was hoping that he could topple the P.A., or that it would collapse from within if Israel's punitive actions continued. But, even as Peres and Arafat met again in Majorca and then in Brussels with European representatives, terror attacks and reprisals continued.

United States Endorses Palestine as a State

At the United Nations in mid-November, President Bush reiterated his support for a Palestinian state but declined to meet Arafat. This was the first time that an American president had actually used Palestine as the name of the state he endorsed, but Bush said Arafat had not done enough to curb terrorist organizations, and the U.S. president rejected the distinction the Palestinian militant groups drew between what they called a national liberation struggle and terrorism as practiced by the September 11 hijackers. The next week, Secretary Powell, in a speech at the University of Louisville, said that the United States was ready to become engaged again and would send two high-level envoys, Anthony Zinni, former U.S. commander of forces in the Middle East, and William Burns, Assistant Secretary of State for the Middle East, to seek a cease-fire, restart negotiations, and help set terms for the creation of a viable Palestinian state and a more secure Israel.

The United States was obviously trying to capitalize on its initial success in driving the Taliban from power in Afghanistan, but the administration recognized that if it were to gain the support of Arab and Muslim countries in the war against terrorism, it had to become more engaged in the Israeli–Palestinian issue. The Europeans also felt strongly that things were spiraling out of control, which is why they had invited Peres and Arafat to meet with EU officials in Brussels. At the UN, there seemed to be an understanding that while they were not directly linked to the Palestinian situation, the September 11 attacks were a reminder of an issue that to many was a cause of greater instability than the threat of Saddam Hussein, whom the Bush administration had targeted as part of its "axis of evil," and against whom the United States was gearing up for possible military action because of Iraq's refusal to readmit UN weapons inspectors.

In the immediate area itself, there was simply more violence, including Palestinian riots against P.A. security forces after they arrested a man accused by Israel of orchestrating terror attacks in Jenin. This was the worst Palestinian–Palestinian violence since early October, when

Arafat forces had opened fire on demonstrators in the Gaza Strip, killing two, to stop a protest against the U.S.-led war in Afghanistan and in support of Osama Bin Laden. Israel demolished homes of suspected terrorists in the Rafah refugee camp in Gaza and on November 25 assassinated Hamas leader Mahmoud Abu Hanoud. Israeli intelligence believed Abu Hanoud had masterminded the attacks on the Tel-Aviv disco, the Sbarro pizzeria in Jerusalem, and a produce market in Jerusalem. This killing would have profound ramifications in the months to come, as Sheikh Yassin, the titular Hamas leader, pledged that Hamas would avenge Hanoud's death.

On the heels of this targeted assassination, Zinni and Burns arrived, just in time to be taken to Afula to see the aftermath of a terror attack there. In their talks, Sharon tried to convince the two Americans that nothing could happen until a new leadership emerged among the Palestinians. In fact, P.A. officials themselves began to have serious doubts about Arafat's effectiveness. These included Muhammad Dahlan, commander of the P.A. preventive security forces in Gaza, who, frustrated by both Sharon and Arafat, resigned his position. It was becoming increasingly clear that any cease-fire would come only with the consent of Hamas and Islamic Jihad. While the U.S. team was in the area, twenty-six Israelis were killed and 190 injured in suicide attacks in fourteen hours. Hamas claimed responsibility, stating they were revenge for Hanoud's death. This unleashed a terrible wave of violence, as Israeli helicopter gunships and tanks attacked P.A. police stations in Gaza and swept through West Bank villages, bombing offices and police stations, and killing several civilians, including children. The P.A. put Sheikh Yassin under house arrest, but this merely resulted in demonstrations against the Authority.

President Bush was putting American prestige on the line for the first time, and Arafat was under pressure to comply with American demands to try to do something. He did say that he would crack down on the terrorists, but it was not at all certain that he could or wished to do so. While still a potent symbol, he appeared to have failed as a politician and leader of government and was in real danger of losing support among his people—and internationally. As the *New York Times* put it, the ongoing violence made Arafat look "at best powerless and at worst complicit."

The continuing violence was also a challenge for Sharon, since it tested his claim that only Israeli force and preemption could prevent terror attacks. Hamas was demonstrating, however, that it could strike in the heart of Jerusalem or Haifa or anywhere, despite Israeli closures, checkpoints, targeted assassinations, and arrests. Nevertheless, the United States stood squarely on Israel's side and virtually gave Sharon *carte-blanche* to retaliate. Powell suggested that this was a last chance for Arafat to demonstrate that he could rein in the extremists and be a true partner for peace. The U.S. position toward Arafat had vacillated after 9/11, with the administration at first reluctant to extend the war on terrorism to Palestinian groups because of its need for broad support in the Arab world. But the suicide missions during the Zinni/Burns mission turned this attitude around.

Israel Pronounces P.A. as an Entity that Supports Terror

Israel had no such hesitation and pronounced the P.A. as a terror-supporting entity. After several more suicide incidents in mid-December, including a Hamas bombing of a bus in the West Bank and the gunning down of surviving passengers as they tried to flee, Sharon's cabinet declared that as far as Israel was concerned, Arafat was irrelevant, and that there would be no more contact with him. Under tremendous international pressure, the P.A. police, despite fierce resistance, tried to hunt down militants in Gaza. On December 16, demonstrating that he still exercised some authority, Arafat called for a cease-fire that held for almost a month.

During this time, however, Israel intercepted the *Karine-A*, an Iranian-funded ship owned and partially crewed by P.A. naval police carrying 50 tons of weapons, including armor piercing weapons, mines, rockets, and high explosives, bound for the Palestinian Authority. Although at first he denied it, Arafat later took responsibility for the *Karine-A* shipment. After the seizure of the ship, Israel bulldozed the runway at the Gaza International Airport and destroyed more than 50 houses in the Rafah refugee camp, leaving more than 500 people homeless. The continuing Israeli blockade of the territories, which cut the West Bank and Gaza into disconnected enclaves, had already severely disrupted the Palestinian economy, increased unemployment and left many Palestinians impoverished. The cease-fire was broken in early January with the killing of four Israeli soldiers, and shortly afterwards, Israel assassinated Raed Karmi, leader of the al-Aqsa Brigades in Tulkarm.

After six Israelis were killed at a Bar Mitzvah celebration in Hadera, the Israel Defense Forces, for the first time since the beginning of the Intifada, temporarily took over an entire town—Tulkarm—where they bombed the police station and rounded up militants. They also made incursions into Nablus and killed four senior members of the Izz ad-Din al-Qassem group, part of Hamas's military arm, and destroyed what they said was a bomb-making lab. Jenin was also considered a factory for suicide bombers, and the Israelis repeatedly bombarded it, destroying police headquarters, prisons, the governor's administrative offices, and its military courtroom. Observers began to question how the Israelis could hold the P.A. responsible for exercising authority and ensuring order when they were destroying P.A. institutions and infrastructure.

January 2002 saw some of the worst terrorist incidents in Israel proper, with several bombings on Jaffa Road in Jerusalem, and in a crowded pedestrian mall in Tel Aviv. At the end of the month, Sharon held his first meeting with senior Palestinian leaders, including Ahmed Qurei and Mahmoud Abbas, and in early February, Arafat in an opinion piece in the *New York Times* denounced terror. The article was in English, but the following week, from his besieged headquarters in Ramallah, he issued a call, in Arabic, for a million martyrs to march on Jerusalem. One U.S. commentator observed that Arafat was acting as a matchmaker for Bush and Sharon, and it was not surprising that when Sharon and the U.S. president next met in the Oval office, Bush was more receptive to Sharon's insistence that Arafat was irrelevant to any peace negotiations.

In March 2002, 250 Palestinians and 124 Israelis died, in one of the worst months in an ever-worsening situation. During the first part of the month, there were suicide bombings within Israel proper, and at checkpoints. Israel moved in and out of the territories and killed many Palestinians, including civilians. In mid-month, Admiral Zinni returned to the area and met with Arafat, and Vice President Cheney also arrived for talks with Israeli leaders but not with Arafat. Cheney's tour of the Middle East was, in part, to try to win Arab support for a possible U.S. attack against Iraq, but he was notably unsuccessful.

The Saudi Plan

At the end of March, there was an Arab summit in Beirut. Arafat did not attend because he was afraid that Sharon would not let him come back. Egyptian president Mubarak and Jordan's King Abdullah II also did not attend, nor did leaders of almost half the twenty-two member states. At the meeting, the Saudis were poised to discuss a peace initiative, which had been leaked in February in a *New York Times* editorial by Thomas Friedman. In the absence of important Arab states, the initiative was left dangling, although the next month Crown Prince Abdullah met with President Bush at the president's ranch in Crawford, Texas, and presented his eight-point plan. He also impressed upon Bush the seriousness of the situation and what it meant for the Arab world. The Saudi plan was basically a land for peace proposal that was not new, but the Saudis were suggesting that the Arab countries might normalize relations with

Israel if Israel returned to the June 1967 borders. While the Arab summit was convening in Beirut, Zinni, who had arranged a rare joint session of Israeli and Palestinian security chiefs, was making some progress toward another cease-fire. Any hopeful signs, however, were dashed by the so-called "Passover massacre" at the end of March, when at least twenty-nine Israelis were killed in a suicide blast in Netanya as they sat down to a Passover seder. On the heels of that incident, Sharon launched "Operation Defensive Shield," in which Israeli troops moved into and reoccupied all the major Palestinian population centers. Arafat's compound in Ramallah, the *Mukata a,* was heavily damaged, and Arafat was confined to just a few rooms.

President Bush initially supported the Israeli assault but then urged Israel to withdraw and sent Colin Powell back to the area. Powell met with Arafat in his besieged compound, a kind of victory for Arafat, since for months the United States had been backing his isolation, but he insisted there could be no cease-fire until Israel ended its military operations and withdrew from the cities and towns it was occupying.

Israel continued to destroy Palestinian infrastructure and to hunt down Palestinian militants. Tanzim faction leader Marwan Barghouti, widely seen as Arafat's successor as head of Fatah, now regarded by Israel as a terrorist, was arrested, as were other wanted men. The Israelis sometimes met fierce resistance, as for example, in the so-called "Jenin massacre." Almost 59 Palestinians, including women and children, as well as 23 Israeli soldiers, died in door-to-door fighting in the refugee camp in that city between April 3 when Israeli forces entered the camp and April 18 when the tanks withdrew. A later UN inquiry into the events at Jenin concluded that despite the high number of deaths, no massacre had occurred. In Bethlehem, Palestinian fighters, including thirteen accused by Israel of terrorism, had taken refuge in the Church of the Nativity. After a thirty-nine day standoff, some Palestinian fighters were sent into exile to Gaza, and the thirteen wanted men were sent to Cyprus or other countries willing to accept them. A compromise was also reached in Ramallah, where Israel lifted the siege of Arafat after six wanted men were transferred to international custody. After this six-week military offensive against the Palestinian militias, Israel began a general pull-back but continued to carry out arrests and raids at will.

A consensus was emerging all around that Arafat must be replaced, and that reform in the Palestinian Authority was essential. Palestinian legislators themselves clearly desired reform. They chafed at the lack of promotion, as the old guard refused to let go of their portfolios, and at the absence of elections, which had not been held since 1996, when Palestinians voted for Arafat as president and for the current eighty-eight members of the legislative council. Arafat himself oversaw something like twenty-eight ministries, there were multiple security agencies, and there was virtually no fiscal accountability. In a speech to his parliament in mid-May, which was rather coolly received, Arafat admitted mistakes and pledged reform, but he gave no details. He did sign a measure granting judicial independence, after ignoring it for eighteen months, and he later signed a Basic Law that had been voted on by the legislature and had sat on his desk for the previous five years. As part of a reform package adopted by the legislators themselves, Arafat was asked to disband the current cabinet and present a new, smaller one to parliament for approval within forty-five days; to call for elections for the parliament and president by spring 2003, preferably sooner; and to reduce the number of Palestinian security services.

The cycle of violence continued, however, with many suicide bombings for which Hamas, Islamic Jihad or the al-Aqsa Brigades claimed responsibility. One involved a teenager who exploded a car next to a bus in northern Israel, killing sixteen. He had been taught to drive just two days earlier. These incidents cast a pall over the arrival of Burns and then Tenet to the area. Both men met with Arafat, and Arafat told Tenet he would revamp the security forces to reduce the number from more than a dozen to six. In June, Arafat convened a new, streamlined cabinet, and on June 13, after six days of mediation by Tenet, Israelis and Palestinians accepted another cease-fire.

Israel Begins to Build a "Security Fence"

On June 17, Israel began to build what it called a "security fence" along the West Bank, initially running roughly near the old green line that marked the pre-June 1967 borders. (See Map 13–1.) There was much debate in Israel about the fence, with many hoping it would keep terrorists out, and others concerned that it would isolate Jewish settlements and represent a border that might become permanent. Palestinians were outraged at what they saw as another attempt by Israel to create facts on the ground and as a pretext for seizing Palestinian land and further extending its territory. Almost simultaneously the 69th suicide bombing in 21 months occurred. After another blast at a Jerusalem bus stop, Israel again occupied selected areas and vowed to stay as long as the terror continued. A group of 55 Palestinian politicians and intellectuals, in a letter published in the English-language *al-Quds* newspaper, now decried the violence and suicide attacks and the damage they did to the Palestinian cause, but they were denounced by Hamas leader Abdul Aziz al-Rantisi.

On June 24, 2002, in a major policy speech by George Bush, the U.S. president publicly endorsed the idea of an independent Palestinian state living side by side with Israel. Bush, however, without mentioning Arafat by name, called for a new and different Palestinian leadership. While telling the Palestinians they must earn such a state, he also called on Israel to end the occupation and cease building settlements. With pressures internally and externally mounting for reform, Arafat announced that elections would be held for president and parliament in January 2003. Palestinians themselves, like Khalil Shikaki, a political science professor at Bir Zeit University and director of the Palestinian Center for Policy and Survey Research in Ramallah, advocated a parliamentary, rather than a presidential, system.

Although these moves provided some hope for change, actual conditions on the ground continued to deteriorate, as the Palestinian death rate climbed, as suicide attacks against Israelis continued, and as building of the security fence and settlements continued. On the evening of July 22–23, Israel dropped a one-ton bomb on the apartment of Salah Shehada, the Hamas military leader in Gaza City, killing him, his guard and thirteen others, including nine children. This derailed discussions of West Bank Tanzim leaders and Hamas officials from Gaza, assisted by the EU, to try to work out a unilateral cease-fire agreement. Learning of this initiative, P.A. figures had tried a parallel initiative under Muhammad Dahlan, former Gaza security chief. Egypt had agreed to help pressure Hamas to stop terrorist attacks, and Jordanian and Saudi diplomats lent their support. The Israeli bombing shattered all these efforts, as well as provoking an angry response from Bush. It also precipitated a terrorist bombing incident at the Hebrew University in Jerusalem a few days later, which Sheikh Yassin linked to the Shehada killing. Hamas and Islamic Jihad also rejected efforts by other Palestinian factions to declare a policy of ending suicide bombings and other attacks on Israeli citizens and limiting them to soldiers and settlers.

Nevertheless, for the next five weeks or so, there was relative calm, during which there were some Israeli pullbacks. Palestinian leaders had begun publicly to demand an end to suicide attacks and Israelis were beginning to believe that their harsh methods were taking a toll on Palestinian militants and providing Israel with some security. The Palestinians themselves were beginning to challenge Arafat, even as Israeli tanks and bulldozers battered his Ramallah headquarters and left him pretty much confined to one section of the compound. In early September, pressured by the Palestinian Legislative Council, he accepted the resignation of his entire cabinet. The 72 members present determined to pass a vote of no-confidence, prompting the cabinet to submit its resignation. Arafat set a January 20, 2003, date for elections. The deputies said their fight was not with Arafat but "to affirm democratic institutions." Even Fatah members blasted the corruption and ineffectiveness of the P.A., and many legislators declared their support for a prime minister and the relegating of Arafat to a symbolic presidential role. However, Hamas and Islamic Jihad had their own agenda, and they continued to carry out suicide missions in Israel.

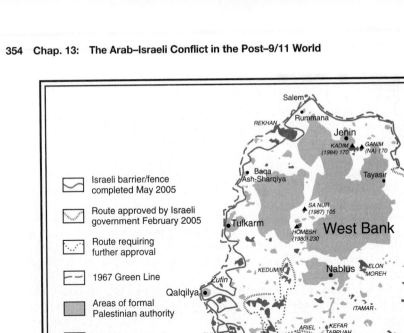

Israeli barrier/fence completed May 2005

Route approved by Israeli government February 2005

Route requiring further approval

1967 Green Line

Areas of formal Palestinian authority

Palestinian cities/towns

Israeli settlement areas

Israeli settlements evacuated August 2005

Salem
REKHAN
Rummana
Jenin
KADIM (1984) 170
GANIM (NA) 170
Baqa Ash-Sharqiya
Tayasir
SA NUR (1987) 105
Tulkarm
HOMESH (1980) 230
West Bank
KEDUMIN
Nablus
ELON MOREH
Zufin
Qalqilya
ITAMAR
ELKANA
ARIEL
KEFAR TAPPUAH
SHILO
HALAMISH
ATERET
BET EL
TALMON
MODI'IN ILLIT
Ramallah
GIVAT ZE'EV
ISRAEL
Jerusalem
MA'ALE ADUMIM
Jericho
Jordan Valley
Jordan River
ETZION BLOC
Bethlehem
Dead Sea
TEKOA
ASFAR
ADORA
Hebron
KIRYAT ARBA
KARMEL
ESHKOLOT
METZADOT YEHUDA

0   Km   20
0   Miles   10

MAP 13–1   West Bank showing Israeli security fence/barrier September 2005

President Yasser Arafat (L) and Prime Minister-elect Mahmoud Abbas (R) (also known as Abu Mazen) speak to the Palestinian Legislative Council meeting, which voted to approve Abbas's new cabinet to replace Arafat's government. Abbas resigned on September 6, 2003, citing lack of support from the Palestinian Authority parliament.

The Quartet "Road Map" to Peace

William J. Burns arrived in the region in October to try to persuade leaders of both sides to accept an evolving "road map" crafted by the "Quartet" of the U.S., UN, Russia, and the EU to achieve peace and establish a Palestinian state next to Israel by 2005. (See Document 13–1.) In the first phase of a three-year, three-phase process, the Palestinian leadership would create the post of prime minister, draft a constitution, and declare an immediate end to the armed Intifada and acts of violence against Israelis. The Israelis would ease curfews and other restrictions on Palestinians, halt attacks in civilian areas, withdraw to positions held on September 28, 2000 (prior to the outbreak of the Intifada), and cease all settlement construction. After Palestinian parliamentary elections, a second stage would last from June to December of 2003, in which negotiations would begin for the creation of an independent Palestinian state with provisional borders and attributes of sovereignty, with other issues to be worked on, such as regional water resources, the environment, economic development, refugees, and arms control. In the last stage, 2004 to 2005, Israelis and Palestinians would start negotiations toward a final settlement and final borders, and the Quartet would meet to endorse the agreement. A final, permanent status resolution creating the Palestinian state would be reached in 2005, and the Israeli occupation that began in 1967 would come to an end.

Although endorsed in general by many on both sides, others echoed the comments of Yossi Beilin, who noted that the plan shared one of the flaws of the Oslo accords, namely an "interim period." Such a period, Beilin argued, would give the "lunatics" on both sides the chance to torpedo the plan.

In late October 2002, Arafat's new cabinet was approved by the Palestinian Legislative Council 56 to 18. Although trimmed to nineteen members, it included only three new faces, including a new interior minister responsible for the overhaul of the security services and a new finance minister. While this was a kind of vote of confidence for Arafat, Sharon was experiencing problems with his cabinet. Defense Minister Binyamin Ben-Eliezer resigned in a dispute over funding for settlements, which his Labor party had wanted cut, and Labor left the government, taking away its twenty-five seats. Shaul Mofaz, the army chief-of-staff, was tapped as the new defense minister. Left with a minority government, Sharon informed Israeli president Moshe Katsav on November 5 that he requested the dissolution of the Knesset and elections within 90 days. Then, he issued an invitation to his Likud rival Binyamin Netanyahu to replace Shimon Peres as foreign minister, an invitation that Netanyahu, possibly to Sharon's surprise, promptly accepted.

New Israeli elections were scheduled for January 28, 2003. Shortly after the previous election, the Knesset had voted overwhelmingly to abandon the direct election of the prime minister, and the upcoming election would be a reversion to the previous practice of voting only for a party, whose head, if the party received a plurality of votes, would then assemble a coalition government. The Labor party chose Amram Mitzna, mayor of Haifa, as its new leader. A decorated combat hero, Mitzna called for unilateral withdrawal from part, but not all, of the West Bank if peace talks proved impossible, and the evacuation of some settlements. In the Likud party primaries, although Netanyahu had declared that if he were elected, he would simply oust Arafat, Sharon scored a decisive victory, probably helped by the unwillingness of Israelis to change horses in midstream while terror continued. There were ambushes, bus bombings, and in Kenya, two coordinated attacks on Israelis. Terrorists fired shoulder-launched missiles at an Israeli passenger jet, narrowly missing the target, minutes before three suicide bombers blew themselves up at the entrance of an Israeli-owned hotel, killing thirteen, including ten Kenyans. Arafat's top deputy, Mahmoud Abbas (Abu Mazen), meanwhile, said that the armed uprising against Israel had been a mistake for the Palestinians and must be stopped, because it held up Palestinian independence and had led to a reoccupation of Palestinian areas by Israeli troops.

On December 20, 2002, the United States joined the other members of the Quartet in calling for a Palestinian state in three years, although there was disagreement on how quickly to press the plan on the Israelis and the Palestinians. Sharon had earlier tentatively backed the plan but couched his endorsement in terms of strict conditions, including Arafat's removal and strict limits on Palestinian security forces, and the cessation of all attacks on Israelis. While the European leaders were anxious for the plan to be formally adopted and published immediately, the United States insisted that this not occur until after the Israeli elections. It was clear that conditions on the ground would influence those elections, but as suicide attacks resumed in early January, it was not certain if these would encourage the Israeli right-wing, or if they would call attention to flaws in Sharon's military strategy. The Israeli army made its deepest incursion into Gaza since 1994, provoked by Palestinian rocket attacks across the border, but Palestinian factional leaders meeting in Cairo rejected a proposal drafted by Egypt and endorsed by Arafat that called for a halt to Palestinian attacks in the territories and in Israel.

In the elections held on January 28, 2003, Ariel Sharon won an overwhelming victory, with the Likud party ending up with forty Knesset seats, up from nineteen in the previous election. He assembled a coalition consisting of Likud, the secular Shinui party, the National Union party, virulently opposed to the creation of a Palestinian state and not averse to expelling Arafat, and with the National Religious party, fervent supporters of the settlements, as the final partner. Shas was cut out. Netanyahu was replaced as foreign minister by Silvan Shalom but appointed finance minister, and Shaul Mofaz retained the defense portfolio. While still demolishing homes of West Bank and Gaza families of militants and approving more settlements, Sharon resumed direct contact with senior Palestinian officials about the possibility of a cease-fire.

Arafat took the first step in the Quartet demands for political, financial, and security reform by announcing that he would appoint a prime minister. It is possible that he gave in on this issue because he felt he had to make changes in advance of a U.S.-led coalition war against Iraq lest there be no Palestinian regime left to reform. Or, perhaps it was because he feared he would be treated like Saddam Hussein. There was certainly the fear among the Palestinian leadership that Sharon would use an American war on Iraq as an excuse to pull the curtain down finally on Oslo, either by forcibly evicting Arafat or reoccupying the Gaza Strip, as he had already reoccupied the West Bank. Indeed, Israel pursued Hamas leaders in Gaza, and in March moved into the Strip in an open-ended mission. There is no doubt that Sharon desired his own version of "regime change," just as the United States was preparing the ground for an assault against Saddam. Would Arafat's concessions to the Quartet encourage the world to exert pressure on Sharon to desist?

The Bush administration, meanwhile, had been unsuccessful in securing Arab support for an attack against Iraq. In fact, on the Arab "street," anti-Americanism was running rampant. At the same time as the United States geared up for regime change in Iraq, Bush needed Sharon to keep Israel out of the fray. The U.S. president, prodded by British Prime Minister Tony Blair, and under pressure from the Europeans and the Arab nations, in an effort to placate hostile Arab opinion, in his first significant speech about the Israeli–Palestinian conflict since the previous June, said in February that ousting Saddam could bring stability to the Middle East and set the stage for peace between Israel and "a truly democratic Palestinian state." On March 14, on the eve of the Iraq war, which began on March 19, Bush, as a gesture to Blair and also to further mollify the Arabs, announced that he was prepared to move ahead with the Road Map.

As the brief but highly destructive war in Iraq was unleashed on March 19, Arafat signed legislation to create the post of prime minister. The Palestinian parliament and members of his own Fatah faction forced him to withdraw a proposal to restrict the prime minister's power. In a stormy session on March, 10 it was agreed that Arafat would retain power to appoint and dismiss the prime minister, but that only the prime minister could form the cabinet, a crucial step in reforming the various ministries.

As the designated Prime Minister Mahmoud Abbas (Abu Mazen) tried to assemble his cabinet, the World Bank, meanwhile, published a report about the Palestinian economy, noting a 53 percent unemployment rate; a two-year 40 percent drop in Gross National Income; a 25 to 30 percent decline in per capita food consumption in the previous two years, with child malnutrition rates climbing; and 60 percent of the population living on less than $2 a day. The Israeli economy was also said to be in steep decline, and for the first time, the Bank said that political progress was indispensable to a resumption of economic and social development in both Israel and the Palestinian areas.

Although Arafat and Abbas quarreled bitterly over some of Abbas's cabinet choices, including Muhammad Dahlan to be in charge of security affairs, on April 29 the legislature approved the new cabinet 51 to 18, with three abstentions. That paved the way for the presentation of the Quartet road map, which international mediators launched just after Abbas was sworn in on April 30. Simultaneously, suicide bombers killed three Israelis at a beachfront bar in Tel Aviv, the 89th such attack since the beginning of the Intifada. As of that date, 2287 Palestinians had been killed and 763 Israelis. Colin Powell arrived to meet with Sharon and Abbas, but not with Arafat. In talks with Sharon, he raised the issue of settlements, which Sharon dismissed, although he said he might ease restrictions on Palestinians if terrorism stopped. In his meetings with Powell, Abbas said that he was ready to disarm terrorist groups provided Israel also took action on the peace plan. And Javier Solana, EU foreign policy chief, also met with Abbas, as well as Arafat, to promote the road map.

On May 17, Sharon and Abbas met for the highest level talks in two years. Saeb Erekat, a chief Palestinian negotiator, had not been invited to be part of the delegation meeting with Sharon and submitted his resignation, a possible sign of a split between the old and new guards. In the talks between Sharon and Abbas, Sharon offered to withdraw the army from centers of most Palestinian cities in the West Bank and from the northern Gaza Strip, in exchange for a commitment to crack down on terrorism from those areas; but Abbas insisted that Sharon formally accept the road map in its entirety first, so the talks were inconclusive.

Even as the talks were being held, or probably because they were being held, a new wave of suicide bombings occurred, five in three days, which caused Sharon to cancel his scheduled trip to the United States to meet with President Bush. Israel immediately sealed off the borders along the West Bank and Gaza Strip and took over the Gaza town of Beit Hanoun, from which rockets had been fired on the Israeli town of Sderot. That had not prevented the female bomber who blew up herself and three Israelis at the entrance of a shopping mall in Afula from slipping through anyway. Israel had taken more than 5000 Palestinians into custody, conducted nighttime sweeps of suspected militants, kept its army in or on the fringes of Palestinian cities in the West Bank, carried out targeted assassinations, and demolished homes. There is no doubt that the punitive actions had some success, and that hundreds of attacks were averted, but all these measures seemed only to have provoked and emboldened the militants, while imposing crushing burdens on the Palestinian population.

Understanding that the two sides were not about to budge, the United States promised that it would "recognize" a written list of fourteen Israeli reservations about the Road Map. With this assurance that the United States would address Israeli concerns, the Israeli cabinet voted 12 to 7, with 4 abstentions, to accept the Road Map. The cabinet's vote marked the first time an Israeli government formally accepted the principle of a Palestinian state. In defending himself the next day, May 26, the veteran hawk Ariel Sharon told stunned Likud legislators: "You cannot like the word, but what is happening is an occupation—to hold 3.5 million Palestinians under occupation, I believe that is a terrible thing for Israel and for the Palestinians." He continued: "I want to say clearly that I have come to the conclusion that we have to reach a [peace] agreement." The next day, however, under intense criticism, he backtracked, saying "We are not occupiers, this is the birthplace of the Jewish people, and in diplomatic terms these are territories in dispute between two peoples."

Encouraged by these developments, however, President Bush announced that he would hold a summit with Abbas and Sharon, hosted by King Abdullah II, on June 4 at the Jordanian port city of Aqaba. This would follow a meeting with Arab leaders at the Egyptian resort town of Sharm al-Sheikh. Clearly, the American president was now becoming personally involved, and expectations were raised all around. In advance of the president's visit, Sharon and Abbas met again on May 29. Sharon agreed to lift restrictions on Palestinians, and Abbas reiterated his determination to fight terror. Sharon said that if Abbas were indeed successful, and there was quiet, Israel would participate in negotiations to form a provisional Palestinian state as soon as possible. Sharon said he would pull the Israeli forces out of West Bank cities and would turn security control over to Palestinians in the northern Gaza Strip.

He also promised to lift border restrictions in both areas. Additionally, Israel would reinstate 25,000 work permits for Palestinians cut off for months from their jobs in Israel. Encouraged also by the fact that the new Palestinian finance minister, Salaam Fayyad, had begun to reform the finances and allowed two international firms to audit the finances, Sharon said he would turn over to the P.A. about $35 million each month in tax money frozen since the beginning of the Intifada. Palestinian officials would be allowed to travel freely between the West Bank and Gaza, and Israel would release about 100 detained militants. These concessions followed a promise from Abbas to work forcefully to end terrorist attacks and to secure a cease-fire from Hamas. Hamas leaders in Gaza told Western newspapers that if Abbas could get prisoners released and attacks on militants ended, they would consider a temporary truce. The al-Aqsa

Martyrs' Brigades, however, rejected "the road map to hell and any cease-fire until the rights of the Palestinian people are restored without any condition."

On June 3, President Bush arrived in Sharm al-Sheikh for the meeting of Arab leaders that included President Mubarak, King Abdullah II of Jordan, Crown Prince Abdullah of Saudi Arabia, King Hamad of Bahrain, and Mahmoud Abbas. The Arab leaders endorsed the Road Map, condemned terror and violence and called upon Israel to "rebuild trust and restore normal Palestinian life." The meeting helped to elevate the status of Abbas, as Arafat remained technically sidelined. President Bush was certainly putting his own prestige on the line, and many have asked why. As noted in *The Economist*, the war with Iraq placed America in a position to exert pressure on rejectionist countries like Syria and Iran, which had sponsored and supported terrorist groups and actions against Israel. Washington hoped that removing an immediate threat from those countries would make it more possible for Israel to compromise and more difficult for Palestinian militants to achieve their aims by violence. And it gave Bush an opportunity to try to convince the Arab and Muslim world that the war against Iraq and against terrorism was not a war against Islam.

The following day, Bush met in Aqaba with Abbas and Sharon. Abbas, afterward, issued a strong statement, which he had worked out with the Americans, renouncing terror, calling for an end to the armed Intifada and pledging a cessation of terrorist activities against Israelis anywhere. Sharon, in acknowledging that there would be a Palestinian state, said that he would order the dismantling of "illegal" outposts. Bush, seeking to allay fears that there would be no follow-up to the American initiative, assured the parties that he was committed to working for a peace between Israel and the Palestinians, that he would dispatch a team headed by John Wolf, a State Department official, to monitor progress, and that Condoleeza Rice, the National Security Advisor, and Colin Powell would act as his surrogates in the area.

The Road Map Comes to a Dead End

Within a few days, however, Arafat stated that Abbas has made too many concessions at Aqaba, and Abdul Aziz Rantisi, the Hamas spokesman, announced that Hamas would not hold any truce or cease-fire talks with Abbas. Accusing Abbas of being too conciliatory toward Israel and not insisting on the Palestinian right of return, the right of resistance against occupation, the end of Israel's assassination policy, and the release of substantial numbers of prisoners, Hamas vowed to continue the Intifada. On June 6, three terrorists dressed in Israeli army uniforms, one each from Hamas, Islamic Jihad, and the al-Aqsa Brigades, carried out a suicide mission against an Israeli army post in Gaza and killed five soldiers. Abbas condemned the attack but said that he would never use force against the militants for fear of causing a civil war. Clearly, Abbas was caught between the demands of the terrorist groups, the Israelis, and the Americans. Although obligated under the Road Map to put an end to violence against Israelis, without a power base of his own, and with many of the security services still under Arafat's control, he was in a much more difficult position than Sharon.

Sharon, at least, had the majority of Israelis supporting him, and he made a gesture of compliance with the Road Map by dismantling ten "illegal" outposts in the West Bank. In retaliation for the terrorist attack at the Erez checkpoint, however, Israel attempted a targeted assassination of Rantisi, firing a missile from a helicopter gunship on his vehicle as it was passing through an intersection in Gaza City. Although injured, he was able to escape, but his bodyguard and a bystander were killed, and many Palestinians were injured. From his hospital bed, Rantisi vowed revenge. President Bush, in a strong reprimand to Israel, condemned the attack on Rantisi. Within days, however, a Hamas suicide bomber dressed as an orthodox Jew blew up a bus in central Jerusalem, killing sixteen and injuring more than a hundred. Israel then launched helicopter gunship attacks in Gaza City, killing some Hamas officials along with several civilians, and injuring scores more. In one week alone, the combined Israeli–Palestinian death toll climbed past fifty.

As Condoleeza Rice prepared to visit the area, Egypt tried unsuccessfully to get the militant groups to agree to a cease-fire. Interestingly, it was Marwan Barghouti, working with a mobile phone from his Israeli prison cell, and with Israel's complicity, who steered the al-Aqsa Brigades, Hamas, and Islamic Jihad toward a truce. On June 29, the groups agreed to a "Hudna" for three months (a "Hudna" may be described as a truce of fixed duration). Israel was deeply suspicious of what it feared would simply be a temporary cessation of violence while the militants regrouped and rearmed. And it is possible that the groups were gambling that, in fact, Abbas would not be able to get concessions from Israel, their cease-fire would provide an excuse for his not going after the terrorist infrastructure, the Road Map would fail, and a negotiated settlement, which they continued to reject, would be impossible.

Offering Abbas some cover, the White House invited him to Washington, where President Bush said he trusted him and offered funds to the Palestinian Authority. He also spoke out against Israel's fence and against settlements, but said that Israel could not be expected to release prisoners who might commit terrorist activities again. Israel, meanwhile, had withdrawn from Bethlehem and northern Gaza, and on the eve of his own visit to Washington, Sharon announced that about 550 of roughly 5000 prisoners would be released, which the Palestinians dismissed as being not adequate and mere window dressing. Sharon also said that some road blocks in the West Bank would be removed, and that more "unauthorized" outposts would be dismantled. On the other hand, there was no sign of a letup in building activity in other settlements, and the majority of road blocks and checkpoints remained.

During the summer of 2003, although there were incidents on both sides, a kind of eerie calm prevailed—until August 19, when a terrible bus bombing in Jerusalem claimed the lives of twenty-two Israelis, including six children. The Hamas man who exploded himself, a father of two himself, in his videotaped will, said that the bombing was in retaliation for Israel's assassination of an Islamic Jihad leader the previous week. Israel immediately froze security talks and the planned withdrawal from any additional West Bank cities, and closed off the West Bank and Gaza. Israel also killed a top political leader of Hamas in Gaza, Ismail Abu Shanab, and on August 21, Hamas and Islamic Jihad announced that the truce was over. The gloves were off, as Israel announced that if the P.A. did not crack down on these groups, Israel would.

Meanwhile, Arafat and Abbas appeared to be engaged in a destabilizing power struggle. The two men were particularly at loggerheads over who should control the security services, and how or if they should be combined, a key provision of the U.S.-backed peace plan. Clearly in an attempt to undermine Abbas, Arafat appointed Jibril Rajoub, previously West Bank security chief and an adversary of Muhammad Dahlan, as National Security Advisor to preside over a new National Security Council that Arafat would direct. Even Colin Powell called on Arafat to let Abbas have some free rein, but that would not have served Arafat's purposes. In early September, Abbas asked the P.A. parliament either to support him or deprive him of his post, and on September 6, he resigned. A few hours later, Israel dropped a 550 pound bomb on a Gaza City apartment in a botched attempt to kill Hamas leaders including Sheikh Yassin and Mohammed Deif, number one on Israel's most wanted list, as part of a new approach to eradicate the Hamas infrastructure—a policy of all-out war against Hamas adopted following the August 19 bus bombing in Jerusalem.

Arafat's nomination to replace Abbas was an ally, speaker of the Palestinian parliament, Abu Alaa, or Ahmed Qurei, who had helped put together the Oslo accords in 1993. A few days later, President Bush declared that Arafat had "failed as a leader." Responding to Bush, Qurei told *The Associated Press*: "This is a regrettable statement that does not serve the peace processs . . . Arafat is the elected leader of the Palestinian people and represents the will of these people . . . President Bush and the American administration [should] respect the will of the Palestinian people."

But on September 11, 2003, the Israeli security cabinet declared that Arafat was a "complete obstacle to any reconciliation between Israel and the Palestinians," and said the government would work to "remove" this obstacle "in a manner and time of its choosing." Ehud Olmert, the deputy prime minister, even called for Arafat to be killed. Israeli forces confined Arafat to his headquarters—the *mukataa*—in Ramallah. There were extraordinary demonstrations in Ramallah and throughout the Palestinian territories supporting Arafat, who defiantly declared to thousands of supporters that Palestine was "*terra sancta*." Israel's cabinet announcement served only to enhance his stature and restore him once again to center stage despite an IMF audit of the Palestinian Authority that showed that Arafat had diverted some $900 million in public funds to a bank account he controlled. Faced with almost universal international condemnation of the threat against Arafat, on September 15 Foreign Minister Silvan Shalom declared Israel had no plans to kill Arafat, although U.S. President George Bush stated Arafat had "stalled" the Road Map.

The Road Map faced many problems, as Dennis Ross and virtually every commentator noted. There was no way to set in motion the many obligations either side was supposed to take, there was no way to judge performance and no monitoring ability, and there was lack of clarity. How did one distinguish between a social service agency and a terrorist organization? What was the real number of settler outposts? How could the two sides agree on what each would do, when, and where? It was clear that the Road Map was going nowhere and that for all intents and purposes it had collapsed.

Debate over the effectiveness of the government's strategy continued in Israel, but on October 1, the Knesset approved the extension of its "security fence" or barrier,* which at some points would extend into the West Bank for ten miles or more. Ninety miles of the projected 385-mile barrier had already been completed; however, as the peace process stalled and the al-Aqsa Intifada escalated, Prime Minister Sharon sought to include more West Bank settlements within the fence and to increase the number of new homes within them. On October 2, tenders were called for a further 600 new homes, 530 to be built at Beitar Illit, southwest of Jerusalem. In a mild rebuke, the United States announced that $300 million would be deducted from the $3 billion annual loan package to Israel—the amount already spent on construction of the fence.

Meanwhile, violence continued. In response to suicide bombings at a popular café in Jerusalem and a restaurant jointly owned by an Arab and a Jew in Haifa, Israel launched an air strike against an alleged Palestinian military training camp in Syria nine miles north of Damascus. This was the first attack on Syrian soil by Israeli forces in twenty years, and although the situation quieted down, fears were raised that the Israel–Palestinian conflict might once again spread beyond Israel's borders. Missiles were also fired at the homes of Hamas and Islamic Jihad activists in the Gaza Strip but no casualties were reported. Denouncing these actions, Arafat declared a state of emergency and Qurei formed an emergency cabinet.

Israel continued its policy of seeking out those it believed responsible for attacks against its citizens. In mid-October, it launched a major military operation on the border of the southern Gaza Strip at Rafah to uncover suspected smuggling tunnels under what is known as the Philadelphi Route. The Gaza–Egypt border runs through the middle of the town of Rafah, and the Philadelphi Route is a narrow strip of land along the Gaza side of the border. Under the 1993 Oslo accords, it was controlled by Israel. More than ten Palestinians were killed and many more injured in the raid as Israeli forces blew up at least 85 houses. Five subsequent air attacks aimed at activist leaders killed a dozen Palestinian civilians and brought international criticism. Palestinian Prime Minister Qurei sought a truce among the Palestinian factions but could

---

* The Israelis describe the structure as a security fence, the Palestinians call it a separation barrier or wall. We shall use the terms fence and barrier interchangeably.

not satisfy Israeli or world opinion that he was capable of reining them in. Hamas leader Abdul Aziz al–Rantisi offered some hope when he declared that Hamas militants would no longer target Israeli civilians in Israel, but talks in the Egyptian capital, Cairo, in early December failed to produce agreement among the various factions to establish a truce.

On November 12, the Palestinian Legislative Council approved a new government and cabinet headed by Prime Minister Qurei. The mainstream Fatah faction of the PLO dominated the Legislative Council with 66 of the 85 seats, and 15 of the 24 ministers making up the new government were members of Fatah. In an effort better to control the various groups responsible for security, as well as the militants, a Supreme National Security Council was created with both Arafat and Qurei as members, in an attempt to lessen Arafat's sole control over security matters. Nevertheless, the 74-year-old Arafat appeared to remain in firm control over the appointment of security officials.

With Arafat *persona non grata*, the principals not talking to each other, and the United States preoccupied with the ongoing conflict in Iraq, it was not surprising that there were grassroots efforts at rapprochement, which signified the intense desire of ordinary Israelis and Palestinians at least to continue a dialogue. Private peace talks led to the announcement in mid-October that opposition politicians (including former Israeli Justice Minister Yossi Beilin) together with Palestinian negotiators (including former Palestinian Information Minister Yasser Abed Rabbo) had drawn up their own peace plan. The fifty-page plan, which became known as the Geneva accord, was officially launched in that city in early December in the presence of prominent international peace advocates. Its proposals included an Israeli withdrawal from much of the West Bank and the Gaza Strip in return for the waiving of the right of return to Israel for 3.8 million Palestinian refugees. It envisaged a Palestinian state in approximately 97.5 percent of the West Bank, with some land swaps that would enable Israel to retain some of the larger settlement blocs, and with shared sovereignty of Jerusalem, including the holy sites of Judaism and Islam. Sharon immediately rejected the initiative outright, describing it as "a stab in the back." The P.A. gave it very token support, but the Palestinian militant factions also rejected it. Despite endorsement by Egypt, the plan received little support from the Arab League. Those outside the region however, the EU and the United States especially, were far more enthusiastic about the Geneva initiative.

Meanwhile, on November 19, the UN Security Council passed Resolution 1515 endorsing the "Road Map," and Sharon spoke halfheartedly about restoring the process, but he did little to stop the construction of illegal outposts in the West Bank, which under the terms of the Road Map were to be dismantled. Nor did he try to prevent the further expansion of settlements in the occupied territories. Israel's chief of staff, Moshe Ya'alon, criticized Sharon for his harsh policy toward the Palestinians, arguing that it only served to feed anti-Israeli feeling and activity among Palestinians, although Shin Bet (Israel's internal security service) disagreed.

The level of violence overall lessened in the second half of 2003 and early 2004 compared with levels in 2001 and 2002. Conflict had intensified in the Gaza Strip with numerous Palestinians and Israeli settlers and soldiers killed, but despite a suicide bombing in December and another in late January 2004 that claimed eleven lives, the number of attacks within Israel's pre-June 1967 borders in the first half of 2004 declined, and the number of Israeli fatalities was 80 percent lower than at the height of violence that broke out in September 2000. Israelis argued that this demonstrated the efficacy of the Israeli military offences, including the targeted killings of radical Palestinian Islamist leaders, in weakening the ability of Palestinians to launch strikes. The decline in successful attacks in Israel was also attributed to the effectiveness of the security fence in separating Israelis and Palestinians. Another factor leading to the relative easing of violence was that popular support for armed struggle against Israel had declined among the Palestinians, who had seen their homes, economy, and fragile infrastructure destroyed in the ongoing violence.

Sharon's Unilateral Gaza Withdrawal Plan

At the urging of Egyptian President Hosni Mubarak and the United States, the 76-year-old Israeli Prime Minister Sharon agreed to meet with his Palestinian counterpart, Prime Minister Ahmed Qurei, for the first time on March 16, 2004. On March 14, however, two teenage boys from the Gaza Strip blew themselves up, killing ten Israelis and wounding eight in a double suicide attack in the southern industrial port city of Ashdod. Militant Palestinian groups had vowed retaliation after Israel had killed fourteen people in a Gaza raid on March 7. Qurei condemned the bombings, for which Hamas and Islamic Jihad claimed responsibility, but thousands of Palestinians marched in Gaza to celebrate the event. Sharon called off the talks. He was, he stated, unwilling to resume peace talks with the new Palestinian leadership. In fact, beginning in December 2003, on a number of occasions, he and Deputy Prime Minister Ehud Olmert had publicly floated the idea of a unilateral withdrawal from Gaza. It was clear by late spring of 2004 that Sharon's disengagement plan called for the dismantling of all twenty-one Jewish settlements in the approximately 137 square mile Gaza Strip and the evacuation of the 8,000 plus settlers, along with the Israeli forces protecting them, as well as the dismantling of four small settlements in the northern West Bank. (See Map 12–1 and Document 13–2.) Israel would retain control of the border between Gaza and Egypt and would continue to control the airspace and the seacoast off of Gaza. In addition, Palestinian refugees would have no right of return to Israel.

Had Sharon been swayed by the demographic argument about the threat to the Jewish majority in the state, or by the isolation of Israel in the world community and the possible loss of American support, or by what appeared to be the inexorable drift of events? Whatever the motivation, he had caught everyone off-balance and, according to one commentator, completely recast the Israeli political and diplomatic agenda. Although he had presided over the evacuation of the Jewish settlement of Yamit in the Sinai after the peace treaty with Egypt, he was considered the architect of the settlement policy and, as infrastructure minister in Netanyahu's cabinet, the promoter of isolated settlements that would make it impossible for Israel to return territory in the West Bank. There was no indication that Sharon himself had come to believe that a Palestinian state was inevitable, and, indeed, his stated determination that Israel would continue to control the coastline, airspace, and borders of Gaza would preclude the development of a viable Palestinian entity. Many Palestinians now believed that giving up Gaza was simply a pretext for holding on to the West Bank, or at the very least, the major settlement blocs.

Sharon's dramatic disengagement plan met with fierce opposition from settlers and some leading members of his own Likud party, as well as by Palestinians and other Arab leaders including Egyptian President Hosni Mubarak. The army, through Defense Minister Shaul Mofaz, was strongly behind a complete withdrawal from Gaza, as were the majority of the Israeli population. However, the initiative threatened the stability of Sharon's coalition. Extreme nationalist and religious right-wing members of the coalition and Likud party were opposed to ceding any territory Israel had occupied since 1967 to the Palestinians, and they opposed evacuating any settlements anywhere. They saw the plan as the first step to further territorial concessions.

The Labor party and the Left were unhappy about the unilateral nature of the proposals. They feared that Sharon's plan would further hinder resumption of bilateral peace negotiations with the Palestinians, and they were suspicious of the prime minister's territorial ambitions. Was it, they wondered, a plan that would restrict a future Palestinian state to the Gaza Strip and a greatly truncated West Bank? Sharon's decision to implement his plan unilaterally was also problematic in that, by avoiding negotiations with the Palestinians for evacuating the Gaza settlements, Israel received no *quid pro quo* toward peace. The Geneva accord, in contrast, offered Israel security arrangements, an end to claims, and an end to the conflict in exchange for withdrawal from the settlements.

There were a number of troubling issues surrounding Sharon's Gaza plan besides the actual evacuation of settlements. There was the question of compensation for the evacuated settlers, the arrangements for post-withdrawal security, the disposition of the settlements' infrastructure, freedom of movement for Palestinians between Gaza and the West Bank, and between Gaza and Egypt, as well as into Israel, to name but a few.

The question of compensation was perhaps the easiest to resolve. Within a short time the Knesset agreed on a figure of as much as $300,000 to be paid to each of the approximately 1600 families. This was small comfort, however, to many who had lived in settlements for close to thirty years and had built homes and livelihoods there. While most settlers insisted that they would not resort to violence in being uprooted, there were many who said they would passively resist their removal, and there were some rabbis who encouraged religious soldiers and reservists not to obey orders forcibly to remove the settlers. "Jews do not expel Jews" became the mantra of those opposing the disengagement plan—orange their color of protest. Sharon, "the bulldozer," who had fought in all of Israel's wars, who had become prime minister promising Israelis security, who was known to distrust and even hate the Arabs, was now vilified by many in his own party and on the right of the political spectrum. The withdrawal was seen as a religious betrayal and cowardly surrender to Palestinian terrorism, and many Israelis believed that quitting Gaza was just the thin edge of a wedge that would eventually see Israel having to give up much, and perhaps all, of the West Bank as well. In addition, some Israelis expressed concern that a withdrawal from Gaza while the Intifada continued would encourage Palestinian militants bent on the use of force—the "reward for terrorism" argument. They feared it would set a precedent for the West Bank and another Intifada as, they believed, the Lebanese pullout had led to the al-Aqsa Intifada and ultimately the Gaza withdrawal.

There was particular concern about security in relation to the Gaza–Egypt border. Israel hoped that Egypt would secure this border, and in June, Foreign Minister Shalom flew to Cairo to discuss possible arrangements. Egypt was reluctant to be seen collaborating with Israel but did agree to patrol the Egyptian side of the border. Israeli security chiefs were especially worried about the smuggling of arms into the Gaza strip by Palestinian militants through tunnels under the Philadelphi Route. During the previous year, as noted above, Israel had destroyed a number of Rafah houses in which tunnel entrances were found.

The P.A. and some Israelis were also concerned that the Israeli withdrawal from Gaza would leave the area without effective government, creating greater instability. The P.A. had not been able to establish firm control of the territory, and Hamas and Islamic Jihad might take the opportunity to extend their support among the population. The assassination of Sheikh Ahmad Yassin, 66, founder and supreme leader of Hamas by an Israeli missile on March 21 as he left his Gaza City mosque, and the assassination of his successor Dr. Abdul Aziz Rantisi, a pediatrician and co-founder of Hamas, less than four weeks later on April 17, just days after Bush had endorsed Sharon's controversial plans, did not help allay these fears. Israel estimated that Hamas had been responsible for around 425 attacks that killed more than 375 people. Israel justified its policy of targeted assassinations on the ground that the P.A. would not, or could not, prevent attacks against Israelis by terrorists.

And, how would Gaza function economically? The RAND Corporation estimated that the Palestinian population of the West Bank and Gaza will nearly double in fifteen years to 6.6 million, including some 600,000 refugees who might return. If Israel continued to prohibit the Palestinians from operating a seaport or airport in Gaza, it would be extremely difficult to import and export goods. What would happen to the Erez Industrial Park, with its 200 factories, both Israeli and Palestinian owned, and its 5000 workers? How would borders and crossing points be managed? The former head of the World Bank, James Wolfensohn, was appointed as special coordinator to help the P.A. run Gaza, and Shimon Peres was also asked to help deal with economic issues affecting Gaza after the Israelis left.

The overriding concern of most Palestinians, however, was that Sharon's Gaza disengagement would distract attention from what they saw as his strategic goal of consolidating Israel's control over the West Bank. They believed that he was prepared to sacrifice the civilian settlements in Gaza to preserve the other Israeli settlements in the heart of the West Bank on the Palestinian side of the separation barrier. These settlements will be protected by confining and controlling the Palestinians through a combination of electronic sensors, roadblocks, and checkpoints that will create additional barriers within the external separation barrier.

Hoping he had sufficient support within the Likud party—the party he help found in 1979—Sharon scheduled a party referendum on his plan for May, prior to presenting it to the cabinet. Meanwhile, he sought to strengthen his position with U.S. support for the withdrawal plan. In mid-April, he visited Washington to gain White House endorsement. American efforts to engage in the peace process were hampered because the majority of the Arab and Muslim world remained furious with the United States because of its war against Iraq, another Arab country. Bush's apparent embrace of Sharon, whom he had called "a man of peace" also added to Arab hostility and suspicion of the United States. At the Bush-Sharon meeting in April, the president endorsed the idea of Israel's withdrawal from Gaza, calling it "historic and courageous." He also said that the United States would not object to Israel's retaining some West Bank settlements, and that it was unrealistic to expect that negotiations for a Palestinian state would lead to a full and complete return to the 1949 armistice lines. He also conceded that resettling Palestinian refugees in Israel was not viable. These concessions were laid out in letters exchanged between the two leaders, and they enraged the Arab and Muslim world.

This apparent new policy was seen as a clear shift from the previous American position that issues like borders and the "right of return" were to be resolved in final-status talks, and these nods to Sharon were immediately denounced by Palestinian Prime Minister Ahmed Qurei, who angrily said that "'Bush is the first U.S. president to give legitimacy to Jewish settlements on Palestinian land. We reject this." Bush insisted that Sharon's withdrawal and the new American approach were meant to bring Israelis and Palestinians closer to the final status talks, and that they did not set back the "Road Map" plans favored by the United States. The U.S. president played lip service to the validity of the international Road Map, but few doubted that it had collapsed. In these circumstances, it was not surprising that Sharon's plan received cautious approval among European powers.

No doubt in part to allay fears that he was going soft on security issues, Sharon ordered Israeli troops into Rafah once again. In the largest military incursion into the Gaza Strip since the 1967 war ("Operation Rainbow in the Cloud"), launched on May 18, around 1,000 Israeli soldiers reportedly destroyed residential dwellings leaving more than 1,000 Palestinians homeless in and around Rafah (population about 90,000), searching for Palestinian tunnels used to smuggle arms. The operation that lasted almost two weeks attracted considerable international and domestic criticism. The UN Security Council was prompted to pass yet another resolution condemning Israel on May 19 (UN Security Council Resolution 1544, 2004). According to UNWRA (the UN Works and Relief Agency), more than 17,000 Palestinians had lost their homes through Israeli demolition since the outbreak of the second Intifada in September 2000. Palestinian militants responded with a series of rocket attacks on the southern Israeli town of Sderot, prompting Israeli troops to occupy the northern Gaza Strip between Beit Hanoun and the Jabalya refugee camp.

Sharon suffered a political setback in the Likud party referendum held in May. Although only just over half of the members participated, 60 percent of them voted in a nonbinding vote against the disengagement plan. Nevertheless, Sharon survived a vote of no-confidence in the Knesset, and defiantly told his Likud and other opponents that he could always form a government of national unity with the Labor Party. To emphasize his determination to press ahead with his plan, on June 4, two days before the cabinet was to vote on the issue, Sharon removed two hard-line National Union Party members from the 23-member cabinet. On June 6, exactly thirty-seven years after Israel seized control of Gaza on the second day of the June 1967 war, the now 21-member cabinet voted 14 to 7 in principle to withdraw from the Strip, in a slightly altered plan. However, within a few days, with the loss of support of all seven National Union Party members and the defection of two National Religious Party cabinet members, the prime minister's coalition consisted of only 59 of the 120-member Knesset (40 from Likud, 15 from the secularist centrist Shinui Party, and 4 from the NRP). This was not the first time an Israeli prime minister had led a minority government, and Sharon's position as leader of the government was not immediately threatened, as he could rely on the support of the Labor party (19 seats), at least in the short term. And he needed it. Sharon survived two votes of no-confidence in the Knesset on the day after the cabinet vote on disengagement.

In mid-June, Sharon's position as prime minister was strengthened with the good news that Attorney General Menachem Mazuz had decided that he would not indict the prime minister or his sons, whom the state prosecutor in March had recommended be charged for bribery and corruption in what had become known as the Greek Island affair. Sharon had been under a cloud since the end of October 2003, when he had been questioned by police regarding allegations that while foreign minister in a previous Likud government he had given political favors to a political supporter in return for payments to his son Gilad.

Controversy over the Security Barrier and Targeted Killings

Israel felt the heat of international scrutiny over its security fence and the question of nuclear weapons in June and July 2004. On June 30, the Israeli Supreme Court, in a case brought by Arab villagers (and no doubt keen to preempt the World Court—formerly the International Court of Justice—in The Hague, The Netherlands), ruled that a 20-mile section of the proposed 385-mile security fence being built in the West Bank would have to be rerouted because it violated the human rights of some 35,000 local Palestinians near Jerusalem. Broadly popular in Israel for preventing terror attacks in the north where it was completed, the barrier was adamantly opposed by the Palestinians. On July 1, the court ordered the temporary suspension of the barrier near Har Homa just southeast of Jerusalem. On July 9, the World Court in its nonbinding verdict on the construction of Israel's security barrier, stated that its route inside occupied territory breached international law. The ruling was rejected by Prime Minister Sharon, but Attorney General Mazuz called for the government to alter the route of the proposed barrier to comply with Israel's Supreme Court ruling handed down ten days earlier. However, the government was determined that the large Jewish settlement blocs of Ma'ale Adumim and Gush Etzion would remain on the Israeli side of the barrier.

A few weeks later, on July 20, a United Nations General Assembly resolution, which passed 150 to 6, with 10 abstentions, called on Israel to obey the World Court ruling and tear down the barrier. Along with the Israeli Supreme Court decision, the World Court and UN declarations were a victory for the Palestinians, who continue to see the barrier as a land grab that slices up their territory and makes a coherent state more difficult to achieve. Despite international criticism, the majority of the Israeli public support the construction of the fence, believing it is one of the major reasons for the decrease in Palestinian attacks within Israel.

Israel's secrecy surrounding its nuclear weapons was an especially sensitive issue, especially given the world's (and Israel's) interest in the nuclear programs of Iran and North Korea. On July 6–8, the UN International Atomic Energy Agency (IAEA) visited Israel but Israeli officials refused to confirm or deny possession of nuclear weapons. In late July, the Supreme Court refused Mordechai Vanunu, who had leaked the details of Israel's nuclear program and been jailed, permission to travel outside Israel for at least a year, and in November he was rearrested and held for seven days under house arrest on suspicion of leaking "national secrets" in talks with foreign journalists.

Palestinian militants resumed their attacks within Israel in July and August. Several Israelis were killed when the al-Aqsa Martyrs' Brigade exploded a bomb near a bus in central Tel Aviv on July 11. On August 31, more than sixteen people were killed and over one hundred injured when Hamas suicide bombers blew up two buses in Beersheba in southern Israel. Israel responded by closing the city of Hebron and launching tank and aerial attacks on a suspected Hamas training center in Gaza City, killing fourteen and wounding thirty in the largest attack in the Gaza Strip since Operation Rainbow in May. Israel also issued warnings to Syria, which it claimed harbored and encouraged leading Hamas figures.

At the end of September, Israel launched a large fifteen-day incursion (code-named "Operation Days of Penitence") into the northern Gaza Strip to put an end to rocket attacks into Israel. At least 66 Palestinian militants and around 50 civilians were killed in an attack that took place in and around the Jabalya refugee camp. Over 230 houses were destroyed and hundreds of hectares of agricultural land bulldozed. News organizations estimated that up to 3334 Palestinians and 1017 Israelis had died in the four years since the outbreak of the second Intifada in September 2000, and that more than 620 of the Palestinian and 110 of the Israeli dead were children age 17 and under. Sharon defended IDF actions, arguing that the targeted assassinations and forays into Palestinian neighborhoods decimated terrorist leadership, and that the road blocks intercepted hundreds of would-be suicide bombers. Israel paid a price, though, in anti-Israel sentiment, increasing anti-Semitism, especially in Europe, and calls for boycotts of Israeli universities and academics.

Sharon hunkered down, seeking to further his Gaza withdrawal plans while pacifying opponents. He was besieged on all sides. On August 24, a week after the Likud party voted to reject his proposal to form a coalition with the Labor party, he announced plans to build more than 1500 new homes in the West Bank. His strategy was to deflect discontent with his Gaza withdrawal by strengthening Israel's hold on the West Bank, especially the settlement blocs close to Jerusalem. This announcement met with an immediate rebuke from UN Secretary General Kofi Annan, who called on Israel to stop the expansion of settlements in the Palestinian territories. Nor did the proposed additional homes silence domestic opposition. On September 12, thousands of Jewish settlers demonstrated at the Western ("Wailing") Wall in Jerusalem demanding a referendum on the plan. Two days later the Security Cabinet approved a compensation package in which each settler family would receive between $200,000 and $400,000 to relocate, and on October 24, the compensation package for the 8,000 Jewish settlers was approved by the whole cabinet. On October 25, the Knesset passed Sharon's plan to dismantle all twenty-one settlements in the Gaza Strip and four in the northern West Bank by a margin of 67 votes to 45. The Knesset approved the compensation package on November 3, conditional upon approval of the budget in 2005.

While Sharon struggled to keep his government functioning, Arafat was himself facing a virtual uprising against his leadership in Gaza. Violent protests broke out, which began when Palestinians affiliated with Fatah kidnapped four French workers and two Palestinian police commissioners, saying they would not release them unless Arafat tackled corruption in the P.A. by, among other things, sacking the Old Guard. The hostages were released the next morning, but Prime Minister Qurei described Gaza as being in "an unprecedented state of chaos." Arafat said that he would consolidate the dozen or so security forces of about 40,000 men into three, but that he would keep control, instead of turning it over to his prime minister. This caused Qurei to tender his resignation, which Arafat, however, would not accept. When Arafat named his cousin Musa, former head of military intelligence in Gaza, as public security chief, thousands of Palestinians protested in front of the Legislative Council headquarters, P.A. offices in Khan Younis were burned, and the al-Aqsa Martyrs' Brigades rejected the appointment. (Musa Arafat was assassinated in September 2005 by unknown Palestinians.) It seemed clear that lawlessness was increasing as different parties, groups, and factions began to try to strengthen their positions before Israel's withdrawal. There were no clear directives from Arafat, and corruption ran rampant. It is almost certain that Muhammad Dahlan, the former P.A. security chief in Gaza was behind the protest demonstrations. Dahlan had come out in favor of the Israeli withdrawal because he said it would allow Palestinians to show they could govern themselves, and he called for Palestinian elections.

The demonstrations in Gaza sputtered out, and evidently there was a rapprochement between Dahlan and Arafat, but the tensions continued to simmer. The prospect of Israeli withdrawal had set off a struggle of Palestinians for control, both within Fatah itself and between Fatah and the more radical factions of Hamas and Islamic Jihad. The major source of conflict was between those who continued to represent a "liberation movement," and those whose main concern was state-building. It was noteworthy, however, that Hamas agreed to take part in local elections scheduled to take place for the first time since 1976 in the territories.

Israel had destroyed much of Hamas's organization in the West Bank and much of its infrastructure in Gaza and, through its policy of targeted assassinations, had removed its most visible leaders. Hamas's basic ideology, however, remained unchanged, as illustrated in the two bus bombings in Beersheba it carried out in late August, presumably in revenge for the Israeli assassinations earlier in the year of Sheikh Yassin and Abdul Aziz al-Rantisi.

Before the al-Aqsa Intifada, some 30,000 of the 1.4 million Palestinians in Gaza had worked in Israel, but that had trickled to just a few thousand. In the fall of 2004, the average daily wage in Gaza was about $12.00 a day, and unemployment was estimated by *The Economist* as being as high as 60 percent. Those working had an average of 7.7 dependents. On the West Bank, with its 1.8 million Palestinians, some 160 checkpoints, as well as the security barrier, had restricted movement and hampered daily life. There was also a breakdown of law and order as in Gaza, and the police and security forces were equally corrupt and ineffective.

Death of Yasser Arafat: Mahmoud Abbas Elected President of P.A.

In November 2004, as George W. Bush won reelection in the U.S. presidential election, Yasser Arafat lay ill and dying in a Paris hospital. Sick and frail, the 75-year-old Arafat finally succumbed on November 11. An official funeral service was held in Cairo, his place of birth, on November 12, attended by heads of state of many Arab nations and most European foreign ministers. Arafat's body was then flown to Ramallah to be buried, not in Jerusalem as he had wished. He was buried in the compound of the mukataa where he had been under siege by Israel for the last three years of his life. Twenty thousand grieving mourners surged into the compound, although his widow Suha was not there. Forty days of mourning followed.

"Mr. Palestine" was dead. Arafat will be remembered for his failures as well as his accomplishments. He achieved much for his people and made a separate Palestinian identity a reality. His was a liberation movement that achieved world recognition, and he was always its symbol and spokesman. But Arafat had not been able, or perhaps had not wanted, to engage in state-building. He kept his cards close to his chest, lacked a clear ideology except for revolution and liberation, and was unwilling to share power or resources. As long as he lived, there could never be true democracy or power-sharing in the Palestinian Authority, no way to tackle corruption or to build viable institutions, and he left behind a highly factionalized movement.

To most observers, especially in Israel and the United States, his abrupt departure from the negotiating table at Camp David II suggested his inability to seize clear opportunities, when presented, to further his goal of an independent state of Palestine. Despite his avowed shift from embracing armed struggle to advocating diplomatic means to achieve a Palestinian state, most Israelis, except perhaps for the ever-optimistic Shimon Peres, and the dovish Left, had never trusted Arafat, had never considered him anything but a terrorist, and his unleashing of the al-Aqsa Intifada, they said, proved them right. The second Intifada certainly destroyed the peace camp in Israel. So deep was this hatred and fear of Arafat among Israelis that the only Israeli leader to sign a peace accord with him, Yitzhak Rabin, was shot and killed by a Jewish right-wing extremist. With Arafat's death, however, opportunities for negotiations to resume between Israel and the Palestinian Authority appeared to open up, if ways could be found to realize them.

Mahmoud Abbas was selected as the new head of the PLO, and on December 23 some 140,000 Palestinians voted for around 800 candidates in municipal elections in the West Bank in the first local elections since 1976. Fatah candidates were returned in over half (16) of the councils, although Hamas won in nine. (Hamas did even better in 10 municipalities in the Gaza Strip in January 2005.) Abbas, along with seven other candidates, then kicked off a two-week electoral campaign in advance of presidential elections to be held in January. He reiterated Palestinian demands: that Israel withdraw from all the occupied territory; that East Jerusalem become the capital of a Palestinian state; and that the "right of return" of Palestinian refugees be recognized. Probably to appease his more militant critics, he also called Israel "the Zionist enemy."

On January 9, 2005, Abbas won the presidential election after a 66 percent voter turnout with close to 70 percent of the vote. This was hailed as a true democratic election, and it was noteworthy that, in fact, he did not receive the customary 99 percent of the vote, and that there were other viable candidates. The election was boycotted by Hamas and Islamic Jihad on the grounds that an election held under occupation was not free and fair. In the Gaza Strip, where Hamas had most of its supporters, it is estimated that about half of the eligible voters voted.

It was widely speculated, however, that had he not withdrawn his candidacy in order to avoid a split in Fatah, Marwan Barghouti, currently imprisoned in Israel after being convicted for a number of killings, might have won the election. During the second Intifada, Barghouti became increasingly popular as a leader of the Fatah Tanzim militia, an organization that carried out bombings under the name of the al-Aqsa Martyrs' Brigades. On June 6, 2004, he had been sentenced to five life sentences for five murders, and 40 years imprisonment for attempted murder. Barghouti declared his candidacy just before the registration deadline expired but unexpectedly retired from the race on December 12. With his withdrawal, Mahmoud Abbas was assured of victory.

President Bush stated that the election marked an essential step toward the goal of Palestinian statehood and promised to help the new president in a renewed push for peace talks with Israel. Sharon congratulated Abbas on his victory and urged the new Palestinian leader to invest efforts to end attacks on Israelis. The EU also praised the election.

Critics insisted that Abbas's goals were the same as Arafat's, and that only the tactics were different. They noted that he had publicly questioned the utility of the Intifada and disavowed violence and suicide attacks against Israelis not because they were wrong, but because they hurt the Palestinian cause and gave Israel a pretext to reoccupy the territories. Shortly after he assumed the presidency, however, reciprocal measures began to be seen. Abbas ordered the security forces to try to prevent attacks against Israel, and Israel resumed security contacts with the Palestinians, although Sharon said political contacts would not be resumed until Abbas acted against Hamas and Islamic Jihad. Abbas was not prepared to do this, saying that trying to dismantle the extremist organizations by force would unleash a civil war. Instead, he went to Gaza to talk to Hamas and Islamic Jihad leaders about a cease-fire and about bringing Hamas into the political process. While Israel kept insisting that he dismantle the infrastructure of terrorism and do something to reform the security forces, Abbas also felt that he could not be seen to be doing Israel's bidding. He did order hundreds of Palestinian security forces to deploy in northern Gaza to try to prevent the launching of mortars and Qassam rockets toward Israeli targets, and Israel responded by partially reopening the Rafah crossing between Egypt and Gaza.

Sharon's minority coalition Likud government had collapsed on December 1, because of differences over the budget and the subsequent sacking of the five cabinet ministers belonging to the Shinui Party. He was left reliant upon only the 40 members of his Likud party. The Israeli prime minister was not the only Israeli politician facing rebellion with his party, however. In late August, Peres faced opposition from within the Labor party over joining Sharon in a unity government. But on December 17, Sharon reached agreement with Peres to form a new coalition government with eight Labor ministers. Peres was to be second deputy prime minister, and the coalition was joined by the five member ultra-orthodox United Torah Judaism. Sharon's position was far from secure however. The Knesset only narrowly approved the new coalition government on January 10, 2005, as 13 "rebel" members of the Likud party voted against the government in protest over the disengagement plan. Two days later, the first reading of the 2005 budget was passed. Thousands of settlers once again held demonstrations, this time outside the Knesset. The budget was finally passed (58 to 36) on March 29 with the support of the opposition Shinui party just two days before the budget deadline date. If the Knesset had failed to pass the budget by March 31, Sharon would have had to resign and call elections, possibly killing the Gaza plan.

Tensions eased between Israel and the Palestinian Authority. In late January 2005, Israel said that it would stop marking Palestinian militants for death, and this move apparently prompted the extremists to suspend attacks on Israelis while talks continued with Abbas about a longer-term cease-fire at least until the Palestinian legislative elections scheduled in July. At the urging of Egyptian President Mubarak, Sharon agreed to meet Abbas on February 8, at Sharm al-Sheikh. On February 1, the Israeli attorney general declared unlawful a government decision to seize land around Jerusalem from Palestinian owners, and in a goodwill gesture, on February 3, the Israeli Cabinet agreed to release 900 Palestinian prisoners (mostly administrative detainees, a large number of whom were members of Abbas's Fatah faction) and to pull troops back from West Bank towns, including Jericho. Israel held around 8,000 Palestinians on security-related charges, and Abbas was under intense pressure at home to have them freed. Bush promised funds to help the process.

At their Sharm al-Sheikh meeting hosted by Mubarak and attended also by King Abdullah II of Jordan, Sharon and Abbas announced a mutual cease-fire, agreed to halt all acts of violence against each other, and spoke of a new opportunity for peace and calm. Perhaps more important, they agreed to coordinate efforts on the Gaza and West Bank disengagement and to work together on security coordination. Hamas said that Abbas's statement was a unilateral declaration by the P.A. and that it was not binding on them, but after Abbas spent five days in Gaza negotiating with Hamas leaders, they agreed to a temporary period of quiet.

Significantly, no American mediator was present at this meeting, but both Egypt and Jordan stated they would soon return their ambassadors to Israel. It should be noted that the summit dealt with issues of Israeli security, but not with the settlements or the barrier, although both leaders talked about reviving the Road Map. Sharon not only agreed to release the 900 prisoners, but also to discuss with a joint commission the release of another 2000 or so in jail since before Oslo. He also announced that Israel would allow exiled militants involved in the siege at the Church of the Nativity in Bethlehem in spring 2002 to return to their hometowns. Thirteen of them, once branded as "senior terrorists," had been deported to Europe, another twenty-six to Gaza. Further, he said that Israel would pull back from and give the Palestinian security forces control over the major West Bank cities, and that more work permits would be given to Gazans. In another significant move, shortly after this summit, Shaul Mofaz, Israel's defense minister, ordered a halt to the policy of demolishing the homes of Palestinian militants. It is estimated by B'Tselem, the Israeli human rights group, that Israel had destroyed about 675 homes since the start of the Intifada. The first 500 Palestinian prisoners were released on February 21, and on June 2 another 400 prisoners were released as promised.

Subsequent to these events, both Jordan and Egypt returned their ambassadors to Israel after a four-year absence. Ahmed Qurei won the support of his Fatah party for a new 24-member cabinet of professionals and technocrats, seventeen of whom had had no prior high-level political experience, tasked to institute changes in Palestinian political life. Most were experts in their respective fields and held doctorates or medical, law, or engineering degrees. Initially, Qurei had presented a cabinet stacked with old-guard Arafat loyalists, which lawmakers, complaining of corruption and mismanagement, vetoed. Although not in the Cabinet, Saeb Erekat remained as the Palestinian chief negotiator with Israel. Nabil Shaath was appointed a deputy prime minister and information minister.

The new government was tested rather early when a suicide bomber killed four at a seaside Tel Aviv club on February 25. It was the first attack against Israeli civilians since November, when three were killed at a food market in Tel Aviv. Saeb Erekat condemned the act and called it an attempt to undermine Palestinian national interests, and Abbas called it an "act of sabotage." Despite the attack, Israeli troops went ahead with the planned transfer of security control to the P.A. in Jericho in mid-March, in what was expected to be the beginning of the process of returning the five major West Bank towns to Palestinian control, although several weeks later, the return of Bethlehem, Qalqilya, and Ramallah was frozen after Israel said that in Jericho and Tulkarm the P.A. did not live up to its promise to disarm wanted militants.

Hamas, meanwhile, confirmed publicly that it would participate in Palestinian legislative elections scheduled for July 17, ending a ten-year boycott of the Palestinian Authority. Regarding both Israel and the P.A. as illegitimate, Hamas had not taken part in elections in 1996 since the P.A. was an outcome of the 1993 Oslo accords that Hamas rejected. A Hamas spokesman said that the group would run on a platform "of the legitimate rights of the Palestinian people and protecting the program of resistance as a strategic choice until the occupation is swept away." At a two-day meeting in Cairo, Abbas met with thirteen of the Palestinian factions, which agreed to extend their informal truce through the rest of the year.

In February, Sharon won two significant votes. The Knesset passed the Evacuation Compensation Law on February 16, and on February 20, the Cabinet by a vote of 17 to 5 gave final approval for the withdrawal from Gaza and the four West Bank settlements, and also approved the final route of the security fence in the West Bank. The revised route of the barrier, which was closer to the Green Line, focused on the southern West Bank and reduced the amount of West Bank land on the Israeli side from 15 percent to 7–8 percent. As expected, it incorporated Ma'ale Adumim, Ariel, and Gush Etzion, and a large majority of the 240,000 settlers in the West Bank as well as the more than 200,000 Israelis living in the eastern part of Jerusalem annexed after 1967. *The New York Times* estimated that 99.5 percent of Palestinians would live outside the barrier in 92 percent of the West Bank, with 74 percent of Israeli settlers inside it—before any final negotiations. The other 26 percent of Israelis would have to move or live within a Palestinian state. Fewer than 10,000 Palestinians would be inside the barrier. Under the compensation plan, most Gaza families would receive $200,000 to $400,000 and could move anywhere in Israel or to one of the West Bank settlements that would remain under Israeli sovereignty. Netanyahu and Natan Sharansky, Minister for Diaspora Affairs and Jerusalem, voted against the withdrawal, and both eventually left the Cabinet.

Withdrawal of settlements was to begin on July 20; however, because the work would have begun during a mourning period before a Jewish fast day, Sharon announced a three-week delay until August 15 to begin the withdrawal. Meanwhile, at its annual convention on March 3 the Likud party voted to hold a national referendum on the withdrawal. Sharon ignored the vote, which he considered a last-ditch delaying tactic. "I will not allow the extremist margins to dictate our policy," he told the party. A few weeks later, on March 21, the government announced plans to build an additional 3,500 housing units in a 4.6 square mile area known as E-1 within the extended municipal boundaries of the settlement at Ma'ale Adumim. Should the construction of these houses go ahead (not recognized under international law, but approved by Israeli authorities) they would link the settlement to Jerusalem, creating Israeli territorial contiguity in an area the status of which is supposed to be discussed in peace negotiations with the Palestinians. An Israeli report—the Sasson report—made public in March also criticized the government for its support of around 105 illegal West Bank outposts, many of which had been built in the previous three years and were thereby prohibited under the Road Map.

On April 11, Prime Minister Sharon visited president Bush at the president's ranch in Crawford, Texas. The visit was complicated by Israel's announcement about the additional homes to be built in Ma'ale Adumim. Sharon, although rebuked by Bush, said that since the Road Map was not yet in force because the Palestinians had not dismantled the terror organizations, it was his understanding that Washington would allow construction within existing built-up areas, but not outside. Bush again urged Sharon to halt settlement expansion in the West Bank, and under intense U.S. pressure, Sharon later froze plans to expand Ma'ale Adumim. Meanwhile, the first disengagement steps were taken on April 20 with the removal of military equipment from southern Gaza.

In local elections at the beginning of May, Fatah won in at least 45 of 84 municipalities, but Hamas won in 23, including Rafah and Bureij, results challenged by Fatah. Independents or no clear winner accounted for the remaining sixteen. Problems also surfaced within Fatah regarding the impending elections for a new Palestinian legislature. President Abbas and Prime Minister Qurei were engaged in a struggle for control of the Legislative Council. On May 18, the legislature voted for a new law providing that two-third of the seats be filled from local constituencies and one-third from national party lists, but Abbas refused to sign the law. He wanted all 132 seats in a new legislature to be filled through a system of party lists, in order to reduce the influence of powerful local families and clans upon which many Fatah legislators relied. Qurei resisted the reforms proposed by Abbas and supported the Fatah old guard.

Abbas visited Washington at the end of May seeking U.S. assurances of help in halting Israeli settlement activity. It was his first meeting at the White House as president of the P.A. Bush renewed his demand that Israel stop expanding settlements in contested areas and announced that he would send Secretary of State Condoleeza Rice to Jerusalem and Ramallah before Israel's scheduled Gaza withdrawal to urge Israeli and Palestinian restraint. The president also pledged $50 million in direct aid (instead of through NGOs) to the P.A. for new housing and infrastructure projects. Praising Abbas as "a man of courage," Bush reiterated that long-term issues regarding a future Palestinian state, including its boundaries, would have to be negotiated between the two sides and not imposed by Israel, although Abbas remained concerned about Bush's letter to Sharon about final borders reflecting certain "realities" in the West Bank.

The Bush administration had reservations about Abbas's unwillingness to go after the militants and to draw Hamas into the political process. Officially, the United States continued to label Hamas, like Hizbullah, a terrorist organization, which it refused to recognize. Abbas, however, continued to insist that his tactics had helped reduce violence, thus making peace negotiations more possible.

Initially unable to reach a compromise on a new election law, in early June Abbas announced that he would postpone the planned July Palestinian legislative elections. In mid-June, the Palestinian parliament finally passed a compromise election law creating a mixed system, with half the legislators to be chosen by districts and the other half from a national slate of party candidates. The number of delegates would be increased to 132 from the current 88. The elections were rescheduled for late January 2006.

On June 21, 2005, Sharon and Abbas met for the first time in over four months. Secretary of State Rice had been in Jerusalem two days before, insisting both sides work together on the disengagement plan, but the talks between the two leaders were a bust. They met for two hours, with the Palestinians insisting on freedom of movement in and out of Gaza and the use of an airport and seaport, the release of prisoners, and key Palestinian towns on the West Bank handed back to their control, and Israel insisting again that first all Palestinian attacks against Israel had to stop. A joint press conference was cancelled. At a somewhat lower level, Israelis and Palestinians, with U.S. approval, agreed that Israel would demolish the Gaza houses to make way for more suitable housing for the Palestinians, although the question of how to dispose of the rubble from the demolition was left unresolved.

To accommodate the settlers leaving Gaza, on June 26 the Israeli cabinet approved a plan for a new community along the southern Mediterranean coast, just north of Ashkelon, to be called Nitzanim, on land part of which is a nature reserve. The land was to be sold at cut-rate prices and would be in addition to the compensation offered to a family. Environmentalists and beach lovers opposed this move, and there were objections as well to offering the settlers land for a fraction of the cost of comparable real estate in the vicinity. The main settlers' council, Yesha, was also "dismissive," but some families accepted this option.

As the date for the pull-out approached, however, violence began to escalate. On July 12, in the second suicide bombing since the "truce" in February, a Palestinian suicide bomber from Islamic Jihad killed himself and five Israelis at a busy intersection outside a shopping mall in Netanya. In an apparent linked incident, a truck laden with gas canisters exploded inside the main entrance of Shavei Shomron, a West Bank settlement about twenty miles east of Netanya. Two days later, an Israeli woman was killed and another Israeli wounded when a Qassam rocket fired from Gaza landed on a house in the kibbutz of Netiv Haasara. This was supposedly in retaliation for the arrest by Israel after the Netanya attack of several Islamic Jihad militants in the West Bank and killing of one of them. The Palestinian authorities said that Hamas was responsible for the rocket attack and later clashed with Hamas militants, although both Hamas and the al-Aqsa Brigades claimed responsibility. After Palestinian fighters unleashed another barrage of rockets and mortars from Gaza, Israeli helicopters fired missiles killing seven Hamas militants in a series of air strikes on Gaza City and Khan Younis. Hamas threatened revenge for the air strikes, which seemed to signal a resumption by Israel of targeted killings, which it had agreed to stop in February.

Violence also pitted Palestinians against Palestinians, as Abbas attempted to curb the activities of armed groups. Clashes erupted in Gaza City in the worst internal fighting in recent years, after Palestinian security forces raided a neighborhood searching for militants suspected of firing rockets. Militants later torched a police station and set a police armored personnel carrier and three jeeps on fire. Two boys were killed in the crossfire, and there were heavy exchanges of fire. Militants meanwhile continued to attack Israeli targets, launching dozens of mortar shells and rockets from across the Gaza Strip.

As these events were occurring, three bills were introduced in the Knesset to delay the withdrawal decision, but they were defeated, thus removing the last possible barrier to Israel's pull-back scheduled for August 15. By mid-July, about 10 percent of the Israeli greenhouses in Gaza had been dismantled, but there were efforts underway to preserve the remaining ones in order to assure jobs and production for the Palestinians. An agreement was eventually brokered by James Wolfensohn, the Bush administration's Middle East envoy and former head of the World Bank, for a private Israeli foundation to buy the greenhouses for $14 million. Wolfensohn contributed $500,000 of his own money, and rounded up American and other donors to provide the rest. According to the *New York Times*, the agreement left intact 90 percent of the approximately 1000 greenhouses in Gush Katif, the main settlement cluster in Gaza. The greenhouses employed around 4000 Palestinians, and it was hoped that they would provide jobs for an additional 6000 in the local economy. Among the unresolved issues was whether Israel could or would find a way to let Palestinian goods in sealed containers move from Gaza into Israel without being unloaded and reloaded again on Israeli trucks.

As the date for the withdrawal approached, protest rallies in Israel began to attract ever larger crowds, many chanting "Jews do not expel Jews" and most wearing the symbolic orange signifying support for the settlers and opposition to the withdrawal. In southern Israel, soldiers and police blocked the route into Gaza, and police prevented many buses and cars from traveling to the demonstrations from other parts of Israel. In one particularly large demonstration, and perhaps responding to the charge that their actions were undemocratic, the police did allow the demonstrators to spend the night in Kfar Maimon, close to the border with Gaza. The army, however, moved in to evict about 150 right-wing protesters who were holed up in the Palm Beach hotel in Gaza for a month or so, using it as a headquarters for resistance. Despite the official closure of Gaza to Israelis not already living there, several thousand protesters, intent on preventing the forcible removal of the settlers, continued to infiltrate the area, being housed by some of the settlers or setting up makeshift campsites.

Sharon stood firm and was supported by the vast majority of police and military forces, as well as the majority of Israelis. In the first week of August, however, Finance Minister Benjamin Netanyahu, in a move anticipated and encouraged by the Israeli right-wing, resigned his cabinet post in protest over the Gaza withdrawal. Communal anger also threatened to get out of control in early August when a disgruntled Jewish extremist and army deserter shot and killed a number of Israeli Arabs on a bus in northern Israel and was in turn murdered by an angry crowd of passengers and bystanders.

At midnight on August 14, Gaza was sealed off, and the settlers who had not already left were given 48 hours to leave voluntarily before forcible evictions were to take place. Many in the northern Gaza Strip left of their own accord, and others in some of the settlements also prepared to leave. Settlers at Neve Dekalim, a holdout, said they would resist, and there were some who said they would resist with violence if necessary. After the 48 hours, the army and police moved in to evict forcibly those settlers and protesters who remained. Immediately following the evacuations of Nissanit and Dugit in the northern Gaza Strip, bulldozers razed more than thirty homes, marking the first large-scale demolitions during the disengagement.

Hamas proclaimed victory, saying it was their actions that caused the Israelis to leave, and many Palestinians believed, or preferred to believe, that was the case, which is exactly what many in Israel who opposed the withdrawal feared—and also believed or preferred to believe. Some Israelis feared that the evacuation of Gaza would be interpreted by radical Palestinians as a reward for terrorism, which would encourage them to continue their violent activities in the West Bank. Indeed, Hamas leaders vowed that they would not lay down their arms until all of Palestine had been liberated. Abbas, meanwhile, issued statements urging Palestinians not to attack the Israelis, or loot, or otherwise impede the evacuations, and by and large the Palestinians did nothing to interfere with the process.

Evacuation Completed

Except for some isolated incidents, the withdrawal was carried off peacefully. Emotional and prayerful scenes took place throughout Gaza, and the residents of Katif, prior to their departure, hung a sign on the gate: "We shall return soon." On Monday August 22, the last of the settlements, Netzarim, was evacuated. The eighty original families, along with twenty recent arrivals, held a ceremony and communal worship service before leaving peacefully. Netzarim had long been a symbol and flashpoint for both Israelis and Palestinians. Isolated and hard to defend, the central Gaza enclave was frequently the target of daily Palestinian rifle fire. Settlers placed signs throughout Israel proclaiming "It is at Netzarim that Israel will triumph." In the first month of the al-Aqsa Intifada, Netzarim junction was the site of an Israeli–Palestinian exchange of fire, which killed 12-year-old Mohammed al-Durra, who became the central Palestinian icon of the uprising.

By Monday evening, August 22, Dan Harel, the evacuation military commander, announced that the army and police had completed their task, and that no Israeli civilians remained in Gaza. The evacuation had taken place with relatively little violent confrontation.

Southern district police commander Uri Bar-Lev estimated that the number of illegal infiltrators who had managed to penetrate the area before the evacuation began was less than 1500, despite the predictions of some that between 5000 and 8000 infiltrators would confront security forces. During the pullout, 949 arrests were made and 701 detainees who were not involved in violence against security forces were released. At the end of the Gaza operations, 310 disengagement opponents remained in prison.

Stiffer resistance was expected to the dismantling of the four northern West Bank settlements, where around 2,100 opponents had illegally infiltrated Sanur and Homesh, the first two settlements listed for evacuation. Army-backed police arrested 87 right-wing activists en-route to the settlements, and protesters firebombed an Israel Defense Forces communications position near Homesh. The protesters also spread spikes on the road, puncturing the tires of military vehicles summoned to the site. An IDF vehicle was attacked near the Kedumim junction near the settlements during a violent demonstration, but resistance was overcome, and the settlements were emptied.

Meanwhile, Egyptian security forces backed by armored vehicles were deployed in the Sinai Peninsula on a massive sweep through the desert region in search of terrorists. Since October 2004, a number of deadly attacks had taken place in the Sinai, beginning with hotel bombings in the resort of Taba. In July, dozens were killed in three blasts that targeted Sharm al-Sheikh, the highly popular resort at the southern tip of the Sinai, and in early August a bomb in northern Sinai hit a vehicle carrying peacekeepers of the Multinational Force and Observers, which helps to monitor the 1979 Egypt–Israeli peace agreement.

During the Gaza evacuation, 750 Egyptian security forces took up positions along the Gaza–Egypt border in the area of Rafah's Philadelphi route to monitor arms smuggling. Like Israel, Egypt, concerned about its own Muslim extremists and the influence of the Muslim Brotherhood, viewed with some trepidation the possible takeover in Gaza of Hamas and Islamic Jihad should Abbas and the P.A. not prevail.

By September 12, the IDF had completed the demolition of Jewish houses and military outposts and, leaving more than twenty synagogues intact, withdrew completely from the Gaza Strip, handing it over to the Palestinian Authority. The orderly Israeli military departure was followed shortly after by chaotic scenes of Palestinians celebrating on the beach front, and ugly scenes of Palestinians setting alight some of the settlement synagogues. Despite efforts by Palestinian security forces to prevent it, the celebrations were accompanied by widespread uncontrolled looting. The deputy Palestinian finance minister reported that about 30 percent of the greenhouses that had been turned over sustained various degrees of damage. The 38-year era of Israeli settlement in the Gaza Strip had come to an end.

Conclusion

Implications of Gaza Withdrawal

Many questions remain. How the disengagement will be judged retrospectively is difficult to assess. Will Gaza be a successful model for future Palestinian independence? What will happen in the West Bank? Will violent conflict between Israel and Palestinians continue and if so, on what scale?

The Palestinian Authority viewed the withdrawal with cautious optimism. President Abbas called upon Palestinians to celebrate a "great historic victory," and urged them to lay down their arms and look forward to a normal life living in peace like other peoples. But after years of virtually continuous warfare the P.A. faced enormous problems. It cannot build economic prosperity or security without outside assistance. It wants, and needs, the support of Israel—and that of the United States and EU—to create an independent modern economy, but it cannot be seen to be cooperating too fully with its former enemy. Hamas, already popular among Gaza Palestinians because of its social services and its stand against corruption, claimed Israel's departure a victory not for the P.A. but for their armed struggle, which it has vowed to continue. The P.A., however, cannot afford to lose the support of the population to extremist elements. It hopes that the economic plan under formulation by James Wolfensohn will assist in raising the standard of living of Palestinians and strengthen Abbas in the face of Hamas. The challenge is for Abbas to keep his promise to maintain "one authority, one law and one armed force." The political process can then continue. It is in Israel's interest to assist the P.A. and the Palestinians, because a Gaza Strip rife with privation and poverty would pose a danger to Israel. Another avenue for the Palestinian Authority is stronger and closer ties with Egypt and with Jordan—an idea strengthened by the fact that the wife of King Abdullah II, Queen Rania, is a Palestinian.

However, Palestinians fear that Israel will maintain control over Gaza's territorial, sea, and air space, and all border crossings. They will not be permitted to rebuild the airport. The Israeli army and security services will continue to control entry and exit from the area into the West Bank and Israel. Palestinians believe that by creating delays at the borders, Israeli forces will prevent their produce from reaching domestic and export markets in fresh condition, thereby rendering them uncompetitive. Many are apprehensive that Gaza will become a vast prison under the external control of the IDF, which will retain the right to intervene. Some ray of hope did appear in November 2005, however, when the U.S. Secretary of State Condoleeza Rice brokered a deal between the P.A. and Israel that resulted in the reopening of the border crossing between Gaza and Egypt, to be managed by the P.A. with EU monitors present. A Gaza seaport will also be rebuilt.

Within Israel, opinions differ over the question of Israel's future security. Contrary to opponents of the disengagement, like former Finance Minister Netanyahu, many government officials are convinced that the disengagement has already enhanced Israel's security. Israel with the Gaza settlements was weaker than Israel without them, they argue. To begin with, they point out, no more Israelis will be killed in the Strip, and the substantial expense of maintaining a reinforced division to safeguard the settlements there will be saved. Although they do not expect terrorism to disappear, it will take place in the West Bank, where the Israel Defense Forces have greater operational flexibility. At the same time, the expectation that terrorist incidents will proliferate in the West Bank has led to an almost unanimous agreement that the security fence must be completed. The announcement by Hamas that they will not give up their armed struggle until all of Palestine is liberated is taken seriously by most Israelis. There is also the widely held view that pressure will be put on Israel to make further territorial concessions, even if President Abbas takes no further steps to dismantle the Palestinian-armed factions.

Although many Israelis fear that Gaza will become a launching pad for unrestrained rocket attacks across the border, Mofaz has stated that Israel has sufficient economic and military resources to deter such attacks. The hope is that the more the Palestinian economy develops, the more susceptible the Palestinians will become to economic pressures. And, he notes—stating the obvious—Israel has the military means to exercise pressure from outside the Gaza Strip. If Gaza does become an exporter of terrorism, the IDF will return.

Threat of Civil War in Israel Refuted

The evacuation of the Gaza Strip and the four northern West Bank settlements had profound implications for Israel domestically. The 2005 Gaza evacuation refuted prophecies of a civil war. It also disproved the claim that the IDF and police did not have the power to evacuate settlements. For years, the dread of civil war had been a central element in Israeli thinking about the future of the settlements. Both opponents and supporters of the settlements had manipulated this threat. The former were genuinely concerned about a split in the nation, and the latter used it to deepen the occupation. Many Israelis remember the threat of civil war that forced Yitzhak Rabin in 1994 to reverse his decision to uproot the seven Jewish families of the Tel Rumeida settlement in Hebron following Baruch Goldstein's massacre of twenty-nine Palestinian worshipers in the Ibrahimi mosque.

Sharon had been on both sides of the national debate. In opposition, he joined those who threatened to "set the country on fire" if the government moved against settlers. As a member of the government, he contributed more than most politicians to establishing new outposts and expanding existing settlements. Yet it was Ariel Sharon who sent in the bulldozers to destroy the Gaza settlements, against the will of the majority of his Likud party.

The Israeli newspaper *Ha'aretz* editorialized that messianic rabbis had transformed the struggle over the Gaza settlements from a legitimate political dispute into an all-out war between the state and religion. Yet despite the pressure and what *Ha'aretz* called the "the spiritual terrorism" of right-wing rabbis and zealots, little resistance was recorded; bloody violence was directed, whenever it took place, at Arabs. Most of the religious public in Israel did not want to disengage from the Zionist state and were not planning to turn it into a theocratic state by means of a demographic victory. The disengagement demonstrated that it was still possible for most religious Israelis to share their lives with the secular majority.

The United States was optimistic about the future following Israel's withdrawal from the Gaza Strip. Secretary of State Condoleezza Rice welcomed the completion of Israel's withdrawal from Gaza and called for international cooperation to help restore the Palestinian economy and security forces. "This is an historic moment for both sides, and the commitment of both sides to a successful disengagement process has been impressive," Rice stated. Abbas announced that the United States had pledged an additional $30 million to support Palestinian water projects. He noted that Washington had already made good on its promise to provide $50 million for housing projects to create new jobs, and Palestinian negotiator Saeb Erekat said the two sides agreed that "Gaza will not be first and last."

The Gaza withdrawal has enabled Israel to gain some moral high ground. To the EU and the United States, Israel has proved that it is capable of deciding to evacuate settlements and implementing the decision, which had previously been in doubt. Many outside and inside Israel view Israel's departure from the Gaza Strip as one stage in a process that has to continue in the West Bank as well, although they will continue to tie this to a Palestinian commitment to halt all acts of terror.

The challenge for the P.A. is to demonstrate that it is capable of controlling the Palestinian parties dedicated to the use of violence, and that it is committed to the continuation of the peace process.

The challenge for Israel is to create a public majority that will support another withdrawal, and, according to Shimon Peres and the new leader of Labor, Amir Peretz, who was elected in the party primary in November, this would be Labor's election campaign platform. Sharon, himself, who indicated that a peace deal might necessitate further withdrawals, faced a serious political challenge from Benjamin Netanyahu, who declared his intention to contest Sharon's leadership of the Likud. Remarking that life in Likud had become "unbearable," on November 21, Sharon asked President Katsav to dissolve the Knesset. Sharon then announced his intention to form a centrist party called Kadima, throwing the Israeli political situation into turmoil. New elections were scheduled for March 28, 2006, with Sharon hoping to put together an alliance that would enable him to continue the peace process.

Initial signs were not encouraging on either side after the Gaza and West Bank withdrawals. Immediately upon the completion of the evacuations, Sharon ordered the expropriation of Palestinian lands on which the separation fence is to be built around the Ma'ale Adumim settlement bloc east of Jerusalem. In the past year alone, even after factoring in the evacuation of the twenty-one settlements in Gaza and four in the West Bank, the population of West Bank settlements grew by nearly 13,000 people, increasing the number of Jews living in the West

Bank to around 250,000, and Sharon never disguised his intention to make Ma'ale Adumim part of Israel and "territorially contiguous with Jerusalem."

There is no doubt that the decision to expropriate additional Palestinian land, taken at this particular time, was seen as provocative by the P.A. and the Palestinians. "Israel's insistence on expanding settlements represents a declaration of war against the Palestinians because it aims to prevent the establishment of a Palestinian state by reinforcing and prolonging occupation," Palestinian cabinet minister Ghassan al-Khatib said. Sharon subsequently bowed to U.S. pressure and halted this action.

At almost the same time, an attempted suicide bombing in Beersheba severely wounded two Israeli security guards and injured forty-six others. And Muhammad Deif, commander of Hamas's armed Izzedine al-Qassam Brigades, and one of Israel's most wanted men, issued a video in which he warned the P.A. against trying to confiscate Hamas's weapons. Addressing both the P.A. and Israel, he called for a continuation of armed struggle until the "occupied motherland" was completely liberated.

How the dramatic events of the recent past will play out remains to be seen, although there seems no end to the violence in sight. Nevertheless, there is no doubt that, once again, we are at a turning point in the Arab–Israeli conflict.

Suggestions for Further Reading

BEILIN, YOSSI, *The Path to Geneva: The Quest for a Permanent Agreement, 1996–2004*, RDV Books, 2004.

ENDERLIN, CHARLES, *Shattered Dreams: The Failure of the Peace Process in the Middle East, 1995–2002*, New York, Other Press, 2002.

KERSHNER, ISABEL, Barrier: The Seam of the Israeli–Palestinian Conflict, Palgrave Macmillan, 2005.

KIMMERLING, BARUCH, AND MIGDAL, JOEL, *The Palestinian People: A History*, Cambridge, Harvard University Press, 2003.

ROSS, DENNIS, *The Missing Peace*, New York, Farrar, Straus and Giroux, 2004.

 DOCUMENT 13–1

A Performance-Based Roadmap to a Permanent Two-State Solution to the Israeli–Palestinian Conflict

The following is a performance-based and goal-driven roadmap, with clear phases, timelines, target dates, and benchmarks aiming at progress through reciprocal steps by the two parties in the political, security, economic, humanitarian, and institution-building fields, under the auspices of the Quartet [the United States, European Union, United Nations, and Russia]. The destination is a final and comprehensive settlement of the Israel–Palestinian conflict by 2005, as presented in President Bush's speech of 24 June, and welcomed by the EU, Russia and the UN in the 16 July and 17 September Quartet Ministerial statements.

A two-state solution to the Israeli–Palestinian conflict will only be achieved through an end to violence and terrorism, when the Palestinian people have a leadership acting decisively against terror and willing and able to build a practicing democracy based on tolerance and liberty, and through Israel's readiness to do what is necessary for a democratic Palestinian state to be established, and a clear, unambiguous acceptance by both parties of the goal of a negotiated settlement as described below. The Quartet will assist and facilitate implementation of the plan, starting in Phase I, including direct discussions between the parties as required. The plan establishes a realistic timeline for implementation. However, as a performance-based plan, progress will require and depend upon the good faith efforts of the parties, and their compliance with each of the obligations outlined below. Should the parties perform their obligations rapidly, progress within and through the phases may come sooner than indicated in the plan. Noncompliance with obligations will impede progress.

A settlement, negotiated between the parties, will result in the emergence of an independent, democratic, and viable Palestinian state living side by side in peace and security with Israel and its other neighbors. The settlement will resolve the Israel–Palestinian conflict, and end the occupation that began in 1967, based on the foundations of the Madrid Conference, the principle of land for peace, UNSCRs 242, 338 and 1397, agreements previously reached by the parties, and the initiative of Saudi Crown Prince Abdullah—endorsed by the Beirut Arab League Summit—calling for acceptance of Israel as a neighbor living in peace and security, in the context of a comprehensive settlement. This initiative is a vital element of international efforts to promote a comprehensive peace on all tracks, including the Syrian–Israeli and Lebanese–Israeli tracks.

The Quartet will meet regularly at senior levels to evaluate the parties' performance on implementation of the plan. In each phase, the parties are expected to perform their obligations in parallel, unless otherwise indicated.

PHASE I: ENDING TERROR AND VIOLENCE, NORMALIZING PALESTINIAN LIFE, AND BUILDING PALESTINIAN INSTITUTIONS — PRESENT TO MAY 2003

In Phase I, the Palestinians immediately undertake an unconditional cessation of violence according to the steps outlined below; such action should be accompanied by supportive measures undertaken by Israel. Palestinians and Israelis resume security cooperation based on the Tenet work plan to end violence, terrorism, and incitement through restructured and effective Palestinian security services. Palestinians undertake comprehensive political reform in preparation for statehood, including drafting a Palestinian constitution, and free, fair and open elections upon the basis of those measures. Israel takes all necessary steps to help normalize Palestinian life. Israel withdraws from Palestinian areas occupied from September 28, 2000 and the two sides restore the status quo that existed at that time, as security performance and cooperation progress. Israel also freezes all settlement activity, consistent with the Mitchell report. . . .

PHASE II: TRANSITION — JUNE 2003–DECEMBER 2003

In the second phase, efforts are focused on the option of creating an independent Palestinian state with provisional borders and attributes of sovereignty, based on the new constitution, as a way station to a permanent status settlement. As has been noted, this goal can be achieved when the Palestinian people have a leadership acting decisively against terror, willing and able to build a practicing democracy based on tolerance and liberty. With such a leadership, reformed civil institutions and security structures, the Palestinians will have the active support of the Quartet and the broader international community in establishing an independent, viable, state.

Progress into Phase II will be based upon the consensus judgment of the Quartet of whether conditions are appropriate to proceed, taking into account performance of both parties. Furthering and sustaining efforts to normalize Palestinian lives and build Palestinian institutions,

Phase II starts after Palestinian elections and ends with possible creation of an independent Palestinian state with provisional borders in 2003. Its primary goals are continued comprehensive security performance and effective security cooperation, continued normalization of Palestinian life and institution-building, further building on and sustaining of the goals outlined in Phase I, ratification of a democratic Palestinian constitution, formal establishment of office of prime minister, consolidation of political reform, and the creation of a Palestinian state with provisional border. . . .

PHASE III: PERMANENT STATUS AGREEMENT AND END
OF THE ISRAELI–PALESTINIAN CONFLICT—2004—2005

Progress into Phase III, based on consensus judgment of Quartet, and taking into account actions of both parties and Quartet monitoring. Phase III objectives are consolidation of reform and stabilization of Palestinian institutions, sustained, effective Palestinian security performance, and Israeli–Palestinian negotiations aimed at a permanent status agreement in 2005. . . .

Released on April 30, 2003

 DOCUMENT 13-2

The Cabinet Resolution Regarding the Disengagement Plan,
June 6, 2004, as Published by the Israeli Prime Minister's Office

Revised Disengagement Plan

Main Principles

1. Background—Political and Security Implications
  The State of Israel is committed to the peace process and aspires to reach an agreed resolution of the conflict based upon the vision of US President George Bush. The State of Israel believes that it must act to improve the current situation. The State of Israel has come to the conclusion that there is currently no reliable Palestinian partner with which it can make progress in a two-sided peace process. Accordingly, it has developed a plan of revised disengagement (hereinafter—the plan), based on the following considerations:
One. The stalemate dictated by the current situation is harmful. In order to break out of this stalemate, the State of Israel is required to initiate moves not dependent on Palestinian cooperation.
Two. The purpose of the plan is to lead to a better security, political, economic and demographic situation.
Three. In any future permanent status arrangement, there will be no Israeli towns and villages in the Gaza Strip. On the other hand, it is clear that in the West Bank, there are areas which will be part of the State of Israel, including major Israeli population centers, cities, towns and villages, security areas and other places of special interest to Israel.
Four. The State of Israel supports the efforts of the United States, operating alongside the international community, to promote the reform process, the construction of institutions and the improvement of the economy and welfare of the Palestinian residents, in order that a new Palestinian leadership will emerge and prove itself capable of fulfilling its commitments under the Roadmap.

Five. Relocation from the Gaza Strip and from an area in Northern Samaria should reduce friction with the Palestinian population.

Six. The completion of the plan will serve to dispel the claims regarding Israel's responsibility for the Palestinians in the Gaza Strip.

Seven. The process set forth in the plan is without prejudice to the relevant agreements between the State of Israel and the Palestinians. Relevant arrangements shall continue to apply.

Eight. International support for this plan is widespread and important. This support is essential in order to bring the Palestinians to implement in practice their obligations to combat terrorism and effect reforms as required by the Roadmap, thus enabling the parties to return to the path of negotiation.

2. Main Elements
The Gaza Strip

1) The State of Israel will evacuate the Gaza Strip, including all existing Israeli towns and villages, and will redeploy outside the Strip. This will not include military deployment in the area of the border between the Gaza Strip and Egypt ("the Philadelphi Route") as detailed below.

2) Upon completion of this process, there shall no longer be any permanent presence of Israeli security forces in the areas of Gaza Strip territory which have been evacuated.

The West Bank

3) The State of Israel will evacuate an area in Northern Samaria (Ganim, Kadim, Sa-Nur and Homesh), and all military installations in this area, and will redeploy outside the vacated area.

4) Upon completion of this process, there shall no longer be any permanent presence of Israeli security forces in this area.

5) The move will enable territorial contiguity for Palestinians in the Northern Samaria area.

6) The State of Israel will assist, together with the international community, in improving the transportation infrastructure in the West Bank in order to facilitate the contiguity of Palestinian transportation.

7) The process will facilitate normal life and Palestinian economic and commercial activity in the West Bank.

3.3 The intention is to complete the planned relocation process by the end of 2005.

The Security Fence:

The State of Israel will continue building the Security Fence, in accordance with the relevant decisions of the Government. The route will take into account humanitarian considerations.

3. Security Situation Following the Relocation
One. The Gaza Strip:

1) The State of Israel will guard and monitor the external land perimeter of the Gaza Strip, will continue to maintain exclusive authority in Gaza air space, and will continue to exercise security activity in the sea off the coast of the Gaza Strip.

2) The Gaza Strip shall be demilitarized and shall be devoid of weaponry, the presence of which does not accord with the Israeli-Palestinian agreements.

3) The State of Israel reserves its fundamental right of self-defense, both preventive and reactive, including where necessary the use of force, in respect of threats emanating from the Gaza Strip.

Two. The West Bank:

1) Upon completion of the evacuation of the Northern Samaria area, no permanent Israeli military presence will remain in this area.

2) The State of Israel reserves its fundamental right of self-defense, both preventive and reactive, including where necessary the use of force, in respect of threats emanating from the Northern Samaria area.

3) In other areas of the West Bank, current security activity will continue. However, as circumstances require, the State of Israel will consider reducing such activity in Palestinian cities.

The State of Israel will work to reduce the number of internal checkpoints throughout the West Bank.

4. *Military Installations and Infrastructure in the Gaza Strip and Northern Samaria*
In general, these will be dismantled and evacuated, with the exception of those which the State of Israel decides to transfer to another party.

5. *Security Assistance to the Palestinians*
The State of Israel agrees that by coordination with it, advice, assistance and training will be provided to the Palestinian security forces for the implementation of their obligations to combat terrorism and maintain public order, by American, British, Egyptian, Jordanian or other experts, as agreed therewith.

No foreign security presence may enter the Gaza Strip and/or the West Bank without being coordinated with and approved by the State of Israel.

6. *The Border Area Between the Gaza Strip and Egypt (Philadelphi Route)*
The State of Israel will continue to maintain a military presence along the border between the Gaza Strip and Egypt (Philadelphi Route). This presence is an essential security requirement. At certain locations, security considerations may require some widening of the area in which the military activity is conducted.

Subsequently, the evacuation of this area will be considered. Evacuation of the area will be dependent, inter alia, on the security situation and the extent of cooperation with Egypt in establishing a reliable alternative arrangement.

If and when conditions permit the evacuation of this area, the State of Israel will be willing to consider the possibility of the establishment of a seaport and airport in the Gaza Strip, in accordance with arrangements to be agreed with Israel.

7. *Real Estate Assets*
In general, residential dwellings and sensitive structures, including synagogues, will not remain. The State of Israel will aspire to transfer other facilities, including industrial, commercial and agricultural ones, to a third, international party which will put them to use for the benefit of the Palestinian population that is not involved in terror.

The area of the Erez industrial zone will be transferred to the responsibility of an agreed upon Palestinian or international party.

The State of Israel will explore, together with Egypt, the possibility of establishing a joint industrial zone on the border of the Gaza Strip, Egypt and Israel.

8. *Civil Infrastructure and Arrangements*
Infrastructure relating to water, electricity, sewage and telecommunications will remain in place.

In general, Israel will continue, for full price, to supply electricity, water, gas and petrol to the Palestinians, in accordance with current arrangements.

Other existing arrangements, such as those relating to water and the electro-magnetic sphere shall remain in force.

9. Activity of Civilian International Organizations

The State of Israel recognizes the great importance of the continued activity of international humanitarian organizations and others engaged in civil development, assisting the Palestinian population.

The State of Israel will coordinate with these organizations arrangements to facilitate their activities.

The State of Israel proposes that an international apparatus be established (along the lines of the AHLC), with the agreement of Israel and international elements which will work to develop the Palestinian economy.

10. Economic Arrangements

In general, the economic arrangements currently in operation between the State of Israel and the Palestinians shall remain in force. These arrangements include, inter alia:

One. The entry and exit of goods between the Gaza Strip, the West Bank, the State of Israel and abroad.

Two. The monetary regime.

Three. Tax and customs envelope arrangements.

Four. Postal and telecommunications arrangements.

Five. The entry of workers into Israel, in accordance with the existing criteria.

In the longer term, and in line with Israel's interest in encouraging greater Palestinian economic independence, the State of Israel expects to reduce the number of Palestinian workers entering Israel, to the point that it ceases completely. The State of Israel supports the development of sources of employment in the Gaza Strip and in Palestinian areas of the West Bank, by international elements.

11. International Passages

a. The International Passage Between the Gaza Strip and Egypt

1) The existing arrangements shall continue.

2) The State of Israel is interested in moving the passage to the "three borders" area, south of its current location. This would need to be effected in coordination with the Government of Egypt. This move would enable the hours of operation of the passage to be extended.

b. *The International Passages Between the West Bank and Jordan:*

The existing arrangements shall continue.

12. Erez Crossing Point

The Erez crossing point will be moved to a location within Israel in a time frame to be determined separately by the Government.

13. Conclusion

The goal is that implementation of the plan will lead to improving the situation and breaking the current deadlock. If and when there is evidence from the Palestinian side of its willingness, capability and implementation in practice of the fight against terrorism, full cessation of terrorism and violence and the institution of reform as required by the Road Map, it will be possible to return to the track of negotiation and dialogue.

Conclusion

The Changing Character of the Arab–Israeli Conflict

The character, conduct, and focus of the Arab–Israeli conflict, and the ways the participants perceived themselves and others, have altered significantly in the course of the past half century. In the twenty years following the establishment of the Jewish state, the main issue for Israel was its continuing existence and security in the face of unrelenting hostility from Palestinian Arab refugees and the neighboring Arab states. After 1967, it was how to recognize and satisfy the national aspirations of the Palestinians. For the Arabs of the former Palestine mandate, the issues were their displacement after 1948 and how to realize their desire for a viable national state of their own. To the Arabs of the region, the creation of the Jewish state had been another example of Western colonialism and of a Western challenge to Islam, but the wars of 1948–1949, 1956, 1967, and 1973 made the continuation of the Jewish state unmistakably clear to friend and foe alike. With Israel in occupation of the West Bank and the Gaza Strip, by the early 1970s, the conflict focused on the future status of the Palestinian Arab population in the occupied territories. This was a concern reflected in the world community as well.

At first, following the wars of 1967 and 1973, the UN Security Council—in Resolutions 242 and 338—contented itself with broad and ambiguous resolutions concerning the settlement of the conflict, referring only to the existing states and calling for a solution to the refugee problem. A distinct change of attitude occurred in the United Nations, however. In addition to attempting to resolve issues among the nations of the regions, the United Nations now acknowledged the Palestinian Arabs as a distinct entity, not just as refugees. After 1974, following the lead of the Arab League, the United Nations passed a number of resolutions acknowledging the right of the Palestinians to self-determination and recognizing the PLO as the sole legitimate representative of the Palestinian people.

The Arab states continued to oppose Israel's presence, especially its occupation of territories captured in the 1967 war. After failing to achieve results through war in 1973, however, Egypt signed the Camp David accords in September 1978 and a peace treaty with Israel in 1979, recognizing the Jewish state in return for Israel's return of the Sinai Peninsula. The Camp

David accords also included the proposal that "Egypt, Israel, Jordan and the representatives of the Palestinian people should participate in negotiations on the resolution of the Palestinian problem in all its aspects"—but the other Arab states refused to endorse the accords. U.S. President Ronald Reagan, in peace proposals announced in September 1982, stated that self-government by the Palestinians of the West Bank and Gaza in association with Jordan offered the best chance for a durable, just, and lasting peace. The Palestinians repeatedly indicated that they regarded the PLO as their representative, but Israel refused to recognize or negotiate with the PLO, since the PLO, in Israel's eyes, was a terrorist organization that failed to recognize both Israel's right to exist and Security Council Resolutions 242 and 338.

In taking this stand, Israel had the support of the United States throughout the 1970s and most of the 1980s. Meanwhile, the PLO had been unable to act independently of the Arab governments to achieve anything for the Palestinian people, and its unwillingness to compromise, as well as Chairman Yasser Arafat's personal vicissitudes and the challenges to his leadership within the PLO, resulted in a crisis of confidence among the population in the territories. Taking matters into their own hands during the Intifada, the Palestinians in the territories moved from being pawns to being participants in the resolution of the conflict. The PLO quickly attempted to take control of the Intifada, although its leadership role was questioned, especially by the more radical Palestinians, and increasingly by the more religious Muslim militants.

In July 1988, King Hussein relinquished all claims to the West Bank. Up to this point, Jordan, although nominally at war with Israel, had been primarily concerned with incorporating western Palestine within the kingdom, and Jordan was as reluctant as Israel to acknowledge Palestinian national identity. Indeed, as we have seen, King Hussein retaliated for Palestinian military challenges to his position. Following a brief but bloody civil war in 1970, he expelled PLO leaders and their followers, forcing them to flee to Lebanon. The result was the disruption of Lebanon's economy and fragile political balance. Civil war resulted, and Syria, which always saw itself as a player in Lebanon, soon became involved. Moreover, the presence of the PLO leadership in Lebanon shifted the conflict between Israel and Palestinian groups to southern Lebanon. In 1982, Israel invaded Lebanon with catastrophic results for Lebanese and Palestinian civilians— and worldwide condemnation for the Israelis. It also resulted in the relocation of the PLO leaders to Tunis.

In late 1988, however, as a result of the new conditions created by the Intifada and Hussein's renunciation of claims to the West Bank, Arafat for the first time endorsed a two-state solution to the Israeli–Palestinian conflict. While issuing a Palestinian declaration of independence, he also took the first steps toward recognizing Israel and accepting UN Security Council Resolutions 242 and 338. The United States then opened a dialogue with the PLO and urged Israel to negotiate directly with the organization.

The 1991 Gulf War briefly distracted the players in the Arab–Israeli conflict, but it had important consequences. Within ten months of its ending, the major antagonists in the conflict met in a historic peace conference in Madrid, Spain. Bilateral negotiations between Israel and the Arabs, and multilateral talks involving many other nations, were set in motion. Although there was some progress in the bilateral talks, there were no breakthroughs. Meanwhile, Israeli and PLO representatives had held secret negotiations in and around Oslo, Norway, which came to fruition with statements of mutual recognition and the signing of an Israel–PLO peace accord in September 1993. Implementation of the agreement proceeded, with an accord on Gaza and Jericho in 1994 and the signing of an interim agreement on Palestinian autonomy in the rest of the West Bank in September 1995. In May 1996, an initial session was held on "final status" issues. By October 1994, Jordan and Israel had ended their state of war and signed a peace treaty, and several other Arab states had opened low-level relations with the Jewish state. Despite outbursts of violence and apparent setbacks, such as the Israeli elections in May 1996, which replaced the Labor government elected in 1992 with a coalition headed by Likud leader Benjamin Netanyahu, Israel and the Arabs were in the process of normalizing relations.

That process continued with a protocol on Hebron in January 1997, and the Wye River Memorandum of September 1998, which dealt with further Israeli redeployments from the West Bank, to take place in accord with Palestinian efforts to curb violence and terrorism. A partial Israeli withdrawal began, and the Palestine National Council in December voted to nullify those articles in the PLO Covenant calling for Israel's destruction; but further movement was suspended over Israeli accusations of Palestinian noncompliance. Netanyahu's government fell over both domestic issues and the desire of the majority of Israelis to proceed with the peace process, and new elections were called in Israel.

Ehud Barak was elected overwhelmingly in May 1999 on a platform of withdrawing Israeli troops from southern Lebanon and accelerating the peace process. Talks were resumed between Israel and Syria, but these foundered again over how to achieve simultaneously Israeli objectives of a peace treaty and security, and those of Syria for full Israeli withdrawal from the Golan Heights and a return to the pre-1967 borders.

Meanwhile, Barak continued to pursue the Palestinian track, and at Sharm al-Sheikh in September 1999, he and Arafat set February 13, 2000, as a target date for a framework agreement on all final status issues, and September 13, 2000, as the deadline for a final peace agreement. Although negotiators continued to meet, there was little progress. Finally, at the prodding of President Clinton, the two leaders agreed to attend a summit at Camp David in July 2000. Although the Israelis and Palestinians made some effort to reconcile their differences with American assistance, the wide gulf between their "red lines" on borders, refugees, and especially Jerusalem was not able to be bridged. Negotiations did continue, however, since both sides realized that the September date was looming, and that without some resolution of the issues, violence could very well break out.

That violence did erupt with the outbreak of the al-Aqsa Intifada after a visit of Ariel Sharon to the Temple Mount/Haram al-Sharif on September 28. What followed became essentially a war. At President Clinton's urging, there were important last-ditch efforts by Palestinian and Israeli negotiators in January, 2001 that nearly resulted in agreement on most of the major issues. Clinton was a lame-duck president, however, Barak's government had collapsed, and in February 2001, Ariel Sharon was elected prime minister of Israel, signaling a new phase in the conflict. Hardliners had gained control of both sides, and the peace process was clearly in question. Events such as September 11, 2001, and the self-declared and so-called United States Global War on Terrorism, the U.S.-led War on Afghanistan and War in Iraq removed whatever slight restraints there were on both Israelis and Palestinians. The distinction, however narrow, between civilian and combatant all but disappeared in the next few years, as increasing numbers on both sides died through Palestinian suicide bombings and Israeli tank and missile strikes. Hamas and Islamic Jihad called for more "martyrs" on the one side, and the religious/nationalist parties on the other called for more Jewish settlements. Suicide attacks continued, Israeli checkpoints and roadblocks proliferated, illegal settlements sprang up, and Israel began building a separation "fence" or "wall." The extremists on both sides became more entrenched than ever, as the Oslo process, a casualty of increasing violence, struggled to stay relevant.

Although initially the new Bush administration had adopted a "hands-off" approach to the Arab-Israeli conflict, the U.S. President's "War on Terror" increasingly involved him in the Israeli-Palestinian situation. While he staunchly supported Ariel Sharon and Israeli policies, he also endorsed the idea of a Palestinian state, and along with the UN, the EU and Russia sponsored a "Road Map" to peace to try to achieve a two-state solution by 2005. Despite the President's personal involvement, which included a summit between Sharon and Palestinian Prime Minister Mahmoud Abbas, and meetings with Arab leaders, his war in Iraq eroded American credibility in the Arab and Muslim world. Moreover, the Road Map was compromised by divisive internal struggles within the Palestinian Authority and within Israel, and by the ability of extremists to undermine any moves toward compliance.

The Palestinian Authority lost the capacity to control its militant factions, even if it had the will—something the Israelis doubted as long as Arafat was at the helm; and Sharon's political fate seemed to be dependent upon the support of right-wing parties, even if he were willing to accept a viable Palestinian state—something the Palestinians doubted. The death of Yasser Arafat in November 2004, the election of Mahmoud Abbas as Palestinian president, and Sharon's unilateral withdrawal of Israeli settlements in the Gaza Strip in August, 2005 appeared to present new opportunities and to offer at least a glimmer of light at the end of the tunnel.

In a sense, the conflict has come full circle. The essential questions today appear to be those posed in the 1880s where our story began, and again in 1947 and 1948 when the fledgling UN General Assembly met to determine the future of the British mandate: How can Palestine, the area to the West of the River Jordan, be shared between Jews and Arabs? Until the issues between Israelis and Palestinians are resolved to the satisfaction of both parties, there will be no rest. Israel and its neighbors may sign peace treaties, but neither Israelis nor Palestinians will live peaceful, secure, and prosperous lives until they recognize and acknowledge each other's legitimate concerns and make the painful compromises necessary to resolve their differences through political rather than through military means. It may be useful at this point, then, to consider some of the issues still outstanding as of this writing.

Outstanding Issues in the Conflict

Israel and the Palestinians

The current outstanding issues between Israel and the Palestinians were identified and delineated at Oslo. Most commentators agree that the creation of a Palestinian state alongside Israel in the future is the most likely outcome. However, the boundaries of the Palestinian and Israeli states, and the relationship between the two entities—and their neighbors—are far from clear. The major concerns of both sides revolve around security, the status of Jerusalem, the future of the Jewish settlements in the West Bank, the return of, or compensation owed to, the Palestinian refugees, and the allocation of water resources.

Palestinian Statehood   For the Palestinians, the issue is, as noted above, statehood rather than autonomy. But in the meantime, what does autonomy entail until statehood is achieved? Despite Israel's withdrawal from the Gaza Strip, Palestinians do not feel free from Israeli reprisal air-raids and targeted assassinations in Gaza, or from oppressive closures, checkpoints and Israeli intrusions in the West Bank. As long as Israel insists on responsibility for overall security, including the checking of persons, vehicles, and weapons at all points of entry in and out of Israel from Gaza, and the Israeli army feels free to enter any area of the West Bank when it chooses, Palestinians still regard themselves as an occupied people. Although many Palestinians question the ability of the Palestinian Authority to control the extremist groups and govern democratically, honestly, and efficiently, clearly their aspirations are for complete independence in all of the occupied territory. Despite paying lip service to the idea, the Israeli government under Sharon showed little sign of accommodating the Palestinian desire to achieve statehood. Palestinians are convinced, moreover, that Jewish settlers in the West Bank and their extreme religious and nationalist supporters will never give up an inch of what they call the Land of Israel, and, unlike the situation in Gaza, will fight to retain it.

For their part, most Israelis believe that the fall 2000 outbreak of violence revealed that even if the present Palestinian leadership under Mahmoud Abbas meant what it said about living together with Israel, the widespread popular hostility to Israel, the uncompromising ideology of groups like Hamas and Islamic Jihad, and the personal, factional, and class-based rivalries within the Palestinian community itself preclude any peaceful cooperation with the Jewish state. While it may have been plausible prior to 2000 to say that the majority of Israelis, like the majority of the Palestinians, appeared willing to take the necessary risks and make the compromises essential for peace, the al-Aqsa Intifada and its aftermath produced skepticism and disillusion, and Israelis remain concerned with what they consider an existential threat to their security.

Israeli Security   For Israel, security arrangements remain a fundamental issue. Despite its overwhelming military superiority and the unlikelihood of a full-scale attack that could seriously threaten its territorial integrity, there is apprehension that in essentially agreeing in peace talks to return to an approximation of the pre-1967 borders, they created a dangerous situation. The 2000 Intifada, however, indicated to most observers that the location of borders was not the only consideration in provoking violence against Israeli citizens and settlers by Palestinian religious or political extremists. The presence and expansion of Israeli West Bank settlements, and Israel's harsh policies in the territories, were also a source of resentment and conflict, while Hamas and Islamic Jihad remained committed to the destruction of the Jewish state. Sharon's decision to enhance Israel's security by withdrawing from the provocative settlements in the Gaza Strip, and especially his decision to build a "security fence" was widely approved by Israelis. As long as Palestinian attacks on Israelis continue, most of the population regard the security fence, and its completion, as essential to their security and argue that modifications can be made only when the security situation stabilizes. Palestinians, however, call the fence a barrier or wall. Built almost entirely on West Bank land, it creates a reality, they say, that precludes the possibility of two viable states because it will prevent the emergence of a contiguous Palestinian polity.

Jewish Settlements   As we have seen, there are two dimensions to the questions surrounding the future of the Jewish settlements in the West Bank. The first is the relationship between the Israeli government and the settlers. The second is the negotiation between the Israeli government and the Palestinian Authority over the future of the settlements. Not surprisingly, the question of the right of Israelis to build settlements in the occupied territories has been part of the political discourse in Israel since 1967. The Sharon government's evacuation of settlers from the Gaza Strip and from four West Bank settlements was achieved with far less disruption than anticipated given the opposition generated by previous proposals to give up settlements. At the same time, Sharon indicated that he would seek to annex portions of the West Bank around Jerusalem and closest to the "green line" containing the largest group of Jewish settlements. This plan, now a central element in Israeli policy, is viewed by many Israelis as a legitimate and necessary compromise between the need to satisfy the settlers and their supporters and the almost certain reality that the remainder of the West Bank will eventually be handed over to the Palestinians. The Palestinians rejected this general idea at the Camp David summit in July 2000 and have continued adamantly to oppose it, insisting that all the settlements in the West Bank and Gaza were illegal under international law and that the entire West Bank must be returned to them. (See West Bank Map 12–4.)

Palestinian Refugees   Various estimates place the number of Palestinian refugees, most of whom left Israel after 1948, and their descendants at between 3 and 4 million. About 2.7 million live on the West Bank and in Gaza, and about a million are in camps run by international UNRWA and other agencies in the West Bank, Gaza, Jordan, Lebanon, and Syria. While Palestinians in Jordan were given the option of citizenship and now comprise over 66 percent of the Jordanian population, and although refugees in Syria and elsewhere have had opportunities to integrate into their host countries, those in Lebanon have largely been confined to camps, and the Lebanese government has continued to be hostile to their presence, denying them citizenship and economic opportunity.

The Palestinian position on the refugees has always been that, in accordance with UN Resolution 194, they must have the right to return to Israel and, moreover, that Israel must accept responsibility for their plight. Israel has continued to insist that the refugees fled or were expelled for many reasons, and it has refused to admit legal or moral responsibility for their fate. Israel early on adopted the principle of compensation as a way of resolving the issue. In various peace negotiations since Oslo, Israel has proposed allowing only approximated 100,000 refugees to return to Israel as part of a family reunification program and has requested international aid to compensate, rehabilitate and relocate the rest. It has been estimated that such an aid package could cost in the billions of dollars, and that in any final deal between Israel and the Palestinians, the Palestinians would ask the United States for at least $40 billion, much of it for refugee assistance. At the Camp David II summit, the "right of return" of Palestinian refugees to Israel became an irresolvable issue. In January 2001, at Taba, the two sides discussed both the principle itself and possible ways to implement in but did not come to any agreement. At most, Israel was prepared to acknowledge that refugees would be allowed to return, but only to those areas of the occupied territories that might be included in a Palestinian state. Sharon rejected the "right of return" to Israel out of hand, a stand supported by the Bush administration.

Jerusalem The status of Jerusalem is one of the most emotionally charged issues to be resolved. Palestinians have claimed East Jerusalem, including the Old City, with its religious sites, as the capital of an independent Palestinian state, while Israel has vowed never to divide or relinquish control of what it calls its eternal capital.

The key to understanding what is happening in relation to Jerusalem is to recognize that there are different geographical concepts used by the two sides when they speak of the city. The Israelis conquered and annexed East Jerusalem in 1967 and have steadily expanded the municipal boundaries of the city, which now include several Jewish neighborhoods to the North, East and South. Although the project has been postponed, it is almost certain that Israel will also attempt to link the extended Jerusalem municipality with Ma'ale Adumim, one of the largest Jewish settlements on the West Bank. The Arab population within this area is approximately 230,000. The P. A. recognizes neither Israel's annexation of East Jerusalem nor its expansion into what it considers Palestinian land on the West Bank.

The Palestinians consider Jerusalem as part of a region that includes, besides East Jerusalem *per se*, the Arab neighborhoods, towns and villages surrounding the city (excluding Ramallah and Bethlehem). This area, which they consider integral to the city includes, for example, 90 per cent of the town of Abu Dis, which straddles Israel's Jerusalem municipality line. The Arab population in this larger, regional definition is about 328,000. (See Map 12–3.)

It has been suggested that the demands of both sides could be met through agreement to accept each other's terminology. Thus, Jerusalem could be the eternal and undivided capital of Israel, at the same time that it could be the capital of the state of Palestine, which would be called al-Quds (the Arabic name for the city.) At one point, concurrent with a general peace plan conceived by Yossi Beilin and Abu Mazen (Mahmoud Abbas) in 1995, a Palestinian parliament house located at Abu Dis was envisaged.

As noted earlier, at the second Camp David summit in 2000, Israel was prepared to turn over Abu Dis to the Palestinians and to give the Palestinians autonomy in parts of East Jerusalem, as well as the right to fly the Palestinian flag over the Muslim and Christian holy places in the Old City. But Israel would not turn over sovereignty of all of East Jerusalem to the Palestinians. The Clinton "bridging proposals" of December 2000, and the January 2001 Taba talks proposed Arab sovereignty over the Arab neighborhoods and Jewish sovereignty over the Jewish neighborhoods of the city, with various options proposed for the Old City and the Holy Places.

According to one suggestion, the Holy Places would be considered to be under divine sovereignty. A similar "peace plan" conceived by former Shin Bet chief Ami Ayalon and al-Quds University president Sari Nusseibeh in 2002 also envisaged Arab control over Arab neighborhoods and Jewish control over Jewish ones, with both sides defined as "guardians" of their holy places. The unofficial Geneva Accord of 2003 also divided Jerusalem on a demographic basis, and suggested using "a visible color-coding scheme . . . in the Old City to denote the sovereign areas of the respective Parties." It called for Palestinian sovereignty over the Temple Mount/Haram al-Sharif, but Israeli sovereignty over the Jewish quarter of the Old City and the Western, or Wailing, Wall. It is clear that if there is an eventual peace agreement, there will be a compromise with regard to Jerusalem, and that sovereignty will be shared, although the modalities will undoubtedly continue to be a subject of extended discussion and debate.

Lebanon

Israel's precipitous withdrawal from Lebanon created new security concerns for Israel and brought problems in its wake for the countries involved. With its "security buffer" eliminated, Israel worried about the immediate threat of rocket attacks and terrorist activity by Hizbullah, as well as by Palestinians in southern Lebanon. In early August 2000, after verifying Israel's withdrawal from Lebanon, UNIFIL forces moved into southern Lebanon, and a few days later the Lebanese government announced that it would begin deploying about 1,000 men tasked by the Interior Ministry to keep law and order in areas that had been patrolled by Hizbullah after the Israelis left. These measures, however, did not deter cross border rocket attacks. The Lebanese government neither disarmed Hizbullah nor prevented Hizbullah from maintaining a presence in southern Lebanon, and Iran indicated that it would continue to arm and support Hizbullah against Israel. The new battleground between Israel and Hizbullah has become the Shebaa farms area, which Lebanon claims is part of its territory and therefore an area from which Israel should have withdrawn. Israel insists that the Shebaa farms belongs to Syria as part of the Golan Heights and is therefore negotiable only with Syria. The UN sided with Israel on this issue, but it is a flashpoint and an excuse for Hizbullah, supported by Syria for its own purposes, to continue its armed struggle against Israel.

Israel believes that its withdrawal from southern Lebanon weakened its ability to gather intelligence information about Hizbullah groups. Perhaps a greater danger for Israel, and for the P.A., to come out of Israel's Lebanon withdrawal, however, is that the apparent success of Hizbullah militancy obviously led many Palestinians to believe that terrorist attacks and guerrilla warfare are more effective than negotiation. The outbreak of the al-Aqsa intifada suggests that Palestinian militants adopted these tactics to try to achieve their own goals, and according to one Palestinian poll in September 2005, 84% of Palestinians believed that Israel's unilateral withdrawal from the Gaza Strip and the four West Bank settlements was a direct result of the suicide bombings, rocket attacks and other acts of terrorism that the militant groups carried out during the previous five years.

The situation of the approximately 370,000 Palestinian refugees in Lebanon is an important issue also awaiting resolution. Lebanon never absorbed them, and the Palestinians do not necessarily want to stay there. They are predominantly Sunni, and the Muslim majority in Lebanon is now Shiite. The Palestinians in Lebanon are fairly well-armed, as noted by Lebanese President Lahoud, and some Israel defense officials are concerned that these men might be manipulated by Syria, whose troops occupied some of the camps until April 2005. Syria encourages the Palestinians in Lebanon to follow the Hizbullah model of armed struggle.

At present, Lebanon's internal political situation remains volatile and uncertain. Former Prime Minister Rafik Hariri was assassinated on February 14, 2005, in a massive bombing in Beirut by, it was widely assumed, pro-Syrian supporters of President Lahoud. The Syrian government denied any role, but within days of the killing, it faced widespread criticism in Lebanon that at one point involved hundreds of thousands of protestors. Following intense domestic and international pressure, Syria withdrew its troops in April after 29 years of occupation. In October, 2005, a UN investigative commission headed by Detlev Mehlis issued a report implicating senior members of Syria's security services, including Syrian President Bashar Assad's brother and brother-in-law, in Hariri's assassination. Although Syria still wields considerable influence in Lebanon, and the popular euphoria faded following a series of bombings in Beirut, the Mehlis findings could have dire consequences both for President Lahoud and for the Syrians.

The Syrian Track

President Hafez al-Assad's desire to regain all of the Golan Heights for Syria led him to consider the possibility of negotiations with Israel, but as we have seen, Syria and Israel remained far apart on the question of "full peace for full withdrawal," the formula arrived at when Yitzhak Rabin was prime minister. Benjamin Netanyahu and the Likud considered the Golan essential for Israel's security, and they rejected the idea of returning any part of it to Syria. Assad hosted Abu Nidal and the rejectionist factions of the PLO, and Syria provided the headquarters for Hamas outside the territories and controlled the situation in Lebanon. Ehud Barak made it a priority of his new administration to reactivate the Syrian track, but negotiations that were initiated by President Clinton in the winter of 1999–2000 faltered over the same issues as before.

The death of Hafez al-Assad, in early June 2000, once again pushed the Syrian–Israeli relationship into the background. Assad was a known factor, Bashar, his son and successor, was not. Although educated in and familiar with the West, the extent of his control of Syria's government and policies remains unclear. At first, his priorities were to ensure his own position and that of the minority Alawite sect of which he is the leader. He also continued to retain control in Lebanon, where he oversaw Syrian policy during the last years of his father's rule. Syria has become marginalized, however, not only with regard to the Arab-Israeli conflict, but also in terms of the role the U.S. seems determined to play in the Middle East since the September 11, 2001 attacks. While not named by President Bush as part of an "axis of evil," the U.S. increasingly regards Syria as a supporter of terrorist groups and as a conduit for Iraqi insurgents. There are many who speculate that if the United States ultimately succeeds in its effort at regime change and "democratization" in Iraq, Syria will be the next target. The October 2005 UN report on the Hariri assassination was welcome news to the Bush administration, which immediately called for punitive action against Syria. The report has compromised Syria's continued role in Lebanon and its support of Hizbullah, while also perhaps threatening the future of Bashar Assad himself. Needless to say, negotiations on the Golan Heights are off the table for the time being.

Economic Issues

There are also outstanding economic issues. In the early 1990s, both the Israelis and the Palestinians recognized that they could not afford the economic costs of the continuing level of violence in the occupied territories and especially in the Gaza Strip. The future of Gaza became critical. The heightened level of violence, loss of life, curfews, closures, and strikes that resulted from the first Intifada, the events of the Gulf War, the rise of Islamic extremism, and Israeli hardline policies exacted a heavy price on both sides. Israel believed that it had become too dependent on the 150,000 Palestinians who traveled to Israel each day to work; neither could it ease the growing poverty nor contain the levels of violence in the 135-square-mile area through means of curfews or military force. The P.A. and the Palestinians realized that the population of Gaza could not exist economically without Israel; there was no self-sufficient economic infrastructure in the squalid, overcrowded refugee camps.

The Israeli–Palestinian rapprochement and the establishment of the Palestinian Authority did not bring about an alleviation of the situation. In Gaza, hardship and distress resulted from the vicious cycle of terrorism and Israeli closures, which virtually sealed the borders and prevented Palestinians from reaching their jobs in Israel. Moreover, although the P.A. counted heavily on the contribution of donor funds, in both Gaza and the West Bank, mismanagement, corruption, instability, and uncertainty prevented all but a trickle of the pledged funds from being disbursed. The al-Aqsa intifada and Israel's response brought about more economic distress for Gaza, and it remains to be seen how the P.A. will manage the economy there now that the Israelis have evacuated all their settlements and withdrawn their troops.

There are many other outstanding economic issues, including the divisibility and use of the available water supplies, the nature of the physical connection between the West Bank and Gaza, and between Israel and what may become a Palestinian state, joint economic ventures, and trade and currency arrangements.

Most observers believe that economics is the key to the permanent success of any Israel–Palestinian rapprochement as well as normal relations between Israel and the other Arab states. The 1993 Declaration of Principles provided for joint economic committees, free-trade zones, and cooperation on energy, water, and electricity; and discussions on some of these issues began between Palestinian and Israeli representatives. The economic linkages between Jordan and Israel continue to be worked out largely through the medium of a trilateral Israel–Jordan–U.S. economic committee, although there have been bilateral negotiations, too, on a number of issues. Regional economic matters were being negotiated in the multilateral talks that continued on a wide range of issues until the events of fall 2000. The working group on regional economic development, as early as November 1993, adopted the "Copenhagen Action Plan," comprising thirty-five projects in various fields, including highway construction, electricity grids, energy, tourism, agriculture, financial markets, and investment opportunities. A Monitoring Committee was established to monitor the implementation of the Copenhagen plan, to formulate a regional agenda, and to set priorities for the working group. All this activity is now in abeyance, although both Israel and the Arabs have an interest in seeing that international investment, both private and governmental, flows into the area and helps to create conditions beneficial to all the countries of the region.

These are not easy matters to anticipate, of course. There is also fear on the part of some Arabs that Israel, with its economic superiority, high technology, advanced planning, and managerial skills, will dominate the region economically. The merchant, business, banking, industrial, and agricultural sectors in the neighboring Arab states worry about their ability to compete with Israel in a deregulated economy. They are concerned about the possible social and cultural—even political—impact of their joining a globalized economy.

Regionally, the allocation and development of the scarce water resources, and issues surrounding hydro-politics, remain sources of potential conflict, although the multilateral working group on water worked on these issues, and Jordan and Israel have resolved some of their differences. One of the problems confronting negotiators is that international law is unclear concerning disputes over water rights and such questions as the relationship between water and territory.

There are two conflicting claims: the upstream states claim that the water is theirs by "sovereign right," and the downstream states claim that they have historic or natural rights to the water. Both claims have been drawn upon in the negotiations of the past few years. Discussions between Israel, Jordan, and the Palestinians over water resources focused on access to the Jordan River and on the extent of tapping to be allowed in West Bank aquifers by the Palestinians. The Palestinian Authority will almost certainly demand the right to tap more water from the West Bank aquifers to promote and expand its agriculture than Israel presently allows the Palestinians. The World Health Organization estimates that 26.5 gallons of potable water per person is needed daily to meet minimal health and sanitation standards. In the West Bank (and until recently in Gaza), where Israel controls most of the water resources, the average consumption is 18.5 gallons per person daily. This contrasts with daily water consumption in Jewish settlements of about 74 gallons per person. The disparity is aggravated by the drainage of aquifers for Israeli industry and agriculture. Some of these problems may be alleviated by the construction of a huge water desalinization plant near Ashkelon that will produce 100 million cubic meters of water a year in two identical, adjacent facilities. The plant will provide additional water not only for Israel but also potentially for Gaza, five miles away. One unit has been completed, and another is expected to be finished in the near future. Water, however, will remain a point of dispute not only for Israel, the P.A., and Jordan, but also for Israel and Syria over water from the Sea of Galilee.

America's ongoing war in Iraq has the potential to undermine or destabilize peace treaties signed by Jordan and Egypt with Israel, and it now has serious implications as well for Syria, Lebanon, and Iran. Iran, through its military power, nuclear pretensions, and the leadership and other support it provides to Hizbullah, Hamas, Islamic Jihad and Islamic extremists in other countries, is committed to the reversal of any movement toward Arab–Israeli peace. Indeed, in October 2005, its new president, extremist Mahmoud Ahmadinejad, called for Israel to be wiped off the map.

In the final analysis, the future of the Arab-Israeli conflict depends on the response of both Israelis and Arabs to the imponderable, existential, questions that have been at the heart of the conflict from the beginning, but which now have a special relevance as Israel has celebrated close to sixty years of statehood. Just how does Israel see itself in relation to the Palestinians and the Arab states, and, in turn, how do the Palestinians, and Arab states, view Israel and see themselves in relation to the Jewish state?

It appears that if and when negotiations resume, they will take a form very different from the Oslo process. Nevertheless, there can be no denying the importance of agreements reached and the decisions made in the past few years. Although Oslo did not break down the mutual hatred and distrust built up by decades of war and violence, it was a landmark event heralding the start of a new era in relationships among Israel, the Palestinians, and the other Arab countries. The Oslo process transformed the face of the Arab–Israeli conflict. The change in attitude of both sides in reaching those agreements was as revolutionary as it was unprecedented and unexpected. For the Israelis to accept the PLO as more than just a group of terrorists, and to recognize that nations, including Israel, sometimes act extralegally, and for the PLO and other Arab states, both formally and informally, to recognize the Jewish state and accept the futility of using force to achieve their goals, were major breakthroughs.

While the Arab states accept that peace treaties with Israel may be inevitable, many are not yet ready for normalization of relations and have doubts about the implications for their own societies of a more economically and militarily advanced Jewish state in their midst. For its part, Israel seems unable to free itself from anxiety and fear of the Arabs, despite its overwhelming military superiority, including the possession of atomic weapons and its close relationship with the United States.

The violence that flared late in 2000 between Israel and the Palestinians indicated that the two sides were still far apart on the issues that divide them, and that suspicion, fear, hostility, and passion are never far from the surface. Palestinian Authority President Yasser Arafat did not live to see the establishment of a Palestinian state. Nor has his successor, Mahmoud Abbas, brought an end to Palestinian violence. Israeli Prime Minister Ariel Sharon gambled in unilaterally withdrawing settlers from the Gaza Strip, and thereby appeared to have strengthened his tenuous hold on leadership in Israel. However, he gave every indication of preferring unilateral action to meaningful negotiations and, like Abbas, his own political future was by no means certain. Both leaders were in a somewhat precarious position, and the character of the conflict was as much dependent on their fate as on the policies they might have wished to implement.

"Peace" in this most unpredictable and intractable conflict is very fragile, however; and it can only be hoped that this next generation of Israelis and Arabs, free of the paralyzing history and memories of their parents and grandparents, will succeed in building bridges of cooperation that will finally bring this conflict to an end. Perhaps a new generation who have experienced only the suffering conflict brings will emerge to replace the battle-hardened veterans who cannot forget their pyrrhic victories.

Postscript: January 2006

In view of developments between December 2005 and January 2006, we thought it necessary to add the following postscript.

Relations between Israel and the Palestinians deteriorated during December 2005. Following Israel's disengagement, the Gaza Strip descended into virtual lawlessness as the P.A., under Abbas, lost control of the several militant groups. There were suicide bombings, and Islamic Jihad fired Qassam rockets from Gaza into Israeli border towns. Israel reentered northern Gaza, established a security zone, launched major heliocopter rocket attacks against suspected bomb factories, and resumed targeted assassinations of terrorist leaders. On the West Bank, Israel continued to expropriate Palestinian land, expand settlements, extend the security barrier, and establish a dual road network that greatly complicated Palestinian travel. The Israeli Defense Forces also periodically prohibited residents of Tulkarm, Nablus, and Jenin, now controlled by Hamas local governments, from travelling freely from the northern parts of the West Bank to points southward.

Politically, there were important developments as well. President Abbas seemed unable even to control Fatah groups who resorted to storming government buildings and kidnappings to extort jobs and to protest Fatah policies. In mid-December, members of the Fatah "young guard" formed a breakaway party called "al-Mustaqbal" (the "future") but were persuaded to return to the fold after extracting certain concessions from Abbas. In early January 2006, P.A. security forces briefly lost control of the Rafah crossing in a factional fight that broke down the gates and allowed a number of Palestinians freely to enter Egypt.

Israelis and many worldwide were dismayed to hear on January 4, 2006, that the 77- year-old Israeli Prime Minister Ariel Sharon, who had been hospitalized briefly for a minor stroke in mid-December, had suffered a massive cerebral hemorrhage and was rushed to Jerusalem's Hadassah Hospital in the middle of the night where he underwent lengthy surgery to stem massive bleeding. It became immediately apparent that even if he survived, there was no chance that he would return to politics.

The majority of Israelis responded to news of Sharon's stroke with shock, fear, or both. Sharon's sudden exit from the political arena prompted lengthy retrospectives of the prime minister's career, and prognostications about Israel's future and that of the Arab–Israeli conflict. In recent years, Sharon had achieved almost mythical status among Israelis. Sharon was eulogized (as was also the case with assassinated Prime Minister Yitzhak Rabin) as the uncompromising general who had become a peace hero. Many Israelis believed or hoped that, had his stroke not defeated him, Sharon would have brought peace with the Palestinians and clear and recognized borders. It had been widely speculated that with an expected electoral victory in March 2006, there would be further Israeli withdrawals, to lines of Israel's choosing, on the West Bank. The sense of loss was intensified by this thwarted hope, or illusion. Many Israelis failed to notice that Sharon was very close to achieving his goal of unilaterally removing the Arab demographic threat, a goal that might provide the security Israel sought, but a goal that had little to do with peace with the Palestinians.

Palestinian and Arab reactions were mixed. Hamas and Islamic Jihad extremists and most of the Arab population in Gaza and the West Bank celebrated Sharon's misfortune, welcoming the departure of the person they regarded as the arch-enemy of the Palestinians and the architect of the settlement movement. Concerned moderates, like P.A. leaders Abbas and Erekat, expressed their sympathy, no doubt worried that an even more hard-line Israeli leader like Benjamin Netanyahu would take Sharon's place.

The immediate question for Israelis was whether, or if, Kadima ("Forward") could survive the loss of its founder. Was there a new Israeli "center" that Kadima could appeal to—and if so, what did it believe in? Ehud Olmert was immediately appointed acting prime minister of a caretaker government and quickly established himself as the undisputed leader of Kadima. The 60-year-old hawkish, experienced, and decisive Olmert, a former mayor of Jerusalem, was the first to speak out in favor of replacing the Road Map with unilateralism, even before Sharon announced the Gaza disengagement. He represented a continuation of Israeli policies. As Sharon remained critically ill in a coma, campaigning for the scheduled March 28 Israeli general elections briefly went on hold, resuming on January 13. In Likud party primaries held on January 13, Netanyahu was reelected as uncontested leader. Those Likud members who had joined Sharon's new party and ministry, but who returned to Likud, and those "rebels" who had most vociferously opposed Sharon's Gaza withdrawal were placed much lower on Likud's electoral list as punishment. Polls, however, indicated that Likud would win only around 13 seats in the 120 seat Knesset, with 42 to 43 seats for Kadima, and with around 20 for Labor. (Kadima actually won a plurality of 29 seats in the elections.)

Meanwhile, factional disputes over the selection of candidates and what parties could participate in the January 25, 2006, Palestinian parliamentary elections added to the sense of chaos within the Palestinian community. Hamas, regarded as a terrorist organization by Israel and the United States, decided to enter the elections, and polls predicted that it could take more than a third of the legislature's 132 seats, putting it in a strong position to push its opposing views on peace, security, and the role of Islam in political life.

Campaigning for the elections continued but with some confusion over whether or not Palestinians living in East Jerusalem would be permitted to vote, and, if so, where. Sharon had initially refused to permit the 100,000 eligible East Jeruslaem Arabs to participate in the elections as it was anticipated that Hamas would make a strong showing. P.A. officials, fearing that Fatah would lose ground to Hamas, threatened to call off the elections if Palestinians in East Jerusalem were prevented from voting. Under pressure from the United States, anxious to advance the democratization process in the Middle East, and concerned that it would be blamed if the elections were cancelled, Israel relented, although Olmert told President Bush that there could be "no progress with an administration in which there are terrorist organizations as members." On January 14, the Israeli Cabinet determined that it would enable elections to be held at five post office locations, as had been done in the 1996 elections, but it would not permit any Hamas candidates to campaign in East Jerusalem, nor would they be allowed to post or distribute campaign material in Jerusalem.

In an extraordinary outcome, Hamas won a stunning victory in the January 25 elections for the 132 seat Palestinian Legislative Council, winning 76 seats and ending the domination of Fatah, which had held 55 of the 88 seats in the outgoing parliament. Fatah won only 43 seats, with the remainder going to independents and smaller parties. An estimated 78 percent of the 1.3 million eligible voters took part in peaceful, orderly polling across the West Bank, East Jerusalem, and the Gaza Strip. Exploiting Palestinian disgust and anger at the widespread corruption and incompetence of Fatah, Hamas captured almost all of the sixteen constituencies in the West Bank and Gaza, and in the Jerusalem district. Prime Minister Qurei and the cabinet submitted their resignations to Abbas, chairman of the non-sovereign Palestinian Authority, who called upon Hamas to form a government. Hamas leaders floated the idea of a national unity government with Fatah, perhaps hoping it could deal with domestic issues, while leaving thornier issues of relations with Israel and the United States to Fatah. Humiliated, Fatah leaders immediately rejected this suggestion. Abbas insisted that negotiations with Israel could be carried on through him as leader of the PLO to bypass a Hamas-led government.

The surprising (even to Hamas) outcome of the democratically held elections will have profound implications for the Palestinians, Israel, the United States and the Middle East in general. The election result added chaos to an already uncertain and fragile environment. The

Palestinians will look to Hamas to prove that it can govern rather than merely act as a violent opposition. Although Hamas was expected to honor the cease-fire it agreed to in February 2005, Hamas spokesmen indicated that, unlike Fatah, they were unwilling to negotiate with Israel on security or economic matters, or to recognize the Jewish state. Political leader Mahmoud Zahar, speaking in Gaza, stated that Hamas would not engage with Israel and would seek closer relations with Arab states. Some Fatah militants refused to accept the election outcome and violent clashes took place in the Palestinian territories.

Israelis were divided, some hoping that a Hamas-dominated government could act pragmatically and realistically; most others believing that Hamas would never renounce its basic ideology. Acting Prime Minister Olmert made it clear that Israel would not accept the new government, or any government that included Hamas in its present form. Israel's control of movement of the Palestinian population, and its control of the external and internal borders of Palestinian enclaves will not be affected by the election result. With any negotiations toward peace on indefinite hold, and the possibility of a two-state solution deferred, it seemed likely that Israel would continue its policy of unilateral separation from the Palestinians, with a view toward determining final borders between itself and the Palestinians. Israel threatened to withhold a $50 million transfer of tax and customs receipts to the new administration, and the United States and its allies threatened to withhold more than $250 million in aid.

President Bush and the U.S. administration were clearly shocked when the election results were announced. While hailing "democracy" and the "will of the people," Bush stated that the United States would not recognize a Hamas-led government unless the group renounced violence and recognized Israel's right to exist.

Clearly, we have arrived at yet another turning point in a conflict that continues to confound and amaze.

GLOSSARY

'Abd   Arabic for "slave" or "servant." Often used in compound names (Abdullah, or Servant of Allah).

Alawi (or Alawite)   Small Shia offshoot found primarily in Syria and eastern Turkey. Syrian president Assad is an Alawite.

Aliyah   Hebrew "to go up" or to ascend. Refers to immigration to Palestine and later Israel.

AMAL   Arabic meaning "hope." Acronym for Units of the Lebanese Resistance. Sometimes called the Movement of the Deprived and Dispossessed. Shiite movement started by Imam Musa al-Sadr in Lebanon in 1974. With his disappearance in 1978, the movement has been led by Nabih Berri.

Ashkenazim   Jews of European (including Russian) background.

Ayatollah   Arabic for "sign" of God. Title of highest rank among Twelver Shiites.

Baath   Arabic meaning "renaissance." The Arab Renaissance party, a pan-Arab party advocating Arab freedom, Arab socialism, and Arab unity. Became important from the 1950s on, particularly in Syria and Iraq.

Bricha   Hebrew meaning "flight." Organized, illegal mass movement to lead Jewish Holocaust survivors out of Europe to Palestine.

Caliph   Arabic for "successor" or "deputy," referring to the leaders of the Islamic community after the death of the Prophet Muhammad. After the death of the fourth caliph, Ali, the Caliphate was the institution accepted by the majority of the Muslims, called Sunnis.

Dar al-Harb   Arabic for "House of War"—that territory not under Islamic rule.

Dar al-Islam   Arabic for "House of Islam"—those areas ruled under the aegis of Islam.

Dhimmis   Subject but protected or tolerated minorities living under Islam, particularly people of a "book" or scripture such as Christians and Jews. These groups were allowed to live as self-governing autonomous communities but were subject to high taxation, various humiliations, and an inferior position.

Diaspora   The dispersion of the Jewish people after the destruction of the Second Temple in 70 C.E.

Druze (or Druse)   Eleventh-century Shiite offshoot that developed its own rituals and practices. Secretive and close-knit communities found in Lebanon, Syria, Jordan, and Israel.

Emir, or Amir   Arabic for "prince." Used as a title of rank.

Eretz Yisrael   Hebrew for the "Land of Israel," referring to the biblical borders of the Kingdom of Israel including "Judea" and "Samaria" (the West Bank of the Jordan River).

FATAH   Arabic for "conquest." Also a reverse acronym for the "Palestine Liberation Movement." Originally dedicated to armed struggle against Israel in order to liberate Palestine, it was founded in 1959 in Kuwait. It launched its first raid against Israel on January 1, 1965, from Syrian territory. After the 1967 war, Fatah emerged as the predominant Palestinian group, and in 1969 its leader, Yasser Arafat, was chosen as chairman of the PLO. Although its emphasis, strategy, and tactics have changed over the years, and although Arafat's relationship with various Arab rulers has fluctuated, Fatah remains the largest PLO group.

Fedayeen   Arabic plural meaning "those who sacrifice themselves," referring to those who fight for the faith against the enemies of Islam.

Fellahin   Arabic plural for "peasants."

Haganah   Hebrew for "defense." At first, the underground Jewish defense organization during the mandate period. Merged into the Israel Defense Forces (IDF) in 1948 when Israel was founded.

Hajj   The pilgrimage of Muslims to Mecca. One of the five pillars of the faith.

HAMAS   Arabic word meaning "zeal." Acronym for the Islamic Resistance Movement. Militant armed wing of the Muslim Brotherhood in the West Bank and Gaza formed at the beginning of the Intifada in 1987. A Sunni group, but eventually accepted assistance from Shiite Iran. Became leader of ten Islamic and Palestinian rejectionist factions at start of Madrid peace talks in 1991. Opposed to 1993 Israel–PLO Accord and rejects existence of the Jewish state.

Herut   Hebrew meaning "freedom." Revisionist Zionist party led by Menachem Begin after 1948. An important opposition party in the Knesset, its platform called for a Jewish state on both sides of the Jordan River. Became part of a Right-Center coalition called the Likud ("Unity") in 1973.

Histadrut   Jewish labor or trade-union federation both during and after the mandate period.

Hizbullah   Arabic for "Party of God." Umbrella group for radical Shiite factions in Lebanon, including Islamic Jihad and others. Carried out kidnappings and hostage-taking of Westerners and attacks against Israel's "security zone" in southern Lebanon.

Hudna   In Muslim jurisprudence a temporary truce or cease-fire with a non-Muslim enemy not to exceed ten years.

IDF   Israel Defense Forces.

Imam   Arabic for "prayer leader." Also title of leader recognized by Shiites as the legitimate head of the Islamic community.

Intifada   Arabic for "shaking off." Refers to movement of civil disobedience in Gaza Strip and West Bank, which began in 1987 as Palestinians attempted to end Israeli occupation. The second, or al-Aqsa, intifada, began in September 2000.

Irgun (Irgun Zvai Leumi, or ETZEL, its initials)   Hebrew for "National Military Organization." Military arm of Revisionist Zionist movement, created in 1937. Taken over in Palestine by Menachem Begin in 1942. Opposed to "accommodationist" tactics of mainstream Jewish Agency and its defense organization, the Haganah. Carried out attacks against British military and immigration authorities in Palestine, including blowing up a wing of the King David Hotel in 1946. Disbanded by Ben-Gurion in 1948 and merged with IDF.

Islam   Arabic for "submission." A Muslim is one who submits to the will of the one true God, Allah.

Jihad   Arabic meaning to "strive" or to "struggle." Can be interpreted as the internal effort to be a good Muslim, or as a defensive struggle against those who threaten Islam, or as an offensive war against unbelievers.

Khedive   Honorific title of rulers of Egypt in the nineteenth and twentieth centuries acting as representatives of the Ottoman sultan.

Kibbutz   Cooperative agricultural village with common ownership of land.

Knesset   The Israeli parliament.

LEHI   Hebrew initials for "Fighters for the Freedom of Israel." Also known as the Stern Gang. Group under Avraham Stern that broke away from the Irgun to undertake terrorist attacks against both military and civilian targets during the British mandate period in Palestine.

Likud   Meaning "unity," the Likud bloc of Right and Centrist parties came into being in Israel late in the summer of 1973. Likud won its first election in 1977, and Menachem Begin became prime minister.

Mapai   "The Workers' Party of the Land of Israel," Mapai was a Socialist-Zionist party founded in 1930 that played the dominant role in the political, economic, and cultural life of the Yishuv and immediately after the establishment of Israel in 1948. In 1969, it entered into a parliamentary alignment with other Left and Left-of-Center parties called the Labor Alignment.

Maronite   Christian group that migrated from Syria to northern Lebanon. Made contact with Rome during the Crusades but established formal links with the Vatican only in the eighteenth century. The Maronites have their own Patriarch and liturgy. From the mandate period on, the president of Lebanon was a Maronite Christian.

Millet   Self-governing, autonomous religious (non-Muslim) community within various Muslim empires in the medieval and early modern periods.

Moshav   Cooperative agricultural village with individual land holding and income permitted.

Mufti   An Islamic judge or legal scholar who can issue a *fetwa*, or legal pronouncement, based on his knowledge of the sources of the Sharia, the corpus of Islamic law. The honorific title grand mufti of Jerusalem was bestowed on Hajj Amin al-Husseini by the British during the mandate period, giving him a certain measure of political power within the mandate area.

OAPEC   Organization of Arab Petroleum Exporting Countries.

OPEC   Organization of Petroleum Exporting Countries.

Poalei Zion   Hebrew for "Workers of Zion," the Labor Zionist movement that predominated in the prestate history of Israel and in Israeli politics (as the Mapai party) until 1977.

Pogrom   Sudden outbreak against or massacre of Jews, especially in Russia under the czars.

Qur'an (or Koran)   The word of Allah revealed to Muhammad. The holy book of Islam.

Sanjak   Ottoman administrative unit.

Sephardim   Non-European Jews, especially those who lived under Islamic rule, such as the Jews of Spain (Sepharad).

Sharia   The corpus of Islamic law.

Shaykh (Sheikh)   Patriarchal leader of a tribe. Also used as a title of rank or honor.

Shia (or Shii, or Shiite)   Arabic for "party," referring to the party, or partisans, of Ali and his family as the legitimate leaders of the Islamic community after the death of Muhammad. Ali was Muhammad's cousin, and through his marriage to Fatima, the prophet's son-in-law and the father of Hassan and Hussein, the only grandsons of Muhammad to reach maturity. There are three major branches of Shiism, the Fivers, Seveners, and Twelvers, and several offshoots of these.

Stern Gang   See LEHI.

Sunni (or Sunnite)   Referring to the way or custom of the majority. The majority group in Islam that followed the principle of designation or election in the selection of leaders of the Islamic community after the death of Muhammad.

Talmud   Consisting of the Mishnah, or oral law compiled by the rabbis after the destruction of the Second Temple, and the Gemarah, which is commentary on the Mishnah, the Talmud is primarily, but not exclusively, a body of Jewish law.

Torah   The Five Books of Moses. Literally, "teachings."

Ulema   From the Arabic word *ilm*, or knowledge. Islamic lawyers, jurists, scholars, and teachers.

Umma   The Islamic community of believers.

UNDOF   United Nations Disengagement Observer Forces on the Golan Heights.

UNEF   United Nations Emergency Forces.

UNGA   United Nations General Assembly.

UNIFIL   United Nations Interim Forces in Lebanon.

UNRWA   United Nations Relief and Works Agency.

Vilayet   Ottoman province.

Yishuv   Hebrew word referring to the Jewish community in Palestine before the establishment of Israel.

Zaim   Arabic for a "leader." Referring to a notable who represents and mediates for the group. In Lebanon, acknowledged leaders of the various feudal and sectarian groups. A kind of "godfather."

GUIDE TO PRONUNCIATION

[This is intended as an approximate guide to the rendering in English of foreign terms]

a as in h**a**t · i as in b**i**t · u as in b**u**t · th as in **th**ink
ah as in f**a**ther · ī as in b**i**te · ū as in t**u**ne · dh as in **th**ere
ā as in h**a**te · ir as in f**ire** · ūr as in l**ure** · ch as in Ba**ch**
ār as in h**are** · · · (Johann Sebastian)

e as in b**e**ll · o as in n**o**t · oo as in p**u**t · z as in i**ts**
ē as in b**e** · ō as in n**o**te · o͞o as in b**oo**n ·
ēr as in d**eer** · or as in m**ore** · ou as in n**ow**, **ou**t ·
ë as in b**i**rd, h**e**rd · · ·

401

PHOTO CREDITS

INDEX